HOW TO PREPARE FOR THE
Graduate Record Examinations®

Morris Bramson
Morton Selub
Lawrence Solomon

Books for Professionals
Harcourt Brace Jovanovich, Publishers
San Diego   New York   London

Printed in the United States of America

Library of Congress Cataloging-in-Publication Data

Bramson, Morris.
  How to prepare for the graduate record examinations.

  (Books for professionals)
  1. Graduate record examination — Study guides.
I. Selub, Morton.   II. Solomon, Lawrence.   III. Title.
IV. Series.
LB2367.4.B73 1987   378′.1662   86-25669
ISBN 0-15-600702-9

Third edition

  C D E

Table of Contents

PART VI   PRACTICE EXERCISES IN MATHEMATICS BY TOPICS

PART VII   PRACTICE TESTS FOR THE GRE

PART VIII   VOCABULARY LIST FOR THE GRE

PART 1
Description of the GRE General Test

Format of the GRE General Test

Section of Test	Number of Questions	Time Allowed
Section I: Verbal	7 Sentence Completions 9 Analogies 11 Reading Comprehension 11 Antonyms	30 minutes
Section II: Analytical	25 Analytical Ability Questions (Analytical Reasoning and Logical Reasoning)	30 minutes
Section III: Quantitative	15 Quantitative Comparisons 15 Data Interpretation and Discrete Quantitative Questions	30 minutes
Section IV: Analytical	25 Analytical Ability Questions (Analytical Reasoning and Logical Reasoning)	30 minutes
Section V: Verbal	7 Sentence Completions 9 Analogies 11 Reading Comprehension 11 Antonyms	30 minutes
Section VI: Quantitative	15 Quantitative Comparisons 15 Discrete Quantitative and Data Interpretation Questions	30 minutes
Section VII: Verbal *or* Quantitative *or* Analytical	Varies with type of questions	30 minutes

Total Time = 210 minutes or 3 ½ hours

As the table above shows, the GRE (Graduate Record Examinations) General Test consists of seven sections, each of which is 30 minutes long. You should be prepared to spend four hours taking the GRE. This period includes time to complete registration before the test begins and to take a short break in the middle of the exam.

Each test contains two verbal sections, each consisting of 38 questions; two mathematical sections (called "quantitative" sections by the test makers), each consisting of 30 questions; and two analytical sections, each consisting of 25 questions. The seventh section may be verbal, quantitative, or analytical. This section is experimental; that is, it consists of questions the test makers are trying out for future editions of the test. The seven sections may appear in any order on the test you receive. Furthermore, several editions of the test are used during one session. The test your neighbor has will not be the same as yours.

Your answers on the experimental section do not count toward your final score. However, the experimental section looks just like the regular sections, and since the various sections may appear in any order on any test, you will not know which is the experimental one. If, for example, your edition of the test contains three quantitative sections, you will know that one of them is the experimental section, but you will have no way of knowing which one. In addition, since you are allowed to see only one section of the test at a time, you won't know until toward the end if the test has three quantitative sections; the experimental one may be far behind you by then. That is why you must do your best on every section.

Scoring of the GRE

The system of scoring used for the GRE imposes *no penalty* for an incorrect answer. Your score is based simply on the number of questions you answer correctly. It is therefore advisable to answer all questions on the examination. If you do not know the answer to a question, make an educated guess. Try to eliminate some of the choices and make a selection from those remaining. You risk nothing by guessing. A general test-taking strategy to keep in mind is to go through an entire section answering the questions you can answer without much effort and then go back and spend extra time working on the tougher questions. In the closing moments, guess the answers to any remaining questions.

The number of correct answers on the two verbal sections is your *verbal raw score*. It can vary from 0 to 76. The number of correct answers on the two quantitative sections is your *quantitative raw score*. It can vary from 0 to 60. Finally, the number of correct answers on the two analytical sections is your *analytical raw score*. It can vary from 0 to 50.

Your three raw scores are then converted by statistical methods to *scaled scores* to make it simple to compare the scores of different editions of the GRE; a scaled score on one edition of the test is comparable to the same scaled score on other editions.

The scaled scores range from 200 to 800. However, these scores are not commonly below 300 or above 700. The average score is 500, and about two-thirds of all test takers score between 400 and 600.

At the beginning of Section VII of this book you will find a chart for converting your raw scores on the practice tests to scaled scores. You can thus compare your results from one practice test to the next and monitor your progress. Your scaled scores will give you a good approximation of how you will do on the actual GRE.

When evaluating your work on the practice tests, consider a scaled score above 630 as excellent and one between 500 and 629 as good. A score between 480 and 500 indicates that you rank at about the midpoint of the range of scores.

Types of GRE Verbal Ability Questions

The four types of GRE verbal ability questions test the extent of your vocabulary and the degree to which you can read with understanding. The four types of questions are:

> Antonyms
> Analogies
> Sentence Completions
> Reading Comprehension

The antonym and analogy questions are used to test your vocabulary, and the sentence completions and reading comprehension questions are used to test your reading ability. Each type of verbal question is examined in detail in Part II of this book.

Types of GRE Quantitative Ability Questions

Three types of questions are posed in the quantitative ability sections of the GRE. These types of questions are:

> Quantitative Comparison
> Discrete Quantitative
> (self-contained problems to be solved)
> Data Interpretation

The quantitative ability questions test your skills in arithmetic (including your understanding of integers, fractions, percentages, and averages), elementary algebra (including your understanding of formulas, linear equations, and simple quadratic equations), and informal geometry (including your understanding of angle relationships, right-triangle relationships, area, perimeter, and volume). Your ability to interpret graphs and tables is also tested.

Each type of quantitative ability question is examined in detail in Part III of this book. For a review of the various mathematical topics tested in these sections, see Parts V and VI.

Types of GRE Analytical Ability Questions

The two types of questions that appear in the analytical ability section of the GRE test your reasoning skills. These types of questions are:

Analytical Reasoning
Logical Reasoning

No knowledge of formal or symbolic logic is required for success on these questions. Each question contains all the information you will need to solve it. Both types of questions are examined in detail in Part IV of this book.

PART II
Strategies for the Verbal Ability Questions

The GRE Verbal Ability Questions: What They Are Like, What They Test

Part II of this book will describe the four types of GRE verbal questions and then provide detailed instructions for answering each type of question. When you complete your study of Part II, you will be ready to face the verbal sections of the GRE with the confidence it takes to work effectively and score high on them.

As mentioned in Part I, the four types of questions in the verbal section of the GRE are:

Antonyms
Analogy/Word Relationships
Sentence Completions
Reading Comprehension

Each verbal section consists of 7 sentence completions, 9 analogies, 11 reading comprehension questions, and 11 antonyms, in that order, for a total of 38 questions.

ANTONYM QUESTIONS—OPPOSITES

When you think of vocabulary tests, you probably think of definitions or synonyms. The GRE vocabulary question, however, does not ask you for a synonym; it asks you to select an opposite, or antonym, for a given word. As shown in the following example, you will be given a word printed in capital letters, five words or phrases that are lettered (a) to (e), and the task of selecting the lettered word or phrase that is *most nearly opposite* in meaning to the capitalized word.

WEAK

(a) simple
(b) soft
(c) deft
(d) strong
(e) heavy

Answer: (d)

This simple example is intended to illustrate the nature of the antonym question, not to test your vocabulary power. The antonym for *weak* is, of course, *strong*.

The GRE is not likely to test you on words as familiar as the one in the previous example; it will test you on the wide range of words that you, as either a college student or a graduate, would be expected to have encountered in your recreational reading and course work. Some words will be more familiar to you than others; some may be completely unfamiliar.

The antonym questions are intended to test the extent of your knowledge of vocabulary, your skill in differentiating among shades of meaning, and your ability to reason.

In subsequent pages, you will find suggestions for enlarging your vocabulary, advice on avoiding the pitfalls built into this question category, and instruction that will help you improve your performance in selecting opposites. In Part VIII you will find an extensive vocabulary list for study.

ANALOGY QUESTIONS—WORD RELATIONSHIPS

In the analogy/word relationship question, you are given a pair of capitalized words and five other pairs of words lettered (a) through (e); you are expected first to find a relationship between the two capitalized words and then to select a lettered pair of words that are related to one another in a way that is *most similar* to the way in which the capitalized pair is related.

Note carefully how the analogy question is written. The two words of each pair are separated by a colon, as follows: "chef : recipe," "doctor : diagnosis." The colon here is a kind of shorthand for the phrase "is related to." Another symbol, a pair of colons, separates the capitalized pair of words from the five pairs of lettered choices. The double colon here means "in the same way that," or words to that effect.

Substitute the words for the colon symbols, and the analogy question reads, "The first word of the capitalized pair is related to the second word of that pair in the same way that the first word of one of the lettered pairs is related to its second word." The sample question that follows illustrates the format and nature of the analogy question:

TALL : SHORT ::   (a) fire : water
(b) skilled : deft   (c) hot : cold
(d) now : later   (e) hard : rock

Answer: (c)

Tall and *short* are adjectives used to describe opposite physical dimensions. Similarly, *hot* and *cold* are adjectives used to describe opposite physical properties. Choice (c) is, therefore, the correct answer.

Fire and *water* are in opposition—water quenches fire—but they are not words that describe opposite qualities. The words in choice (b) are synonyms. In choice (e), the first word describes a physical quality of the item denoted by the second word. In neither (b) nor (e) is the relationship similar to that in the given pair. The words in choice (d) are not opposites—*earlier*, not *now*, is the opposite of *later*. Furthermore, neither word describes physical qualities. The answer to the sample question should be stated as follows: *Tall* is the opposite of *short* in the same way that *hot* is the opposite of *cold*.

The relationship in the sample question is easily perceived. Actual test questions will cover a fairly wide range of relationship types and will vary in their levels of difficulty.

The analogy question tests your ability to see relationships between words, distinguish among different types of relationships, and recognize similarities between relationships. This question also tests your vocabulary, your general knowledge, and your ability to think logically.

Later in Part II you will be given examples of the types of word relationships you are likely to encounter on the GRE and instruction on how to solve them effectively. You will also learn strategies and techniques that will permit you to work more quickly and effectively, with greater confidence and security about your ability to deal with this type of question.

SENTENCE COMPLETION QUESTIONS

The sentence completion question of the GRE tests your ability in several areas: vocabulary, correct usage, sentence structure, logical thinking, and reading comprehension.

For this type of question, you are given a sentence with one or two blanks in it where key words have been removed. From among five choices, lettered (a) through (e), you are asked to select the word or words that, when substituted for the blanks, *best complete the meaning of the sentence*. The words that you select must be suitable from the point of view of meaning, correct usage, and grammatical aptness. With the blanks filled, the sentence must be coherent and logical. Each sentence contains all the information necessary for answering the question. Here is an example of the sentence completion question:

> The trustees of the Orchestral Society had hoped to reap substantial benefits through the sale of the paintings that Mr. Cooper had – – –, but the proceeds from the auction, which was poorly attended because of the blizzard, were – – –.
>
> (a) retained . . . unworthy
> (b) lent . . . confiscated
> (c) bequeathed . . . disappointing
> (d) assembled . . . enormous
> (e) appraised . . . taxable
>
> Answer: (c)

This incomplete sentence, as it stands, has structural, logical, and informational clues to help us fill in the blanks and complete it. The word "but" is a reversal indicator; it is a structural clue that implies that the trustees' hopes for substantial benefits were not fulfilled. Furthermore, the sentence informs us that attendance at the auction was poor. That information, coupled with the implication of the reversal indicator, leads us to conclude that the proceeds were low and, therefore, *disappointing* rather than *enormous*.

What of the other possibilities? Choices (*a*) and (*b*) can be eliminated. The trustees would not sell paintings that were *lent* to them, nor would they sell paintings that Mr. Cooper had *retained*—presumably for himself. As for choice (*e*), there is nothing in the sentence to support that choice. With the blanks filled in by the words in choice (*c*), the completed sentence is logical, grammatical, meaningful, and correct.

Later in Part II you will learn about the importance of indicator words, sentence logic, linguistic elements, contextual clues, and correct usage in determining the proper choice of answer for the sentence completion question. You will also find a discussion of appropriate questions to ask yourself when working on these questions.

READING COMPREHENSION QUESTIONS

You are probably already familiar with the reading comprehension question because it appears on many standardized tests. In this part of the GRE, you are given a passage to read and are asked to answer a number of questions dealing with the material in that passage. The questions use the same format found in the other verbal sections: each question is followed by answer choices lettered (*a*) through (*e*). You must select, solely on the basis of the contents of the passage, the one that best answers that question.

The reading passages come from four disciplines: the social sciences, biological sciences, physical sciences, and humanities. Some of the questions are concerned with identifying stated information and specific details in the passage, while others deal with implied or tacit ideas, opinions, or materials. Some ask for identification of the main idea or the central thrust of the passage, while others ask about supporting arguments or ideas. Some are concerned with the author's purpose, point of view, reasoning, or argumentation, and others ask you to apply to other issues the author's point of view as expressed or implied in the passage.

No prior knowledge of the material in a passage is needed to answer its questions; each passage contains all the necessary information. The following sample reading passage and questions are representative of the type of material you will encounter on the exam:

In the Great Lakes, the life cycles of individual organisms provide a number of fascinating, although brief, scenarios. But together, all the agents of change among the plants, birds, and fish become a full-length play on the massive stage of the Great Lakes basin.

Several important props must be described before we get to the play's narrative. One is the relative shallowness of the lakes, scraped out some 10,000 to 15,000 years ago by receding ice sheets. Another is the size of these inland seas, so enormous that the earth's rotation plays, through the Coriolis force, a major role in the dynamics of the Great Lakes, as it does in the oceans. And because the lakes all outflow either into each other or into the Saint Lawrence River and differ in surface size and in volume, they all have different water residence times.

1. Which of the following are (is) directly stated in the passage?
    I. The Great Lakes all flow directly into the Saint Lawrence River.
    II. The Great Lakes basin is vast, but it is not very deep.
    III. The props needed for a full-length play about the Great Lakes would require a massive stage.

    (a) I only
    (b) II only
    (c) III only
    (d) I and II only
    (e) I, II, and III

2. From the information given in the passage, we can infer that
    (a) the birds and fish of the Great Lakes are unique organisms
    (b) the Coriolis force pushed the ice sheets back
    (c) the Great Lakes are as large as any of the oceans
    (d) water residence time is the length of time that a particular particle of water spends in one of the lakes before it flows out of that lake
    (e) water residence time varies from 10,000 to 15,000 years according to particular lake conditions

3. This passage is probably part of
    (a) a newspaper article on the decline in fish production in the Great Lakes
    (b) an article on the natural history of the Great Lakes
    (c) a prospectus offering waterfront land for real estate development
    (d) a treatise on the Coriolis force
    (e) a water pollution study with emphasis on the Great Lakes
                            Answers: 1. (b) 2. (d) 3. (b)

In question 1, item I is not stated in the passage. The last sentence says that the lakes outflow *into each other* or into the Saint Lawrence River. Item III represents a mistaken notion of what the passage actually says. The Great Lakes region forms a massive stage figuratively; the idea of stage, play, and props is not to be taken literally. Item II is supported by the last sentence in paragraph one and the second sentence in paragraph two. Since only item II is directly stated in the passage, the correct answer is choice (b).

In question 2, the statement in choice (d) can be inferred from the last sentence of the passage. The author concludes, "... they all have different water residence times," directly after stating "... because the lakes all ... differ in surface size and in volume ...," thus tying size and volume together to the idea of outflow. We can draw the conclusion that any particular particle of water remains (resides) in any of the lakes a longer or shorter period of time depending upon the size of that lake and the rate of its outflow, and that "water residence time" is what we call that period of time. Choice (d) is, therefore, the correct answer.

Nothing in the passage deals with fish production or water pollution, and the Coriolis force is mentioned only once, so choices (a), (d), and (e) in question 3 have no support. We can eliminate choice (c), since the entire thrust of the passage is toward consideration of the Great Lakes as an environment for plant and animal life, not real estate development. We can deduce that choice (b) is the answer to question 3 from the formality of the language; the presence of a continuous thread dealing with "plants," "organisms," "birds," and "fish"; and the attention to the geological beginnings of the Great Lakes. These all indicate the likelihood that the passage is part of an article dealing with natural history.

Later in Part II you will find detailed information on the types of reading passages you are likely to encounter on the GRE, and you will be introduced to a wide variety of question types. We will, of course, present various strategies for attacking the reading comprehension question successfully.

The GRE Antonym Question and the Importance of Vocabulary Study

WHY YOU SHOULD STUDY VOCABULARY . . . STARTING NOW

Is it too late to study vocabulary? Some people say there is little point in studying vocabulary for the GRE. They contend that vocabulary development is a long-term, ongoing process and that it's not possible for those who have not been working on increasing vocabulary all along to improve their word power overnight. Don't listen to them! It is far better for you to do something about vocabulary than to do nothing. And the time to do it is now!

No matter what you may hear to the contrary, it is possible to learn a large number of new words in a comparatively short period of time. If you have six months before you take the GRE, you can learn literally thousands of words. If you have six weeks, you still can add a sizable number of new words to your working vocabulary. Even if you have only a little time, don't despair; learn as many new words as you can. Every word that you learn represents a possible point added to your raw score, and every point counts.

Star athletes win important events because they have trained rigorously. Great virtuosos practice continually to prepare for important concerts.

Train for the GRE as people do for any other competitive event. Be as well prepared as possible when you sit down to take the exam.

Although the GRE is indeed competitive, doing your personal best is also important. Maybe you can't score 800, but don't let that discourage you. If you improve just a little on each part of the exam, your overall score can grow dramatically. For example, if you are at the 500 level now, all you need to reach 550 is a few more correct answers: just 5 more in the verbal ability sections and 3 more in each of the quantitative ability and analytical ability sections. It doesn't take too much more to improve by 100 points, and jumping 150 or 200 points is not impossible.

The next section, which will thoroughly explain how to approach and deal with the antonym question, will be followed by a complete outline of suggestions for strengthening your vocabulary. Part VIII of the book offers a lengthy list of words that you might find in portions of the GRE.

ANSWERING THE ANTONYM QUESTION

Successful test takers know the importance of understanding the question before undertaking to answer it. Familiarize yourself beforehand with the general nature of the directions for each type of question on the GRE. Don't wait until the bell rings for the start of the test to figure out what you are supposed to do. However, no matter how well you think you know the directions, be sure to skim them again when you take the actual test, just to be sure that no changes have been made.

The sample directions below are very similar to those on recent Graduate Record Examinations:

Directions: In each of the questions below, a capitalized word is followed by five words or phrases lettered (a) through (e). Select the word or phrase most nearly OPPOSITE in meaning to the capitalized word.

The wording of the directions on the test may vary slightly from the above, but the general sense will remain the same. Your task is to find, among the choices offered, the word that is *most nearly opposite* in meaning to the given word. This means that your choice does not have to be absolutely opposite in meaning to the given word, just that it must be the word, from among the choices, that is most nearly opposite in meaning to the given word. Since the questions may require that you choose among words that are close in meaning, be sure to consider all choices carefully before you make your final selection.

Finding an antonym for the capitalized word starts with thinking of a synonym for that word. If you don't know a word's meaning, you can't select an antonym. The easiest way to express a word's meaning is not through a definition but, rather, through a synonym. To focus your attention on this approach, use the following formula statement:

> Word X means (state a synonym for word X), and the opposite of word X is (state your selection from among the choices).

Try this approach on this sample antonym question:

CONFLICT

(a) adherence
(b) stimulation
(c) joy
(d) intonation
(e) harmony

Answer: (e)

Following the model that we have devised, the formula statement for the sample question would be: "*Conflict* means 'discord' or 'disagreement,' and the opposite of *conflict* is *harmony*."

Here are some thoughts to keep in mind when answering the antonym question:

Alternate definitions. Many words have more than one dictionary definition. The first meaning you assign to a given word may not always be the one that was intended for the question. The next sample question illustrates this point:

FAIR

(a) angry
(b) glum
(c) homely
(d) hopeless
(e) judicial

Answer: (c)

If you have assigned a synonym or meaning to the capitalized word and can't find an opposite among the choices offered, you should consider the possibility that the given word has either one other or several other meanings. Try to bring those meanings to mind.

If your first response was that *fair* means "impartial," "sunny," or "light-colored," the absence of choices such as "biased," "stormy," or "swarthy" should have alerted you to the possibility that some other meaning for *fair* was intended. In this instance, *fair* means "beautiful," as in "Mirror, mirror on the wall, who is the fairest of them all?" The opposite is *homely*, choice (c).

Pronunciation. Some words have more than one pronunciation, with a different meaning for each. Other words are not spelled the way they are pronounced, and you may have heard or used them without ever having seen them in print. In either instance, you may not recognize a word with which you are actually familiar. The next sample question features a word that has two different pronunciations, each associated with a separate meaning:

CONSUMMATE

(a) compact
(b) imperfect
(c) crass
(d) bold
(e) active

Answer: (b)

Consummate, when accented on the first syllable and pronounced to rhyme with "ate," is a verb which means "to bring to completion." When accented on either the first or second syllable and pronounced to rhyme with "it," *consummate* is an adjective which means "perfect" or "superb." When we describe a singer as a "consummate" artist, we are saying that the singer is superb. When we say, "Let's consummate the deal," we mean, "Let's complete the deal." In the sample question, *consummate* means "perfect," and the opposite is *imperfect.* You know that this meaning is intended because none of the answer choices suggests the opposite of "bring to completion," the other meaning of the word.

The next sample question uses a word that is not pronounced the way it is spelled:

INDICT

(a) exonerate
(b) cross-examine
(c) prevail
(d) respond
(e) deny

Answer: (a)

Indict means to "to accuse of wrongdoing," and the opposite is *exonerate*, which means "to clear of blame." *Indict* is pronounced "indite." A person with only a spoken knowledge of the word might not recognize it in print, since it is spelled as if it would rhyme with "predict."

If you don't recognize a word at first, try pronouncing it several different ways. You may discover a pronunciation that makes the word familiar to you.

Antonyms. The GRE antonym question asks you to find an opposite for the capitalized word. There are no synonyms among the choices offered. (Please note, however, that among the antonym questions on the simulated examinations in this book, the authors *have* placed synonyms among the choices as a study aid to help you build your vocabulary skills.)

Formula statement. Remember to use the formula statement: "*Consummate* means 'perfect' or 'superb,' and the opposite is *imperfect*."

Degrees of oppositeness. Few pairs of words in the English language are absolute synonyms—that is, words that are synonymous in all their meanings. "Sick" and "ill" are synonyms, and you may say, interchangeably, "I am sick," or "I am ill." However, you may not say, "A sick wind blows no good," nor can you say, "I'm ill and tired of your complaints."

Similarly, few words are exact opposites—that is, words that are opposed in all their meanings. It is important to remember that you are directed to find a word that is *most nearly opposite* in meaning to the given word. Try this example:

CONCEAL

(*a*) harvest
(*b*) depose
(*c*) revere
(*d*) espouse
(*e*) unveil

Answer: (*e*)

Conceal means "to cover" or "to remove from sight," and the opposite is *unveil*, which means "to reveal" or "to disclose." Although *unveil* is indeed an opposite of *conceal*, words such as "expose" or "reveal" are also opposite in meaning to *conceal* and in some contexts are even more nearly opposite than *unveil*. However, they are not among the choices offered. Choice (*e*) is *most nearly opposite* in meaning to the given word. Here is another antonym question:

FRESH

(*a*) able
(*b*) worn
(*c*) nutritious
(*d*) unsuitable
(*e*) untutored

Answer: (*b*)

Fresh can mean "not worn," and the opposite is *worn*. You may feel that "stale" would be the best opposite for *fresh*, but "canned," "trite," "adulterated," "salt" (as in "salt water"), and several other words are also acceptable opposites for the capitalized word. Of the choices offered, however, only *worn* satisfies the question. As always, in this question type, your answer need not be a perfect opposite; it is enough if your choice is the one that is most nearly the opposite in meaning to the capitalized word.

HOW TO FIGURE OUT THE MEANING WHEN YOU AREN'T SURE YOU KNOW THE WORD

If you have a fairly large vocabulary, and if you have studied and practiced the approaches and suggestions covered in the preceding section of this book, you should do well on the antonym part of the GRE. However, even if you do not have a vocabulary deficiency, you will come across unfamiliar words, or words of which you are uncertain. What do you do then?

Rule No. 1 is: Never concede any points. Rule No. 2 is: Always obey Rule No. 1. You need every point you can get, and there are methods for unlocking the meanings of words, even those words you think you do not know. Let's look at some of these approaches.

Word origins. Knowledge of a foreign language can be extremely useful in the decoding of English words, since English is a language rich with borrowings from other tongues. If you know some Latin, you can easily figure out that "somnambulist" is a synonym for "sleepwalker," that "precursor" is almost a direct translation of "forerunner," and that "remunerate" means "repay." Thousands of English words have been derived from the Latin, and you will find it helpful to think of the Latin connection when you come across words that, at first encounter, seem unfamiliar.

If you are a student of any of the Romance languages, such as Spanish, Italian, or French, you should have little difficulty with "savant," which means "one of extensive learning," since it comes from the participle of the French verb *savoir*, "to know." Knowing that *verde* in Spanish means "green," you should conclude that "verdure" means "greenery." Familiar with *vendre*, the French for "sell," you should grasp that "vendor" means "seller." So, too, with *gauche*—"clumsy," *naitre*—"nascent," and *pouvoir*—"puissant."

Almost any other language with which you are familiar—including Greek, German, or the Scandinavian tongues—can also prove helpful. You will find that the meanings of many English words derived from those languages become clear if you connect them to words of the language of their origin. However, the foreign language connection will be fruitful only if you develop an awareness of the relationship between English and other languages.

Parts of speech. Often you may find yourself puzzling over the meaning of a particular word, certain that you know it, yet unable to "get" the meaning. Your puzzlement may stem from the fact that the word before you is a word you know that has been transformed into a different part of speech. "Predacious," for instance, is an adjective derived from the noun "predator." "Nutrient" is a noun with the same root as "nutritious." In either instance, if you know one of the forms, you have a clue to the meaning of the second. You may be able to define the verb "decant" by thinking of the noun "decanter" and decode "heterogeneity" if you realize that it is a noun directly related to the adjective "heterogeneous."

Words in context. The brain is like a marvelous computer: almost everything you have ever read or heard is in your brain's memory banks awaiting retrieval. The problem lies in finding the correct "button" to activate the retrieval process. Sometimes you can't recall the information that is lodged in your brain. Sometimes, in fact, you are not even aware of having the information stored away.

Free association is a method that often works to bring those "hidden" words to the fore. If the word seems familiar but you can't recall its meaning, try to remember when you heard it, where you heard it, where you saw it, who said it, or, perhaps, a fragment of the context in which the word was said or written. Recall, if you can, the sentence that included the word in question or, failing that, a phrase of which the word was a part.

Take the word "decant" as an example. Almost every high school student, aware of it or not, has heard that word. Sometime, in a science class that you took, a teacher held up a flask with fluid in it and said, "Now I'm going to decant the liquid from this flask into a beaker with acid in it," and proceeded to pour the liquid. If you can remember that moment when you work on the antonym section of the actual GRE, you will probably be able to figure out what "decant" means by using the answer choices as clues.

If the word "covert" sticks in your brain but refuses to reveal its meaning, try to visualize your favorite anchorperson talking about the "covert operations of the CIA," or conjure up the image of a headline about the "covert activities of terrorist organizations." Those associations, coupled with the answer choices, should help you find the correct antonym. If you also use foreign word origins, you will remember that the French *couvert* means "covered," and the word's meaning will open up to you, especially if one of the choices is "overt," which is closely related to the French *ouvert*, meaning "open."

Is the word "incontrovertible" a puzzler? Try jogging your memory for a contextual clue; have you ever heard the phrase "incontrovertible evidence"? Combine the contextual clue with the parts-of-speech approach to work out the answer. "Controvertible" is an adjective that is related to "controversy," which means "dispute." Taking word-building elements into account—the prefix "in" means "not"—you can conclude that "incontrovertible" means "not able to be disputed." One of the answer choices is certain to be a word like "disputable," or "questionable," or "arguable."

Word-building elements. The use of roots, stems, prefixes, and suffixes for vocabulary detective work is considered valuable by some, and highly overrated by others. If you know how to use these word-building elements, by all means use them, but only as one more weapon in your arsenal.

You may find it useful to know that "tele-" in "telepathy" is a combining form taken from the Greek and that it means "distant" or "transmission over a distance." But be aware that "tele-" in "teleological" is a combining form that means "complete" or "end" (purpose) and derives from a different Greek word.

You may find it confusing that "ped-" in "pedagogue" is not the same stem as "ped-" in "pedant." The former prefix means "child," whereas the latter means "foot." Thus, a "pedagogue" is a "teacher or leader of children," and a "pedant" is "one who makes an ostentatious display of learning" (literally, "a servile follower, walking closely in the steps of another"). To complicate matters further, "ped-" in "pedal" has the same meaning as "pod-" in "podiatry," except that the former is derived from the Latin, while the latter derives from the Greek. Using roots and stems as your primary approach to finding word meanings is risky. It is best to use word-building elements in conjunction with other suggested methods.

All the methods we have outlined can help you with words that are at least slightly familiar to you, but they can't help you much with words you really don't know at all. These ancillary, or auxiliary, methods for unraveling the meanings of words are useful, but your best bet, your basic approach, should be *knowing the words*! To do well on the antonym question of the GRE, you would be well advised to strengthen your vocabulary. You should find the next section very helpful in this regard.

HOW TO IMPROVE YOUR VOCABULARY IN A LIMITED TIME—F.E.P. (FOR EXAM PURPOSES)

No matter how powerful your vocabulary may be, you can improve it markedly between now and exam time. The extent of the improvement will depend directly upon the time you are willing to spend on this study project, but you can learn dozens or even hundreds of new words in a matter of weeks. This new knowledge, you should understand, will be strictly F.E.P.—for exam purposes.

Learning vocabulary F.E.P. involves memorizing lists of words. This technique will prepare you to successfully answer short-answer, multiple-choice vocabulary questions on the GRE, such as the antonym questions and, to a lesser extent, the sentence completion and analogy questions. This kind of learning is short-term learning to meet a specific short-term goal. When you stop reviewing the material, it will quickly fade from memory. If, however, you want to integrate those new words into your permanent vocabulary, you can do so by using them frequently in your everyday conversation and writing.

Here is a program for improving your vocabulary for the GRE. If you work at it, you will get good results.

1. Obtain the necessary supplies. You will need two paperback books: a good dictionary (get one even if you already have a large hardbound desk or unabridged dictionary at home—carrying one of those around would be quite a task) and a thesaurus (a collection of synonyms and antonyms). You will also need some packs of 3- by 5-inch index cards and a small memo book.

2. Keep lists of unfamiliar words you come across in the course of each day. You will find unfamiliar words in the word lists in this book, in your school textbooks, in your recreational reading, and in newspapers and magazines. You will hear unfamiliar words in class, on radio and TV programs, at the movies and the theater, as well as in the conversations around you. Whenever you see or hear an unfamiliar word, jot it down in your memo book.

3. At the end of the day or whenever you have a chance, transfer the words from your memo book to the index cards, one word to a card. Print each word in large, clear letters in the center of the card. Look up the word in the dictionary and read the definitions; then look up the word in the thesaurus.

4. To reinforce learning, write the sentence in which you saw or heard the word directly under the printed word on the front of the card.

5. On the other side of the index card, across the top, print several synonyms of the new word. Along the bottom of the card, print several antonyms of the new word. Use the same color pen or pencil to enter all synonyms and a different color to enter all antonyms.

6. Carry the index cards around with you and use them as flash cards. Whenever you have some spare time—while waiting at the dentist's office, riding the train or bus, or studying in the library—go over your index cards. Look at a word without referring to the back and try to recall as many of its synonyms and antonyms as you can. Check your recall against the entries on the back; then go on to the next card. When you feel you have mastered a particular word, put the card into the "inactive" file. Go over the inactive file periodically. If words in the inactive file are fading from your memory, return them to the "active" file.

7. Bundle the cards in small packs of ten or fifteen. Go over a small pack four or five times in repeat drills. Don't go over your entire list each time.

8. Shuffle the cards frequently so that your learning does not become dependent on the order of the cards.

9. Having someone else go over the cards with you can eliminate some of the monotony of this kind of drill work. Ask friends or relatives to help you.

10. Use the new words in conversation and in writing as frequently as possible. If you are concerned about the possibility that you may embarrass yourself by using a word incorrectly, try this only with family or good friends.

The official GRE test guide suggests that you engage in word games and read some moderately complex books or magazine articles on topics with which you are unfamiliar. Those suggestions are good for general educational and intellectual growth, but they are not specific prescriptions for helping you prepare for the exam. You should take direct steps, such as the previously mentioned method of studying vocabulary, to increase your vocabulary F.E.P.

You will find an extended vocabulary list in Part VIII of this book. The list has not been graded according to level of difficulty, because for all practical purposes, there are no difficult words, only familiar and unfamiliar ones. Any word you know is an easy one for you. Any word you don't know is a difficult one for you.

No single list of words can be considered comprehensive for GRE preparation. Use the materials in this book, your own list of words, lists from school, and any other vocabulary materials you can obtain. Your only limit should be the time you have to spend on this portion of your test preparation.

The GRE Analogy Question

We advise that you familiarize yourself with the test directions for each part of the GRE well before taking the test. Time is of the essence during the exam. Work out the intent of the analogy question now, not during the exam. Of course you should skim the directions at test time to make certain that no substantial changes have been made, but you should already be completely familiar with the general requirements of the directions.

The wording of the following directions is very similar to that used for analogy questions in recent Graduate Record Examinations:

Directions: In each of the questions below, a related pair of words or phrases in capital letters is followed by five pairs of words or phrases lettered (a) through (e). Select the pair that expresses a relationship that is MOST similar to that of the capitalized pair.

While the wording of the directions on the GRE may vary slightly from that of the directions given here, the substance is the same. Your task is to find, among the lettered choices, that pair of words or phrases that forms a relationship most similar to that of the given, capitalized pair. The sample that follows illustrates the format of the analogy/word relationship question:

DARK : LIGHT ::
(a) sweet : soft
(b) brittle : bright
(c) warm : cool
(d) brilliant : radiant
(e) constant : continuous

Answer: (c)

The capitalized words *dark* and *light* are separated by a colon. The colon, you will recall, is used as a symbol to indicate that word A is related to word B. The capitalized pair is separated from the five choices by a double colon which says "in the same way that" or words to that effect. Substituting the words for the symbols, you can phrase the helpful formula statement: "*Dark* is related to *light* in the same way that the words in one of the lettered choices are related to each other."

It is not enough, however, to say that word A is related to word B. It is essential to say *how* the words are related to each other. The analogy/word relationship question requires that you identify the significant relationship existing between two words of a capitalized pair and then find an analogous or similar relationship among the lettered choices.

HOW TO ANSWER THE ANALOGY/WORD RELATIONSHIP QUESTION

What do the terms "word relationship" and "analogy" mean, as used in this type of question? "Word relationship" refers to the nature of the connection linking the two words of a pair. The connection may be their likeness, their difference, the way in which they identify each other, or any other link between them. "Analogy," as used here, refers to the similarity or likeness between the word relationship of one pair and the word relationship of another pair.

To answer the analogy/word relationship question, you must first identify the significant relationship between the capitalized words and then find an analogous relationship between the words of one of the other pairs of answer choices. In the sample in the section above, the relationship between *dark* and *light* is antonymous—they are opposite in meaning; the relationship between *warm* and *cool*, in choice (*c*), is also antonymous. The two pairs therefore are said to be analogous, or parallel in meaning.

The analogy/word relationship question is best expressed in a statement that clearly indicates the relationship between the capitalized words and links that relationship to a similar statement about one of the pairs of choices. Note how this approach is applied in the next sample:

SWEATER : WOOL ::
(*a*) jacket : vest
(*b*) footwear : sneakers
(*c*) jewelry : adornment
(*d*) shoe : leather
(*e*) ring : diamond

Answer: (*d*)

The relationship between the capitalized words can be stated thus: "A *sweater* is usually made of *wool*." The relationships between the words of the answer choices can be expressed by the following statements:

(a) A *jacket* is a part of a suit, and so is a *vest*.
(b) *Footwear* is a general class of apparel, of which *sneakers* are one type.
(c) *Jewelry* is ornamentation worn for *adornment*.
(d) A *shoe* is usually made of *leather*.
(e) A *ring* may have a *diamond* as ornamentation.

The relationship between the words of the capitalized pair is that the first is a product and the second is the primary material of which that product is made. Only statement (d) describes a similar relationship: "A *sweater* is usually made of *wool*, just as a *shoe* is usually made of *leather*."

One of the problems you will face in the analogy/word relationship question is that a pair of words can be related in different ways. For example, recall the first sample pair at the beginning of this section: *dark* and *light*. You could have made these observations about the pair:

1. Both words are adjectives.
2. Both words deal with the same subject.
3. Each word expresses comparative extremes of intensity.

But you could not have said which one of the three observations was the most significant expression of the relationship between the two words until after you had examined the five answer choices.

Significance is the key word in determining the answer to this type of question. The test makers try to present pairs of words that are related in a significant way. The significant way in which *dark* and *light* are related is not that they are adjectives but, rather, that they are words that deal with opposite aspects of the same subject. Each word in choice (a) deals with a different physical quality, as does each word in choice (b). Both words in choice (d) deal with the same subject, but they do not represent extremes or opposites. The words in choice (e) are not opposites. Only in choice (c) is the relationship significantly similar, or analogous, to that of the given pair. The words deal with the same physical quality—temperature—and they are opposite in meaning.

Consider another analogy/word relationship question:

SURGEON : SCALPEL ::
(a) carpenter : cabinet
(b) architect : plans
(c) musician : instrument
(d) baker : oven
(e) sculptor : chisel

Answer: (e)

A *surgeon* uses a *scalpel* as a tool or instrument. Among the choices, similar statements can be made only for the pairs of words in choices (c) and (e):

(c) A *musician* uses an *instrument* as a tool or instrument.
(e) A *sculptor* uses a *chisel* as a tool or instrument.

Since you are directed to select the pair that expresses a relationship that is most similar to that of the capitalized pair, you must determine which of the two pairs is the more similar.

Surgeon and *scalpel* are very specific terms: a surgeon is a particular kind of doctor, and a scalpel is a particular kind of surgical instrument. *Musician* and *instrument* are general terms. If, instead of "musician" and "instrument," the choice had been "percussionist" and "kettle drums," the relationship would have been closer. *Sculptor* and *chisel* are as specific as the terms in the capitalized pair, and the relationship is similar to that of the capitalized pair: A *surgeon* uses a *scalpel* as a tool or instrument in the same way that a *sculptor* uses a *chisel* as a tool or instrument.

Here are some points to remember when working on the analogy questions:

The statement you make should use the words in the same order in which they appear in the question. If a pair appears in the question as "surgeon : scalpel," do not reverse the order in your statement by saying, "A *scalpel* is an instrument used by a *surgeon*." If you are careless in expressing the relationships in the correct order, you may misconstrue the nature of the relationship. Routinize the format of your formula statement: Always use the terms of each pair in the same order in which they are given in the question.

Be sure that the types of words used in your answer choice correspond to the types of words in the capitalized pair. A general term in the given pair should be matched by a general term in the answer choice, and a specific term in the given pair should be matched by a specific term in the answer choice.

The following sample illustrates this point:

TREE : MAPLE ::   (a) wild : rose
(b) kitten : cat   (c) horse : purebred
(d) dog : poodle   (e) shrub : plant

Answer: (d)

Your statement for the word relationship between the terms of the capitalized pair should be, "One type of *tree* is the *maple*." You should keep in mind that the first word, *tree*, is a general term, while the second word, *maple*, is a specific one. Therefore, you should look among the choices for a pair with a general term as the first word and a specific term as the second. Of the answers given, only choice (d) has a general term as the first word and a specific term as the second word. Thus, your formula statement should read, "One type of *tree* is the *maple*, in the same way that one type of *dog* is the *poodle*."

Do not express the analogy problem as if it were a ratio problem. The analogy/word relationship question, despite its format, is *not* a ratio problem; it is a verbal problem. Saying that *dark* is to *light* as *warm* is to *cool* does not state the relationships between the words, nor does it show how they are analogous. Always use the formula statement approach. It expresses the relationship between the capitalized words, thus making it easier to recognize a similar relationship among the answer choices.

Be prepared to reexamine and rephrase the formula statement if you find that two or more of the pairs of choices seem to be analogues of the capitalized pair. The test constructors intend only one answer choice to be the correct analogue. If you have found more than one analogue, you have not determined the most significant relationship between the capitalized words, or you have not stated the relationships of the various answer choices correctly.

The next sample question should clarify this point:

PITCHERS : THROW ::   (*a*) runners : train
(*b*) base runners : slide   (*c*) gymnasts : tumble
(*d*) skaters : pirouette   (*e*) bicyclists : pedal

Answer: (*e*)

If your statement about the capitalized pair is, "*Pitchers throw*," you will find that all five answer choices seem equally valid: *runners train, base runners slide, gymnasts tumble, skaters pirouette,* and *bicyclists pedal.* These statements are all similar to the first statement.

Obviously, all five of the answer choices cannot be correct. Either your statement is wrong, or you have not uncovered the most significant aspect of the relationship between *pitchers* and *throw*.

The initial statement is correct as far as it goes, but it does not make clear that throwing is the most significant aspect of the pitcher's job or that throwing involves an object. Runners train, base runners slide, gymnasts tumble, and skaters pirouette, but those are not their principal activities. Pitchers throw (a ball) as their principal activity. If you broaden your view of the relationship of the capitalized words to include these points, your formula statement will correctly read, "*Pitchers throw* balls as their principal activity, just as *bicyclists pedal* bicycles as their principal activity."

In the course of examining the sample questions, you probably noticed that once you understood the nature of the relationship between the words in the capitalized pair, you found it much easier to select the correct answer. A helpful approach to understanding relationships is to group them according to type.

Fortunately for our purposes, most analogy/word relationships on the GRE fall into a comparatively small number of categories. Knowing the categories, and being able to recognize which one a particular capitalized pair belongs to, is a great help in answering analogy questions.

CATEGORIES OF WORD RELATIONSHIPS FOR THE GRE ANALOGY QUESTION

Word relationships have general patterns that can be categorized. Using word relationship categories to answer analogy questions is efficient and productive. Instead of trying to match the relationship of the capitalized pair with that of each answer choice, identify the category of the given pair and then check to see which answer choice falls into the same category. You will find that almost every word relationship you encounter on the GRE will fall into one of a small number of categories. We will now describe these very useful categories, give examples of them, and explain the answers to the sample problems.

1. Degree of Difference Relationship

The Degree of Difference Relationship is one in which two words are similar in meaning but different in degree. One of the words may be stronger, harsher, or more intense than the other word.

The degree of difference must always flow in the same direction in the answer pair as it does in the capitalized pair. If the first term in the capitalized pair is the stronger term of the two, the first term in the answer pair must also be the stronger of the two.

Remember too that if two or more answers have the correct word relationship in an analogy showing degree of difference, the best choice is the one in which the degree of difference is relatively the same as the degree of difference in the capitalized pair.

FREQUENTLY : ALWAYS :: (*a*) seldom : never
(*b*) shaky : stable   (*c*) never : rarely
(*d*) late : punctual   (*e*) seldom : always

Answer: (*a*)

The words in the capitalized pair both deal with interval of occurrence but differ in degree. Note especially that the second word is an absolute and that the degree of difference flows from the less intense word to the absolute.

The pairs in choices (*b*) and (*d*) can be eliminated because they represent antonymous relationships rather than a degree of difference. In choice (*c*), there is a degree of difference between the first and second words, but it flows in the wrong direction: from the absolute to the less intense.

The words in choices (*a*) and (*e*), like the capitalized pair, deal with interval of occurrence with a degree of difference, but the degree of difference in choice (*e*) is greater than that in the capitalized pair. In fact, the words are very close to being opposites. In choice (*a*), however, the degree of difference is very much the same as in the capitalized pair, and the difference flows toward the absolute word. The formula statement is,

"*Frequently* differs in degree from *always* in the same way that *seldom* differs in degree from *never*."

2. Cause and Effect Relationship

As you might expect from the name, the Cause and Effect Relationship is one in which the action or nature of the first word results in the effect denoted by the second word. Sometimes the relationship is reversed, and the first word denotes the effect and the second, the cause.

The order of words in the answer choice must always match the order of words in the capitalized pair: If the order of the words in the capitalized pair is cause first and effect second, the order of the words in the answer choice must be the same; if the order is effect and then cause in the capitalized pair, the order in the answer choice must also be effect and then cause.

Here is an example of the Cause and Effect Relationship:

> SHOOT : KILL :: (*a*) vex : harm
> (*b*) demobilize : arrive   (*c*) capture : escape
> (*d*) insult : humiliate   (*e*) skip : skid
>
>   Answer: (*d*)

The formula statement for this question is, "If you *shoot* someone, you may *kill* him, in the same way that if you *insult* someone, you may *humiliate* him."

A Cause and Effect Relationship need only have a probable or possible link—shooting does not always lead to killing—but the nature of the link between cause and effect must be the same for both halves of the formula statement. In other words, a possible or probable link between the capitalized words should be matched by a possible or probable link between the answer words, and an inevitable link between the words of the first pair should be matched by an inevitable link between the words of the second pair.

3. Whole and Part, Part and Whole, and Part and Part Relationships

If the first word of the capitalized pair denotes something of which the second word is a component or part, the category into which the pair falls is the Whole and Part Relationship. If the first word denotes something that is a part of what the second word denotes, the category is the Part and Whole Relationship. If both words denote things that are part of a larger thing, the category they fall into is the Part and Part Relationship.

This sample question demonstrates the Whole and Part Relationship:

> SLEIGH : RUNNER :: (*a*) violin : winds
> (*b*) automobile : wheel   (*c*) fringe : carpet
> (*d*) thorn : tendril   (*e*) bacon : eggs
>
>   Answer: (*b*)

The part on which a *sleigh* moves is the *runner*, just as the part on which an *automobile* moves is the *wheel*.

In this sample question, the first word, *sleigh*, is the whole, and the second word, *runner*, is a part of that whole. Only in choice (*b*) does the first word denote a whole and the second, a part. In choice (*d*) both words denote plant parts. In choice (*e*) each word can denote either a whole or a part, depending upon whether we look at it as a single dish or as a component of "bacon and eggs."

Consider this example of the Part and Whole Relationship:

CONTROL COLUMN : AIRPLANE :: (*a*) deck : ship
(*b*) engine : locomotive   (*c*) keel : boat
(*d*) propeller : airplane   (*e*) helm : sailboat

Answer: (*e*)

In this question, all the choices fit into the Part and Whole Relationship. The directions for the analogy question ask you to select the lettered pair of words or phrases that expresses a relationship *most similar* to that of the capitalized pair. To identify the pair that is most similar, you must determine which part has a relationship to the whole that is most like the one between *control column* and *airplane*. To do this, you must define the part and its function rather closely. The statement should be, "The *control column* is the part of the *airplane* that governs the rudder and helps turn the plane, in the same way that the *helm* is the part of the *sailboat* that governs the rudder and helps turn that craft."

Here is a sample question that illustrates the Part and Part Relationship:

HOOF : ANTLER :: (*a*) paw : mane
(*b*) pistol : trigger   (*c*) claw : fender
(*d*) cushion : couch   (*e*) fur : coat

Answer: (*a*)

Hoof and *antler* are each part of a deer, in the same way that *paw* and *mane* are each part of a lion.

4. Function, Action, Composition, Etc., Relationships

This category covers several similar types of relationships, including the following:

a. The first term describes the function of the second.
b. The first term describes an act of the second.
c. The first term describes a device used by the second.
d. The first term describes the composition of the second.
e. The first term describes a product of the second.

In all instances, of course, the terms of any pair can be reversed. In other words, the first term can be an agent whose act is described by the second term, and so on. Some examples of relationships in this category are:

a. CHOP : AX *Chop* describes a function of an *ax*.
b. DAREDEVIL : STUNT A *daredevil* may perform a *stunt*.
c. BOW : ARCHER A *bow* is a weapon (tool) used by an *archer*.
d. ASPHALT : ROADS *Asphalt* is used to make *roads*.
e. DIE : TOOLMAKER A *die* is cut (made) by a *toolmaker*.

A subdivision of this category, the Associational Relationship, is a catchall to cover relationships between words that are commonly associated with one another. "Gourmet : truffles" forms an associational relationship. A *gourmet* is a connoisseur of fine foods, and *truffles* is the name of a food highly prized by gourmets. If you can't fit a relationship into any other category, use your background and your intuition to think of a way in which the words are associated. Just putting them into a sentence may be enough to set you on the right track. Be flexible in applying this category—and all others—but be precise in framing the formula statement.

Let's look at a sample question for the Function Relationship:

GENERALS : COMMAND :: (*a*) senators : filibuster
(*b*) teachers : moralize   (*c*) representatives : legislate
(*d*) judges : condemn   (*e*) waiters : order

Answer: (c)

Generals, as one of their primary functions, *command*, just as *representatives*, as one of their primary functions, *legislate*. Senators may filibuster on occasion, but that is not their primary function. In choice (*d*), the second term describes one function of judges but not a primary function. As their primary function, judges preside over trials and deliver decisions. The correct answer is choice (*c*).

5. Characterization Relationship

In the Characterization Relationship, one term characterizes the other in some way. The characterization can be one that describes a trait that you usually associate with the thing characterized—for example, "inventor : ingenious" or "artist : imaginative"—or it can be a characterization that is opposite to that which we usually associate with the thing described—for example, "autocrat : egalitarian" or "friend : treacherous."

If the relationship in the capitalized pair is one in which the characterization is of the former type, then you must look for a similar characterization among the answer choices. If the capitalized pair consists of an opposite characterization, you must look for an opposite characterization relationship among the choices.

DIPLOMAT : TACTLESS :: (a) autocrat : peremptory
(b) charlatan : guileful   (c) chauvinist : intolerant
(d) gymnast : agile   (e) coward : intrepid

Answer: (e)

The relationship in the capitalized pair is the opposite of what we would normally expect: Diplomats are usually thought of as being tactful, not tactless. Similarly, cowards are usually fearful, not intrepid. Therefore, choice (e) is the correct answer. In all the other choices, the second term provides a characterization that we usually associate with the first term. The statement for this question should be, "A *diplomat* is not usually *tactless*, just as a *coward* is not usually *intrepid*."

Here is another example of the Characterization Relationship:

HOST : HOSPITABLE ::   (a) optimist : pessimistic
(b) humanitarian : altruistic   (c) idealist : cynical
(d) pragmatist : impractical   (e) skeptic : credulous

Answer: (b)

Choice (b) is the correct answer. A *humanitarian* is, by definition, concerned with the welfare of mankind, and *altruistic* means unselfishly devoted to others. On the basis of those meanings, you can say, "A *host* can be characterized as *hospitable*, just as a *humanitarian* can be characterized as *altruistic*." The other choices are all opposite characterizations and therefore incorrect.

6. Classification Relationship

When the first word of a pair is classified by the second word, or vice versa, the pair fits into the Classification Relationship category. The Classification Relationship can also be termed the Defining Relationship; one word of a pair defines the other.

RATTLESNAKE : REPTILE :: (a) cow : herd
(b) chimpanzee : animal   (c) human : mammal
(d) flounder : invertebrate   (e) lobster : seafood

Answer: (c)

A *rattlesnake* is classified as a *reptile*, just as a *human* is classified as a *mammal*. Choice (a) is an example of the Part and Whole Relationship, not the Classification Relationship: A *cow* is one part of a *herd* of cows. *Chimpanzee* in choice (b) is a type of *animal*, but this classification is much more general than the one expressed in the capitalized pair. In choice (d), *flounder* is incorrectly classified as an *invertebrate*. It is actually a vertebrate. *Lobster* in choice (e) is indeed *seafood*, but this classification is not analogous to the biological classification in the capitalized pair. Choice (c) is the correct answer.

7. Sequential Relationship

In this category, the first word denotes an item that usually follows or is followed by the item denoted by the second word. Don't confuse this relationship with the Cause and Effect Relationship. In the Sequential Relationship there is no causal factor.

TUESDAY : MONDAY ::   (a) happy : gift
(b) August : July   (c) second : third
(d) hour : minute   (e) ignite : flame

                                                          Answer: (b)

Tuesday follows *Monday*, just as *August* follows *July*. In choice (c), the order is wrong; *second* does not follow *third*. Choice (e) is incorrect for more than one reason: The relationship is causal, rather than sequential, and the order is not, as in the capitalized pair, in reverse sequence.

8. Synonymous Relationship

The Synonymous Relationship, as the name indicates, is one in which the two words of the pair are similar in meaning. When the capitalized pair in an analogy question consists of synonyms, look for the synonymous pair among the answer choices.
Here is a sample question that illustrates the Synonymous Relationship:

CORPULENT : OBESE ::   (a) hard : heavy
(b) bold : bald   (c) grim : grime
(d) slim : slender   (e) stout : stern

                                                           Answer: (d)

Corpulent and *obese* both mean "very fat" and are synonyms in the same way that *slim* and *slender*, meaning "thin," are synonyms.
Analogy questions are based heavily on vocabulary. You must, therefore, be prepared to use all the techniques you would use for the antonym question. Be especially alert to the possibility that words have secondary meanings.

9. Antonymous Relationship

In the Antonymous Relationship, the two words of the capitalized pair are opposites. Therefore, the correct answer choice will also be a pair of opposites.

Analyze the following sample question:

MOROSE : CHEERFUL ::   (*a*) dim : intemperate
(*b*) portly : diminutive   (*c*) anon : shortly
(*d*) reticent : loquacious   (*e*) cranky : vexatious

Answer: (*d*)

Morose is the opposite of *cheerful*, just as *reticent* is the opposite of *loquacious*. Choice (*d*) is the correct answer.

WINNING STRATEGIES FOR SOLVING THE GRE ANALOGY/WORD RELATIONSHIP QUESTION

Keep in mind the following strategies when you answer the GRE analogy/word relationship question. If you follow these suggestions, you will greatly improve your chances of successfully answering this type of question on the actual exam.

Use the word relationship category approach to the GRE analogy question. This approach is probably the most important strategy at your disposal. It is usually faster and easier to determine the category of a given pair than it is to construct a statement about it. Furthermore, as soon as you have identified the category, you are in the advantageous position of knowing specifically what you are looking for: degree of difference, characterization, cause and effect, or another type of relationship. Your efforts are therefore focused, and you can solve the problem more effectively and efficiently.

Use the formula statement as a crucial element of your overall attack on the question. Remember that the words in your statement must appear in the order that they appear in the question. Your statement about the words in the capitalized pair must highlight the most significant aspect of their relationship. The balancing statement about the words in your answer choice should be structured just like the statement about the capitalized words. If the two halves of your formula statement, the one dealing with the capitalized pair and the one dealing with the answer pair, are phrased in exactly the same way, and if you cannot make the same statement about any of the other answer choices, you almost certainly have the correct answer.

Keep parts of speech parallel. If the capitalized pair consists of two words of the same part of speech (two nouns, two adjectives, two adverbs, etc.), both words of your answer pair will be the same part of speech.

If the capitalized pair consists of words of different parts of speech—noun and verb, noun and adjective, or any other combination of parts of speech—the pair in your answer choice will consist of the same parts of speech as those in the capitalized pair, in the same order.

Watch carefully for certain strong clues such as very specific terms, very general terms, and function terms. A specific term in the capitalized pair will almost certainly be matched by a specific term in the corresponding term of your answer choice. So, too, with the other strong clues.

If you are unable to find an answer pair that parallels the capitalized pair, try one of the following:

a. Reexamine the capitalized relationship; you may have missed the significant aspect.
b. Take a fresh look at the capitalized words *and* the answer choices; words have several meanings, and you may be applying the wrong one.
c. Restate the formula, trying a slightly different approach.

The category approach is highly useful, but it isn't perfect. For example, some word relationships will be variations of the categories named in this section. If you cannot fit the capitalized pair into any category, you can still make the formula statement. If you can't make a significant statement, make any relational statement. If you can eliminate two of the answer choices by this method, at least you will be in a position to make a viable guess.

The GRE Sentence Completion Question

The task that the GRE sentence completion question sets for you is simple, but it tests a number of areas. You are given a sentence with one or two blanks where words have been omitted, and five words or pairs of words lettered (*a*) through (*e*). You are asked to select a lettered word or pair of words to fill the blanks and complete the sentence. You must complete the sentence so that it is logical, coherent, and meaningful, and your answer choice must meet the requirements of style, diction, and usage.

The GRE sentence completion question tests your ability to grasp the meaning of a sentence in which one or more words are missing. It also tests your mastery of vocabulary as demonstrated by your ability to choose words that complete the sentence so that it is logical and meaningful. Finally, the question tests your understanding of sentence structure and the interrelationships among various parts of a sentence.

Of the five answer choices offered, only one can fill in the blanks so that the completed sentence meets the criteria set forth. Selecting the correct answer is not a guessing game; all the information you need for making the correct choice is contained in the incomplete sentence. But you must be able to analyze and utilize the clues.

You should first familiarize yourself with the question format, the directions for the question, and the scope and nature of the task. The directions and the sentence completion question that follow are very similar in format and wording to what has appeared on recent editions of the test:

> Directions: Each of the sentences below has one or more blank spaces indicating where a word or words have been omitted. Each sentence is followed by five words or sets of words lettered from (a) to (e). Select the lettered word or set of words that, inserted to replace the blanks, BEST completes the meaning of the sentence as a whole.
>
> The ancient city of Pompeii lay – – – in the shadow of Mount Vesuvius for more than 1700 years under a deep layer of volcanic – – –.
>
> (a) discretely . . . heat
> (b) comatose . . . eruption
> (c) buried . . . debris
> (d) sheltering . . . lava
> (e) despairing . . . activity
>
> Answer: (c)

As you can see, two words have been omitted from this sentence. You must select the lettered pair of words that, when substituted for the blanks, completes the sentence so that it is logical and meaningful and satisfies the requirements of correct diction and usage.

The incomplete sentence in the sample question tells you a great deal even before you fill in the blanks: for seventeen centuries, Pompeii lay under a deep layer of something volcanic. "Deep layer" is a significant phrase that can help you eliminate some of the second word choices. Use substitution to check their appropriateness: "Lay under a deep layer of volcanic heat"? *Heat, activity,* and *eruption* are not usually described as forming layers. Pompeii may have lain under a deep layer of *debris* or *lava* but not under the others.

Though *lava* seems a possible choice for the second blank, it can be eliminated for two reasons: The first word in choice (d), *sheltering,* doesn't fit from the point of view of usage or meaning, and "volcanic *lava*" is a redundancy. Lava, by definition, is volcanic.

Debris is the only word that seems to fit the second blank. Does the first word of choice (c) fit the first blank? Of course; Pompeii could properly be described as having lain *buried* if it was under a deep layer of volcanic *debris.*

The remaining choices make no sense at all. The sentence as completed by choice (c) satisfies all the criteria established for this type of question.

APPROACHES TO THE GRE SENTENCE COMPLETION QUESTION

Unlike the antonym and analogy questions, the GRE sentence completion question does not lend itself to a single check for correctness. For the antonym question, all you need ask is whether or not your answer choice is an opposite of the capitalized word; for the analogy question, you need only ask if the relationship of the capitalized pair is parallel to the relationship of the answer pair. For the sentence completion question, however, you must deal with greater subtleties of language and structure, but there are ways of approaching each question that will help you uncover clues more readily.

Before we explore the helpful strategies available to you, let us point out your major resource for answering sentence completion questions: your own sense of language. The ability to close gaps in linguistic structures such as sentences is almost, but not quite, intuitive. Almost everyone has the ability to complete sentences. You have probably done so in conversation with others many times. Your clues are usually the context of the conversation, the structure of the sentence, and the direction of movement of the words just prior to the pause in the other person's speech. The approaches we will now look at build on these elements.

Contextual Clues

In terms of the sentence completion question, context is the incomplete sentence itself. Context can tell you something about the setting of the sentence's action, or the nature of the subject, or the period of time that is being written about. In the following example, contextual clues give you background information that leads you directly to the answer.

> Every year thousands of Moslems make a(n) – – – to the holy city of Mecca.
>
> (a) expedition
> (b) tour
> (c) excursion
> (d) junket
> (e) pilgrimage
>
> Answer: (e)

Each of the five answer choices for this question denotes some sort of trip. Since only one of the words can be correct, you must ask yourself two questions: How do these trips differ from one another? and Which one best completes the sentence?

In answer to the first question, an *excursion* is a pleasure trip, an *expedition* is a journey for a specific purpose (like exploration), a *junket* is a trip at public cost, a *pilgrimage* is a long journey to a shrine, and a *tour* is a trip or excursion that is usually circular and ends back at its starting point.

Now we are ready to answer the second question. Two significant words in the sentence, "Moslems" and "Mecca," are contextual clues that should help you decide the nature of the trip. Mecca, according to the sentence, is a holy city. You can deduce that the trip the Moslems make to Mecca is a *pilgrimage*, a long journey to a shrine.

If you were not able to infer, on the basis of contextual clues, that the trip many Moslems make is a pilgrimage, you could have determined the correct answer on the basis of the demands of diction and usage. People make a tour *of*, not *to*, a place; they *go on*, not *make*, an excursion or junket; and they *mount, launch, form,* or *organize*, not *make*, an expedition. Of the choices, the only kind of trip people *make* is a *pilgrimage*. From the standpoint of correctness of diction and usage, the correct answer is choice (*e*).

Expectation Intensifiers

Certain words in our language act as signals. Their presence at the beginning of a sentence permits us to anticipate how the sentence will conclude. We have labeled one such class of words "expectation intensifiers." When you come across an expectation intensifier in a sentence, you can be fairly sure that the expectation of one part of the sentence will be met in the other part of the sentence.

Here are some examples of expectation intensifiers:

therefore	since	consequently
because	thus	as a result

The following sentence completion question uses an expectation intensifier:

He labored industriously at the job for long, weary hours, giving – – – of his energy and loyalty, no matter how great the demands; as a result, when the plant superintendent's position fell vacant, he was – – – nominated by the directors.

(*a*) grudgingly . . . thoughtlessly
(*b*) sparingly . . . almost
(*c*) some . . . again
(*d*) unstintingly . . . unanimously
(*e*) freely . . . reluctantly

Answer: (*d*)

The first half of the sentence tells you how hard the subject worked. Certainly, no one could work like that *grudgingly* or *sparingly*. Those adverbs do not fit the context. The only two choices that have first words that are suitable for the first blank are (*d*) and (*e*).

The second part of the sentence starts with "as a result." What outcome would you expect from unstinting or freely given loyalty and hard work? Try the two endings: he was "reluctantly nominated," or "unanimously nominated." If he had been reluctantly nominated, it would have been *despite* having worked so hard, not *as a result* of having worked so hard. You must conclude that the correct answer is choice (*d*).

The expectation intensifier "as a result" tells you that the subject of the sentence, through his actions—as described in the first part of the sentence—caused the outcome described in the second part of the sentence.

The following sentences illustrate how expectation intensifiers prepare us for the expected:

- Because he was always prepared, he was the only one who passed the surprise exam.
- He drank heavily, ate all the wrong foods, and skipped most of the training drills; consequently, he was dropped from the team.
- He was a brilliant scholar and an outstanding athlete; therefore, we were not surprised when he received a Rhodes scholarship.

In each of the above, the expectation intensifier tells you to anticipate that the end result will not be a surprise.

Reversal Indicators

Just as some words serve as expectation intensifiers, certain others signal that you are going to see a reversal of what you would ordinarily expect. When these words appear in a sentence, they indicate that there was, is, or will be, a reversal of expectations. Listed below are some reversal indicators:

although	notwithstanding	still
despite	nevertheless	yet
however	even though	but

The following sentence completion question uses a reversal indicator:

His most recent novel was a commercial – – –, even though the leading critics of the literary establishment – – – him to the skies for his glowing insights and masterful characterizations.

(a) failure ... praised
(b) venture ... exposed
(c) success ... extolled
(d) advertisement ... panned
(e) project ... launched

Answer: (a)

The reversal indicator "even though" tells you that there are only two logical possibilities: Either the novel was a success "even though" the critics panned it, or the novel was a failure "even though" the critics praised it. The only other possibility is that the sentence is meant to be ironic, but no clues support this idea.

The latter part of the sentence indicates that the critics praised the novelist. They could not have *panned*, *launched*, or *exposed* him because *launched* and *exposed* make no sense when inserted in the second blank, and *panned* in this context is not idiomatic—the idiom is "praised to the skies," not "panned to the skies." Besides, the critics would not pan a writer for "glowing insights and masterful characterizations"; they would praise him.

The only conclusion you can arrive at is that his novel was a commercial *failure* even though the critics *praised* him to the skies. The correct answer is choice (*a*).

Stylistic Clues

Certain elements of style and grammatical structure can serve as useful clues for solving the sentence completion question. When writers use series of phrases that have repetitious aspects, you can tell how to fill in a blank by noting the structure of the phrases that precede and follow it. Sometimes the presence of a colon can indicate that a series of similar words, phrases, or clauses will follow to enlarge on or give examples of what has already been written.

The following sentence completion question contains such stylistic clues:

Quentin was an enigma to the rest of us: smiling and relating amusing anecdotes one moment; sneering and hurling malicious barbs the next; philosophical and – – – one day; hail-fellow-well-met and outgoing the next; unfeeling and flinty sometimes; warmly – – – and giving at other times.

(*a*) pragmatic . . . withdrawn
(*b*) depressed . . . distant
(*c*) introspective . . . sympathetic
(*d*) thoughtful . . . hostile
(*e*) taciturn . . . loquacious

Answer: (*c*)

The sentence starts by telling you that Quentin was an enigma, and the colon leads you to expect a series of remarks or examples that will illustrate this. The two contrasting phrases that follow show that Quentin's behavior was unpredictable. Since they are first in a series of such phrases, you can assume that the writer, for reasons of style and consistency, will follow with other phrases consisting of contrasting remarks that will illustrate Quentin's enigmatic behavior. So, if Quentin was hail-fellow-well-met and outgoing one day, he would undoubtedly be philosophical and *introspective* another day; if he was unfeeling and flinty sometimes, he had to be warmly *sympathetic* and giving at other times.

Some grammatical constructions indicate that linked words must be similar in nature: "not only – – – but also – – –." Other constructions indicate that words must be opposites: "not – – – but rather – – –."

Although Roger is generally considered to be a highly opinionated person who brooks no opposition, he does not – – – but rather – – – those who, on principle, disagree with his views.

(a) despise . . . admires
(b) value . . . compels
(c) crush . . . dazzles
(d) single out . . . isolates
(e) attack . . . reveals

Answer: (a)

Your innate sense of language structure can sometimes help you find the answer to the sentence completion question. In the sample above, if you say, "he does not blank but rather blanks," you can sense the opposing character of the missing words. The only words among the choices that are in opposition to each other are those in choice (a). Recognizing that "although" is a reversal indicator will help you see that choice (a) is the correct answer. You would usually expect that someone who brooks no opposition would have contempt for those who disagree with him. The reversal indicator tells you to expect the opposite.

Logical Analysis

Logical analysis requires that you examine a sentence clause by clause, phrase by phrase, and sometimes word by word to understand each of its components and establish the interrelationships of the parts.

Let's analyze the following sentence completion question:

In late autumn, bears store a(n) – – – of fat in and around the muscles of their bodies, as a form of insurance against the rigors of winter, to help guarantee their – – – through their long hibernation.

(a) abundance . . . appetite
(b) oversupply . . . termination
(c) plenitude . . . emergence
(d) hoard . . . survival
(e) minimum . . . decease

Answer: (d)

The clause that starts with "bears" tells you that bears store fat. The next phrase tells you why: It is insurance against the rigors of winter. The infinitive phrase says that storing the fat helps to guarantee something.

Logic tells you that insurance serves a useful purpose and that a guarantee is meant to protect one's best interests. An animal that is hibernating has no need for a guaranteed *appetite*. As for *emergence*, animals don't emerge "through" their hibernation but, rather, "after." Certainly, bears would not want to guarantee their own *termination*, nor their *decease*. The only word that fits the bears' self-interest is *survival*, the second word in choice (*d*). Since the first word of choice (*d*), *hoard*, fits the first blank of the sentence, choice (*d*) must be the correct answer.

It is impossible to prescribe a simple approach to logical analysis. The approach will vary according to the structure of each individual sentence. You must strive to understand each part of the sentence, try to make connections between sentence elements, and use common sense.

SUMMARIZING THE VARIOUS APPROACHES TO THE GRE SENTENCE COMPLETION QUESTION

The preceding approaches to the GRE sentence completion question will be useful in many instances, but they cannot help you with all sentence completions. You should always be aware of the value of contextual clues, expectation intensifiers, reversal indicators, and stylistic clues. In addition, you should look carefully at the structure of the sentence, the logic of the language, the vocabulary used in the sentence, and any other aspect of writing that offers itself for examination.

Logic can tell you that a sentence, although grammatically correct, does not make sense. Attention to diction and usage can tell you that a word choice is incorrect. The simple fact that words take different prepositions can be of importance. For instance, if you filled a blank with the word choice "concerned," so that the sentence then read, "He felt concerned of the outcome . . . ," you would know the choice was wrong: "Concerned" does not take the preposition "of."

If your language sense is well developed, you may be able to complete the sentence with words of your own without referring to the answer choices. If you can do so and arrive at a meaningful completed sentence, the words you inserted will serve to guide you to the correct answer among the choices offered.

No matter how you arrive at your choice of an answer on the GRE sentence completion question, ask yourself these questions before accepting your choice as correct:

- Does the sentence, with the blanks filled, make a meaningful statement?
- Are the words that fill the blanks correct as to diction and usage?
- Does the completed sentence meet the criteria of standard written English? Is it the kind of sentence that an educated English-speaking person would write?

If you can't answer yes to each of these questions, you'd better take another look at the choices.

The GRE Reading Comprehension Question

The reading comprehension question of the GRE contains much more material than the other verbal question types. When you work the reading comprehension problem, you do not deal with the meaning of a single word, as you do in the antonym question, or the relationship between a pair of words, as you do in the analogy question, or even the analysis of an unfinished sentence, as you do in the sentence completion question. Instead, you answer several questions based on a reading passage of 300–550 words taken from published materials.

Before you consider how best to approach the reading comprehension question, you should follow our standard procedure of familiarizing yourself with the content and format of the directions. The sample directions that follow are closely patterned after those that have appeared on the GRE in the past:

> Directions: In the series of selections below, each passage is followed by questions based on its contents. Read the passage and choose the best answer for each question based on the contents of the passage. The questions must be answered on the basis of what is stated or implied in the reading passage.

Remember that you are to judge the correctness of an answer on the basis of what is *stated* or *implied* in the passage. This means that even if the information runs counter to what you believe to be correct, base your answer on what the passage says, *not* on what you have read elsewhere and *not* on what you believe to be true.

Familiarize yourself with these directions now. Do not wait until test time to wrestle with what they mean. The wording of the actual test directions will differ somewhat from the wording used here, but the general sense will remain the same. To be on the safe side, when you actually take the GRE, read the directions quickly just to make sure that there have been no changes.

The reading passages that you will encounter on the GRE have been taken from published materials dealing with:

> *Biological Sciences*: zoology, ecology, botany, etc.
> *Social Studies*: history, anthropology, sociology, government, etc.
> *Humanities*: art, music, literature, philosophy, etc.
> *Physical Sciences*: physics, chemistry, astronomy, etc.

Do not be alarmed if you have no background knowledge in the subject area covered by a passage. Each passage will contain all the background and information you need to answer the questions that follow it.

The source of the materials for the passages is of interest only to the extent that you are now able to anticipate the kind of material you will find on the test.

A SAMPLE READING PASSAGE AND SOME SAMPLE QUESTIONS

The format and structure of the reading comprehension question is illustrated in the sample passage and the questions that follow. This sample passage is somewhat shorter than the usual passage on the GRE, but in terms of the type of material used and the nature of the questions, it is typical of the easier passages on the exam. In the practice tests in this book you will find more difficult samples drawn from a variety of sources, with questions that will cover the range of difficulty you can expect to encounter on the GRE. These questions will include all the types of reading comprehension questions you will need to be familiar with.

Just for good measure, and because your guess is apt to be as sound as mine, here are a few current theories about the origin of the Basques. Some of the professors who distill racial theories out of skulls and gutturals believe them to be connected with those Berbers whom I mentioned several chapters ago as the possible descendants of one of the earliest tribes of prehistoric Europeans, the so-called Cromagnon race. Others claim that they are the survivors who saved themselves on the European continent when the romantic island of Atlantis disappeared beneath the waves of the ocean. Still others hold that they have always been where they are now and don't bother to ask where they came from. Whatever the truth, the Basques have shown remarkable ability in keeping themselves aloof from the rest of the world. They are very industrious. More than a hundred thousand of them have migrated to South America. They are excellent fishermen and sailors and iron workers, and they mind their own business and keep off the front page of the newspapers.

1. Which of the following does the author suggest is the correct origin of the Basques?
   (a) They are the survivors of Atlantis.
   (b) They are connected with the Berbers.
   (c) Their guttural language comes from the skullmen.
   (d) They are descendants of the Cromagnons.
   (e) The author isn't sure of their origin.

2. The author's main purpose in this passage seems to be to
   (a) explain the origin of the species
   (b) trace the ancestry of the Basques
   (c) characterize the Basques without much concern for theoretical speculation as to their origin
   (d) establish the link between the Berbers and the Cromagnons
   (e) advocate the belief that Atlantis is not just a romantic myth

3. The word "distill," as used in the second sentence of the passage, most nearly means
   (a) vaporize and then condense, as for purification or concentration
   (b) obtain, extract, or condense by or as if by distillation

(c) infuse

(d) instill

(e) let fall in drops

The answers to the sample questions will be explained in detail later in this section. First, let us consider how to approach the reading comprehension questions. If you do not have a method that works for you, or if you feel insecure with the method you are now using, here is an approach that has been used by many with great success on reading comprehension questions.

AN APPROACH TO THE GRE READING COMPREHENSION QUESTIONS

The five-step approach to the GRE reading comprehension questions that we will now outline is very efficient in terms of the speed with which it permits you to answer questions. It is goal oriented. Is your goal comprehension of the passage, or is it answering all the questions? Comprehension of the passage does not mean you will be able to answer all the questions. This method does not deny the need for comprehension; it simply focuses on what you need for the GRE. If you grasp the passage's content completely but cannot answer the questions, you have not achieved your goal. If you answer all the questions correctly but don't completely understand the passage, you *have* achieved your goal.

Your first reaction after reading the following description of this reading question approach may be that it is time-consuming. It is not. With very little practice you will find that this technique is a time saver.

Step No. 1. Read the Questions Quickly.

Skim over the questions at a moderately fast rate. Determine from this quick inspection which questions seem to deal with materials directly stated in the passage, which seem to call for the use of inference, which seem to ask you to make evaluations, and so on.

Read the questions quickly! Step No. 1 is a preliminary step. Don't spend too much time on it. You will be rereading the questions in a subsequent step.

The purpose of Step No. 1 is to give you an idea of what you should be looking for as you read the passage.

Step No. 2. Read the Passage at Your Fastest Rate.

Read the passage at your fastest rate of reading—short of skimming— without worrying about full comprehension at this point.

As you read, try to keep the questions in mind, and if you come across material that seems related to any of the questions, hold the place in the passage with your finger or mark it with a pencil, and go back to check the question's wording.

If the material seems applicable, (1) mark the question number in the margin of the passage alongside the relevant part, and (2) circle your provisional answer choice under the question.

Resume reading where you had left off, and repeat the process outlined above.

Don't worry if you can't recall all the questions while you are doing this first reading!

Don't worry if you can't find materials relating to all of the questions during this first reading!

The purpose of Step No. 2 is to let you get an overview of the structure of the passage and to familiarize you with the relative position, in the passage, of key words, key facts, key ideas.

Step No. 3. Reread the Questions at Your Best Rate for Comprehension, and Check Materials in Known Locations in the Passage.

Reread the questions one at a time. This time, as you read, do so at your best rate of reading for comprehension. If after you have read a question you have an idea of the location in the passage of material that answers that question, find that place and reread the material to see if it is relevant and answers the question. If it does, mark the answer in the appropriate place on your answer sheet.

If you have no idea as to the location in the passage of material that is relevant to that question, go on to the next question! Don't skim through the passage on "fishing expeditions" in search of answer material unless you have a fairly good idea of where that material is placed in the passage. Skimming without strong ideas as to the location of relevant materials is an uneconomical use of time.

Where you have already noted relevant material during Step No. 2, check the question and the applicable portion of the passage quickly and enter your answer on your answer sheet.

The purpose of Step No. 3 is to permit you to go through the more accessible questions quickly so that you may concentrate on the more taxing questions during the next two steps.

Step No. 4. Reread the Passage at Your Best, Most Comfortable Rate of Reading for Comprehension.

This step will be your second and final complete reading of the passage. This time read the passage at your most comfortable rate of reading for comprehension, but don't backtrack as you read.

As you read, keep the unanswered questions in mind, following the same process as in Step No. 2. If you come across material that seems related to the question, hold the place in the passage with your finger or mark it with a pencil, and go back to check the question's wording.

If the material seems applicable, (1) mark the question number in the margin of the passage alongside the relevant part, and (2) circle the provisional answer choice under the question.

Resume reading where you had left off, and repeat the process outlined above.

Resist the temptation to abandon this approach! Don't backtrack! Don't skim! Keep on reading!

The aim of Step No. 4 is different from that of Step No. 2. You already have some idea of the overall structure of the passage; your second, more thoughtful reading should permit you to pick up more subtle clues. Furthermore, you should now have fewer questions to concentrate on since you probably have already answered one or two in previous steps.

Step No. 5. Reread Those Questions That Are Still Unanswered, and Proceed as in Step No. 3.

This step calls for a third rereading of the questions that you have not as yet succeeded in answering.

Follow the procedures in Step No. 3: If after you have read a question you have an idea of the location in the passage of material relevant to the question, go to that location, reread the material to make sure that it is applicable and, if it is, enter the answer in the appropriate place on your answer sheet.

If you can't readily connect the question to material you can locate in the passage, don't start skimming in a random search.

Read on for further clues about answering GRE reading comprehension questions.

ADDITIONAL SUGGESTIONS FOR ANSWERING GRE READING COMPREHENSION QUESTIONS

The five steps we have discussed provide a structured basic approach to the reading comprehension question of the GRE, but there are other procedures, techniques, and approaches to the question that you should bear in mind.

Certain types of questions may better be answered after you have completed the five steps: *main idea* questions, *best title* questions, *style* questions, *author's purpose* or *application of author's principles* questions, and certain *inference* questions. In the course of following the five-step basic approach, you will probably be able to answer easy and moderately difficult questions of the type mentioned, but you may have to try other approaches for the more resistant questions.

Main Idea Questions

Save consideration of "main idea" questions until you have gone through the five-step basic approach. Then ask yourself one or both of the following questions: "In a short phrase or sentence, what is the *topic* of this passage?" and "How would I summarize this passage most succinctly, that is, in the fewest possible words?" The answer to either of those two questions would provide a good clue to the GRE main idea question, which is usually phrased, "What is the main point of this passage?"

One point to remember when trying to determine the main point of the passage is that the answer choices will very often include statements that present minor or secondary points of the passage. Just because a choice may state a point that is contained in the passage does not make that choice correct. Ask yourself, "Does this choice correctly answer the question, 'What is the *main point* of this passage?'"

Frequently, in passages that consist of several paragraphs, the answer choices offered for a main idea question will give the main point of one or more paragraphs. The main point of the passage has to include and encompass the main points of all the paragraphs combined, not just the main points of one or some of the paragraphs of the passage. To be the correct choice for the main idea question or, for that matter, any other question, the answer must be completely correct, not partially correct.

Best Title Questions

The "best title" type of question is another form of main idea question which often confuses GRE test takers, many of whom are not aware that the word "title," as used in this question, does not have the meaning that we usually attribute to this word—that is, the name by which a book, play, story, essay, or other piece of writing is known. As used in the GRE reading comprehension question, the word "title" means the phrase or sentence that best summarizes what the passage as a whole is about.

Best title questions are usually worded: "Which of the following would be the most appropriate title for the passage?" or "Which of the titles below best describes the content of the passage?" In either case, the question is not really concerned about a title in the sense of a catchy or interest-provoking name for the passage. Rather, the question seeks the answer to the unstated or implied question, "Which of the following phrases or sentences best summarizes what this passage, as a whole, is about?"

As in the main idea question, do not accept as an answer a sentence or phrase that tells what *part* of the passage is about. What is only partially true is, in this case, not an acceptable answer. When deciding what the passage as a whole is about, be sure that you do not select a summary statement that sums up only a part of the passage. Select a statement, phrase, or sentence that sums up the *entire* passage.

Questions Calling for Information Directly Stated in the Passage

A common type of question is one that asks you to identify or locate information directly stated in the passage. Questions that ask who, what, where, or when—those questions that ask for dates, places,

---

names, and quantities—can usually be answered by locating and identifying information that is directly stated in the passage.

The fact that a question's answer is directly stated in the passage does not necessarily mean that finding that answer will always prove easy. You must be aware that the question may often paraphrase what is in the passage, thus making identification of the information more difficult. For instance, suppose the question read:

> Which of the following personality traits was most highly regarded by the ancient Greeks?
> (a) courtesy
> (b) cunning
> (c) generosity
> (d) loyalty
> (e) fortitude

You would be looking for the mention of those traits as you read the passage. However, you would be well advised to keep in mind the possibility that those traits might be mentioned through the use of paraphrase or synonym. Thus, unless you were watching for words or phrases that mean the same as "courtesy," "cunning," "generosity," "loyalty," or "fortitude," you might not be able to locate the answer to the question. In the passage, "courtesy" could be written as "politeness" or "civility" or "polite behavior." Similarly, "cunning" could be described as "guile," "generosity" as "munificence," "loyalty" as "fidelity," or "fortitude" as "stoicism." Be aware, then, that in looking for a particular key word you should be prepared to recognize the meaning of that word even when it is contained in the form of a paraphrase or a synonym.

As always, be sure to read the question carefully to be certain that your choice of an answer meets the demands of the question. A choice that offers a verbatim (word-for-word) piece of information from the passage is not necessarily the correct choice merely because it contains true statements. To be correct, the information in your selected answer must respond to the question.

Inference Questions

Some of the questions in the reading comprehension portion of the GRE cannot be answered by referring to directly stated material in the reading passage. These questions can be answered only by inference.

Inference is the process of arriving at a conclusion by indirect means: reading between the lines, using logical reasoning, or linking circumstantial evidence together to build a rational conclusion. Inference is the interpretation of indirect statements, hints, suggestions, and the like.

In some instances, indirect evidence is so strong that you can arrive at a conclusion that is as unmistakably correct as if the evidence had been directly stated. In other instances, you may only be able to say that you arrived at a logical and probable conclusion, one that seems more nearly correct than any other. Remember that instructions for GRE questions usually ask you to choose the best answer available, even if that answer is not a perfect one.

Application of the Author's Principles Questions

Some questions ask you to predict how the author of the passage would act, what position he would take, what his attitude or approach would be in a hypothetical (imaginary or conjectural) situation. You should assume that there is enough evidence in the passage to permit you to determine the author's attitudes, views, or beliefs so that you have a basis for concluding what his probable behavior would be in other situations.

If the author rhapsodizes about nature and the great outdoors, you can probably predict that, given a choice, he would prefer a backpacking vacation to one spent at the gaming tables of Las Vegas. If his passage is a tirade against rigid controls on personal freedoms, you can assume that he would favor the American or the British form of government to that run by a totalitarian elite.

To apply the author's principles, then, you must first determine from the evidence in the passage what he advocates in the concrete situation described, and then you can apply that knowledge to the hypothetical, or imaginary, situation. In a sense, the question that seeks to apply the author's principles is related to the inference question, since you must draw conclusions from indirect evidence.

Author's Style or Mood Questions

Some reading comprehension questions ask you to identify the author's mood, attitude, or style. Such questions are best answered after you have completed the other questions, because your response must be based on an overall understanding of the passage rather than on individual bits of evidence. While it is true that an author may be very blunt about his attitude in a particular matter, very often his overall attitude or mood is revealed more subtly or indirectly. Read carefully and note value-packed words or sentence constructions.

In order to evaluate or determine an author's style of writing, you must be familiar with some of the words used to describe style. Examples of these words are "formal," "informal," "florid," "understated," "scholarly," "hyperbolic," and so forth.

"Informal writing" is writing that employs colloquial expressions, idiomatic terms, everyday language, and comparatively uncomplicated sentence structure. "Scholarly language" is formal writing that uses high-level vocabulary in complex sentence structures, technical terms, and carefully qualified statements. A "florid" style is one that uses very ornate language, flowery adjectives, and literary-sounding figures of speech.

"Understated writing" is writing in which the author plays down what he is saying so that he sounds unexcited or cool. "Hyperbole," on the other hand, is the use of great exaggeration, as in the expression, "I've told you a million times . . ." or "He hit the ball a mile."

Familiarizing yourself with different writing styles will help you to determine an author's mood or attitude and to gain a better understanding of the reading passage.

ANSWERING THE SAMPLE QUESTIONS

Let's return to the sample passage on the Basques on page 43. After you have read the questions, as suggested in Step No. 1 of the suggested approach to the reading question, you start on Step No. 2, the first reading of the passage. If question 1 has stuck in your mind, the word "origin" in the first sentence should trigger a reaction. As soon as you see that word, you should look back at the question. You would probably quickly realize that the author is saying that although there are theories about the origin of the Basques, he doesn't know which of them is correct. You would put a number "1" in the margin next to the first sentence and circle choice (e) as a tentative answer to the question.

Question 2 is an author's purpose question, and you should be able to answer it after you have completed Step No. 2 or Step No. 4. You probably would note after the first reading that (d) is only a distraction, since the passage deals mainly with Basques—the Berbers and Cromagnons being mentioned only in passing. Similarly, the reference to Atlantis is only marginal. You would know already, after having answered question 1, that the passage is not trying to trace the ancestry of the Basques, since the author has said that your guess is as good as his in deciding which theory is correct. Choice (a) is a deliberately misleading one, because the phrase "the origin of the species" usually refers to Darwinian evolutionary theory, and the passage is not about evolution. We can conclude that the author considers most of the passage unimportant except the portion beginning, "Whatever the truth . . ." The answer, therefore, is (c).

In question 3, you are given several dictionary meanings for the word "distill" and are asked which meaning applies in the context of the passage. That the professors "distill" theories out of "skulls and gutturals" implies that they start with bone structures and language sounds, and that from evidence about these, they arrive at their theories. Choice (a) gives a meaning that describes a physical process. Choice (b) gives a similar meaning but suggests that the word can be used figuratively, for it says, ". . . as if by distillation." You can see that the professors don't arrive at their theories by vaporizing bones and then condensing that vapor in a literal sense, but they could do so in a figurative sense. The answer to the question is choice (b).

PART III

Strategies for the Quantitative Ability Questions

The GRE Quantitative Ability Questions: What They Are Like, What They Test

Part III of this book describes the three types of GRE quantitative ability (or mathematical) questions and provides some techniques for answering each type. You should keep in mind that, unlike the verbal ability questions, the quantitative ability questions may test your skill on any GRE mathematical topic. For example, a quantitative comparison section may present you with problems involving fractions, percentages, exponents, averages, and areas. In other words, the *format* of a question does not tell you what to expect regarding its *content*. For that reason you will find separate sections (Parts V and VI) for review and practice of the various mathematical topics tested on the GRE. Use those sections to sharpen your mathematical skills. This section is meant to sharpen your test-taking skills by telling you exactly what to expect in the quantitative sections of the GRE.

As mentioned in Part I, the three types of questions in the quantitative ability section of the GRE are:

> Quantitative Comparison
> Discrete Quantitative
> Data Interpretation

Each quantitative ability section consists of 30 problems, of which 15 are quantitative comparison problems. On recent editions of the GRE, the remaining 15 questions have been divided into 5 data interpretation problems and 10 discrete quantitative problems.

The quantitative ability sections test your ability to solve problems using arithmetic, algebra, and informal geometry.

The arithmetic tested includes the addition, subtraction, multiplication, and division of whole numbers, fractions, and decimals. The exam also tests your knowledge of averages; percents; and the properties of odd and even integers, prime numbers, and factors of integers.

The algebra tested includes formulas and linear equations, exponents and roots, the combination of signed numbers, factorable quadratic equations, and the solution of verbal problems using algebraic techniques. Negative or fractional exponents are not tested on the GRE.

The geometry on the GRE is informal in the sense that it does not stress ability to construct proofs, knowledge of theorems, or conversion of one unit of measure to another. It does test angle relationships; right-triangle relationships; parallel line theorems; and the measurement of area, volume, and perimeter.

See Part V of this book if you need to review any or all of these topics and follow up, if necessary, by working the appropriate problems in Part VI.

The makers of the GRE deliberately construct the quantitative ability questions to be solved through insight and mathematical reasoning, not through lengthy calculations. If you can determine the concept the question is designed to test, you should be able to solve it quickly. If you find yourself filling up the margins of your test book with calculations, you are probably missing something; stop and try to find a different approach to the problem. However, never spend an excessive amount of time on a single problem. Remember that you have an average of one minute to spend on each quantitative ability problem. Continue through the section, solving the problems you can. Then, as time allows, go back to the tough problems. If you can't solve a problem by trying different approaches, make a reasonable guess. Remember, you risk nothing by guessing.

The GRE Quantitative Comparison Question

The GRE quantitative comparison questions are probably unlike any you have ever seen in your mathematics courses. Take the time now to learn how they work, so that during the test you can concentrate on solving them.

In each quantitative comparison question you are given two quantities arranged in two columns, A and B. Your task is simple: compare the quantities and decide whether one is greater than the other, they are equivalent, or their relationship cannot be determined from the information given. If the quantity in Column A is the greater of the two quantities, mark answer choice (*a*). If the quantity in Column B is the greater, mark answer choice (*b*). If the two quantities are equivalent, mark answer choice (*c*). If you determine that not enough information is given in the problem to make the comparison, mark answer choice (*d*). Note that there are only four answers to choose from in the quantitative comparison sections. Never fill in answer choice (*e*) on your answer sheet while working on these problems.

Sometimes information or a figure is centered between the columns above the two quantities. Always consider this information carefully and thoroughly when comparing the quantities in the columns. The test makers do not include this information as a false lead; it always has some bearing on the problem.

The quantitative comparison questions, even more than the other types of questions, test your mathematical reasoning and insight. It's not simply a matter of solving two problems and then seeing which answer is greater. The quantities given in Columns A and B look like the answers to problems already solved, yet you will still have to compare them. Some strategies to help you do this are listed here.

- Don't waste time working out extended calculations. Instead, think about the mathematical concept being tested. If you can determine the concept, you can usually solve the problem with a minimum of arithmetic. For instance, if you are given $(-12)^6$ in Column A and $(-12)^7$ in Column B, you could spend a lot of time working out the multiplication. But the smart test taker will recognize that what is really being tested is the property of powers of negative numbers. If you know that negative numbers raised to even powers are always positive and negative numbers raised to odd powers are always negative, you will quickly see that the correct choice is (a).

- Be sure to consider all types of real numbers when considering the given quantities, especially fractions and negative numbers. For example, 2^3 is greater than 2^2, but $(1/2)^3$ is less than $(1/2)^2$. So don't jump to a conclusion if you are given x^3 in Column A and x^2 in Column B. Anytime you have a problem in which you can determine that in some cases quantity A is greater than quantity B and in other cases quantity B is greater than quantity A, the correct answer choice is (d).

- If there are no variables in the given quantities, then a real value can always be established for the quantities. Therefore, the correct answer for quantities involving no variables can never be (d). It must be (a), (b), or (c).

- Don't rely on the appearance of the figures given with the problems; use only the definite factual information the figures contain. Don't assume, for instance, that an angle is 90 degrees or that a triangle is equilateral unless it is marked as such. If you feel that the given figure is confusing, sketch another in your test book. Just make sure that you use only the factual material given.

Below you will find directions for the quantitative comparison questions, some sample questions, and explanations of the answers to the questions. As always, familiarize yourself with the directions now but scan them again at test time to make sure they have not changed.

Directions: The following questions each consist of two quantities, one in Column A and one in Column B. Compare the two quantities and choose answer

- (a) if the quantity in Column A is greater;
- (b) if the quantity in Column B is greater;
- (c) if the two quantities are equal;
- (d) if the relationship cannot be determined from the information given.

All letters such as x, y, and n represent real numbers. A symbol appearing in both columns represents the same quantity in Column A as it does in Column B.

In some questions, information concerning one or both of the quantities to be compared is centered above the two columns.

Figures are generally not drawn to scale, unless otherwise stated. You may assume these figures lie in a plane, unless it is indicated they represent solid figures.

Lines that appear to be straight may be assumed to be straight lines.

Example: <u>Column A</u>   <u>Column B</u>

                50% of 40   40% of 50

Solution: Since 50% = 1/2, the quantity in Column A has a value of 20. Since 40% = 2/5, the quantity in Column B has a value of 20. Therefore, the quantities in the two columns are equal and the correct answer is choice (c).

Example: <u>Column A</u>   <u>Column B</u>

$$m < 0, \ n < 0, \text{ and } m \neq n$$

$$\frac{m^2 - n^2}{m - n} \qquad\qquad m - n$$

Solution: Since $m^2 - n^2 = (m + n)(m - n)$, you can reduce the fraction in Column A to $m + n$ by canceling out $m - n$, a factor common to both the numerator and the denominator. Now, since m and n are both negative, $m + n$ is less than $m - n$. Therefore, the quantity in Column B is greater than the quantity in Column A and the correct answer is choice (b).

Example: <u>Column A</u>   <u>Column B</u>

$$5x = 3t$$
$$3y = 2t$$

            x y

Solution: You can solve the first equation for x in terms of t, and you can solve the second equation for y in terms of t. However, since you don't know whether t is positive, negative, or zero, you cannot compare x with y. Therefore, the correct answer is choice (d), the relationship cannot be determined from the information given.

Example: <u>Column A</u>   <u>Column B</u>

The sum of the degree measures of the exterior angles of a regular 6-sided polygon	The sum of the degree measures of the exterior angles of a triangle

Solution: The sum of the degree measures of the exterior angles of *any* polygon, no matter how many sides it has, is 360. Since a triangle is a polygon, the quantities in the two columns are equal and the correct answer is choice (c).

Example: <u>Column A</u>   <u>Column B</u>

              $\sqrt[3]{345}$ $\sqrt{47}$

Solution: Start with the quantity in Column B. Since $\sqrt{47} < \sqrt{49}$ and since $\sqrt{49} = 7$, you know that $\sqrt{47} < 7$. Now consider the quantity in Column A. Since $7^3 = 343$ and since $343 < 345$, you know that $\sqrt[3]{345} > 7$. Therefore the quantity in Column A is greater and the correct answer is choice (a).

The GRE Discrete Quantitative Question

"Discrete quantitative" is just an elaborate way of saying individual math problems to be solved. These problems are "discrete" in the sense that each contains all the information needed to solve it. Your task is simply to select the correct answer. These questions are much more traditional than the quantitative comparison problems and more like the multiple-choice questions you have answered on mathematics tests. Each discrete quantitative question has five answers to choose from; remember that you must consider choice (e) again.

The discrete quantitative questions require a bit more mathematical manipulation than the quantitative comparison questions. As with any group of problems, you will find that some are very simple and straightforward and take little time and effort to solve. Others require more effort to read, understand, set up, and solve. It is all right to spend a little extra time doing arithmetic on these latter problems as long as you bear in mind that you have an average of one minute to spend on each problem and that extra time spent in one place will have to be made up elsewhere.

Here are two strategies to keep in mind when working on the discrete quantitative questions:

- Read each question carefully to determine exactly what is being asked. Don't determine how many miles a train has traveled, for instance, when the question asks how many miles the train has left to go. Both numbers are probably given in the answer choices, so be careful.
- Scan the answer choices offered before you start working on a problem. This will give you an idea of the sort of answer you should be looking for (a decimal notation, a fraction, a quantity rounded to the nearest multiple of 1,000, and so on) and may also give you a clue as to how to solve the problem. For example, if all the answers are different powers of the same base, you may realize that the problem is asking you to factor an expression.

On the facing page are sample directions for the discrete quantitative questions, followed by some sample questions with explanations of how to solve them. Familiarize yourself with the directions now, but scan them again at test time for any changes.

Directions: For each of the following problems, select the best answer from among the five choices given.

Example: If 5½% of $x = 11$, then $x =$

(a) 180   (b) 200   (c) 220   (d) 240   (e) 275

Solution: Change 5½% to 0.055:

$$0.055x = 11 \qquad \text{(Multiply by 1000)}$$
$$55x = 11000$$
$$x = 200$$

The answer is (b).

Example: Find the value of $\sqrt[3]{3^5 + 3^5 + 3^5}$.

(a) 4   (b) 5   (c) 6   (d) 8   (e) 9

Solution: $\sqrt[3]{3^5 + 3^5 + 3^5} = \sqrt[3]{3 \times 3^5}$
$$= \sqrt[3]{3^6}$$
$$= 3^2$$
$$= 9$$

The answer is (e).

Example: If $y^2 - 4y - 5 = 0$, what is the value of $(y - 2)^2$?

(a) −1   (b) 3   (c) 5   (d) 9   (e) none of these

Solution: First, factor the quadratic equation and solve for y:

$$y^2 - 4y - 5 = 0$$
$$(y - 5)(y + 1) = 0$$

Thus, $y = 5$ or $y = -1$. Substitute each value for y in the second equation:

$$(y - 2)^2 = (5 - 2)^2 \qquad (y - 2)^2 = (-1 - 2)^2$$
$$= (3)^2 \qquad\qquad\qquad = (-3)^2$$
$$= 9 \qquad\qquad\qquad\quad = 9$$

The answer is (d).

Example: An angle of a triangle is equal to the average of the other two angles of the triangle. If this angle measures $y°$, then what is the value of y?

(a) 54   (b) 58   (c) 60   (d) 65   (e) 68

Solution: Let the other two angles of the triangle be $x°$ and $z°$. Then $y = (x + z) \div 2$ and $x + y + z = 180$. Substitute $x + z = 180 - y$ in the first equation and solve for the value of y:

$$y = \frac{x + z}{2}$$

$$y = \frac{(180 - y)}{2}$$

$$3y = 180$$

$$y = 60$$

The answer is (c).

The GRE Data Interpretation Question

The GRE data interpretation question is based on information presented in tables or graphs. Each table or graph is followed by a set of questions that test your ability to analyze and synthesize the information given and to winnow out the information you need to solve the problems.

The test makers seem to favor graphs over tables. When interpreting graphs, you should keep in mind that different types are used for different purposes. *Circle graphs* are commonly used to show distribution. *Line graphs* are frequently used to represent change in a particular variable or variables. *Bar graphs* are used mainly for comparisons.

Here are some strategies for answering the data interpretation questions:

- Answer the data interpretation questions on the basis of the data given, your knowledge of mathematics, and common facts (for example, the number of inches in a foot). Don't bring any outside information you may have or know to bear on these problems.
- Scan each graph or table quickly to get an idea about it. Then read the questions closely to see what they ask for. When you return to the graph or table, you should have a better idea about the kind of information it provides.
- Some questions may seem too long to work on at one time; break these questions down into parts and then substitute values from the table or graph for each part. When you put the parts back together, the question should make much more sense. Use your test book to jot down notes.
- Again, avoid long calculations. Use estimates and round off large numbers.
- Remember that data in graphs or tables are arranged to have a *visual* meaning. Whenever you can, interpret the data visually. For instance, a quick glance at a bar graph might give you a general idea of the value of the data, whereas you might spend a lot of time trying to figure out the precise value mathematically.

• When reading across a table or graph, make sure you don't read a value from the wrong place. Use the edge of your answer sheet as a straightedge.

The directions for the data interpretation questions are the same as those for the discrete quantitative questions. Some sample data interpretation questions, with explanations of how to solve them, are given below.

Questions 1–4 refer to the following table:

Deaths per 100,000 People in County X from Selected Causes

Year	Pneumonia	Tuberculosis	Cancer	Accidents
1981	78	60	55	67
1982	101	59	59	75
1983	100	57	61	80
1984	125	56	57	91
1985	98	50	58	75

1. If 1,200 people died in County X from accidents in 1983, the population of County X that year was approximately

(a) 96,000   (b) 150,000   (c) 960,000   (d) 1,500,000
(e) It cannot be determined from the information given.

Solution: The table tells us that 80 people per 100,000 died from accidents in 1983. We may then set up the proportion

$$\frac{80}{100,000} = \frac{1,200}{x}$$

where x is the population of County X in 1983. Thus,

$$80x = 1,200 \times 100,000$$
$$x = 1,500,000$$

Therefore, the answer is (d).

2. The total death rate in County X in 1985 was approximately 14 deaths for every 1,000 living persons. What percentage of the total deaths were due to cancer?

(a) 1.2   (b) 3.6   (c) 4.1   (d) 6.4   (e) 4

Solution: Fourteen deaths per 1,000 is equal to 1,400 deaths per 100,000. Since there were 58 deaths per 100,000 due to cancer, the percentage of deaths due to cancer was

$$\frac{58}{1,400} \approx 0.041 = 4.1\%$$

Therefore, the answer is (c).

3. During the five years shown in the table, what was the approximate percentage decrease in deaths per 100,000 people due to tuberculosis in County X?

(a) 34   (b) 32   (c) 23   (d) 17
(e) It cannot be determined from the information given.

Solution: Deaths per 100,000 due to tuberculosis went from 60 in 1981 to 50 in 1985. This was a decrease of 10. Thus,

$$\frac{10}{60} = \frac{1}{6} = 16\frac{2}{3}\% \approx 17\%$$

Therefore, the answer is (d).

4. During the five years shown in the table, what was the approximate average annual number of deaths due to pneumonia in County X?

(a) 93   (b) 89   (c) 86   (d) 78
(e) It cannot be determined from the information given.

Solution: Since we do not know the population of County X for every year in the five-year period, we cannot determine the number of deaths due to pneumonia every year. Hence, we cannot determine the average annual number of deaths due to pneumonia in County X. The answer is (e).

Questions 5–7 refer to the following graph:

The Budget Dollar

Fiscal Year (1985)

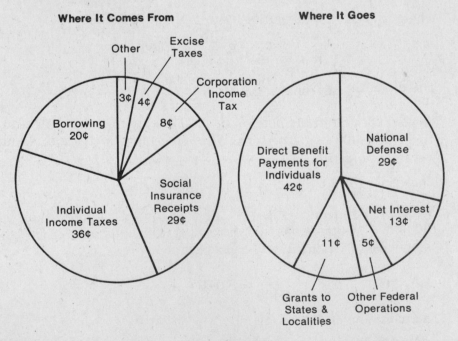

5. If the budget for national defense for fiscal year 1985 was $305 billion, what was the approximate total budget expenditure for that year (in billions of dollars)?

(a) 620   (b) 780   (c) 1,050   (d) 1,140
(e) It cannot be determined from the information given.

Solution: Since 29¢ of every dollar was spent on national defense in 1985, 29% of the total budget equals $305 billion. Thus,

$$0.29x = 305$$
$$x = \frac{305}{0.29} \approx 1,050$$

Therefore, the answer is (c).

6. In 1985, the amount of direct benefit payments for individuals was approximately what percent greater than the amount collected from individual income taxes?

(a) 16.7   (b) 15   (c) 13.5   (d) 12
(e) It cannot be determined from the information given.

Solution: The amount of direct benefit payments was 42¢ per dollar. The individual income tax was 36¢ per dollar. Thus, $42 - 36 = 6$. What percent of 36¢ is 6¢?

$$\frac{6}{36} = \frac{1}{6} = 16\frac{2}{3}\% \approx 16.7\%$$

Therefore, the answer is (a).

7. According to the graph, approximately how much more corporation income tax, in cents per dollar, was collected in 1985 than in 1984?

(a) 3   (b) 4   (c) 5   (d) 6
(e) It cannot be determined from the information given.

Solution: According to the graph, the money collected for 1985 from corporation income tax was estimated to be 8¢ per dollar, but no such information is given for 1984. Thus, no comparison can be made. The answer is (e).

PART IV
Strategies for the Analytical Ability Questions

The GRE Analytical Ability Questions: What They Are Like, What They Test

At least two sections of the GRE deal with analytical ability. Each section contains 25 questions. These questions are broken down into two types:

Analytical Reasoning
Logical Reasoning

The 19 or 20 analytical reasoning questions in each section, which appear in groups of 3 to 7 questions, ask you to analyze a fictional situation. The 5 or 6 logical reasoning questions, which appear singly or in groups of 2 or 3 questions, relate to a brief argument with certain logical features. The two question types are intermingled in each section and are not identified by type. Both types measure your ability to analyze unfamiliar situations, think clearly and logically, detect unstated assumptions underlying arguments, and so on, *without* presupposing any specialized knowledge of logic or any other field.

The directions are straightforward. You have 30 minutes to answer 25 questions, so you have 1.2 minutes for each question. You should leave the most time-consuming questions for last. Individual questions related to a single situation may vary in difficulty, so don't let one difficult question cause you to skip an entire group of questions. In general, the questions in a group are independent of each other; you do not need to answer one to solve the others.

The two types of questions are discussed in more detail below. Sample questions and explanations of how to solve them are provided.

The GRE Analytical Reasoning Question

Analytical reasoning questions refer to sets of statements or conditions that define a fictitious problem or situation. The statements may define the positions of people around a table, the order of a series of events, various permissible groupings among people, or other sets of relationships among things. The questions test your ability to draw logical conclusions from information presented and to synthesize that information in order to deduce the actual structure of or interrelationships among things, times, events, and so on. Basically, you are asked to analyze unfamiliar situations in a clear, logical manner.

Each set of statements or conditions is followed by from two to seven questions. The questions are independent of each other; that is, you do not need to answer any one in order to solve the others. Furthermore, each question usually is totally self-contained; if it presents any new information, the information pertains to that question and no other. Hence, usually you may answer the questions in a set in any order you choose.

As mentioned above, these questions do not require any specialized knowledge of logic, mathematics, or any other field. All you need is the ordinary background information and skills that a college student is expected to have.

The most common question types involve:

- determining the physical or temporal order of things (for example, X is next to Y; Y is two steps from Z)
- ranking things according to one or two qualities (for example, John is taller and lighter than Ken; Ken is shorter and heavier than Steven)
- determining the composition of groups (for example, Susan will not play with Jane; Helen will not play with Susan)
- ascertaining family relationships (for example, X is married to Y and is Z's aunt; Z is A's brother and is B's son)

In a given situation, not all relationships may be defined. For instance, you may be able to deduce the relative weights of six athletes but not that of a seventh. In some situations the information will be given only in relative terms; in others you will deal with absolute values (such as numbers). The data may be definite (X is on first base), indefinite (A is either blue or red), or conditional (if Y is hot, then B is cold). You may be given some information that is superfluous—that is, the questions may be answered without it—but there will be no internal contradictions.

Also note these points:

- Only common sense is needed. This is not the case with the questions that test mathematical or verbal ability.
- Some questions in a group may be easy, and some hard. Work on the most time-consuming ones last.
- Some questions will be difficult, but the situations are not designed to trick or confuse you. Avoid reading unintended subtleties into the information presented.
- Pay special attention to qualifying words like *always*, *never*, *all*, *none*, *many*, *usually*, and *most*. They can crucially alter the meaning of a statement.
- Study the information presented very carefully, paying attention to all key words, before going on to the questions. Often you can figure out the entire structure of relationships so that all the questions in the group become relatively easy to solve.
- With most analytical ability questions, a diagram or table will help you to order your thinking. Such aids may suggest themselves to you as you study the information presented for each question set. As you work the problems in this book, you will develop insight into the types of questions that are more easily solved with such aids.

- The more complex situations generally are followed by a greater number of questions, so these problems are, on the average, no more time-consuming *per question* than are simpler question sets with fewer questions.

Here are some typical analytical reasoning questions with explanatory answers:

Questions 1–3 refer to the following:

The maple is taller than the birch and older than the elm.
The birch is taller than the oak and younger than the elm.
The elm is shorter than the birch and younger than the oak.
The oak is shorter than the elm and older than the maple.

1. Which tree is the tallest?

   (a) the maple
   (b) the birch
   (c) the elm
   (d) the oak
   (e) It cannot be determined from the information given.

2. The elm tree is younger than

   (a) the oak only
   (b) the maple only
   (c) the birch only
   (d) the oak and the maple only
   (e) the oak, the maple, and the birch

3. Which of the facts presented is not needed to list all the trees named in the correct order according to height and age?

   (a) The maple is taller than the birch.
   (b) The elm is shorter than the birch.
   (c) The oak is shorter than the elm.
   (d) The elm is younger than the oak.
   (e) The oak is older than the maple.

Answers:

1. Using capital letters to designate the trees, we find the following height relationships: M > B, B > O, B > E, and E > O. Therefore, the trees are, from tallest to shortest, M, B, E, and O. Since the maple is the tallest, choice (a) is correct.

2. The following age relationships are known: M > E, E > B, O > E, and O > M. Therefore, the trees are, from oldest to youngest, O, M, E, and B. Since both the oak and the maple are older than the elm, choice (d) is correct.

3. The information that the elm is younger than the oak is not needed. The other three statements dealing with age are enough to determine the order of all four trees: oak older than maple, maple older than elm, elm older than birch. It follows that the elm is younger than the oak. All four statements about height are necessary to determine the relative heights of the trees. The answer is (d).

This set of questions, with the exception of question 3, should have been relatively easy for you to solve. Now try another set of analytical reasoning questions.

Questions 4–6 refer to the following:

Six cars are parked in a parking lot in a single row.
The blue car is two spaces from the green car.
The yellow car is three spaces from the red car.
The black car is at one end of the row.
The white car is next to the red car.
The green car is three spaces from the black car.
The blue car is not next to the black car.

4. The white car is next to

(a) the blue car
(b) the black car
(c) the green car
(d) the yellow car
(e) either the blue car or the green car

5. The car farthest from the green car is

(a) the blue car
(b) the black car
(c) the red car
(d) the yellow car
(e) the white car

6. Two cars exchange positions in the lot in such a way that the green car is next to the red car and the white car is three spaces from the black car. Which of the following is (are) true?

   I. The white car is next to the yellow car.
  II. The green car is not next to the yellow car.
 III. The red car is one of the ones that moved.

(a) I only
(b) II only
(c) I and II only
(d) I and III only
(e) I, II, and III

Answers:

4. The cars may be arranged in their proper order by following any of several lines of reasoning. One such logical path is as follows:

STATEMENT: DEDUCTION:

Black is at one end.   ——— ——— ——— ——— ——— Bk
Green is 3 from black.   ——— ——— G ——— ——— Bk
Blue is 2 from green.   Bl ——— G ——— ——— Bk

or

——— ——— G ——— Bl Bk
Blue is not next to black. Bl ——— G ——— ——— Bk
White is next to red.   Bl ——— G W R Bk

or

Bl ——— G R W Bk
Yellow is 3 from red.   Bl Y G W R Bk

Notice that the chart indicating the positions of the cars takes shape gradually as each statement is considered. Also note that in this case it is helpful to consider the statements in an order different from that in which they are presented.

   The finished chart shows that the white car is next to the green one, so that (c) is the correct choice.

5. The finished chart shows that the car farthest from the green car is the black car. The answer is (b).

6. The arrangement that fits the conditions described is Bl–Y–W–G–R–Bk. Statements I and II, then, are true, but statement III is false, since the two cars that have exchanged positions are the green car and the white one. The answer is (c).

Questions 7–10 refer to the following:

For a certain sport, a team of three players is to be chosen from a group of eight players, subject to the following conditions:

(1) If neither A nor B plays, then C must play.
(2) B refuses to play with H.
(3) If C plays, then D does not play.
(4) If E plays, then F must also play.
(5) If G does not play, then H and either A or B must play.

7. Which of the following may be deduced from the conditions given?

   (a) If A and B do not play, D does not play.
   (b) If G plays, H does not play.
   (c) If either A or B plays, then C does not play.
   (d) If E does not play, then F does not play.
   (e) If H plays, then G does not play.

8. On how many different teams may E play?

    (*a*) 0   (*b*) 1   (*c*) 2   (*d*) 3   (*e*) 5

9. Which of the following teams may be chosen without violating any of the conditions given?

    I. ACG
   II. CFG
  III. BDF

    (*a*) I only
    (*b*) III only
    (*c*) I and II only
    (*d*) II and III only
    (*e*) I, II, and III

10. If F is injured and unable to play, how many different teams may be chosen?

    (*a*) 3   (*b*) 6   (*c*) 9   (*d*) 12   (*e*) 15

Answers:

7. Condition (1) says that any team without A and B must contain C, while condition (3) says that any team containing C must omit D. It therefore follows that any team without A and B must also omit D. Choice (*b*) is wrong because, while H must play if G does *not* play, no result follows from the fact that G plays. Choice (*e*) draws the same erroneous conclusion, although its logical form is different. Choices (*c*) and (*d*) are incorrect for similar reasons; they do not follow from the conditions given. The answer is (*a*).

8. All teams with E must also have F. The question is with whom E and F can play. This matter is easily settled when it is noted that if G does not play, both H and A must play. If G plays, the team is complete. However, if A and B don't play, C must. Therefore E cannot be on any team. The answer is (*a*).

9. Statements I and II give possible teams. Statement III gives BDF, a team that cannot exist, since any team without G must contain H. Since only statements I and II are true, choice (*c*) is the correct answer.

10. Until you reached this question, you did not have to come up with any complete list of possible teams. This is necessary now. If time is short, you might skip this problem and go on to the next question. If you have time to answer it, you should first list all teams containing A, then all teams containing B but not A, then all teams containing C but neither A nor B, and so on. The final list of possible teams is: ABG, ACG, ACH, ADG, ADH, AGH, BCG, BDG, and CGH. There

are, then, nine possible teams without F, making (c) the correct choice.

Questions 11–14 refer to the following:

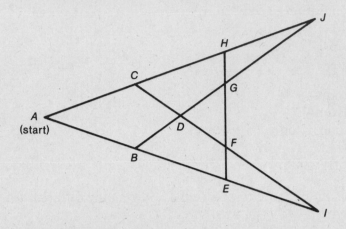

The diagram above represents a system of corridors through which a hungry rat must pass in order to reach food. The lettered points A through J represent food stations. Starting at A, the rat must follow the paths represented by the solid lines in order to reach the food stations. Movement back toward A is not permitted, although vertical movement, such as from G to F, is permitted. The rat may not pass through each food station more than once.

11. How many different paths lead to D?

(a) 1   (b) 2   (c) 3   (d) 4   (e) 5

12. If the first move is to C, then how many different paths lead to H?

(a) 1   (b) 2   (c) 3   (d) 4   (e) 5

13. Counting A and I, what is the *greatest* number of food stations that the rat may visit if it starts at A and ends at I?

(a) 4   (b) 5   (c) 6   (d) 7   (e) 8

14. How many different routes between A and I utilize six moves?

(a) 1   (b) 2   (c) 3   (d) 4   (e) 5

Answers:

11. Remember that A has been designated as the starting point. There are only two possible paths to D, namely A–C–D and A–B–D. The answer is (b).

12. Three paths begin with A–C and lead to H. These are A–C–H, A–C–D–G–H, and A–C–D–F–G–H. The answer is (c).

13. The greatest number of lettered food stations traversed between *A* and *I* is seven, answer choice (*d*). See answer 14 for a description of these routes.

14. Three possible routes between *A* and *I* utilize the maximum number of lettered areas (seven) and moves (six), so (*c*) is the correct answer choice. The routes are *A–C–H–G–F–E–I*, *A–C–D–G–F–E–I*, and *A–B–D–G–F–E–I*.

Questions 15–16 refer to the following:

Four people competing in a logic championship make the following statements:

Alfred: "Barry is the champion."
Barry: "Charlene is the champion."
Charlene: "I'm not the champion."
Dora: "I'm not the champion."

15. If only *one* of these statements is true, then who is the champion?

   (*a*) Alfred
   (*b*) Barry
   (*c*) Charlene
   (*d*) Dora
   (*e*) It is impossible for only one of the contestants' statements to be true.

16. If only *one* of the contestants' statements is false, then who is the champion?

   (*a*) Alfred
   (*b*) Barry
   (*c*) Charlene
   (*d*) Dora
   (*e*) It is impossible for only one of the contestants' statements to be false.

Answers:

15. These questions may be solved by trial and error. Let us assume, as question 15 asks, that only one of the four contestants' statements is true. We must take each contestant's statement to see what would follow if it were the only true one:

   Case 1: Alfred's statement true. That would make Barry champion. In that case, however, both Charlene's and Dora's statements also would be correct, since neither would be champion. Thus, Barry cannot be champion, for that would be consistent with three of the contestants' statements.

Case 2: Barry's statement true. With Charlene champion, Dora's statement would also be true. Thus, Charlene cannot be champion, for that would be consistent with two of the contestants' statements.

Case 3: Charlene's statement true. Since case 1 has already eliminated Barry as champion, if Charlene were correct that someone else is the champion, then that person would have to be either Alfred or Dora. If the champion were Alfred, then Dora would also be telling the truth; this eliminates him. But if the champion were Dora, no other statement would be true. *Thus, Dora being champion would be consistent with only one true statement.*

Case 4: Dora's statement true. The analysis of cases 1, 2, and 3 has eliminated Alfred, Barry, and Charlene from being champion.

The discussion proves that if only one statement is true, then it is Charlene's, and Dora is the champion. This makes choice (*d*) correct.

16. A process similar to that followed in question 15 may be used to answer this question, which assumes one false statement. A simpler way to answer the question is to note that case 1 in the previous answer involves three true statements and one false statement. Thus, Barry being champion fits the criterion of this question, and (*b*) is correct.

Questions 17–20 refer to the following:

Four horses were about to run a race. One of the jockeys made the following predictions prior to the start of the race:

1. There will be no ties for first, second, or third place.
2. Man O' War will beat Citation.
3. If Man O' War wins, then Secretariat will finish last.
4. If Secretariat finishes second, then Citation will finish first or third.
5. If Secretariat finishes third, then Man O' War will be last.
6. If Secretariat wins, then Citation will be second.
7. If Nashua does not finish second, then Citation will not finish second, either.

Amazingly, every prediction proved true!

17. Considering only statements 2, 3, and 4, how many different ways could the four horses have finished the race?

    (*a*) 2   (*b*) 5   (*c*) 6   (*d*) 7   (*e*) 8

18. Who finished first?

    (*a*) Secretariat
    (*b*) Citation

(c) Nashua
(d) Man O' War
(e) There is insufficient information to answer the question.

19. Who finished third?

    (a) Secretariat
    (b) Citation
    (c) Nashua
    (d) Man O' War
    (e) There is insufficient information to answer the question.

20. Consider an eighth true statement in addition to the seven the jockey made:

    8. If Nashua does not win, then Man O' War will finish third.

    Which of the following choices best expresses the relationship between this and the jockey's seven statements?

    (a) This statement is consistent with the others but adds no new information.
    (b) This statement contradicts statement 2.
    (c) This statement contradicts the combined meaning of statements 5 and 6.
    (d) This statement is contradictory to the jockey's predictions but does not contradict any one or two of them taken alone.
    (e) This statement adds new information that allows the second place finisher to be deduced.

Answers:

17. In a complicated situation such as this, it is best to start with any definite relationships that are given. In this case, only statement 2 gives a definite relation; the others are conditional in one way or another. One way to evaluate statements 2, 3, and 4 is to remember that Man O' War beat Citation. Furthermore, in the case in which Man O' War beat everybody and won, Secretariat finished last.

    A preliminary table showing the relations expressed in statements 2 and 3 may be drawn. The horses will be abbreviated as follows: Man O' War = MAN; Citation = CIT; Nashua = NAS; and Secretariat = SEC.

1	2	3	4
MAN			SEC
	MAN	CIT	
	MAN		CIT
		MAN	CIT

These meet the criteria of MAN beating CIT and of SEC finishing last if MAN won. The table may be fleshed out by adding the other horses.

1	2	3	4
MAN	CIT	NAS	SEC
MAN	NAS	CIT	SEC
SEC	MAN	CIT	NAS
NAS	MAN	CIT	SEC
SEC	MAN	NAS	CIT
NAS	MAN	SEC	CIT
SEC	NAS	MAN	CIT
NAS	SEC	MAN	CIT

Statement 4 must now be considered. The final possibility, with SEC second, does not meet the criterion expressed in statement 4. This leaves seven possible combinations meeting the constraints of statements 2, 3, and 4. Therefore, choice (*d*) is correct.

18. In order to solve this problem, let's list the seven possibilities from the preceding answer and then apply statements 1, 5, 6, and 7. The seven possibilities have been designated A through G:

	1	2	3	4
A	MAN	CIT	NAS	SEC
B	MAN	NAS	CIT	SEC
C	SEC	MAN	CIT	NAS
D	NAS	MAN	CIT	SEC
E	SEC	MAN	NAS	CIT
F	NAS	MAN	SEC	CIT
G	SEC	NAS	MAN	CIT

Statement 5 eliminates possibility F. Statement 6 eliminates possibilities C, E, and G. A, B, and D are the only remaining possibilities:

	1	2	3	4
A	MAN	CIT	NAS	SEC
B	MAN	NAS	CIT	SEC
D	NAS	MAN	CIT	SEC

Statement 7 dictates that if Nashua was not second, then Citation also was not second. This eliminates possibility A but leaves B and D. A review of all the statements will show that both B and D are possible finishes; the winner was either Man O' War or Nashua. Uncertainty about which of the two horses was the winner makes choice (*e*) correct.

19. Possibilities B and D both show Citation finishing third; this makes (b) correct.

20. This is a tricky question. Let us review the two possibilities consistent with statements 1–7.

	1	2	3	4
B	MAN	NAS	CIT	SEC
D	NAS	MAN	CIT	SEC

The hypothetical eighth statement concerns possibility B, the one in which Nashua did not win. Certainly this eighth prediction contradicts B; however, it says nothing about the case in which Nashua wins. This eighth statement is consistent with possibility D and allows the second place finisher to be known (Man O' War). This makes choice (e) the correct answer.

Questions 21–24 refer to the following:

The symbols A, B, and C correspond to the symbols W, X, and Y, though not necessarily in that order. The following statements apply to their relationship:

I. If A is not X, then C is not Y.
II. If B is Y, then A is X.
III. If C is not W, then B is Y.

21. Considering statements I and II *only*, which of the following must then be true?

(a) B is Y, C is W, and A is X.
(b) A is not W.
(c) A is X.
(d) A is W or Y, and C is W or X.
(e) B is not Y, A is not W, and C is not X.

22. Considering *only* statement III, how many different ways may A, B, and C correspond to W, X, or Y?

(a) 1   (b) 2   (c) 3   (d) 4   (e) 5

23. Considering statements I, II, and III together, choose the *most inclusive* true statement from among the following.

(a) B is Y, C is W, and A is X.
(b) A is X.
(c) B is X.
(d) C is W.
(e) A is X, B is W, and C is Y.

24. Which deduction may be made from statements I, II, and III?

(a) If B is Y, then C is W.
(b) If B is X, then C is Y.
(c) If C is W, then A is X.
(d) If C is W, then A is Y.
(e) If A is X, then B is W.

Answers:

21. Consideration of statements I and II only allows the following relationships to be deduced. From statement II, we can say that if B is Y, then A is X, and therefore C must be W. In table form:

A	B	C
X	Y	W

Statement I says that if A is *not* X, then C is not Y. If A were W, C could not be Y. This would leave B as being Y, which would violate the statement that if B is Y, then A must be X. This reasoning demonstrates that A cannot be W. Therefore, (b) is the correct answer choice.

We may demonstrate that the other choices are incorrect by listing all the possible relations between the symbols. The following four possibilities exist:

A	B	C
X	Y	W
X	W	Y
Y	X	W
Y	W	X

Note that statements I and II exclude no possibilities, except those in which A is W.

22. This question asks for the number of possible relationships between the symbols under the constraints of statement III only. One way to answer this is to construct another table, beginning with the different possibilities for C.

A	B	C
X	Y	W
Y	X	W

The above is clearly possible because statement III says nothing about the case in which C is W. The next step is simply to write down the possibilities in which C is X or Y (that is, *not* W) and in which B *is*

Y. There is only one relationship that meets these criteria:

A	B	C
W	Y	X

Altogether three possible combinations are allowed by statement III, making (c) correct.

23. This question asks for information about all three statements considered together. There are many ways to see which relationships satisfy all criteria. One way is to juxtapose the allowed possibilities from statements I and II with those from statement III. Any possibility found on both lists is therefore acceptable under the constraints of all three statements taken together. Here are the allowed relationships:

Statements I & II			Statement III		
A	B	C	A	B	C
X	Y	W	X	Y	W
X	W	Y	Y	X	W
Y	X	W	W	Y	X
Y	W	X			

The only relationships seen on both lists are:

A	B	C
X	Y	W
Y	X	W

In both of these possibilities, C is W, making (d) the most inclusive true statement.

24. This question is a reward for having worked through these complicated relationships. It is clear from the above list that only choice (a) presents a true statement of the relations between the symbols.

In general you will find that a difficult set of questions such as this usually has at least one easier question within it to allow you to make up the extra amount of time you have expended on working out the other problems in the set.

The GRE Logical Reasoning Question

The logical reasoning questions present brief arguments, opinions, or attempts at persuasion. You are asked to understand the logical features of these arguments, such as the underlying assumptions of the argument; points that would strengthen or weaken the argument; the validity of the evidence used to support the argument; the structure or method by which the argument is constructed; and the inferences that may be accurately drawn from the argument. There are one to three questions per argument.

The arguments may deal with any subject matter. They may include readings in social science, natural science, or the humanities; advertisements; speeches; and other forms of argument. No specific knowledge of any field is required, however. You are asked to apply a common-sense understanding of logic; you do not need to know advanced logical techniques and specialized terminology. If, as is likely, you have no formal training in logic, it is not worthwhile for you to acquire it in order to improve your score on the GRE.

Also keep in mind the following points:

- Read each argument and question very carefully, so that you understand exactly what is being argued and what is being asked. For example, if an illogical argument is presented, you may be asked to identify the flaw in the argument, to recognize information that would strengthen the argument, or to find another argument that makes the same logical mistake.
- Pay particular attention to key words such as *always, never, all, none, many, usually,* and *most.* They are crucial to logical argument. Take them literally. Remember: a single exception is enough to disprove a statement using *all* but not to disprove one using *most.*
- Assume nothing to be true except what is proven or such generally accepted facts as that the Earth is round or that $2 + 2 = 4$.
- Remember that an invalid argument remains invalid even if a conclusion drawn from it happens to be correct. Conversely, if valid reasoning based on an unsound premise leads to an unsound conclusion, you are expected to recognize the weakness of the premise.

Here are some examples of logical reasoning questions, with full explanations of how to solve them:

1. Being old is no handicap in politics. Senator Allen just won reelection at the age of 82.

   All of the following, *if true,* are valid objections to the above argument *except:*

   (a) Senator Allen was first elected to the Senate at the age of 34.
   (b) An image of youthful vigor is an important asset to a political career.
   (c) Most politicians over the age of 65 lose their elections.
   (d) Senator Allen's majority decreased markedly in each of his last two elections.
   (e) The great majority of today's successful politicians are young.

   Answer: The argument supports an assertion ("Being old is no handicap in politics") with one isolated example (Senator Allen). This sort of reasoning can be attacked in many ways. Choice (b) undermines the assertion by stating an advantage of youth over age. Choice (c) similarly attacks the statement by presenting contradictory data. Choice (d) weakens the supporting example by suggesting that as Senator Allen has aged, his electoral support has diminished. Choice (e) is a reasonable objection, suggesting that if most successful politicians are young, there must be some relative disadvantage to old age. Choice (a), however, merely gives an example of one successful young politician (who happens to be the senator mentioned in the argument). Since the argument did not claim that youth is a significant *disadvantage* in politics, this choice does not seriously weaken the author's reasoning.

2. Most cars that have been driven more than 100,000 miles run poorly; therefore, if the car I own has not been driven many miles, it will not run poorly.

   In its logical features, the preceding argument most resembles which of the following?

   (a) Either your car or my car runs poorly; since your car runs well, my car runs poorly.
   (b) Most old cars run poorly, but mine runs well.
   (c) Most wars last longer than one year; therefore, at least one war takes place every year.
   (d) Most priests are honest; therefore, if you are not a priest, you are dishonest.
   (e) Most horses are brown; therefore, if you bet on a horse, it is probably not black.

   Answer: The argument is illogical because it asserts that since most "A's" (old cars) do "B" (run poorly), then not having "A" will guarantee that "B" will not occur. In basic logical terms, it says: "If A implies B, then not-A implies not-B." Only choice (d) follows the same formula as the original argument.

3. Helen must be dishonest; she rose very quickly in business.

   The above conclusion would be valid only if it were true that

   (a) all females in business are dishonest
   (b) only dishonest people are in business
   (c) dishonest people rise quickly only in business
   (d) no honest women rise very quickly in business
   (e) some honest people outside of business may rise very quickly

   Answer: The argument clearly implies that because Helen advanced very quickly in business, she must be dishonest. For this implication to be correct, it must be true that the only way a woman can rise very quickly in business is by being dishonest. This is stated by choice (d).

Choice (*a*) is incorrect because the statement refers not to all business-women but only to those who are successful; choice (*b*) is incorrect for basically the same reason. Choices (*c*) and (*e*) are incorrect because they deal with an irrelevant subject, namely, the honesty or dishonesty of people *outside* the world of business.

4. The price of oil is dropping. This decline in price will spark an economic boom that will last for ten years.

An unstated assumption of the preceding argument is that

(*a*) oil prices will decline markedly
(*b*) no one will be hurt by a decline in oil prices
(*c*) oil companies have been making too much money
(*d*) the decline in oil prices will last about ten years
(*e*) oil is priced too high for the good of the economy

Answer: The argument is that declining oil prices spur the economy. An obvious underpinning of the argument is that the current oil price is higher than it should be for the welfare of the economy. Choice (*e*) expresses this. The other choices are not implicit in the argument.

5. Theater critic: "The play *Darkness at Midnight* is great. Everyone should rush out and purchase a ticket to it."

Which of the following statements best expresses the critic's opinion?

(*a*) She liked the play.
(*b*) The play will be touring nationwide soon, allowing everyone a chance to see it in person.
(*c*) The play is top-notch and has general appeal.
(*d*) To not see *Darkness at Midnight* would verge on being unpatriotic or antisocial.
(*e*) The critic has never seen a better play.

Answer: This question asks us to make some simple deductions. Certainly the critic felt the play was excellent. Since she urged "everyone" to buy a ticket, she must have felt the play had general appeal. Choice (*c*) expresses these views well.

Although (*a*) is true, saying that the critic *liked* the play does not convey the extent of her views. On the other hand, (*e*) overstates the critic's expressed views; the statement does not imply that the play is the best one she has ever seen. Choice (*b*) plays on the critic's statement that everyone should purchase a ticket to *Darkness at Midnight*, but it is not reasonable to take this statement literally. The word *everyone* does not refer to the entire country's population, and the statement does not suggest that the play will tour nationwide. Choice (*d*) is implausible; the critic's effusive praise of the play does not make a value judgment about those who do not see the play.

6. We now know that even a moderately elevated blood cholesterol level significantly increases the risk of cardiac disease in an individual. Americans eat a cholesterol-rich diet. If the amount of cholesterol the American diet contains were markedly reduced, the incidence of heart disease in Americans would also be markedly reduced.

Which of the following statements is *least* important in critically assessing the above argument?

(a) Lowered cardiac risk might raise the risk of other health problems.
(b) There is a link between diet and blood cholesterol levels.
(c) There is a link between blood cholesterol levels and body tissue.
(d) A "significantly" increased risk of cardiac disease is quantitatively important.
(e) Because of their diet, Americans are highly susceptible to cardiac disease.

Answer: The point raised by choice (a) may be valid, but it is not relevant to a critical assessment of the argument. The other choices point to important relationships within the logical structure of the argument.

7. Ty Cobb, who played baseball many years ago, was the greatest overall baseball player ever. He obtained 4,191 hits.

Which of the following beliefs is implicit in the above assertion?

(a) A single greatest athlete can be identified.
(b) Modern players are easy to compare with players from earlier times.
(c) Many other great players are overrated.
(d) No one has obtained more than 4,191 hits.
(e) Anyone who has obtained fewer than 4,191 hits is inferior to Ty Cobb as a baseball player.

Answer: It is easy to see that (e) is a true statement; the assertion is that *everyone* is inferior to Ty Cobb as a baseball player.

It is possible to err in answering this question because it is choice (e), the last one most people read, that is correct. Some of the other choices are effective "distracters," as misleading incorrect choices are called by specialists in test construction. Choice (a) is incorrect because it refers to a "greatest athlete," whereas the assertion refers only to baseball players. Choice (b) is wrong because it asserts that comparison between modern and old-time players is easy, whereas the assertion implies only that comparison is possible, not that it is necessarily easy. Choice (c) is not plausible. Choice (d) is also poor; the assertion does not imply that the greatest baseball player is the one with the greatest number of career hits; it simply states that the (allegedly) greatest player achieved 4,191 hits.

PART V

Review of Mathematics for the GRE

This part is a review of the mathematics tested in the quantitative sections of the GRE. The review is arranged by topic—signed numbers, fractions, decimals, percentages, and so on. Review the topics in which you feel weak. Then sharpen your skills by working out the practice exercises provided in Part VI. For your convenience, the practice exercises are also arranged by topic.

Signed Numbers

A *positive number* is a number whose value is greater than 0 (for example, +6, which is usually written as 6). A *negative number* is a number whose value is less than 0 (for example, −6). The *absolute value* of a number is its magnitude regardless of its sign; for example, the absolute value of both +6 and −6 is 6. The symbol for absolute value is two parallel lines on either side of a number; for example, $|-2|$ means "the absolute value of negative 2," which equals 2.

To add numbers with the same sign, follow these two steps:

1. Add the absolute values of the numbers.
2. Affix the sign the numbers have in common to the sum.

Example: $(-3) + (-7) = -10$

To add numbers with different signs, follow these two steps:

1. Subtract the number with the smaller absolute value from the number with the greater absolute value.
2. Affix the sign of the number with the greater absolute value to the difference.

Example: $(-7) + (+3) = -4$

To subtract one signed number from another, follow these two steps:

1. Change the sign of the subtrahend (the number being subtracted).
2. Add the two numbers, following the steps above.

Example: $(+7) - (-3) = (+7) + (+3) = +10$

To multiply or divide two signed numbers, multiply or divide their absolute values. Then affix a sign to the result according to the following rules:

1. If the two numbers have the *same* sign, the result is *positive*. For example, $(-8)(-5) = +40$; $(-40) \div (-8) = +5$.
2. If the two numbers have *different* signs, the result is *negative*. For example, $(-9)(+6) = -54$; $(-54) \div (+9) = -6$.

To multiply two or more signed numbers, remember these rules:

1. An *even* number of negative factors yields a *positive* product. For example,

$$(-2)^2 = (-2)(-2) = +4; (-2)^4 = (-2)(-2)(-2)(-2) = +16$$

2. An *odd* number of negative factors yields a *negative* product. For example,

$$(-2)^3 = (-2)(-2)(-2) = -8$$
$$(-2)^5 = (-2)(-2)(-2)(-2)(-2) = -32$$

Fractions

A *fraction* is basically a division problem. The fraction 9/3, for example, means "9 divided by 3." The top number in a fraction (in this case 9) is called the *numerator*; the bottom number (in this case 3) is called the *denominator*. The denominator indicates the number of parts into which something has been divided; the numerator indicates how many of these parts have been taken.

There are several types of fractions. A *simple* (or *common*) *fraction* is a fraction whose numerator and denominator are both whole numbers (for example, 3/4). A *complex fraction* is a fraction whose numerator or denominator is also a fraction (for example, ½/3).

A *proper fraction* is a fraction whose numerator is less than its denominator (for example, 3/7). A proper fraction has a value less than 1. An *improper fraction* is a fraction whose numerator is either equal to or greater than its denominator (for example, 5/5 or 8/5). Improper fractions have a value equal to or greater than 1.

A *mixed number* is a number that represents the sum of an integer, or whole number, and a fraction (for example, 3½, which means "3 + ½"). A mixed number is another way of expressing an improper fraction that has a value greater than 1. The improper fraction 9/5, for instance, can be expressed as a mixed number simply by carrying out the indicated division: $9 \div 5 = 1 + \frac{4}{5}$, or 1⅘.

Equivalent fractions are fractions that have the same value but different forms. The fractions 1/2, 2/4, 3/6, and 4/8, for example, are equivalent fractions (1/2 = 2/4 = 3/6 = 4/8). Two fractions are equivalent if their cross products are equal—that is, if the product of the numerator of the first and the denominator of the second is equal to the product of the denominator of the first and the numerator of the second.

Example: $\frac{1}{2} = \frac{3}{6}$ since $1 \times 6 = 2 \times 3$

You can change the form of a fraction without changing its value by multiplying or dividing both the numerator and the denominator by the same number.

Example: $\dfrac{3}{4} = \dfrac{3 \times 3}{4 \times 3} = \dfrac{9}{12}$ $\dfrac{9}{12} = \dfrac{9 \div 3}{12 \div 3} = \dfrac{3}{4}$

A fraction whose numerator and denominator are not evenly divisible by any common whole number except 1 is said to be expressed in *lowest terms*. The fraction 3/4, for instance, is said to be expressed in lowest terms because 3 and 4 are not divisible by any common whole number except 1.

To reduce a fraction to lowest terms, divide both the numerator and the denominator by their greatest common factor—that is, by the largest number that will divide both evenly.

Example: To reduce 12/30 to lowest terms, divide 12 and 30 by 6, the largest number that will divide both evenly:

$$\frac{12 \div 6}{30 \div 6} = \frac{2}{5}$$

Example: To reduce $12x/15x$ to lowest terms, divide $12x$ and $15x$ by $3x$, their greatest common factor:

$$\frac{12x \div 3x}{15x \div 3x} = \frac{4}{5}$$

To express two or more fractions in like terms, follow these three steps:

1. Find the lowest common denominator of the fractions. The lowest common denominator is the least common multiple of all the denominators—that is, the smallest number that all the denominators will divide evenly.
2. Multiply the denominator of each fraction by the number that will produce the lowest common denominator.
3. Multiply the numerator of each fraction by the same number as the denominator.

Example: To express the fractions 1/2, 3/4, 5/9, and 7/12 in like terms, first find the least common multiple of 2, 4, 9, and 12. That's 36. Then multiply, as shown here:

$$\frac{1 \times 18}{2 \times 18} = \frac{18}{36} \qquad \frac{3 \times 9}{4 \times 9} = \frac{27}{36} \qquad \frac{5 \times 4}{9 \times 4} = \frac{20}{36} \qquad \frac{7 \times 3}{12 \times 3} = \frac{21}{36}$$

To add or subtract fractions, follow these four steps:

1. Express all the fractions in like terms—that is, in terms of their lowest common denominator.

2. Add or subtract the numerators.
3. Place the result over the lowest common denominator.
4. Reduce the fraction to lowest terms.

Example: $\dfrac{1}{2} + \dfrac{3}{4} + \dfrac{5}{9} + \dfrac{7}{12} = \dfrac{18}{36} + \dfrac{27}{36} + \dfrac{20}{36} + \dfrac{21}{36} = + \dfrac{86}{36} = \dfrac{43}{18} = 2\dfrac{7}{18}$

Example: $\dfrac{m}{2} - \dfrac{m}{5} = \dfrac{5m}{10} - \dfrac{2m}{10} = \dfrac{3m}{10}$

To multiply fractions, follow these four steps:
1. Simplify the problem by canceling—that is, by dividing any numerator and any denominator by the largest number that divides both evenly.
2. Multiply the numerators.
3. Multiply the denominators.
4. Place the product of the numerators over the product of the denominators.

Example: To multiply 4/5 by 25/6, first cancel by dividing 4 and 6 by 2 and dividing 5 and 25 by 5. Then multiply:

$$\dfrac{\overset{2}{\cancel{4}}}{\underset{1}{\cancel{5}}} \times \dfrac{\overset{5}{\cancel{25}}}{\underset{3}{\cancel{6}}} = \dfrac{2 \times 5}{1 \times 3} = \dfrac{10}{3} = 3\dfrac{1}{3}$$

Example: To multiply $a^2/6$ by $9/a$, first cancel by dividing a^2 and a by a and dividing 6 and 9 by 3. Then multiply:

$$\dfrac{\overset{a}{\cancel{a^2}}}{\underset{2}{\cancel{6}}} \times \dfrac{\overset{3}{\cancel{9}}}{\underset{1}{\cancel{a}}} = \dfrac{a \times 3}{2 \times 1} = \dfrac{3a}{2}$$

To divide fractions, invert the divisor (the fraction you're dividing by); then multiply.

Example: $\dfrac{5}{8} \div \dfrac{15}{4} = \dfrac{\overset{1}{\cancel{5}}}{\underset{2}{\cancel{8}}} \times \dfrac{\overset{1}{\cancel{4}}}{\underset{3}{\cancel{15}}} = \dfrac{1}{6}$

Example: $\dfrac{\frac{1}{2}}{\frac{2}{3}} = \dfrac{1}{2} \div \dfrac{2}{3} = \dfrac{1}{2} \times \dfrac{3}{2} = \dfrac{3}{4}$

To convert a mixed number into an improper fraction, follow these three steps:

1. Multiply the whole number by the denominator of the fraction.
2. Add the product to the numerator.
3. Place the sum over the denominator.

Example: $5\dfrac{2}{3} = \dfrac{(5 \times 3) + 2}{3} = \dfrac{15 + 2}{3} = \dfrac{17}{3}$

It's often necessary and usually convenient to convert mixed numbers into improper fractions before you perform arithmetic operations on them.

To compare the values of two fractions, follow these three steps:

1. Multiply the numerator of the first fraction by the denominator of the second fraction.
2. Multiply the numerator of the second fraction by the denominator of the first fraction.
3. Compare the two products. The *numerator* that yields the greater product marks the fraction with the greater value.

Example: To determine whether 4/7 is greater than 5/9, first multiply 4 by 9 and get 36; then multiply 5 by 7 and get 35, as shown here:

$$36 \longleftarrow \dfrac{4}{7} \times \dfrac{5}{9} \longrightarrow 35$$

Since 36 is greater than 35, 4/7 is greater than 5/9.

Decimals

A *decimal fraction* is a fraction whose denominator is some power of 10 (such as 10, 100, 1000, and so on). A decimal fraction is written with a decimal point. For example, the form 0.423 is equivalent to 423/1000. In a decimal fraction, the number to the right of the decimal point represents the numerator of the fraction, and the number of places to the right of the decimal point represents the power of 10 in the denominator. One place represents 10^1, or 10; two places represent 10^2, or 100; three places represent 10^3, or 1000; and so on. Thus, 0.4 = 4/10, 0.42 = 42/100, and 0.423 = 423/1000. Adding zeros to the right side of a decimal fraction does not alter its value. Thus, 0.42300 = 0.423.

A *mixed decimal*, like a mixed number, is the sum of an integer, or whole number, and a decimal fraction (for example, 5.75, which means "5 + 0.75"). In a mixed decimal, the number to the left of the decimal point represents the whole number, and the number to the right of the decimal point represents the decimal fraction. We usually refer to mixed decimals and decimal fractions as simply decimals.

To add or subtract decimals, follow these three steps:

1. Write the decimals vertically, making sure that the decimal points are lined up directly under one another. (Add zeros as necessary to prevent careless errors in alignment.)
2. Add or subtract as with whole numbers.
3. Place a decimal point in your answer directly beneath the decimal points in the numbers you're adding or subtracting.

Example: 5.78 + 23.1 + 8.734 =

$$
\begin{array}{r}
5.780 \\
23.100 \\
+\ 8.734 \\
\hline
37.614
\end{array}
$$

Example: 21.78 − 9.3 =

$$
\begin{array}{r}
21.78 \\
-\ 9.30 \\
\hline
12.48
\end{array}
$$

To multiply decimals, follow these two steps:

1. Multiply as with whole numbers.
2. Add the decimal places in all the factors and place a decimal point that many places to the left in your product.

Example:

$$
\begin{array}{r}
4.426 \quad \text{(3 decimal places)} \\
\times\ 0.34 \quad \text{(2 decimal places)} \\
\hline
17704 \\
1\ 3278 \\
\hline
1.50484 \quad \text{(5 decimal places)}
\end{array}
$$

To multiply a decimal by a power of 10, just move the decimal point one place to the *right* for each zero in the power of 10.

Example: Since there are two zeros in 100, to multiply 3.875 by 100, just move the decimal point in 3.875 two places to the right:

$$3.875 = 387.5$$

Example: Since there are three zeros in 1000, to multiply 8.4 by 1000, first add two zeros to the right of the 4 in 8.4: 8.400. Then move the decimal point three places to the right:

$$8.400 = 8400$$

Remember that there is a decimal point after the last (or ones) digit of every whole number, even if it's not expressed.

To divide decimals, follow these four steps:

1. Move the decimal point in the divisor (the number you're dividing by) enough places to the right to make it a whole number.
2. Move the decimal point in the dividend (the number you're dividing) the same number of places to the right.
3. Divide as with whole numbers.
4. Place a decimal point in the quotient (the answer) directly above the decimal point in the dividend.

Example: $0.25\overline{)0.045} = 0.25\overline{)0.045} = 25\overline{)4.50} =$

$$
\begin{array}{r}
0.18 \\
25\overline{)4.50} \\
2\,5 \\
\hline
2\,00 \\
2\,00 \\
\hline
0
\end{array}
$$

To divide a decimal by a power of 10, just move the decimal point one place to the *left* for each zero in the power of 10.

Example: $18.3 \div 100 = 18.3 = 0.183$

$8.5 \div 1000 = 008.5 = 0.0085$

To convert a decimal into a fraction, follow these three steps:

1. Take the number to the right of the decimal point and make it the numerator of the fraction.
2. Count the number of places to the right of the decimal point, multiply 10 by itself that many times (raise 10 to that power), and write the result as the denominator of the fraction.
3. Reduce the fraction to lowest terms:

Example: $0.15 = \dfrac{15}{100} = \dfrac{15 \div 5}{100 \div 5} = \dfrac{3}{20}$

To convert a fraction into a decimal, just divide the numerator by the denominator.

Example: $\dfrac{3}{8} = 3 \div 8 = 0.375$

Percentage

Percent means "out of one hundred." A *percentage* is a decimal fraction whose denominator is 100. A percentage is written with a percent sign. For example, the form 15% means 0.15 or 15/100.

Percentages have decimal and fractional equivalents. Some of the common equivalents, which you should learn before you take the GRE, are shown in the following table.

Percentage	Decimal	Fraction
5%	0.05	$\frac{1}{20}$
10%	0.10	$\frac{1}{10}$
12½%	0.125	$\frac{1}{8}$
15%	0.15	$\frac{3}{20}$
16⅔%	0.1666 . . .	$\frac{1}{6}$
20%	0.20	$\frac{1}{5}$
25%	0.25	$\frac{1}{4}$
30%	0.30	$\frac{3}{10}$
33⅓%	0.333 . . .	$\frac{1}{3}$
37½%	0.375	$\frac{3}{8}$
40%	0.40	$\frac{2}{5}$
50%	0.50	$\frac{1}{2}$
60%	0.60	$\frac{3}{5}$
62½%	0.625	$\frac{5}{8}$
66⅔%	0.666 . . .	$\frac{2}{3}$
75%	0.75	$\frac{3}{4}$
80%	0.80	$\frac{4}{5}$
90%	0.90	$\frac{9}{10}$

To convert a percentage into a decimal, move the decimal point two places to the left and drop the percentage sign.

Example: 34% = 0.34; 4.7% = 0.047; 135% = 1.35

To convert a decimal into a percentage, move the decimal point two places to the right and add a percentage sign.

Example: 0.45 = 45%; .032 = 3.2%; 3 = 300%

To convert a percentage into a fraction, drop the percentage sign, place the percentage over a denominator of 100, and reduce the fraction to lowest terms.

Example: $75\% = \frac{75}{100} = \frac{3}{4}$

To convert a fraction into a percentage, divide the numerator by the denominator, move the decimal point in the quotient two places to the right, and add a percentage sign.

Example: $\dfrac{7}{8} = 7 \div 8 = 0.875 = 87.5\%$, or $87\frac{1}{2}\%$

To find a percentage of a number, convert the percentage into a decimal or a fraction and then multiply.

Example: What is 8% of 45?

Solution: To find 8% of 45, first convert 8% into its decimal equivalent, 0.08, and then multiply it by 45:

$$\begin{array}{r} 45 \\ \times\ 0.08 \\ \hline 3.60 \end{array}$$

Thus, 8% of 45 is 3.6.

Example: If a salesperson receives a $12\frac{1}{2}\%$ commission on everything she sells, what is her commission on sales totaling $2560?

Solution: Convert $12\frac{1}{2}\%$ to its fractional equivalent, ⅛. Then multiply:

$$\frac{1}{8} \times \frac{2560}{1} = 320$$

Thus, the salesperson's commission is $320.

To find what percentage one number is of another, follow these three steps:

1. Express the problem in the form "x is what percentage of y."
2. Divide x by y.
3. Move the decimal point in the quotient two places to the right and add a percentage sign.

Example: What percentage of 60 is 15?

Solution: (1) Reword the problem: 15 is what percentage of 60? (2) Divide 15 by 60: $15 \div 60 = 0.25$. (3) Move the decimal point two places to the right and add a percentage sign: 25%.

To solve a percentage problem in the form "x is $y\%$ of what number," where x and y are given, follow these two steps:

1. Convert the percentage into a decimal or a fraction.
2. Divide the known number by the decimal or fraction.

Example: 42 is 30% of what number?

Solution: (1) Convert 30% into a fraction: 30% = ³⁄₁₀. (2) Divide 42 by ³⁄₁₀:

$$42 \div \frac{3}{10} = \frac{42}{1} \times \frac{10}{3} = 140$$

To find the percentage of an increase or decrease in a quantity, follow these three steps:

1. Subtract to find the amount of the increase or decrease.
2. Divide the amount of the increase or decrease by the *original* quantity.
3. Move the decimal point in the quotient two places to the right and add a percentage sign.

Example: Last week the price of coffee went up from $5 a pound to $6 a pound. By what percentage did the price of coffee increase?

Solution: (1) Subtract $5 from $6 to find the amount of the increase: $6 − $5 = $1. (2) Divide $1 by $5 (the original price): $1 ÷ $5 = 0.20. (3) Move the decimal point two places to the right and add a percentage sign: 20%.

There are many types of percentage problems. The following examples illustrate the range of percentage problems that you may encounter on the GRE. Some of the examples require the use of algebra. If you have trouble following the solutions, review "Operations with Algebraic Expressions" and "Equations and Formulas," two other topics covered in this math review.

Example: The profit on a washing machine is 40% of the cost of the machine. If the cost of the machine is $180, what is the selling price of the machine?

Solution: One way to solve this problem is to find 40% of $180 and then add the result to $180. But there's a faster way. If the profit is 40% of the cost, then the selling price is 100% of the cost plus 40% of the cost, or 140% of the cost. Since 140% = 1.4, the selling price of the machine is 1.4 × $180 = $252.

Example: A dealer buys a typewriter at a wholesale price of $120 and sells it at a retail price of $160. What percentage of the retail price of the typewriter is the dealer's profit?

Solution: If the retail price is $160 and the wholesale price is $120, then the dealer's profit is $160 − $120 = $40. To find what percentage the profit is of the retail price, divide $40 by $160: $40 ÷ $160 = 1/4 = 25%.

Example: If a store is offering a 15% discount on all its radios, how much will a customer pay for a radio that regularly sells for $80?

Solution: If the store is offering a 15% discount, then the customer will pay 100% − 15% = 85% of the regular price. Since 85% = 0.85, the customer will pay 0.85 × $80 = $68.

Example: A woman paid $45 for a dress that was marked down 25%. What was the original price of the dress?

Solution: If the dress was marked down 25%, the woman paid 75%, or 3/4, of the original price. To find the original price, divide the price she paid by 3/4:

$$45 \div \frac{3}{4} = \frac{45}{1} \times \frac{4}{3} = 60$$

The original price was $60.

Example: The sales representative for a company earns a commission of $r\%$ on the sale of s dollars of the company's products. In terms of r and s, what is the sales representative's commission?

Solution: Convert the percentage into a fraction: $r\% = r/100$. Then multiply the fraction by s, the dollar value of the sales: $r/100 \times s = rs/100$.

Example: A woman had $5200. She invested part of it at a simple interest rate of 6% a year and the rest of it at a simple interest rate of 7% a year. If her interest on the investments after one year was $343, how much money did she invest at each rate?

Solution: Let x equal the amount of money the woman invested at 6%. Then $5200 − x$ = the amount she invested at 7%. You know that the interest on the amount invested at 6% plus the interest on the amount invested at 7% equals $343, the total interest for the year. To find the interest on the amount invested at 6%, convert 6% to a decimal and multiply it by x: $0.06(x) = 0.06x$. To find the interest on the amount invested at 7%, convert 7% to a decimal and multiply it by $5200 − x$: $0.07(5200 − x) = 364 − 0.07x$. Now, set up the equation and solve for x:

$$
\begin{aligned}
0.06x + (364 - 0.07x) &= 343 \\
0.06x + 364 - 0.07x &= 343 && \text{(Multiply by 100)} \\
6x + 36400 - 7x &= 34300 && \text{(Subtract 36400)} \\
6x - 7x &= -2100 && \text{(Combine like terms)} \\
-x &= -2100 && \text{(Multiply by −1)} \\
x &= 2100
\end{aligned}
$$

Thus, the woman invested $2100 at 6% and $5200 − $2100 = $3100 at 7%.

Example: How many gallons of water must be evaporated from 100 gallons of a 3% salt solution in order to produce a 5% solution?

Solution: Let x equal the number of gallons of water to be evaporated from the solution. Then $100 - x =$ the number of gallons in the final solution. You know that the amount of salt in the original solution and the amount of salt in the final solution will be equal. To find the amount of salt in the original solution, convert 3% to a decimal and multiply it by 100: $0.03(100) = 3$. To find the amount of salt in the final solution, convert 5% to a decimal and multiply it by $100 - x$: $0.05(100 - x) = 5 - 0.05x$. Now set the two amounts equal and solve for x:

$$3 = 5 - 0.05x \quad \text{(Subtract 5)}$$
$$-2 = -0.05x \quad \text{(Divide by } -0.05)$$
$$40 = x$$

Thus, to reduce the concentration of salt in the solution from 5% to 3%, 40 gallons of water must be evaporated.

Exponents and Roots

The expression 5^3, which is read "5 to the third power" or "5 cubed," means "multiply 5 by itself three times." Thus the expression 5^3 has a value of $5 \times 5 \times 5 = 125$.

In general, the expression b^n, where n is a positive integer greater than or equal to 1, represents the product of n factors, each factor equal to b. In the expression b^n, n is called the *exponent* and b is called the *base*. The expression itself is called the nth power of b.

There are several laws that govern operations with exponents. Following are the ones you should know for the GRE:

1. $b^0 = 1 \quad (b \neq 0)$
2. $b^1 = b$
3. $b^2 \times b^3 = b^{(2+3)} = b^5$
4. $\dfrac{b^4}{b^2} = b^{(4-2)} = b^2 \quad (b \neq 0)$
5. $(b^4)^2 = b^{(4 \times 2)} = b^8$
6. $(ab)^n = a^n b^n$
7. $\left(\dfrac{a}{b}\right)^n = \dfrac{a^n}{b^n}$

The first law tells you that, with the exception of 0, any number raised to the zero power equals 1. Thus, $1^0 = 1$, $2^0 = 1$, $3^0 = 1$, and so on. The second law tells you that any number raised to the first power equals itself. Thus, $1^1 = 1$, $2^1 = 2$, $3^1 = 3$, and so on. The third and fourth laws tell you how to multiply and divide numbers that have exponents. Notice that the laws apply only to numbers that have the same base. Here are examples of how the third and fourth laws work:

Example: $(-3)^2 \times (-3) = (-3)^{(2+1)} = (-3)^3 = (-3) \times (-3) \times (-3) = -27$

Example: $\dfrac{7^8}{7^6} = 7^{(8-6)} = 7^2 = 7 \times 7 = 49$

The fifth law tells you how to raise a power to another power. Here is an example of how the fifth law works:

Example: $(2^3)^2 = 2^{(3 \times 2)} = 2^6 = 2 \times 2 \times 2 \times 2 \times 2 \times 2 = 64$

Finally, the sixth and seventh laws tell you how to raise the power of an expression in parentheses. Here are examples of how these laws work:

Example: $(4a)^2 = 4^2 \times a^2 = 16a^2$

Example: $\left(\dfrac{2}{3}\right)^3 = \dfrac{2^3}{3^3} = \dfrac{2 \times 2 \times 2}{3 \times 3 \times 3} = \dfrac{8}{27}$

As the last example illustrates, raising a number to a power doesn't always increase its value. Here are some rules to remember about the peculiarities of exponents:

1. When 0 and 1 are raised to any power, no matter how large, they remain the same. Thus, $0^0 = 0^{100} = 0$; $1^0 = 1^{100} = 1$.
2. When fractions with a value less than 1 are raised to a power, they decrease in value. Thus, $(1/2)^2 = 1/4$.
3. When a negative number is raised to an even power, it becomes positive. Thus, $(-4)^2 = 16$.
4. When a negative number is raised to an odd power, it remains negative. Thus, $(-4)^3 = -64$.

The opposite of raising a number to a power is finding a root of a number. A root is designated by a *radical sign*, which looks like this: $\sqrt{}$. The *square root* of a number a, which is designated as $\sqrt{a}$, is the number that when squared (that is, raised to the second power) equals a. For example, $\sqrt{16} = 4$, since $4^2 = 16$. The *cube root* of a number a, which is designated as $\sqrt[3]{a}$, is the number that when cubed (that is, raised to the third power) equals a. For example, $\sqrt[3]{27} = 3$, since $3^3 = 27$.

Numbers have negative square roots as well as positive square roots. For instance, since 3^2 and $(-3)^2$ both equal 9, 9 has two square roots, 3 and -3. However, by mathematical convention, $\sqrt{a}$ always designates the positive square root of a. The negative square root of a is designated as $-\sqrt{a}$.

Just as there are several laws that govern operations with exponents, so there are several laws that govern operations with radicals. Following are the ones you should know for the GRE:

1. $\sqrt{a} \times \sqrt{a} = a$
2. $\sqrt{ab} = \sqrt{a} \times \sqrt{b}$
3. $\sqrt{\dfrac{a}{b}} = \dfrac{\sqrt{a}}{\sqrt{b}}$
4. $\sqrt{a} + \sqrt{a} = 2\sqrt{a}$
5. $\dfrac{a}{\sqrt{b}} = \dfrac{a}{\sqrt{b}} \times \dfrac{\sqrt{b}}{\sqrt{b}} = \dfrac{a\sqrt{b}}{b}$

The first law simply tells you that $(\sqrt{a})^2 = a$, which should make sense. For instance, since $\sqrt{4} = 2$ and since $2 \times 2 = 4$, $\sqrt{4} \times \sqrt{4} = 4$. The second and third laws tell you how to simplify radicals—that is, how to express them in their simplest form by "removing" perfect squares. Here are two examples of how the second and third laws work:

Example: $\sqrt{300} = \sqrt{100 \times 3} = \sqrt{100} \times \sqrt{3} = 10\sqrt{3}$

Example: $\sqrt{\dfrac{8}{9}} = \dfrac{\sqrt{8}}{\sqrt{9}} = \dfrac{\sqrt{4 \times 2}}{3} = \dfrac{2\sqrt{2}}{3}$

The fourth law tells you that you can add or subtract radicals if (and only if) they are alike. Here is an example of how the fourth law works:

Example: $\sqrt{75} + 2\sqrt{3} = \sqrt{25 \times 3} + 2\sqrt{3} = (\sqrt{25} \times \sqrt{3}) + 2\sqrt{3} = 5\sqrt{3} + 2\sqrt{3} = 7\sqrt{3}$

Finally, the last rule tells you how to eliminate a radical from the denominator of a fraction. Here's an example:

Example: $\dfrac{1}{\sqrt{2}} = \dfrac{1}{\sqrt{2}} \times \dfrac{\sqrt{2}}{\sqrt{2}} = \dfrac{\sqrt{2}}{2}$

In addition to these five laws, you should know the following common square roots and cube roots for the GRE:

$\sqrt{2} \approx 1.4$	$\sqrt{25} = 5$	$\sqrt{100} = 10$
$\sqrt{3} \approx 1.7$	$\sqrt{36} = 6$	$\sqrt{121} = 11$
$\sqrt{4} = 2$	$\sqrt{49} = 7$	$\sqrt{144} = 12$
$\sqrt{9} = 3$	$\sqrt{64} = 8$	$\sqrt[3]{8} = 2$
$\sqrt{16} = 4$	$\sqrt{81} = 9$	$\sqrt[3]{27} = 3$

Operations with Algebraic Expressions

In algebra, we use letters to represent numbers. These letters are called *variables*. Fixed numerical values are called *constants*. For example, in the expression $7x^2y$, the number 7 is a constant and the letters x and y are variables. Since there is no sign of operation between the number and the letters, we consider the number and the letters to be multiplied. The number and the letters are then called the *factors* of the product. Thus, the factors of $7x^2y$ are 7, x, x, and y. If we cannot factor these numbers and letters any further, we call these the *prime factors* of the expression.

Each factor of a particular product is called the *coefficient* of the other factors. In the expression $7x^2y$, 7 is the *numerical coefficient* of x^2y, and x, x, and y are the *literal coefficients* of 7. In general, when we refer to the coefficient of an algebraic product, we mean the numerical coefficient.

An *algebraic term* is any variable, any constant, or any product or quotient of one or more variables or constants. For example, x, 3, $3xy$, and x/y are all algebraic terms. *Like terms* are terms that contain exactly the same variable(s) raised to exactly the same power(s). For example, a and $2a$ are like terms; so are ab^2 and $4ab^2$. Like terms can be combined (added or subtracted). *Unlike terms* are terms that do not contain exactly the same variable(s) raised to exactly the same power(s). For example, $2a$ and $2ab$ are unlike terms; so are a and a^2, a^2b and ab^2. Unlike terms cannot be combined.

An algebraic expression that consists of only one term is called a *monomial*. Examples are $7x^2y$, $3ab$, $9m$, and $k/4$. An algebraic expression that is the sum or difference of two monomials is called a *binomial*. Examples are $3r + 7s$, $a^2 - b^2$, and $7x^2y + 5$. An algebraic expression that is the sum or difference of three terms is called a *trinomial*. Examples are $5r^2 - 10rs + 4s^2$ and $4x^2 - 5x + 6$. Monomials, binomials, and trinomials are all specific types of *polynomials*.

To add or subtract polynomials, follow these two steps:

1. Add or subtract the numerical coefficients of the like terms.
2. Place the result in front of the common literal factor(s).

Example: $(7m^2 + 2km - 3k^2) + (3m^2 - 5km + 2k^2) =$
$(7m^2 + 3m^2) + (2km - 5km) + (-3k^2 + 2k^2) =$
$10m^2 - 3km - k^2$

To multiply two monomials, follow these two steps:

1. Multiply the numerical coefficients to form the numerical coefficient of the product.
2. Multiply the variables to form the literal part of the product.

Example: $(-4a^3b)(3a^2b^2) = (-4 \times 3)(a^3 \times a^2)(b \times b^2)$
$= -12a^5b^3$

To multiply a polynomial by a monomial, multiply each term of the polynomial by the monomial.

Example: $3a(2r - 5s) = 3a(2r) - 3a(5s)$
$$= 6ar - 15as$$

Example: $8x(x^2 - 5x + 2) = 8x(x^2) - 8x(5x) + 8x(2)$
$$= 8x^3 - 40x^2 + 16x$$

To multiply two polynomials, follow these two steps:

1. Multiply each term of the first polynomial by each term of the second.
2. Combine like terms (if any) algebraically.

Example: $(2r - 3)(r^2 - 5rs) = 2r(r^2) - 2r(5rs) - 3(r^2) + 3(5rs)$
$$= 2r^3 - 10r^2s - 3r^2 + 15rs$$

Example: $(2y + 4)(3y - 5) = 2y(3y) - 2y(5) + 4(3y) - 4(5)$
$$= 6y^2 - 10y + 12y - 20$$
$$= 6y^2 + 2y - 20$$

To divide one monomial by another, follow these two steps:

1. Divide the numerical coefficients to form the numerical coefficient of the quotient.
2. Divide the variables to form the literal part of the quotient.

Example: $\dfrac{10x^2y^3z^5}{-5xy^2z^3} = \dfrac{10}{-5} \times \dfrac{x^2}{x} \times \dfrac{y^3}{y^2} \times \dfrac{z^5}{z^3}$
$$= -2xyz^2$$

To divide a polynomial by a monomial, divide each term of the polynomial by the monomial.

Example: $\dfrac{x^6 - 7x^5 + 4x^4}{x^2} = \dfrac{x^6}{x^2} - \dfrac{7x^5}{x^2} + \dfrac{4x^4}{x^2}$
$$= x^4 - 7x^3 + 4x^2$$

To factor a polynomial—that is, to express a polynomial as the product of a monomial factor and another factor—follow these three steps:

1. Find a monomial factor that is common to all the terms of the polynomial. The common monomial factor may be a constant, a variable, or a product of the two.

2. To find the second factor, divide each term of the polynomial by the common monomial factor.
3. Rewrite the polynomial as the product of the common monomial factor and the second factor.

Example: In the polynomial $3x^2 + 6xy + 12x$, the constant 3 and the variable x are both common factors of $3x^2$, $6xy$, and $12x$. Therefore the polynomial can be rewritten as the product of $3x$ and another factor. To find the other factor, divide each term of the polynomial by $3x$: $3x^2 \div 3x = x$; $6xy \div 3x = 2y$; $12x \div 3x = 4$. The result is $x + 2y + 4$. Since the polynomial $3x^2 + 6xy + 12x$ is the product of $3x$ and $x + 2y + 4$, it can be rewritten as $3x(x + 2y + 4)$.

To factor a trinomial of the form $x^2 + ax + b$, where x is a variable and a and b are constants, follow these three steps:

1. Set up two binomials with x as the first term in each: $(x \quad)(x \quad)$.
2. Through trial and error, find two numbers whose sum is a and whose product is b.
3. Make one of the numbers the second term of the first binomial; make the other number the second term of the second binomial.

Example: To factor $x^2 - 7x + 12$, start by setting up two binomials whose first terms are x: $(x \quad)(x \quad)$. Then, find two numbers whose sum is -7 and whose product is 12. Those numbers are -3 and -4. Make -3 the second term of one binomial (it doesn't matter which) and -4 the second term of the other: $(x - 3)(x - 4)$. To check your results, multiply the two binomials: $(x - 3)(x - 4) = x^2 - 4x - 3x + 12 = x^2 - 7x + 12$.

To factor a binomial of the form $x^2 - y^2$, just remember this: A binomial that is the difference between two squared terms is the product of the sum and the difference of the square roots of the two terms. In other words, $x^2 - y^2 = (x + y)(x - y)$.

Example: $9x^2 - 49 = (3x + 7)(3x - 7)$

To reduce an algebraic fraction to lowest terms, follow these two steps:

1. Factor the numerator and the denominator.
2. Cancel any factors that are common to both the numerator and the denominator.

Example: $\dfrac{3a^2b}{6ab} = \dfrac{3ab(a)}{3ab(2)} = \dfrac{a}{2}$

Example: $\dfrac{x^2 - 25}{x^2 - 8x + 15} = \dfrac{(x + 5)\cancel{(x - 5)}}{(x - 3)\cancel{(x - 5)}}$

$$= \dfrac{x + 5}{x - 3}$$

To multiply algebraic fractions, follow these three steps:

1. Factor the numerators and denominators of the fractions, if possible.
2. Cancel any factor that is common to both a numerator and a denominator.
3. Multiply the remaining factors of the numerators to form the numerator of the product; multiply the remaining denominators to form the denominator of the product.

Example: $\dfrac{3a + 9}{15a} \times \dfrac{a^2}{a^2 - 9} = \dfrac{\cancel{3}(a + 3)}{\cancel{3}(5)\cancel{(a)}} \times \dfrac{a\cancel{(a)}}{\cancel{(a + 3)}(a - 3)}$

$$= \dfrac{a}{5(a - 3)}$$

To divide algebraic fractions, simply invert the divisor (the fraction you're dividing by); then multiply, following the three steps above.

Example: $\dfrac{(a + 1)^2}{b^2} \div \dfrac{6a + 6}{9b^2} = \dfrac{(a + 1)^2}{b^2} \times \dfrac{9b^2}{6a + 6}$

$$= \dfrac{(a + 1)\cancel{(a + 1)}}{\cancel{b}\cancel{(b)}} \times \dfrac{3\cancel{(3)}\cancel{(b)}\cancel{(b)}}{2\cancel{(3)}\cancel{(a + 1)}}$$

$$= \dfrac{3(a + 1)}{2}$$

To add or subtract algebraic fractions, follow these four steps:

1. Find the lowest common denominator of the fractions.
2. Express each fraction in terms of the lowest common denominator.
3. Add or subtract the numerators, as indicated, and place the sum or difference over the lowest common denominator.
4. Reduce the fraction to lowest terms, if possible.

Example: $\dfrac{5}{rs} + \dfrac{9}{st} = \dfrac{t(5)}{t(rs)} + \dfrac{r(9)}{r(st)}$

$$= \dfrac{5t}{rst} + \dfrac{9r}{rst}$$

$$= \dfrac{5t + 9r}{rst}$$

Example:
$$\frac{2a-5}{3a}+\frac{3a+2}{5a}=\frac{5(2a-5)}{5(3a)}+\frac{3(3a+2)}{3(5a)}$$

$$=\frac{10a-25}{15a}+\frac{9a+6}{15a}$$

$$=\frac{10a-25+9a+6}{15a}$$

$$=\frac{19a-19}{15a}$$

Example:
$$\frac{p-1}{2}-\frac{p-5}{8}=\frac{4(p-1)}{4(2)}-\frac{p-5}{8}$$

$$=\frac{4p-4}{8}-\frac{p-5}{8}$$

$$=\frac{4p-4-p+5}{8}$$

$$=\frac{3p+1}{8}$$

Ratio and Proportion

A *ratio* is a way of comparing two quantities. For example, if a girl is 5 feet tall and a boy is 6 feet tall, the ratio of the girl's height to the boy's height is 5 to 6. A ratio is commonly expressed in either of two forms: 5 : 6 or 5/6. As the second form suggests, a ratio is really just another name for a fraction. In other words, it is the quotient of one number divided by another.

Example: In a class of 30 students, there are 20 boys and 10 girls. Find the ratio of boys to girls, the ratio of boys to students, and the ratio of girls to students.

Solution: The ratio of boys to girls is 20/10, which can be reduced to 2/1. The ratio of boys to students is 20/30, which can be reduced to 2/3. And the ratio of girls to students is 10/30, which can be reduced to 1/3.

Example: A rod 14 meters long is divided into two pieces. If the ratio of the two pieces is 3 to 4, what is the length of the shorter piece?

Solution: Let $3x$ equal the length of the shorter piece and $4x$ equal the length of the longer piece. You know that the two pieces together are 14 meters long, so set the sum of their lengths equal to 14 and solve for x:

$$3x + 4x = 14$$
$$7x = 14 \quad \text{(Divide by 7)}$$
$$x = 2$$

If $x = 2$, then the length of the shorter piece is $3 \times 2 = 6$ meters.

A *proportion* is an equality between two ratios. A proportion is commonly expressed in either of two forms: $4/5 = 8/10$ or $4 : 5 = 8 : 10$. The four elements in a proportion (in this case 4, 5, 8, and 10) are called the *terms* of the proportion. In the proportion $4 : 5 = 8 : 10$, the middle terms (5 and 8) are known as the *means* and the outer terms (4 and 10) are known as the *extremes*. In any proportion, the product of the means is equal to the product of the extremes. Thus, if $a : b = c : d$, then $bc = ad$. This equality makes it possible to find the fourth term of any proportion if the other three terms are known.

Example: If $8 : x = 6 : 21$, what is the value of x?

Solution: Express the two ratios in fractional form, cross multiply to find the product of the means and the product of the extremes, set the two products equal, and solve for x:

$$\frac{8}{x} = \frac{6}{21} \quad \text{(Cross multiply)}$$
$$6x = 168 \quad \text{(Divide by 6)}$$
$$x = 28$$

There are two types of proportion: direct proportion and inverse proportion. In a *direct proportion*, quantities vary in the same direction—that is, they increase or decrease together. The distance you travel, for example, will increase as the number of hours you travel increases. Thus time spent traveling and distance traveled are directly proportional. When you're working with a direct proportion, set up your equation so that the corresponding quantities are *directly* across from one another on either side of the equal sign:

$$\frac{\text{Fewer hours} \leftrightarrow \text{Shorter distance}}{\text{More hours} \leftrightarrow \text{Longer distance}}$$

Example: According to the weather bureau, 2 inches of snow have fallen in the last 5 hours. If snow continues to fall at the same rate, how much snow will fall in 8 hours?

Solution: If snow falls at a constant rate, then the amount of snow that falls is directly proportional to the length of time that it snows. Let x

equal the number of inches that will fall in 8 hours. Then set up a direct proportion, cross multiply, and solve for x:

$$\frac{2}{x} = \frac{5}{8} \quad \text{(Cross multiply)}$$

$$5x = 16 \quad \text{(Divide by 5)}$$

$$x = 3\frac{1}{5}$$

In an *inverse proportion*, quantities vary in opposite directions—that is, as one increases, the other decreases. For example, the number of hours it will take you to get somewhere will increase as the speed at which you travel decreases. Thus, time spent traveling and speed of travel are inversely proportional. When you're working with an inverse proportion, you must *invert* one of the ratios—that is, you must set up your equation so that the corresponding quantities are *diagonally* across from one another on either side of the equal sign:

$$\frac{\text{Fewer hours}}{\text{More hours}} = \frac{\text{Slower speed}}{\text{Faster speed}}$$

Example: Six men work at the same rate. If it takes four of the men 12 days to do a job, how long will it take all six of them to do the same job?

Solution: If they all work at the same rate, it will take six men less time to do the job than it takes four men. So the number of men working is inversely proportional to the number of days required to complete the job. Let x equal the number of days it will take six men to do the job. Then set up an inverse proportion, cross multiply, and solve for x:

$$\frac{4}{6} = \frac{x}{12} \quad \text{(Cross multiply)}$$

$$6x = 48 \quad \text{(Divide by 6)}$$

$$x = 8$$

Notice that the ratio of the number of men, which is 4/6 or 2/3, is the *inverse* of the ratio of the number of days it takes to do the job, which is 12/8 or 3/2.

Example: A large gear with a diameter of 5 inches drives a smaller gear with a diameter of 2 inches. When the large gear turns through 20 revolutions, how many revolutions does the smaller gear turn through?

Solution: The smaller gear turns through a greater number of revolutions than the larger gear, so the number of revolutions is inversely proportional to the size of the gear. Let x equal the number of revolutions that the smaller gear turns through. Then set up an inverse proportion, cross multiply, and solve for x:

$$\frac{5}{2} = \frac{x}{20} \quad \text{(Cross multiply)}$$

$$2x = 100 \quad \text{(Divide by 2)}$$

$$x = 50$$

Proportions are frequently useful in solving geometry problems. Here is one example:

Example: In the following figure, corresponding angles are equal, as marked. What is the length of x?

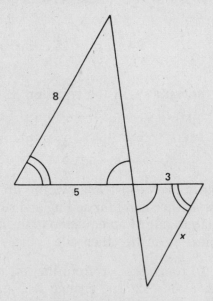

Solution: If the corresponding angles of two triangles (or any two similar figures) are equal, then the corresponding sides of the two triangles (or similar figures) are directly proportional. Thus:

$$\frac{x}{8} = \frac{3}{5} \quad \text{(Cross multiply)}$$

$$5x = 24 \quad \text{(Divide by 5)}$$

$$x = 4\frac{4}{5}$$

Equations and Formulas

An *equation* is a statement that two expressions are equal. Most equations include one or more variables, or unknowns. To solve an equation is to find a numerical value for each variable that satisfies (or works out in) the equation. Such a value is called a *solution*, or *root*, of the equation. The basic principle for solving equations is this: Whatever you do to one side of an equation, you must do to the other side.

There are several basic techniques for solving equations:

1. *Isolating the variable on one side of the equal sign.* One of your first objectives in solving an equation is to isolate all the terms containing the variable (the unknown) on one side of the equal sign (usually the left) and all the numbers (the knowns) on the other side of the equal sign (usually the right). Ordinarily you can achieve this objective by adding the same quantity to both sides of the equation or by subtracting the same quantity from both sides of the equation.

   Example: To isolate the variable in the equation $4x = 15 - x$, add x to both sides:

   $$4x + x = 15 - x + x$$
   $$5x = 15$$

   To isolate the variable in the equation $3x = 2x + 5$, subtract $2x$ from both sides:

   $$3x - 2x = 2x + 5 - 2x$$
   $$x = 5$$

2. *Transposing a term from one side of an equation to the other.* Transposing is shorthand for adding and subtracting. To transpose a term from one side of an equation to the other, simply change its sign and move it to the other side.

   Example: To transpose -6 from the left to the right side of the equation $2x - 6 = 12 + x$, change its sign from -6 to $+6$ and move it:

   $$2x = 12 + x + 6$$
   $$2x = 18 + x$$

   (This operation is equivalent to adding 6 to both sides of the equation.) To transpose x from the right to the left side of the same equation, change its sign from $+x$ to $-x$ and move it:

   $$2x - x = 18$$
   $$x = 18$$

   (This operation is equivalent to subtracting x from both sides of the equation.)

3. *Clearing an equation of fractions.* To clear an equation of fractions, multiply each term on both sides of the equation by the lowest common denominator of all the fractions.

Example: The lowest common denominator of the fractions in the following equation is 15:

$$\frac{4x + 1}{3} - \frac{2x + 1}{5} = \frac{3}{5}$$

To clear the equation of fractions, multiply each term on both sides by 15 (cancel before you multiply):

$$15\left(\frac{4x + 1}{3}\right) - 15\left(\frac{2x + 1}{5}\right) = 15\left(\frac{3}{5}\right)$$
$$5(4x + 1) - 3(2x + 1) = 3(3)$$
$$20x + 5 - 6x - 3 = 9$$

4. *Cross multiplying.* Cross multiplying is generally the simplest way of solving an equation that is set up in the form of a proportion. To cross multiply, multiply the numerator on each side of the equation by the denominator on the opposite side.

Example: The following equation is set up in the form of a proportion:

$$\frac{x}{8} = \frac{11}{2}$$

To solve it, multiply x by 2 and 8 by 11; then set the products equal and divide both sides of the equation by 2:

$$2x = 88$$
$$x = 44$$

5. *Multiplying an equation by* -1. Occasionally you will encounter (or end up with) an equation like the following: $-x = -7$. To find the value of $+x$ rather than $-x$, multiply both sides of the equation by -1. Multiplying an equation by -1 changes the sign of every term on both sides of the equation.

Example: To find the value of x, given the equation $-x = -7$, multiply both sides of the equation by -1:

$$-1(-x) = -1(-7)$$
$$+x = +7$$

These techniques work on *literal equations*—equations that consist of letters only—as well as they do on regular equations.

Example: To solve the following literal equation for x, simply add b to both sides and then divide both sides by a:

$$ax - b = c$$
$$ax = b + c$$
$$x = \frac{b + c}{a}$$

Most formulas, such as $D = RT$ (Distance = Rate × Time) and $A = bh$ (Area = base × height), are literal equations. You can use the same techniques on them that you use on regular equations.

> **Example:** To solve the formula $D = RT$ for R, just divide both sides by T. The result is
>
> $$\frac{D}{T} = R$$
>
> which means that Rate = Distance ÷ Time.

Most of the equations that you encounter on the GRE will be equations of the *first degree*—that is, equations that include no variables with exponents greater than 1. All of the equations in the examples above are equations of the first degree. However, you will also be expected to know how to solve simple quadratic equations. *Quadratic equations* are equations of the second degree—that is, equations that include variables with exponents of 2. Every quadratic equation has two roots, which may, in some cases, be equal.

A quadratic equation that has a second-degree term and a constant term but no first-degree term is called an *incomplete quadratic equation*. The equation $x^2 = 49$ is an example of an incomplete quadratic equation. To solve an incomplete quadratic equation like this, take the square root of both sides, remembering that a square root can be either positive or negative. Thus, $x = \pm\sqrt{49} = \pm7$. The two roots of the equation are $+7$ and -7. Here is another, slightly different, example in which the constant is not a perfect square:

> **Example:** $r^2 = 12$
> $$\sqrt{r^2} = \pm\sqrt{12}$$
> $$r = \pm\sqrt{4 \times 3}$$
> $$r = \pm2\sqrt{3}$$

As this example illustrates, square roots are usually expressed in simplest form.

A quadratic equation that has a second-degree term, a first-degree term, and a constant term is called a *complete quadratic equation*. The equation $x^2 + x = 6$ is an example of a complete quadratic equation. The only complete quadratic equations that you will encounter on the GRE will be factorable.

To solve a factorable quadratic equation, follow these four steps:

1. Transpose the three terms to the left side of the equation (if necessary) and set the resulting trinomial equal to 0.
2. Arrange the trinomial so that the powers of the variable are in descending order.

3. Factor the trinomial into two binomials.
4. Set each binomial factor equal to 0 and solve the two resulting equations. The solutions are the two roots of the equation.

Example: To solve the equation $x^2 + x = 6$, first subtract 6 from both sides and then factor the trinomial on the left side:

$$x^2 + x - 6 = 0$$
$$(x + 3)(x - 2) = 0$$

Since the product of the two binomial factors is 0, one or the other of them (or both) must have a value of 0. Thus:

$$x + 3 = 0 \quad \text{or} \quad x - 2 = 0$$
$$x = -3 \quad \text{or} \quad x = 2$$

The two roots of the equation are -3 and 2. To check, substitute each root for x in the equation and work it out.

The equations we've looked at so far have been equations in one variable. For the GRE you also need to be able to solve simultaneous equations in two variables. There are two methods for solving simultaneous equations in two variables: the substitution method and the addition-or-subtraction method.
To solve two simultaneous equations by the substitution method, follow these three steps:

1. Use algebraic techniques to solve one equation for one variable in terms of the second.

   Example: Given the simultaneous equations $x + 4y = 2$ and $2x - 7y = -1$, solve the first equation for x in terms of y:

   $$x + 4y = 2$$
   $$x = 2 - 4y$$

2. Substitute the result of step 1 in the second equation and solve for the numerical value of the second variable.

   Example: Continuing the example above, substitute $2 - 4y$ for x in the second equation and solve for y:

   $$2(2 - 4y) - 7y = -1$$
   $$4 - 8y - 7y = -1$$
   $$-15y = -5$$
   $$y = \frac{1}{3}$$

3. Substitute the result of step 2 in either equation and solve for the numerical value of the first variable.

Example: Continuing the previous example, substitute 1/3 for y in the first equation and solve for x:

$$x + 4\left(\frac{1}{3}\right) = 2$$
$$3x + 4 = 6$$
$$3x = 2$$
$$x = \frac{2}{3}$$

To solve two simultaneous equations by the addition-or-subtraction method, follow these three steps:

1. Add or subtract the two equations so that you eliminate one variable.

Example: Given the simultaneous equations $2x - y = 12$ and $x + y = 15$, add the two equations to eliminate y:

$$2x - y = 12$$
$$+\ \ x + y = 15$$
$$\overline{3x + 0 = 27}$$

2. Solve the equation resulting from step 1 for the numerical value of the remaining variable.

Example: Continuing the example above, solve $3x + 0 = 27$ for x:

$$3x + 0 = 27$$
$$3x = 27$$
$$x = 9$$

3. Substitute the result of step 2 in either equation and solve for the numerical value of the second unknown.

Example: Continuing the example above, substitute 9 for x in the second equation and solve for y:

$$9 + y = 15$$
$$y = 6$$

The addition-or-subtraction method works only if the coefficient of one of the variables is the same in both equations—regardless of its sign. (In the example above, the coefficient of y in both equations is 1: -1 in the first equation, $+1$ in the second.) In some cases, you have to multiply or divide one of the equations before you can use the addition-or-subtraction method.

Example: Given the simultaneous equations $2x + 6y = 10$ and $3x + 3y = 9$, you have to multiply the second equation by 2 and make it $6x + 6y = 18$ before you can subtract the first equation from it. Remember, to subtract, change the sign of each term and then add:

$$\begin{array}{r} 6x + 6y = 18 \\ + \; -2x - 6y = -10 \\ \hline 4x + 0 = 8 \end{array}$$

Motion Problems

The basic formula for motion problems is

$$\text{Distance} = \text{Rate} \times \text{Time}$$

or, in shorthand,

$$D = RT$$

If R is in miles per hour and T is in hours, then D is in miles. The motion formula has two variations, which may be more appropriate for some problems:

$$R = \frac{D}{T} \qquad T = \frac{D}{R}$$

Here are a few examples of simple motion problems:

Example: A collegiate track star runs 1 mile in 4 minutes. What is his rate in miles per hour?

Solution: Since you're asked to find the track star's rate in miles per hour, first express 4 minutes as a fraction of 1 hour (60 minutes):

$$\frac{4}{60} = \frac{1}{15}$$

Then substitute the two values you're given into the rate formula and solve for R:

$$R = \frac{D}{T}$$
$$= \frac{1}{\frac{1}{15}}$$
$$= \frac{1}{1} \times \frac{15}{1}$$
$$= 15$$

The track star's rate is 15 miles per hour.

Example: A woman drives 120 miles to a destination in 2 hours and then drives home in another 3 hours. What is her average speed for the round trip?

Solution: To find the woman's average speed, or rate, use the following variation on the rate formula:

$$\text{Average rate} = \frac{\text{Total distance}}{\text{Total time}}$$

Thus:

$$R = \frac{120 + 120}{2 + 3}$$
$$= \frac{240}{5}$$
$$= 48$$

The woman's average rate, or speed, is 48 miles per hour.

Example: If a pilot flies a plane d miles at a rate of m miles per minute, in terms of d and m, how many hours does a flight take?

Solution: Since you're asked to find the number of *hours* a flight takes, first express the pilot's rate in miles per hour rather than miles per minute by multiplying m by 60 and getting $60m$. Then substitute the literal values you're given into the time formula:

$$T = \frac{D}{R}$$
$$= \frac{d}{60m}$$

A flight takes $d/60m$ hours.

Some motion problems are more complex than the previous examples. For more complex motion problems, drawing a diagram or making a chart is often helpful. Here are two examples:

Example: Two cars start out from the same town at the same time and travel in opposite directions on a straight road. If one car travels at a rate of 50 miles per hour and the other car travels at a rate of 60 miles per hour, in how many hours will they be 495 miles apart?

Solution: To help yourself visualize the problem, first draw a diagram:

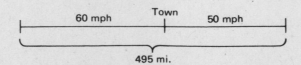

As the diagram illustrates, the distance the first car travels plus the distance the second car travels equals 495 miles. Let h equal the number of hours the cars travel. Then the distance the first car travels is $50h$, and the distance the second car travels is $60h$. Set up the equation and solve for h:

$$50h + 60h = 495$$
$$110h = 495$$
$$h = 4\frac{1}{2}$$

The two cars will be 495 miles apart in 4½ hours.

Example: A man leaves home and travels in his car at 40 miles per hour. Thirty minutes later, his wife leaves home and follows him in her car at 50 miles per hour. How many hours will the wife travel before she catches up with her husband?

Solution: Let h equal the number of hours the wife travels (since that's what you're looking for). Then $h + 1/2 =$ the number of hours the husband travels (since he travels 30 minutes longer). Now, make a chart like the one below and fill in everything you know:

	Rate $\times$	Time $=$	Distance
Wife	50	h	$50h$
Husband	40	$h + 1/2$	$40h + 20$

You know that the husband and the wife both travel the same distance. Therefore:

$$50h = 40h + 20$$
$$10h = 20$$
$$h = 2$$

The wife will travel 2 hours before she catches up with her husband.

Work Problems

The basic formula for solving work problems is very similar to the basic formula for solving motion problems:

$$\text{Work done} = \text{Rate} \times \text{Time}$$

Work rates are usually expressed in terms of the job to be done. For example, if it takes a painter 5 days to paint a room, then the painter's rate of work is 1/5 of the job per day.

Example: A clerk can type a report in 30 minutes. At this rate, what part of the report can the clerk type in *m* minutes if $m < 30$?

Solution: If the clerk can type the report in 30 minutes, then the clerk's rate of work is 1/30 of the report per minute. In *m* minutes, then, the clerk can type $m \times 1/30 = m/30$ of the report.

Many work problems involve fractional parts of a job that are completed at different rates. In such problems, the fractional parts must add up to 1 (the whole job).

Example: One tractor can plow a field in 16 hours. Another tractor can plow the same field in 20 hours. How many hours will it take to plow the field if both tractors work together?

Solution: The rate of the first tractor is 1/16 of the field per hour. The rate of the second tractor is 1/20 of the field per hour. Let *h* equal the number of hours that the two tractors will plow. Then the first tractor will plow $h \times 1/16 = h/16$ of the field, and the second tractor will plow $h \times 1/20 = h/20$ of the field. Since the sum of the work done by the two tractors must equal 1 (the whole job), you can set up the following equation:

$$\frac{h}{16} + \frac{h}{20} = 1$$

To solve an equation like this, first clear it of fractions by multiplying each term on both sides by 80, the lowest common denominator of the two fractions:

$$80\left(\frac{h}{16}\right) + 80\left(\frac{h}{20}\right) = 80(1)$$
$$5h + 4h = 80$$

Then solve for *h*:

$$9h = 80$$
$$h = 8\frac{8}{9}$$

Example: It takes 4 hours for an old machine and a new machine working together to complete a job. If it takes the old machine 12 hours to complete the job by itself, how long does it take the new machine to complete the job by itself?

Solution: If it takes the old machine 12 hours to complete the job by itself, then in 4 hours the old machine does 4/12, or 1/3, of the job. Let *h* equal the number of hours it takes the newer machine to complete the job by itself. Then in 4 hours the new machine does $4/h$ of the job. You know that in 4 hours the two machines together complete the entire job, so set up the equation and solve for h:

$$\frac{1}{3} + \frac{4}{h} = 1 \quad \text{(Subtract 1/3)}$$

$$\frac{4}{h} = \frac{2}{3} \quad \text{(Cross multiply)}$$

$$2h = 12 \quad \text{(Divide by 2)}$$

$$h = 6$$

Average Problems

An *average* is the sum of a set of values divided by the number of values in the set. For example, the sum of 29, 11, 18, 46, 3, 104, and 41 is 252; therefore, the average of these seven numbers is $252 \div 7 = 36$. Another name for the average of a group of values is the *mean*, or *arithmetic mean*.

The basic formula for solving average problems is this:

$$\text{Average value} = \frac{\text{Sum of values}}{\text{Number of values}}$$

If you're given a set of values and you're asked to find the average, use this basic formula.

Example: The temperatures recorded one cold morning in various parts of the county were as follows: $13°$, $6°$, $-4°$, $0°$, and $-5°$. What was the average temperature in the county that morning?

Solution: Let a equal the average temperature. Then plug the information you're given into the basic formula for solving average problems:

$$a = \frac{13 + 6 + (-4) + 0 + (-5)}{5}$$

$$= \frac{10}{5}$$

$$= 2$$

The average temperature was $2°$.

If you're given the average and you're asked to find a missing value from a given set of values, first find the sum of all the values by using this variation on the basic formula:

$$\text{Sum of values} = \text{Average value} \times \text{Number of values}$$

Then subtract the sum of the known values from the sum of all the values to find the missing value.

Example: Nancy's grades on four out of five math tests have been 77, 82, 86, and 88. If she wants her average on all five tests to be 85, what score must she earn on the fifth test?

Solution: If Nancy wants her average score on five tests to be 85, then she must earn a total of $85 \times 5 = 425$ points on the tests. So far she has earned $77 + 82 + 86 + 88 = 333$ points. So she must earn $425 - 333 = 92$ points on the fifth test.

If you're given two averages—the average for one set of values and the average for a second set of values—and you're asked to find the combined average of the two sets, use the variation on the basic formula to find the sum of each set of values. Then add the two sums together and divide the combined sum by the total number of values in both sets.

Example: Twenty of the thirty students in a history class scored an average of 78 points on a test. If the remaining ten students scored an average of 90 points on the test, what was the average score for the entire class?

Solution: Since more students scored 78 points than 90 points, the class average must be closer to 78 than to 90. Therefore, you cannot find the class average simply by adding 78 and 90 and dividing the sum by 2. To find the class average, you must find the sum of the scores of all the students in the class, and then you must divide that sum by 30, the total number of students in the class. To find the sum of the scores of all the students in the class, first find the sum of the scores of the twenty students who averaged 78:

$$78 \times 20 = 1560$$

Then find the sum of the scores of the ten students who averaged 90:

$$90 \times 10 = 900$$

Finally, add the two sums together and divide by 30:

$$\frac{1560 + 900}{30} = \frac{2460}{30} = 82$$

Integer Problems

The set of *integers* is made up of the set of positive whole numbers, the set of negative whole numbers, and zero. The numbers 6, 7, 8, 9, and 10 are called *consecutive integers*, since they follow in natural order. Any group of consecutive integers may be represented as $n, n + 1, n + 2$, and so on.

If x is an integer divisible by another integer y, then x is said to be a multiple of y and y is said to be a factor of x. A number that has no other factors besides itself and 1 is a *prime number*. The numbers 7, 11, and 19 are all prime numbers. The number 1, though divisible only by itself and 1, is not considered a prime number. Numbers that are not prime numbers are called *composite numbers*. The number 15, for instance, is a composite number since it has factors other than 1 and 15. Those factors are 3 and 5.

Any integer that has 2 as a factor (that is, any integer that is divisible by 2) is an *even integer*. An even integer may be represented as $2n$, where n is any integer. The numbers -4, -2, 0, 2, and 4 are called *consecutive even integers*. Any integer that does not have 2 as a factor (that is, any integer that is not divisible by 2) is an *odd integer*. An odd integer may be represented as $2n + 1$, where n is any integer. The numbers 3, 5, 7, and 9 are called *consecutive odd integers*. The rules that govern the multiplication and addition of odd and even integers are as follows:

$$\text{even} \times \text{even} = \text{even} \qquad \text{even} + \text{even} = \text{even}$$
$$\text{odd} \times \text{odd} = \text{odd} \qquad \text{odd} + \text{odd} = \text{even}$$
$$\text{even} \times \text{odd} = \text{even} \qquad \text{even} + \text{odd} = \text{odd}$$

These rules also apply to the division and subtraction of odd and even integers.

Here are a few examples of the types of integer problems you may encounter on the GRE:

Example: If k is any integer, which of the following must also be an integer?

(a) $\dfrac{k}{3}$

(b) $\dfrac{k + 1}{3}$

(c) $\dfrac{k + 2}{3}$

(d) $\dfrac{3k - 1}{3}$

(e) $\dfrac{3k + 3}{3}$

Solution: Since you're looking for the expression that *must* be an integer, no matter what integer k is, you can solve this problem fairly easily by substituting simple integral values for k in each of the answer choices. If $k = 1$, for instance, neither (a) nor (b) will be an integer. If $k = 2$, neither (c) nor (d) will be an integer. So the correct answer must be (e). You can see that it is if you simplify the expression:

$$\frac{3k + 3}{3} = \frac{3(k + 1)}{3} = k + 1$$

If k is an integer, then $k + 1$ must also be an integer.

Example: A haberdasher sells neckties for $7 each and shirts for $12 each. If he sells $95 worth of ties and shirts, what is the least number of ties he could have sold?

(a) 3   (b) 4   (c) 5   (d) 6   (e) 7

Solution: The quickest way to solve a problem like this is through the process of elimination. You know that the amount of money spent on shirts must be divisible by $12, so multiply each answer by $7 and subtract the result from $95. With choice (a), the amount of money spent on shirts would be $95 − $21 = $74, which is not divisible by $12. With choice (b), the amount of money spent on shirts would be $95 − $28 = $67, which is not divisible by $12. With choice (c), the amount of money spent on shirts would be $95 − $35 = $60, which *is* divisible by $12. Therefore choice (c) must be the correct answer.

Example: If n is any integer, which of the following must be an *even* integer?

(a) $2n + 3$
(b) $2n - 1$
(c) $3n$
(d) $2n + 4$
(e) $6n - 3$

Solution: Since it is the product of 2 and another integer, you know that $2n$ must be an even integer. If $2n$ is an even integer, then $2n + 3$ must be an odd integer, since even + odd = odd; $2n - 1$ must be an odd integer, since even − odd = odd; and $6n - 3$, which is equivalent to $3(2n - 1)$, must also be an odd integer, since odd × odd = odd. Of the two remaining choices, $3n$ may be either an even integer or an odd integer, depending on the value of n. So the correct answer is $2n + 4$, which must be an even integer, since even + even = even.

Angle Relationships

Angles are defined by their size and by their relationship to other angles. An *acute angle* has a measure greater than 0° but less than 90°. A *right angle* has a measure of 90°. Two angles that together have a measure of 90° are called *complementary angles*. An *obtuse angle* has a measure greater than 90° but less than 180°. A *straight angle* (which looks like a straight line) has a measure of 180°. Two angles that together have a measure of 180° (that is, two angles that together form a straight line) are called *supplementary angles*.

To solve the geometry problems on the GRE, you need to know a few basic facts about angles and angle relationships:

1. If two lines intersect, the four angles formed are either equal or supplementary. The angles opposite one another, which are called *vertical angles*, are equal. The angles next to one another are supplementary.

2. If two parallel lines are intersected by a third line, called a *transversal*, the eight angles formed are either equal or supplementary. For example, if line *PQ* is parallel to line *RS*, then angles 1 and 2, which are called *corresponding angles*, are equal, and angles 2 and 3, which are called *alternate interior angles*, are also equal. The angles that are not equal, such as the angles next to one another, are supplementary.

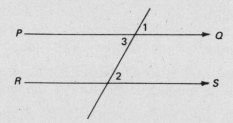

3. If two sides of a triangle are equal, the angles opposite these sides are also equal. In triangle *PQR*, for example, if *PQ* = *PR*, as shown, then angle *Q* = angle *R*. The reverse is also true; in other words, if angle *Q* = angle *R*, then *PQ* = *PR*. A triangle that has two equal sides is called an *isosceles triangle*.

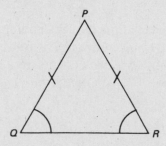

4. The sum of the measures of the three interior angles of a triangle is 180°.

Example: In triangle *RST*, if *RS* = *RT* and angle *T* has a measure of 70°, as shown, what is the measure of angle *R*?

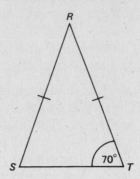

Solution: If *RS* = *RT*, then angle *S* has the same measure as angle *T*. To find the measure of angle *R*, just multiply 70° by 2 and subtract the product from 180°:   180° − (70° × 2) = 180° − 140° = 40°.

5. If a triangle is *equilateral*—that is, if all three of its sides are the same length—then each angle has a measure of 60°.

6. The two acute angles in a right triangle, which is a triangle with a right angle, are complementary. The sum of their measures is 90°.

Example: If the acute angles of a right triangle are in the ratio of 2 to 3, what is the degree measure of the smaller angle?

Solution: If the angles are in the ratio of 2 to 3, you can represent them as $2x$ and $3x$. You know that the sum of their degree measures is 90, so set up the equation and solve for x:

$$2x + 3x = 90$$
$$5x = 90$$
$$x = 18$$

If $x = 18$, then the degree measure of the smaller angle is $2 \times 18 = 36$.

7. If the vertex of an angle is at the center of a circle, then the angle is called a *central angle* and its measure is equal to the measure of the arc it intercepts. (An *arc* is a portion of a circle.) In circle *O*, for example, angle *POQ* is a central angle. Its measure is equal to the measure of arc *PQ*.

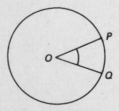

Example: Circle *O* has a radius of 9. If angle *POQ* measures 40°, what is the length of arc *PQ*?

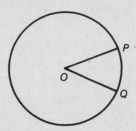

Solution: Arc *PQ* is intercepted by central angle *POQ*, so its measure is the same as the measure of angle *POQ*, which is 40°. You know that there are 360 degrees of arc in a circle, so an arc of 40° is 40/360 = 1/9 of the circumference of a circle. To find the circumference of a circle of radius 9, recall the formula $C = 2\pi r$, where *r* is the radius of the circle:

$$C = 2\pi r$$
$$= 2\pi 9$$

Therefore the length of arc *PQ* is

$$\frac{1}{9} \times 2\pi 9 = 2\pi$$

Since π has an approximate value of 3.14 (or 22/7), arc *PQ* has an approximate length of $2 \times 3.14 = 6.28$.

8. If the vertex of an angle lies on a circle, then the angle is said to be *inscribed* in the circle and its measure is equal to half the measure of the arc it intercepts. Angle *RST*, for example, is an inscribed angle. Its measure is equal to half the measure of arc *RT*.

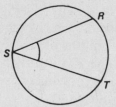

Example: Arc *GF* in circle *O* has a measure of 130°, as shown. What is the value of *x*?

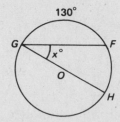

Solution: Since angle *FGH* is an inscribed angle, its measure ($x°$) is half the measure of arc *FH*. To find the measure of arc *FH*, recall that there are 180 degrees of arc in a semicircle. If arc *GF* = 130°, then arc *FH* = 180° − 130° = 50°. Therefore, $x = 50 \div 2 = 25$.

9. A line that intersects a circle at one and only one point is called a *tangent*. If a radius is drawn to the point at which a tangent intersects a circle, two right angles are formed and the radius is said to be *perpendicular* to the tangent. For example, if line *S* is tangent to circle *O* at point *T*, then radius *OT* is perpendicular to line *S*.

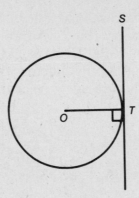

Right-Triangle Relationships

A *right triangle* is any triangle that has a 90° angle. An *isosceles right triangle* is a right triangle with two equal sides and two equal angles. The two equal angles in an isosceles right triangle each measure 45°.

The two shorter sides of a right triangle are called the *legs*. The longest side, which is the side opposite the right angle, is called the *hypotenuse*. The relationship between the lengths of the legs and the hypotenuse of a right triangle is expressed in the *Pythagorean theorem*, which states that the square of the length of the hypotenuse is equal to the sum of the squares of the lengths of the legs. Thus:

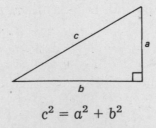

$$c^2 = a^2 + b^2$$

Certain "standard" right triangles turn up frequently on the GRE. Two of them have sides that are in whole-number proportions. These are the 3-4-5 and the 5-12-13 right triangles, so called because their sides are in the ratio of 3 to 4 to 5 and 5 to 12 to 13, respectively.

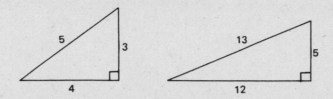

In general, if the legs of a right triangle have lengths of $3k$ and $4k$, where k is some number greater than 0, then the hypotenuse has a length of $5k$. If the legs have lengths of $5k$ and $12k$, then the hypotenuse has a length of $13k$.

Example: A 39-foot ladder leaning against a building reaches a point 36 feet high on the building. How many feet from the foot of the building is the foot of the ladder?

Solution: If you draw a sketch, you'll see that the ladder, the building, and the ground form a right triangle:

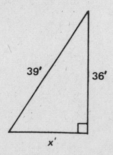

Since $39 = 13 \times 3$ and $36 = 12 \times 3$, this right triangle is the $5k$-$12k$-$13k$ right triangle and $k = 3$. Therefore, the foot of the ladder is $5 \times 3 = 15$ feet from the foot of the building.

Two other "standard" right triangles are the 30°-60°-90° triangle and the 45°-45°-90° triangle. As the following figure illustrates, the sides of the 30°-60°-90° triangle are in the ratio of a to $a\sqrt{3}$ to $2a$, where a is some number greater than 0.

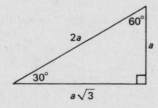

Notice that in the 30°-60°-90° triangle the hypotenuse ($2a$) is twice as long as the shorter leg (a).

Example: What is the height of an equilateral triangle of side 10?

Solution: The height divides an equilateral triangle into two 30°-60°-90° triangles, as shown in the following figure:

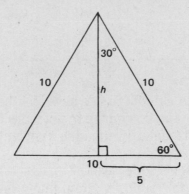

Thus the height (h) of the triangle is $5\sqrt{3}$.

As the following figure illustrates, the sides of the 45°-45°-90° triangle are in the ratio of a to a to $a\sqrt{2}$, where a is some number greater than 0.

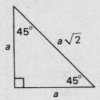

Example: What is the length of the diagonal of a square of side 7?

Solution: A diagonal divides a square into two 45°-45°-90° triangles, as shown in the following figure:

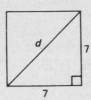

Thus the diagonal (d) of the square has a length of $7\sqrt{2}$.

Area Problems

The unit of area is a square whose side is a unit of length; examples are the square inch, the square yard, and the square meter. The area of a surface is the number of units of area it contains. The formulas for finding the areas of common plane geometrical figures are shown here:

Rectangle

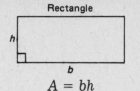

$$A = bh$$

Square

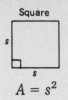

$$A = s^2$$

Triangle

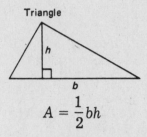

$$A = \frac{1}{2}bh$$

Circle

$$A = \pi r^2$$

Parallelogram

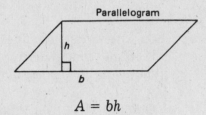

$$A = bh$$

Here are some examples of the types of area problems you may encounter on the GRE:

Example: A circle is inscribed in a square of side 4. What is the ratio of the area of the square to the area of the circle?

Solution: If the circle is inscribed in the square, then the radius of the circle is 2, as shown in the following figure:

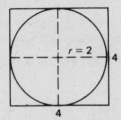

A circle of radius 2 has an area of $\pi r^2 = \pi 2^2 = 4\pi$. A square of side 4 has an area of $s^2 = 4^2 = 16$. Therefore, the ratio of the area of the square to the area of the circle is

$$\frac{16}{4\pi} = \frac{4}{\pi}$$

Example: If the area of an isosceles right triangle is 50, what is the length of the hypotenuse of the triangle?

Solution: As the following figure shows, the base and the height of an isosceles right triangle are equal:

Let x equal the length of the base and the height of the triangle. Then plug what you know into the formula for finding the area of a triangle and solve for x:

$$50 = \frac{1}{2}(x)(x)$$

$$50 = \frac{x^2}{2}$$

$$x^2 = 100$$

$$x = 10$$

You know that the sides of an isosceles right triangle, which is a 45°-45°-90° triangle, are in the ratio of a to a to $a\sqrt{2}$, so the length of the hypotenuse of the triangle is $10\sqrt{2}$.

Example: How many square yards of carpeting are needed to cover the floor of a room that is 20 feet long and 14 feet wide?

Solution: You're asked to find the number of square *yards*, not the number of square feet, so first convert 20 feet to 20/3 yards and 14 feet to 14/3 yards. Then multiply to find the area of the room in square yards:

$$\frac{20}{3} \times \frac{14}{3} = \frac{280}{9} = 31\frac{1}{9}$$

Notice that you cannot multiply 20 by 14 and then divide by 3. If you do, your answer will be way off because a square yard is not equivalent to 3 square feet. A square yard is 3 feet square, which means that it is 3 feet on each side. Thus 1 square yard = 3 feet × 3 feet = 9 square feet.

Geometry of Solids

A *solid* is any closed three-dimensional figure with plane (two-dimensional) surfaces as sides. A *face* is any of the plane surfaces that form the sides of a solid. An *edge* is the line formed when two sides of a solid meet. The *surface area* of a solid is the sum of the areas of all of the sides, or faces, of the solid. The surface area of a solid is measured in square units. The *volume* of a solid is the amount of space contained within or occupied by the solid. The volume of a solid is measured in cubic units.

A *rectangular solid* is a three-dimensional figure whose sides are all rectangles. The solid shown here is a rectangular solid:

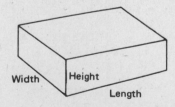

A rectangular solid has six faces and twelve edges. The volume of a rectangular solid is given by the formula Volume = length × width × height, or, in shorthand, $V = LWH$.

> **Example:** What is the volume of a box that is 3 feet long, 2 feet wide, and 18 inches high?

> **Solution:** First express the height of the box in feet: 18 inches = 3/2 feet. Then multiply the length by the width and the height:

$$V = LWH$$
$$= 3 \times 2 \times \frac{3}{2}$$
$$= 9$$

The volume of the box is 9 cubic feet.

A *cube* is a rectangular solid whose sides are all squares of the same size. The solid shown here is a cube:

Cube

Like any other rectangular solid, a cube has six faces and twelve edges. The edges of a cube are all equal. The volume of a cube is given by the formula Volume = edge cubed, or, in shorthand, $V = e^3$.

> **Example:** The total surface area of a cube is 96 square centimeters. What is the volume of the cube?

> **Solution:** The total surface of a cube is the sum of the areas of the six faces. Since the six faces are all the same size, the area of each face is $96 \div 6 = 16$. A cube with a face of area 16 has an edge of $\sqrt{16} = 4$. Therefore the volume of the cube is $4^3 = 64$ cubic centimeters.

A *right circular cylinder* is a three-dimensional figure whose two bases are circles of the same size. The solid shown here is a right circular cylinder:

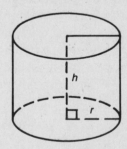

The volume of a right circular cylinder is given by the formula $V = \pi r^2 h$, where r is the radius of the circular bases of the cylinder and h is the height of the cylinder.

> **Example:** The radius of the base of a right circular cylinder is 5 centimeters. If the height of the cylinder is 14 centimeters, what is the volume of the cylinder?

> **Solution:** $V = \pi r^2 h$
> $= \pi \times 5^2 \times 14$
> $= \pi \times 25 \times 14$
> $= 350\pi$

Since π has an approximate value of 22/7, the cylinder has an approximate volume of $350 \times 22/7 = 1100$ cubic centimeters.

Coordinate Geometry

The *rectangular coordinate system* is used to locate points in a plane and to graph linear equations, which are equations with variables of the first degree, or first power, only. The rectangular coordinate system consists of a background grid and two perpendicular number lines that intersect at the zero point on each, as shown in the following figure:

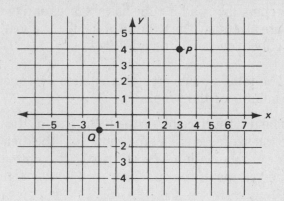

The point at which the two number lines intersect is known as the *origin*. The horizontal number line is known as the *x-axis*. The vertical number line is known as the *y-axis*. The numbers to the right of the origin on the *x*-axis and above the origin on the *y*-axis are positive. The numbers to the left of the origin on the *x*-axis and below the origin on the *y*-axis are negative.

Each point in the coordinate plane is defined by an *ordered pair* of real numbers, called *coordinates*. Ordered pairs, or coordinates, are written in the form (x, y).

The first coordinate, called the *x-coordinate* or *abscissa*, defines the distance of a point from the origin along the *x*-axis. The second coordinate, called the *y-coordinate* or *ordinate*, defines the distance of a point from the origin along the *y*-axis.

> ***Example:*** The coordinates (3, 4) define the point that is three units to the right of the origin on the *x*-axis and four units above the origin on the *y*-axis. That point is labeled *P* on the preceding graph. The coordinates $(-2, -1)$ define the point that is two units to the left of the origin on the *x*-axis and one unit below the origin on the *y*-axis. That point is labeled *Q* on the preceding graph.

To locate a point in the coordinate plane, follow these three steps:

1. Find the point designated by the *x*-coordinate on the *x*-axis and draw an imaginary line perpendicular to the *x*-axis through it.
2. Find the point designated by the *y*-coordinate on the *y*-axis and draw an imaginary line perpendicular to the *y*-axis through it.
3. Find and plot the point you're looking for at the intersection of the two imaginary lines.

To find the distance between any two points *P* and *Q* in the coordinate plane, use the formula

$$PQ = \sqrt{(x_1 - x_2)^2 + (y_1 - y_2)^2}$$

where (x_1, y_1) are the coordinates of point *P* and (x_2, y_2) are the coordinates of point *Q*.

> ***Example:*** If the coordinates of point *P* are (3, 4) and the coordinates of point *Q* are $(-2, -1)$, what is the distance between the two points?
>
> ***Solution:*** $PQ = \sqrt{(x_1 - x_2)^2 + (y_1 - y_2)^2}$
> $= \sqrt{[3 - (-2)]^2 + [4 - (-1)]^2}$
> $= \sqrt{5^2 + 5^2}$
> $= \sqrt{50}$
> $= \sqrt{25 \times 2}$
> $= 5\sqrt{2}$

To find the midpoint *M* of a line segment *PQ* in the coordinate plane, use the formula

$$M = \left(\frac{x_1 + x_2}{2}, \frac{y_1 + y_2}{2}\right)$$

where (x_1, y_1) are the coordinates of point *P* and (x_2, y_2) are the coordinates of point *Q*.

Example: If the coordinates of point P are (6, 5) and the coordinates of point Q are (2, 1), what is the midpoint of line segment PQ?

Solution: $M = \left(\dfrac{x_1 + x_2}{2}, \dfrac{y_1 + y_2}{2} \right)$

$= \left(\dfrac{6 + 2}{2}, \dfrac{5 + 1}{2} \right)$

$= (4, 3)$

To graph a linear equation in two variables, such as $x + 6 = 2y$, follow these six steps:

1. Use standard algebraic techniques to isolate one of the variables on the left side of the equation (for example, if $x + 6 = 2y$, then $x = 2y - 6$).
2. Assign any convenient value to the second variable (for example, $y = 4$) and solve to find the corresponding value of the first variable (for example, if $y = 4$, then $x = 2(4) - 6 = 2$).
3. Write down the corresponding values of the two variables in the form of an ordered pair (for example, [2, 4]).
4. Repeat the procedure twice so that you have three different ordered pairs, or coordinates.
5. Locate the points defined by the three ordered pairs in the coordinate plane.
6. Connect the points. The line thus formed is the graph of the equation.

To find the area of a figure in the coordinate plane, determine the dimensions of the figure and then plug those dimensions into the basic formula for finding the area of the figure.

Example: The coordinates of the vertices of triangle PQR are (4, 3), (2, 1), and (7, 1). What is the area of the triangle?

Solution: Sketch the triangle, as shown here:

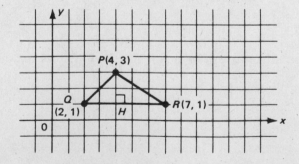

Since the base of the triangle is parallel with one of the axes, determining the dimensions of the triangle is a simple matter. The base, as you can see, is 5 units (the difference between the x-coordinates of R and Q). The height is 2 units (the difference between the y-coordinates of P, at the apex, and Q and R at the base). Therefore, the area of the triangle is

$$\frac{1}{2}\,bh = \frac{1}{2} \times 5 \times 2 = 5$$

Inequalities

An *inequality* is simply a statement that one expression is not equal to another. There are four basic inequality signs:

$>$ is greater than	$\geq$ is greater than or equal to
$<$ is less than	$\leq$ is less than or equal to

The statement $5 > 2$ means that 5 is greater than 2. Another way of saying the same thing is $2 < 5$, which means that 2 is less than 5. The statement $3x \leq 6$ means that $3x$ is less than or equal to 6. Another way of saying the same thing is $6 \geq 3x$, which means that 6 is greater than or equal to $3x$.

The inequality $x > 4$ is satisfied for all values of x greater than 4. Thus, all values of x greater than 4 are called the *solution set* for the inequality $x > 4$. To find the solution set for an inequality, remember these basic principles:

1. You can add the same quantity to or subtract the same quantity from both sides of an inequality without altering its solution set.
2. You can multiply or divide both sides of an inequality by the same positive quantity without altering its solution set.
3. You can multiply or divide both sides of an inequality by the same negative quantity without altering its solution set *if you change the direction of the inequality*.

Example: To find the solution set of the inequality $3y + 5 > 17$, first subtract 5 from both sides and then divide both sides by 3:

$$3y + 5 > 17$$
$$3y > 12$$
$$y > 4$$

Example: To find the solution set of the inequality $3t < 5t - 16$, first subtract $5t$ from both sides and then divide both sides by -2, remembering to reverse the sign of the inequality:

$$3t < 5t - 16$$
$$-2t < -16$$
$$t > 8$$

There are a few basic geometric inequalities that you should know for the GRE:

1. The sum of the lengths of two sides of a triangle is greater than the length of the third side.

   Example: What is the range of values for x in the following figure?

   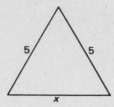

   Solution: Since the length of the third side of a triangle must be less than the sum of the lengths of the other two sides, you know that x must have a value less than 10. Since the length of any side of a triangle must be positive (it cannot be negative), you also know that x must be greater than 0. Therefore you can express the range of values for x as $0 < x < 10$.

2. If two sides of a triangle are unequal, the angles opposite these sides are unequal and the greater angle lies opposite the longer side. The converse is also true.

   Example: In triangle PQR, if $QR > PQ$, then angle $P >$ angle R. Conversely, if angle $P >$ angle R, then $QR > PQ$.

   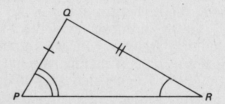

3. The measure of an exterior angle of a triangle is greater than the measure of either remote interior angle. In fact, the measure of an exterior angle of a triangle is equal to the sum of the measures of the two remote interior angles.

   Example: In triangle RST, the measure of exterior angle x is greater than the measure either of remote interior angle R or of remote interior angle S. In fact, the measure of exterior angle x is equal to the sum of the measures of remote interior angles R and S.

   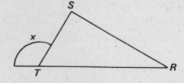

PART VI
Practice Exercises
in Mathematics
by Topics

This part consists of practice exercises designed to help you sharpen your quantitative skills for the GRE. It includes a set of exercises corresponding to each of the topics covered in the preceding math review. In addition, it includes a set of data interpretation exercises and a set of quantitative comparison exercises. Explanatory answers for all exercises begin on page 171.

Signed Numbers

1. $(4) + (-7) - (-11) =$

   (a) -14 (b) -8 (c) 0 (d) $+8$ (e) $+22$

2. $(-5) + (-9) - (23) + (2) =$

   (a) -35 (b) -17 (c) $+11$ (d) $+13$ (e) $+37$

3. $(8) - (-4) + (-10) - (-19) =$

   (a) -25 (b) -24 (c) -17 (d) $+13$ (e) $+21$

4. $9(6 - 8) - (-3) =$

   (a) -21 (b) -18 (c) -15 (d) $+15$ (e) $+18$

5. $(-4 + -1)(3 - 7) =$

   (a) -50 (b) -20 (c) $+12$ (d) $+20$ (e) $+30$

6. $(-8 \times 10) \div (4 - 6) =$

   (a) -82 (b) -40 (c) -8 (d) $+8$ (e) $+40$

7. $(-18.4) + (3.7) =$

   (a) -22.1
   (b) -14.7
   (c) -1.47
   (d) $+1.47$
   (e) $+14.7$

8. If the temperature was $-27.5°$ yesterday and $+4.7°$ this morning, how much did the temperature rise?

   (a) $2.28°$
   (b) $3.22°$
   (c) $22.8°$
   (d) $31°$
   (e) $32.2°$

9. What is the product of -8.7 and -3.4?

   (a) -30
   (b) -29.58
   (c) -2.958
   (d) $+2.958$
   (e) $+29.58$

10. $(-92.4) \div (+4) =$

   (a) -23.1
   (b) -2.31
   (c) -0.231
   (d) $+2.31$
   (e) $+23.1$

Fractions

1. The fraction $\dfrac{24}{32}$ expressed in lowest terms is

   (a) $\dfrac{12}{16}$ (b) $\dfrac{6}{8}$ (c) $\dfrac{3}{4}$ (d) $\dfrac{6}{16}$ (e) $\dfrac{3}{8}$

2. Change $\dfrac{19}{5}$ to a mixed number.

   (a) $5\dfrac{1}{5}$ (b) $3\dfrac{4}{5}$ (c) $4\dfrac{4}{5}$ (d) $15\dfrac{4}{5}$ (e) $\dfrac{5}{19}$

3. 40 is what part of 64?

   (a) $\dfrac{3}{8}$ (b) $\dfrac{5}{12}$ (c) $\dfrac{7}{8}$ (d) $\dfrac{5}{12}$ (e) $\dfrac{5}{8}$

4. Change $9\dfrac{2}{3}$ to an improper fraction.

   (a) $\dfrac{14}{3}$ (b) $\dfrac{21}{3}$ (c) $\dfrac{21}{2}$ (d) $\dfrac{29}{3}$ (e) $\dfrac{54}{3}$

5. $\dfrac{2}{3} + \dfrac{3}{4} =$

   (a) $1\dfrac{5}{12}$ (b) $\dfrac{5}{7}$ (c) $\dfrac{12}{17}$ (d) $\dfrac{5}{12}$ (e) $\dfrac{7}{12}$

6. $14\frac{1}{2} - 9\frac{2}{3} =$

   (a) $5\frac{5}{6}$ (b) $5\frac{1}{3}$ (c) $4\frac{1}{3}$ (d) $3\frac{2}{3}$ (e) $4\frac{5}{6}$

7. 9 inches is what part of a foot?

   (a) $\frac{2}{3}$ (b) $\frac{3}{4}$ (c) $\frac{7}{12}$ (d) $\frac{5}{6}$ (e) $\frac{4}{5}$

8. Divide 27 by $2\frac{1}{4}$.

   (a) $60\frac{3}{4}$ (b) $13\frac{1}{2}$ (c) 12   (d) $12\frac{3}{4}$ (e) $13\frac{3}{4}$

9. A man owned $\frac{3}{8}$ of a business and sold $\frac{2}{3}$ of his share. What part of the entire business did he sell?

   (a) $\frac{5}{11}$ (b) $\frac{5}{24}$ (c) $\frac{6}{11}$ (d) $\frac{1}{4}$ (e) $\frac{9}{16}$

10. $10\frac{2}{3}$ ounces is what fractional part of a pound?

    (a) $\frac{2}{3}$ (b) $\frac{3}{4}$ (c) $\frac{5}{6}$ (d) $\frac{4}{7}$ (e) $\frac{5}{8}$

11. 81 is $\frac{3}{4}$ of what number?

    (a) $60\frac{3}{4}$ (b) 112   (c) 102   (d) 108   (e) $90\frac{2}{3}$

12. A strip of metal $7\frac{1}{8}$ inches long is to be divided into 6 equal parts. How long, in inches, will each part be?

    (a) $1\frac{7}{48}$ (b) $1\frac{1}{6}$ (c) $\frac{11}{16}$ (d) $1\frac{3}{8}$ (e) $1\frac{3}{16}$

13. An oil tank is $\frac{5}{8}$ full. When 6 gallons of oil are removed, the tank is $\frac{1}{4}$ full. What is the total capacity of the tank in gallons?

    (a) 14   (b) 16   (c) 18   (d) 20   (e) 24

14. $5\dfrac{2}{5} \times 6\dfrac{2}{3} =$

    (a) 24   (b) 30   (c) 36   (d) 39   (e) 42

15. $\dfrac{5x}{8} - \dfrac{x}{2} =$

    (a) $\dfrac{4x}{6}$ (b) $\dfrac{2x}{3}$ (c) $\dfrac{3x}{8}$ (d) $\dfrac{x}{8}$ (e) $\dfrac{x}{2}$

16. Reduce $\dfrac{12k}{18k}$ to lowest terms.

    (a) $\dfrac{2}{3}$ (b) $\dfrac{2k}{3}$ (c) $\dfrac{4}{6}$ (d) $\dfrac{6k}{9}$ (e) $\dfrac{3k}{4}$

17. $\dfrac{3}{4}$ is what fractional part of $1\dfrac{1}{8}$?

    (a) $\dfrac{27}{32}$ (b) $\dfrac{5}{8}$ (c) $\dfrac{6}{11}$ (d) $\dfrac{7}{12}$ (e) $\dfrac{2}{3}$

18. A man has completed $\dfrac{5}{8}$ of a job in 10 days. If he continues to work at the same rate, how many more days will it take him to finish the job?

    (a) 5   (b) 6   (c) 7   (d) $7\dfrac{1}{2}$ (e) 8

19. A boy spent \$2.70, which was $\dfrac{5}{9}$ of what he had originally. How much did he have originally?

    (a) \$4.86   (b) \$1.50   (c) \$2.45   (d) \$3.85   (e) \$4.84

20. $\dfrac{7y}{4} - \dfrac{3y}{2} + \dfrac{5y}{8} =$

    (a) $\dfrac{3y}{4}$ (b) $\dfrac{9y}{8}$ (c) $\dfrac{9y}{10}$ (d) $\dfrac{7y}{8}$ (e) $\dfrac{5y}{8}$

Decimals

1. A man's temperature rose one day from 98.6° to 102.4°. How many degrees did it rise?

    (a) 2.2   (b) 2.4   (c) 3.4   (d) 3.8   (e) 4.2

2. $.0057 \times 1000 =$

   (a) 57   (b) 5.7   (c) .57   (d) .057   (e) 570

3. Write the decimal .625 as a common fraction in *lowest* terms.

   (a) $\dfrac{12}{100}$ (b) $\dfrac{625}{1000}$ (c) $\dfrac{62}{100}$ (d) $\dfrac{125}{200}$ (e) $\dfrac{5}{8}$

4. Write the fraction $\dfrac{7}{20}$ as a decimal.

   (a) .35   (b) .7   (c) .27   (d) .53   (e) .72

5. Which of the following has the *largest* value?

   (a) .3   (b) .33   (c) .303   (d) .033   (e) .333

6. Bill buys 8 rolls at 12¢ each, 4 pounds of beef at $1.12 a pound, and 3 quarts of milk at 47¢ a quart. How much change does he get back from a 20 dollar bill?

   (a) $6.85   (b) $8.42   (c) $13.15   (d) $14.12   (e) $14.87

7. $\dfrac{1}{3}$ is what *decimal* part of $\dfrac{5}{6}$?

   (a) .28   (b) .32   (c) .36   (d) .40   (e) .56

8. Which of the following is the closest approximation of the product of .51, .75, .375, and .667?

   (a) $\dfrac{3}{32}$ (b) $\dfrac{3}{16}$ (c) $\dfrac{3}{4}$ (d) $\dfrac{7}{16}$ (e) $\dfrac{5}{16}$

9. Dividing by .04 is the same as multiplying by

   (a) $\dfrac{1}{25}$ (b) $\dfrac{1}{4}$ (c) 4   (d) 25   (e) 400

10. $1.25 \times .60 =$

    (a) .075   (b) $\dfrac{3}{4}$ (c) $\dfrac{4}{5}$ (d) 75   (e) $7\dfrac{1}{2}$

11. If a strip of metal is 0.28 feet long, its length in *inches* is

    (a) less than 2

    (b) between 2 and $2\dfrac{1}{2}$

(c) between $2\frac{1}{2}$ and 3

(d) between 3 and 4

(e) more than 4

12. If $\frac{13}{10}y = .039$, then $y =$

(a) .03   (b) .3   (c) 1.2   (d) 1.6   (e) 3

13. $\frac{7}{.7 \times .7} =$

(a) $\frac{7}{100}$ (b) $\frac{7}{10}$ (c) $\frac{100}{7}$ (d) 7   (e) 70

14. If $.3p - 1.2 = 4.8$, then $p =$

(a) 2   (b) 20   (c) 200   (d) .2   (e) .02

15. If $31,000 = 3.1 \times 10^x$, then $x =$

(a) 2   (b) 3   (c) 4   (d) 5   (e) 6

Percentage

1. Find 30% of 42.

(a) 126   (b) 1.26   (c) 12.6   (d) 1260   (e) .126

2. A team played 40 games one season and won 24 of them. What percent of its games did the team win?

(a) 24   (b) 32   (c) 40   (d) 48   (e) 60

3. 75% equals how many twelfths?

(a) 6   (b) 7   (c) 8   (d) 9   (e) 10

4. 120% of 40 =

(a) 48   (b) 50   (c) 52   (d) 54   (e) 56

5. 15 is 60% of what number?

(a) 22   (b) 25   (c) 28   (d) 30   (e) 32

6. The price of coffee dropped from $4.20 a pound to $3.15 a pound. What was the percent decrease?

(a) 20   (b) 23   (c) 25   (d) 27   (e) 30

7. 0.8% is the same as 1 out of every

   (a) 90   (b) 100   (c) 110   (d) 115   (e) 125

8. In 1970, the rainfall in city X was 80% of the normal level. If the rainfall that year was 36 inches, how many inches of rainfall per year is normal for city X?

   (a) 30   (b) 32   (c) 34   (d) 45   (e) 48

9. What is 40% of $\frac{5}{6}$?

   (a) $\frac{1}{3}$ (b) $\frac{4}{25}$ (c) $\frac{5}{24}$ (d) $\frac{10}{3}$ (e) $\frac{100}{3}$

10. 8 ounces is what percent of 15 pounds?

   (a) $3\frac{1}{3}$ (b) $18\frac{1}{3}$ (c) 30   (d) $33\frac{1}{3}$ (e) $53\frac{1}{3}$

11. If x is 40% of y, then y is what percent of x?

   (a) 120   (b) 130   (c) 140   (d) 210   (e) 250

12. A tank contains 60 gallons of oil, which is 40% of its capacity. How many gallons can the tank hold?

   (a) 130   (b) 150   (c) 160   (d) 180   (e) 240

13. What percent of 25 is p?

   (a) $\frac{p}{4}$ (b) $\frac{p}{25}$ (c) $4p$ (d) $\frac{4p}{25}$ (e) $\frac{p}{16}$

14. How many liters of pure acid are there in 8 liters of a 20% solution of acid?

   (a) 1.2   (b) 1.4   (c) 1.5   (d) 1.6   (e) 2.4

15. A man buys a $60 radio at a discount of 25%. How much does he pay for it?

   (a) $40   (b) $45   (c) $48   (d) $50   (e) $52

16. Beef loses 20% of its weight when roasted. How many pounds of raw beef must be roasted to yield 6 pounds of roast beef?

   (a) 6.5   (b) 6.8   (c) 7.2   (d) 7.5   (e) 8.2

17. If the ratio of nurses to doctors in a hospital is 7 to 1, what percent of the staff is nurses?

(a) $87\frac{1}{2}$ (b) $83\frac{1}{3}$ (c) 86   (d) $83\frac{2}{3}$ (e) 78

18. 2 is what percent of $4t$?

(a) $\frac{t}{50}$ (b) $\frac{50}{t}$ (c) $2t$ (d) $\frac{1}{2t}$ (e) $200t$

19. An article costing C dollars is sold for a gain of $r\%$ on the cost. What is the selling price of the article?

(a) $\frac{rC}{100}$

(b) $C(1 + r)$

(c) $\frac{C(1 + r)}{100}$

(d) $C\left(1 + \dfrac{r}{100}\right)$

(e) $r + \dfrac{rC}{100}$

20. A 10-quart solution of alcohol and water is 30% alcohol. If 2 quarts of water are added, what percent of the resulting solution is alcohol?

(a) 20   (b) 24   (c) 25   (d) 26   (e) 30

21. A suit costing $160 is sold for $120. What is the percent loss on the cost?

(a) $33\frac{1}{3}$ (b) 25   (c) 40   (d) 35   (e) 20

22. How many ounces of water must be added to 8 ounces of a 25% solution of salt and water in order to obtain a 10% solution?

(a) 8   (b) 9   (c) 10   (d) 12   (e) 14

23. If a poster is reduced by 10% of its height and 30% of its width, what percent of its original size will it be?

(a) 3   (b) 37   (c) 70   (d) 57   (e) 63

24. Mr. Malkin has $10,000 invested. Part of the sum is invested at a simple annual interest rate of 8%, and the rest is invested at a simple annual interest rate of 6%. The annual income from the 8% investment is $240 more than the annual income from the 6% investment. How much does Mr. Malkin have invested at 8%?

(a) $4,000   (b) $5,000   (c) $6,000   (d) $6,500   (e) $7,000

25. The price of a piece of property was reduced by 15% to $76,500. What was the original price of the property?

(a) $85,000
(b) $90,000
(c) $96,000
(d) $98,000
(e) $98,500

Exponents and Roots

1. $r^3 \times r^5 =$

(a) r^{15} (b) $2r^8$ (c) r^{16} (d) r^8 (e) $8r$

2. $(2p^2)^3 =$

(a) $2p^6$ (b) $8p^6$ (c) $8p^5$ (d) $2p^5$ (e) $6p^6$

3. If $x < -1$, then which of the following expressions has the greatest value?

(a) $\dfrac{1}{x^2}$ (b) x^5 (c) $\left(\dfrac{1}{x}\right)^3$ (d) x^2 (e) x^4

4. Divide $15c^6d^5$ by $-5c^2d^2$.

(a) $-3c^4d^3$
(b) $-3c^3d^3$
(c) $3c^4d^3$
(d) $-3c^3d^4$
(e) $-3c^4d$

5. $\sqrt{36r^5} =$

(a) $6r^2$ (b) $6r^3$ (c) $6r^2\sqrt{r}$ (d) $6r\sqrt{r}$ (e) $6r^4\sqrt{r}$

6. $\sqrt[3]{-\dfrac{1}{8}} =$

(a) $\dfrac{1}{2}$ (b) $\dfrac{1}{4}$ (c) $-\dfrac{1}{4}$ (d) -2 (e) $-\dfrac{1}{2}$

7. If 57 million $= 5.7 \times 10^n$, then $n =$

(a) 5   (b) 6   (c) 7   (d) 8   (e) 9

8. $\sqrt{200} - \sqrt{50} =$

(a) $\sqrt{150}$ (b) 5   (c) $\sqrt{40}$ (d) $5\sqrt{2}$ (e) 2

9. $\dfrac{(5r^2s^3)^3}{5r^2s^5} =$

(a) r^4s^4 (b) $25r^3s$ (c) $25r^4s^4$ (d) r^3s (e) $5r^3s$

10. If $2^p = q$, then $2^{p+1} =$

(a) $q + 1$ (b) $q + 2$ (c) $2q$ (d) q^2 (e) $q^2 + 1$

Operations with Algebraic Expressions

1. Add $4x + 2y$ to $x - 4y$.

(a) $5x - 2y$
(b) $5x + 2y$
(c) $3x - 2y$
(d) $3x + 2y$
(e) $4x - 2y$

2. $(-5r^3s)(3rs^4) =$

(a) $-15r^3s^4$
(b) $-15r^4s^4$
(c) $-15r^4s^5$
(d) $15r^4s^5$
(e) $15r^3s^4$

3. Divide $45x^3y^5$ by $-5x^2y^3$.

(a) $9xy^2$ (b) $-9xy^2$ (c) $-9y^2$ (d) $-40xy^2$ (e) $40xy^2$

4. Divide $(9x^3 - 6x^2 + 3x)$ by $3x$.

(a) $6x^2 - 2x + 1$
(b) $3x^2 - 3x + 1$
(c) $3x^2 - 2x + 3$
(d) $3x^2 - x$
(e) $3x^2 - 2x + 1$

5. The sum of two binomials is $3x^2 - 5x$. If one of the binomials is $2x^2 - x$, what is the other?

(a) $5x^2 - 6x$
(b) $5x^2 - 4x$
(c) $x^2 - 6x$
(d) $x^2 - 4x$
(e) $x^2 + 4x$

6. Factor $x^2 - 36$.

    (a) $(x + 6)(x - 6)$
    (b) $(x + 18)(x - 18)$
    (c) $(x - 6)(x - 6)$
    (d) $(x + 6)(x + 6)$
    (e) $(x - 9)(x + 4)$

7. Express $(r - 1)(r + 2)$ as a trinomial.

    (a) $r^2 - 2$
    (b) $r^2 - r - 2$
    (c) $r^2 + r + 2$
    (d) $r^2 + r - 2$
    (e) $r^2 - 2r - 2$

8. Factor $3y^2 - 48$ completely.

    (a) $3(y^2 - 16)$
    (b) $3(y - 4)(y + 4)$
    (c) $3(y - 4)(y - 4)$
    (d) $3(y + 4)(y + 4)$
    (e) $3(y + 8)(y - 8)$

9. Multiply $(2a - b)$ by $(2a + b)$.

    (a) $4a^2 - 2ab - b^2$
    (b) $4a^2 + 2ab - b^2$
    (c) $4a^2 - b^2$
    (d) $4a^2 + b^2$
    (e) $4a^2 - 4ab - b^2$

10. Express $(2p + 1)(3p - 2)$ as a trinomial.

    (a) $6p^2 + p - 2$
    (b) $6p^2 + p + 2$
    (c) $6p^2 + 7p - 2$
    (d) $6p^2 - 7p - 2$
    (e) $6p^2 - p - 2$

11. Factor $3ax + 3ay + 6a$ completely.

    (a) $3a(x + y + a)$
    (b) $3a(x + y + 2)$
    (c) $a(3x + 3y + 6a)$
    (d) $3(ax + ay + 2a)$
    (e) $3a(x + y + 3a)$

12. Factor $m^2 + 5m - 24$ completely.

    (a) $(m - 8)(m - 3)$
    (b) $(m + 8)(m + 3)$
    (c) $(m + 12)(m - 2)$
    (d) $(m + 8)(m - 3)$
    (e) $(m - 8)(m + 3)$

13. Reduce $\dfrac{27xy^3}{45x^2y}$ to lowest terms.

    (a) $\dfrac{3y}{5x^2}$ (b) $\dfrac{3y^2}{5}$ (c) $\dfrac{3y}{5x}$ (d) $\dfrac{9y^2}{15x}$ (e) $\dfrac{3y^2}{5x}$

14. Reduce $\dfrac{r^2 - 25}{r^2 - 2r - 15}$ to lowest terms.

    (a) $\dfrac{5}{3}$ (b) $\dfrac{r + 5}{r - 3}$ (c) $\dfrac{r + 5}{r + 3}$ (d) $\dfrac{r - 5}{r + 3}$ (e) $\dfrac{5r}{3}$

15. $\dfrac{12c}{5d} \times \dfrac{15d^2}{36c^2} =$

    (a) $\dfrac{c}{d}$ (b) $\dfrac{d}{c}$ (c) $\dfrac{3d}{c}$ (d) $\dfrac{d}{3c}$ (e) $\dfrac{c}{3d}$

16. $\dfrac{a^2 + 2ab + b^2}{a^2 - b^2} \times \dfrac{6a}{3a + 3b} =$

    (a) $\dfrac{2}{a - b}$ (b) $\dfrac{a}{a - b}$ (c) $\dfrac{2a}{a + b}$ (d) $\dfrac{2a}{a - b}$ (e) $\dfrac{2a}{b - a}$

17. $8st \div \dfrac{24s}{t} =$

    (a) $\dfrac{t}{3s}$ (b) $\dfrac{3s}{t}$ (c) $\dfrac{t^2}{3}$ (d) $\dfrac{3}{t^2}$ (e) $\dfrac{st}{3}$

18. $\dfrac{m^2 - 25}{18} \div \dfrac{m - 5}{27} =$

    (a) $\dfrac{3(m - 5)}{2}$ (b) $\dfrac{3(m + 5)}{2}$ (c) $\dfrac{2(m + 5)}{3}$ (d) $\dfrac{3m}{2}$ (e) $\dfrac{2m}{3}$

Ratio and Proportion

1. What is the ratio of 9 inches to 2 feet?

    (a) $9 : 2$ (b) $2 : 9$ (c) $3 : 8$ (d) $8 : 3$ (e) $3 : 4$

2. Two girls divide $1.60 in the ratio of 5 to 3. How much more does one girl get than the other?

    (a) $.40   (b) $.50   (c) $.60   (d) $.80   (e) $1.00

3. The weight of 15 feet of wire is 6 pounds. How many pounds will 25 feet of this same wire weigh?

    (a) 8   (b) 8.5   (c) 9   (d) 9.5   (e) 10

4. At a certain time of day, a vertical yardstick casts a 20-inch shadow. How tall, in feet, is a flagpole that casts a shadow of 15 feet at the same time?

    (a) 20   (b) 22   (c) 25   (d) 27   (e) 30

5. A gear 12 centimeters in diameter is turning a gear 18 centimeters in diameter. When the smaller gear has made 42 revolutions, how many has the larger one made?

    (a) 24   (b) 28   (c) 50   (d) 63   (e) 72

6. An inch is to a foot as how many feet is to a yard?

    (a) 4   (b) 3   (c) $1\frac{1}{4}$ (d) $\frac{5}{8}$ (e) $\frac{1}{4}$

7. If 6 boys can paint their clubroom in 8 hours, how many hours will it take 10 boys working at the same rate?

    (a) $13\frac{1}{3}$ (b) $8\frac{1}{4}$ (c) $4\frac{4}{5}$ (d) $4\frac{1}{2}$ (e) $4\frac{1}{4}$

8.

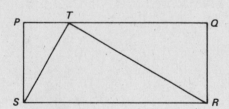

    In the figure above, what is the ratio of the area of triangle RST to the area of rectangle $PQRS$?

    (a) $1:2$ (b) $1:3$ (c) $1:4$ (d) $1:1$ (e) $2:1$

9. Of the following, which *cannot* be the ratio of the lengths of the sides of a triangle?

    (a) $3:4:5$
    (b) $2:3:5$
    (c) $3:3:4$
    (d) $1:1:1$
    (e) $6:7:8$

10. Two out of every 5 players on a baseball team are rookies. If the team has 15 players who are *not* rookies, what is the total number of players on the team?

   (a) 6   (b) 18   (c) 25   (d) 27   (e) 30

11. If the ratio of p to q is 2 to 3 and the ratio of q to r is 1 to 2, then the ratio of p to r is

   (a) $1:1$ (b) $3:1$ (c) $1:2$ (d) $1:3$ (e) $2:5$

12. A board is cut into three pieces whose lengths are in the ratio $3:4:5$. If the piece of medium length is 10 feet long, what is the length in feet of the original board?

   (a) 28   (b) 30   (c) 32   (d) 34   (e) 36

Equations and Formulas

1. If $8x + 3 = 27$, then $x - 2 =$

   (a) 0   (b) 1   (c) 2   (d) 3   (e) 4

2. If $2y + 7 = y - 9$, then $y =$

   (a) -2 (b) $+2$ (c) $+16$ (d) -16 (e) $-5\frac{1}{3}$

3. If $F = \frac{9}{5}C + 32$ and $F = 77$, then $C =$

   (a) 25   (b) 45   (c) 54   (d) 60   (e) 81

4. If $\frac{r}{3} + \frac{r}{4} = \frac{7}{12}$, then $r =$

   (a) 0   (b) 1   (c) $1\frac{1}{4}$ (d) $2\frac{1}{12}$ (e) 3

5. If $ax = 5 + bx$, then $x =$

   (a) $\frac{a - b}{5}$ (b) $\frac{5}{a + b}$ (c) $\frac{a}{b} - 5$ (d) $\frac{a + b}{5}$ (e) $\frac{5}{a - b}$

6. If $3x - y = 30$ and $5x - 3y = 10$, then $y =$

   (a) 10   (b) 20   (c) 30   (d) 40   (e) 50

7. If $P = EI$ and $E = IR$, find P in terms of E and R.

   (a) $\frac{E^2}{R}$ (b) E^2R (c) $\frac{R}{E^2}$ (d) $\frac{E}{R}$ (e) $\frac{R}{E}$

8. If $7p - 8 = 6 + 7q$, then $p - q =$

    (a) 0   (b) 1   (c) 2   (d) -2 (e) $\dfrac{2}{7}$

9. If $5y = \dfrac{45}{y}$, then $y =$

    (a) $+3$ only
    (b) -3 only
    (c) $+9$ only
    (d) $+3$ or -3
    (e) -9 only

10. The formula $h = 16t^2$ represents the distance h, in feet, that an object falls from rest after t seconds. In how many seconds will an object fall 400 feet?

    (a) 2   (b) 3   (c) $3\sqrt{2}$ (d) $2\sqrt{3}$ (e) 5

11. If $y^2 - 10y - 24 = 0$, then $y =$

    (a) 6 or 4
    (b) -6 or $+4$
    (c) -6 or $+2$
    (d) 12 or -2
    (e) -12 or $+2$

12. If $x^2 - 4x = 12$, then $x =$

    (a) -6 or $+2$
    (b) 6 or -2
    (c) 4 or -3
    (d) -4 or $+3$
    (e) 12 or 1

13. Find the values of x and y if $2x + y = 24$ and $4x - y = 12$.

    (a) $x = 6$, $y = 12$
    (b) $x = 12$, $y = 6$
    (c) $x = -6$, $y = 12$
    (d) $x = 6$, $y = -12$
    (e) $x = -6$, $y = -12$

14. Find the values of a and b if $a - 2b = -1$ and $2a + 3b = 12$.

    (a) $a = -3$, $b = 2$
    (b) $a = 3$, $b = -2$
    (c) $a = -3$, $b = -2$
    (d) $a = 3$, $b = 2$
    (e) $a = 4$, $b = -1$

Motion Problems

1. A man drives 261 miles in $4\frac{1}{2}$ hours. What is his average speed in miles per hour?

   (a) 50   (b) 52   (c) 54   (d) 56   (e) 58

2. A jet plane flies at 450 miles per hour from 2:30 P.M. to 6 P.M. How many miles does it fly?

   (a) 1500   (b) 1540   (c) 1575   (d) 1600   (e) 1635

3. How many minutes does it take to travel 1 mile at 45 miles per hour?

   (a) $1\frac{1}{3}$ (b) $1\frac{2}{3}$ (c) $1\frac{3}{4}$ (d) 2   (e) $2\frac{1}{4}$

4. A plane flies k kilometers in h hours. What is its average speed in kilometers per hour?

   (a) kh (b) $\dfrac{h}{k}$ (c) $\dfrac{2k}{h}$ (d) $\dfrac{k}{h}$ (e) $\dfrac{2h}{k}$

5. A girl rides her motorcycle at the rate of 45 miles per hour. What is her rate in feet per second? (5,280 feet = 1 mile)

   (a) 60   (b) 66   (c) 70   (d) 76   (e) 88

6. It takes Bill 14 minutes to bicycle 1 mile to school and 16 minutes to return. What is his average speed in miles per *hour* for the round trip?

   (a) 2   (b) 3   (c) 4   (d) 5   (e) 6

7. A bus travels a distance of 120 miles at 60 miles per hour and then returns at 40 miles per hour. What is the average speed in miles per hour for the round trip?

   (a) 42   (b) 44   (c) 46   (d) 48   (e) 50

8. Ralph runs 320 yards in 30 seconds. If he runs the first 200 yards in 20 seconds, what is his average speed, in yards per second, for the remainder of the distance?

   (a) 10   (b) 11   (c) 12   (d) $12\frac{2}{3}$ (e) $13\frac{1}{4}$

9. Two planes leave the same airport at the same time and travel in opposite directions, one at 550 miles per hour and the other at 300 miles per hour. In how many hours will they be 2550 miles apart?

   (a) 2.5   (b) 3   (c) 3.4   (d) 3.8   (e) 4

10. Jim started walking at 3 miles per hour. Helen started bicycling from the same place $2\frac{1}{2}$ hours later and followed the same route. If Helen was traveling at a rate of 8 miles per hour, in how many hours did she overtake Jim?

(a) $1\frac{1}{2}$ (b) $1\frac{3}{4}$ (c) 2   (d) $2\frac{1}{4}$ (e) $2\frac{1}{2}$

Work Problems

1. Ben can complete a job in t hours. If he works at a steady rate, what part of the job can he complete in 3 hours, if $t > 3$?

(a) $\dfrac{t}{3}$ (b) $\dfrac{3}{t}$ (c) $3t$ (d) $t + 3$ (e) $3 - t$

2. Marian can do a certain job in 12 hours. What part of the job can she do in n hours, if $n < 12$?

(a) $12 - n$ (b) $n + 12$ (c) $\dfrac{4n}{3}$ (d) $\dfrac{12}{n}$ (e) $\dfrac{n}{12}$

3. It takes Mort x hours to paint his house. How much of his house can he paint in n hours, if $n < x$?

(a) $\dfrac{x}{n}$ (b) $\dfrac{x}{n - x}$ (c) $\dfrac{n}{x}$ (d) $x - n$ (e) $\dfrac{x}{x - n}$

4. Maria can do a job in 2 hours. Henry can do the same job in 3 hours. If they work together, how many hours will it take them to do the job?

(a) $1\frac{1}{5}$ (b) $1\frac{5}{6}$ (c) $1\frac{1}{2}$ (d) $1\frac{2}{3}$ (e) $1\frac{3}{4}$

5. Dan can wax a car in 6 hours. Pete can wax the same car in 4 hours. How many hours will it take to wax the car if the two boys work together?

(a) 2   (b) $2\frac{1}{4}$ (c) $2\frac{1}{2}$ (d) $2\frac{2}{5}$ (e) $2\frac{4}{5}$

6. It takes 6 hours for one pipe to fill a tank and 8 hours for another pipe to empty it. If both pipes are open, how many hours will it take to fill the tank?

(a) 7   (b) $14\frac{3}{5}$ (c) 24   (d) $21\frac{1}{2}$ (e) $18\frac{2}{3}$

7. Mr. Lee can do a certain job in x hours. His son takes twice as long to do the job. Working together, they can do the job in 6 hours. How many hours does it take Mr. Lee to do the job alone?

(a) $7\frac{1}{2}$ (b) $8\frac{1}{4}$ (c) $8\frac{1}{2}$ (d) $8\frac{2}{3}$ (e) 9

Average Problems

1. Arthur receives grades of 72, 77, 82, 83, and 91 in five subjects. What is his average?

(a) 78   (b) 79   (c) 80   (d) 81   (e) 82

2. Temperature readings at a ski slope were taken every hour for six hours one afternoon. The readings were 12°, 11°, 7°, 4°, −2°, and −8°. What was the average temperature in degrees?

(a) 3   (b) $3\frac{1}{2}$ (c) 4   (d) $4\frac{1}{2}$ (e) 5

3. Marlene gets grades of 79, 83, 86, and 89 on four math tests. What grade must she get on her fifth test to average 85?

(a) 86   (b) $86\frac{2}{5}$ (c) 87   (d) $87\frac{1}{2}$ (e) 88

4. If a, b, c, d, and e are five consecutive odd numbers, their average is

(a) a (b) b (c) c (d) d (e) e

5. Fifty students had an average of 80. Thirty other students had an average of 86. Find the average of all the students.

(a) $81\frac{1}{4}$ (b) $81\frac{3}{4}$ (c) 82   (d) $82\frac{1}{4}$ (e) $83\frac{1}{2}$

6. Dan has 50 minutes to do 30 problems. He does the first 20 problems in 45 seconds each. What is the average number of minutes he can spend on each remaining problem?

(a) $1\frac{1}{4}$ (b) $2\frac{1}{3}$ (c) $2\frac{2}{3}$ (d) $3\frac{1}{2}$ (e) $3\frac{3}{4}$

7. What is the average of n, $n + 1$, $n + 2$, $n + 3$, $n + 4$, and $n + 5$?

(a) $n + 2$

(b) $n + 2\frac{1}{2}$

(c) $n + 3$

(d) $6n + 15$

(e) $n + 3\frac{1}{2}$

8. If the average of r and s is 9, and $t = 18$, what is the average of r, s, and t?

(a) 12 (b) $12\frac{1}{2}$ (c) $12\frac{2}{3}$ (d) 13 (e) $13\frac{1}{2}$

9. A class of 20 students has an average of p on a particular test. One student then has her grade raised by 10 points. What is the new class average?

(a) $p + 10$ (b) $p + 2$ (c) $p + 1$ (d) $p + \frac{1}{2}$ (e) $p + \frac{1}{4}$

10. The average of 10 scores is x and the average of another 20 scores is y. What is the average of all 30 scores?

(a) $10x + 20y$

(b) $x + 2y$

(c) $\dfrac{x + 2y}{30}$

(d) $\dfrac{10x + 20y}{3}$

(e) $\dfrac{x + 2y}{3}$

Integer Problems

1. If k is any integer, which of the following must also be an integer?

(a) $\dfrac{k}{3}$ (b) $\dfrac{k + 1}{3}$ (c) $\dfrac{k + 3}{3}$ (d) $\dfrac{3k - 1}{3}$ (e) $\dfrac{3k + 3}{3}$

2. For any integer t, which of the following must be an even integer?

(a) $2t + 2$ (b) $2t + 1$ (c) $2t - 1$ (d) $2t + 3$ (e) $t + 2$

3. If $p = \frac{2}{3}q$ and q is a positive integer, which of the following could be the value of p?

   (a) $\frac{3}{2}$ (b) $\frac{4}{3}$ (c) 3   (d) 5   (e) $2\frac{1}{2}$

4. Which of the following is a product of 17 and an integer?

   (a) 171   (b) 1712   (c) 1724   (d) 1734   (e) 1707

5. Which of the following is *not* the product of two consecutive odd integers?

   (a) 15   (b) 63   (c) 99   (d) 143   (e) 153

6. Which of the following *cannot* be written as the sum of two prime numbers?

   (a) 10   (b) 14   (c) 17   (d) 20   (e) 30

7. If p is a positive integer divisible by 6, which of the following must also be divisible by 6?

   (a) $p + 48$ (b) $\frac{p}{6}$ (c) $2p - 1$ (d) $3p + 2$ (e) $\frac{p}{3}$

8. For which of the following values of y will $36y^2 + 36y + 36$ be an integer?

   (a) $\frac{1}{4}$ (b) $\frac{1}{3}$ (c) $\frac{1}{9}$ (d) $\frac{1}{5}$ (e) $\frac{1}{8}$

9. If a carton containing a dozen eggs is dropped, which of the following *cannot* be the *ratio* of broken eggs to whole eggs?

   (a) $2:1$ (b) $3:1$ (c) $3:2$ (d) $5:1$ (e) $7:5$

10. A clerk in a fruit store sells peaches for 15¢ each and oranges for 20¢ each. If he sells \$3.00 worth of peaches and oranges, what is the *least* number of peaches he could have sold?

   (a) 4   (b) 5   (c) 6   (d) 7   (e) 8

Angle Relationships

1. In triangle RST, $RT = ST$ and angle $T = 70°$. What is the number of degrees in angle R?

   (a) 50   (b) 55   (c) 60   (d) 65   (e) 70

2. If the angles of a triangle are in the ratio 3 : 4 : 5, what is the difference in degrees between the largest and smallest angles?

    (a) 15   (b) 22   (c) 30   (d) 35   (e) 40

3. What is the number of degrees in the angle between the hands of a clock at 12 : 30?

    (a) 145   (b) 150   (c) 155   (d) 160   (e) 165

4. If a wheel has 24 spokes evenly spaced from one another, how many degrees are there in the angle formed by two consecutive spokes?

    (a) 15   (b) 18   (c) 20   (d) 22   (e) 24

5. A string of length 3π is laid along the circumference of a circle of radius 4. How many degrees are there in the arc covered by the string?

    (a) 150   (b) 135   (c) 120   (d) 105   (e) 90

6.

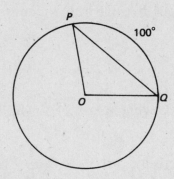

    In circle O above, arc PQ has a measure of 100°, as shown. What is the degree measure of angle PQO?

    (a) 30   (b) 37   (c) 40   (d) 45   (e) 50

7.

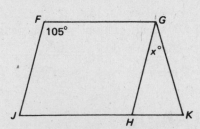

    In the figure above, $FGHJ$ is a parallelogram. If $GH = GK$, what is the value of x?

    (a) 25   (b) 30   (c) 35   (d) 40   (e) 45

8. In parallelogram $RSTV$, angle $R = 2n°$. What is the degree measure of angle S?

(a) $90 + 2n$
(b) $180 - n$
(c) $180 + 2n$
(d) $180 - 2n$
(e) $4n$

9.

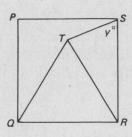

In the figure above, $PQRS$ is a square and QRT is an equilateral triangle. What is the value of y?

(a) $55°$ (b) $60°$ (c) $65°$ (d) $70°$ (e) $75°$

10.

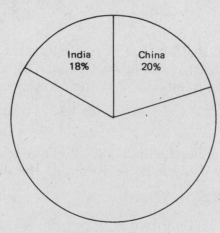

World Population

In the circle graph above, how many degrees are there in the central angle of the sector for China?

(a) 68 (b) 70 (c) 72 (d) 74 (e) 76

Right-Triangle Relationships

1. A rectangle has a diagonal of 26 feet and a height of 10 feet. What is the length, in feet, of the base of the rectangle?

(a) 21 (b) 22 (c) 23 (d) 24 (e) 25

2. A 20-foot ladder is placed against a building so that the foot of the ladder is 12 feet from the foot of the building. How many feet up the building does the ladder reach?

   (a) 14   (b) 15   (c) 16   (d) 17   (e) 18

3. The perimeter of a square is 16. What is the length of the diagonal of the square?

   (a) 4   (b) $4\sqrt{2}$ (c) $4\sqrt{3}$ (d) $2\sqrt{2}$ (e) $2\sqrt{3}$

4. In isosceles triangle PQR, base QR has length 16 and sides PQ and PR each have length 17. What is the height of the triangle?

   (a) 15   (b) $8\sqrt{2}$ (c) $8\sqrt{3}$ (d) $\sqrt{353}$ (e) 14

5. The lengths of the legs of a right triangle are $\dfrac{3}{4}$ and 1. What is the length of the hypotenuse of the triangle?

   (a) $\sqrt{2}$ (b) 2   (c) $1\dfrac{1}{2}$ (d) $\dfrac{\sqrt{5}}{2}$ (e) $1\dfrac{1}{4}$

6. Circle O has a radius of 7 inches. Point P is 25 inches from the center of circle O. If a tangent is drawn from point P to circle O, what is the distance in inches from point P to the point of tangency?

   (a) $12\sqrt{2}$ (b) 20   (c) 22   (d) 24   (e) $10\sqrt{3}$

7. If a ship sails 60 miles due south, 90 miles due east, and 60 miles due south again, how many miles is it from its starting point?

   (a) 120   (b) 135   (c) 150   (d) 160   (e) $100\sqrt{3}$

8. A right triangle has a leg of length 3. If the angle opposite that leg measures 30°, what is the length of the other leg of the triangle?

   (a) $3\sqrt{2}$ (b) $3\sqrt{3}$ (c) $\dfrac{3}{2}$ (d) 5   (e) 6

9.

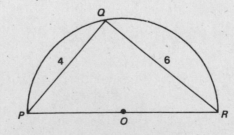

In semicircle PQR, $PQ = 4$ and $QR = 6$. What is the radius of the semicircle?

(a) $2\sqrt{13}$ (b) 8   (c) 4   (d) $\sqrt{13}$ (e) $\frac{1}{2}\sqrt{13}$

10. A square is inscribed in a circle of diameter 10. What is the length of the side of the square?

(a) $5\sqrt{3}$ (b) $5\sqrt{2}$ (c) 8   (d) $10\sqrt{2}$ (e) $4\sqrt{3}$

Area Problems

1. What is the price per square foot of carpet that sells for $10.80 per square yard?

(a) $1.20   (b) $1.80   (c) $3.25   (d) $3.50   (e) $3.70

2. If one circle has a diameter twice as large as the diameter of a smaller circle, what is the ratio of the area of the larger circle to the area of the smaller circle?

(a) 2:1   (b) 4:1   (c) 6:1   (d) 3:2   (e) 8:1

3. The length of a rectangle is 3 centimeters more than its width. If the perimeter of the rectangle is 58 centimeters, what is the area of the rectangle in square centimeters?

(a) 104   (b) 143   (c) 162   (d) 186   (e) 208

4.

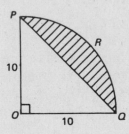

In the figure above, arc PQ is a quarter of a circle of radius 10. What is the area of the shaded region?

(a) $50 - 25\pi$
(b) $50\pi - 50$
(c) $25\pi - 50$
(d) $50\pi - 100$
(e) $50 - 50\pi$

5. If the area of a square is $49t^2$, the perimeter of the square is

(a) $49t$ (b) $36t$ (c) $28t^2$ (d) $28t$ (e) $14t$

6.

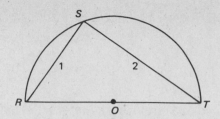

In the figure above, *RST* is a semicircle with center *O*. The area of the semicircle is

(a) $\dfrac{5\pi}{2}$ (b) $\dfrac{5\pi}{4}$ (c) $\dfrac{\pi\sqrt{5}}{2}$ (d) $\dfrac{25\pi}{8}$ (e) $\dfrac{5\pi}{8}$

7. The length and width of a rectangle are respectively 8 centimeters larger and 4 centimeters shorter than the side of a square of equal area. What is the length, in centimeters, of the side of the square?

(a) 4   (b) 8   (c) 12   (d) 24   (e) 40

8.

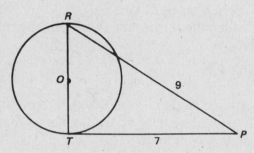

In the figure above, *PT* is tangent to circle *O*. If *PT* = 7 and *PR* = 9, as shown, what is the area of circle *O*?

(a) 4π (b) $\pi\sqrt{32}$ (c) 8π (d) 16π (e) 32π

9. A square has a side of *p* inches. Its sides are then increased by *q* inches each to form a new square. By how many square inches is the area of the original square increased?

(a) $q^2 + 2pq$ (b) q^2 (c) $q^2 - 2pq$ (d) pq (e) $2p + 2q$

10. If the length of a rectangle is increased by 20% and the width is increased by 10%, by what percent is the area of the rectangle increased?

(a) 15   (b) 24   (c) 30   (d) 32   (e) 40

Geometry of Solids

1. A truck can hold 3 cubic yards of sand. If a cubic foot of sand weighs 80 pounds, the weight of a truckload of sand, in pounds, is

(a) 240   (b) 270   (c) 2160   (d) 6480   (e) 6820

2. A rectangular tank is 14 feet long, 7 feet wide, and 6 feet deep. How many cubic feet of water will it hold if it is filled to within 6 inches of the top?

(a) 330   (b) 430   (c) 539   (d) 637   (e) 686

3. A ton of coal occupies 35 cubic feet. If a coal bin is 8 feet long and 5 feet wide, how many feet deep must it be to hold 6 tons of coal?

(a) $5\frac{1}{4}$ (b) 6   (c) $6\frac{2}{7}$ (d) $6\frac{2}{3}$ (e) 7

4. If the edge of a cube is doubled, its volume is multiplied by

(a) 2   (b) 3   (c) 4   (d) 6   (e) 8

5. The faces of a cube with an edge of 3 inches are all painted. The cube is then cut into smaller cubes, each with an edge of 1 inch. How many of the 1-inch cubes have paint on one face only?

(a) 4   (b) 6   (c) 8   (d) 10   (e) 12

6. The three dimensions of a rectangular solid are p, $2p$, and $3p$. What is the total surface area of the solid?

(a) $11p^2$ (b) $14p^2$ (c) $6p^3$ (d) $20p^2$ (e) $22p^2$

7. The formula for finding the volume of a cone is $V = \frac{1}{3}Bh$, where B represents the area of the circular base and h represents the height of the cone. If the volume of a cone is 96π and the height is 8, what is the radius of the circular base?

(a) 6   (b) 7   (c) $7\frac{1}{2}$ (d) 8   (e) 9

8. What is the surface area, in square inches, of a cube whose volume is 27 cubic inches?

(a) 27   (b) 36   (c) 54   (d) 68   (e) 72

9. A rectangular 5-gallon oil can is 11 inches long and 10 inches high. How wide, in inches, is the can if there are 231 cubic inches in 1 gallon?

(a) 10   (b) $10\frac{1}{2}$ (c) 11   (d) $11\frac{1}{2}$ (e) 12

10. Cubes with an edge of 1 inch are used to form a cube with an edge of 1 foot. How many of the small cubes does the bottom layer of the large cube contain?

(a) 12   (b) 24   (c) 48   (d) 144   (e) 152

11. A right circular cylinder has a height of 4 inches and a base with a diameter of 7 inches. What is the volume of the cylinder in cubic inches?

(a) 1372π (b) 196π (c) 98π (d) 49π (e) 28π

12. A cylindrical can has a height of 9 inches and a circular base with a diameter of 14 inches. If there are 231 cubic inches in 1 gallon, approximately how many gallons does the can hold?

(a) 3   (b) 4   (c) 4.5   (d) 6   (e) 6.75

Coordinate Geometry

1.

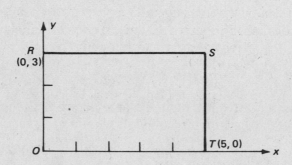

What is the perimeter of rectangle ORST in the figure above?

(a) 16   (b) 14   (c) 11   (d) 8   (e) 6

2.

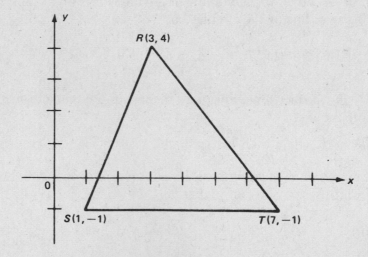

What is the area of triangle RST in the figure above?

(a) 8   (b) 12   (c) 15   (d) 18   (e) 9

3. The x-axis is shifted to a new position such that the points H, J, and K assume new coordinates as follows:

Point	Original Coordinates	New Coordinates
H	$(3, 5)$	$(3, 2)$
J	$(4, 2)$	$(4, -1)$
K	$(2, 6)$	$(2, 3)$

If the original coordinates of P were $(5, 1)$, which of the following are the new coordinates of P?

(a) $(2, -2)$
(b) $(5, 4)$
(c) $(8, 1)$
(d) $(8, -2)$
(e) $(5, -2)$

4.

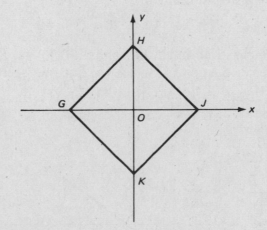

In the figure above, $GHJK$ is a square of area 49. What are the coordinates of K?

(a) $\left(\dfrac{7}{2}\sqrt{2}, 0\right)$

(b) $(7, 0)$

(c) $\left(0, \dfrac{7\sqrt{2}}{2}\right)$

(d) $\left(0, -\dfrac{7}{2}\sqrt{2}\right)$

(e) $(7\sqrt{2}, 0)$

5.

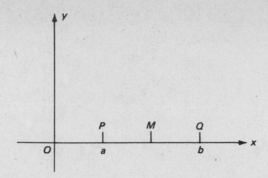

In the figure above, points P and Q are a and b units, respectively, from origin O. If M is the midpoint of PQ, how many units from the origin is point M?

(a) $\dfrac{a - b}{2}$ (b) $\dfrac{a + b}{2}$ (c) $\dfrac{b - a}{2}$ (d) $a + \dfrac{b}{2}$ (e) $b + \dfrac{a}{2}$

6. The coordinates of the vertices of a triangle are $(0, 5)$, $(0, -3)$, and $(4, 3)$. What is the area of the triangle?

(a) 16   (b) 20   (c) 24   (d) 28   (e) 32

7. A straight line passes through the points $R(0, 8)$ and $S(6, 4)$. What are the coordinates of the point at which the line intersects the x-axis?

(a) $(0, 12)$ (b) $(9, 0)$ (c) $(10, 0)$ (d) $(11, 0)$ (e) $(12, 0)$

8.

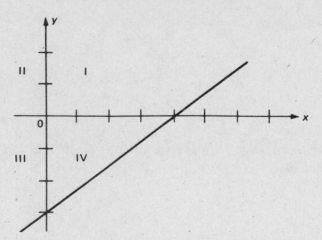

The figure above shows the graph of a linear equation. Which of the following describes the y-coordinates of those points on the graph that lie in quadrant IV?

(a) $0 < y < 4$
(b) $-3 < y < 0$
(c) $y < 0$
(d) $y > -3$
(e) $-4 < y < 0$

9.

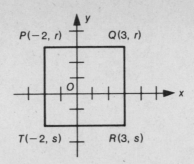

What is the area of *PQRT* in the figure above?

(a) $5(r - s)$
(b) $5(r + s)$
(c) $3r + 2s$
(d) $3r - 2s$
(e) $r - s$

10.

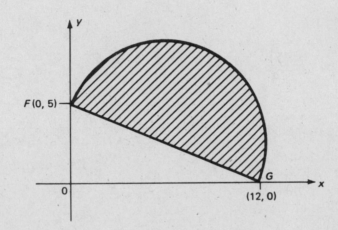

What is the area of the shaded semicircular region in the figure above?

(a) $\dfrac{13\pi}{4}$ (b) $\dfrac{169\pi}{4}$ (c) $\dfrac{169\pi}{8}$ (d) $\dfrac{13\pi}{2}$ (e) 26π

Inequalities

1. If $2x + 2 > 10$, then which of the following must be true?

(a) $x < 8$
(b) $x < 6$
(c) $x > 4$
(d) $x > 5$
(e) $x > 6$

2. If $9 < y^2 < 64$, then

   (a) $3 < y < 8$
   (b) $3 < y^2 < 8$
   (c) $\dfrac{1}{8} < y^2 < \dfrac{1}{3}$
   (d) $-8 < y^2 < -3$
   (e) $\sqrt{3} < y < \sqrt{8}$

3. Which of the following is equivalent to $\dfrac{p}{3} - 2 > 5$?

   (a) $p > \dfrac{7}{3}$ (b) $p > \dfrac{5}{3}$ (c) $p > 9$ (d) $p > 15$ (e) $p > 21$

4. If p and q are integers and $2p - q > 2p + q$, then

   (a) $q > 0$ (b) $q < 0$ (c) $p = q$ (d) $p > q$ (e) $q > p$

5.

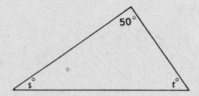

   In the figure above, if $s < 50 < t$, then

   (a) $t < 80$
   (b) $s + t < 130$
   (c) $50 < t < 80$
   (d) $t > 80$
   (e) $t > 100$

6. If $(r - s)^2 < r^2 + s^2$, then

   (a) $r^2 < s^2$ (b) $s^2 < r^2$ (c) $r > s$ (d) $s > r$ (e) $rs > 0$

7. If n is an integer and $\dfrac{1}{5} < \dfrac{1}{n+1} < \dfrac{1}{3}$, then

   (a) $n < 4$ (b) $n > 4$ (c) $n = 4$ (d) $n = 3$ (e) $n = \dfrac{1}{4}$

8. If $-4 < p < 5$ and $-2 < q < 0$, then which of the following is true for all possible values of $(p - q)$?

   (a) $-6 < (p - q) < 5$
   (b) $-4 < (p - q) < 5$
   (c) $-2 < (p - q) < 5$
   (d) $-6 < (p - q) < 7$
   (e) $-4 < (p - q) < 7$

9.

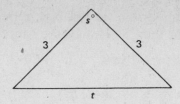

In the figure above, if $90 < s < 180$, then

(a) $0 < t < 3\sqrt{2}$
(b) $3 < t < 3\sqrt{2}$
(c) $6 < t < 6\sqrt{2}$
(d) $3\sqrt{2} < t < 6$
(e) $3 < t < 6$

10. If $0 < r < s < 1$, then which of the following is true?

(a) $r + s > 1$

(b) $\dfrac{1}{r} > \dfrac{1}{s}$

(c) $r^2 + s^2 > 1$
(d) $rs > 1$
(e) $-s > -r$

Data Interpretation

Questions 1–4 refer to the following circle graph.

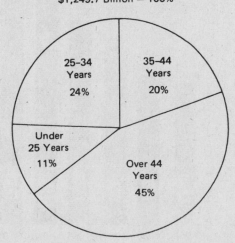

Personal Income, 1975
$1,249.7 Billion = 100%

1. According to the graph, what was the approximate personal income, in billions of dollars, of the 35–44 age group in 1975?

    (a) 180   (b) 220   (c) 250   (d) 280   (e) 310

2. About how many degrees are there in the central angle of the sector on the graph that represents the 1975 personal income of those under 25 years of age?

    (a) 31   (b) 34   (c) 37   (d) 40   (e) 43

3. According to the graph, which of the following represents the ratio of the personal income of the over-44 age group to the personal income of the 35–44 age group in 1975?

    (a) 2:1   (b) 3:2   (c) 5:2   (d) 8:5   (e) 9:4

4. If total personal income in 1975 was 20% greater than it was in 1972, then according to the graph, what was the approximate total personal income, in billions of dollars, in 1972?

    (a) 1100   (b) 1040   (c) 1000   (d) 960   (e) 900

Questions 5–9 refer to the following bar graph.

Total and Percent of U.S. Gross National Product Spent on Health 1960–1973

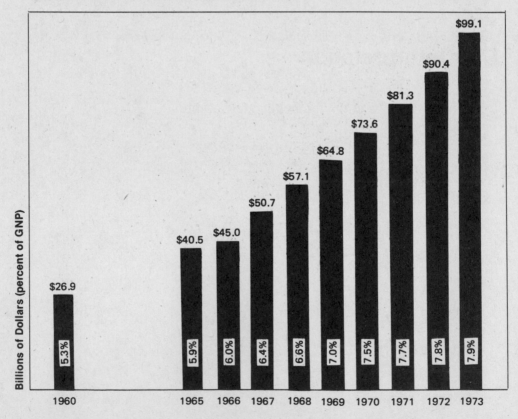

5. According to the graph, the ratio of total health expenditures in 1973 to total health expenditures in 1960 was approximately

(a) 3:1   (b) 4:1   (c) 3:2   (d) 7:3   (e) 5:2

6. If the population of the United States of America was about 215 million in 1973, then according to the graph, what was the approximate cost per capita for health and medical care that year?

(a) $465   (b) $510   (c) $550   (d) $590   (e) $615

7. According to the graph, what was the approximate gross national product, in billions of dollars, in 1965?

(a) 500   (b) 550   (c) 590   (d) 630   (e) 680

8. According to the graph, during what 3-year period did the proportion of the gross national product spent on health care remain steadiest?

(a) 1965–1967
(b) 1967–1969
(c) 1969–1971
(d) 1971–1973
(e) 1968–1970

9. According to the graph, by approximately what percent did health care expenditures increase from 1972 to 1973?

(a) 8.9   (b) 9.6   (c) 10.4   (d) 11.2   (e) 12.0

Questions 10–13 refer to the following line graph.

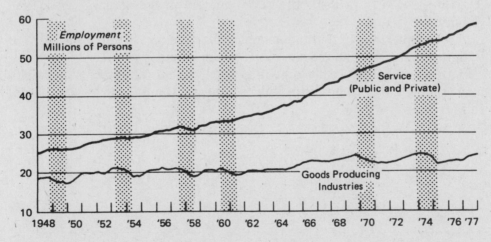

10. According to the graph, approximately what was total employment, in millions, in both service and goods-producing industries at the end of 1965?

(a) 51   (b) 54   (c) 57   (d) 63   (e) 66

11. For the entire period shown on the graph, the increase in employment in service industries was about how many times greater than the increase in employment in goods-producing industries?

    (a) 2   (b) 3   (c) 5   (d) 10   (e) 12

12. According to the graph, which of the following is closest to the ratio of the number of service workers to the number of goods-producing workers at the end of 1970?

    (a) 2:1   (b) 3:2   (c) 5:3   (d) 5:2   (e) 4:3

13. According to the graph, at the end of what year did the number of service workers show an increase of 100% over the number of service workers at the start of 1948?

    (a) 1970   (b) 1972   (c) 1974   (d) 1975   (e) 1976

Quantitative Comparisons

The following questions each consist of two quantities, one in Column A and one in Column B. Compare the two quantities and choose answer

(a) if the quantity in Column A is greater;
(b) if the quantity in Column B is greater;
(c) if the two quantities are equal;
(d) if the relationship cannot be determined from the information given.

All letters such as x, y, and n represent real numbers. A symbol appearing in both columns represents the same quantity in Column A as it does in Column B.

In some questions, information concerning one or both of the quantities to be compared is centered above the two columns.

Figures are generally not drawn to scale, unless otherwise stated. You may assume these figures lie in a plane, unless it is indicated they represent solid figures.

Lines that appear to be straight may be assumed to be straight lines.

	Column A	Column B
1.	$2 \times 3 \times 4 \times 5$	110
2.	25^2	5^4
3.	$3y - 1$	$3y + 1$

	Column A	Column B

$$0 < p < q$$

4. $3p$ q

$$r - 10 = 15$$

5. $r + 5$ 30

6.

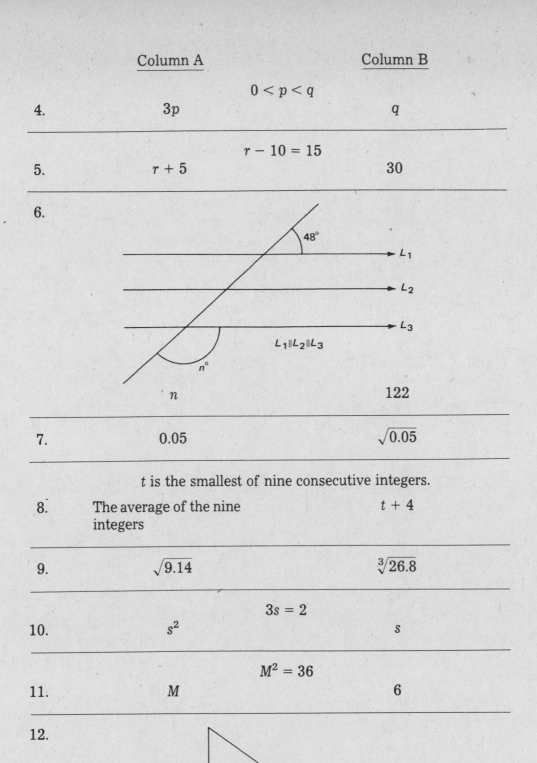

$L_1 \| L_2 \| L_3$

    n 122

---

7. 0.05 $\sqrt{0.05}$

---

t is the smallest of nine consecutive integers.

8. The average of the nine integers $t + 4$

---

9. $\sqrt{9.14}$ $\sqrt[3]{26.8}$

$$3s = 2$$

10. s^2 s

$$M^2 = 36$$

11. M 6

12.

p 5

	Column A	Column B

Column A   **Column B**

$$0 < m + n < 1$$

13. n 1

___

14. $\dfrac{1}{3} - \dfrac{1}{6}$ $\dfrac{1}{6} - \dfrac{1}{12}$

___

15.   Area of a square with side $\dfrac{3}{4}k$ Area of a circle with diameter k

___

16. $3\sqrt{11}$ 11

___

$$5r = 4k$$
$$4s = 3k$$

17. r s

___

18.

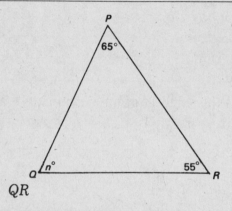

       QR PR

___

g and h are positive integers.

19. $\dfrac{gh - 3}{gh}$ $\dfrac{g - \dfrac{3}{h}}{g}$

___

20.

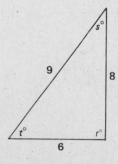

       r $s + t$

Explanatory Answers

SIGNED NUMBERS

1. (d) $(4) + (-7) - (-11) =$
$4 - 7 + 11 = +8$

2. (a) $(-5) + (-9) - (23) + (2) =$
$-5 - 9 - 23 + 2 = -35$

3. (e) $(8) - (-4) + (-10) - (-19) =$
$8 + 4 - 10 + 19 = +21$

4. (c) $9(6 - 8) - (-3) =$
$9(-2) + 3 =$
$-18 + 3 = -15$

5. (d) $(-4 + -1)(3 - 7) =$
$(-5)(-4) = +20$

6. (e) $(-8 \times 10) \div (4 - 6) =$
$(-80) \div (-2) = +40$

7. (b) $(-18.4) + (3.7) = -14.7$

8. (e) The temperature rose $27.5° + 4.7° = 32.2°$.

9. (e) $(-8.7) \times (-3.4) = +29.58$

10. (a) $(-92.4) \div (+4) = -23.1$

FRACTIONS

1. (c) $\dfrac{24}{32} = \dfrac{24 \div 8}{32 \div 8} = \dfrac{3}{4}$

2. (b) Divide 19 by 5:
$$\dfrac{19}{5} = 19 \div 5 = 3\dfrac{4}{5}$$

3. (e) $\dfrac{40}{64} = \dfrac{40 \div 8}{64 \div 8} = \dfrac{5}{8}$

4. (d) Multiply 9 by 3 and add 2:
$$9\dfrac{2}{3} = \dfrac{(9 \times 3) + 2}{3} = \dfrac{29}{3}$$

5. (a) $\dfrac{2}{3} + \dfrac{3}{4} = \dfrac{2 \times 4}{3 \times 4} + \dfrac{3 \times 3}{4 \times 3}$
$= \dfrac{8}{12} + \dfrac{9}{12}$
$= \dfrac{17}{12} = 1\dfrac{5}{12}$

6. (e) Since 2/3 cannot be subtracted from 1/2 with a positive difference, we borrow $1 = 2/2$ from 14. Thus, we get
$$13\dfrac{3}{2} - 9\dfrac{2}{3} = 13\dfrac{9}{6} - 9\dfrac{4}{6}$$
$$= 4\dfrac{5}{6}$$

7. (b) There are 12 inches in 1 foot. Thus:
$$\dfrac{9}{12} = \dfrac{9 \div 3}{12 \div 3} = \dfrac{3}{4}$$

8. (c) $27 \div 2\dfrac{1}{4} = 27 \div \dfrac{9}{4}$
$= \dfrac{\overset{3}{27}}{1} \times \dfrac{4}{\underset{}{9}}$
$= 12$

9. (d) $\dfrac{\overset{}{2}}{3} \times \dfrac{3}{\underset{4}{8}} = \dfrac{1}{4}$

10. (a) There are 16 ounces in a pound. Thus:
$$\dfrac{10\dfrac{2}{3}}{16} = \dfrac{32}{3} \div \dfrac{16}{1}$$
$$= \dfrac{\overset{2}{32}}{3} \times \dfrac{1}{\underset{}{16}}$$
$$= \dfrac{2}{3}$$

11. (d) $81 = \dfrac{3}{4}x$

$$x = 81 \div \dfrac{3}{4}$$

$$= \dfrac{\overset{27}{\cancel{81}}}{1} \times \dfrac{4}{\cancel{3}}$$

$$= 108$$

12. (e) $7\dfrac{1}{8} \div 6 = \dfrac{57}{8} \div \dfrac{6}{1}$

$$= \dfrac{\overset{19}{\cancel{57}}}{8} \times \dfrac{1}{\underset{2}{\cancel{6}}} = 1\dfrac{3}{16}$$

13. (b) Let x equal the capacity of the tank in gallons. Then set up the equation, multiply both sides by 8, and solve for x:

$$\dfrac{5}{8}x - 6 = \dfrac{1}{4}x$$
$$5x - 48 = 2x$$
$$5x - 2x = 48$$
$$3x = 48$$
$$x = 16$$

14. (c) $5\dfrac{2}{5} \times 6\dfrac{2}{3} = \dfrac{\overset{9}{\cancel{27}}}{\cancel{5}} \times \dfrac{\overset{4}{\cancel{20}}}{\cancel{3}}$

$$= 36$$

15. (d) $\dfrac{5x}{8} - \dfrac{x}{2} = \dfrac{5x}{8} - \dfrac{4x}{8} = \dfrac{x}{8}$

16. (a) $\dfrac{12k}{18k} = \dfrac{12k \div 6k}{18k \div 6k} = \dfrac{2}{3}$

17. (e) $\dfrac{\dfrac{3}{4}}{1\dfrac{1}{8}} = \dfrac{3}{4} \div \dfrac{9}{8}$

$$= \dfrac{\cancel{3}}{\cancel{4}} \times \dfrac{\overset{2}{\cancel{8}}}{\underset{3}{\cancel{9}}} = \dfrac{2}{3}$$

18. (b) If the man has done 5/8 of the job in 10 days, then his rate is 1/8 of the job every 10/5 = 2 days. Thus, it will take him $3 \times 2 = 6$ days to perform the remaining 3/8 of the job.

19. (a) Let x equal the amount the boy originally had. Then:

$$\dfrac{5}{9}x = 2.70$$

$$x = 2.70 \div \dfrac{5}{9}$$

$$= \dfrac{\overset{.54}{\cancel{2.70}}}{1} \times \dfrac{9}{\cancel{5}} = 4.86$$

20. (d) $\dfrac{7y}{4} - \dfrac{3y}{2} + \dfrac{5y}{8} = \dfrac{14y}{8} - \dfrac{12y}{8} + \dfrac{5y}{8}$

$$= \dfrac{14y - 12y + 5y}{8}$$

$$= \dfrac{7y}{8}$$

DECIMALS

1. (d) $\begin{array}{r} 102.4 \\ -\ 98.6 \\ \hline 3.8 \end{array}$

2. (b) To multiply .0057 by 1000, move the decimal point three places to the right and get 5.7.

3. (e) $.625 = \dfrac{625}{1000} = \dfrac{625 \div 125}{1000 \div 125} = \dfrac{5}{8}$

4. (a) $\dfrac{7}{20} = \dfrac{7 \times 5}{20 \times 5} = \dfrac{35}{100} = .35$

5. (e) Just as $333 > 330 > 303 > 300 > 33$, so $.333 > .330 > .303 > .300 > .033$.

6. (c) Bill spends $8 \times \$0.12 = \$0.96$ on rolls, $4 \times \$1.12 = \$4.48$ on beef, and $3 \times \$0.47 = \$1.41$ on milk, for a total of $6.85. His change is therefore $20.00 - \$6.85 = \$13.15$.

7. (d) $\dfrac{\dfrac{1}{3}}{\dfrac{5}{6}} = \dfrac{1}{\cancel{3}} \times \dfrac{\cancel{6}^{2}}{5} = \dfrac{2}{5} = .40$

8. (a) Convert the decimals into fractions: $.51 \approx 1/2$, $.75 = 3/4$, $.375 = 3/8$, $.667 \approx 2/3$. Then multiply:

$$\dfrac{1}{\cancel{2}} \times \dfrac{3}{4} \times \dfrac{3}{8} \times \dfrac{\cancel{2}}{3} = \dfrac{3}{32}$$

9. (d) Since $.04 = 4/100 = 1/25$, dividing by .04 is equivalent to multiplying by 25.

10. (b) $1.25 \times .60 = .75 = \dfrac{3}{4}$

11. (d) $0.28 \times 12 = 3.36$

12. (a) $\dfrac{13}{10} y = .039$ (Multiply by 10)

    $13y = .39$ (Divide by 13)

      $y = .03$

13. (c) $\dfrac{7}{.7 \times .7} = \dfrac{7}{.49} = \dfrac{700}{49} = \dfrac{100}{7}$

14. (b) To solve for p, multiply both sides of the equation by 10, add 12 to both sides, and then divide both sides by 3:

    $.3p - 1.2 = 4.8$
    $3p - 12 = 48$
     $3p = 60$
      $p = 20$

15. (c) Since the decimal place in 3.1 must be moved four places to the right to make it 31,000, the correct exponent for 10 is 4: $31,000 = 3.1 \times 10^{4}$.

PERCENTAGE

1. (c) $0.30 \times 42 = 12.6$

2. (e) $\dfrac{24}{40} = \dfrac{6}{10} = 60\%$

3. (d) $75\% = \dfrac{3}{4} = \dfrac{3 \times 3}{4 \times 3} = \dfrac{9}{12}$

4. (a) $1.20 \times 40 = 48$

5. (b) Let x equal the number. Then, since $60\% = 3/5$:

$$15 = \dfrac{3}{5} x \quad \left(\text{Multiply by } \dfrac{5}{3} \right)$$
$$25 = x$$

6. (c) The price decreased $4.20 - \$3.15 = \$1.05$ a pound. Thus:

$$\dfrac{1.05}{4.20} = \dfrac{105}{420} = \dfrac{1}{4} = 25\%$$

7. (e) $0.8\% = \dfrac{.8}{100} = \dfrac{8}{1000} = \dfrac{1}{125}$

8. (d) Let x equal normal rainfall in inches. Then, since $80\% = 4/5$:

$$\dfrac{4}{5} x = 36 \quad \left(\text{Multiply by } \dfrac{5}{4} \right)$$
$$x = 45$$

9. (a) $40\% = 2/5$. Thus:

$$\dfrac{2}{5} \times \dfrac{5}{6} = \dfrac{1}{3}$$

10. (a) Let $x\%$ equal the unknown percent. Convert 8 ounces into 0.5 pounds. Then set up a proportion and solve for x:

$$\frac{0.5}{15} = \frac{x}{100} \quad \text{(Cross multiply)}$$

$$15x = 50 \quad \text{(Divide by 15)}$$

$$x = 3\frac{1}{3}$$

11. (e) If $x = 40\%y = 2/5$ of y, then $y = 5/2x = 2.5x = 250\%$ of x.

12. (b) Let x equal the total number of gallons the tank holds. Then, since $40\% = 2/5$:

$$\frac{2}{5}x = 60 \quad \left(\text{Multiply by } \frac{5}{2}\right)$$

$$x = 150$$

13. (c) Let $x\%$ equal the unknown percent. Then set up a proportion and solve for x:

$$\frac{p}{25} = \frac{x}{100} \quad \text{(Cross multiply)}$$

$$25x = 100p \quad \text{(Divide by 25)}$$

$$x = 4p$$

14. (d) $.20 \times 8 = 1.6$

15. (b) If the man gets a 25% discount, then he pays 75%, or 3/4, of the original price. Thus:

$$\frac{3}{4} \times \$60 = \$45$$

16. (d) The weight of the cooked roast is 80% of the weight of the raw roast. Let x equal the weight of the raw roast. Then:

$$.8x = 6 \quad \text{(Multiply by 10)}$$

$$8x = 60 \quad \text{(Divide by 8)}$$

$$x = 7.5$$

17. (a) Out of every 8 staff members, 7 are nurses: $7/8 = 87\frac{1}{2}\%$.

18. (b) $$\frac{2}{4t} = \frac{x}{100} \quad \text{(Cross multiply)}$$

$$4tx = 200 \quad \text{(Divide by } 4t)$$

$$x = \frac{50}{t}$$

19. (d) The selling price is the cost plus $r\%$, or $r/100$, of the cost:

$$C + \frac{r}{100} \times C = C + \frac{rC}{100}$$

$$= C\left(1 + \frac{r}{100}\right)$$

20. (c) There are $.30 \times 10 = 3$ quarts of alcohol in the original 10-quart solution, and there will be 3 quarts of alcohol in the resulting 12-quart solution. Thus:

$$\frac{3}{12} = \frac{1}{4} = 25\%$$

21. (b) The loss is $\$160 - \$120 = \$40$. Thus:

$$\frac{40}{160} = \frac{1}{4} = 25\%$$

22. (d) An 8-ounce solution that is 25%, or 1/4, salt contains $1/4 \times 8 = 2$ ounces of salt. The new solution will contain the same amount of salt. Let x equal the number of ounces of water to be added in order to obtain a solution that is 10%, or 1/10, salt. Then:

$$\frac{2}{8 + x} = \frac{1}{10} \quad \text{(Cross multiply)}$$

$$8 + x = 20 \quad \text{(Subtract 8)}$$

$$x = 12$$

23. (e) When reduced, the poster will be 100% − 10% = 90%, or 9/10, of its original height and 100% − 30% = 70%, or 7/10, of its original width. Therefore, it will be

$$\frac{9}{10} \times \frac{7}{10} = \frac{63}{100} = 63\%$$

of its original size.

24. (c) Let x equal the amount invested at 8%. Then $10,000 - x =$ the amount invested at 6%. The annual income from the amount invested at 8% is $.08x$. The annual income from the amount invested at 6% is $.06(10,000 - x) = 600 - .06x$. Thus:

$$.08x = 600 - .06x + 240$$
$$.14x = 840$$
$$x = 6000$$

25. (b) The reduced price is 100% − 15% = 85% of the original price. Let x equal the original price. Then:

$$.85x = 76,500$$
$$x = 90,000$$

EXPONENTS AND ROOTS

1. (d) $r^3 \times r^5 = r^{3+5} = r^8$

2. (b) $(2p^2)^3 = 2^3 \times p^{2\times3} = 8p^6$

3. (e) Suppose $x = -2$. Then $1/x^2 = 1/4$; $x^5 = -32$; $(1/x)^3 = -1/8$; $x^2 = 4$; and $x^4 = 16$.

4. (a) $\dfrac{15c^6d^5}{-5c^2d^2} = -3c^4d^3$

5. (c) $\sqrt{36r^5} = \sqrt{36r^4}\sqrt{r}$
$$= 6r^2\sqrt{r}$$

6. (e) $\sqrt[3]{-\dfrac{1}{8}} = -\dfrac{1}{2}$

7. (c) Since $57,000,000 = 5.7 \times 10^7$, $n = 7$.

8. (d) $\sqrt{200} - \sqrt{50} = \sqrt{100}\sqrt{2}$
$$- \sqrt{25}\sqrt{2}$$
$$= 10\sqrt{2} - 5\sqrt{2}$$
$$= 5\sqrt{2}$$

9. (c) $\dfrac{(5r^2s^3)^3}{5r^2s^5} = \dfrac{125r^6s^9}{5r^2s^5} = 25r^4s^4$

10. (c) Since $2^{p+1} = 2^p \times 2$, if $2^p = q$, then $2^{p+1} = 2q$.

OPERATIONS WITH ALGEBRAIC EXPRESSIONS

1. (a) $4x + 2y$
   $\underline{+\ x - 4y}$
   $5x - 2y$

2. (c) The product of -5 and 3 is -15. The product of r^3 and r is r^4. The product of s and s^4 is s^5. Therefore:

$$(-5r^3s)(3rs^4) = -15r^4s^5$$

3. (b) $\dfrac{45x^3y^5}{-5x^2y^3} = \dfrac{45}{-5} \times \dfrac{x^3}{x^2} \times \dfrac{y^5}{y^3} = -9xy^2$

4. (e) $\dfrac{9x^3 - 6x^2 + 3x}{3x} = \dfrac{9x^3}{3x} - \dfrac{6x^2}{3x} + \dfrac{3x}{3x}$
$$= 3x^2 - 2x + 1$$

5. (d) To find the other binomial, subtract $2x^2 - x$ from $3x^2 - 5x$. To subtract $2x^2 - x$, change the sign of each term and add:

$$3x^2 - 5x$$
$$\underline{+\ -2x^2 +\ x}$$
$$x^2 - 4x$$

6. (a) $x^2 - 36 = x^2 - 6^2$
$= (x + 6)(x - 6)$

7. (d) Multiply each term of the first binomial by each term of the second binomial:
$$(r - 1)(r + 2) =$$
$$r(r + 2) - 1(r + 2) =$$
$$r^2 + 2r - r - 2 = r^2 + r - 2$$

8. (b) $3y^2 - 48 = 3(y^2 - 16)$
$= 3(y - 4)(y + 4)$

9. (c) Multiply each term of the first binomial by each term of the second binomial:
$$(2a - b)(2a + b) =$$
$$2a(2a + b) - b(2a + b) =$$
$$4a^2 + 2ab - 2ab - b^2 = 4a^2 - b^2$$

10. (e) Multiply each term of the first binomial by each term of the second binomial:
$$(2p + 1)(3p - 2) =$$
$$2p(3p - 2) + 1(3p - 2) =$$
$$6p^2 - 4p + 3p - 2 = 6p^2 - p - 2$$

11. (b) $3ax + 3ay + 6a = 3a(x + y + 2)$

12. (d) To factor $m^2 + 5m - 24$, find two factors of -24 that add up to $+5$. Those factors are $+8$ and -3. Therefore:
$$(m^2 + 5m - 24) = (m + 8)(m - 3)$$

13. (e) $\dfrac{27xy^3}{45x^2y} = \dfrac{27xy^3 \div 9xy}{45x^2y \div 9xy}$
$= \dfrac{3y^2}{5x}$

14. (c) $\dfrac{r^2 - 25}{r^2 - 2r - 15} = \dfrac{(r + 5)(r - 5)}{(r + 3)(r - 5)}$
$= \dfrac{r + 5}{r + 3}$

15. (b) $\dfrac{12c}{5d} \times \dfrac{15d^2}{36c^2} = \dfrac{d}{c}$

16. (d) Factor as shown; then cancel and multiply:
$$\dfrac{a^2 + 2ab + b^2}{a^2 - b^2} \times \dfrac{6a}{3a + 3b} =$$
$$\dfrac{(a + b)(a + b)}{(a + b)(a - b)} \times \dfrac{3(2a)}{3(a + b)} = \dfrac{2a}{a - b}$$

17. (c) $8st \div \dfrac{24s}{t} = \dfrac{8st}{1} \times \dfrac{t}{24s} = \dfrac{t^2}{3}$

18. (b) Factor as shown; then invert, cancel, and multiply:
$$\dfrac{m^2 - 25}{18} \div \dfrac{m - 5}{27}$$
$$= \dfrac{(m + 5)(m - 5)}{9 \times 2} \times \dfrac{9 \times 3}{(m - 5)}$$
$$= \dfrac{3(m + 5)}{2}$$

RATIO AND PROPORTION

1. (c) There are $2 \times 12 = 24$ inches in 2 feet. Thus, the ratio of 9 inches to 2 feet is
$$\dfrac{9}{24} = \dfrac{9 \div 3}{24 \div 3} = \dfrac{3}{8}$$

2. (a) Let $5x$ equal the larger share and $3x$ equal the smaller share. Then:
$$5x + 3x = 1.60$$
$$8x = 1.60$$
$$x = .20$$
If $x = .20$, then $5x = 1.00$ and $3x = .60$. So the larger share is $\$1.00 - \$.60 = \$.40$ greater than the smaller share.

3. (e) Length and weight are directly proportional. Let x equal the weight of the longer wire. Then:

$$\frac{15}{6} = \frac{25}{x}$$
$$15x = 150$$
$$x = 10$$

4. (d) The height of the object and the length of the shadow are directly proportional. Let x equal the height of the flagpole. Then:

$$\frac{36}{20} = \frac{x}{15}$$
$$\frac{9}{5} = \frac{x}{15}$$
$$5x = 135$$
$$x = 27$$

5. (b) The size of the gear and the number of revolutions it makes are inversely proportional. Let x equal the number of revolutions the larger gear makes. Then:

$$\frac{12}{18} = \frac{x}{42}$$
$$\frac{2}{3} = \frac{x}{42}$$
$$3x = 84$$
$$x = 28$$

6. (e) The ratio of 1 inch to 12 inches (1 foot) is directly proportional to the ratio of x feet to 3 feet (1 yard). Thus:

$$\frac{1}{12} = \frac{x}{3}$$
$$12x = 3$$
$$x = \frac{1}{4}$$

7. (c) The number of boys is inversely proportional to the number of hours it will take to paint the club-room. Let x equal the number of hours it will take 10 boys. Then:

$$\frac{6}{10} = \frac{x}{8}$$
$$\frac{3}{5} = \frac{x}{8}$$
$$5x = 24$$
$$x = 4\frac{4}{5}$$

8. (a) The formula for finding the area of a triangle is $A = 1/2bh$. The formula for finding the area of a rectangle is $A = bh$. Since triangle RST and rectangle $PQRS$ have the same base and the same height, the ratio of the area of RST to the area of $PQRS$ is $1:2$.

9. (b) The sum of the lengths of any two sides of a triangle must be greater than the length of the third side. Therefore, the sides of a triangle cannot be in the ratio $2:3:5$.

10. (c) If 2 out of every 5 players are rookies, then 3 out of every 5 players are nonrookies. Let x equal the total number of players on the team. Then:

$$\frac{3}{5} = \frac{15}{x}$$
$$3x = 75$$
$$x = 25$$

11. (d) The ratio of p to r is the product of the ratio of p to q and the ratio of q to r, as shown here:

$$\frac{p}{\cancel{q}} \times \frac{\cancel{q}}{r} = \frac{p}{r}$$

The ratio of p to q is 2 to 3 and the ratio of q to r is 1 to 2. Therefore:

$$\frac{2}{3} \times \frac{1}{\cancel{2}} = \frac{1}{3}$$

12. (b) Let the lengths of the three pieces be $3x$, $4x$, and $5x$. Then the total length is $12x$. You know that the piece of medium length is 10 feet long. Thus:

$$4x = 10$$

$$x = 2\frac{1}{2}$$

If $x = 2\frac{1}{2}$, then $12x = 30$.

EQUATIONS AND FORMULAS

1. (b) $8x + 3 = 27$ (Subtract 3)
$8x = 24$ (Divide by 8)
$x = 3$

If $x = 3$, then $x - 2 = 1$.

2. (d) $2y + 7 = y - 9$ (Subtract y)
$y + 7 = -9$ (Subtract 7)
$y = -16$

3. (a) Substitute 77 for F in the formula and solve for C:

$$77 = \frac{9}{5}C + 32 \quad \text{(Subtract 32)}$$

$$45 = \frac{9}{5}C \qquad \left(\text{Multiply by } \frac{5}{9}\right)$$

$$25 = C$$

4. (b) Clear the equation of fractions by multiplying both sides by 12, the lowest common denominator. Then solve for r:

$$\frac{r}{3} + \frac{r}{4} = \frac{7}{12}$$

$$4r + 3r = 7$$

$$7r = 7$$

$$r = 1$$

5. (e) Subtract bx from both sides of the equation so that all the terms containing x are on the same side of the equal sign:

$$ax = 5 + bx$$

$$ax - bx = 5$$

Then factor out x and divide both sides by $a - b$:

$$x(a - b) = 5$$

$$x = \frac{5}{a - b}$$

6. (c) To find x, first multiply the first equation by -3:

$$-3(3x - y = 30) = -9x + 3y$$
$$= -90$$

Then add the two equations together:

$$
\begin{array}{r}
-9x + 3y = -90 \\
+ \quad 5x - 3y = 10 \\
\hline
-4x = -80 \\
x = 20
\end{array}
$$

To find y, substitute 20 for x in the first equation (the original one):

$$3(20) - y = 30$$
$$60 - y = 30$$
$$-y = -30$$
$$y = 30$$

7. (a) Solve the second equation for I:

$$E = IR$$

$$\frac{E}{R} = I$$

Then substitute E/R for I in the first equation:

$$P = EI = E \times \frac{E}{R} = \frac{E^2}{R}$$

8. (c) $\quad 7p - 8 = 6 + 7q$
$ 7p - 7q = 14$
$ 7(p - q) = 14$
$ p - q = 2$

9. (d) $5y = \dfrac{45}{y}$

$$5y^2 = 45$$
$$y^2 = 9$$
$$y = \pm\, 3$$

10. (e) Substitute 400 for h in the formula and solve for t:

$$h = 16t^2$$
$$400 = 16t^2$$
$$25 = t^2$$
$$5 = t$$

(Note that if $t^2 = 25$, then $t = +5$ or -5. However, time cannot be negative. Therefore, in this problem, $t = +5$ only.)

11. (d) Find two factors of -24 that add up to -10. Those factors are -12 and $+2$. Thus:

$$y^2 - 10y - 24 = 0$$
$$(y - 12)(y + 2) = 0$$

Set each binomial factor equal to 0 and solve to find the two roots of the equation:

$$y - 12 = 0 \quad \text{or} \quad y + 2 = 0$$
$$y = 12 \quad \text{or} \quad y = -2$$

12. (b) First, transpose 12 to the left side of the equation:

$$x^2 - 4x - 12 = 0$$

Second, find two factors of -12 that add up to -4. Those factors are -6 and $+2$. Thus:

$$(x - 6)(x + 2) = 0$$

Third, set each binomial factor equal to 0 and solve to find the two roots of the equation:

$$x - 6 = 0 \quad \text{or} \quad x + 2 = 0$$
$$x = 6 \quad \text{or} \quad x = -2$$

13. (a) To find the value of x, add the two equations together:

$$\begin{array}{r} 2x + y = 24 \\ +\ 4x - y = 12 \\ \hline 6x \quad\ = 36 \\ x \quad\ = 6 \end{array}$$

To find the value of y, substitute 6 for x in the first equation:

$$2(6) + y = 24$$
$$12 + y = 24$$
$$y = 12$$

14. (d) To find the value of b, multiply the first equation by -2:

$$-2(a - 2b = -1) = -2a + 4b$$
$$= 2$$

Then add it to the second equation:

$$\begin{array}{r} -2a + 4b = 2 \\ +\ \ 2a + 3b = 12 \\ \hline 7b = 14 \\ b = 2 \end{array}$$

To find the value of a, substitute 2 for b in the first equation (the original one):

$$a - 2(2) = -1$$
$$a - 4 = -1$$
$$a = 3$$

MOTION PROBLEMS

1. (e) To find average speed, or rate, divide distance by time:

$$261 \div 4\tfrac{1}{2} = \dfrac{261}{1} \times \dfrac{2}{9} = 58$$

2. (c) The plane flies for $3\tfrac{1}{2}$, or $7/2$, hours. To find distance, multiply rate by time:

$$450 \times \dfrac{7}{2} = 1575$$

3. (a) Set the problem up in the form of a proportion: 1 mile is to x minutes as 45 miles is to 60 minutes (1 hour). Thus:

$$\frac{1}{x} = \frac{45}{60}$$
$$45x = 60$$
$$x = 1\frac{1}{3}$$

4. (d) $R = \dfrac{D}{T}$

$ = \dfrac{k}{h}$

5. (b) Her rate in miles per minute is 45/60. To find her rate in feet per second, multiply her rate in miles per minute by 5280/60:

$$\frac{45}{60} \times \frac{5280}{60} = \frac{3}{4} \times \frac{88}{1} = 66$$

6. (c) To find the average speed, divide the total distance by the total time. The total distance is 2 miles. The total time is 30 minutes, or 1/2 hour. Thus:

$$2 \div \frac{1}{2} = \frac{2}{1} \times \frac{2}{1} = 4$$

7. (d) The first half of the round trip takes 120/60 = 2 hours. The second half takes 120/40 = 3 hours. To find the average speed, divide the total distance (240 miles) by the total time (5 hours): 240/5 = 48 miles per hour.

8. (c) If he runs 200 yards in 20 seconds, then he runs the remaining 120 yards in 10 seconds: 120/10 = 12 yards per second.

9. (b) Let t equal the number of hours the two planes travel. Then the distance traveled by the one plane is $550t$ and the distance traveled by the other plane is $300t$. The two distances together add up to 2550 miles, so set up the equation and solve for t:

$$550t + 300t = 2550$$
$$850t = 2550$$
$$t = 3$$

10. (a) Let t equal the time that Helen travels. Then the distance Helen travels is $8t$. Let $t + 2\frac{1}{2}$ equal the time that Jim travels. Then the distance Jim travels is $3(t + 2\frac{1}{2}) = 3t + 15/2$. The distance that Helen travels is equal to the distance that Jim travels, so set up the equation and solve for t:

$$8t = 3t + \frac{15}{2}$$
$$5t = \frac{15}{2}$$
$$10t = 15$$
$$t = 1\frac{1}{2}$$

WORK PROBLEMS

1. (b) If Ben can complete the job in t hours, then in 1 hour he can complete $1/t$ of the job and in 3 hours he can complete $3/t$ of the job.

2. (e) Marian can do 1/12 of the job in 1 hour, so she can do $n/12$ of the job in n hours.

3. (c) Mort's rate is $1/x$ of the house per hour. In n hours, then, he can paint n/x of the house.

4. (a) Let x equal the number of hours it will take Maria and Henry to do the job together. Maria's rate is 1/2 the job per hour, so in x hours she will do $x/2$ of the job. Henry's rate is 1/3 of the job per hour, so in x hours he will do $x/3$ of the job. Set the sum of their work equal to 1 (the whole job) and solve for x:

$$\frac{x}{2} + \frac{x}{3} = 1$$
$$3x + 2x = 6$$
$$5x = 6$$
$$x = 1\frac{1}{5}$$

5. (d) Let x equal the number of hours it will take the two boys to wax the car. Dan waxes 1/6 of the car per hour, so in x hours he will wax $x/6$ of the car. Pete waxes 1/4 of the car per hour, so in x hours he will wax $x/4$ of the car. Set the sum of their work equal to 1 and solve for x:

$$\frac{x}{6} + \frac{x}{4} = 1$$
$$2x + 3x = 12$$
$$5x = 12$$
$$x = 2\frac{2}{5}$$

6. (c) In 1 hour, 1/6 of the water needed to fill the tank will flow in and 1/8 of the water needed to empty the tank will flow out. In x hours, $x/6$ of the water needed to fill the tank will flow in and $x/8$ of the water needed to empty the tank will flow out. Thus:

$$\frac{x}{6} - \frac{x}{8} = 1$$
$$4x - 3x = 24$$
$$x = 24$$

7. (e) Mr. Lee's rate is $1/x$ of the job per hour, so in 6 hours he does $6/x$ of the job. His son's rate is $1/2x$ of the job per hour, so in 6 hours his son does $6/2x$, or $3/x$, of the job. Set the sum of their work equal to 1 and solve for x:

$$\frac{6}{x} + \frac{3}{x} = 1$$
$$6 + 3 = x$$
$$9 = x$$

AVERAGE PROBLEMS

1. (d) Add the five grades: $72 + 77 + 82 + 83 + 91 = 405$. Then divide the sum by 5: $405 \div 5 = 81$.

2. (c) The sum of the six temperatures is $24°$, so the average temperature is $24° \div 6 = 4°$.

3. (e) To get an average of 85 on 5 tests, Marlene needs grades totaling $85 \times 5 = 425$. So far she has earned grades totaling $79 + 83 + 86 + 89 = 337$. Therefore, she must earn a grade of $425 - 337 = 88$ on her fifth test.

4. (c) Since the numbers are all evenly spaced, the average must be equal to the middle one, c.

5. (d) The 50 students who averaged 80 earned $50 \times 80 = 4000$ points. The 30 students who averaged 86 earned $30 \times 86 = 2580$ points. Therefore, all 80 students together averaged

$$\frac{4000 + 2580}{80} = \frac{6580}{80}$$
$$= 82\frac{1}{4}$$

6. (d) Dan does the first 20 problems in $20 \times 3/4 = 15$ minutes. Therefore, he has 35 minutes left to do the remaining 10 problems. That's an average of $35/10 = 3\frac{1}{2}$ minutes for each problem.

7. (b) The sum of the six numbers is $6n + 15$. Therefore, the average is

$$\frac{6n + 15}{6} = \frac{6n}{6} + \frac{15}{6} = n + 2\frac{1}{2}$$

8. (a) If the average of r and s is 9, then the sum of r and s is $2 \times 9 = 18$. If $t = 18$, then the sum of r, s, and t is 36 and the average of r, s, and t is $36 \div 3 = 12$.

9. (d) If 20 students averaged p points on a test, then together they scored a total of $20p$ points. If one grade was then raised 10 points, the total increased to $20p + 10$, and the average increased to

$$\frac{20p + 10}{20} = \frac{20p}{20} + \frac{10}{20} = p + \frac{1}{2}$$

10. (e) If the average of 10 scores is x, then the sum of the scores is $10x$. If the average of 20 scores is y, then the sum of the scores is $20y$. If the sum of 30 scores is $10x + 20y$, then the average of the scores is

$$\frac{10x + 20y}{30} = \frac{x + 2y}{3}$$

INTEGER PROBLEMS

1. (e) If k is an integer, then choice (e) must also be an integer since

$$\frac{3k + 3}{3} = \frac{3(k + 1)}{3} = k + 1$$

The other choices may or may not be integers, depending on the value of k.

2. (a) If t is an integer, then $t + 1$ must be an integer and $2(t + 1)$, or $2t + 2$, must be an even integer.

3. (b) Solve for q:

$$p = \frac{2}{3}q$$

$$\frac{3}{2}p = q$$

If q is an integer, then p must be some number that when multiplied by 3/2 will yield an integer. Of the choices, only 4/3 will yield an integer when multiplied by 3/2.

4. (d) $1734 = 17 \times 102$

5. (e) Choice (e), 153, is not the product of two consecutive odd integers. The other choices are: $15 = 3 \times 5$; $63 = 7 \times 9$; $99 = 9 \times 11$; $143 = 11 \times 13$.

6. (c) Choice (c), 17, cannot be written as the sum of two prime numbers. The other choices can be: $10 = 3 + 7$; $14 = 3 + 11$; $20 = 3 + 17$; $30 = 7 + 23$.

7. (a) Let p equal $6k$, where k is an integer. Then $p + 48 = 6k + 48 = 6(k + 8)$, which is divisible by 6. This is not true of the other choices.

8. (b) You know from looking at the answer choices that y is a fraction. In order for $36y^2 + 36y + 36$ to be an integer, both the denominator of the fraction and the square of the denominator of the fraction must be factors of 36. Both 3 and $3^2 = 9$ are factors of 36.

9. (c) The number of broken eggs must be an integer and the number of whole eggs must be an integer. Therefore, the sum of the two numbers in the ratio must divide 12 (a dozen) evenly. The sum of 3 and 2 does not divide 12 evenly.

10. (a) When the amount spent on peaches is subtracted from $3.00, the difference must be divisible by 20¢ (the price of one orange). So use the process of elimination. Four peaches will cost $.60, leaving $2.40, which is divisible by 20¢. Since 4 is the least of the numbers given as choices, it must be the answer.

ANGLE RELATIONSHIPS

1. (b) Sketch the triangle and you will see that angle R is opposite side ST and angle S is opposite side RT. If $RT = ST$, then angle R = angle S. You know that the third angle, angle T, measures 70°. You also know that the three angles of a triangle add up to 180°. Therefore, the degree measure of angle R is

$$\frac{180 - 70}{2} = \frac{110}{2} = 55$$

2. (c) Let the angles be $3x$, $4x$, and $5x$. Then set their sum equal to 180 and solve for x:

$$3x + 4x + 5x = 180$$
$$12x = 180$$
$$x = 15$$

If $x = 15$, then the difference in degrees between the largest angle and the smallest angle, which is $2x$, must be $2 \times 15 = 30$.

3. (e) There are $360° \div 12 = 30°$ between the successive numbers on the face of a clock. At 12:30 the small hand of a clock is halfway between 12 and 1 and the large hand is pointing directly at 6, so the two hands are 5½ numbers apart. Thus:

$$5\frac{1}{2} \times 30 = \frac{11}{2} \times \frac{30}{1} = 165$$

4. (a) $\dfrac{360°}{24} = 15°$

5. (b) The circumference of the circle is $2\pi r = 2\pi 4 = 8\pi$. Thus, a string 3π long will cover 3/8 of the circle:

$$\frac{3}{8} \times 360° = 135°$$

6. (c) Angle PQO is one of the three angles in triangle OPQ. Since $OP = OQ$, angle PQO and angle QPO, a second angle in the triangle, are equal. The third angle, angle POQ, is a central angle, so its measure is the same as the measure of the arc it intercepts. You know that the measure of the arc it intercepts is 100°. Therefore, the degree measure of angle PQO is

$$\frac{180 - 100}{2} = \frac{80}{2} = 40$$

7. (b) If $FGHJ$ is a parallelogram, then angle GHJ = angle F = 105°. If angle $GHJ = 105°$, then angle $GHK = 180° - 105° = 75°$. If $GH = GK$, then angle GKH = angle $GHK = 75°$. Therefore, $x = 180° - 2(75°) = 180° - 150° = 30°$.

8. (d) The angles next to one another in a parallelogram are supplementary. Therefore, if angle $R = 2n°$, then angle $S = 180° - 2n°$.

9. (e) If $PQRS$ is a square, then $QR = RS$ and angle $QRS = 90°$. If QRT is an equilateral triangle, then $QR = RT$ and angle $QRT = 60°$. Therefore, $RS = RT$, angle $RTS =$ angle $RST = y°$, and angle $SRT = 90° - 60° = 30°$. Thus, the value of y is

$$\frac{180 - 30}{2} = \frac{150}{2} = 75$$

10. (c) The number of degrees in the central angle is 20%, or 1/5, of the number of degrees in the entire circle:

$$\frac{1}{5} \times 360 = 72$$

RIGHT-TRIANGLE RELATIONSHIPS

1. (d) The diagonal of a rectangle divides the rectangle into two congruent right triangles. A right triangle with a hypotenuse of 26 feet and a leg of 10 feet has a second leg of 24 feet, since it is twice the size of the standard 5-12-13 right triangle. Therefore, the base of the rectangle is 24 feet.

2. (c) The ladder, the ground, and the building form a right triangle with a hypotenuse of 20 feet and a leg of 12 feet. A right triangle with a hypotenuse of $4 \times 5 = 20$ feet and a leg of $4 \times 3 = 12$ feet has a second leg of $4 \times 4 = 16$ feet, since it is four times as large as the standard 3-4-5 right triangle.

3. (b) A square with a perimeter of 16 has a side of $16 \div 4 = 4$. A square with a side of 4 has a diagonal of $4\sqrt{2}$.

4. (a) The height divides the triangle into two congruent right triangles, each with a hypotenuse of 17 and a leg of $16 \div 2 = 8$, as shown in the following figure:

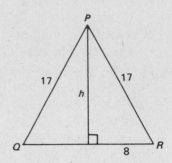

To find the length of the other leg, which is the height (h) of triangle PQR, use the Pythagorean theorem:

$$h^2 + 8^2 = 17^2$$
$$h^2 + 64 = 289$$
$$h^2 = 225$$
$$h = 15$$

5. (e) Let h equal the length of the hypotenuse. Then plug the information you're given into the Pythagorean theorem and solve for h:

$$h^2 = \left(\frac{3}{4}\right)^2 + 1^2$$
$$h^2 = \left(\frac{3}{4}\right)^2 + \left(\frac{4}{4}\right)^2$$
$$h^2 = \frac{9}{16} + \frac{16}{16}$$
$$h^2 = \frac{25}{16}$$
$$h = \frac{5}{4}$$
$$h = 1\frac{1}{4}$$

6. (d) Draw a sketch, as shown here:

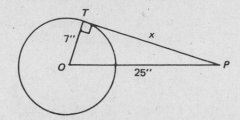

A radius drawn to the point of tangency is perpendicular to the tangent, so triangle OTP is a right triangle with a hypotenuse of 25 inches and a leg of 7 inches. To find the length of the other leg in inches, use the Pythagorean theorem:

$$x^2 + 7^2 = 25^2$$
$$x^2 + 49 = 625$$
$$x^2 = 576$$
$$x = 24$$

7. (c) Sketch the ship's route, as shown here:

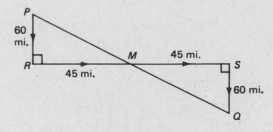

As you can see in the figure, triangle PRM and triangle QSM are congruent right triangles. To find the length of the hypotenuse of each triangle, notice that the legs have lengths of $3 \times 15 = 45$ and $4 \times 15 = 60$. This means that the triangles are each 15 times larger than the standard 3-4-5 right triangle, which means in turn that the hypotenuse of each triangle

has a length of $5 \times 15 = 75$. Therefore the ship is $2 \times 75 = 150$ miles from its starting point.

8. (b) The triangle is a 30°–60°–90° triangle whose sides are in the ratio $a : a\sqrt{3} : 2a$. If the side opposite the 30° angle has a length of 3, then the side opposite the 60° angle, which is the other leg of the triangle, has a length of $3\sqrt{3}$.

9. (d) If angle PQR is inscribed in a semicircle, then it intercepts an arc of 180° and it measures $180° \div 2 = 90°$. If angle PQR measures 90°, then triangle PQR is a right triangle. If a right triangle has legs of lengths 4 and 6, then it has a hypotenuse (PR) of length

$$PR^2 = 4^2 + 6^2$$
$$PR^2 = 16 + 36$$
$$PR^2 = 52$$
$$PR = \sqrt{4 \times 13}$$
$$PR = 2\sqrt{13}$$

Finally, if PR has a length of $2\sqrt{13}$, then OR, the radius of the circle, has a length of

$$\frac{2\sqrt{13}}{2} = \sqrt{13}$$

10. (b) A square inscribed in a circle has a diagonal equal in length to the diameter of the circle, as shown in the following figure:

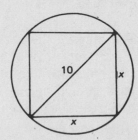

The diagonal of a square divides the square into two congruent 45°-45°-90° triangles whose sides are in the ratio $x : x : x\sqrt{2}$. You know that $x\sqrt{2} = 10$. Therefore:

$$x = \frac{10}{\sqrt{2}} = \frac{10 \times \sqrt{2}}{\sqrt{2} \times \sqrt{2}} = \frac{10\sqrt{2}}{2}$$
$$= 5\sqrt{2}$$

AREA PROBLEMS

1. (a) Since 1 square yard is 3 feet by 3 feet, it is equivalent to 9 square feet. Thus, if 1 square yard of carpet costs $10.80, then 1 square foot costs $10.80 ÷ 9 = $1.20.

2. (b) If the ratio of the diameters of two circles is 2:1, then the ratio of the areas of the two circles is $2^2 : 1^2$, or 4:1.

3. (e) The perimeter of a rectangle is equal to the sum of twice the length and twice the width. Let x equal the width and $x + 3$ equal the length. Then:

$$2x + 2(x + 3) = 58$$
$$2x + 2x + 6 = 58$$
$$4x = 52$$
$$x = 13$$

A rectangle with a width of 13 centimeters and a length of $13 + 3 = 16$ centimeters has an area of $13 \times 16 = 208$ square centimeters.

4. (c) The area of the shaded region is 1/4 of the area of a circle of radius 10 minus the area of a triangle of base 10 and height 10. First, find the area of a circle of radius 10:

$$A = \pi r^2 = \pi 10^2 = 100\pi$$

Second, divide that area by 4:

$$100\pi \div 4 = 25\pi$$

Third, find the area of a triangle of base 10 and height 10:

$$A = \frac{1}{2}bh = \frac{1}{2} \times 10 \times 10 = 50$$

Finally, subtract the area of the triangle from the area of 1/4 of the circle:

$$25\pi - 50$$

5. (d) A square with an area of $49t^2$ has a side of $\sqrt{49t^2} = 7t$ and a perimeter of $4 \times 7t = 28t$.

6. (e) Since angle RST intercepts an arc of 180° (half a circle), it measures $180° \div 2 = 90°$. So triangle RST is a right triangle. To find the length of RT, which is the diameter of the semicircle, use the Pythagorean theorem:

$$RT^2 = 1^2 + 2^2$$
$$RT^2 = 1 + 4$$
$$RT^2 = 5$$
$$RT = \sqrt{5}$$

Now, if the diameter of the semicircle is $\sqrt{5}$, then the radius is $\sqrt{5}/2$. Therefore, the area of the semicircle is

$$\frac{1}{2}\pi r^2 = \frac{1}{2}\pi\left(\frac{\sqrt{5}}{2}\right)^2 = \frac{1}{2}\pi\frac{5}{4} = \frac{5\pi}{8}$$

7. (b) Let s equal the side of the square. Then $s + 8 = $ the length of the rectangle and $s - 4 = $ the width of the rectangle. You know that the areas of the two figures are equal, so set up the equation and solve for s:

$$(s + 8)(s - 4) = s^2$$
$$s^2 + 4s - 32 = s^2$$
$$4s = 32$$
$$s = 8$$

8. (c) A radius drawn to the point of tangency is perpendicular to the tangent. Therefore, angle RTP is a right angle and triangle RTP is a right triangle. To find the length of RT, which is the diameter of circle O, use the Pythagorean theorem:

$$9^2 = 7^2 + RT^2$$
$$81 = 49 + RT^2$$
$$32 = RT^2$$
$$\sqrt{32} = RT$$

A circle with a diameter of $\sqrt{32}$ has a radius of $\sqrt{32}/2$. Therefore, its area is

$$\pi r^2 = \pi \left(\frac{\sqrt{32}}{2}\right)^2 = \pi \frac{32}{4} = 8\pi$$

9. (a) The area of the original square is p^2 square inches. The area of the enlarged square is $(p + q)^2 = p^2 + 2pg + q^2$ square inches. The difference is $2pq + q^2$ square inches.

10. (d) If the length of the original rectangle is l, then the length of the enlarged rectangle is 120% of l, or $1.2l$. If the width of the original rectangle is w, then the width of the enlarged rectangle is 110% of w, or $1.1w$. Since $1.2l \times 1.1w = 1.32lw$, or 132% of lw, the area of the enlarged rectangle is 32% greater than the area of the original rectangle.

GEOMETRY OF SOLIDS

1. (d) A cubic yard is 3 feet × 3 feet × 3 feet = 27 cubic feet, so there are $3 \times 27 = 81$ cubic feet in 3 cubic yards. If 1 cubic foot of sand weighs 80 pounds, then 81 cubic feet weigh $80 \times 81 = 6480$ pounds.

2. (c) If the tank is filled to within 6 inches of the top, then the depth of the water will be 5½, or 11/2, feet. Therefore, the number of cubic feet of water in the tank will be

$$14 \times 7 \times \frac{11}{2} = 539$$

3. (a) Six tons of coal will occupy $6 \times 35 = 210$ cubic feet. Let d equal the depth of the coal bin in feet. Then:

$$8 \times 5 \times d = 210$$
$$40d = 210$$
$$d = 5\frac{1}{4}$$

4. (e) If the edge of a cube is 1, the volume of the cube is $1^3 = 1$. If the edge of a cube is 2, then the volume of the cube is $2^3 = 8$. Therefore, if the edge of a cube is doubled, the volume of the cube is multiplied by 8. (In general, if the ratio of the corresponding lengths of two similar figures is $1:2$, then the ratio of the corresponding areas is $1^2:2^2$, or $1:4$, and the ratio of the volumes is $1^3:2^3$, or 1 to 8.)

5. (b) The following figure shows three of the six 1-inch cubes that have paint on only one face. The other three are in the centers of the three faces of the 3-inch cube that are not showing.

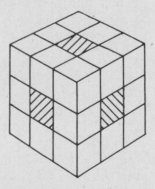

6. (e) The total surface area is the sum of the areas of the six faces of the solid. Two of the faces have an area of $p \times 2p = 2p^2$, two have an area of $p \times 3p = 3p^2$, and two have an area of $2p \times 3p = 6p^2$. Therefore, the total surface area is

$$2(2p^2) + 2(3p^2) + 2(6p^2) =$$
$$4p^2 + 6p^2 + 12p^2 = 22p^2$$

7. (a) Plug the information you're given into the formula and solve for B:

$$V = \frac{1}{3}Bh$$

$$96\pi = \frac{1}{3}B \times 8 \quad \text{(Divide by 8)}$$

$$12\pi = \frac{1}{3}B \quad \text{(Multiply by 3)}$$

$$36\pi = B$$

If the area of the circular base is 36π, then the radius of the base is $\sqrt{36} = 6$.

8. (c) A cube with a volume of 27 cubic inches has an edge of $\sqrt[3]{27} = 3$. The area of each of the six faces of a cube with an edge of 3 is $3^2 = 9$. Therefore, the total surface area of the cube is $6 \times 9 = 54$ square inches.

9. (b) If there are 231 cubic inches in 1 gallon, then there are $5 \times 231 = 1155$ cubic inches in 5 gallons. Let w equal the width of the can in inches. Then:

$$11 \times 10 \times w = 1155$$
$$110w = 1155$$
$$w = 10\frac{1}{2}$$

10. (d) Since there are 12 inches in 1 foot, it takes $12 \times 12 = 144$ cubes with an edge of 1 inch to make one layer of a cube with an edge of 1 foot.

11. (d) The radius of the base of the cylinder is 7/2. The height of the cylinder is 4. Thus:

$$V = \pi r^2 h$$
$$= \pi \times \left(\frac{7}{2}\right)^2 \times 4$$
$$= \pi \times \frac{49}{4} \times 4$$
$$= 49\pi$$

12. (d) Since $V = \pi r^2 h$ and since π has an approximate value of 22/7, the volume of the can in cubic inches is approximately

$$\frac{22}{7} \times 7^2 \times 9 = 22 \times 7 \times 9$$
$$= 1386$$

Since 231 cubic inches = 1 gallon, the can holds approximately $1386 \div 231 = 6$ gallons.

COORDINATE GEOMETRY

1. (a) One dimension of the rectangle is the difference between the y-coordinates of the two points given: $3 - 0 = 3$. The other dimension is the difference between the x-coordinates: $5 - 0 = 5$. Therefore, the perimeter of the rectangle is

$$(2 \times 3) + (2 \times 5) = 6 + 10 = 16$$

2. (c) The base of the triangle is the difference between the x-coordinates of points T and S: $7 - 1 = 6$. The height of the triangle is the difference between the y-coordinates of

point *R* and points *S* and *T*: $4 - (-1) = 4 + 1 = 5$. Therefore, the area of the triangle is

$$\frac{1}{2} \times 6 \times 5 = 15$$

3. (e) The difference between the *x*-coordinates of the points is 0. The difference between the *y*-coordinates is -3. Therefore, if the original coordinates of point *P* were $(5, 1)$, the new coordinates are $(5, -2)$.

4. (d) If the area of square *GHJK* is 49, then the side of the square has a length of $\sqrt{49} = 7$ and the diagonal of the square has a length of $7\sqrt{2}$. Since the *x*-axis bisects diagonal *HK*, *OK* has a length of $7\sqrt{2}/2$. Therefore, the coordinates of point *K* are

$$\left(0, -\frac{7}{2}\sqrt{2}\right)$$

5. (b) The distance *OM* is the average of the distance *OP* and *OQ*. Thus:

$$OM = \frac{a + b}{2}$$

6. (a) Since the *x*-coordinates of two of the vertices are 0, you know that one side of the triangle lies along the *y*-axis. Call that side the base. Its length is the difference between the *y*-coordinates of the two vertices: $5 - (-3) = 5 + 3 = 8$. The height of the triangle is then the difference between the *x*-coordinate of the third vertex and the *x*-coordinates of the two vertices at the base: $4 - 0 = 4$. Therefore the area of the triangle is

$$\frac{1}{2} \times 8 \times 4 = 16$$

7. (e) The *y*-coordinate of the point at which the line intersects the *x*-axis is 0. To find the *x*-coordinate, draw a sketch, as shown here:

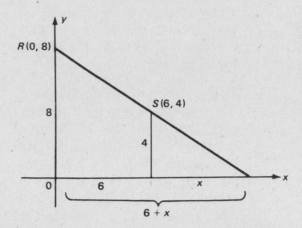

The *x*-coordinate of the point is the sum of 6 and *x*. To find the value of *x*, notice that there are two triangles in the sketch, one with a base of *x* and a height of 4 and one with a base of $6 + x$ and a height of 8. Since the corresponding angles of these triangles are equal, the corresponding sides of the triangles are proportional. Thus:

$$\frac{4}{8} = \frac{x}{6 + x}$$
$$\frac{1}{2} = \frac{x}{6 + x}$$
$$2x = 6 + x$$
$$x = 6$$

If $x = 6$, then $6 + x = 12$. The coordinates of the *x*-intercept are $(12, 0)$.

8. (b) The range of values is defined by the *y*-coordinates of the points at which the line intersects the two axes. It intersects the *y*-axis at $y = -3$. It intersects the *x*-axis at $y = 0$. Therefore, $-3 < y < 0$.

9. (a) One dimension of $PQRT$ is the difference between the y-coordinates of the vertices at the top and the bottom: $r - s$. The other dimension is the difference between the x-coordinates of the vertices on the right and the left: $3 - (-2) = 3 + 2 = 5$. Therefore, the area of $PQRT$ is $5(r - s)$.

10. (c) The diameter of the semicircle is the hypotenuse of a right triangle with legs of 5 and 12. A right triangle with legs of 5 and 12 has a hypotenuse of 13, since it is the standard 5-12-13 right triangle. A semicircle with a diameter of 13 has a radius of 13/2. Therefore, its area is

$$\frac{1}{2} \times \pi \times \left(\frac{13}{2}\right)^2 = \frac{1}{2} \times \pi \times \frac{169}{4}$$

$$= \frac{169\pi}{8}$$

INEQUALITIES

1. (c) $2x + 2 > 10$ (Subtract 2)
$\qquad 2x > 8$ (Divide by 2)
$\qquad x > 4$

2. (a) Take the positive square root of each term:

$$9 < y^2 < 64$$
$$3 < y < 8$$

3. (e) $\dfrac{p}{3} - 2 > 5$ (Multiply by 3)

$\qquad p - 6 > 15$ (Add 6)
$\qquad p > 21$

4. (b) $2p - q > 2p + q$ (Subtract 2p)
$\qquad -q > q$ (Add q)
$\qquad 0 > 2q$ (Divide by 2)
$\qquad 0 > q$

If $0 > q$, then $q < 0$.

5. (d) You know that $s + t + 50 = 180$, so $s + t = 130$. If $s < 50$, then t must be greater than 80.

6. (e) Start by squaring the left side of the inequality:

$$(r - s)^2 < r^2 + s^2$$
$$r^2 - 2rs + s^2 < r^2 + s^2$$

Then subtract $r^2 + s^2$ from both sides:

$$-2rs < 0$$

Finally, divide both sides by -2, remembering to reverse the direction of the inequality:

$$rs > 0$$

7. (d) If n is an integer, then $n + 1$ must also be an integer. The only integer between 3 and 5 is 4. Therefore:

$$n + 1 = 4$$
$$n = 3$$

8. (e) To find the bottom of the range of values for $p - q$, subtract the greatest possible value of q from the least possible value of p:

$$(p - q) > -4 - 0$$
$$> -4$$

To find the top of the range of values for $p - q$, subtract the least possible value of q from the greatest possible value of p:

$$(p - q) < 5 - (-2)$$
$$< 5 + 2$$
$$< 7$$

Thus, $-4 < (p - q) < 7$.

9. (d) If s were 90, then the triangle would be a 45°-45°-90° triangle with sides in the ratio of $a : a : a\sqrt{2}$, and t would have a value of $3\sqrt{2}$. But $s > 90$; therefore,

$t > 3\sqrt{2}$. Since the sum of the lengths of any two sides of a triangle must be greater than the length of the third side, t must be less than $3 + 3$. Therefore $3\sqrt{2} < t < 6$.

10. (b) If r and s are both proper fractions, if r and s are both positive, and if $r < s$, then

$$\frac{1}{r} > \frac{1}{s}$$

If you do not see this, substitute simple values for r and s, such as 1/4 and 1/2, and work it out. You'll get 4 and 2, respectively.

DATA INTERPRETATION

1. (c) Round $1,249.7 billion to $1250 billion. Then multiply by 1/5 (20%). The result is $250 billion.

2. (d) $0.11 \times 360° = 39.6° \approx 40°$

3. (e) $\dfrac{45}{20} = \dfrac{9}{4}$

4. (b) If total personal income in 1975 was 20% greater than it was in 1972, then total personal income in 1975 was 100% + 20% = 120% of total personal income in 1972. Let x equal total personal income in 1972. Then:

$$1.2x = 1249.7$$
$$x \approx 1040$$

5. (b) $\dfrac{99.1}{26.9} \approx \dfrac{4}{1}$

6. (a) $\dfrac{\$99.1 \text{ billion}}{215 \text{ million}} \approx \dfrac{\$100,000}{215}$

$$= \dfrac{\$20,000}{43} \approx \$465$$

7. (e) According to the graph, $40.5 billion was spent on health care in 1965, and $40.5 billion was 5.9% of the gross national product that year. Let x equal the gross national product in billions of dollars in 1965. Then:

$$.059x = 40.5$$
$$x \approx 680$$

8. (d) According to the graph, between 1971 and 1973 the percentage of gross national product spent on health care increased by only 0.2, from 7.7% to 7.9%.

9. (b) According to the graph, health care expenditures increased from $90.4 billion to $99.1 billion, or $8.7 billion, from 1972 to 1973. Therefore, they increased

$$\frac{8.7}{90.4} \approx .096 = 9.6\%$$

10. (d) According to the graph, employment in service industries at the end of 1965 was about 40 million and employment in goods-producing industries was about 23 million, for a total of about 63 million.

11. (c) During the period covered on the graph, employment in the goods-producing industries increased from about 18 million to about 24 or 25 million, or about 6 or 7 million. Employment in the service industries increased from about 25 million to about 58 million, or about 33 million. So the increase in employment in the service industries was about 5 times greater.

12. (a) According to the graph, at the end of 1970 there were about 47 million service workers and about 23 million goods-producing workers. A ratio of 47 to 23 is approximately equal to a ratio of 2 to 1.

13. (b) According to the graph, there were 25 million service workers at the start of 1948. Since 100% of 25 is 25, look for the year when there were 50 million service workers. That was the end of 1972.

QUANTITATIVE COMPARISONS

1. (a) Column A has a value of $2 \times 3 \times 4 \times 5 = 6 \times 20 = 120$, which is greater than 110.

2. (c) $25^2 = (5^2)^2 = 5^4$

3. (b) No matter what value $3y$ has, $3y + 1$ will always be 2 greater than $3y - 1$.

4. (d) If p were 1 and q were 2, $3p$ would be greater than q. However, if p were 1 and q were 5, $3p$ would be less than q. Hence, the relationship cannot be determined.

5. (c) If $r - 10 = 15$, then $r = 25$ and $r + 5 = 30$. Therefore, the amounts in the two columns are equal.

6. (a) If the three lines are parallel, then the angle marked $n°$ is supplementary to the angle marked 48°. Therefore, $n = 180 - 48 = 132$, which is greater than 122.

7. (b) The square root of 0.05 is greater than 0.2, since $0.2 \times 0.2 = 0.04$.

Therefore, $\sqrt{0.05} > 0.05$. Remember this: The square root of a number between 0 and 1 is always greater than the number, and the square of a number between 0 and 1 is always less than the number.

8. (c) The integers are $t, t + 1, t + 2, \ldots, t + 8$. The average of a group of consecutive integers is the middle integer, which in this case is $t + 4$.

9. (a) Since $3^2 = 9$ and $9.14 > 9$, Column A has a value a little greater than 3. Since $3^3 = 27$ and $26.8 < 27$, Column B has a value a little less than 3.

10. (b) If $3s = 2$, then $s = 2/3$ and $s^2 = 4/9$, which is less than 2/3, or 6/9.

11. (d) If $M^2 = 36$, then $M = \pm6$. Since M may have a value of $+6$ or -6, the relationship between M and 6 cannot be determined.

12. (b) To find the value of p, use the Pythagorean theorem:
$$p^2 + 11^2 = 12^2$$
$$p^2 + 121 = 144$$
$$p^2 = 23$$
$$p = \sqrt{23}$$
Since $5 = \sqrt{25}$ and since $\sqrt{25} > \sqrt{23}, 5 > p$.

13. (d) As long as their sum is between 0 and 1, m and n may be any numbers. Consider some possibilities: $m = 10$ and $n = -9\frac{1}{2}$; $m = -1/2$ and $n = 1$; $m = -100$ and $n = 100.1$. Therefore, the correct answer is choice (d): the relationship between n and 1 cannot be determined.

14. (a) Express the fractions in both columns in terms of their lowest common denominator, 12. Then subtract as indicated and compare the results. You'll find that Column A has a value of 2/12 and Column B has a value of 1/12. Therefore, Column A is greater.

15. (b) The area of the square is

$$\left(\frac{3}{4}k\right)^2 = \frac{9k^2}{16}$$

The area of the circle is

$$\pi\left(\frac{k}{2}\right)^2 = \frac{\pi k^2}{4} \approx \frac{3.14k^2}{4} \approx \frac{12k^2}{16}$$

Therefore, the area of the circle is greater than the area of the square.

16. (b) Since $3\sqrt{11} = \sqrt{9} \times \sqrt{11}$ and since $11 = \sqrt{11} \times \sqrt{11}$, Column B is greater.

17. (d) In order to make the comparison, you must know the value of k. If $k = 0$, then $r = s$. If $k > 0$, then $r > s$. If $k < 0$, then $r < s$.

18. (a) QR is opposite an angle measuring 65°. PR is opposite an angle measuring $180° - (65° + 55°) = 180° - 120° = 60°$. Since $65° > 60°$, $QR > PR$.

19. (c) Multiply both the numerator and the denominator in Column B by h and you'll get the fraction in Column A:

$$\frac{g - \dfrac{3}{h}}{g} \times \frac{h}{h} = \frac{gh - 3}{gh}$$

20. (b) If r were 90, then the triangle would be twice the size of the standard 3-4-5 right triangle and its longest side would be 10. Since the longest side of the triangle is less than 10, r must be less than 90 and $s + t$ must be greater than 90.

PART VII
Practice Tests
for the GRE

The four practice tests in this part of the book are similar in form and content to the actual GRE General Test that is currently given. As you finish each test, check your answers against those in the answer key. For those questions you answered incorrectly, look over the explanatory answers that follow each test and answer key.

If you find that you are having difficulty with a particular topic in the quantitative section, review this topic in Part V, the mathematics review section, and work out the problems related to this topic in Part VI. Similarly, if you are having difficulty with areas of the verbal section, look over suggestions related to this area in Part II, the verbal practice section. For additional help with the analytical ability portion of the test, review the illustrations and suggestions made in Part IV.

You can determine your raw score on each section of the test by following the scoring directions on page 3. You may then evaluate this score by studying the score conversion chart on page 198.

We believe that going through these tests in this manner will help you become more familiar with the GRE General Test and help you to continually improve your GRE score.

Test-Taking Suggestions

Before starting the tests, review these suggested test-taking techniques:

- Remember that you have a limited time to complete each section of the GRE. Try to develop a pace that will permit you to finish each section without loss of accuracy. Do not spend too much time on any single question; make a notation of those questions you find difficult and return to them if and when you finish the section.
- Before you take the actual GRE, make sure that you thoroughly understand the directions for each type of test question. Then skim the directions at test time to make sure that they are the instructions you already know.
- Since there is no penalty for a wrong answer, answer every question even if you must guess. Eliminate any answer that is clearly wrong and make an educated guess from among the remaining choices.
- Make sure that the number of each question you are answering matches the corresponding number on the answer sheet. The number of answer spaces on the answer sheet may be more than the number of questions in a particular section, so ignore any extra spaces. If you erase an answer, do it thoroughly.
- Avoid using time unnecessarily. It is wise not to check problems in a quantitative section until you have finished the section. Make quick, simple diagrams and figures if they are helpful in solving a problem. If a diagram for a particular problem accompanies the problem, write directly on it; do not start drawing another diagram.

- Do not become alarmed if you cannot answer some questions or if you do not finish every section. You may still score well on the GRE.
- Bring a watch with you to check your pace. In some sections, the easier questions appear first, so you should do these rapidly in order to conserve time for the more difficult questions that come later.

Self-Appraisal and Score Conversion Chart

When you finish each test, figure your raw scores according to the scoring instructions on page 3 of this book. Use the number of correct responses in sections I and II to obtain your raw verbal score, the number of correct responses in sections III and IV for your raw quantitative score, and the number of correct responses in sections V and VI for your raw analytical score (remember that section VII is an experimental section and does not count toward your score). Then enter your scores here.

	Verbal	Quantitative	Analytical
Test 1	_____	_____	_____
Test 2	_____	_____	_____
Test 3	_____	_____	_____
Test 4	_____	_____	_____

CONVERTING RAW SCORES TO SCALED SCORES

With the aid of statistical processes, the raw score is converted to a score scaled from 200 to 800. The scale conversion varies in different years for different tests. To determine your approximate score on the practice tests in this book, arrive at your raw score as explained above. Then find your raw score and its scaled equivalent in the Score Conversion Chart on the next page.

SELF-APPRAISAL

In evaluating your achievement on the practice tests, consider a converted score of 650–800 as excellent and 500–649 as good. A score of 500 on the conversion scale indicates that you rank close to the midpoint of the range of scores. If you score below 500 on any of the three parts of the test, you should undertake further review and practice in those particular areas. By recording your scores from the chart on this page, you will be able to monitor your progress.

SCORE CONVERSION CHART

Raw Scores	Scaled Scores			Raw Scores	Scaled Scores		
	Verbal	Quanti-tative	Analyt-ical		Verbal	Quanti-tative	Analyt-ical
76	800			38	420	530	690
75	800			37	420	520	680
74	800			36	410	500	660
73	790			35	400	490	650
72	780			34	390	480	630
71	770			33	380	460	610
70	760			32	370	450	600
69	750			31	360	440	580
68	740			30	360	430	570
67	730			29	350	420	550
66	720			28	340	410	530
65	710			27	340	390	520
64	690			26	330	380	510
63	680			25	330	370	500
62	670			24	320	360	490
61	660			23	310	350	470
60	650	800		22	300	340	450
59	640	800		21	290	330	440
58	620	790		20	280	320	420
57	610	780		19	270	310	410
56	600	770		18	260	300	400
55	580	760		17	250	290	380
54	570	750		16	240	280	370
53	560	740		15	230	270	360
52	550	730		14	220	250	340
51	540	720		13	210	230	330
50	530	710	800	12	200	220	310
49	520	690	800	11	200	210	300
48	510	680	800	10	200	200	290
47	500	670	790	9	200	200	270
46	490	660	780	8	200	200	260
45	480	640	770	7	200	200	250
44	470	620	760	6	200	200	230
43	460	600	750	5	200	200	220
42	450	590	740	4	200	200	210
41	440	580	730	3	200	200	200
40	430	560	710	2	200	200	200
39	430	550	700	1	200	200	200
				0	200	200	200

Answer Sheet—Practice Test 1

When you have chosen your answer to any question, blacken the corresponding space on the answer sheet below. Make sure your marking completely fills the answer space. If you change an answer, erase the previous marking completely.

Section I

1 Ⓐ Ⓑ Ⓒ Ⓓ Ⓔ	11 Ⓐ Ⓑ Ⓒ Ⓓ Ⓔ	21 Ⓐ Ⓑ Ⓒ Ⓓ Ⓔ	30 Ⓐ Ⓑ Ⓒ Ⓓ Ⓔ
2 Ⓐ Ⓑ Ⓒ Ⓓ Ⓔ	12 Ⓐ Ⓑ Ⓒ Ⓓ Ⓔ	22 Ⓐ Ⓑ Ⓒ Ⓓ Ⓔ	31 Ⓐ Ⓑ Ⓒ Ⓓ Ⓔ
3 Ⓐ Ⓑ Ⓒ Ⓓ Ⓔ	13 Ⓐ Ⓑ Ⓒ Ⓓ Ⓔ	23 Ⓐ Ⓑ Ⓒ Ⓓ Ⓔ	32 Ⓐ Ⓑ Ⓒ Ⓓ Ⓔ
4 Ⓐ Ⓑ Ⓒ Ⓓ Ⓔ	14 Ⓐ Ⓑ Ⓒ Ⓓ Ⓔ	24 Ⓐ Ⓑ Ⓒ Ⓓ Ⓔ	33 Ⓐ Ⓑ Ⓒ Ⓓ Ⓔ
5 Ⓐ Ⓑ Ⓒ Ⓓ Ⓔ	15 Ⓐ Ⓑ Ⓒ Ⓓ Ⓔ	25 Ⓐ Ⓑ Ⓒ Ⓓ Ⓔ	34 Ⓐ Ⓑ Ⓒ Ⓓ Ⓔ
6 Ⓐ Ⓑ Ⓒ Ⓓ Ⓔ	16 Ⓐ Ⓑ Ⓒ Ⓓ Ⓔ	26 Ⓐ Ⓑ Ⓒ Ⓓ Ⓔ	35 Ⓐ Ⓑ Ⓒ Ⓓ Ⓔ
7 Ⓐ Ⓑ Ⓒ Ⓓ Ⓔ	17 Ⓐ Ⓑ Ⓒ Ⓓ Ⓔ	27 Ⓐ Ⓑ Ⓒ Ⓓ Ⓔ	36 Ⓐ Ⓑ Ⓒ Ⓓ Ⓔ
8 Ⓐ Ⓑ Ⓒ Ⓓ Ⓔ	18 Ⓐ Ⓑ Ⓒ Ⓓ Ⓔ	28 Ⓐ Ⓑ Ⓒ Ⓓ Ⓔ	37 Ⓐ Ⓑ Ⓒ Ⓓ Ⓔ
9 Ⓐ Ⓑ Ⓒ Ⓓ Ⓔ	19 Ⓐ Ⓑ Ⓒ Ⓓ Ⓔ	29 Ⓐ Ⓑ Ⓒ Ⓓ Ⓔ	38 Ⓐ Ⓑ Ⓒ Ⓓ Ⓔ
10 Ⓐ Ⓑ Ⓒ Ⓓ Ⓔ	20 Ⓐ Ⓑ Ⓒ Ⓓ Ⓔ		

Section II

1 Ⓐ Ⓑ Ⓒ Ⓓ Ⓔ	11 Ⓐ Ⓑ Ⓒ Ⓓ Ⓔ	21 Ⓐ Ⓑ Ⓒ Ⓓ Ⓔ	30 Ⓐ Ⓑ Ⓒ Ⓓ Ⓔ
2 Ⓐ Ⓑ Ⓒ Ⓓ Ⓔ	12 Ⓐ Ⓑ Ⓒ Ⓓ Ⓔ	22 Ⓐ Ⓑ Ⓒ Ⓓ Ⓔ	31 Ⓐ Ⓑ Ⓒ Ⓓ Ⓔ
3 Ⓐ Ⓑ Ⓒ Ⓓ Ⓔ	13 Ⓐ Ⓑ Ⓒ Ⓓ Ⓔ	23 Ⓐ Ⓑ Ⓒ Ⓓ Ⓔ	32 Ⓐ Ⓑ Ⓒ Ⓓ Ⓔ
4 Ⓐ Ⓑ Ⓒ Ⓓ Ⓔ	14 Ⓐ Ⓑ Ⓒ Ⓓ Ⓔ	24 Ⓐ Ⓑ Ⓒ Ⓓ Ⓔ	33 Ⓐ Ⓑ Ⓒ Ⓓ Ⓔ
5 Ⓐ Ⓑ Ⓒ Ⓓ Ⓔ	15 Ⓐ Ⓑ Ⓒ Ⓓ Ⓔ	25 Ⓐ Ⓑ Ⓒ Ⓓ Ⓔ	34 Ⓐ Ⓑ Ⓒ Ⓓ Ⓔ
6 Ⓐ Ⓑ Ⓒ Ⓓ Ⓔ	16 Ⓐ Ⓑ Ⓒ Ⓓ Ⓔ	26 Ⓐ Ⓑ Ⓒ Ⓓ Ⓔ	35 Ⓐ Ⓑ Ⓒ Ⓓ Ⓔ
7 Ⓐ Ⓑ Ⓒ Ⓓ Ⓔ	17 Ⓐ Ⓑ Ⓒ Ⓓ Ⓔ	27 Ⓐ Ⓑ Ⓒ Ⓓ Ⓔ	36 Ⓐ Ⓑ Ⓒ Ⓓ Ⓔ
8 Ⓐ Ⓑ Ⓒ Ⓓ Ⓔ	18 Ⓐ Ⓑ Ⓒ Ⓓ Ⓔ	28 Ⓐ Ⓑ Ⓒ Ⓓ Ⓔ	37 Ⓐ Ⓑ Ⓒ Ⓓ Ⓔ
9 Ⓐ Ⓑ Ⓒ Ⓓ Ⓔ	19 Ⓐ Ⓑ Ⓒ Ⓓ Ⓔ	29 Ⓐ Ⓑ Ⓒ Ⓓ Ⓔ	38 Ⓐ Ⓑ Ⓒ Ⓓ Ⓔ
10 Ⓐ Ⓑ Ⓒ Ⓓ Ⓔ	20 Ⓐ Ⓑ Ⓒ Ⓓ Ⓔ		

Section III

1 Ⓐ Ⓑ Ⓒ Ⓓ Ⓔ	9 Ⓐ Ⓑ Ⓒ Ⓓ Ⓔ	17 Ⓐ Ⓑ Ⓒ Ⓓ Ⓔ	24 Ⓐ Ⓑ Ⓒ Ⓓ Ⓔ
2 Ⓐ Ⓑ Ⓒ Ⓓ Ⓔ	10 Ⓐ Ⓑ Ⓒ Ⓓ Ⓔ	18 Ⓐ Ⓑ Ⓒ Ⓓ Ⓔ	25 Ⓐ Ⓑ Ⓒ Ⓓ Ⓔ
3 Ⓐ Ⓑ Ⓒ Ⓓ Ⓔ	11 Ⓐ Ⓑ Ⓒ Ⓓ Ⓔ	19 Ⓐ Ⓑ Ⓒ Ⓓ Ⓔ	26 Ⓐ Ⓑ Ⓒ Ⓓ Ⓔ
4 Ⓐ Ⓑ Ⓒ Ⓓ Ⓔ	12 Ⓐ Ⓑ Ⓒ Ⓓ Ⓔ	20 Ⓐ Ⓑ Ⓒ Ⓓ Ⓔ	27 Ⓐ Ⓑ Ⓒ Ⓓ Ⓔ
5 Ⓐ Ⓑ Ⓒ Ⓓ Ⓔ	13 Ⓐ Ⓑ Ⓒ Ⓓ Ⓔ	21 Ⓐ Ⓑ Ⓒ Ⓓ Ⓔ	28 Ⓐ Ⓑ Ⓒ Ⓓ Ⓔ
6 Ⓐ Ⓑ Ⓒ Ⓓ Ⓔ	14 Ⓐ Ⓑ Ⓒ Ⓓ Ⓔ	22 Ⓐ Ⓑ Ⓒ Ⓓ Ⓔ	29 Ⓐ Ⓑ Ⓒ Ⓓ Ⓔ
7 Ⓐ Ⓑ Ⓒ Ⓓ Ⓔ	15 Ⓐ Ⓑ Ⓒ Ⓓ Ⓔ	23 Ⓐ Ⓑ Ⓒ Ⓓ Ⓔ	30 Ⓐ Ⓑ Ⓒ Ⓓ Ⓔ
8 Ⓐ Ⓑ Ⓒ Ⓓ Ⓔ	16 Ⓐ Ⓑ Ⓒ Ⓓ Ⓔ		

Section IV

1 Ⓐ Ⓑ Ⓒ Ⓓ Ⓔ	9 Ⓐ Ⓑ Ⓒ Ⓓ Ⓔ	17 Ⓐ Ⓑ Ⓒ Ⓓ Ⓔ	24 Ⓐ Ⓑ Ⓒ Ⓓ Ⓔ
2 Ⓐ Ⓑ Ⓒ Ⓓ Ⓔ	10 Ⓐ Ⓑ Ⓒ Ⓓ Ⓔ	18 Ⓐ Ⓑ Ⓒ Ⓓ Ⓔ	25 Ⓐ Ⓑ Ⓒ Ⓓ Ⓔ
3 Ⓐ Ⓑ Ⓒ Ⓓ Ⓔ	11 Ⓐ Ⓑ Ⓒ Ⓓ Ⓔ	19 Ⓐ Ⓑ Ⓒ Ⓓ Ⓔ	26 Ⓐ Ⓑ Ⓒ Ⓓ Ⓔ
4 Ⓐ Ⓑ Ⓒ Ⓓ Ⓔ	12 Ⓐ Ⓑ Ⓒ Ⓓ Ⓔ	20 Ⓐ Ⓑ Ⓒ Ⓓ Ⓔ	27 Ⓐ Ⓑ Ⓒ Ⓓ Ⓔ
5 Ⓐ Ⓑ Ⓒ Ⓓ Ⓔ	13 Ⓐ Ⓑ Ⓒ Ⓓ Ⓔ	21 Ⓐ Ⓑ Ⓒ Ⓓ Ⓔ	28 Ⓐ Ⓑ Ⓒ Ⓓ Ⓔ
6 Ⓐ Ⓑ Ⓒ Ⓓ Ⓔ	14 Ⓐ Ⓑ Ⓒ Ⓓ Ⓔ	22 Ⓐ Ⓑ Ⓒ Ⓓ Ⓔ	29 Ⓐ Ⓑ Ⓒ Ⓓ Ⓔ
7 Ⓐ Ⓑ Ⓒ Ⓓ Ⓔ	15 Ⓐ Ⓑ Ⓒ Ⓓ Ⓔ	23 Ⓐ Ⓑ Ⓒ Ⓓ Ⓔ	30 Ⓐ Ⓑ Ⓒ Ⓓ Ⓔ
8 Ⓐ Ⓑ Ⓒ Ⓓ Ⓔ	16 Ⓐ Ⓑ Ⓒ Ⓓ Ⓔ		

Section V

1 Ⓐ Ⓑ Ⓒ Ⓓ Ⓔ	8 Ⓐ Ⓑ Ⓒ Ⓓ Ⓔ	14 Ⓐ Ⓑ Ⓒ Ⓓ Ⓔ	20 Ⓐ Ⓑ Ⓒ Ⓓ Ⓔ
2 Ⓐ Ⓑ Ⓒ Ⓓ Ⓔ	9 Ⓐ Ⓑ Ⓒ Ⓓ Ⓔ	15 Ⓐ Ⓑ Ⓒ Ⓓ Ⓔ	21 Ⓐ Ⓑ Ⓒ Ⓓ Ⓔ
3 Ⓐ Ⓑ Ⓒ Ⓓ Ⓔ	10 Ⓐ Ⓑ Ⓒ Ⓓ Ⓔ	16 Ⓐ Ⓑ Ⓒ Ⓓ Ⓔ	22 Ⓐ Ⓑ Ⓒ Ⓓ Ⓔ
4 Ⓐ Ⓑ Ⓒ Ⓓ Ⓔ	11 Ⓐ Ⓑ Ⓒ Ⓓ Ⓔ	17 Ⓐ Ⓑ Ⓒ Ⓓ Ⓔ	23 Ⓐ Ⓑ Ⓒ Ⓓ Ⓔ
5 Ⓐ Ⓑ Ⓒ Ⓓ Ⓔ	12 Ⓐ Ⓑ Ⓒ Ⓓ Ⓔ	18 Ⓐ Ⓑ Ⓒ Ⓓ Ⓔ	24 Ⓐ Ⓑ Ⓒ Ⓓ Ⓔ
6 Ⓐ Ⓑ Ⓒ Ⓓ Ⓔ	13 Ⓐ Ⓑ Ⓒ Ⓓ Ⓔ	19 Ⓐ Ⓑ Ⓒ Ⓓ Ⓔ	25 Ⓐ Ⓑ Ⓒ Ⓓ Ⓔ
7 Ⓐ Ⓑ Ⓒ Ⓓ Ⓔ			

Section VI

1 Ⓐ Ⓑ Ⓒ Ⓓ Ⓔ	8 Ⓐ Ⓑ Ⓒ Ⓓ Ⓔ	14 Ⓐ Ⓑ Ⓒ Ⓓ Ⓔ	20 Ⓐ Ⓑ Ⓒ Ⓓ Ⓔ
2 Ⓐ Ⓑ Ⓒ Ⓓ Ⓔ	9 Ⓐ Ⓑ Ⓒ Ⓓ Ⓔ	15 Ⓐ Ⓑ Ⓒ Ⓓ Ⓔ	21 Ⓐ Ⓑ Ⓒ Ⓓ Ⓔ
3 Ⓐ Ⓑ Ⓒ Ⓓ Ⓔ	10 Ⓐ Ⓑ Ⓒ Ⓓ Ⓔ	16 Ⓐ Ⓑ Ⓒ Ⓓ Ⓔ	22 Ⓐ Ⓑ Ⓒ Ⓓ Ⓔ
4 Ⓐ Ⓑ Ⓒ Ⓓ Ⓔ	11 Ⓐ Ⓑ Ⓒ Ⓓ Ⓔ	17 Ⓐ Ⓑ Ⓒ Ⓓ Ⓔ	23 Ⓐ Ⓑ Ⓒ Ⓓ Ⓔ
5 Ⓐ Ⓑ Ⓒ Ⓓ Ⓔ	12 Ⓐ Ⓑ Ⓒ Ⓓ Ⓔ	18 Ⓐ Ⓑ Ⓒ Ⓓ Ⓔ	24 Ⓐ Ⓑ Ⓒ Ⓓ Ⓔ
6 Ⓐ Ⓑ Ⓒ Ⓓ Ⓔ	13 Ⓐ Ⓑ Ⓒ Ⓓ Ⓔ	19 Ⓐ Ⓑ Ⓒ Ⓓ Ⓔ	25 Ⓐ Ⓑ Ⓒ Ⓓ Ⓔ
7 Ⓐ Ⓑ Ⓒ Ⓓ Ⓔ			

Section VII

1 Ⓐ Ⓑ Ⓒ Ⓓ Ⓔ	8 Ⓐ Ⓑ Ⓒ Ⓓ Ⓔ	14 Ⓐ Ⓑ Ⓒ Ⓓ Ⓔ	20 Ⓐ Ⓑ Ⓒ Ⓓ Ⓔ
2 Ⓐ Ⓑ Ⓒ Ⓓ Ⓔ	9 Ⓐ Ⓑ Ⓒ Ⓓ Ⓔ	15 Ⓐ Ⓑ Ⓒ Ⓓ Ⓔ	21 Ⓐ Ⓑ Ⓒ Ⓓ Ⓔ
3 Ⓐ Ⓑ Ⓒ Ⓓ Ⓔ	10 Ⓐ Ⓑ Ⓒ Ⓓ Ⓔ	16 Ⓐ Ⓑ Ⓒ Ⓓ Ⓔ	22 Ⓐ Ⓑ Ⓒ Ⓓ Ⓔ
4 Ⓐ Ⓑ Ⓒ Ⓓ Ⓔ	11 Ⓐ Ⓑ Ⓒ Ⓓ Ⓔ	17 Ⓐ Ⓑ Ⓒ Ⓓ Ⓔ	23 Ⓐ Ⓑ Ⓒ Ⓓ Ⓔ
5 Ⓐ Ⓑ Ⓒ Ⓓ Ⓔ	12 Ⓐ Ⓑ Ⓒ Ⓓ Ⓔ	18 Ⓐ Ⓑ Ⓒ Ⓓ Ⓔ	24 Ⓐ Ⓑ Ⓒ Ⓓ Ⓔ
6 Ⓐ Ⓑ Ⓒ Ⓓ Ⓔ	13 Ⓐ Ⓑ Ⓒ Ⓓ Ⓔ	19 Ⓐ Ⓑ Ⓒ Ⓓ Ⓔ	25 Ⓐ Ⓑ Ⓒ Ⓓ Ⓔ
7 Ⓐ Ⓑ Ⓒ Ⓓ Ⓔ			

Practice Test 1

GRE Practice Test 1

SECTION I

Time—30 minutes
38 Questions

For each of the numbered questions in this section, choose the best answer according to the instructions, and blacken the correspondingly numbered blank space on the answer sheet.

Each of the sentences below has one or more blank spaces indicating where a word or words have been omitted. Each sentence is followed by five words or sets of words lettered from (a) to (e). Select the lettered word or set of words that, inserted to replace the blanks, BEST completes the meaning of the sentence as a whole.

1. His theories, though criticized by economists of more orthodox bent, have had enormous − − − on government fiscal policy.

   (a) restraint
   (b) impact
   (c) acceptance
   (d) tension
   (e) reliance

2. Unwilling to admit that his program of tax abatement had failed to achieve its goal, the mayor attempted to − − − the attention of the electorate from the problem by − − − the issue with irrelevant statistics.

   (a) capture . . . complicating
   (b) focus . . . confuting
   (c) divert . . . obfuscating
   (d) remove . . . buttressing
   (e) compelling . . . falsifying

3. To be a truly great writer, it is not enough to write from − − −; it is also necessary to write with − − −.

   (a) enterprise . . . money
   (b) reading . . . conflict
   (c) loneliness . . . style
   (d) materialism . . . facts
   (e) experience . . . inspiration

4. Although many people advocate personal sacrifice for the public good, their – – – often ends at the point where the call for their personal – – – begins.

   (a) temperance . . . resentment
   (b) altruism . . . involvement
   (c) intention . . . supplication
   (d) participation . . . invocation
   (e) contention . . . dispersal

5. Her credentials for the position were – – – in every respect but one: she could not speak a word of Turkish!

   (a) impeccable
   (b) essential
   (c) inconsequential
   (d) pedestrian
   (e) unacceptable

6. Even though he had planned carefully for almost every conceivable – – –, his ambitious project wound up a dismal failure when a(n) – – – power outage brought all the machinery to a complete standstill.

   (a) day . . . inevitable
   (b) facet . . . insufficient
   (c) succession . . . opportune
   (d) possibility . . . automatic
   (e) eventuality . . . unanticipated

7. His attitude toward social welfare legislation, based entirely on his perception of himself as a self-made man, – – – him the support of the voters in the state's economically depressed urban areas.

   (a) earned
   (b) cost
   (c) divested
   (d) evoked
   (e) replicated

In each of the questions below, a related pair of words or phrases in capital letters is followed by five pairs of words or phrases lettered from (a) to (e). Select that lettered pair that expresses a relationship that is MOST similar to that of the capitalized pair.

8. TRICKLE : TORRENT : : (a) decay : rot
   (b) contribution : bequest (c) zephyr : gale
   (d) imprint : emboss (e) gust : gusset

9. JUDGE : ADJUDICATE : :
   (a) researcher : emendate (b) mediator : reconcile
   (c) appellant : implore (d) administrator : regulations
   (e) lawyer : interrogate

10. FLOTILLA : PT BOATS : : (a) ligature : wound
    (b) sonar : submarine (c) salvo : broadside
    (d) empire : sovereign (e) squadron : cavalry

11. INTIMIDATE : WHEEDLE : : (a) revile : impugn
    (b) defile : rebuke (c) coordinate : disinter
    (d) impetuous : resolute (e) extol : disparage

12. PUSILLANIMOUS : CRAVEN : :
    (a) indefatigable : malingerer (b) cantankerous : humbug
    (c) obstreperous : peacemaker (d) deluded : paranoid
    (e) independent : parasite

13. EVASION : SUSPICION : : (a) inanity : humor
    (b) banter : passion (c) disdain : corruption
    (d) horror : sympathy (e) remorse : absolution

14. CONVULSION : SPASM : : (a) dispassion : emotion
    (b) fury : ire (c) imbroglio : rodomontade
    (d) amusement : laugh (e) triumph : rout

15. TRILOGY : NOVEL : : (a) fabric : weaving
    (b) rice : paddy (c) serial : episode
    (d) gun : cartridge (e) teeth : gums

16. INVENTORY : STOCK : : (a) repertory : operas
    (b) cracker : barrel (c) catalog : classification
    (d) symptoms : ailment (e) dossier : suspects

In the series of selections below, each passage is followed by questions based on its contents. Read the passage and choose the best answer for each question based on the contents of the passage. The questions must be answered on the basis of what is stated or implied in the reading passage.

In the collected body of writing we call literature, there may be distinguished two separate groupings, capable of blending, but also fitted for reciprocal repulsion. There is first the literature of knowledge, and secondly the literature of power. The function of the first is to teach; the function of the second is to move. The first is a rudder, the second an oar or sail. The first speaks to the mere discursive understanding; the second speaks ultimately to the higher understanding or reason, but always through the affections of pleasure and sympathy. Whenever we talk in ordinary language of seeking information or gaining knowledge, we understand the words as connected with absolute novelty. But it is the grandeur of all truth which can occupy a very high place in human interests, although it may not be absolutely novel even to the meanest of minds.

What do we learn from *Paradise Lost*? Nothing at all. What do we learn from a cookbook? Something new, something we did not know before, in every paragraph. But would we therefore put the wretched cookbook on a higher level of estimation than the divine poem? What we owe to Milton is not any knowledge, of which a million separate items are still but a million advancing steps on the same earthly level; what we owe is power, that is, exercise and expansion of your own latent capacity of sympathy with the infinite, where every pulse and each separate influx is a step upwards—a step ascending as upon Jacob's ladder from earth to mysterious altitudes above the earth. All the steps of knowledge, from first to last, carry us farther on the same plane, but could never raise us one foot above your ancient level on earth; whereas, the very first step of power is flight—an ascending into another element where earth is forgotten.

17. The main purpose of this passage is to

    (a) differentiate between the attainment of factual knowledge and the arrival at philosophical understanding
    (b) disparage intellectual activities and the attainment of learning
    (c) encourage mysticism as a desirable philosophical goal
    (d) inspire writers to produce more practical books
    (e) indicate the importance of even such mundane books as cookbooks

18. Which of the following statements can be inferred from the passage?

    (a) We stand to gain most from the reading of political treatises.
    (b) The first step on the moon was mankind's most important moment.
    (c) A recipe for bread is worth a thousand poems.
    (d) Great literature must address itself to fundamental philosophical truths rather than to material progress.
    (e) The function of poetry is to elevate the relationship between the practical arts and everyday life.

19. According to the passage, Milton's *Paradise Lost* could be characterized as

    (a) pedantic
    (b) literature of knowledge
    (c) a kind of philosophical cookbook
    (d) infinitely complex in structure
    (e) expressive of the grandeur of truth

Radiation occurs from three natural sources: radioactive material in the environment, such as in soil, rock, or building materials; cosmic rays; and substances in the human body, such as radioactive potassium in bone and radioactive carbon in tissues. These natural sources account for an exposure of about 100 millirems a year for the average American.

The largest single source of man-made radiation is medical x-rays, yet most scientists agree that hazards from this source are not as great as those from weapons-test fallout, since strontium-90 and carbon-14 become incorporated into the body, hence delivering radiation for an entire lifetime. The issue is, however, by no means uncontroversial; indeed, the last two decades have witnessed intensified examination and dispute about the effects of low-level radiation, beginning with the United Nations Scientific Committee on the Effects of Atomic Radiation, which reported in 1958: "Even the smallest amounts of radiation are liable to cause deleterious genetic and perhaps also somatic effects."

A survey conducted in Britain confirmed that an abnormally high percentage of patients suffering from arthritis of the spine who had been treated with x-rays contracted cancer. Another study revealed a high incidence of childhood cancer in cases where the mother had been given prenatal pelvic x-rays. These studies have pointed to the need to re-examine the assumption that exposure to low linear energy transfer presented only a minor risk.

Recently, examination of the death certificates of former employees of a West Coast plant which produces plutonium for nuclear weapons revealed markedly higher rates for cancers of the pancreas, lung, bone marrow and lymph systems than would have been expected in a normal population.

While the National Academy of Sciences committee attributes these differences to chemical or other environmental causes, rather than radiation, other scientists maintain that any radiation exposure, no matter how small, leads to an increase in cancer risk. It is believed by some that a dose of one rem, if sustained over many generations, would lead to an increase of one percent in the number of serious genetic defects at birth, a possible increase of 1,000 disorders per million births.

In the meantime, regulatory efforts have been disorganized, fragmented, and inconsistent, characterized by internecine strife and bureaucratic delays. A Senate report concluded that coordination of regulation among involved departments and agencies was not possible because of jurisdictional disputes and confusion. One Federal agency has been unsuccessful in its efforts to obtain sufficient funding and manpower for the enforcement of existing radiation laws, and the chairperson of a panel especially created to develop a coordinated Federal program has resigned.

20. According to the passage, scientists generally agree that

(a) man-made radiation accounts for 100 millirems per person
(b) the last two decades have witnessed intensified low-level radiation
(c) radioactive fallout constitutes a far greater threat than low-level radiation from medical x-rays.
(d) cosmic rays and other man-made radiation can be ignored
(e) linear energy transfer presents only a minor risk

21. The primary purpose of the passage is to

(a) explain the difference between natural and man-made radiation
(b) arouse concern about the risks connected with the use of producers of low-level radiation, such as medical x-rays
(c) criticize the United Nations Scientific Committee on the Effects of Atomic Radiation
(d) advocate limiting the use of atomic-weapons testing since the fallout is extremely hazardous
(e) publicize the results of a recent British medical survey

22. Which of the following items does the author present to support the quotation at the end of the second paragraph?

I. Strontium-90 and carbon-14 become incorporated into the body and deliver radiation for an entire lifetime.
II. An abnormally high percentage of patients with arthritis of the spine who were treated with x-rays subsequently contracted cancer.
III. There is a high incidence of cancer among children of mothers who had been given prenatal pelvic x-rays.

(a) I only
(b) II only
(c) I and II only
(d) II and III only
(e) I, II, and III

23. It can be inferred that the chairperson, mentioned in the last paragraph, who resigned from the panel to develop a coordinated federal program for radiation regulation probably did so because

(a) he disagreed with the findings of the Senate committee
(b) regulatory efforts have been balked by disputes, confusion, and bureaucratic delays
(c) his agency could not obtain funding or manpower for implementation of existing laws
(d) he supported the position of the National Academy of Sciences committee and opposed regulation of radiation exposure
(e) he was disorganized and inconsistent in operating his bureau

24. Of the following, the sources of radiation that are natural are

   (a) radioactive potassium in bone, strontium-90, uranium ore
   (b) carbon-14 in tissues, cosmic rays, x-rays
   (c) cosmic rays, radioactive potassium in bones, radioactive carbon in tissues
   (d) plutonium, radioactive material in rock, strontium-90
   (e) x-rays, carbon-14, plutonium

25. Which of the following are not supported by the passage?

   (a) The average American receives an exposure to radiation of 100 millirems a year.
   (b) Higher rates of cancer of the pancreas, lung, and bone marrow and lymph systems were found among employees in a West Coast plutonium producing plant.
   (c) Even a relatively small dose of radiation, sustained over a number of generations, could lead to an increased number of serious genetic defects.
   (d) The United Nations Scientific Committee on the Effects of Atomic Radiation seems to disagree with most scientists on the hazards involved in the use of low-level radiation.
   (e) The National Academy of Sciences committee does not feel that radiation in the West Coast plant caused the markedly higher rates for cancers of the pancreas, lung, bone marrow and lymph systems.

26. Some scientists believe that a dose of one rem, continued over a period of generations, would

   (a) raise the strontium-90 levels in the body, but otherwise have little effect
   (b) relieve the acute suffering of those afflicted with arthritis of the spine without side effects
   (c) have the effect of increasing by one percent the cases of genetic defects of a serious order
   (d) in the long run have little impact on the regulatory efforts of federal agencies
   (e) cause an additional 1,000 disorders per million cases of cancer of the bone marrow and lymph systems

27. It can be inferred from this passage that

   (a) the causes of particular types of cancers can be readily ascertained by identifying the source of radiation
   (b) the amount of low-level radiation in the nation has increased measurably since 1958

(c) controversial appointments have been made to several of the investigative panels of the Senate

(d) scientists, by and large, are unconcerned about environmental aspects of cancer causation

(e) the committees on radiation effects of the National Academy of Sciences and of the United Nations are in disagreement on the impact of low linear energy transfer

In each of the questions below, a capitalized word is followed by five words or phrases lettered (a) through (e). Select the word or phrase most nearly OPPOSITE in meaning to the capitalized word.

Since some of the questions require that you distinguish fine shades of meaning, consider all choices carefully before you select your answer.

28. PRODIGAL

(a) son
(b) portent
(c) hoarder
(d) prominence
(e) goad

29. ABORTIVE

(a) trivial
(b) fruitful
(c) lustful
(d) durable
(e) furtive

30. FACTITIOUSLY

(a) judiciously
(b) veritably
(c) identically
(d) pretentiously
(e) cautiously

31. DOMINION

(a) contribution
(b) loyalty
(c) anarchy
(d) submission
(e) empire

32. SUBLIME

(a) greasy
(b) poetic
(c) underscore
(d) acidic
(e) vulgar

33. VULPINE

(a) artless
(b) ingenious
(c) critical
(d) sophisticated
(e) obese

34. DILATORY

(a) wide-eyed
(b) peevish
(c) unflagging
(d) overt
(e) lazy

35. ELITE

(a) type
(b) hoi polloi
(c) elegance
(d) conceit
(e) rival

36. PRECOCIOUS

    (*a*) vain
    (*b*) cautious
    (*c*) antecedent
    (*d*) retarded
    (*e*) pretty

37. RADICAL

    (*a*) secondary
    (*b*) square
    (*c*) theorem
    (*d*) forcible
    (*e*) uncommon

38. DEROGATORY

    (*a*) inflammatory
    (*b*) depilatory
    (*c*) interrogative
    (*d*) commendatory
    (*e*) commemorative

STOP! Work only on this section until the time allowed is over.

SECTION II

Time—30 minutes
38 Questions

For each of the numbered questions in this section, choose the best answer according to the instructions, and blacken the correspondingly numbered blank space on the answer sheet.

Each of the sentences below has one or more blank spaces indicating where a word or words have been omitted. Each sentence is followed by five words or sets of words lettered from (*a*) to (*e*). Select the lettered word or set of words that, inserted to replace the blanks, BEST completes the meaning of the sentence as a whole.

1. They stood in the middle of the crowded thoroughfare, engrossed in one another, completely – – – of the throngs of people who swarmed around them.

   (*a*) aware
   (*b*) oblivious
   (*c*) contemptuous
   (*d*) terrified
   (*e*) concerned

2. War and peace are mutually – – – states of being, and a war to preserve peace is not a paradox; it is a – – –.

   (*a*) attractive . . . reversal
   (*b*) exclusive . . . repercussion
   (*c*) opposed . . . discontinuance
   (*d*) incompatible . . . contradiction
   (*e*) reconcilable . . . preemption

3. The reckless drive toward – – – of the totalitarian alliance of the Axis probably would have succeeded if their leaders had not overreached themselves by drawing the United States into the war as early as they did.

   (*a*) vindication
   (*b*) oblivion
   (*c*) conquest
   (*d*) self-realization
   (*e*) hegemony

4. For those who believe in the – – – theory of history, every – – – is *ipso facto* testimony to behind-the-scenes intrigue and plotting.

   (*a*) great man . . . defection
   (*b*) conspiracy . . . coincidence
   (*c*) deterministic . . . reversal
   (*d*) revolutionary . . . defeat
   (*e*) Marxist . . . confession

5. To describe Hilbert as a – – – would not be wide of the mark when you consider how wont he was to – – – with friend or foe, with or without provocation.

   (*a*) curmudgeon . . . quarrel
   (*b*) renegade . . . revile
   (*c*) controversialist . . . tergiversate
   (*d*) misanthrope . . . fraternize
   (*e*) xenophobe . . . clash

6. Although the injury appeared – – –, the examination by the ophthalmologist revealed that he would need immediate surgery to save his sight.

   (*a*) superficial
   (*b*) hereditary
   (*c*) self-inflicted
   (*d*) infected
   (*e*) intermittently

7. While it is true that the children have been placed in – – – groupings within each grade level, there are significant – – – in learning ability from child to child within each of those groupings.

   (*a*) chronological . . . losses
   (*b*) temporary . . . impairments
   (*c*) heterogeneous . . . changes
   (*d*) homogeneous . . . differences
   (*e*) small . . . growths

In each of the questions below, a related pair of words or phrases in capital letters is followed by five pairs of words or phrases lettered from (*a*) to (*e*). Select that lettered pair that expresses a relationship that is MOST similar to that of the capitalized pair.

8. EMBROIL : STRIFE : : (*a*) arbitrate : settlement
   (*b*) infiltrate : cull (*c*) indemnify : reduction
   (*d*) predicate : conclusion (*e*) counteract : performance

9. IMPASSE : CONCEDE : : (*a*) latitude : resistance
   (*b*) touchdown : penalty (*c*) agreement : dissent
   (*d*) revolution : outbreak (*e*) schism : diverge

10. PRIMEVAL : MEDIEVAL : : (*a*) gorilla : monk
(*b*) thorn : rose (*c*) show : ice
(*d*) evolution : revelation (*e*) dinosaur : dragon

11. METER : POETRY : : (*a*) symptoms : illness
(*b*) ideals : idealism (*c*) wolf : predator
(*d*) inflection : acting (*e*) water : sailing

12. MERCENARY : GENEROUS : :
(*a*) destroy : improvise (*b*) exclusive : circle
(*c*) clique : unrestricted (*d*) fiery : aquiver
(*e*) delinquent : untoward

13. ENFEEBLE : EXHAUST : : (*a*) strengthen : abuse
(*b*) enervate : deplete (*c*) invigorate : drain
(*d*) supply : supplant (*e*) discover : abandon

14. MOUNTEBANK : QUACKERY : :
(*a*) jackanape : mummery (*b*) raconteur : testimony
(*c*) huckster : thievery (*d*) embezzler : fraud
(*e*) politician : nonfeasance

15. PEDANT : ERUDITION : : (*a*) carpenter : cabinetry
(*b*) prude : modesty (*c*) ballerina : ballet
(*d*) diplomat : blunt (*e*) enemy : graciousness

16. CAPRICIOUS : RELIABILITY : :
(*a*) extemporaneous : predictability
(*b*) volatile : changeability (*c*) arbitrary : whimsicality
(*d*) tenacious : practicality (*e*) heated : steaming

In the series of selections below, each passage is followed by questions based on its contents. Read the passage and choose the best answer for each question based on the contents of the passage. The questions must be answered on the basis of what is stated or implied in the reading passage.

It has become apparent that the morality of individuals is far more consistent and far less conditional than the morality of groups. The individual may, through sensitivity or reasoning, judge a situation objectively, even when that situation impinges on self-interest.

The social group, binding together the natural human impulses of individuals, tends to diminish rational constraints, particularly in pursuit of its goals. Empathy with the needs of others, existent in the individual, disappears in the egoism of the group. The restraint of impulse is served by the cumulative ruthlessness of self-centered drives. Spontaneity becomes irresponsibility; confidence becomes arrogance: such is the potency and moral poverty of social groups.

The tension created by this dichotomy is inevitable. The rational individual attempts to resist the incursions of his self-consciousness, but is simultaneously drawn, by common cause or purpose, into the larger community. He must subjugate internal moral constraints to the group need for unquestioning support. Eventually he may identify so completely that he arrogates to himself the responsibility to purge others of their individualism.

17. According to the author of this passage, social groups

   (a) harness their impulses through rational constraints
   (b) are objective in their evaluation of situations that impinge on their self-interest
   (c) subjugate their spontaneity to the demands of individual conscience
   (d) demand unquestioning allegiance to the beliefs and goals of the group
   (e) give their support unstintingly to their members' efforts at self-realization, even when those efforts conflict with the views of the group

18. How can the author's point of view, as expressed in the passage, best be capsulized?

   (a) The power of the group is not only greater than that of the individual, but also more wisely used.
   (b) Social groups restrain their natural impulses for the greater good of all.
   (c) Group behavior tends to be far less responsive to moral considerations than individual behavior tends to be.
   (d) The fullest growth of individual expression comes through the liberating influence of the social group.
   (e) The social group is far more objective than the individual.

19. In the light of the views expressed in the passage, it could be inferred that the type of local government the author would prefer is

   (a) election of officials running on specific political platforms
   (b) appointment of local officials by trustees representing the boards of community and civic associations
   (c) a city-manager type of government
   (d) town meetings with secret ballot
   (e) election of officials by qualified taxpayers

   The reasons organisms age have been much discussed. Some have claimed that senescence is a mechanism for culling the aged from the population to prevent overcrowding. Others have believed aging to be the unavoidable outcome of tissue metabolism. Still others have felt the question of senescence to be largely irrelevant since few wild organisms ever reach the senile stage. Modern evolutionary theory has a rationale for senescence which has a firm theoretical base: natural selection of individuals.

One should be skeptical of the claim that organisms deteriorate with age as an inevitable outcome of living. Considering the complex morphogenetic changes many organisms undergo during development, it would seem that maintaining what has been formed should be relatively simple. A valid theory of senescence must explain why salmon usually deteriorate rapidly and die after spawning, at an age of two or three, while trees and tortoises may live for hundreds of years without degenerating.

Senescence, in and of itself, can never help the individual's Darwinian fitness. All else being equal, an organism's chances of perpetuating its genes are better if it is healthy rather than sick, alive rather than dead. If senescence is to be compatible with natural selection, there must be some concomitant benefit associated with it that outweighs its disadvantage. Since Darwinian fitness is measured by total reproduction, the advantage must be that senescence is inextricably tied up with reproductive effort.

Consider that all organisms have a finite probability of dying of natural causes within any given time period. This puts a premium on reproducing sooner rather than later. In other words, an organism's Darwinian fitness tends to be enhanced by not deferring reproduction till a later time, for that organism might be killed or injured in the interim. The degree of risk an organism is subject to determines how much pressure there is to reproduce soon.

An insect, for example, may have a ten percent chance of being killed each day; it is not surprising that insects have high reproductive rates, and high rates of senescence. Tortoises, on the other hand, have heavy shells which presumably provide efficient protection against predation and injury; because their mortality risk is low, they are able to rely on long lives and can defer reproduction until times are most favorable. Their senescence rates are low.

If an organism is able to have more offspring as it ages, it experiences an evolutionary pressure opposing that caused by mortality. In such cases, low senescence rates are favored to take advantage of the increased reproductive rate at future times. This theory would predict that female fish which produce more eggs as they grow older and larger would age at a much slower rate than male fish whose sperm production does not rise with size.

This line of reasoning suggests that when organisms have little or no chance of reproducing, they tend to die early as a result of physical degenerative changes called senescence. But how, then, does this hypothesis explain the continued survival of humans well past reproductive age? Why do human females live long lives after menopause has marked the end of their ability to bear further offspring? There are at least two explanations. One is that this situation is an evolutionary anomaly: primitive people rarely lived past fifty. But a more complete explanation is that postreproductive people can advance their reproductive fitness through parental and grandparental care of their descendants: by furnishing advice, food, protection, a place in society, among other things, they can greatly advance the future reproduction of their already existing descendants.

20. The author's purpose in this passage is to

    (a) demonstrate the validity of Darwin's theories on evolution and the origin of species

    (b) propose a rescarch study of senescence and its causes as related to reproduction

    (c) pose iconoclastic questions

    (d) compare the deterioration of the salmon with that of the tortoise

    (e) suggest an explanation for varying rates of senescence in different species

21. Which statement is neither supported nor contradicted by the passage?

    (a) A person with three children has greater Darwinian fitness, all else being equal, than a person with two children.

    (b) Female fish live longer, on the average, than male fish.

    (c) High reproductive rates and high rates of senescence are frequently linked in a species.

    (d) Species secure from predation and injury can be expected to enjoy high rates of senescence and low rates of reproduction.

    (e) Salmon, unlike tortoises and trees, tend to have high rates of senescence.

22. According to this passage, organisms deteriorate and die

    (a) simply because they are worn out from old age

    (b) as a result of the principle of Darwinian fitness

    (c) when they have fulfilled their primary function, providing for the survival of the species

    (d) in a random fashion, not governed by any consistent principle

    (e) after spawning, or as a result of predation and injury

23. In the light of the final statement in the third paragraph of the passage, which of the following would best satisfy the idea of Darwinian fitness?

    (a) Early betrothal

    (b) Prohibition of divorce

    (c) Encouragement of adoption

    (d) Celibacy, as practiced by the Shakers

    (e) Increased use of fertility drugs

24. Low rates of senescence are often linked with delayed or protracted reproductive capacity. Which of the following statements contradicts that observation?

(*a*) Reproductive capacity of humans ends before senescence sets in.
(*b*) Male fish whose sperm production does not rise with size age more quickly than female fish whose fertility increases with size and age.
(*c*) Salmon spawn at an early age and then die after spawning.
(*d*) Insects with high mortality rates have high reproductive rates.
(*e*) Tortoises have low rates of senescence.

25. Which of the following statements is neither expressed nor implied in the passage?

(*a*) It would appear to the author that organisms ought to be able to maintain themselves without deteriorating through age.
(*b*) Senescence makes no sense in terms of the theory of natural selection.
(*c*) It is more desirable for organisms, by and large, to reproduce at an early stage of life rather than a late one.
(*d*) The less danger there is of an organism's dying, the less pressure on it for early reproduction.
(*e*) One explanation of the survival of women well past childbearing age is that their doing so is an evolutionary aberration.

26. According to the passage, senescence must have some benefit that outweighs its disadvantage. Which of the following is an advantage of senescence?

(*a*) The drive for early reproduction in slow-aging organisms
(*b*) Low senescence rates that take advantage of increased future reproductive rate
(*c*) Reduced size of male fish
(*d*) Survival of salmon after birth
(*e*) The slow locomotion of the tortoise

27. The author believes the following about senescence:

I. It is an inevitable outcome of tissue metabolism.
II. Organisms that have little likelihood of reproducing tend to die early as a result of senescence.
III. Human survival past the active reproductive stage does not contradict the idea of senescence as inextricably tied up with reproductive effort.

(*a*) I only
(*b*) II only
(*c*) II and III only
(*d*) I and II only
(*e*) I, II, and III

In each of the questions below, a capitalized word is followed by five words or phrases lettered (a) through (e). Select the word or phrase most nearly OPPOSITE in meaning to the capitalized word.

Since some of the questions require that you distinguish fine shades of meaning, consider all choices carefully before you select your answer.

28. VENIAL

(a) judicial
(b) offensive
(c) heinous
(d) immortal
(e) salable

29. LACONIC

(a) voluble
(b) lazy
(c) snaky
(d) milky
(e) explicatory

30. VITIATED

(a) mixed
(b) vitrified
(c) negated
(d) transposed
(e) purified

31. CALUMNIATE

(a) fatten
(b) extol
(c) duplicate
(d) add
(e) collide

32. CHARY

(a) pessimistic
(b) trustful
(c) weary
(d) humanitarian
(e) celibate

33. ENDEMIC

(a) arrested
(b) prehistoric
(c) fluid
(d) ubiquitous
(e) epicene

34. OBLOQUY

(a) encomium
(b) reproach
(c) precision
(d) abstruseness
(e) obscurity

35. EMPYREAL

(a) dusky
(b) commanding
(c) terrestrial
(d) pure
(e) enchanted

36. SANCTION

(a) enjoin
(b) treaty
(c) purify
(d) hinder
(e) neglect

37. EMPIRICAL

(a) experimental
(b) theoretical
(c) psychological
(d) objectionable
(e) thoughtful

38. INTOLERANT

(a) permissive
(b) conducive
(c) participatory
(d) excessive
(e) condemnatory

STOP! Work only on this section until the time allowed is over.

SECTION III

Time—30 minutes
30 Questions

The following questions each consist of two quantities, one in Column A and one in Column B. Compare the two quantities and on the answer sheet blacken oval

(*a*) if the quantity in Column A is greater;
(*b*) if the quantity in Column B is greater;
(*c*) if the two quantities are equal;
(*d*) if the relationship cannot be determined from the information given.

All letters such as x, y and n represent real numbers. A symbol appearing in both columns represents the same quantity in Column A as it does in Column B.

In some questions, information concerning one or both of the quantities to be compared is centered above the two columns.

Figures are generally not drawn to scale, unless otherwise stated. You may assume these figures lie in the plane, unless it is indicated they represent solid figures.

Lines that appear to be straight may be assumed to be straight lines.

Column A		Column B
1. The average of $(60 + 3)$ and $(60 - 3)$		The average of 58, 59, 60, 61, 62
2. 3×97		$300 - 8$
3. $3y + 2$	$6y + 4 = 14$	$\dfrac{20}{3}$
4. The area of a square with a side of 3		The area of a triangle with a base of 3
5. $\dfrac{\sqrt{5}}{5}$		$\dfrac{1}{\sqrt{5}}$
6. $1 + \dfrac{x}{y}$	$x, y \neq 0$	$1 + \dfrac{y}{x}$
7. 6% of 80		10% of 50

	Column A	**Column B**

8.

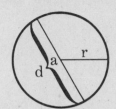

a = area of circle
d = diameter, r = radius

| $\dfrac{a}{d}$ | $\dfrac{a}{r}$ |

9.
$$p \times q = 0$$

| p | q |

10.
$$\frac{k}{3} = \frac{m}{5}$$

| 5k | 3m |

11. $2\sqrt{5}$ | 5

12.

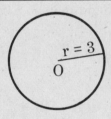

r = 3

| A (area of circle) | C (circumference) |

13.

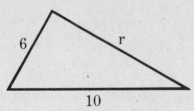   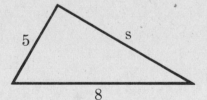

| The minimum possible value of r | The minimum possible value of s |

14. Percent increase in size of class that was raised from 30 to 36 students | Percent decrease in size of class that was reduced from 36 to 30

15.
$$u^2 = 9$$

| u | 3 |

Solve each of the following problems based on the information provided. Then indicate the best answer on your answer sheet.

16. 12 is what percent of 300?

   (a) 2
   (b) 4
   (c) 6
   (d) 8
   (e) 12

17. If 3/4 of a certain number is 2/3, what is 3/8 of the number?

   (a) 1/3
   (b) 2/3
   (c) 1/4
   (d) 5/8
   (e) 4/9

18. The altitude to the hypotenuse of a right triangle

   (a) is also a median
   (b) is also an angle bisector
   (c) divides the triangle into two equal areas
   (d) divides the triangle into two similar triangles
   (e) divides the triangle into two congruent triangles

19.

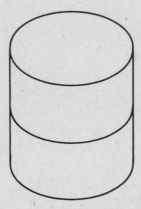

A vertical, cylindrical oil tank is one-half full. When 12 gallons of oil are added, the tank is 5/8 full. What is the capacity of the tank in gallons?

   (a) 74
   (b) 79
   (c) 84
   (d) 90
   (e) 96

20. A taxi service charges 50¢ for the first quarter mile of a ride and 20¢ for each additional quarter mile. What is the fare in cents for a trip of n miles, where n is greater than 1/4 mile?

(a) 40 + 20n
(b) 50 + 20 (n − 1)
(c) 50n + 20 (n − 1/4)
(d) 50 + 20 (4n − 1)
(e) 50 + 20 (n − 1/4)

Questions 21–24 refer to the following graphs.

Medical Care By Type of Service

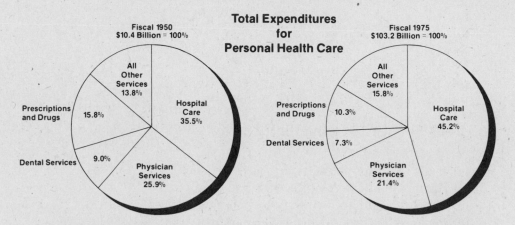

21. What was the increase or decrease in expenditures for dental services from 1950 to 1975?

(a) + $ 1.76 billion
(b) − $ 1.76 billion
(c) − $ 176 million
(d) + $ 6 billion
(e) + $ .66 billion

22. The consumer price index rose by about 280% from 1950 to 1975. What percent of the increase in hospital care expenses is attributable to inflation?

(a) 15%
(b) 25%
(c) 35%
(d) 45%
(e) 55%

23. What item increased least in dollar amount from 1950 to 1975?

(a) Hospital care
(b) Prescriptions and drugs

(c) Dental services
(d) Other services
(e) Physician services

24. By what factor did the expenditure for hospital care increase from 1950 to 1975?

(a) 5
(b) 13
(c) 18
(d) 26
(e) 30

25.   (Figure is not
                                                                    drawn to scale.)

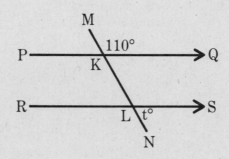

In the figure above, PQ ∥ RS. Then t =

(a) 60
(b) 70
(c) 75
(d) 80
(e) 110

26. $\dfrac{8}{0.2 \times 0.2} =$

(a) 200
(b) 20
(c) 2
(d) 1/20
(e) 1/200

27. If the volume of a cube is 125, then the total surface area of the cube is

(a) 100
(b) 125
(c) 150
(d) 175
(e) 200

28.

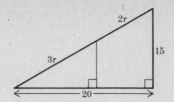

In the triangle above, r =

(a) 3
(b) 4
(c) 10
(d) 6
(e) 5

29. If p + q is 150% of q, then p is what percent of q?

(a) 10%
(b) 15%
(c) 25%
(d) 50%
(e) 75%

30. If $T = \dfrac{R}{1 - kx}$, x =

(a) $1 - \dfrac{R}{Tk}$

(b) $\dfrac{T - R}{Tk}$

(c) $\dfrac{T - R}{k}$

(d) $\dfrac{T}{k} - \dfrac{R}{Tk}$

(e) $T - \dfrac{R}{Tk}$

STOP! Work only on this section until the time allowed is over.

Time — 30 minutes
30 Questions

The following questions each consist of two quantities, one in Column A and one in Column B. Compare the two quantities and on the answer sheet blacken oval

   (*a*) if the quantity in Column A is greater;
   (*b*) if the quantity in Column B is greater;
   (*c*) if the two quantities are equal;
   (*d*) if the relationship cannot be determined from the information given.

All letters such as x, y and n represent real numbers. A symbol appearing in both columns represents the same quantity in Column A as it does in Column B.

In some questions, information concerning one or both of the quantities to be compared is centered above the two columns.

Figures are generally not drawn to scale, unless otherwise stated. You may assume these figures lie in the plane, unless it is indicated they represent solid figures.

Lines that appear to be straight may be assumed to be straight lines.

Column A	Column B

1.

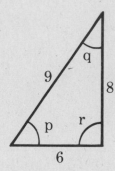

(Figure is not drawn to scale.)

$p + q$ r

---

2. $f > 0, g > 0, f > g$

$f - g$ $\dfrac{f^2 - g^2}{f - g}$

Column A	Column B

3.

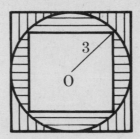

Area shaded vertically (‖‖‖‖)	Area shaded horizontally (≡)

Questions 4–8 refer to the figure below.

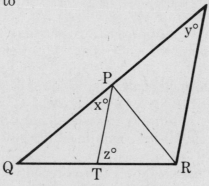

PT bisects angle QPR
PT is parallel to RS

4. x   y

5. z   x

6. PS   PR

7. PQ   PR

8. $\dfrac{PQ}{PS}$ $\dfrac{TQ}{TR}$

9. The number of tangents to a circle from a point outside the circle.   The number of common tangents to two circles.

10. $a = \dfrac{b}{b-2}$, $b \neq 2$

$\dfrac{b}{2}$ $\dfrac{a}{a-1}$

	Column A	Column B

Column A   **Column B**

11. $u > v$

u^2 v^2

12. The probability of getting 2 heads on 2 tosses of a coin   The probability of getting 5 heads on 5 tosses of a coin

13. Length of the hypotenuse of a right triangle with legs 5 and 10   Length of the side of a square of area of 130

14. $\dfrac{1}{3} + \dfrac{1}{9} + \dfrac{1}{27}$ $\dfrac{1}{2}$

15. $\sqrt{.09}$ The value of $\dfrac{\pi}{10}$ to the nearest tenth

Solve each of the following problems based on the information provided. Then indicate the best answer on your answer sheet.

Questions 16–19 refer to the following graph:

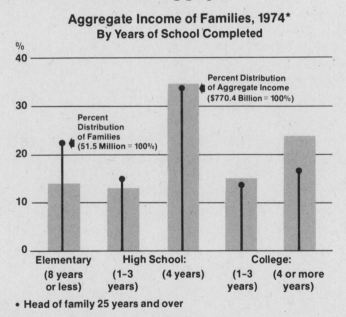

Aggregate Income of Families, 1974*
By Years of School Completed

16. What percent of family heads in the United States had completed high school in 1974?

    (*a*) 33%
    (*b*) 43%
    (*c*) 50%
    (*d*) 62%
    (*e*) 87%

17. How much money was earned by college graduates (4 or more years) in the United States in 1974?

    (a) $300 billion
    (b) $185 billion
    (c) $135 billion
    (d) $9 billion
    (e) $205 billion

18. How much did the average head of family who had not been to high school earn in 1974?

    (a) $9,100
    (b) $8,100
    (c) $10,100
    (d) $11,100
    (e) $7,100

19. What group earned the most total income in 1974?

    (a) High school: 1–3 years
    (b) High school: 4 years
    (c) College: 1–3 years
    (d) College: 4 years
    (e) Elementary

20. A bicycle wheel with a radius of 14 inches travels one mile (5,280 feet). Approximately how many revolutions does the wheel make?

    (a) 780
    (b) 740
    (c) 720
    (d) 560
    (e) 48

21. If a carton containing a dozen eggs is dropped, which one of the following cannot be the ratio of broken eggs to whole eggs?

    (a) 1:2
    (b) 1:3
    (c) 5:7
    (d) 1:4
    (e) 1:5

22.

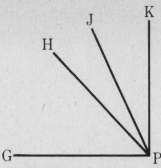

(Figure not drawn to scale.)

In the figure above ∠KPG = 90°, ∠KPH = 40° and ∠GPJ = 65°. How many degrees in ∠HPJ?

(a) 15
(b) 18
(c) 20
(d) 23
(e) 26

23. For any integer n, which of the following must be an odd integer?

I. 2n + 1
II. 2n + 4
III. 2n − 3

(a) I only
(b) II only
(c) III only
(d) I and II only
(e) I and III only

Questions 24–26 refer to the following table:

Year	1950	1955	1960	1965	1970	1975
Population in millions	152	166	181	196	205	213

24. What is the percent increase in population from 1950 to 1975?

(a) 30%
(b) 34%
(c) 37%
(d) 40%
(e) 44%

25. During which five-year period was there the lowest percent increase in population?

(a) 1950–55
(b) 1955–60
(c) 1960–65
(d) 1965–70
(e) 1970–75

26. If the population continues to grow uniformly at the same rate that it grew from 1970–75, what is the projected population in millions for 1980?

(a) 215
(b) 218
(c) 221
(d) 224
(e) 227

27. Anne buys a roast beef and trims away 10% of its weight as excess fat. If the beef loses 20% of its trimmed weight in roasting, what percent of the weight of the original beef remains after roasting?

(a) 48%
(b) 60%
(c) 67%
(d) 70%
(e) 72%

28. The altitude to the base of a triangle is 1¼. If the area of the triangle is 2, then the base =

(a) $1\frac{3}{5}$

(b) $2\frac{1}{4}$

(c) $2\frac{3}{4}$

(d) $3\frac{1}{5}$

(e) $5\frac{1}{8}$

29. In parallelogram PQRS, PQ = 3 and PS = 4. The length of diagonal QS =

(a) 3
(b) 4
(c) 5
(d) 6
(e) It cannot be determined from the information given

30. If p and q are positive integers, and $p^3q^4 = 5000$, then $pq =$

(a) 10
(b) 15
(c) 20
(d) 30
(e) It cannot be determined from the information given

STOP! Work only on this section until the time allowed is over.

SECTION V

Time—30 minutes
25 Questions

In this section a written passage or set of statements precedes each question or group of questions. Choose the best answer to each question. For some questions you may find it useful to draw a diagram, graph, or other problem-solving aid.

Questions 1–4 refer to the following:

(1) A ladder contains evenly spaced rungs.
(2) Rung A is directly above rung D.
(3) Rung C is directly above rung E.
(4) Rung F is four rungs below rung D.
(5) Rung C is two rungs above rung F.

1. Which of the following represents the relative order of the rungs from the lowest to the highest?

   (a) A C E F D
   (b) F E C D A
   (c) A D F C E
   (d) C E F A D
   (e) F E C A D

2. Rungs G and B are two rungs apart. Which statement could *not* be true about their location, if G and B are different from the previously named rungs?

   (a) B is two rungs below A.
   (b) G is one rung above A.
   (c) G is six rungs below A.
   (d) B is below G but above F.
   (e) All of the above are possibly true.

3. Rungs X and Y are added. They are one-and-one-half times as far apart as the original rungs. Which statement implies a situation in which either X or Y has the same location as a previously named rung?

   (a) X is midway between A and the rung above A.
   (b) Y is midway between A and the rung below A.
   (c) X is midway between E and the rung above E.
   (d) Y is midway between E and the rung below E.
   (e) Y is midway between C and the rung above C.

4. If statement (3) were omitted, which of the following statements would provide the equivalent information?

   (a) The ladder has only six rungs, and rung E is below rung D.
   (b) Rung E is below rung C.
   (c) Rung E is between rungs D and C.
   (d) Rung E is above rung F and below rung D.
   (e) The ladder has only six rungs, and rung E is below rung C.

Questions 5–6 refer to the following:

The great influence special interest groups have in Washington perverts the democratic process and should be controlled by laws which let the common man have more of a voice in government.

5. Which of the following points would strengthen the argument above?

   (a) Special interest groups are inevitable in a complex democracy.
   (b) Most people are represented by at least one special interest group.
   (c) Because of special interest groups, the agricultural policies of the United States are often wasteful and self-contradictory.
   (d) Most special interest groups responsibly and persuasively argue their points of view.
   (e) Because of special interest groups, the United States is a friend of countries which are enemies, such as Israel-Egypt and Greece-Turkey.

6. Which of the following points would most weaken the argument above?

   (a) Many good laws have been passed because of special interest groups.
   (b) Laws have been passed which would, if enforced, limit the influence of special interest groups to an acceptable level.
   (c) Some democracies are more influenced by special interest groups than in the United States.
   (d) Special interest groups are inevitable in a complex democracy.
   (e) Polls show that most people feel their opinion is irrelevant to the conduct of national policy.

Questions 7–10 refer to the following:

(1) Some children are putting on a play and are deciding who will be allowed to act in it.
(2) A card may be necessary for permission to act, but only if its possessor is less than five years old.
(3) A card may be obtained by trading a ball for it.
(4) A card may be traded for a doll.
(5) A doll may be traded for a ball.
(6) A ball may be necessary for permission to act, but only if its possessor has previously had a doll.

(7) Either a card, as described in (2), or a ball, as described in (6), is necessary for permission to act.

(8) Only one object is possessed by each child at a given time.

7. The above procedures fail to specify

(a) any means of obtaining a ball
(b) how possession of a ball might lead to permission to act without ever having had a doll
(c) whether anything other than a card or a ball, as described in (7), is necessary for permission to act
(d) alternative uses for a card
(e) alternative uses for a ball

8. Under the rules given, who might receive permission to act?

I. A possessor of a ball who has never received a doll.
II. A six-year-old possessor of a card.
III. A five-year-old possessor of a doll who never receives a card.

(a) I only
(b) I and II only
(c) I and III only
(d) II and III only
(e) I, II, and III

9. Which of the following *cannot* receive permission to act?

I. A four-year-old possessor of a ball who never trades.
II. A 6-year-old possessor of a card who never obtains a ball.
III. A 6-year-old possessor of a doll who never obtains a card.

(a) I only
(b) III only
(c) I and II only
(d) II and III only
(e) I, II, and III

10. From the rules given, it can be inferred that

(a) a four-year-old with a card will receive permission to act
(b) a five-year-old with a card will not be able to get permission to act
(c) for certain children, a card or a ball will be sufficient to receive permission to act
(d) for certain children, a card and a ball will be sufficient to receive permission to act
(e) a six-year-old cannot act without a ball

Questions 11–15 refer to the following:

Six students take a certain achievement test; their ages and scores are recorded.

P is older than U and scored lower than Q.
Q is younger than U and scored higher than R.
R is younger than P and scored higher than P.
S is older than T and scored lower than U.
T is older than P and scored higher than Q.
U is younger than R and scored lower than P.

11. Which student is the oldest?

    (a) P
    (b) Q
    (c) R
    (d) S
    (e) T

12. Which student scored the lowest?

    (a) Q
    (b) R
    (c) S
    (d) T
    (e) U

13. Which student, if any, is younger than P and also scored lower than P?

    (a) Q
    (b) S
    (c) U
    (d) T
    (e) none

14. Which student, if any, is older than R and also scored higher than R?

    (a) P
    (b) Q
    (c) S
    (d) T
    (e) none

15. Which of the facts presented is not needed to determine the relative rankings and ages of all the students mentioned?

    (a) P is older than U.
    (b) U is younger than R.
    (c) P scored lower than Q.
    (d) Q scored higher than R.
    (e) U scored lower than P.

Questions 16–22 refer to the following:

Two identical twins have a very unusual characteristic. One tells nothing but lies on Mondays, Wednesdays, and Fridays, and tells nothing but the truth all other days. The other tells nothing but lies on Tuesdays, Thursdays, and Saturdays, and tells nothing but the truth all other days. Sundays both children speak the truth.

16. Which of the following statements can be deduced from the information presented?

   I. If it is Sunday, the twins will both say so.
   II. If it is not Sunday, one twin will give the correct day and the other will lie about everything.
   III. On any given day, only one twin will give his correct name.

   (a) I only
   (b) I and II only
   (c) I and III only
   (d) II and III only
   (e) I, II, and III

17. If they are heard saying the following on the same day, which logical statement can be deduced?

   Twin A: "It is Thursday."
   "My name is Bill."
   Twin B: "It is Friday."
   "My name is John."

   I. If it is Friday, A's name is not Bill.
   II. It is Friday.
   III. The boys do not behave according to their description.

   (a) I only
   (b) II only
   (c) III only
   (d) I and II only
   (e) II and III only

18. If they are heard saying the following on the same day, which choice presents a correct statement?

   Twin A: "It is Sunday."
   Twin B: "Yesterday was Sunday."
   Twin A: "It is summer."

   (a) It is a summer Sunday.
   (b) It is a summer Monday.
   (c) It is Monday but not summer.
   (d) It is Sunday but not summer.
   (e) It is impossible to determine whether it is Sunday or Monday.

19. According to the information presented, which of the following conversations would be impossible?

   (a) Twin A: "Today you are a liar."
       Twin B: "Today I am a truthteller."
   (b) Twin A: "Today you are a liar."
       Twin B: "You are telling the truth."
   (c) Twin A: "Tomorrow I shall be a liar."
       Twin B: "That's correct."
   (d) Twin A: "Tomorrow you will be a liar."
       Twin B: "Today you are a truthteller."
   (e) Twin A: "Yesterday we were both truthtellers."
       Twin B: "You're lying."

20. Which of the choices for the previous question presents a conversation which could occur on exactly six days of the week?

   (a) Choice (a)
   (b) Choice (b)
   (c) Choice (c)
   (d) Choice (d)
   (e) Choice (e)

21. Twin A says to twin B, "If this were tomorrow, you might say, 'You are a liar.'"

   Which of the following can be concluded from the above statement?

   (a) Twin A's statement is a lie.
   (b) Twin B's statement is true.
   (c) There is at least one day of the week on which twin A could not have made the above statement.
   (d) The above statement by twin A could have been made any day of the week, regardless of whether he was a liar or truthteller.
   (e) If the above statement by twin A were a lie, then twin B would be a truthteller the day after the statement was made.

22. Assume that the twins followed a different set of rules, so that on a given day both told only the truth while the next day both only lied, alternating days of truthtelling and lying. Under these rules, which of the following conversations would be possible?

   (a) Twin A: "Today you are a liar."
       Twin B: "That's correct."
   (b) Twin A: "Today you are a liar."
       Twin B: "That's not so."
   (c) Twin A: "Tomorrow we will be liars."
       Twin B: "Yesterday we were truthtellers."
   (d) Twin A: "Tomorrow we will be liars."
       Twin B: "You're one year older than I am."
   (e) Twin A: "We always tell the truth."
       Twin B: "We sometimes tell the truth."

23. It is entirely possible, though unlikely, that there are dinosaurs surviving in the unexplored wilds of Africa. I say that a major expedition should be mounted to try to settle this question.

An unstated assumption of the above argument is that

(a) dinosaurs are alive somewhere on earth
(b) the importance of finding dinosaurs outweighs the unlikelihood of finding them
(c) if dinosaurs exist in Africa, a major expedition will find them
(d) other types of animals usually thought to be extinct are probably alive somewhere on earth
(e) dinosaurs do not exist anywhere outside of Africa

24. If only the good die young, then only not-good people die old.

Logically, the above statement is most similar to which of the following?

(a) If only intelligent people take this test, then no one who is not intelligent takes this test.
(b) If only insects have six legs, then only mammals have four legs.
(c) If only doctors can prescribe drugs, then pharmacists can not prescribe drugs.
(d) If only small things are beautiful, then only not-small things are ugly.
(e) If (a) implies (b), then not-(b) implies not-(a).

25. There was a mother whose child was suffering from a certain rare kidney disease such that the only way the child could be cured would be for the mother to donate one of her kidneys to the child. The mother refused, and her refusal was upheld by the courts. My opinion is that she was selfish and thus should not have been supported in her decision by the courts.

The argument above is most seriously weakened by the fact that

(a) selfish behavior is not in itself illegal
(b) the donation of a kidney involves a certain risk to the donor
(c) the donation of the kidney might not have saved the child's life anyway
(d) research into other methods of treatment was far advanced at the time the mother made her decision
(e) there is no way to definitely determine that the child's future was hopeless without the kidney donation

STOP! Work only on this section until the time allowed is over.

Time—30 minutes
25 Questions

A written passage or set of statements precedes each question or group of questions in this section. Choose the best answer to each question. For some questions you may find it useful to draw a diagram, graph, or other problem-solving aid.

Questions 1–4 refer to the following:

(1) Six people sat at a circular table in six equally spaced seats.
(2) There were two seats between Frances and Carl.
(3) There was one seat between Dora and Emmett.

1. Which of the following must have been true?

    I. Carl sat next to Emmett.
    II. Dora sat next to Frances.
    III. Alfred, another sitter, sat next to either Dora or Emmett, but not both.

    (a) I only
    (b) III only
    (c) I and II only
    (d) II and III only
    (e) I, II, and III

2. Which of the following must have been true?

    I. If Dora sat next to Carl, then Frances sat next to Betty, another sitter.
    II. If there were two seats between Dora and Betty, then Alfred sat next to Frances.
    III. If there were two seats between Alfred and Dora, then Carl sat next to Emmett.

    (a) I only
    (b) III only
    (c) I and II only
    (d) II and III only
    (e) I, II, and III

3. If a seventh person, George, joined the group with his own chair and sat directly between Carl and Emmett, then

    (a) there was one seat between George and Frances
    (b) Alfred was next to Dora
    (c) there were two seats between George and Dora
    (d) Alfred was next to Frances
    (e) Betty was next to Dora

4. Which of the following could not have been true?

    I. Dora was closer to Carl than Emmett was to Frances.
    II. Dora was farther from Frances than from Carl.
    III. Dora was farther from Carl than from Emmett.

(a) II only
(b) III only
(c) I and III only
(d) II and III only
(e) neither I, II, nor III

Questions 5–7 refer to the following:

In the effort to fire a Civil Service employee, his or her manager may have to spend up to $100,000 of tax money to do so. Since workers know it is so hard for them to be fired, they tend to loaf. This explains in large part why government is so inefficient.

5. It is clear that the author believes that

    I. it is possible to give workers too much job security
    II. more government workers should be fired
    III. most government workers are Civil Service employees

(a) I only
(b) II only
(c) III only
(d) I and II only
(e) I and III only

6. The argument would be most strengthened by pointing out that

(a) workers in private industry are more efficient than are government workers
(b) people are inherently lazy
(c) Civil Service jobs are awarded on merit, without regard to political influence
(d) most Civil Service workers are conscientious
(e) studies show that the easier the firing procedure, the more efficient the worker

7. The argument would be best rebutted by pointing out that

(a) most Civil Service managers do not care about the short-term cost of $100,000 and will fire employees anyway
(b) most Civil Service workers are highly efficient, motivated workers
(c) government is traditionally inefficient
(d) non-Civil Service government workers are more efficient than are Civil Service workers
(e) other countries have inefficient Civil Services and equally complex firing procedures for Civil Service employees

Questions 8–10 refer to the following:

The letters J, K, L, M, N, and P represent six consecutive odd integers, not necessarily in that order.

L is halfway between P and M.
N is four more than K and six less than M.

8. Which of the following statements must be true?

    I. J is between L and M.
    II. N is the average of K and M.
    III. The average of P and J is another member of the original set of six integers.

    (a) I only
    (b) II only
    (c) I and III only
    (d) I and II only
    (e) neither I, II, nor III

9. Which of the following integers may be halfway between K and J?

    (a) P
    (b) L
    (c) N
    (d) M
    (e) none of those mentioned

10. An odd integer not included in the original set of six integers is represented by the letter Q. Which of the following statements about Q could be true?

    (a) Q is five less than K.
    (b) Q is seven more than P.
    (c) Q is four less than P and two more than M.
    (d) Q is the average of the original six numbers.
    (e) Q is 10 more than L.

Questions 11–14 refer to the following:

Three identical boxes each contain two marbles. One contains two black marbles, one contains two white marbles, and one contains one black and one white marble. Once each box was correctly labeled, but now the labels have gotten mixed up so that none is correctly labeled. The labels are abbreviations, so that "B" stand for one black marble and "W" stands for one white marble.

11. If a white ball is drawn from the box labeled BW, then which of the following must be true?

    I. The box labeled BW contained two white marbles.
   II. The box labeled BB contains a black marble.
  III. The box labeled WW contains a white marble.

(a) I only
(b) II and III only
(c) I and II only
(d) I and III only
(e) I, II, and III

12. How many different possible arrangements of the sets of two balls in the three incorrectly labeled boxes exist?

(a) 1
(b) 2
(c) 3
(d) 4
(e) 6

13. If a white ball is drawn from the box labeled BB, then which of the following statements must be false?

    I. The box labeled WW must contain two black balls.
   II. Exactly two possible arrangements of balls in the other two boxes exist.
  III. The box labeled BW contains two balls of the same color.

(a) I only
(b) III only
(c) I and II only
(d) II and III only
(e) I, II, and III

14. Which of the following steps is sufficient by itself to determine the contents of all three boxes?

    I. Draw a ball from the box labeled BB.
   II. Draw a ball from the box labeled WW.
  III. Draw a ball from the box labeled BW.

(a) I only
(b) III only
(c) I or II only
(d) II or III only
(e) I, II, or III

Questions 15–17 refer to the following:

Four men named George, Henry, Isaac, and Jesse, are blindfolded. Each man's chin is then painted either yellow or blue. The men are instructed to raise their hands if, when the blindfolds are removed, they see at least one man with a blue chin. When the blindfolds are removed, Henry sees two men with blue chins and everyone with arms raised.

15. How many men does Jesse see with blue chins?

    (a) 1 only
    (b) 2 only
    (c) 3 only
    (d) 1 or 2 only
    (e) 1, 2, or 3

16. The group is instructed that anyone able to discern the color of his own chin without looking will win ten dollars. However, anyone who guesses wrong will lose twenty dollars. After a long pause, Henry announced that he knows the color of his chin.

It may be inferred that

    (a) Henry's chin is blue
    (b) Henry's chin is yellow
    (c) If Henry cheated, his chin is blue
    (d) since two of the three men Henry sees have blue chins, the chances are his chin is also blue
    (e) since two of the three men Henry sees have blue chins, the chances are his chin is yellow

17. From Henry's ability to answer the question, we can infer that

    (a) greed conquers all
    (b) a cheater can invalidate even the most carefully constructed tests
    (c) the question is impossible to answer with a high degree of certainty
    (d) if Henry's chin were yellow, someone else would be able to answer the question fairly rapidly
    (e) if Henry's chin were blue, someone else would be able to answer the question fairly rapidly

Questions 18–23 refer to the following:

(1) A team of three persons is to be formed so that one person from each of three towns is on the team.
(2) Players A–C are from town I, players D–F are from town II, and players H–J are from town III.
(3) D and H will not play without each other.
(4) A will not play with E.

(5) B and F may play together, but not with J.
(6) Neither C nor I will play with F.

18. To how many different teams may C belong?

   (a) 0
   (b) 1
   (c) 2
   (d) 3
   (e) 4

19. Which of the following statements may be inferred from the conditions given?

   (a) If J plays, then E must play.
   (b) If C plays, then E must play.
   (c) If B plays, then F does not play.
   (d) If E plays, then I must play.
   (e) If C plays, then H does not play.

20. Which of the following teams is (are) possible?

   I. A, D, H
  II. C, E, I
 III. B, F, J

   (a) I only
   (b) III only
   (c) I and II only
   (d) II and III only
   (e) I, II, and III

21. Which player may belong to the smallest number of different possible teams?

   (a) A
   (b) B
   (c) F
   (d) I
   (e) J

22. Which player may belong to the greatest number of different possible teams?

   (a) B
   (b) C
   (c) D
   (d) E
   (e) J

23. Which of the following new conditions would eliminate the greatest number of different possible teams?

(a) A and D refuse to play with each other.
(b) E refuses to play with I or J.
(c) J is injured and is unable to play at all.
(d) A refuses to play with F or E.
(e) C refuses to play with D, F, or J.

24. Since all dogs I have seen have tails, all dogs have tails.

The statement above is logically most similar to which of the following?

(a) Since all fires I have seen are very hot, all fires cause great destruction.
(b) Since all people I have met are friendly, no unfriendly people exist.
(c) Since food is necessary for survival, all people eat.
(d) Since all horses I have seen are fast, all horses run races.
(e) Since all books I have read are paperbacks, hardbound books are not fun to read.

25. The biggest problem in America is the lack of polite, law-abiding behavior. All you have to do is go to Manhattan and observe how many people are illegally driving through red lights to see how bad things are.

The argument above would be most persuasive if it were true that

(a) driving through red lights is impolite as well as illegal
(b) the behavior of Manhattan auto drivers is indicative of the general state of affairs in the nation
(c) America is in a pretty bad state
(d) people who run red lights are responsible for the general state of affairs in the nation
(e) traffic is worse in Manhattan because of the rudeness of many drivers

STOP! Work only on this section until the time allowed is over.

SECTION VII

Time—30 minutes
25 Questions

1. Which of the following is a product of 13 and an integer?

   (a) 131
   (b) 1314
   (c) 1323
   (d) 1326
   (e) 1303

2. $(4r^2s^3)^3 =$

   (a) $16r^6s^9$
   (b) $64r^6s^9$
   (c) $64r^5s^6$
   (d) $64r^5s^9$
   (e) $16r^6s^6$

3. Which of the following fractions is greater than 1/4 and less than 1/3?

   (a) 3/8
   (b) 1/5
   (c) 3/10
   (d) 4/7
   (e) 4/9

4. If $x = -1$, which of the following is the greatest?

   (a) $x^2 - 1$
   (b) $-1/x$
   (c) $1 + x$
   (d) $1/x$
   (e) $1 - x$

5. What is the volume of a cube with a surface area of $54t^2$?

   (a) $27t^3$
   (b) $9t^2$
   (c) $27t^2$
   (d) $9t^3$
   (e) $54t^3$

6. If a 19-cup mixture of powder and water contains one cup of powder, how many cups of powder must be added to get a mixture having powder and water in the ratio of 1:2?

(a) 6
(b) 8
(c) 17
(d) 19
(e) 24

Questions 7–10 refer to the following graphs.

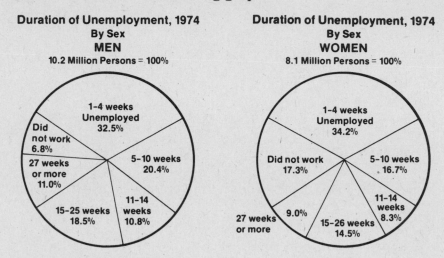

Duration of Unemployment, 1974
By Sex
MEN
10.2 Million Persons = 100%

Did not work 6.8%
1–4 weeks Unemployed 32.5%
5–10 weeks 20.4%
27 weeks or more 11.0%
15–25 weeks 18.5%
11–14 weeks 10.8%

Duration of Unemployment, 1974
By Sex
WOMEN
8.1 Million Persons = 100%

Did not work 17.3%
1–4 weeks Unemployed 34.2%
5–10 weeks 16.7%
27 weeks or more 9.0%
15–26 weeks 14.5%
11–14 weeks 8.3%

7. How many men were unemployed for 15 weeks or more in 1974?

(a) 3.0 million
(b) 4.0 million
(c) 2.7 million
(d) 3.7 million
(e) 3.2 million

8. What percent of the population that was unemployed at all was unemployed for 4 weeks or less?

(a) 62.3%
(b) 66.7%
(c) 72.1%
(d) 59.8%
(e) 33.3%

9. Which of the following groups had the largest number of unemployed persons?

(a) Men 1–4 weeks
(b) Women 1–4 weeks
(c) Men 5–14 weeks

(*d*) Women 5–26 weeks
(*e*) Men and women 15–26 weeks

10. Assuming the worst case (i.e., the maximum number of weeks unemployed), which of the following groups had the greatest number of man-weeks of unemployment?

(*a*) Men 1–4 weeks
(*b*) Men 5–10 weeks
(*c*) Men 11–14 weeks
(*d*) Men 15–26 weeks
(*e*) Women 5–10 weeks

11.

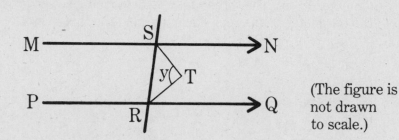

(The figure is not drawn to scale.)

In the figure above, MN is parallel to PQ, ST bisects angle NSR and RT bisects angle SRQ. How many degrees in angle y?

(*a*) 83
(*b*) 90
(*c*) 95
(*d*) 100
(*e*) the measure of the angle cannot be determined from the information given

12. What must be added to $(r^2 + s^2)$ to equal $(r + s)^2$?

(*a*) 0
(*b*) rs
(*c*) – rs
(*d*) – 2rs
(*e*) 2rs

13. Troop A is 11 miles south of a fire tower and troop B is 15 miles east of the tower. Troop A travels at a rate of 2 miles an hour and troop B travels at a rate of 3 miles an hour. If both travel toward the tower for one hour, how many miles apart will they then be?

(*a*) 13
(*b*) 14
(*c*) 15
(*d*) 16
(*e*) It cannot be determined from the information given.

14.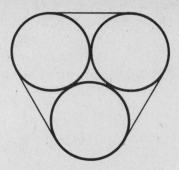

The above diagram represents three circular garbage cans, each of diameter 2 feet. The three cans are all touching as shown. Find, in feet, the perimeter of the rope encompassing the three cans.

(a) 8
(b) $6 + 2\pi$
(c) 6
(d) $8 + 2\pi$
(e) $6 + 4\pi$

15. If $\dfrac{2x + 6}{x^3 + 6x^2 + 5x} = 0$, then x =

(a) -3
(b) 3
(c) 0
(d) -5
(e) -1

16. If p = 2q and q = 3r, find the value of r in terms of p

(a) $\dfrac{3p}{2}$
(b) 3p
(c) 6p
(d) $\dfrac{2p}{3}$
(e) $\dfrac{p}{6}$

17. If a student has an average of 76% on his first two tests and has an average of 85% on the next four tests, what is his final average on all six tests?

(a) 82.0%
(b) 80.5%
(c) 82.5%
(d) 87.3%
(e) 81.6%

18. A 26-foot ladder is placed against a building so that it reaches a height of 24 feet from the ground. How many feet is the foot of the ladder from the building?

   (a) $5\sqrt{2}$
   (b) 5
   (c) 4
   (d) 10
   (e) $2\sqrt{313}$

19.

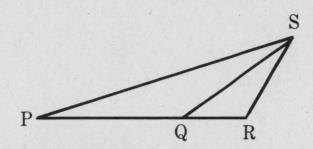

In the figure above, PQ = QS, QR = RS, and angle SRQ = 100°; how many degrees in angle QPS?

   (a) 10
   (b) 15
   (c) 20
   (d) 25
   (e) 30

20.

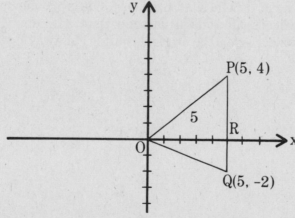

In the figure above, what is the area in square units of triangle OPQ?

   (a) 5
   (b) 8
   (c) 10
   (d) 13
   (e) 15

21. A car averages m miles on g gallons of gasoline. At the same rate, how many miles will the car travel on n gallons?

(a) $\dfrac{mn}{g}$

(b) $\dfrac{n}{mg}$

(c) $\dfrac{g}{mn}$

(d) $\dfrac{gn}{m}$

(e) $\dfrac{mg}{n}$

22. If $y = \dfrac{rs}{1 + x}$, then $x =$

(a) $\dfrac{rs}{y} - y$

(b) $\dfrac{rs - y}{r}$

(c) $\dfrac{y}{rs} - 1$

(d) $\dfrac{rs - 1}{y}$

(e) $\dfrac{rs}{y} - 1$

23. A piece of a square metal shaft p cm. on a side is ground down on a lathe into a cylindrical shaft p cm. in diameter, its length remaining the same. What fractional part of the original shaft is cut away?

(a) $\dfrac{4 - \pi}{\pi}$

(b) 1/2

(c) $\dfrac{\pi}{4}$

(d) $\dfrac{4 - \pi}{4}$

(e) $\dfrac{1 - \pi}{4}$

Questions 24–25 refer to the following circle graph.

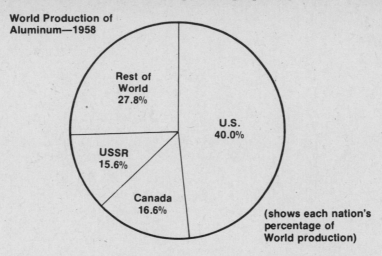

World Production of Aluminum—1958

Rest of World 27.8%

U.S. 40.0%

USSR 15.6%

Canada 16.6%

(shows each nation's percentage of World production)

24. How many degrees are there in the central angle of the sector of the circle representing the United States?

(a) 112
(b) 124
(c) 135
(d) 144
(e) 150

25. If Canada produced .581 million metric tons of aluminum in 1958, what was the world production of aluminum in millions of metric tons in that year?

(a) 2.5
(b) 2.8
(c) 3.0
(d) 3.2
(e) 3.5

STOP! Work only on this section until the time allowed is over.

Answer Key — Practice Test 1

SECTION I

1. *b*	9. *b*	17. *a*	25. *a*	33. *a*
2. *c*	10. *e*	18. *d*	26. *c*	34. *c*
3. *e*	11. *e*	19. *e*	27. *e*	35. *b*
4. *b*	12. *d*	20. *c*	28. *c*	36. *d*
5. *a*	13. *e*	21. *b*	29. *b*	37. *a*
6. *e*	14. *b*	22. *d*	30. *b*	38. *d*
7. *b*	15. *c*	23. *b*	31. *d*	
8. *c*	16. *a*	24. *c*	32. *e*	

SECTION II

1. *b*	9. *c*	17. *d*	25. *b*	33. *d*
2. *d*	10. *e*	18. *c*	26. *b*	34. *a*
3. *c*	11. *d*	19. *d*	27. *c*	35. *c*
4. *b*	12. *c*	20. *e*	28. *c*	36. *a*
5. *a*	13. *b*	21. *b*	29. *a*	37. *b*
6. *a*	14. *d*	22. *c*	30. *e*	38. *a*
7. *d*	15. *b*	23. *e*	31. *b*	
8. *a*	16. *a*	24. *a*	32. *b*	

SECTION III

1. *c*	7. *b*	13. *a*	19. *e*	25. *b*
2. *b*	8. *b*	14. *a*	20. *d*	26. *a*
3. *a*	9. *d*	15. *d*	21. *d*	27. *c*
4. *d*	10. *c*	16. *b*	22. *a*	28. *e*
5. *c*	11. *b*	17. *a*	23. *c*	29. *d*
6. *d*	12. *a*	18. *d*	24. *b*	30. *b*

SECTION IV

1. *a*	7. *d*	13. *b*	19. *b*	25. *e*
2. *b*	8. *c*	14. *b*	20. *c*	26. *c*
3. *b*	9. *d*	15. *c*	21. *d*	27. *e*
4. *c*	10. *c*	16. *d*	22. *a*	28. *d*
5. *a*	11. *d*	17. *b*	23. *e*	29. *e*
6. *c*	12. *a*	18. *a*	24. *d*	30. *a*

SECTION V

1. *b*	6. *b*	11. *d*	16. *b*	21. *e*
2. *a*	7. *c*	12. *c*	17. *a*	22. *d*
3. *e*	8. *e*	13. *c*	18. *c*	23. *b*
4. *e*	9. *c*	14. *d*	19. *b*	24. *d*
5. *c*	10. *e*	15. *c*	20. *a*	25. *a*

SECTION VI

1. *b*	6. *e*	11. *c*	16. *d*	21. *c*
2. *a*	7. *b*	12. *b*	17. *d*	22. *d*
3. *d*	8. *e*	13. *a*	18. *d*	23. *b*
4. *b*	9. *c*	14. *b*	19. *c*	24. *b*
5. *a*	10. *e*	15. *e*	20. *c*	25. *b*

SECTION VII

1. *d*	6. *b*	11. *b*	16. *e*	21. *a*
2. *b*	7. *d*	12. *e*	17. *a*	22. *e*
3. *c*	8. *e*	13. *c*	18. *d*	23. *d*
4. *e*	9. *a*	14. *b*	19. *c*	24. *d*
5. *a*	10. *d*	15. *a*	20. *e*	25. *e*

Explanatory Answers—Practice Test 1

SECTION I

1. (b) The theories could have placed restraints, but they could not have *had* restraint (incorrect usage). Choice (c), acceptance, would have taken the preposition "by."

2. (c) "Capture," "focus," or "remove" the attention from are all examples of incorrect usage. For "capture" the preposition would be "of"; for "focus" the preposition would be "on." The use of "remove" in this case is poor diction. Choice (e), "compelling," is entirely wrong on grammatical grounds.

3. (e) A truly great writer writes both with *inspiration* and from *experience*. This is not the only possible answer but is certainly the best of the choices given.

4. (b) "Although" suggests that people do not necessarily do what they advocate. Though they advocate personal sacrifice—*altruism*—it would seem that they mean this advice only for others; they draw the line where they themselves are asked for personal *involvement*.

5. (a) The sentence implies that she could do everything required except speak Turkish; otherwise her credentials were faultless, or *impeccable*.

6. (e) When people plan, they may plan to include "facets," but they do not plan "for" them; nor would a competent writer plan for every conceivable "day" or "succession." People plan for *eventualities*—contingencies or possible occurrences—and "possibilities." The second word of choice (d), however, "invocation," makes no sense in this context, while the second word of choice (e) does. An *unanticipated* power outage would be an *eventuality* that was not one of the "almost every conceivable" ones that he had planned for, and with the power down, his ambitious project would wind up a failure.

7. (b) A person who perceives himself as a self-made man would very likely take positions that hold that people can overcome societal difficulties. Voters in economically depressed areas would probably vote for someone who proposed governmental assistance for their plight, rather than for someone who held that he had "made it" and so could they. Hence, his position would *cost*, rather than "earn" him their votes.

8. (c) Just as a *trickle* is a much smaller flow of liquid than a *torrent*, so too a *zephyr* is a much milder wind than a *gale*. This is a degree of difference type of analogy.

9. (b) A *judge* is called upon to *adjudicate*—pass judgment on, or settle juridically; similarly, a *mediator* is called upon to *reconcile* the differences between disputants. In both instances the second word is a major function of the first word.

10. (e) A *flotilla* is a naval fighting unit consisting of such small vessels as *PT boats*. Analogously, a *squadron* is a fighting unit made up of *cavalry*. This is a whole and part type of analogy.

11. (e) To *intimidate* is to force someone into an action by inducing fear, while to *wheedle* is to persuade someone by coaxing or flattery. *Extol* and *disparage* are also a pair of opposites, the former meaning to praise highly, the latter to belittle or treat slightingly.

12. (d) A *pusillanimous* person can be characterized as being *craven*; both words mean cowardly. Similarly, a *deluded* person may be characterized as *paranoid*, since a paranoid person does often suffer from delusions.

13. (e) To respond to questions with *evasion* may evoke *suspicion*. Similarly, to exhibit *remorse* may result in *absolution*, or freedom from the consequences of a previous act. This is a cause and effect type of relationship.

14. (b) Both a *convulsion* and a *spasm* are similar in nature, but the former is generally the more violent involuntary muscular contraction. *Fury* and *ire*, too, are very similar, but the former means rage so great that it resembles insanity, while the latter means simply anger or wrath. This is a degree of difference relationship.

15. (c) A *trilogy* is a work consisting of three *novels*. Similarly, a *serial* is a work consisting of a number of installments or *episodes*. This is a whole and part relationship.

16. (a) The *inventory* of a firm is the merchandise or *stock* that it has on hand. The *repertory* of an opera company consists of the *operas* that the company is currently prepared to present.

17. (a) The passage points out several times that factual knowledge is on a lower level than power. The cookbook is factual; *Paradise Lost* represents the literature of power. It is the latter that carries you "into another element" where you are no longer earthbound. Check sentences five and seven in paragraph one, and sentence six and those following in paragraph two.

18. (d) Since the passage minimizes the importance of novelty and factual knowledge—new learning materials and new facts—you can assume that choices (a) and (c) are incorrect. Again, the passage disparages the ultimate value of seeking information, gaining knowledge, and as a corollary even such impressive new undertakings as walking on the moon, so you can assume that it does not consider choices (b) or (e), both quite practical matters, to be of importance. Sentence six in paragraph two, which speaks of expansion of one's latent capacity for sympathy with the infinite, implies the importance of philosophical truths vis-a-vis "a million advancing steps on the same earthly level."

19. (e) The grandeur of truth, referred to in the last sentence of the first paragraph, is obviously connected in the passage with Milton's "divine poem."

20. (c) First sentence, paragraph two, says "... most scientists agree that hazards from this source [man-made radiation through medical x-rays] are not as great as those from weapons-test fallout."

21. (b) The passage spends little time on the difference between man-made and natural radiation, so choice (a) is out. It makes no critical reference to the United Nations committee, so choice (c) is wrong. The passage never mentions limiting weapons testing, so choice (d) is wrong. Choice (e) is also wrong, since the British survey is mentioned only briefly, for another purpose. The passage does, however, point up that though most scientists agree that weapons-test fallout is more dangerous than radiation from medical x-rays, there is enough evidence and enough scientific concern to arouse a demand that something be done about the state of disarray of the regulatory agencies.

22. (d) Strontium-90 and carbon-14 are not mentioned in relation to being present in small amounts. The passage implies that the evidence concerning the possible effects of the small amounts of radiation used in the treatment of arthritis of the spine and for prenatal pelvic examinations supports the statement at the end of the second paragraph.

23. (b) Since the last paragraph starts by speaking of internal fights and bureaucratic delays, it would be logical to assume that the chairperson quit because of "disputes, confusion, and bureaucratic delays." There is no evidence that he agreed or disagreed with the Senate committee (choice (a)). The agency that could not procure manpower or funding for enforcement of existing laws was not the chairperson's panel, choice (c). Choices (d) and (e) are not related to the panel in question.

24. (c) Choice (a) is wrong: strontium-90 is associated with weapons-test fallout. Choice (b) is wrong: carbon-14 is associated with weapons-test fallout also. Choice (d) is wrong: plutonium is manufactured, as the passage points out, and strontium-90, as already pointed out, comes from man-made sources. Choice (e) is wrong as far as carbon-14 and plutonium is concerned. The correct answers found in choice (c) can be found in the opening sentence.

25. (a) The average American receives an exposure to radiation of 100 millirems a year from *natural sources alone*, according to the passage, but the passage does not say how much *total* radiation the average American receives per year.

26. (c) The answer is clearly indicated in the next-to-last paragraph.

27. (e) The committee of the United Nations (see paragraph two) says that even the smallest amounts of radiation can have serious genetic effects. The committee of the National Academy seems to play down the effect of low-level radiation in the two studies cited and attributes somatic and genetic changes to chemical and environmental causes rather than to radiation from man-made sources. None of the other choices are accurate.

28. (c) *Prodigal*—a wastrel or spendthrift; opposite—*hoarder*

29. (b) *Abortive*—unable to germinate; opposite—*fruitful*

30. (b) *Factitiously*—professed or pretended; opposite—*veritably* (truly)

31. (d) *Dominion*—control or domination; opposite—*submission*

32. (e) *Sublime*—elevated in thought; opposite—*vulgar*

33. (a) *Vulpine*—characteristic of a fox (foxy); opposite—*artless*

34. (c) *Dilatory*—inclined to procrastinate; opposite—*unflagging*

35. (b) *Elite*—the highest class; opposite—*hoi polloi* (the common people)

36. (d) *Precocious*—swift in development; opposite—*retarded*

37. (a) *Radical*—root or fundamental; opposite—*secondary*

38. (d) *Derogatory*—disparaging; opposite—*commendatory* (praising)

SECTION II

1. (b) The word "engrossed" indicates that they were so wrapped up in one another that they were unaware, or *oblivious*, of the rest of the world.

2. (d) The fact that a war to preserve peace is not a paradox indicates that it is not a *seeming* contradiction; it is, possibly, an *actual* con-

tradiction. This interpretation makes sense of the sentence using choice (d).

3. (c) Only two of the choices are at all suitable: (c) or (e). Choice (e), however, "hegemony," which speaks of leadership or predominant influence of one state over others, does not go far enough. The Axis powers were not satisfied to have influence over other states; they wanted the finality of conquest.

4. (b) The only choice that makes sense when both words are inserted is choice (b), *conspiracy . . . coincidence*. If every coincidence is seen as evidence of plotting and intrigue, then all such incidents "prove" that history is the record of gigantic conspiracies.

5. (a) A person who *quarrels* with others without provocation is, almost by definition, a *curmudgeon*.

6. (a) The word "although" indicates that what follows in the other part of the sentence will be contrary to what might be expected. The need for surgery to save his sight is opposed to the initial thought that the wound appeared *superficial*, that is, slight or merely external.

7. (d) The construction "While it is true. . ." implies that what follows after will be in spite of the initial statement. Thus, in the correct choice (d), although the children are grouped with others who are essentially like themselves (*homogenous* groupings), there are still *differences* among them within these groupings.

8. (a) To *embroil* someone is to involve him in *strife*. To *arbitrate* is to in-

volve the parties in *settlement* of strife. This is a cause and effect relationship.

9. (*c*) An *impasse* may end if one of the parties will *concede* a point or points to the other. An *agreement* may end if one of the parties to it begins to *dissent*.

10. (*e*) We associate the *primeval* period with the *dinosaur*, and the *medieval* period with the *dragon*.

11. (*d*) *Meter* is one of the techniques employed in the art of *poetry*, just as *inflection* is one of the techniques employed in the art of *acting*.

12. (*c*) A *mercenary* is one who can be characterized as grasping and avaricious rather than *generous*. Similarly, a *clique* can be characterized as exclusive rather than *unrestricted*.

13. (*b*) *Enfeeble* means to weaken, while *exhaust* means to use up. *Enervate* and *deplete* mean the same, respectively, as *enfeeble* and *exhaust*, and their relationship is, therefore, analogous. This is a degree of difference relationship.

14. (*d*) A *mountebank*, by definition, engages in *quackery*. Similarly, an *embezzler* engages in *fraud*.

15. (*b*) A person is called a *pedant* if he indulges in displays of excessive learning or *erudition*. Similarly, a person is called a *prude* if he displays excessive *modesty*.

16. (*a*) *Capricious* behavior is not characterized by *reliability*. *Extemporaneous* actions are not characterized by *predictability*.

17. (*d*) Sentence three in the last paragraph states that the individual must subjugate his internal moral constraints to the group need for unquestioning support, which is just a different way of saying that social groups demand unquestioning allegiance.

18. (*c*) Choice (*c*) is a rephrasing of the opening sentence, which is the topic sentence of the passage. This thought is repeated in paragraph two, which refers to the cumulative ruthlessness of self-centered drives (cumulative on the part of the members of the group), and again in the next-to-last sentence of the passage.

19. (*d*) The form of local government that would be most resistant to group pressures would be town meetings with open discussions and closed ballots. Individuals could best exercise personal judgment and follow their own morality. Under choice (*e*), the taxpayers would probably act as a social group, as would the official bound by political programs devised by special interest groups, as outlined in choice (*b*). Governments under these choices, similarly, would not be as responsive to individual morality. Choices (*a*) and (*c*) would be unlikely to mitigate the ruthlessness of the group. The only type of government the author might not object to would be town meetings with secret ballot, choice (*d*).

20. (*e*) Choice (*a*) is incorrect: the purpose is too broad. The author is not considering Darwin's theories as a whole, but only the question of senescence as it relates to Darwinian

theory. The author makes no proposal for a research study, so choice (*b*) is incorrect. Choice (*c*) is very vague, while choice (*d*) is too narrow: the author only mentions the salmon and the tortoise as examples of rates of senescence in his attempt to explain why rates of senescence vary among many species.

21. (*b*) The passage does not say that female fish live longer than males. It only mentions the specific case of the female living longer than the male under special circumstances. On the other hand, the passage does not say that female fish do *not* live longer than males.

22. (*c*) Choice (*a*) is wrong: In fact, the passage warns the reader to be skeptical of this belief. Choice (*b*) is a vague answer that cannot be applied to this question specifically. Neither (*d*) nor (*e*) is a viable answer. Choice (*c*) is suggested in the third paragraph and again in the last paragraph, first sentence.

23. (*e*) The statement in paragraph three indicates that Darwinian fitness is measured by total reproduction. Choice (*a*), early betrothal, does not necessarily indicate early or frequent reproduction. Choice (*b*), prohibition of divorce, similarly does not guarantee large total reproduction. Choice (*c*) does not answer to the question of increased or high reproduction. Choice (*d*), celibacy, is completely opposed to the notion of Darwinian fitness. Choice (*e*), the use of fertility drugs, would increase rate of reproduction and thus best satisfy the idea of Darwinian fitness as expressed in the passage.

24. (*a*) If humans fit into the pattern suggested, they would still be bearing young at the age of 60 or 70. Since, however, the human female usually is no longer capable of reproducing after middle age, you would expect senescence to increase rapidly thereafter to fit the statement in question.

25. (*b*) The statement in choice (*a*) is expressed in the second sentence of paragraph two. The first two sentences of paragraph four express the thought in choice (*c*). The statement in choice (*d*) is a paraphrase of the first sentence of paragraph six, and the statement in choice (*e*) is expressed in the fifth sentence of the last paragraph. The statement in choice (*b*), however, is the exact opposite of what is expressed throughout the third paragraph.

26. (*b*) Senescence, the passage says, is tied up with reproductive effort. The advantage of a high rate of senescence is a high and early birth effort and rate. The advantage of a low rate of senescence is the opportunity for deferring reproductive efforts to take advantage of favorable future conditions.

27. (*c*) Statement I is not believed by the author (see sentence one of paragraph two). Statement II is contained in the first sentence of the last paragraph. Statement III is explained in the last sentence of the passage. The author believes that the survival of humans past the active reproductive stage is connected with providing favorable conditions for reproduction of their already existing offspring.

28. (*c*) *Venial*—excusable or forgiveable; opposite—*heinous* (totally reprehensible)

29. (a) *Laconic*—expressing much in few words; opposite—*voluble*

30. (e) *Vitiated*—spoiled or corrupted; opposite—*purified*

31. (b) *Calumniate*—slander or make malicious statements about; opposite—*extol* (praise)

32. (b) *Chary*—wary, timid; opposite—*trustful*

33. (d) *Endemic*—indigenous, peculiar to a particular locality; opposite—*ubiquitous* (widespread)

34. (a) *Obloquy*—censure, bad repute; opposite—*encomium* (high praise)

35. (c) *Empyreal*—celestial, pertaining to the sky; opposite—*terrestrial*

36. (a) *Sanction*—approve; opposite—*enjoin* (prohibit or restrict)

37. (b) *Empirical*—derived from experience; opposite—*theoretical*

38. (a) *Intolerant*—bigoted; unwilling to accept differing opinions or ways of behaving; opposite—*permissive* (characteristically permitting or tolerating behavior that others might disapprove or forbid)

SECTION III

1. (c) Both averages equal 60 and are therefore equal.

2. (b) $3 \times 97 = 291$ and $300 - 8 = 292$. Hence the item in Column B is greater.

3. (a) $6y + 4 = 14$
Divide both sides by 2
$3y + 2 = 7$ and $20/3 = 6\frac{2}{3}$
Thus Column A is greater.

4. (d) The area of a triangle $= (1/2)bh$ (base $\times$ height)
Since we do not know the value of h, we cannot determine its area.

5. (c) Rationalize the denominator in Column B:
$$\frac{1}{\sqrt{5}} \times \frac{\sqrt{5}}{\sqrt{5}} = \frac{\sqrt{5}}{5}$$
The items in both columns are equal.

6. (d) We cannot compare the two quantities without knowing the values of x and y.

7. (b) 6% of 80 $= .06 (80) = 4.8$
10% of 50 $= .10 (50) = 5.0$
So the item in Column B is greater.

8. (b) Since $d = 2r$, the denominator of a/d is greater than that in a/r, and therefore $a/d < a/r$.

9. (d) If $pq = 0$, we know only that p or q or both are zero. Since we do not know whether either p or q is positive or negative, we cannot compare them.

10. (c) $\dfrac{k}{3} = \dfrac{m}{5}$
Cross-multiply:
$5k = 3m$

11. (b) $\sqrt{5}$ is slightly more than 2
$\sqrt{5} > 2$
Multiply both sides by $\sqrt{5}$
$\sqrt{5} \times \sqrt{5} > 2\sqrt{5}$
$5 > 2\sqrt{5}$

12. (a) $C = 2\pi r = 2\pi(3) = 6\pi$
$A = \pi r^2 = \pi(3)^2 = 9\pi$
Thus, $A > C$

13. (a) The sum of any two sides of a triangle is greater than the third
side.
In Column A, $r > 4$
In Column B, $s > 3$
So the minimum possible value of
r is greater than the minimum possible value of s.

14. (a) Increase in class size is
$36 - 30 = 6$
Percent increase = $6/30 = 1/5 =$
20%
Decrease in class size is $36 - 30 =$
6
Percent decrease = $6/36 = 1/6 =$
$16\frac{2}{3}\%$
So the item in Column A is greater.

15. (d) If $u^2 = 9$, then u may equal $+3$ or
-3. So we cannot compare the
two quantities in both columns.

16. (b) $\dfrac{12}{300} = \dfrac{4}{100} = 4\%$

17. (a) Let n = the number
then $(3/4)n = 2/3$
$n = 2/3 \times 4/3 = 8/9$
$3/8 \times 8/9 = 1/3$

18. (d) The altitude to the hypotenuse of a
right triangle divides the figure into two right triangles that are similar to the given triangle and are,
therefore, similar to each other.

19. (e) Let x = capacity of tank in gallons
$\dfrac{1}{2}x + 12 = \dfrac{5}{8}x$

Multiply both sides by 8.
$4x + 96 = 5x$
$x = 96$

20. (d) n miles = 4n quarter miles
After paying for the first quarter
mile, there are (4n − 1) quarter
miles to be paid for at the rate of
20¢ each. Thus, Fare = 50 +
20(4n − 1).

21. (d) In 1950, dental services were 9.0%
of 10.4 billion, or about \$.9 billion.
In 1975 they were 7.3% of \$103.2
billion, or about \$7.5 billion. The in-
crease is the difference, about \$6
billion.

22. (a) First, what was the increase in
hospital expenses? In 1950, they
were 35.5% of \$10.4 billion, or
about \$3.7 billion. In 1975 they
were 45.2% of \$103.2 billion, or
about \$46.6 billion. The total in-
crease was about \$43 billion. How-
ever, general prices rose by 280%,
so if hospital expenses did not rise
at all for other reasons, inflation
alone would have caused a price increase of \$3.7 billion times 280%,
to about \$10.4 billion, an increase
of about \$6.7 billion. The \$6.7
billion is about 15% of the total increase of \$43 billion.

23. (c) In these types of problems, where
there are two pie charts for two
years, and the later year has a
much higher total (as here, \$10.4
billion in 1950 and \$103 billion in
1975), in general, the smallest segments will have the smallest
growth in dollars, and the largest
segments will have the largest
growth, in spite of how the actual
percentages change. In other
words, because dental services
here is the smallest item, it is the
best place to start. 9% of \$10 billion
is \$.9 billion in 1950. 7.3% of \$103
billion is about \$7.5 billion in 1975,
for an increase of about \$6.6

billion. Prescriptions were 16% in 1950, or $1.6 billion, and 10% in 1975, or $10.4 billion, an increase of about $8.8 billion. Dental services had the smaller increase, and the other items are not worth checking. Note that prescriptions went from 16% in 1950 to 10% in 1975, a greater decrease in percentage than dental services, which went from 9% to 7%, but this did not matter.

24. (b) In 1975 hospital care was 45% of $103 billion, or about $46 billion. In 1950 it was 35.5% of $10.4 billion, or about $3.6 billion. This is about a 13-fold increase.

25. (b) $\angle KLS = \angle MKQ = 110°$ (corresponding angles) $\angle SLN$ is supplementary to $\angle KLS$, so that
$t = 180 - 110 = 70$

26. (a) $\dfrac{8}{.2 \times .2} = \dfrac{8}{.04} = \dfrac{800}{4} = 200$

27. (c) $e = \text{edge of cube} = \sqrt[3]{125} = 5$
then $S = 6e^2$ (six sides of cube)
$= 6(5)^2$
$= 150$

28. (e) Since the legs of the large right triangle are 15 and 20, the triangle is a 3—4—5 right triangle with all sides multiplied by 5.
Hence, the hypotenuse is 25.
Thus,
$3r + 2r = 25$
$5r = 25$
$r = 5$

29. (d) $p + q = 1.5q$
$p = .5q$
p is 50% of q

30. (b) $\dfrac{T}{1} = \dfrac{R}{1 - kx}$
Cross-multiply:
$R = T - Tkx$
$Tkx = T - R$
$x = \dfrac{T - R}{Tk}$

SECTION IV

1. (a) If the side opposite r were 10, the triangle would be a 6—8—10 or 3—4—5 right triangle, and $\angle r$ would equal 90°. Since the side opposite r is less than 10, r < 90° and thus p + q > 90°. So that p + q > r.

2. (b) $\dfrac{f^2 - g^2}{f - g} = \dfrac{(f + g)(f - g)}{(f - g)}$
$= f + g$
Since f and g are positive quantities,
$f + g > f - g$

3. (b) Vertical shaded area = Large Square − Circle
The large square has a side equal to the diameter of the circle; so its area = $6^2 = 36$.
The area of the circle = $\pi \times 3^2 = 9\pi \approx 28$
Vertical shaded area $\approx 36 - 28 = 8$
Horizontal shaded area = Circle − Small Square
The small square is equal in area to 1/2 the product of its diagonals = $1/2 \times 6 \times 6 = 18$
Horizontal shaded area $\approx 28 - 18 = 10$
Thus, the horizontal shaded area is the greater.

4. (c) x = y since corresponding angles of parallel lines are equal.

5. (a) z is an exterior angle of triangle PQT so that z > x.

6. (c) Since PT bisects ∠QPR, ∠TPR = x; x = y since they are corresponding angles of parallel lines; ∠TPR = ∠PRS since they are alternate interior angles of parallel lines. Thus, ∠PRS = x = y. So that triangle SPR is isosceles with PS = PR.

7. (d) No information is given to compare PQ and PR.

8. (c) Since PT is parallel to RS, PT divides QS and QR into proportional segments.

9. (d) The number of common tangents to two circles cannot be determined unless we know whether or not the circles intersect.

10. (c) If $a = \dfrac{b}{b-2}$, then $ab - 2a = b$,

$ab - b = 2a$, $b(a-1) = 2a$ and

$\dfrac{b}{2} = \dfrac{a}{a-1}$

11. (d) If u and v are positive, then $u^2 > v^2$. However, if $u = 2$ and $v = -3$, $u^2 < v^2$. Thus, not enough information is given to make comparison.

12. (a) It is much more likely that one may get 2 heads on 2 tosses of a coin than 5 heads on 5 tosses of a coin. To see this more clearly, think of getting 50 heads on 50 tosses of a coin, a very unlikely occurrence (low probability).

13. (b) Let hypotenuse = c
$c^2 = 5^2 + 10^2 = 125$
$c = \sqrt{125}$
s = side of square = $\sqrt{130}$
Thus, s > c

14. (b) $\dfrac{1}{3} + \dfrac{1}{9} + \dfrac{1}{27} = \dfrac{9}{27} + \dfrac{3}{27} + \dfrac{1}{27}$

$= \dfrac{13}{27}$

$\dfrac{1}{2} = \dfrac{13\frac{1}{2}}{27} > \dfrac{13}{27}$

15. (c) $\sqrt{.09} = .3$

$\dfrac{\pi}{10} = \dfrac{3.14}{10} = .314$

$= .3$ (to nearest tenth)

16. (d) This question has two tricky points. The first is to tell which part of the graph refers to education and which to income. The line with the bulb on top is the education graph, not the bar. Second, the answer is not simply the high-school/4-years bulb, but the sum of three bulbs: 4 years high school, about 33%; 1–3 years college, about 13%; and 4 or more years college, about 16%, or 62% in total.

17. (b) The bar graph shows about 24%; the overall income total is $770.4 billion; so college graduates earned a total of $185 billion. This time do not add up any graphs.

18. (a) Heads of families who never attended high school comprise about 23% of the total of 51.5 million, or 12 million. They earn about 15% of the total earnings of $770.4 billion, or $108 billion. Therefore their average earnings are $108 billion ÷ 12 million, or about $9,100.

19. (b) Notice that the question did not ask which group had the highest *per capita* income. This type of question is the most sophisticated because it is simpler than it appears. High school grads earned the most total income.

20. (c) $C = 2\pi r$
$= 2 (3.14)(14) = 88$ inches (approx.)

or $C = \dfrac{88}{12}$ feet

No. of revolutions $= 5280 \div \dfrac{88}{12}$

$= 60 \times 12$
$= 720$

21. (d) The number of broken eggs (or whole eggs) must be a whole number. The sum of 1 and 4 is 5 and, since 12 is not divisible by 5, we cannot find two whole numbers in the ratio 1:4 that add up to 12. It is possible to find two such numbers in the four other choices.

22. (a) Let y = no. of degrees in $\angle$HPJ
then $\angle$KPJ $= 40 - y$
$\angle$GPJ $+ \angle$KPJ $= 90$
$65 + (40 - y) = 90$
$40 - y = 25$
$y = 15$

23. (e) $2n + 1$ must be odd since $2n$ is even and 1 more than an even number is odd.
$2n + 4 = 2(n + 2)$ and is thus an even number
$2n - 3$ must be odd since $2n$ is even and 3 less than an even number is odd.
Thus I and III are odd integers.

24. (d) The population increased from 152 to 213, an increase of 61 million. Thus the percent increase $= 61/152 \times 100\% = .40 \times 100\% = 40\%$.

25. (e) The increase from 1970 to 1975 was 8 million.

Percent increase $= \dfrac{8}{205}$,

which is less than 4%.
From 1965 to 1970, the increase was 9 million.

Percent increase $= \dfrac{9}{196} > \dfrac{9}{200}$

or about 4½%.
The other percent increases are larger, so that (e) is the lowest percent increase.

26. (c) The percent increase from 1970 to 1975 was less than 4%. Based on 213 million population in 1975, less than 4% would be about 8 million. Thus the population in 1980 would be 213 + 8 or 221 million.

27. (e) Let n = the original weight of the roast beef. After 10% of n is trimmed away, 90% of n remains, or .9n pounds. If 20% of the trimmed weight is then lost, then 80% remains, or
$.8 (.9n) = .72n$
$= 72\% \, n$

28. (d) $A = \dfrac{1}{2}bh$

$2 = \dfrac{1}{2}b \dfrac{5}{4}$

$2 = \dfrac{5b}{8}$

$5b = 16$

$b = 3\dfrac{1}{5}$

29. (e)

To determine the length of QS, we would also have to know the value of angle P. Therefore, QS cannot be determined from the information given.

30. (a)
$$p^3q^4 = 5000$$
$$p^3q^3(q) = 5000$$
$$(pq)^3(q) = 5000$$

Therefore pq is a quantity which, when cubed, is a factor of 5000. By trial and error, the only solution which satisfies this requirement is
$$pq = 10$$
$$(pq)^3 = 1000; q = 5$$

SECTION V

1. (b) The directions are clear for these four easy questions. The first question may be answered by several similar methods. One involves using information from instruction 2, then from instruction 4, then from instruction 5, and then from instruction 3. The answer evolves as follows.

A____	A____	A____	A____
D____	D____	D____	D____
____	____	____	____
____	C____	C____	
____	____	E____	
F____	F____	F____	
Instruction (2)	(4)	(5)	(3)

The order of rungs, from lowest to highest, is thus F/E/C/D/A.

2. (a) If B is two rungs below A, G is either equivalent to rung A or to rung E. This would violate the question's directions, and thus B cannot be two rungs below A. G could be one rung above A if B is two rungs above G, so that choice (b) is incorrect. If G is six rungs below A, it is one rung below F. B could then be two rungs below G, making choice (c) incorrect. Choice (d) is clearly incorrect; one way to show this is to see that B may be above A, with G two rungs above B.

3. (e) If X is midway between C and the rung above C, then Y must coincide either with D or with E. Choices (a) and (b) are incorrect because the rung not mentioned in the choice could be above the mentioned rung. (c) is wrong because with X half a rung above E, Y could be at the *unnamed* rung between C and D. (d) is incorrect because X could be a rung below F.

4. (e) The diagram above shows the state of knowledge without statement 3: statements 1, 2, 4, and 5 give the locations of rungs A, D, C, and F but not of rung E. Choice (a) does not specify whether E is between D and C or between C and F, and is thus less precise than statement (3). When you note that the number of rungs on the ladder is not specified, you may quickly eliminate choice (b), because it does not prevent E from being below F. Choice (c) locates E in a different location from that implied by statement (3). Choice (d) locates E either between D and C or between C and F, and is thus less precise than statement (3). Choice (e), however, specifies that there are only six rungs and therefore effectively locates rung E between C and F, just as does statement (3). Therefore, (e) is the correct choice.

5. (c) The argument is that special interest groups have too much influence. Pointing out instances in which they have exerted such influence to the nation's detriment strengthens the argument. Choice (c), ascribing "wasteful and

self-contradictory" agricultural policies to the actions of special interest groups, strengthens the argument in this manner. (*a*) and (*b*) are irrelevant to the question of the amount of influence special interest groups have. (*d*) weakens the argument. (*e*) points out examples of policies influenced by special interest groups, but unlike (*c*) does not claim or imply that the policies are detrimental to the country. (*c*) is therefore the best choice.

6. (*b*) The argument claims that because of the great influence of special interest groups, new laws should be passed. Choice (*b*), pointing out that such laws already exist, completely demolishes this argument (assuming the statement in (*b*) is true). (*a*) is not nearly as good a choice, for the argument was not that special interest groups have never been beneficial, only that they pervert the democratic process; pointing out that they can be good does not weaken the argument much. The other choices are irrelevant both to the issues of influence of special interest groups and to the need for new laws.

7. (*c*) The instructions can be written diagrammatically as follows:

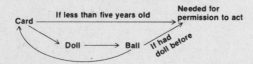

The procedures only state that a card or a ball is necessary for permission to act. They do not state that nothing else is also necessary for permission to act. In other words, a ball or a card is necessary, but not necessarily suffi-

cient, for permission to act. A glance at the diagram shows that the other choices are incorrect. This question is moderately easy.

8. (*e*) Statement I is correct because a possessor of a ball who has never received a doll can trade the ball for a card. If he is less than five, he might then receive permission to act; if not, he can trade the card for a doll and the doll for a ball, and then might receive permission to act. A six-year-old possessor of a card (Statement II) might receive permission to act by trading the card for a doll and the doll for a ball. A five-year-old possessor of a doll might qualify to act simply by trading the doll for a ball; he has no need to ever get a card. Statement III is therefore correct.

9. (*c*) The conditions stipulate that a card is necessary for a child under five to act, so that a 4-year-old possessor of a ball who never trades cannot act. Similarly, those over 6 years of age need a ball to act, so that the child described in statement II also cannot act. A six-year-old who possesses a doll has the potential to possess a ball, and thus might be able to act. Choice (*c*) is therefore correct.

10. (*e*) Statement (7) says that either a card or a ball is needed to act, implying that anyone five years old or older needs a ball to get permission to act. This reasoning shows choice (*e*) to be correct. Choices (*a*)–(*d*) are false because the data do not state definitely who *will* act; the statements state conditions *necessary* for acting but they do not mention whether these

conditions are always *sufficient* to permit a child to act.

11. (*d*) From the information given, we can order the students for each characteristic from low to high as follows:

Age: Q<U<R<P<T<S
Score: S<U<P<R<Q<T

From the age sequence above, we can seen that S is the oldest.

12. (*c*) From the score sequence above, we see that S was the lowest scorer.

13. (*c*) From the age sequence above, we can see that Q, U, and R are younger than P; from the score sequence, that S and U scored lower than P. Thus, U is younger than P and also scored lower than P.

14. (*d*) From the age sequence above, we can see that P, T, and S are older than R; from the score sequence, that Q and T scored higher than R. Thus T is older than R and also scored higher than R.

15. (*c*) We are told in the third ranking statement that P scored lower than R, and in the second statement that R scored lower than Q. Together, these facts imply that P scored lower than Q, making this statement unnecessary to rank the students' scores. All of the other statements are necessary to arrive at the complete rankings.

16. (*b*) The directions are straightforward. If your head is clear, these questions should be moderately easy. Statement I is correct; both children tell the truth on Sundays.

Statement II is correct: on all other days than Sundays, one child lies and the other tells nothing but the truth, so that the truthteller will give the correct day and the liar will lie about everything. Statement III is incorrect, because it refers to Sundays as well as to other days; it would be correct if it referred to days other than Sundays. Both twins give their correct names on Sundays, though, so that the statement is false.

17. (*a*) Since at least one of the boys tells the truth each day, either twin A or twin B is telling the truth. Either it is Thursday and A's name is Bill or it is Friday and B's name is John. If it is Friday, then A is a liar and his name is not Bill. Statement I expresses this deduction, and is therefore correct. Statement II is incorrect because A may be the truthteller, making the day Thursday. Statement III is incorrect; the descriptions of the boys are consistent with the quoted statements in this question.

18. (*c*) If the day is Sunday, both boys would tell the truth and agree that it is Sunday. Since they disagree, it is not Sunday and twin A is therefore lying. Since at least one tells the truth each day, twin B is telling the truth when he states that yesterday was Sunday. Since A is lying, it is not summer. The day is therefore a Monday but not a summer Monday.

19. (*b*) The conversation represented in choice (*b*) is not possible, according to the rules given. The day cannot be Sunday, for then twin B

could not be a liar. Every other day, one twin is a liar and the other a truthteller. If A were telling the truth in saying that B is a liar, B would not be able to make the true statement that A was telling the truth. Conversely, if A were lying in saying that B is a liar, B would not be able to tell the lie that A was making a true statement, for B would be a truthteller and would have to correctly call A a liar.

Choice (a) presents a conversation which could occur any day except Sunday (see question 20). The conversations in (c) and (d) are possible on Sunday. The conversation in (e) is possible four days a week (see question 20).

20. (a) The conversation in choice (a) could not occur on Sunday, for then twin A could not call twin B a liar. It could occur on any of the other six days, however. On days when A is lying, he could dishonestly say that B is a liar; B could then respond truthfully that B is a truthteller that day. On the days when A is a truthteller, he could honestly call B a liar, and B could falsely reply that B was a truthteller that day.

Choice (b) is impossible, as shown above. Choices (c) and (d) could occur on Sunday (but on no other day), making them incorrect. Choice (e) could not occur on Sunday. It could occur on Monday if twin A is telling the truth and B is lying. It could occur on the three other days when A was lying and B was telling the truth. It could not, however, occur on the days when A was telling the truth and B was lying, except for Mon-

day. For this reason, choice (e) is incorrect.

21. (e) This is a difficult problem. Let us examine under what conditions twin A could have made the statement that the following day twin B could call him a liar. On Sunday through Friday, twin A could be telling the truth, to be followed the next day by twin B correctly calling him a liar that day. On Saturday, twin A could be lying, for on Sunday twin B could not call twin A a liar. On the other weekdays, twin A could not be a liar and make that statement, for the following day twin A would be a truthteller and twin B a liar, and twin B could, in fact, say falsely that twin A was a liar. All these facts may be summarized as follows:

Mon–Fri: A = truthteller, B = liar. Next day: A = liar, B = truthteller.

Sun: A, B = truthtellers. Next day: A = liar, B = truthteller.

Sat: A = liar, B = truthteller. Next day: A, B = truthtellers.

The only choice that fits this scheme is (e).

22. (d) If both twins either tell the truth or lie on any given day, they can never disagree in conversation and thus cannot make contradictory statements. The conversation in choice (b) is contradictory. The conversation in choice (a) is impossible because it shows twin A calling twin B a liar while twin B is calling twin A a truthteller;

under the terms of this question, they have to agree. Choice (c) presents a contradiction in that it shows the twins disagreeing about the following day and the previous day; since they alternate days, there should be no such disagreement. Choice (d) is possible if both are lying; twin B's statement is a lie, since A and B are *twins*. Choice (e) is impossible, since twin A's statement is false, while twin B's statement is true.

23. (b) The speaker first raises the possibility of dinosaurs existing somewhere on earth, then asserts that a major expedition should be mounted to answer the question. In a world of infinite resources, it would be sensible to directly test the truth of all possible statements, but the resources of the world are limited. Choice (b) states an unstated assumption of the speaker, that it is worth the effort to try to find the dinosaurs even if success is unlikely. The other choices do not represent assumptions of the speaker; he does not assume that dinosaurs do exist, that they could not exist outside of Africa, that they would necessarily be found if they do exist, or that other species thought extinct are in fact alive.

24. (d) In the first statement, the phrase "good die young" is changed to "not-good die old." The subject, "the good," is negated to "the not-good," and the adjective, "young," is changed to its opposite, "old." Choice (d) has the same characteristics. The subject, "small things," is changed to "not-small things," and the adjective, "beautiful," is

changed to its opposite, "ugly." The other choices do not share these characteristics. Note that the first statement and choice (d) are false statements. If only good people die young, it still may be that good people die old; if the only beautiful things are small, it still may be that some small things are ugly. Choices (a), (c), and (e) can be eliminated because they are true statements.

25. (a) The thrust of the argument is that, because the mother was selfish, the judicial system should have forced her to perform an unselfish act instead. The fact that there is no law against selfish behavior cuts to the heart of the author's argument, and is thus the best answer. The other statements are relevant to the situation, but they do not speak directly to the author's logical train of thought.

SECTION VI

1. (b) From the three statements, four possible arrangements involving Frances (F), Carl (C), Dora (D), and Emmett (E) can be drawn.

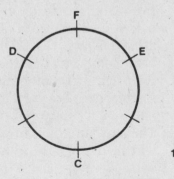

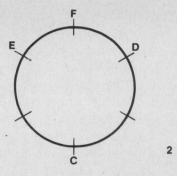

2

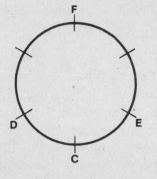

3

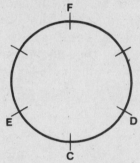

4

Situations 1 and 2 show that Carl need not have sat next to Emmett, so that statement I is wrong. Situations 3 and 4 show that Dora need not have sat next to Frances, so that statement II is incorrect. A glance at all four situations shows that Alfred must have been next to either Dora or Emmett, but not both, so that statement III is correct.

2. (*a*) The only situations in which Dora was next to Carl are 3 and 4; in both of these, Betty must have been next to Frances. Statement I is therefore correct. Situations 1

and 2 show statements II and III to be false. In them, there could be two seats between Dora and Betty without Alfred being next to Frances, contrary to statement II. Also in them, there could be two seats between Alfred and Dora without Carl being next to Emmett, contrary to statement III.

3. (*d*) George could sit between Carl and Emmett only if situation 3 or 4 existed. In either one, Alfred must have been next to Frances. The other choices are incorrect.

4. (*b*) The four possible situations show Dora either closer to Carl than to Emmett or the same distance from both, making statement III false. Examination of the diagrams shows that statements I and II may both be true.

5. (*a*) Statement I is obviously correct. The argument is that Civil Service workers are too secure in their jobs. Statement II does not follow from that argument, which is that firing procedures should be simpler, so that the fear of being fired would lead the workers to be more efficient. This is distinct from the argument that more workers actually should be fired. Statement III, that most government workers are Civil Service workers, does not necessarily follow from the argument. Simply because the author believes that Civil Service is responsible for a large part of governmental inefficiency, he need believe nothing about the relative number of Civil Service workers. An analogy is that an inefficient President could make all of government much more inefficient, and a poorly performing

spark plug could be responsible for an entire car's poor performance.

6. (e) The best answer is that the relationship between ease of firing and work efficiency have been shown to be directly related, as the author claims without proof for Civil Service. (a), (b), and (c) do not speak to the author's argument; (a) in particular is deficient because it does not even refer to Civil Service workers. To the extent that it is relevant, (d) tends to weaken the author's argument.

7. (b) If most Civil Service workers are highly efficient, motivated workers, the central argument concerning firing procedures is irrelevant. (a) is a much weaker rebuttal because $100,000 is still wasted every time an employee is fired. (c) and (e) are irrelevant and (d) strengthens the argument.

8. (e) Since consecutive odd numbers differ by 2, and M is 10 more than K, we can infer that K is the smallest of the six consecutive odd numbers and M is the largest. We may begin to diagram the numbers as follows:

K —— N —— —— M

Since L is halfway between P and M, we may add to the diagram in either of two ways:

K P N L —— M

or

K —— N P L M

Since J is the only number left, the finished series may be either:

K P N L J M .

or

K J N P L M

We thus see that J may or may not be between L and M (I). N is obviously *not* the average of K and M, or it would be halfway between them (II). The average of P and J may or may not be a member of the set; either it would be between N and L, which is impossible, or it would be N itself. Therefore, neither I, II, nor III *must* be true.

9. (c) We can see from the two possible sequences above that N may be halfway between K and J.

10. (e) Q cannot be 5 less than K, since K − 5 would be an even number (a). Likewise, choice (b) cannot be true. From either of the possible positions of P and N, we see that Q cannot be both 4 less than P and 8 more than N (c). The average of the 6 numbers is an even number and cannot equal Q (d). Q can be 10 more than L, since L + 10 is an odd number (e).

11. (c) The key to solving these problems is to remember that the boxes are mislabeled. The labels have not merely been scrambled, but are on incorrect boxes. One important deduction that can be made from this observation is that the box labeled BW contains either two white or two black marbles. Its contents can be determined by one drawing. It contains two of whatever color marble is drawn. The other boxes do not share this quality. Statement I is correct, as mentioned above. The contents of the other boxes may then be easily determined.

Label	BB	BW	WW
Contents	?	2 white	?

Consider the box labeled BB: Since it is mislabeled, it cannot contain two black marbles; since the box labeled BW contains two white marbles, the only possibility is that the BB box contains one white and one black marble. By elimination, the box labeled WW must contain two black marbles.

Statements I and II are true; statement III is false.

12. (b) The following table may be set up to demonstrate that there are only two possible arrangements of balls in boxes agreeing with the condition that each box is mislabeled. The solution may be arrived at more simply, however, by extending the reasoning of the previous explanation. There we say that if the box labeled BW contains two white marbles, the contents of the other boxes are known. Similarly it may be reasoned that if the box labeled BW contains two black marbles, the contents of the other boxes are also known. Since the box labeled BW can only contain either two white or two black marbles, there are only two possible arrangements of marbles in the boxes.

Label

Possible	BB	BW	WW
Contents			
I	BB	BW	WW
II	BB	WW	BW
III	BW	WW	BB
IV	BW	BB	WW
V	WW	BB	BW
VI	WW	BW	BB

It is clear that only possibilities III and V meet the stipulation.

13. (a) Since the boxes are mislabeled, the fact that a white ball is drawn from the box labeled BB adds nothing to the conditions already given. The question can thus be answered by referring to the table in the previous explanatory answer, remembering that only arrangements III and V are possible. Statement I is seen to be false; the box labeled WW may contain either two black balls or one ball of each color. Statements II and III are seen to be correct. Statement I is the only false statement, making choice (a) correct.

14. (b) A glance at the two possible arrangements in the table shows that if even one ball in the box labeled BW is known, then the contents of all boxes are determined. Drawing a ball from either the BB box or the WW box may not settle the issue, for in either possible arrangement, it is possible to draw a white ball from the box labeled BB or a black ball from the box labeled WW. Only statement III presents a way of determining the contents of all the boxes, making choice (b) correct.

15. (e) Jesse may see 1, 2, or 3 people with blue chins. If Henry does not have a blue chin, so that only two people in the group have blue chins, then Jesse sees only one blue chin if his own chin is painted blue. If two people have their chins painted blue and Jesse is not one of them, then he sees two blue chins. If Henry's chin is blue and Jesse's chin is not, he sees three blue chins.

16. (d) Henry is able to determine the color of his chin in the following way.

If his chin is not blue, then only two of the four men have blue chins. One of those men would have looked around and seen only *one* man with a blue chin. That man, in fact, would have his hand raised, however, meaning that he sees someone else with a blue chin. From this observation, one of the two men with the blue chins would have quickly been able to conclude that his own chin was blue. The failure of this to happen allows Henry to conclude that no one is able to look around and see only one blue chin; this means that Henry's chin must also be blue.

17. (*d*) This question is explained by question 16 above.

18. (*d*) The best way to approach this set of questions is to list all possible teams, eliminating those which the conditions make impossible.

From condition (3), the only teams involving players D or H are ADH, BDH, and CDH. The possible teams involving F cannot include H, leaving AFI, AFJ, BFI, BFJ, CFI, and CFJ. Condition (6) eliminates teams combining F with C or I, leaving only AFJ and BFJ. Condition (5) eliminates BFJ, leaving AFJ as the only team that F can play on.

Player E cannot be on A's team, according to condition (4), but can play with B, C, I, or J, giving four possible teams for him to be on: BEI, BEJ, CEI, and CEJ.

The possible teams are: ADH, AFJ, BDH, BEI, BEJ, CDH, CEI, and CEJ.

Since C is on three of these teams, choice (*d*) is correct.

19. (*c*) It is clear from the list of possible teams that if B is a member, then F is not a member, making choice (*c*) correct. It is easy to find teams which make the other choices incorrect.

20. (*c*) Teams ADH and CEI are possible, but not team BFJ, so choice (*c*) is correct.

21. (*c*) Player F can belong to only one possible team, fewer than any other player.

22. (*d*) Player E can belong to four teams, more than anyone else. B, C, D, and J can each belong to three teams.

23. (*b*) It is clear that if E refused to play with I or J, then he could no longer play on any teams, which would eliminate four possible teams. The refusal of A and D to play with each other would eliminate only team ADH. If J could not play, three teams would be eliminated. Only team AFJ would no longer be possible if A refused to play with J. The refusal of C to play with D, F, or J would only eliminate CDH and CEJ as possible teams.

24. (*b*) The stem statement contains an inference about all members of some class from the author's observations of some members of the class. Only (*b*) also contains this inference. It contains the reasoning that since the author has only met friendly people, then only friendly people exist, and therefore no unfriendly people exist. (*a*) is incorrect because the author has observed hot fires, but has inferred great destruction, a

different concept. Similarly, (d) confuses fast horses with race-horses. (e) is not analogous because it generalizes from paper-backs to another class, hardbound books. (c) does not contain any observations and is not at all analogous to the stem statement.

25. (b) The argument seems to be that America is impolite, as exemplified by Manhattan's rude drivers. If it were true that the behavior of Manhattan car drivers reflects the general state of affairs in the nation, then the argument would have some support. Choices (a), (c), and (e) are not relevant to the thrust of the argument. Choice (d) is closer, but overstates the case, by saying that the drivers are *responsible for*, rather than merely *indicative of*, the general state of affairs.

SECTION VII

1. (d) Divide each choice by 13 and find the one with an integral quotient.
$$\frac{1326}{13} = 102$$
The other four choices all have remainders.

2. (b) $(4r^2s^3)^3 = 4^3(r^2)^3(s^3)^3$
$$= 64r^6s^9$$

3. (c) $1/4 = .25$ and $1/3 = .33\frac{1}{3}$
Look for the fraction that has a decimal value between these two values. Since $3/10 = .30$, this choice is the correct answer.

4. (e) Substitute -1 for x in each choice.
$$1 - x = 1 - (-1) = 1 + 1 = 2$$
The other choices yield 0, 1, or -1 so that 2 is the greatest value.

5. (a) The surface area of a cube is given by $S = 6e^2$ where e is the edge of the cube.
Then $54t^2 = 6e^2$
$9t^2 = e^2$
$e = 3t$
$V = e^3 = (3t)^3$
$V = 27t^3$

6. (b) Let x = no. of cups of powder added
$$\frac{1 + x}{18} = \frac{1}{2}$$
$$2 + 2x = 18$$
$$2x = 16$$
$$x = 8$$

7. (d) Don't forget those who did not work at all! Add the percentages: $18.5\% + 11.0\% + 6.8\% = 36.3\%$ times 10.2 million = 3.7 million.

8. (e) It is not correct to add the percentages for men and women: $32.5\% + 34.2\% = 66.7\%$ does not yield an answer. It is necessary to calculate men and women separately: 32.5% of 10.2 million men = 3.3 million; 34.2% of 8 million women = 2.8 million, for a total of 6.1 million, which is about 33% of 18.3 million.

9. (a) First, narrow the choices if possible. Men, 5–14 weeks is 20.4% + 10.8% = 31.2%, which is less than men 1–4 weeks at 32.5% so (c) can be eliminated. Women 5–26 weeks is 16.7% + 8.3% + 14.5% = 39.5%, while women 1–4 weeks is 34.2%, so (b) can be eliminated.
Now some calculations are necessary, but they can be estimated: Men 1–4 weeks is 32.5% of 10.2 million, or about 3.3 million. Women 5–26 weeks is 39.5% of 8.1 million, approximately 40% of

8 million or 3.2 million. The men 15–26 weeks is 18.5% of 10.2 million, or about 1.9 million; women 15–26 weeks is 14.5% of 8.1 million, or about 1.2 million, for a total of 3.1 million. Men 1–4 weeks is the largest group.

10. (d) First eliminate (e) since it is obviously smaller than (b). Next, perform approximate calculations, starting with the most likely answer, men 15–26 weeks: 26 × 18% = 468. Next try 11–14: 14 × 11% = 154. Next 5–10: 10 × 20% = 200; and finally 4 × 33% = 130. Men 15–26 weeks, 468 is the largest. Note that it is not necessary to extend the calculations to calculate the actual man-weeks (i.e., multiply by 10.2 million).

11. (b) Since MN ∥ PQ, ∠NSR +∠SRQ = 180°.
Dividing both sides of this equation by 2, we get 1/2 ∠ NSR + 1/2 ∠SRQ = 1/2 × 180°
or
∠TSR +∠SRT = 90°
In triangle RST, since the sum of two angles is 90°, the third angle is also 90°. Thus, y = 90°

12. (e) $(r + s)^2 = (r + s)(r + s)$
$= r^2 + 2rs + s^2$
Thus 2rs must be added to $r^2 + s^2$ to equal $(r + s)^2$

13. (c)
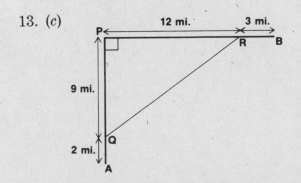

The given figure shows the positions of A and B after traveling for one hour. A moves to Q and B moves to R, so that triangle PQR has legs of 9 and 12 miles. It is a 3—4—5 triangle, with sides multiplied by 3; so that QR = 15.

14. (b)
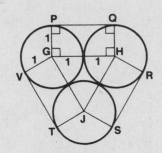

In this illustration, the length of the rope is PQ + $\overparen{PV}$ + VT + $\overparen{TS}$ + SR + $\overparen{QR}$ = 3PQ + 3$\overparen{VP}$. From the rectangle PQHG, PQ = GH = 2. Since triangle GHJ is equilateral, ∠HGJ = 60°. Angles PGH and VGJ are each 90°, so that angle PGV = 360 – 180 – 60 = 120°. Thus, arc PV = 1/3 circumference = 1/3 (2 π) and 3$\overparen{PV}$ = 2π. Thus the length of the rope is 2π + 6.

15. (a) If $\dfrac{2x + 6}{x^3 + 6x^2 + 54}$ = 0, then
2x + 6 = 0
x = −3

16. (e) p = 2q, q = 3r
Substitute q = 3r in first equation.
p = 2(3r) = 6r
Divide both sides by 6.
$r = \dfrac{p}{6}$

17. (a) Average =
$\dfrac{76 + 76 + 85 + 85 + 85 + 85}{6}$
= 82.0%

18. (*d*)

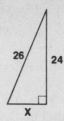

Since $26 = 2 \times 13$ and $24 = 2 \times 12$, the triangle is a 5–12–13 right triangle with each side multiplied by 2. Thus, $x = 2 \times 5 = 10$ feet.

19. (*c*) Since $QR = RS$, $\angle SQR = \angle QSR$ and since $\angle SRQ = 100°$, then $\angle SQR = 40°$. Also, since $PQ = QS$, $\angle P = \angle PSQ$. Angle SQR is an exterior angle of triangle PQS and is therefore equal to $\angle P + \angle PSQ = 2 \angle P$. Thus $\angle P = 20°$.

20. (*e*) $PQ = 4 - (-2) = 4 + 2 = 6$
$OR = 5$
Area of triangle $OPQ =$
$1/2(PQ \times OR)$
$= 1/2 \times 6 \times 5$
$= 15$

21. (*a*) The car travels m/g miles per gallon.
On n gallons, it travels
$$\frac{(m)}{(g)} n = \frac{mn}{g}$$

22. (*e*) $y = \dfrac{rs}{1 + x}$
$y(1 + x) = rs$
$y + xy = rs$
$xy = rs - y$
$x = \dfrac{rs - y}{y} = \dfrac{rs}{y} - 1$

23. (*d*)

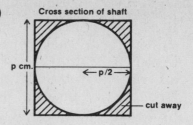

Cross section of shaft

Original cross section area $= p^2$
Final cross section area $=$
$$\pi \left(\frac{p}{2}\right)^2 = \frac{p^2}{4}$$
Area cut away $=$
$$p^2 - \frac{p^2}{4} = p^2 \left(1 - \frac{\pi}{4}\right)$$
Fraction of part cut away $=$
$$1 - \frac{\pi}{4} = \frac{4 - \pi}{4}$$

24. (*d*) Central angle $= 40\%$ of $360°$
$= .4 (360)$
$= 144°$

25. (*e*) Let $x =$ no. of millions of metric tons in world production, then
16.6% of $x = .581$
$1/6 \ x = .581$ (approximately)
$x = 3.486 = 3.5$ (approximately)

Answer Sheet—Practice Test 2

When you have chosen your answer to any question, blacken the corresponding space on the answer sheet below. Make sure your marking completely fills the answer space. If you change an answer, erase the previous marking completely.

Section I

1 Ⓐ Ⓑ Ⓒ Ⓓ Ⓔ	11 Ⓐ Ⓑ Ⓒ Ⓓ Ⓔ	21 Ⓐ Ⓑ Ⓒ Ⓓ Ⓔ	31 Ⓐ Ⓑ Ⓒ Ⓓ Ⓔ
2 Ⓐ Ⓑ Ⓒ Ⓓ Ⓔ	12 Ⓐ Ⓑ Ⓒ Ⓓ Ⓔ	22 Ⓐ Ⓑ Ⓒ Ⓓ Ⓔ	32 Ⓐ Ⓑ Ⓒ Ⓓ Ⓔ
3 Ⓐ Ⓑ Ⓒ Ⓓ Ⓔ	13 Ⓐ Ⓑ Ⓒ Ⓓ Ⓔ	23 Ⓐ Ⓑ Ⓒ Ⓓ Ⓔ	33 Ⓐ Ⓑ Ⓒ Ⓓ Ⓔ
4 Ⓐ Ⓑ Ⓒ Ⓓ Ⓔ	14 Ⓐ Ⓑ Ⓒ Ⓓ Ⓔ	24 Ⓐ Ⓑ Ⓒ Ⓓ Ⓔ	34 Ⓐ Ⓑ Ⓒ Ⓓ Ⓔ
5 Ⓐ Ⓑ Ⓒ Ⓓ Ⓔ	15 Ⓐ Ⓑ Ⓒ Ⓓ Ⓔ	25 Ⓐ Ⓑ Ⓒ Ⓓ Ⓔ	35 Ⓐ Ⓑ Ⓒ Ⓓ Ⓔ
6 Ⓐ Ⓑ Ⓒ Ⓓ Ⓔ	16 Ⓐ Ⓑ Ⓒ Ⓓ Ⓔ	26 Ⓐ Ⓑ Ⓒ Ⓓ Ⓔ	36 Ⓐ Ⓑ Ⓒ Ⓓ Ⓔ
7 Ⓐ Ⓑ Ⓒ Ⓓ Ⓔ	17 Ⓐ Ⓑ Ⓒ Ⓓ Ⓔ	27 Ⓐ Ⓑ Ⓒ Ⓓ Ⓔ	37 Ⓐ Ⓑ Ⓒ Ⓓ Ⓔ
8 Ⓐ Ⓑ Ⓒ Ⓓ Ⓔ	18 Ⓐ Ⓑ Ⓒ Ⓓ Ⓔ	28 Ⓐ Ⓑ Ⓒ Ⓓ Ⓔ	38 Ⓐ Ⓑ Ⓒ Ⓓ Ⓔ
9 Ⓐ Ⓑ Ⓒ Ⓓ Ⓔ	19 Ⓐ Ⓑ Ⓒ Ⓓ Ⓔ	29 Ⓐ Ⓑ Ⓒ Ⓓ Ⓔ	
10 Ⓐ Ⓑ Ⓒ Ⓓ Ⓔ	20 Ⓐ Ⓑ Ⓒ Ⓓ Ⓔ	30 Ⓐ Ⓑ Ⓒ Ⓓ Ⓔ	

Section II

1 Ⓐ Ⓑ Ⓒ Ⓓ Ⓔ	11 Ⓐ Ⓑ Ⓒ Ⓓ Ⓔ	21 Ⓐ Ⓑ Ⓒ Ⓓ Ⓔ	31 Ⓐ Ⓑ Ⓒ Ⓓ Ⓔ
2 Ⓐ Ⓑ Ⓒ Ⓓ Ⓔ	12 Ⓐ Ⓑ Ⓒ Ⓓ Ⓔ	22 Ⓐ Ⓑ Ⓒ Ⓓ Ⓔ	32 Ⓐ Ⓑ Ⓒ Ⓓ Ⓔ
3 Ⓐ Ⓑ Ⓒ Ⓓ Ⓔ	13 Ⓐ Ⓑ Ⓒ Ⓓ Ⓔ	23 Ⓐ Ⓑ Ⓒ Ⓓ Ⓔ	33 Ⓐ Ⓑ Ⓒ Ⓓ Ⓔ
4 Ⓐ Ⓑ Ⓒ Ⓓ Ⓔ	14 Ⓐ Ⓑ Ⓒ Ⓓ Ⓔ	24 Ⓐ Ⓑ Ⓒ Ⓓ Ⓔ	34 Ⓐ Ⓑ Ⓒ Ⓓ Ⓔ
5 Ⓐ Ⓑ Ⓒ Ⓓ Ⓔ	15 Ⓐ Ⓑ Ⓒ Ⓓ Ⓔ	25 Ⓐ Ⓑ Ⓒ Ⓓ Ⓔ	35 Ⓐ Ⓑ Ⓒ Ⓓ Ⓔ
6 Ⓐ Ⓑ Ⓒ Ⓓ Ⓔ	16 Ⓐ Ⓑ Ⓒ Ⓓ Ⓔ	26 Ⓐ Ⓑ Ⓒ Ⓓ Ⓔ	36 Ⓐ Ⓑ Ⓒ Ⓓ Ⓔ
7 Ⓐ Ⓑ Ⓒ Ⓓ Ⓔ	17 Ⓐ Ⓑ Ⓒ Ⓓ Ⓔ	27 Ⓐ Ⓑ Ⓒ Ⓓ Ⓔ	37 Ⓐ Ⓑ Ⓒ Ⓓ Ⓔ
8 Ⓐ Ⓑ Ⓒ Ⓓ Ⓔ	18 Ⓐ Ⓑ Ⓒ Ⓓ Ⓔ	28 Ⓐ Ⓑ Ⓒ Ⓓ Ⓔ	38 Ⓐ Ⓑ Ⓒ Ⓓ Ⓔ
9 Ⓐ Ⓑ Ⓒ Ⓓ Ⓔ	19 Ⓐ Ⓑ Ⓒ Ⓓ Ⓔ	29 Ⓐ Ⓑ Ⓒ Ⓓ Ⓔ	
10 Ⓐ Ⓑ Ⓒ Ⓓ Ⓔ	20 Ⓐ Ⓑ Ⓒ Ⓓ Ⓔ	30 Ⓐ Ⓑ Ⓒ Ⓓ Ⓔ	

Section III

1 Ⓐ Ⓑ Ⓒ Ⓓ Ⓔ	9 Ⓐ Ⓑ Ⓒ Ⓓ Ⓔ	17 Ⓐ Ⓑ Ⓒ Ⓓ Ⓔ	24 Ⓐ Ⓑ Ⓒ Ⓓ Ⓔ
2 Ⓐ Ⓑ Ⓒ Ⓓ Ⓔ	10 Ⓐ Ⓑ Ⓒ Ⓓ Ⓔ	18 Ⓐ Ⓑ Ⓒ Ⓓ Ⓔ	25 Ⓐ Ⓑ Ⓒ Ⓓ Ⓔ
3 Ⓐ Ⓑ Ⓒ Ⓓ Ⓔ	11 Ⓐ Ⓑ Ⓒ Ⓓ Ⓔ	19 Ⓐ Ⓑ Ⓒ Ⓓ Ⓔ	26 Ⓐ Ⓑ Ⓒ Ⓓ Ⓔ
4 Ⓐ Ⓑ Ⓒ Ⓓ Ⓔ	12 Ⓐ Ⓑ Ⓒ Ⓓ Ⓔ	20 Ⓐ Ⓑ Ⓒ Ⓓ Ⓔ	27 Ⓐ Ⓑ Ⓒ Ⓓ Ⓔ
5 Ⓐ Ⓑ Ⓒ Ⓓ Ⓔ	13 Ⓐ Ⓑ Ⓒ Ⓓ Ⓔ	21 Ⓐ Ⓑ Ⓒ Ⓓ Ⓔ	28 Ⓐ Ⓑ Ⓒ Ⓓ Ⓔ
6 Ⓐ Ⓑ Ⓒ Ⓓ Ⓔ	14 Ⓐ Ⓑ Ⓒ Ⓓ Ⓔ	22 Ⓐ Ⓑ Ⓒ Ⓓ Ⓔ	29 Ⓐ Ⓑ Ⓒ Ⓓ Ⓔ
7 Ⓐ Ⓑ Ⓒ Ⓓ Ⓔ	15 Ⓐ Ⓑ Ⓒ Ⓓ Ⓔ	23 Ⓐ Ⓑ Ⓒ Ⓓ Ⓔ	30 Ⓐ Ⓑ Ⓒ Ⓓ Ⓔ
8 Ⓐ Ⓑ Ⓒ Ⓓ Ⓔ	16 Ⓐ Ⓑ Ⓒ Ⓓ Ⓔ		

Section IV

1 ⒶⒷⒸⒹⒺ	9 ⒶⒷⒸⒹⒺ	17 ⒶⒷⒸⒹⒺ	24 ⒶⒷⒸⒹⒺ
2 ⒶⒷⒸⒹⒺ	10 ⒶⒷⒸⒹⒺ	18 ⒶⒷⒸⒹⒺ	25 ⒶⒷⒸⒹⒺ
3 ⒶⒷⒸⒹⒺ	11 ⒶⒷⒸⒹⒺ	19 ⒶⒷⒸⒹⒺ	26 ⒶⒷⒸⒹⒺ
4 ⒶⒷⒸⒹⒺ	12 ⒶⒷⒸⒹⒺ	20 ⒶⒷⒸⒹⒺ	27 ⒶⒷⒸⒹⒺ
5 ⒶⒷⒸⒹⒺ	13 ⒶⒷⒸⒹⒺ	21 ⒶⒷⒸⒹⒺ	28 ⒶⒷⒸⒹⒺ
6 ⒶⒷⒸⒹⒺ	14 ⒶⒷⒸⒹⒺ	22 ⒶⒷⒸⒹⒺ	29 ⒶⒷⒸⒹⒺ
7 ⒶⒷⒸⒹⒺ	15 ⒶⒷⒸⒹⒺ	23 ⒶⒷⒸⒹⒺ	30 ⒶⒷⒸⒹⒺ
8 ⒶⒷⒸⒹⒺ	16 ⒶⒷⒸⒹⒺ		

Section V

1 ⒶⒷⒸⒹⒺ	8 ⒶⒷⒸⒹⒺ	14 ⒶⒷⒸⒹⒺ	20 ⒶⒷⒸⒹⒺ
2 ⒶⒷⒸⒹⒺ	9 ⒶⒷⒸⒹⒺ	15 ⒶⒷⒸⒹⒺ	21 ⒶⒷⒸⒹⒺ
3 ⒶⒷⒸⒹⒺ	10 ⒶⒷⒸⒹⒺ	16 ⒶⒷⒸⒹⒺ	22 ⒶⒷⒸⒹⒺ
4 ⒶⒷⒸⒹⒺ	11 ⒶⒷⒸⒹⒺ	17 ⒶⒷⒸⒹⒺ	23 ⒶⒷⒸⒹⒺ
5 ⒶⒷⒸⒹⒺ	12 ⒶⒷⒸⒹⒺ	18 ⒶⒷⒸⒹⒺ	24 ⒶⒷⒸⒹⒺ
6 ⒶⒷⒸⒹⒺ	13 ⒶⒷⒸⒹⒺ	19 ⒶⒷⒸⒹⒺ	25 ⒶⒷⒸⒹⒺ
7 ⒶⒷⒸⒹⒺ			

Section VI

1 ⒶⒷⒸⒹⒺ	8 ⒶⒷⒸⒹⒺ	15 ⒶⒷⒸⒹⒺ	21 ⒶⒷⒸⒹⒺ
2 ⒶⒷⒸⒹⒺ	9 ⒶⒷⒸⒹⒺ	16 ⒶⒷⒸⒹⒺ	22 ⒶⒷⒸⒹⒺ
3 ⒶⒷⒸⒹⒺ	10 ⒶⒷⒸⒹⒺ	17 ⒶⒷⒸⒹⒺ	23 ⒶⒷⒸⒹⒺ
4 ⒶⒷⒸⒹⒺ	11 ⒶⒷⒸⒹⒺ	18 ⒶⒷⒸⒹⒺ	24 ⒶⒷⒸⒹⒺ
5 ⒶⒷⒸⒹⒺ	12 ⒶⒷⒸⒹⒺ	19 ⒶⒷⒸⒹⒺ	25 ⒶⒷⒸⒹⒺ
6 ⒶⒷⒸⒹⒺ	13 ⒶⒷⒸⒹⒺ	20 ⒶⒷⒸⒹⒺ	
7 ⒶⒷⒸⒹⒺ	14 ⒶⒷⒸⒹⒺ		

Section VII

1 ⒶⒷⒸⒹⒺ	11 ⒶⒷⒸⒹⒺ	21 ⒶⒷⒸⒹⒺ	30 ⒶⒷⒸⒹⒺ
2 ⒶⒷⒸⒹⒺ	12 ⒶⒷⒸⒹⒺ	22 ⒶⒷⒸⒹⒺ	31 ⒶⒷⒸⒹⒺ
3 ⒶⒷⒸⒹⒺ	13 ⒶⒷⒸⒹⒺ	23 ⒶⒷⒸⒹⒺ	32 ⒶⒷⒸⒹⒺ
4 ⒶⒷⒸⒹⒺ	14 ⒶⒷⒸⒹⒺ	24 ⒶⒷⒸⒹⒺ	33 ⒶⒷⒸⒹⒺ
5 ⒶⒷⒸⒹⒺ	15 ⒶⒷⒸⒹⒺ	25 ⒶⒷⒸⒹⒺ	34 ⒶⒷⒸⒹⒺ
6 ⒶⒷⒸⒹⒺ	16 ⒶⒷⒸⒹⒺ	26 ⒶⒷⒸⒹⒺ	35 ⒶⒷⒸⒹⒺ
7 ⒶⒷⒸⒹⒺ	17 ⒶⒷⒸⒹⒺ	27 ⒶⒷⒸⒹⒺ	36 ⒶⒷⒸⒹⒺ
8 ⒶⒷⒸⒹⒺ	18 ⒶⒷⒸⒹⒺ	28 ⒶⒷⒸⒹⒺ	37 ⒶⒷⒸⒹⒺ
9 ⒶⒷⒸⒹⒺ	19 ⒶⒷⒸⒹⒺ	29 ⒶⒷⒸⒹⒺ	38 ⒶⒷⒸⒹⒺ
10 ⒶⒷⒸⒹⒺ	20 ⒶⒷⒸⒹⒺ		

Practice Test 2

GRE Practice Test 2

SECTION I

Time—30 minutes
38 Questions

For each of the numbered questions in this section, choose the best answer according to the instructions, and blacken the correspondingly numbered blank space on the answer sheet.

Each of the sentences below has one or more blank spaces indicating where a word or words have been omitted. Each sentence is followed by five words or sets of words lettered from (a) to (e). Select the lettered word or set of words which, inserted to replace the blanks, BEST fits in with and completes the meaning of the sentence as a whole.

1. The decision of the Supreme Court in the famous case of Brown vs. Board of Education has already – – – a profound change in the fabric of American life.

   (a) imbedded
   (b) undergone
   (c) effected
   (d) implemented
   (e) complied

2. Though they denied the existence of a – – – in their friendship, their increasingly rancorous disputes convinced us that their long – – – would not survive the run of the current production.

   (a) rift . . . collaboration
   (b) drift . . . contract
   (c) pact . . . voyage
   (d) miasma . . . conversation
   (e) letdown . . . separation

3. The problems of adolescence are primarily problems of – – – to changing roles complicated by problems of dramatic physical development.

   (a) adjustment
   (b) containment
   (c) insensitivity
   (d) reversion
   (e) adoption

4. His – – – knew almost no bounds when his team reached the playoffs; but when they pulled away to a commanding lead in the final period of the fourth game, after winning the first three in a row, his elation became – – –.

   (a) humility . . . apparent
   (b) reluctance . . . boring
   (c) sentimentality . . . fantastic
   (d) pride . . . thoughtful
   (e) elation . . . euphoric

5. His adherents were loath to believe the evidence that so clearly – – – his guilt, even though his own testimony all but constituted a confession.

   (a) minimized
   (b) proclaimed
   (c) refuted
   (d) consummated
   (e) impugned

6. Because of unsolved difficulties related to the disposal of nuclear wastes, and fears aroused by the failure of – – – foolproof safety systems, the promise of cheap and – – – electricity through the development of nuclear power has not been realized.

   (a) indubitably . . . alternating
   (b) redundant . . . superfluous
   (c) shockproof . . . unfettered
   (d) allegedly . . . abundant
   (e) monitored . . . fail-safe

7. Though the thrust of his argument went counter to the beliefs of his time and he was forced, at the last, to – – –, his views have prevailed and are accepted now as correct.

   (a) recant
   (b) confess
   (c) retire
   (d) recapitulate
   (e) intervene

In each of the questions below, a related pair of words or phrases in capital letters is followed by five pairs of words or phrases lettered from (a) to (e). Select that lettered pair that expresses a relationship that is MOST similar to that of the capitalized pair.

8. CHOREOGRAPHER : PIROUETTE : :
   (a) composer : chord   (b) batter : balk
   (c) dramatist : critic   (d) banker : debt
   (e) parent : sibling

9. QUIVER : VIBRATE : : (*a*) falsify : reveal
(*b*) portray : portrait (*c*) frighten : terrify
(*d*) inebriate : detoxify (*e*) imperious : deleterious

10. GENERAL : COMMANDS : : (*a*) specific : responses
(*b*) doctor : diagnosis (*c*) clergyman : redeems
(*d*) senator : legislates (*e*) aviator : aerates

11. ANNUL : MARRIAGE : : (*a*) reverse : verdict
(*b*) disavow : guilt (*c*) admit : complicity
(*d*) arrogate : responsibility (*e*) consecrate : house

12. NEMESIS : GUARDIAN ANGEL : :
(*a*) romantic : sophisticate (*b*) mendicant : friar
(*c*) avenger : challenger (*d*) miser : spendthrift
(*e*) gourmet : connoisseur

13. EXPEND : REPLENISH : : (*a*) foment : rebellion
(*b*) exhort : encourage (*c*) augment : oversupply
(*d*) defect : rejoin (*e*) occupy : reoccupy

14. IMMUNE : SUSCEPTIBLE : :
(*a*) cavalier : presumptuous (*b*) valiant : puissant
(*c*) fluent : affluent (*d*) steadfast : headstrong
(*e*) exempt : obliged

15. FERAL : WOLVERINE : :(*a*) attenuated : assassin
(*b*) timorous : milksop (*c*) cavernous : amphitheater
(*d*) rabid : fox (*e*) hereditary : matriarch

16. EQUATION : TERM : : (*a*) rocket : nose cone
(*b*) carburetor : mixture (*c*) formula : constituent
(*d*) binomial : monocular (*e*) verdict : sentence

In the series of selections that follows, each passage is followed by questions based on its content. Read the passage and choose the best answer for each question based on the contents of the passage. The questions must be answered on the basis of what is stated or implied in the reading passage.

The response of adults to the behavior of adolescents is often more strongly influenced by the adults' own needs than by the way the adolescents are acting. A whole range of emotions and feelings from concern to outright hostility is evoked, leading to perceptions and actions which impact on our entire society.

The adult world clings tenaciously to social order, resistive to the young people whose questioning, risk-taking, and spontaneity threaten existing arrangements. Adult fears that adolescents will escape their control, with the concomitant anxiety about unplanned change and disorderliness, lead to determined efforts to restrain young people through familial and societal regulation.

Equally important is the loss of self-esteem that many adults feel when faced with the adolescent challenge to the tenets by which their lives have been ruled. Convinced that success is the measure of worth, unwilling to admit to doubt about the path taken or the value of the prizes secured, the adult defends equally against the serious probing and the ingenuous disaffection. The youth who searches for and attains what his parents had yearned for and then denied themselves, attacks the most vulnerable facet of the adult personality—the fragile self-esteem. It is no wonder, then, that rather than an attempt at loving understanding, the parent responds with bitterness and antagonism.

17. Which of the following, according to the passage, lead the parent to respond with hostility rather than understanding?

   I. Adolescent success in fields or endeavors where the parent had once hoped to achieve success, but which the parent has had to renounce
   II. The reluctance of the parent to subject his or her values to fresh scrutiny
   III. The desire of the parent to have the adolescent achieve success through hard work

   (a) I only
   (b) II only
   (c) III only
   (d) I and II only
   (e) II and III only

18. Which of the following statements is neither expressed nor implied in the passage?

   (a) Adults are uncomfortable in the face of what they perceive as lack of planning by adolescents.
   (b) Adults are willing to tolerate adolescent probing if it is done with thoughtfulness.
   (c) Fear that adolescents will take control of their own lives lead to familial regulation.
   (d) Young people are more inclined to take risks in their approaches to life than adults.
   (e) Although parents may say that they are thinking only of their children's good when they are critical, they are often really thinking of themselves.

19. Which of the statements below offers the best summary of the author's point of view as expressed in the passage?

   (a) Despite their questioning of the values of their elders, adolescents really want the same things their parents have.

   (b) If adolescents only would follow parental advice, societal hostilities would diminish.

   (c) In a spirit of adolescent rebelliousness, young people deliberately prize what their parents scorn.

   (d) Today's adolescents act no differently from the way their parents behaved when they were adolescents.

   (e) The explanation of adult bitterness and antagonism toward youth lies in the regret of parents about dropping that for which they had yearned when they were young, and their reluctance to examine the values of the path they had turned to instead.

In terms of its prevalence, obesity is the leading disease in the United States. Obesity may be defined as a condition of excess adipose tissue, as fatness beyond cultural esthetic norms, or as adipose tissue tending to disrupt good health of mind and body. A common rule of thumb is that people more than 20 pounds above their desirable weights are obese. By this measure, 30 percent of men and 40 percent of women in America are obese. Despite the prevalence of the disease, curative measures are almost impossible for those currently obese; future generations may be spared.

Adipose tissue is a triumph of evolution. Fat yields 9.0 calories per gram, while carbohydrates and protein each yield 4.0 calories per gram, and fat contains much less water than does protein. It is, therefore, much more efficient to store excess energy as fat than as protein. Primitive man, with uncertain food sources, had great need for excess fat, but modern Western man, with predictable food supply and sedentary lifestyle, is burdened by this evolutionary vestige. This is not to say that modern man has no need at all for adipose tissue; on the contrary, he needs it for such important purposes as insulation from cold, and protection of organs from injury.

The problem Americans face is losing excess adipose tissue, and they turn from one fad diet to another. Despite a billion-dollar diet industry, the five-year cure rate of obesity is almost zero. Cancer is more curable. The reasons for this are psychological as well as physiological.

From a physical standpoint, losing a pound or two a week for a few weeks is not difficult, for most of the loss is in the form of protein and water, and protein carries with it four times its weight in water. However, when the body has been in negative nitrogen balance for too long, it acts to correct the situation by taking in as much or more nitrogen than it excretes. Since protein is the only source of nitrogen in the diet, any future weight loss must come from adipose tissue, the very compactness of which makes losing weight a very slow and tedious task. If caloric expenditure exceeds intake by 500 calories, only 62 grams of adipose tissue can be lost as compared with 620 grams of protein and associated water. The body's tendency to return to nitrogen balance can be so strong that the dieter may actually gain weight while still expending more calories than he is ingesting. Faced with a discontinuance of weight loss, or even a weight gain, while still adhering to a previously successful diet tends to lead dieters to suffer depression, hunger, decreased metabolic rate, inactivity, and weakness, which in turn lead to the diet's abandonment. The strong tendency then is for rapid weight gain, probably from numerous psychological factors as well as such physiological ones as increased lipid synthesis.

Obese people tend to be hypertensive, diabetic, and, because they are relatively insensitive to insulin's effects, hyperinsulinemic. Weight loss is associated with improvement in all these categories. Further, obesity is correlated with increased serum lipids (such as cholesterol), a condition which is additionally significant because of its role in atherosclerotic heart disease, by far the leading cause of death in the United States.

While vigorous attempts to reduce obesity in America should be aimed at all affected, the most successful efforts are likely to be those directed toward children. If the advertising and food industries stop trying to sell high-caloric, low-nutritive-value foods to children, if parents reserve sweets as treats for special occasions, and if mothers and fathers are successfully educated to understand that the feeding patterns they impose on their infants and children can determine the adolescent and adult eating habits those children will develop, the future generation may not be as fat as ours is.

20. For which of the following questions does the passage provide an answer through the information it offers?

(a) How do hypertension and atherosclerosis contribute to obesity in modern man?
(b) Why do people very often fail to lose weight even though they are cutting down on caloric intake?
(c) What is the effect of the nitrogen cycle on metabolism and weight loss?
(d) What is the educational role of obese parents in preventing problems of weight control in their children?
(e) What part does metabolic rate play in the utilization of carbohydrates to accelerate weight loss?

21. According to the passage, the role that evolution plays in relation to obesity is that

(a) adipose tissue is a convenient form of body structure in which to store excess energy

(b) modern man uses large amounts of energy, mostly in the form of protein and carbohydrates

(c) the development of a sedentary lifestyle encouraged the ingestion of reduced calories

(d) modern man's body cannot deal with an evolutionary vestige of what was needed by primitive man, the development of adipose tissue for storing energy in the face of an uncertain food supply

(e) primitive man's need for insulation from the cold led to modern man's need for a diet strong in serum lipids

22. A statement that is neither supported or contradicted by the passage is that

(a) dieters need four times as much water as protein for every pound of adipose tissue they wish to expend

(b) adipose tissue is still needed by modern man for certain important purposes

(c) obesity, as a disease, is the number one cause of death in America

(d) the diet industry in the United States has made little progress toward curing obesity

(e) it is not difficult to lose weight at the outset when going on a diet

23. It can be inferred from the passage that

(a) atherosclerotic people also suffer from obesity

(b) following a careful weight-loss diet is the only effective cure for obesity

(c) bringing the body into a condition of negative nitrogen balance will assist the dieter to achieve weight loss

(d) the roots of obesity are to be found in the feeding and eating problems of infancy and childhood

(e) psychiatric treatment can uncover the underlying causes of obesity

24. Overcoming obesity, the passage says, is important for all but one of the following reasons:

(a) Loss of weight is accompanied by lessening of hypertension.

(b) Obesity has a deleterious effect on both physical and mental health.

(c) Obese people tend to cut back on serum lipids, to which they are completely insensitive.

(d) Weight loss is associated with improvement in the case of diabetics.

(e) Obesity is correlated with the presence of increased serum lipids, which in turn plays a significant role in atherosclerotic heart disease, the leading cause of death in the United States.

25. The statement below that is neither expressed nor implied in the passage is that

(a) the food industries have contributed to the incidence of obesity in America
(b) severe weight loss leads to serious psychological and physiological problems
(c) modern Western man's lifestyle is at odds with his evolutionary heritage of a system that finds it efficient to store excess energy as fat
(d) more than one third of American men and women are obese
(e) obesity, the leading disease in the United States, may be difficult to cure, but future generations may not be afflicted by it

26. The author's purpose in writing this passage was to

(a) criticize the billion-dollar diet industry in America
(b) demonstrate that obesity is a genetic disorder
(c) advocate a national crusade against obesity
(d) discourage dependency on fad diets as a method for losing weight
(e) raise the reader's consciousness in regard to the dangers of obesity, and to advocate an educational program to fight it.

27. According to the passage, adipose tissue

(a) is composed mostly of fat and water, with but 4.0% protein or carbo-hydrate in it
(b) to the extent of 62 grams can be lost if caloric intake is 500 calories under caloric expenditure
(c) carries with it four times its weight in water
(d) is a triumph over evolution; man can now do without it
(e) has been found to be related to curable cancer

In each of the following questions, a capitalized word is followed by five words or phrases lettered (a) through (e). Select the word or phrase most nearly OPPOSITE in meaning to the capitalized word.

Since some of the questions require that you distinguish fine shades of meaning, consider all choices carefully before you select your answer.

28. ANIMUS

(a) adjuration
(b) vertebrate
(c) dread
(d) sympathy
(e) bias

29. INTERDICT

(a) sanction
(b) dictate
(c) interpose
(d) disdain
(e) apprehend

30. INADVERTENT

(a) hesitant
(b) perplexed
(c) unadvertised
(d) adapted
(e) premeditated

31. ABORIGINE

(a) unique
(a) decorative
(c) emigrant
(d) obsolescent
(e) unknown

32. CORROBORATIVE

(a) precarious
(b) refutative
(c) governable
(d) collective
(e) convertible

33. NOXIOUS

(a) noisy
(b) harmless
(c) flippant
(d) gaseous
(e) flagrant

34. INIMICAL

(a) amicable
(b) friendless
(c) unusual
(d) imitative
(e) accidental

35. VAINGLORIOUS

(a) empirical
(b) portentous
(c) alluring
(d) unassuming
(e) weak

36. BELLICOSE

(a) pacific
(b) ringing
(c) wordy
(d) blaspheming
(e) archaic

37. SAVANT

(a) deliverer
(b) deceiver
(c) simpleton
(d) gambler
(e) teacher

38. INNOCUOUS

(a) visible
(b) pernicious
(c) vulnerable
(d) intolerable
(e) indecorous

STOP! Work only on this section until the time allowed is over.

SECTION II

Time—30 minutes
38 Questions

For each of the numbered questions in this section, choose the best answer according to the instructions, and blacken the correspondingly numbered blank space on the answer sheet.

Each of the sentences below has one or more blank spaces indicating where a word or words have been omitted. Each sentence is followed by five words or sets of words lettered from (a) to (e). Select the lettered word or sets of words which, inserted to replace the blanks, BEST fits in with and completes the meaning of the sentence as a whole.

1. The rising tide of feminism promised equality to all, regardless of – – –, but she found, as an older woman newly returned to the arena, that her experience and skills were only – – – marketable.

   (a) race . . . inversely
   (b) ability . . . retroactively
   (c) legalisms . . . commercially
   (d) opposition . . . fortuitously
   (e) gender . . . minimally

2. We were taken aback when we learned of his defection, never having suspected that he was anything but loyal, so credible had been his – – – of fidelity and devotion to the cause.

   (a) vociferation
   (b) intimation
   (c) dissimulation
   (d) presumption
   (e) presentiment

3. Abstemious by virtue of his upbringing, he was ill-equipped to cope with temptation, and his descent into gluttony and – – – was swift and – – –.

   (a) felony . . . rewarding
   (b) melancholy . . . mournful
   (c) dissipation . . . precipitous
   (d) telegony . . . merciful
   (e) barratry . . . final

4. Planning large-scale troop movements is fairly routine—you learn about – – – in Officer Candidate School; however, – – – of such movements is something you learn only through experience.

   (a) mobility . . . anticipation
   (b) logistics . . . implementation
   (c) clerical work . . . infiltration
   (d) strategy . . . levitation
   (e) demobilization . . . redeployment

5. He saw himself as a good Samaritan whose – – – advice and assistance, unsolicited though it was, would save us from our own stupidity and incompetence, but we saw him as an – – – meddler.

   (a) grudging . . . insuperable
   (b) intelligible . . . offensive
   (c) redundant . . . unnecessary
   (d) valuable . . . officious
   (e) sparing . . . officious

6. Utility industry leaders, in determining which of the various types of energy sources to develop, make their decision, in the privacy of the boardroom, on the basis of profitability, but publicly they – – – their choice on the basis of lowered rates and increased safety.

   (a) justify
   (b) camouflage
   (c) estimate
   (d) underwrite
   (e) replicate

7. As the FAA investigation of the plane crash revealed, the ground-crew work schedule was so crowded that they could not have conducted more than the most – – – of preflight inspections of the ill-fated aircraft prior to takeoff.

   (a) peremptory
   (b) obvious
   (c) repetitive
   (d) cursory
   (e) thoroughgoing

In each of the questions below, a related pair of words or phrases in capital letters is followed by five pairs of words or phrases lettered from (a) to (e). Select that lettered pair that expresses a relationship that is MOST similar to that of the capitalized pair.

8. CHEERFUL : EUPHORIC : : (a) frenzied : excited
   (b) artificial : artful (c) luscious : delicious
   (d) credible : incredible (e) sorrowful : lugubrious

9. LITMUS : ACID : : (a) oral : intelligence
(b) investigation : suspect (c) gauntlet : ordeal
(d) fingerprint : evidence (e) polygraph : truth

10. DECEIT : OPPROBRIUM : : (a) rectitude : esteem
(b) conceit : insufferable (c) obsession : fixation
(d) forebearance : aversion (e) heresy : disillusion

11. RELUCTANT : PERSUASION : : (a) irate : antagonism
(b) contemplative : meditative (c) vision : acuity
(d) loath : coercion (e) detest : caressing

12. QUIBBLE : AMBIGUITY : : (a) scribble : clarity
(b) nitpick : pettiness (c) perjure : unreliability
(d) babble : prattling (e) squelch : harness

13. ENTOURAGE : ATTENDANT : : (a) factory : assembler
(b) claque : sycophant (c) cortege : funeral
(d) minion : follower (e) myrmidon : hatchet man

14. DISTASTEFUL : ODIOUS : : (a) habitual : occasional
(b) febrile : debilitated (c) fond : devoted
(d) incapacitated : limpid (e) coarse : unrefined

15. QUENCH : THIRST : : (a) slake : amusement
(b) quell : rebellion (c) penetrate : disguise
(d) drub : deponent (e) intensify : search

16. DESICCANT : DEHYDRATES : : (a) ship : navigator
(b) producer : orchestra : (c) prevaricator : lies
(d) promulgator : intercedes (e) vesicant : ameliorates

In the series of selections that follows, each passage is followed by questions based on its content. Read the passage and choose the best answer for each question based on the contents of the passage. The questions must be answered on the basis of what is stated or implied in the reading passage.

A majority taken collectively may be regarded as a being whose opinions and, most frequently, whose interests are opposed to those of another being, which is styled a minority. If it is admitted that a man, possessing absolute power, may misuse that power by wronging his adversaries, why should a majority not be liable to the same reproach? Men are not apt to change their characters by agglomeration; nor does their patience in the presence of obstacles increase with the consciousness of their strength. For these reasons we should not willingly invest any group of our fellows with that unlimited authority which we should refuse to any individual.

One social power must always predominate over others; but liberty is endangered when this power is checked by no obstacles which may retard its course and force it to moderate its own vehemence. Unlimited power is, in itself, a bad and dangerous thing, and no power on earth is so worthy of honor for itself or of reverential obedience to the rights which it represents, that we should admit its uncontrolled and all-predominant authority. When the right and the means of absolute command are conferred on a people or a king, upon an aristocracy or a democracy, a monarchy or a republic, there has been implanted the germ of tyranny.

The main evil of the present democratic institutions of the United States does not arise, as is often asserted in Europe, from their weakness, but from their overpowering strength; the excessive liberty which reigns in that country is not so alarming as is the very inadequate security which exists against tyranny.

When an individual or a party is wronged in the United States, to whom can he apply for redress? If to public opinion, public opinion constitutes the majority; if to the legislature, it represents the majority, and implicitly obeys its injunctions; if to the executive power, it is appointed by the majority, and remains a passive tool in its hands; the public troops consist of the majority under arms; the jury is the majority invested with the right of hearing judicial cases; and in certain states even the judges are elected by the majority. However iniquitous or absurd the evil complained about, no sure barrier is established to defend against it.

17. Of the following statements or phrases, the one which best summarizes the meaning of the passage is

   (a) the tyranny of the majority
   (b) democracy, the triumph of the people
   (c) the pluralist way to govern
   (d) the ballot box and the bullet
   (e) the absolute monarchy versus the silent majority

18. The statement that is supported by the passage is that

   (a) majority rule safeguards the rights of all the people
   (b) individual liberty is incompatible with government
   (c) majority rule, even under a democracy, should have some checks on its power
   (d) no government should be trusted since all governments are equally tyrannical
   (e) minority rule would probably be more responsive to the needs of all the people.

19. According to the author,

    (*a*) the main trouble with the United States is the weakness of its government

    (*b*) the legislature not only represents the governed but also obeys their mandates, which is why it can be responsive to complaints

    (*c*) one social power must always predominate over others, and for that reason there is no point in providing checks and balances in government

    (*d*) excessive liberty in the United States is the major cause for alarm about government under majority rule

    (*e*) the trouble with our government is that nothing holds the majority in check

There is widespread belief that the emergence of giant industries has been accomplished by an equivalent surge in industrial research. A recent study of important inventions made since the turn of the century reveals that more than half were the product of individual inventors working alone, independent of organized industrial research. While industrial laboratories contributed such important products as nylon and transistors, independent inventors developed air conditioning, the automatic transmission, the jet engine, the helicopter, insulin, and streptomycin. Still other inventions, such as stainless steel, television, silicons, and plexiglass were developed through the combined efforts of individuals and laboratory teams.

Despite these findings, we are urged to support monopoly power on the grounds that such power creates an environment supportive of innovation. We are told that the independent inventor, along with the small firm, cannot afford to undertake the important research needed to improve our standard of living while protecting our diminishing resources; that only the prodigious assets of the giant corporation or conglomerate can afford the kind of expenditures that can produce the technological advances vital to economic progress. But when we examine expenditures for research, we find that of the more than $35 billion spent each year in this country, almost two-thirds is spent by the federal government. More than half of this government expenditure is funneled into military research and product development, accounting for the enormous increase in spending in such industries as nuclear energy, aircraft, missiles, and electronics. There are those who consider it questionable that these defense-linked research projects will account for an improvement in the standard of living or, alternately, do much to protect our diminishing resources.

Recent history has demonstrated that we may have to alter our long-standing conception of the process actuated by competition. The price variable, once perceived as the dominant aspect of the competitive process is now subordinate to the competition of the new product, the new business structure, and the new technology. While it can be assumed that in a highly competitive industry not dominated by a single corporation, investment in innovation—a risky and expensive budget item—might meet resistance from management and stockholders who might be more concerned with cost-cutting, efficient organization, and large advertising budgets, it would be an egregious error to assume that the monopolistic producer should be equated with bountiful expenditures for research. Large-scale enterprises tend to operate more comfortably in stable and secure circumstances, and their managerial bureaucracies tend to promote the status quo and resist the threat implicit in change. Furthermore, the firm with a small share of the market will aggressively pursue new techniques and different products, since with little vested interest in capital equipment or plant it is not deterred from investment in innovation. In some cases, where inter-industry competition is reduced or even entirely eliminated, the industrial giants may seek to avoid capital loss resulting from obsolescence by deliberately obstructing technological progress.

The conglomerates are not, however, completely exempt from strong competitive pressures; there are instances in which they, too, must compete, as against another industrial Goliath, and then their weapons may include large expenditures for innovation.

20. According to the passage, important inventions of the twentieth century

    (a) are not necessarily produced as a result of governmental support for military weapons research and development
    (b) came primarily from the huge laboratories of monopoly industries
    (c) were produced at least as frequently by independent inventors as by research teams
    (d) have greater impact on smaller firms than on conglomerates
    (e) sometimes adversely affect our standard of living and diminish our natural resources

21. It is the author's belief, as expressed or implied in the passage, that

    (a) monopoly power creates an environment supportive of innovation
    (b) governmental protection for military research will do much to protect our dwindling resources
    (c) industrial giants, with their managerial bureaucracies, respond more quickly to technological change
    (d) firms with a small share of the market will aggressively pursue innovations because they are not locked into old capital equipment
    (e) the independent inventor cannot afford to undertake the research needed to improve our standard of living

22. Management and stockholders might be deeply concerned with cost-cutting rather than innovation if

(a) their company is faced with strong competition in a field not dominated by one of the industrial giants

(b) they are very stable and secure and hold a monopoly position in their industry

(c) they are part of the military-industrial complex and are the recipients of federal funds for product development

(d) they have produced some of the important inventions of this century

(e) they have little vested interest in capital equipment or plant

23. It can be inferred from the passage that the author

(a) has little confidence in the ability of monopolistic industry to produce the important inventions of the future

(b) would rather see the federal government spend money on social services than on the defense establishment

(c) favors a conservative approach to innovation and places trust in conglomerates to provide efficient production

(d) while admitting that more than half the important inventions of the century were produced by independent inventors, feels that the future lies in the hands of giant industry

(e) believes spinoffs from defense-linked research will account for an improvement in future inventions

24. The amount of money spent by the federal government for non-military research and product development is

(a) more than $36 billion each year

(b) approximately $24 billion each year

(c) more than $18 billion each year

(d) more than $12 billion each year

(e) less than $12 billion each year

25. Which of the following statements is neither expressed nor implied in the passage?

(a) Important inventions have been produced, in the past, by individuals as well as by corporate teams.

(b) The federal government's research funds are funneled into pure research as well as military research.

(c) The development of the automatic transmission is not credited to organized industrial research.

(d) Industrial giants may deliberately suppress innovations to avoid capital loss resulting from obsolescence.

(e) When faced with competition from another monopolistic industrial power, the giant corporation may allot large sums of money for the development of innovations.

26. The author's purpose in this passage is to

   (a) advocate an increase in governmental support of organized industrial research
   (b) point out a common misconception about the relationship between the extent of industrial research and the growth of monopolistic power in industry
   (c) describe the inadequacies of small firms in dealing with the important matter of research and innovation
   (d) show that America's strength depends upon individual ingenuity and resourcefulness
   (e) encourage free market competition among industrial giants

27. Which of the following best supports the thesis that industrial giants do not best serve to provide the innovation we need to improve our standard of living and protect our diminishing resources?

   (a) More than half the important inventions made since the turn of the century were the product of individual inventors working alone, independent of organized industrial research.
   (b) More than half the government expenditure for research goes to military research.
   (c) The missile industry is one that benefits from government spending for research.
   (d) Large-scale enterprises tend to operate more comfortably in stable and secure circumstances.
   (e) Conglomerates are not completely exempt from strong competitive pressures.

In each of the following questions, a capitalized word is followed by five words or phrases lettered (a) through (e). Select the word or phrase most nearly OPPOSITE in meaning to the capitalized word.

Since some of the questions require that you distinguish fine shades of meaning, consider all choices carefully before you select your answer.

28. CHICANERY

   (a) porcelain
   (b) vegetation
   (c) probity
   (d) tomfoolery
   (e) meekness

29. PROPINQUITY

   (a) mystery
   (b) remoteness
   (c) delight
   (d) annoyance
   (e) presence

30. CHOLERIC

   (a) placid
   (b) ill
   (c) faint
   (d) monotonous
   (e) unfriendly

31. TRANQUIL

   (a) tumultuous
   (b) willing
   (c) wayward
   (d) wonted
   (e) lucid

32. MUNIFICENT

(*a*) indigenous
(*b*) slimy
(*c*) mercenary
(*d*) perspicuous
(*e*) parsimonious

33. SPURIOUS

(*a*) willful
(*b*) unambitious
(*c*) authentic
(*d*) antipathetic
(*e*) staid

34. IMPALPABLE

(*a*) touchy
(*b*) discursive
(*c*) relenting
(*d*) tangible
(*e*) virginal

35. PARAMOUNT

(*a*) magnetic
(*b*) subordinate
(*c*) subject
(*d*) lover
(*e*) important

36. DEROGATE

(*a*) acclaim
(*b*) yield
(*c*) empower
(*d*) withhold
(*e*) correspond

37. CONTRAVENE

(*a*) disclaim
(*b*) extirpate
(*c*) efface
(*d*) uphold
(*e*) condemn

38. MORBID

(*a*) deflated
(*b*) insensate
(*c*) replete
(*d*) vigorous
(*e*) wholesome

STOP! Work only on this section until the time allowed is over.

SECTION III

Time—30 minutes
30 Questions

The following questions each consist of two quantities, one in Column A and one in Column B. Compare the two quantities and on the answer sheet blacken oval

    (*a*) if the quantity in Column A is greater;
    (*b*) if the quantity in Column B is greater;
    (*c*) if the two quantities are equal;
    (*d*) if the relationship cannot be determined from the information given.

All letters such as x, y and n represent real numbers. A symbol appearing in both columns represents the same quantity in Column A as it does in Column B.

In some questions, information concerning one or both of the quantities to be compared is centered above the two columns.

Figures are generally not drawn to scale, unless otherwise stated. You may assume these figures lie in a plane, unless it is indicated they represent solid figures.

Lines that appear to be straight may be assumed to be straight lines.

Column A	**Column B**
1. 30% of 40	40% of 30

2.
$$n < 0$$

Column A	Column B
$(3n)^2$	$3n^2$

3.

Radius of circle O	Chord of circle O

4. $\sqrt{8.5}$	$\sqrt[3]{28.2}$

5.

3g   4h

g	h

	Column A	**Column B**

6. The sale price of an $80 radio after a 30% discount | The sale price of an $80 radio after successive discounts of 20% and 10%

---

7. $$3x + 4y = 12$$

x | | y

8.

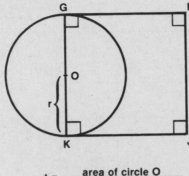

$$t = \frac{\text{area of circle O}}{\text{area of square GHJK}}$$

t | | 3/4

---

9. **A regular n-sided polygon**

The number of degrees in each interior angle of the polygon | The number of degrees in each exterior angle of the polygon

---

10.

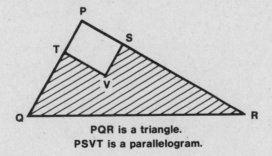

PQR is a triangle.
PSVT is a parallelogram.

Perimeter of PQR | | Perimeter of shaded region

Column A	**Column B**

11.

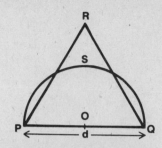

PQR is an equilateral triangle.
PSQ is a semicircle of diameter d.

Area of triangle	Area of semicircle

12. The number of prime factors of 330 | The number of prime factors of 210

13.

$$\frac{p}{7} = \frac{7}{p}$$

$$p < 0$$

$\dfrac{p}{14}$ | $\dfrac{-1}{7}$

14.

$$rst = 0, r > s$$

rt | st

15. y^2 | $y(y + 2)$

Solve each of the following problems based on the information provided. Then indicate the best answer on your answer sheet.

16. If $y + 2/7 = 5/7$, then $y + 1/7 =$

(a) 3/7
(b) 4/7
(c) 5/7
(d) 1
(e) 8/7

17. What is the greatest positive integer that is less than $\sqrt{340}$?

   (a) 15
   (b) 16
   (c) 17
   (d) 18
   (e) 19

18. If p is equal to 11,793 rounded to the nearest thousand and q is 11,793 rounded to the nearest hundred, then p – q is equal to

   (a) 0
   (b) 100
   (c) 200
   (d) 300
   (e) 2000

19. Point R is on one side of a square and point S is on the opposite side. If the perimeter of the square is 36, what is the longest possible length of RS?

   (a) 8
   (b) 9
   (c) $9\sqrt{3}$
   (d) $5\sqrt{2}$
   (e) $9\sqrt{2}$

20. A produce salesman sells apples for 20¢ each and oranges for 25¢ each. If he sells $4.00 worth of apples and oranges, what is the least amount of apples he could have sold? (Zero is not an answer.)

   (a) 2
   (b) 3
   (c) 4
   (d) 5
   (e) 6

Questions 21–24 are based on the following graph:

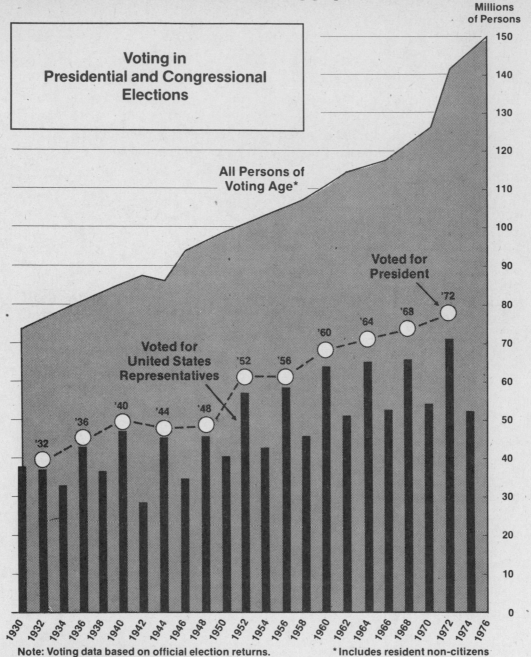

Voting in Presidential and Congressional Elections

Millions of Persons

All Persons of Voting Age*

Voted for President

'72

Voted for United States Representatives

'32 '36 '40 '44 '48 '52 '56 '60 '64 '68

Note: Voting data based on official election returns.

* Includes resident non-citizens

21. What percent of those who voted for President in 1972 voted for a member of the House?

    (*a*) 90%
    (*b*) 80%
    (*c*) 70%
    (*d*) 60%
    (*e*) 50%

22. Which two successive elections showed the largest fall-off of voting for Representatives from a Presidential year to the next election?

   (a) 1956–1958
   (b) 1960–1962
   (c) 1964–1966
   (d) 1968–1970
   (e) 1972–1974

23. Which period experienced the largest growth of voting-age citizens?

   (a) 1966–1968
   (b) 1968–1970
   (c) 1970–1972
   (d) 1972–1974
   (e) 1974–1976

24. What percent of the eligible population voted for President in 1964?

   (a) 47%
   (b) 52%
   (c) 57%
   (d) 63%
   (e) 69%

25. If the circumference of a circle is numerically equal to the area of the circle, the circumference of the circle is

   (a) 4
   (b) 2π
   (c) $\pi\sqrt{2}$
   (d) π
   (e) 4π

26. In which of the following expressions can the 5's be cancelled out without changing the value of the expression?

   (a) $\dfrac{p^5}{q^5}$

   (b) $\dfrac{5p - q}{5}$

   (c) $\dfrac{\dfrac{p}{5}}{\dfrac{5}{q}}$

   (d) $\dfrac{5p^2 + 5q^2}{5}$

   (e) $5p + 5q$

27. Peter lives 3 miles south of the school. Bill, who lives west of the school, finds that the direct distance from his house to Peter's is 1 mile shorter than the distance by way of the school. How many miles west of the school does Bill live?

(a) 3/4
(b) 1¼
(c) 1¾
(d) 2¼
(e) 11

28. If r>s and s>t, which of the following represents the smallest number?

(a) t – r
(b) r – t
(c) s – t
(d) s – r
(e) t – s

29.

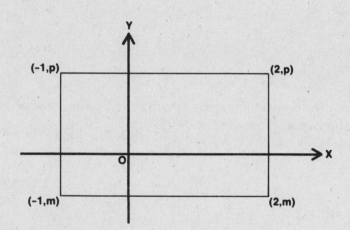

The area of the rectangle in the above figure is

(a) p – m
(b) 3(p – m)
(c) 3(p + m)
(d) p + m
(e) 3(m – p)

30.

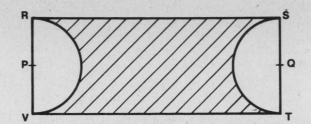

Given rectangle RSTV with semicircles P and Q with diameters of 10, as shown above. If TV = 25, what is the area of the shaded region?

(a) $250 - 20\pi$

(b) $250 - 50\pi$

(c) 225π

(d) $250 - 25\pi$

(e) $250 - \dfrac{25\pi}{2}$

STOP! Work only on this section until the time allowed is over.

Time—30 minutes
30 Questions

The following questions each consist of two quantities, one in Column A and one in Column B. Compare the two quantities and on the answer sheet blacken oval

(*a*) if the quantity in Column A is greater;
(*b*) if the quantity in Column B is greater;
(*c*) if the two quantities are equal;
(*d*) if the relationship cannot be determined from the information given.

All letters such as x, y and n represent real numbers. A symbol appearing in both columns represents the same quantity in Column A as it does in Column B.

In some questions, information concerning one or both of the quantities to be compared is centered above the two columns.

Figures are generally not drawn to scale, unless otherwise stated. You may assume these figures lie in a plane, unless it is indicated they represent solid figures.

Lines that appear to be straight may be assumed to be straight lines.

Column A	**Column B**

Questions 1–3 refer to the figure below.

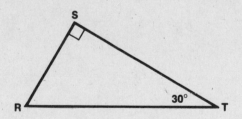

1. RS	ST
2. RS	1/2 RT
3. ST	3/4 RT

Column A	Column B

Questions 4–11 refer to the figure below.

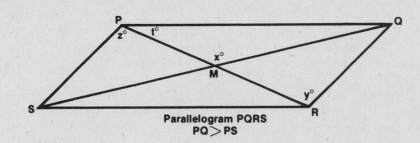

Parallelogram PQRS
PQ > PS

4. Area of △ PMS	Area of △ PMQ
5. RQ	RS
6. x	y
7. y	z
8. t	y
9. Area of △ PQM	1/3 area of PQRS
10. PR	PQ – QR
11. x + t	150

---

12. Number of seconds in 1 day	Number of hours in 20 years

13.
$$\frac{r}{s} = \frac{2}{5} \qquad \frac{s}{t} = \frac{3}{4}$$

1/3	$\frac{r}{t}$

---

14. Four times the surface area of a cube of edge 3	The surface area of a cube of edge 6

15.
$$2r + 5s = 12$$

r	s

Solve each of the following problems based on the information provided. Then indicate the best answer on your answer sheet.

Questions 16–19 refer to the following graph.

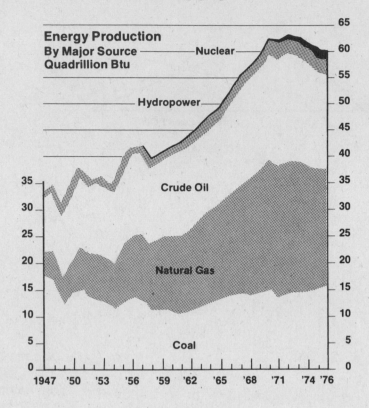

Energy Production By Major Source Quadrillion Btu

16. Approximately how many quadrillion Btu of natural gas were produced in 1967?

    (a) 6
    (b) 10
    (c) 14
    (d) 18
    (e) 22

17. In 1976 approximately what percent of total energy production was from crude oil?

    (a) 10%
    (b) 20%
    (c) 30%
    (d) 40%
    (e) 50%

18. The percent increase in total energy production in 1976 over the total energy production in 1962 is approximately:

    (a) 20%
    (b) 35%

(c) 42%
(d) 45%
(e) 50%

19. Which energy source experienced the greatest increase in production over the years shown on the graph?

(a) Nuclear
(b) Hydropower
(c) Crude oil
(d) Natural gas
(e) Coal

20. The degree measures of the three angles of a triangle are x, y and z. If z is the average of x and y, find the value of z.

(a) 20
(b) 40
(c) 60
(d) 90
(e) It cannot be determined from the information given.

21. A boy starts mowing a lawn at 10 A.M. and by 11:20 A.M. has finished 4/5 of it. If he continues working at the same rate, at what time will he finish mowing the lawn?

(a) 11:36 A.M.
(b) 11:40 A.M.
(c) 11:52 A.M.
(d) 12:00 noon
(e) 12:40 P.M.

Questions 22 and 23 refer to the following graphs.

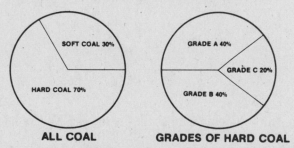

ALL COAL   GRADES OF HARD COAL

22. The graphs above show the distribution of coal production in a certain state. The graph on the left shows the percentages of hard and soft coal, and that on the right shows the distribution of grades of hard coal. What percent of the total production was Grade B hard coal?

(a) 14%
(b) 21%
(c) 28%
(d) 34%
(e) 40%

23. In the circle graph on the left, how many degrees are there in the central angle of the sector for soft coal?

   (a) 108
   (b) 120
   (c) 144
   (d) 160
   (e) 252

24. If a theatre ticket including a 15% tax costs $11.50, then the amount of the tax is

   (a) $.77
   (b) $1.00
   (c) $1.15
   (d) $1.50
   (e) $1.72

25. A cubic centimeter of a certain metal weighs 10 grams. What is the weight in grams of a cube of this metal that is 2 centimeters on each edge?

   (a) 20
   (b) 40
   (c) 50
   (d) 60
   (e) 80

26. N is 5% of

   (a) $\dfrac{N}{20}$
   (b) 5N
   (c) 20N
   (d) $\dfrac{N}{5}$
   (e) 10N

27. At which of the following times will the hands of a clock form an angle of exactly 120°?

   (a) 12:20
   (b) 12:40
   (c) 8:20
   (d) 4:00
   (e) All of the above

28. In the senior class of a certain high school, 140 students study French and 180 study Spanish. If 60 students study both French and Spanish, what is the ratio of the number of students taking Spanish only to the number taking French only?

   (a) 3:2
   (b) 2:1
   (c) 9:7
   (d) 4:3
   (e) 5:3

29. A box contains marbles of three different colors. What is the *least* number of marbles a blindfolded person must pick to be sure that she has at *least four* of the same color?

   (a) 4
   (b) 7
   (c) 9
   (d) 10
   (e) 13

30. A motorist drives 60 miles to the next town at 40 miles per hour and returns at 30 miles per hour. What is his average speed for the round trip in miles per hour?

   (a) $32\frac{3}{7}$

   (b) $34\frac{2}{7}$

   (c) 35
   (d) 37

   (e) $37\frac{1}{2}$

STOP! Work only on this section until the time allowed is over.

SECTION V

Time— 30 minutes
25 Questions

A written passage or set of statements precedes each question or group of questions in this section. Choose the best answer to each question. For some questions you may find it useful to draw a diagram, graph, or other problem-solving aid.

Questions 1–4 refer to the following:

Students in the first year at a particular school may choose from among the following courses: Mathematics; psychology; chemistry or physics, but not both; and French or Spanish, but not both.

A first-year student must also take exactly two of the following three courses: English, history, and sociology.

1. According to the rules listed above, what is the maximum number of courses a first-year student can take?

   (a) six
   (b) seven
   (c) eight
   (d) nine
   (e) ten

2. If a first-year student takes math, physics, and psychology and wishes to take a total of six courses, how many possible combinations of courses can she choose from?

   (a) three
   (b) four
   (c) five
   (d) six
   (e) seven

3. If a first-year student takes mathematics, English, and history and wants to take a total of five courses, how many possible combinations of courses can he choose from?

   (a) four
   (b) five
   (c) six
   (d) seven
   (e) eight

4. A first-year pre-med student wishes to take a total of only three courses. Which courses may she not take together?

   (a) chemistry and English
   (b) sociology and physics
   (c) history and English
   (d) psychology and sociology
   (e) French and psychology

Questions 5–7 refer to the following:

   The earth's resources are being depleted much too fast. To correct this, the United States must keep its resource consumption at present levels for many years to come.

5. The argument above is based on the assumption that

   (a) the world should not increase its present rate of resource consumption
   (b) the United States wastes resources
   (c) the United States uses more resources than any other country
   (d) the United States imports most of the resources it uses
   (e) curbing United States resource consumption will significantly retard world resource depletion

6. The argument would be most strengthened if it were pointed out that

   (a) new resource deposits are constantly being discovered
   (b) the United States uses one-third of all resources used in the world
   (c) other countries need economic development more than the United States does
   (d) other countries have agreed to hold their resource consumption at present levels
   (e) the United States has been conserving resources for several years already

7. The argument would be most weakened if it were pointed out that

   (a) through exploration and technology, using resources can lead to finding more resources
   (b) resources such as oil are irreplaceable
   (c) other countries than the United States waste resources
   (d) an economy cannot survive without using resources
   (e) the United States population is bound to increase in the foreseeable future, and each additional person will consume resources

Questions 8–11 refer to the following:

Seven people seat themselves at two round tables.
    (1) Arthur is next to Caryn.
    (2) Bertha is directly to Glenda's left.
    (3) Don is not next to Bertha.
    (4) Caryn is not at the same table as Fred.
    (5) Fred is not next to Bertha.
    (6) Don is not next to Arthur.
    (7) Bertha is not at Arthur's table.
    (8) Edward is also seated.

8. How many people may be at Arthur's table?

    I. 2
   II. 3
   III. 4

    (a) I only
    (b) III only
    (c) I or II only
    (d) II or III only
    (e) I, II, or III

9. How many different seating combinations are possible, given the conditions above?

    (a) 1
    (b) 2
    (c) 3
    (d) 4
    (e) 6

10. Which of the following is implied by the conditions given?

    (a) Don is next to Glenda.
    (b) Edward is next to Arthur.
    (c) Fred is next to Glenda.
    (d) Edward is next to Bertha.
    (e) Edward is next to Glenda.

11. Which person could leave his or her table without causing any contradiction of the given conditions?

    (a) Arthur
    (b) Bertha
    (c) Edward
    (d) Fred
    (e) Caryn

Questions 12–17 refer to the following:

There are six baseball teams in a league.
The Acorns have better pitching and worse hitting than the Cavaliers.

The Browns have better pitching than the Acorns and worse hitting than the Engineers.

The Cavaliers have worse pitching and worse hitting than the Fowls.

The Diamonds have worse pitching and better hitting than the Cavaliers.

The Engineers have worse pitching than the Diamonds and worse hitting than the Acorns.

The Fowls have worse pitching than the Browns and worse hitting than the Diamonds.

12. Which team has the best pitching?

(a) The Acorns
(b) The Browns
(c) The Cavaliers
(d) The Diamonds
(e) The Fowls

13. Which team has the worst hitting?

(a) The Acorns
(b) The Browns
(c) The Cavaliers
(d) The Engineers
(e) The Fowls

14. Which of the following teams has (have) both better pitching and worse hitting than the Cavaliers?

 I. Acorns
 II. Fowls
III. Browns

(a) I only
(b) II only
(c) I and III only
(d) II and III only
(e) I, II, and III

15. Which of the following teams has (have) both better pitching and worse hitting than the Fowls?

 I. Acorns
 II. Browns
III. Diamonds

(a) I only
(b) II only
(c) III only
(d) I and II only
(e) Neither I, II, nor III

16. Not enough information is provided to determine the relative strength of the pitching of which of the following pairs of teams?

    I. The Acorns and the Browns
   II. The Browns and the Fowls
  III. The Acorns and the Fowls

    (a) I only
    (b) II only
    (c) III only
    (d) II and III only
    (e) Neither I, II, nor III

17. Not enough information is provided to determine the relative strength of the hitting of which of the following pairs of teams?

    I. The Acorns and the Engineers
   II. The Acorns and the Cavaliers
  III. The Engineers and the Fowls

    (a) I only
    (b) II only
    (c) III only
    (d) I and II only
    (e) Neither I, II, nor III

Questions 18–23 refer to the following:

There were three sheep (A, B, C), each on a different ranch (X, Y, Z) with a different owner (D, E, F). One night, each sheep was killed on its owner's ranch by a different wolf (1, 2, 3). The three owners hunted the wolves, and each killed one wolf.

    (1) Sheep A was not on ranch X.
    (2) Wolf 2 killed sheep B.
    (3) Owner D killed wolf 1.
    (4) No owner killed the wolf that killed his own sheep.
    (5) Sheep C was killed on ranch Y.
    (6) Owner D owned sheep A.
    (7) Owner E did not kill the wolf that killed sheep C.

18. It can be inferred from the information presented that

    (a) sheep A was on ranch Z
    (b) sheep C belonged to owner E
    (c) wolf 1 killed sheep A
    (d) wolf 1 killed the sheep on ranch X
    (e) sheep B belonged to owner F

19. Which of the following relationships can be inferred from the information given?

I. Owner D killed the wolf that killed sheep C.
II. Wolf 2 killed the sheep on ranch Z.
III. Owner E killed wolf 2.

(a) I only
(b) III only
(c) I and II only
(d) II and III only
(e) I, II, and III

20. Which of the following statements is inconsistent with the information presented?

(a) Owner E owned sheep B.
(b) Wolf 2 killed the sheep on ranch Y.
(c) Wolf 3 killed sheep A.
(d) Owner F killed wolf 3.
(e) Sheep B lived on ranch X.

21. Which of the following statements, if true, would provide additional information concerning the relationships being described?

I. Owner F did not own ranch Z.
II. Wolf 1 killed the sheep on ranch Y.
III. Owner E owned sheep B.

(a) I only
(b) II only
(c) III only
(d) II and III only
(e) Neither I, II, nor III

22. Which of the following statements is (are) correct?

I. If owner E owned sheep B, then owner F owned ranch Y.
II. If owner F killed wolf 3, then he owned sheep B.
III. If owner E killed wolf 2, then he owned ranch X.

(a) I only
(b) III only
(c) I and II only
(d) II and III only
(e) I, II, and III

23. Which of the numbered statements provides the *least* information concerning the relationships being described?

(a) 1
(b) 2
(c) 3
(d) 6
(e) 7

24. Most people who eat fatty foods get heart disease. If Alan does not eat fatty foods, he will not get heart disease.

   The argument above assumes that

   (a) heavier people are more susceptible to heart disease than lighter people
   (b) cholesterol is the major cause of heart disease
   (c) the major cause of heart disease is the eating of fatty foods
   (d) people suffering from heart disease should reduce their intake of fatty foods
   (e) Alan has enough will power to control his intake of fatty foods

25. If interest rates drop, stock market prices increase.

   The statement above is logically equivalent to which of the following statements?

   (a) If stock market prices increase, interest rates drop.
   (b) If interest rates do not drop, stock market prices do not increase.
   (c) If interest rates do not drop, stock market prices decrease.
   (d) If stock market prices do not increase, interest rates do not drop.
   (e) If interest rates rise, stock market prices decrease.

   STOP! Work only on this section until the time allowed is over.

SECTION VI

Time—30 minutes
25 Questions

A written passage or set of statements precedes each question or group of questions in this section. Choose the best answer to each question. For some questions you may find it useful to draw a diagram, graph, or other problem-solving aid.

Questions 1–3 refer to the following:

A certain science test yields scores that are multiples of 5, ranging from 50 to 100 with a passing grade of 70. The letters Q, R, S, T, and U represent five different passing grades.

Q is 10 points higher than R.
R is 5 points higher than T.
S is 5 points lower than T.
U is 10 points lower than T.

1. What is the correct order of the scores from highest to lowest?

   (a) QTRSU
   (b) RQTSU
   (c) QRTUS
   (d) QSRTU
   (e) QRTSU

2. V is a passing score not equal to any of the above scores. V may fall between scores

   (a) Q and R
   (b) R and T
   (c) T and S
   (d) S and U
   (e) R and S

3. W is a passing score not equal to any of the above scores, which differs from U by 5. W must equal

   (a) 90
   (b) 85
   (c) 80
   (d) 75
   (e) 70

Questions 4–5 refer to the following:

Medical costs have been rising so fast that the country must control them. The only way to do this is to make government responsible for providing all health care.

4. The argument above has as its logical basis which of the following assumptions?

    I. Of all costs, medical costs have been rising fastest.
   II. All citizens are entitled to medical care.
  III. The private sector cannot control medical costs.

    (a) I only
    (b) II only
    (c) III only
    (d) I and II only
    (e) II and III only

5. Of the following, the most effective rebuttal to the argument would be which of the following statements? (Assume the statement's truth.)

    (a) Doctor's fees have not been responsible for most of the increase in medical costs.
    (b) Medical costs have been rising in countries in which the government provides all health care.
    (c) Some private medical insurance plans have kept costs relatively stable.
    (d) Most people are now satisfied with the quality of their medical care.
    (e) The government-owned railroad system loses money.

Questions 6–9 refer to the following:

Five cowboys and five Indians are on opposite sides of a river. Each group wishes to cross to the other side. The only available means of transportation is a canoe that holds no more than three people. Since the cowboys fear the Indians, at no time can the Indians outnumber the cowboys either on one side or in the canoe. Equal numbers of cowboys and Indians are permissible.

When considering possible solutions, ignore consecutive repetitive moves, such as an Indian initially crossing over and then crossing right back by himself.

6. Which of the following is a possible first crossing?

    I. One Indian
    II. Two cowboys
    III. Three Indians

    (a) I only
    (b) III only
    (c) I and II only
    (d) II and III only
    (e) I, II, and III

7. Which of the following must be true in all possible solutions?

    I. The first crossing involves the Indians.
    II. The second crossing involves no cowboys.
    III. The final crossing involves only Indians.

    (a) I only
    (b) III only
    (c) I and III only
    (d) II and III only
    (e) I, II, and III

8. If the final crossing involves only two Indians, then the next-to-final crossing could involve

    (a) one cowboy
    (b) two cowboys
    (c) three cowboys
    (d) one cowboy and two Indians
    (e) two cowboys and one Indian

9. Suppose the first three crossings are: 1) two Indians; 2) three cowboys; 3) one Indian, one cowboy. What is the minimum number of further crossings that would complete the exchange satisfactorily?

    (a) 1
    (b) 2
    (c) 3
    (d) 4
    (e) 6

Questions 10–15 refer to the following:

Three-person work crews are to be chosen from among two groups totaling seven people. Group I consists of A, B, C, and D. Group II consists of E, F, and G. Each group must have at least one representative in any possible work crew. Also,

(1) C refuses to work unless E works.
(2) If A works, then F works.
(3) G will not work if A works.
(4) If C does not work, then B does not work.

10. Which of the following crews may *not* be assembled?

    I. A, C, E
   II. A, F, G
  III. B, D, G

(a) I only
(b) III only
(c) I and II only
(d) II and III only
(e) I, II, and III

11. A crew containing A may also contain

(a) E and F
(b) B and C
(c) D and G
(d) C and E
(e) B and F

12. Which of the following *cannot* work with A?

(a) B
(b) C
(c) D
(d) E
(e) F

13. Which of the following statements are true?

    I. If B works, then E works.
   II. If B works, then D does not work.
  III. C may work with E and F.

(a) I only
(b) III only
(c) I and II only
(d) II and III only
(e) I, II, and III

14. A crew containing F and G could also contain which of the following?

    I. B
   II. C
  III. D

    (*a*) I only
    (*b*) III only
    (*c*) I and II only
    (*d*) II and III only
    (*e*) I, II, and III

15. How many different crews may be assembled according to the conditions given?

    (*a*) 5
    (*b*) 6
    (*c*) 7
    (*d*) 8
    (*e*) 9

Questions 16–21 refer to the following:

(1) Nine cards are arranged in a square in such a way that there are three rows and three columns of three cards each.
(2) The cards are numbered 1–9.
(3) Two cards are considered adjacent only if they are in the same row or column.
(4) All rows add to 15.
(5) 5 is in the center.
(6) 9 is in the same row as 5.
(7) 6 is next to 1.
(8) 4 is in the same column as 9.
(9) Both diagonals add to 15.

16. Which cards must be adjacent?

    (*a*) 1 and 3
    (*b*) 3 and 7
    (*c*) 5 and 2
    (*d*) 5 and 1
    (*e*) 2 and 3

17. Which cards cannot be adjacent?

    (*a*) 5 and 4
    (*b*) 3 and 8
    (*c*) 4 and 8
    (*d*) 6 and 7
    (*e*) 6 and 1

18. The middle column *cannot* add to

    I. 10
    II. 15
    III. 20

    (a) I only
    (b) III only
    (c) I and II only
    (d) I and III only
    (e) II and III only

19. If the column with 6 in it adds to 10, which of the following must be false?

    (a) 6 is adjacent to 2.
    (b) 3 is adjacent to 8.
    (c) One of the columns adds to 20.
    (d) 6 is not next to 7.
    (e) 7 is in the middle column.

20. Which of the numbered statements could be omitted without affecting the total amount of information presented?

    I. Statement (7)
    II. Statement (8)
    III. Statement (9)

    (a) I only
    (b) III only
    (c) I and II only
    (d) II and III only
    (e) Neither I, II, nor III

21. If statement (8) were omitted, which of the following would be correct?

    (a) Both diagonals would still have to add to 15.
    (b) Either one or two diagonals would have to add to 15.
    (c) 7 could be adjacent to 4.
    (d) 4 could be in the same row as 6.
    (e) 3 could be in the same column as 9.

22. John is an economist, but since he does not have much money, he must not be very good at his job.

    The argument above would be most weakened if it were pointed out that

    (a) economists are often relatively poor at the beginning of their careers
    (b) many professors of economics have left lucrative positions in business
    (c) many good economists have lost money through imprudent investments in the stock market

(d) many psychiatrists are not mentally healthy

(e) one can be a good economist without being a good manager of one's personal finances

23. Do you believe that the present inefficient, inhumane welfare system should be replaced by one which meets the human and economic needs of the country and the welfare recipients?

In terms of its logical features, the question above most resembles which of the following?

(a) Do you believe that this beautiful ring is more attractive than that repulsive trinket?

(b) When will we wake up to the fact that it is time to start acting and stop talking?

(c) Do you think this beautiful weather will continue?

(d) Have you ever beaten your wife?

(e) If you get accepted to graduate school, will you attend?

24. All polar bears are said to be white. In support of this claim, I can look outdoors and count many objects that are not white and are also not polar bears. The fact that I live in Texas is immaterial.

The author of the argument above has assumed that

(a) personal examination of the evidence is preferable to any amount of second-hand learning

(b) the claim that all polar bears are white is identical to the claim that all non-white objects are not polar bears

(c) if a statement is true, it is true at all times and in all places

(d) even in Texas, polar bears may be studied in zoos and other scientific facilities

(e) indirect evidence is often the best or only way to demonstrate the truth of an assertion

25. Worldwide famines have always occurred in the past, which indicates that the present widespread abundance of food will not last forever.

Which of the following is not an implicit assumption of the speaker of the argument above?

(a) That which has been will continue to be.

(b) There is no specific evidence to suggest a global famine in the near future.

(c) Famines are purely evil in their effects on humanity.

(d) The future is predictable to at least a limited degree.

(e) A particular future occurrence may be predicted although its timing may be very obscure.

STOP! Work only on this section until the time allowed is over.

SECTION VII

Time—30 minutes
38 Questions

For each of the numbered questions in this section, choose the best answer according to the instructions, and blacken the correspondingly numbered blank space on the answer sheet.

Each of the sentences below has one or more blank spaces indicating where a word or words have been omitted. Each sentence is followed by five words or sets of words lettered from (a) to (e). Select the lettered word or set of words which, inserted to replace the blanks, BEST fits in with and completes the meaning of the sentence as a whole.

1. Defense department experts are asking for sizable budgetary increases for research and development, citing the – – – between our military capability and that of our potential enemies.

    (a) correlation
    (b) void
    (c) relationship
    (d) disparity
    (e) contrast

2. His opening remarks were bound to stir up great – – –, for he had, with great deliberation, taken an – – – position on the question of wage and price control.

    (a) controversy . . . unorthodox
    (b) interest . . . unintended
    (c) expectations . . . untoward
    (d) indifference . . . insidious
    (e) restraint . . . impartial

3. When the president reported to the nation on television, the picture he painted appeared – – – to his viewers as he somberly revealed the precarious position of our beleaguered troops.

    (a) optimistic
    (b) auspicious
    (c) ominous
    (d) believable
    (e) redundant

4. Contrary to the earlier beliefs of scientists, the sun is not an incandescent liquid mass that is rapidly – – – heat; rather, it is a body that runs on an almost – – – amount of atomic fuel.

(a) storing . . . unbelievable
(b) wasting . . . indefinite
(c) reducing . . . infinitesimal
(d) absorbing . . . exhausted
(e) radiating . . . infinite

5. Lester thought they were – – – when they embraced, but the rest of us thought they were genuinely – – – toward one another.

(a) extravagant . . . averse
(b) dissimulating . . . affectionate
(c) ridiculous . . . antagonistic
(d) sublimating . . . inadvertent
(e) embarrassed . . . discomposed

6. Psychological support, such as counseling or group therapy, is virtually as important an aspect of care for the severely disabled as – – –.

(a) preventive medicine
(b) surgery
(c) others
(d) physical rehabilitation
(e) analysis

7. Although the industrial revolution has undoubtedly – – – the standard of living of most of the westernized world and contributed much toward ending hunger and poverty in the highly industrialized nations, it has also – – – a Pandora's box of new ills that have poisoned the air, the land, and the sea and stripped the good earth of some of its goodness.

(a) improved . . . opened
(b) revised . . . devised
(c) raised . . . concealed
(d) impaired . . . exploded
(e) augmented . . . caused

In each of the questions below, a related pair of words or phrases in capital letters is followed by five pairs of words or phrases, lettered from (a) to (e). Select the lettered pair that expresses a relationship that is MOST similar to that of the capitalized pair.

8. RABBLE : PLEBEIAN : : (a) hoi polloi : aristocratic
(b) gentry : reentry (c) intelligentsia : elitist
(d) upper crust : flaky (e) commonality : sincere

9. RECAPITULATE : SYNOPSIZE : : (a) behead : sum up
(b) encumber : burden (c) reconcile : alienate
(d) inveterate : analyze (e) encapsulate : synthesis

10. EMBARRASS : HUMILIATE : :
    (*a*) embezzle : peculate (*b*) invest : speculate
    (*c*) inquire : ask (*d*) annoy : exasperate
    (*e*) whine : grumble

11. EXPLICATE : OBFUSCATE : :
    (*a*) precipitate : deliberate (*b*) ornate : ungulate
    (*c*) convey : accompany (*d*) verify : extract
    (*e*) liquidate : fluoridate

12. ARCHAEOLOGIST : ARTIFACTS : :
    (*a*) curator : museum (*b*) Mozart : symphonies
    (*c*) neurology : medicine (*d*) paleontologist : fossils
    (*e*) podiatrist : feet

13. ANESTHETIC : PAIN : : (*a*) pleasure : satisfaction
    (*b*) liniment : muscle (*c*) novocaine : extraction
    (*d*) insomniac : sleepiness (*e*) stimulant : sluggishness

14. PISTOL : HOLSTER : : (*a*) bracelet : wrist
    (*b*) lorgnette : purse (*c*) looseleaf : binder
    (*d*) thread : needle (*e*) sword : scabbard

15. CONSTELLATION : STAR : : (*a*) sun : orbit
    (*b*) limousine : cortege (*c*) rifleman : platoon
    (*d*) pride : lion (*e*) monopoly : cartel

16. CONTIGUOUS : REMOTE : : (*a*) nonchalant : excitable
    (*b*) tangential : askew (*c*) redolent : odoriferous
    (*d*) distant : nearer (*e*) congruent : similar

In the series of selections that follows, each passage is followed by questions based on its content. Read the passage and choose the best answer for each question based on the contents of the passage. The questions must be answered on the basis of what is stated or implied in the reading passage.

Most arguments about Dreiser's work center around the question of what is the overriding value in a work of art: content or form. His supporters, who included Frank Norris, H. L. Mencken, and even Nobelist Sinclair Lewis, maintained that his courageous truth-telling realism "cleared the trail from Victorian timidity in American fiction to honesty, boldness, and passion of life." They argued that his style, inelegant as it was, represented his subject more appropriately than genteel aestheticism would have done.

Dreiser's antagonists, chiefly critics who embraced the New Humanism, condemned his crude style and his choice of prosaic characters and mundane situations. They attacked his work as vulgar because he used commonplace subjects, and immoral because he questioned accepted values. Some of their animus can be attributed to sharp political differences between them and the writers of so-called proletarian literature, like Farrell, Steinbeck, and Dos Passos. These impassioned critics deplored what they deemed the crude anti-intellectualism of the naturalists. Others, like Kazin and Cowley, wrote about Dreiser's work as if it had emanated without thought, care, or design, mirroring reality and only, as if by accident, unconsciously reaching artistic heights.

The doctrinal dispute continues. The tradition, inherited by Dreiser from Defoe, appears in added strength and new forms in recent works of Truman Capote and Norman Mailer. Prisoners, picketers, slum children and their like become the protagonists of bestselling works, while gossamer tales of modern Brahmins are spun by Jamesian adherents.

17. The author mentions Truman Capote and Norman Mailer as writers who

(a) are exponents of the aesthetic approach to writing
(b) embrace the New Humanism
(c) have praised Dreiser, Farrell, and Steinbeck
(d) deplore the crude anti-intellectualism of the critics
(e) follow in the literary tradition of the naturalists

18. For which of the following did the New Humanists criticize Dreiser?

I. His gossamer tales of modern Brahmins
II. His immorality, as demonstrated by his relationships with proletarian writers
III. His sharp political differences with them

(a) I and II only
(b) II only
(c) none of the above
(d) II and III only
(e) III only

19. It can be inferred from the passage that the author

(a) disagrees with past criticism of Dreiser
(b) prefers style to bold, honest content
(c) admires Kazin and Cowley
(d) joins the New Humanists in characterizing Dreiser as crude
(e) feels that the tradition of Dreiser and Defoe is dead

In the study of language, it has been recognized that words used to convey sensory perceptions, feelings, and emotions carry no meaning of themselves. They can trigger feelings or sensations that the listener has experienced – not more than that. We know that the perception of color varies with light, background, and distance. What is green seen by a colorblind person? Which is the "real" color? Are we not, in asking that question, implying that color exists independent of the observer?

Similarly, when we characterize an individual or a social behavior as "good" or "bad," we are communicating the contention that this evaluation is absolute, objective, and unchanging. Yet it should be apparent that varying observers would present disparate evaluations. We may, then, attempt to win agreement by describing the behavior in question, offering criteria on which judgment was based, indicating that these criteria are personal. This communication style, the semanticist holds, will help bridge the gap between individuals and make it more likely that people will understand each other.

Students of language have experimented with the use of nonsymbolic language as a means of overcoming linguistic barriers. The language of sounds, as in the cases of infants and animals, and the language of facial expression and body pose, have been termed "phatic communion" by Bronislaw Malinowski. We all know people who have good "poker faces." We also know some whose faces communicate – sometimes contradicting their spoken sentiments. Korzybski has pointed out that signal reactions, instantaneous and unmediated, if undifferentiated according to the appropriateness of the situation, reflect immature, impulsive personalities, while the development of the ability to delay response will permit modified, thoughtful symbol behavior, a characteristic of the mature person.

20. The statement that shows the best understanding of the first two sentences of the passage is

(a) colorblind people are not good judges of paintings
(b) bring me a champagne-colored blouse that matches this watch
(c) the perception of color varies with light
(d) modern music is not as good as baroque music
(e) as soon as the room is warm enough, turn the heat off

21. Which of the following does the semanticist maintain will help bridge the communication gap between people, according to the passage?

   I. characterizing behavior in absolute terms
  II. describing behavior objectively
 III. establishing criteria for judging behavior

(a) I only
(b) I and II only
(c) II and III only
(d) III only
(e) I, II, and III

22. According to the passage,

(a) "phatic communion" is the form of communication that children employ with animals
(b) linguistics will overcome the language barrier through the use of symbols

(c) one characteristic of the mature person is the ability to delay response appropriate to the situation

(d) a poker face conceals reactions to threatening stimuli

(e) the behavior of impulsive personalities permits modified reactions

After a major theory has become doctrine, we tend to forget seemingly legitimate objections later shown to be incorrect, remembering only the controversial aspects of those theories. This leads to retrospective arrogance: by aligning ourselves with the victorious doctrine, we disdain those who opposed it.

Although much has been written about the theological conflicts with Darwinian theory, little is known of the powerful scientific objections that modified Darwin's beliefs.

During Darwin's lifetime, the accepted theory of heredity was that of blending inheritance, in which forms intermediate between those of the parents resulted from mating. Mendel's discovery that inheritance was particulate was published, but was unrecognized. Jenkin pointed out that if a rare and favorable mutation occurred, it would soon be obliterated due to "swamping" from repeated crossings from the wild-type form. Disputing Darwin's conception of evolution as proceeding through the natural selection of those with slightly better characteristics than arose randomly, Jenkin concluded that natural selection could not account for the tremendous diversity of life, hypothesizing that large numbers of organisms mutated simultaneously in the same direction—a controlled orthogenetic process resembling a series of "special creations."

Since "special creationism" was an ideological target of Darwin's, he found himself in a quandary. Although he did not abandon his theory, he admitted that natural selection played a much smaller part in evolution than he had previously claimed. He also embraced the Lamarckian concept that somatic changes in parents are transmitted to their offspring, thus providing a mechanism by which an entire population could change in the same direction at once.

Another potent objection came from the physicists led by Lord Kelvin, who contested the assumption of previous geologists and biologists that life had existed for billions of years, if not infinitely. How, these iconoclasts questioned, could evolution proceed by slow steps in millions of years, and how could advanced forms, recently evolved, show such great differences? The Kelvinists, basing their conclusions on the assumption that the sun was an incandescent liquid mass rapidly radiating heat, calculated that the age of the earth was between twenty and forty million years.

Darwin was forced to admit that their calculations were correct and their premises rational, and to adjust his theory. He proposed that change had occurred much more rapidly in the past than in the present, where species seemed static, and that more advanced forms varied more rapidly than lower forms. This provided further reason to advocate Lamarck's theory of inheritance, because that could account for the rapid change.

It is interesting to note that both these retreats of Darwin were later shown to be faulty. The discovery that the sun runs on a nearly infinite amount of atomic fuel totally invalidated Kelvin's argument. Mendel was "rediscovered" in the twentieth century, when it was pointed out that the particulate nature of inheritance meant that favorable mutation could not only persist, but could rapidly become prevalent.

23. The author's major premise can be understood to say that

    (a) Darwin's theory of evolution explains natural selection
    (b) objections are forgotten after a theory is accepted
    (c) present scientific beliefs are subject to future disproof
    (d) religious objections prevented the acceptance of Darwin's theory
    (e) the arrogance of scientists suppresses opposing viewpoints, and creates fallacious theories

24. A statement which is neither supported nor contradicted in this passage is

    (a) Contrary to Lord Kelvin's beliefs, the sun is not losing energy.
    (b) The word "rediscovered" is in quotation marks because Mendel's work on heredity was virtually ignored at the time that he first published it.
    (c) Scientists sometimes modify their theories in response to criticisms that are actually incorrect.
    (d) Important discoveries that conflict with accepted belief are sometimes ignored when they are first set forth.
    (e) The concept of the particulate nature of inheritance, when it was finally understood, had very little importance for the Darwinians.

25. It can be inferred from this passage that

    I. the theory of blending inheritance would conflict with current beliefs on inherited traits
    II. Lamarck was refuted by twentieth-century adherents to the Mendelian view
    III. the age of the earth, according to Kelvin and the other physicists, determines the amount of genetic variation

    (a) I only
    (b) II only
    (c) II and II only
    (d) I, II, and III
    (e) I and II only

26. In response to contemporary scientific objections raised against his theories, Darwin

(a) embraced the doctrine of "special creationism"
(b) referred to Mendel's findings to buttress his own theory of evolution
(c) accepted Lamarck's theory of transmitted characteristics
(d) retreated to a stance little different from that of Jenkin
(e) admitted that his ideas were based largely on Kelvin's theories

27. Which of the following concepts most clearly supports Darwin's conception of evolution?

(a) The age of the earth was calculated by the Kelvinists to be between twenty and forty million years.
(b) A rare and favorable mutation would soon be obliterated due to "swamping" from repeated crossings from the wild-type form.
(c) Somatic changes in parents are transmitted to their children.
(d) The particulate nature of inheritance means that favorable mutations may rapidly become prevalent.
(e) Large numbers of organisms are thought to have mutated simultaneously in a series of "special creations."

In each of the questions below, a capitalized word is followed by five words or phrases lettered (a) through (e). Select the word or phrase most nearly OPPOSITE in meaning to the capitalized word.

Since some of the questions require that you distinguish fine shades of meaning, consider all choices carefully before you select your answer.

28. PROFLIGATE

(a) proficient
(b) contaminated
(c) archaic
(d) virtuous
(e) inept

29. CIRCUMSCRIBED

(a) recycled
(b) unchecked
(c) natural
(d) precise
(e) delineated

30. PROFOUND

(a) effete
(b) feckless
(c) superficial
(d) superfluous
(e) reticent

31. LITTORAL

(a) figurative
(b) nescient
(c) prosaic
(d) inland
(e) argumentative

32. FLAMBOYANT

(a) extinguished
(b) austere
(c) reminiscent
(d) distinguished
(e) extraordinary

33. KNAVISH

(a) unscrupulous
(b) disloyal
(c) unconcerned
(d) spare
(e) unexceptionable

34. BLOWZY

    (*a*) dapper
    (*b*) frosty
    (*c*) clumsy
    (*d*) elegaic
    (*e*) incontinent

35. FUGITIVE

    (*a*) corrupt
    (*b*) warden
    (*c*) permanent
    (*d*) pervasive
    (*e*) stagnant

36. ENGROSSED

    (*a*) refined
    (*b*) befouled
    (*c*) distracted
    (*d*) embossed
    (*e*) unencumbered

37. SEPULCHRAL

    (*a*) hypocritical
    (*b*) cheerful
    (*c*) noxious
    (*d*) hidden
    (*e*) overt

38. INSIPID

    (*a*) testy
    (*b*) innocuous
    (*c*) sapient
    (*d*) revolting
    (*e*) transparent

STOP! Work only on this section until the time allowed is over.

Answer Key—Practice Test 2

SECTION I

1. *c*	9. *c*	17. *d*	25. *b*	33. *b*
2. *a*	10. *d*	18. *b*	26. *e*	34. *a*
3. *a*	11. *a*	19. *e*	27. *b*	35. *d*
4. *e*	12. *d*	20. *b*	28. *d*	36. *a*
5. *b*	13. *d*	21. *d*	29. *a*	37. *c*
6. *d*	14. *e*	22. *a*	30. *e*	38. *b*
7. *a*	15. *b*	23. *d*	31. *c*	
8. *a*	16. *c*	24. *c*	32. *b*	

SECTION II

1. *e*	9. *e*	17. *a*	25. *b*	33. *c*
2. *c*	10. *a*	18. *c*	26. *b*	34. *d*
3. *c*	11. *d*	19. *e*	27. *d*	35. *b*
4. *b*	12. *b*	20. *c*	28. *c*	36. *a*
5. *d*	13. *b*	21. *d*	29. *b*	37. *d*
6. *a*	14. *c*	22. *a*	30. *a*	38. *e*
7. *d*	15. *b*	23. *a*	31. *a*	
8. *e*	16. *c*	24. *e*	32. *e*	

SECTION III

1. *c*	7. *d*	13. *b*	19. *e*	25. *e*
2. *a*	8. *a*	14. *d*	20. *d*	26. *d*
3. *d*	9. *d*	15. *d*	21. *a*	27. *b*
4. *b*	10. *c*	16. *b*	22. *e*	28. *a*
5. *a*	11. *a*	17. *d*	23. *c*	29. *b*
6. *b*	12. *c*	18. *c*	24. *d*	30. *d*

SECTION IV

1. *b*	7. *c*	13. *a*	19. *d*	25. *e*
2. *c*	8. *b*	14. *c*	20. *c*	26. *c*
3. *a*	9. *b*	15. *d*	21. *b*	27. *d*
4. *c*	10. *a*	16. *d*	22. *c*	28. *a*
5. *b*	11. *d*	17. *c*	23. *a*	29. *d*
6. *a*	12. *b*	18. *b*	24. *d*	30. *b*

SECTION V

1. *a*	6. *b*	11. *d*	16. *c*	21. *c*
2. *d*	7. *a*	12. *b*	17. *e*	22. *c*
3. *e*	8. *a*	13. *b*	18. *a*	23. *e*
4. *e*	9. *b*	14. *c*	19. *a*	24. *c*
5. *e*	10. *d*	15. *b*	20. *b*	25. *d*

SECTION VI

1. *e*	6. *b*	11. *a*	16. *d*	21. *a*
2. *a*	7. *c*	12. *a*	17. *a*	22. *e*
3. *e*	8. *c*	13. *e*	18. *d*	23. *a*
4. *c*	9. *b*	14. *b*	19. *e*	24. *b*
5. *c*	10. *e*	15. *e*	20. *c*	25. *c*

SECTION VII

1. *d*	9. *b*	17. *e*	25. *e*	33. *e*
2. *a*	10. *d*	18. *c*	26. *c*	34. *a*
3. *c*	11. *a*	19. *a*	27. *d*	35. *c*
4. *e*	12. *d*	20. *b*	28. *d*	36. *c*
5. *b*	13. *e*	21. *c*	29. *b*	37. *b*
6. *d*	14. *e*	22. *c*	30. *c*	38. *c*
7. *a*	15. *d*	23. *b*	31. *d*	
8. *c*	16. *a*	24. *a*	32. *b*	

Explanatory Answers — Practice Test 2

SECTION I

1. (c) "Imbed" is incorrect; it means to fix into a surrounding mass, or place in a bed. To imbed in a fabric is unsuitable. The only word that makes sense is *effected*, which means brought about.

2. (a) They denied something that is probably unpleasant. The only possibilities are a *rift*, or a "let-down." "Separation," the word paired with the latter, makes no sense at all, but *collaboration*, the word paired with the former, does.

3. (a) The context implies that adolescents must cope with changing roles. *Adjustment* is the only word that fits.

4. (e) His team's reaching the playoffs would make him feel "pride" or *elation*, not "humility," "reluctance," or "sentimentality." After three victories in a row, he would have felt extremely happy; his elation would not have become "thoughtful" but *euphoric*, which means an intense feeling of well-being.

5. (b) What kind of evidence would a man's adherents be loath (reluctant) to hear? Evidence that *proclaimed* his guilt.

6. (d) A truly foolproof safety system cannot fail; only one that claims to be foolproof, one that is *allegedly* foolproof, can.

7. (a) If his beliefs went counter to those of his time, what might he have been forced to do? While either "retire" or *recant* could complete the sentence grammatically, the former does not respond to the question of the man's position on his views, while the latter fits in with the final statement that his views are now accepted as correct, which implies that he had probably recanted.

8. (a) A *choreographer*—composer of dance—would score a *pirouette* as an element of a dance composition. In similar fashion, a *composer* of music would score a *chord* as an element of a musical composition. This is a function relationship.

9. (c) To *quiver* is to shake with a slight but rapid motion, that is, to *vibrate*. To *frighten* is to scare, throw into a fright, or *terrify*. Although each pair of words expresses a synonymous relationship, they also express degree of difference relationships as used in certain contexts.

10. (d) A *general*, as one of his primary functions, *commands*. Similarly, a *senator legislates*. This is a function relationship.

11. (a) To *annul* a *marriage* is to cancel it. To *reverse* a *verdict* is to annul or cancel it.

12. (d) A *nemesis* is an agent of punishment or retribution, the opposite of

a *guardian angel*. Similarly, a *miser* is the opposite of a *spendthrift*.

13. (*d*) To *expend* means to use up, whereas to *replenish* is to refill or resupply. To *defect* is to desert, whereas to *rejoin* is to come back into the company of those one has left. This is an opposites relationship.

14. (*e*) *Immune* and *susceptible* are opposites, the former meaning protected from, the latter meaning vulnerable to. *Exempt* and *obliged*, too, are opposites. *Exempt* means free from obligation or liability to which others are subject; *obliged* means subject to comply or perform.

15. (*b*) *Feral* means uncultivated, wild, not domesticated, and it could characterize a *wolverine*, an animal of the weasel family. *Timorous*, which means fearful or timid, could characterize a *milksop*, a weak, effeminate youth. This is a characterization relationship.

16. (*c*) One of the components of an *equation* is a *term*. Similarly, one of the components of a *formula* is a *constituent*. This is a whole and part relationship.

17. (*d*) Statement I is contained in the next-to-last sentence, which is followed by the sentence "It is no wonder . . . the parent responds with bitterness and antagonism." Statement II is expressed a couple of sentences earlier on, ". . . unwilling to admit to doubt about the path taken or the value of the prizes secured, the adult defends. . ." Statement III is not found in the passage.

18. (*b*) The passage actually says that the adult defends against serious probing as well as against ingenuous disaffection. It is clear, therefore, that adults would not accept even thoughtful probing.

19. (*e*) This summary statement is a paraphrase of the second paragraph.

20. (*b*) Choice (*a*) is incorrect because the passage indicates the reverse: obesity contributes to hypertension and atherosclerosis. Choice (*c*) is incorrect; the passage does not discuss the nitrogen cycle. The passage does not discuss obese parents vis-a-vis obese children, so choice (*d*) is incorrect. The passage does not deal with the role of carbohydrates in connection with obesity, so choice (*e*) is wrong. The answer to the question of choice (*b*) can be found in the passage, in the fourth paragraph, starting with the words, "However, when the body has been in negative nitrogen balance. . . ."

21. (*d*) Primitive man evolved as an organism capable of storing excess energy against times when food would not be available. This physical evolvement has left man with a system for storing fat which modern Western man no longer needs, and which contributes to obesity.

22. (*a*) No reference is made to the need for water in relation to expending adipose tissue. Choice (*b*) is supported by paragraph two. Choice (*c*) is contradicted at the end of the next to the last paragraph, where atherosclerotic heart disease is called the number one cause of

death in the U.S. Choice (*d*) is supported in paragraph three. Choice (*e*) is supported by the first sentence in the fourth paragraph.

23. (*d*) The last paragraph suggests that children with good eating habits probably will not become obese. You can infer that bad eating habits are a root cause of obesity. As to choice (*a*), although obesity may be accompanied by increased serum lipids and, therefore, a tendency toward atherosclerosis, the converse is not necessarily correct, and the passage does not suggest it to be so. The article suggests that good eating habits, not dieting, are the answer to obesity, so choice (*b*) is wrong. Choice (*c*) is not in any way implied in the passage.

24. (*c*) Evidence for choices (*a*), (*b*), (*d*), and (*e*) are contained in paragraphs five, one, five, and five respectively. Choice (*c*) states the opposite of what the passage notes in paragraph five.

25. (*b*) Obesity is mentioned as disrupting good health of mind and body. No such problems are attributed to weight loss in the passage. Choice (*a*) is implied in sentence two of paragraph six; choice (*c*) is expressed in sentence four, paragraph two; choice (*d*) appears in the first paragraph—women comprise more than half the population. If 40 percent of women and 30 percent of men are obese, then at least 35 percent of all American men and women are obese; choice (*e*) is clearly expressed in the last sentence.

26. (*e*) The author barely, if at all, criticizes the diet industry, so choice (*a*) is incorrect. The ability to store excess energy in the form of adipose tissue is suggested as being an evolutionary vestige; the passage does not suggest that the storage of excessive adipose tissue is a genetic disorder, so choice (*b*) is incorrect. Choice (*c*) is incorrect; no mention is made of a national crusade of any sort. Choice (*d*) is wrong; the passage barely mentions fad diets, but makes no judgments concerning them. What the passage does do is stress the difficulty of losing weight, explain the problems related to obesity, and suggest that parents be educated to understand good eating habits for their children.

27. (*b*) In paragraph four, the passage explains the relationship between caloric reduction and weight loss, as given in choice (*b*). See paragraph two for correction of choice (*a*), paragraph four for the correction of choice (*c*), paragraph two for the correction of choice (*d*), and paragraph three to see the basis for the error in choice (*e*).

28. (*d*) *Animus*—hostile feeling; opposite—*sympathy*

29. (*a*) *Interdict*—prohibit; opposite—*sanction*

30. (*e*) *Inadvertent*—unintentional; opposite—*premeditated*

31. (*c*) *Aborigine*—original inhabitant; opposite—*emigrant*

32. (*b*) *Corroborative*—confirming; opposite—*refutative* (proving false)

33. (b) *Noxious*—harmful; opposite—
harmless

34. (a) *Inimical*—hostile; opposite—*amicable*

35. (d) *Vainglorious*—excessively proud,
pompous; opposite—*unassuming*

36. (a) *Bellicose*—pugnacious, eager to
fight; opposite—*pacific*

37. (c) *Savant*—one of profound learning; opposite—*simpleton*

38. (b) *Innocuous*—harmless, inoffensive; opposite—*pernicious* (ruinous, injurious, hurtful)

SECTION II

1. (e) Since it is feminism that promises
equality to all, it must be
regardless of *gender*. Skills from
the past, however, might be only
minimally marketable.

2. (c) He had succeeded in convincing
others of his loyalty by feigning,
that is, *dissimulating* fidelity and
devotion to the cause.

3. (c) The sentence indicates that he descended into gluttony and something related. *Dissipation* is the
only word meaning dissolute behavior like gluttony. The second
word, *precipitous*, which means
abrupt or perpendicular, fits the
sense of the sentence.

4. (b) *Logistics* is the branch of military
science that deals with the movement of supplies and personnel.
Implementation means execution

or putting into effect, and it would
be best learned through experience.

5. (d) A person who is objectionably forward in giving unwanted advice or
assistance could be characterized
as *officious* or offensive. Choice (b)
is eliminated because "intelligible,"
which means comprehensible, is a
poor choice to describe assistance.
Choice (e), too, is unacceptable because the sentence clearly implies
that his advice was not sparing.
Furthermore, the sentence speaks
of how he saw his advice, and since
he was offering it freely and
thought it would save people from
themselves, he must have thought
it *valuable*.

6. (a) To *justify* means to show why an
act is defensible or blameless. The
industry leaders would not want to
proclaim that they had made their
decision simply on the basis of profitability. They would want to show
that their motive was the good of
the public. *Justify* is the correct
word of choice.

7. (d) If the ground crew was working on
a very crowded schedule, it is reasonable to assume that they could
not have made a thoroughgoing inspection, but rather a *cursory*, that
is, superficial one that was performed rapidly without noticing
details.

8. (e) A *cheerful* person is in good spirits;
an *euphoric* person has an exaggerated feeling of well-being. A
sorrowful person is gloomy; a *lugubrious* person is exaggeratedly
gloomy. This is a degree of difference relationship.

9. (e) *Litmus* is used to test for *acid*. A *polygraph* is used to test for *truth*. Function relationship.

10. (a) One who practices *deceit* may suffer censure, or *opprobrium*. One who adheres to *rectitude* in his actions earns the *esteem* of others.

11. (d) If someone is merely *reluctant*, *persuasion* may be all it takes to change his mind. If one however is *loath* to do something, it may take *coercion*, or the use of force to change his mind.

12. (b) To *quibble* is to use *ambiguity* to deal with a point at issue. To *nit-pick* is to engage in *pettiness* in an argument.

13. (b) A member of an *entourage* is an *attendant*. A member of a *claque* is a *sycophant* or servile flatterer. Whole and part relationship.

14. (c) Something *distasteful* may be offensive, but not as offensive as something *odious*. To be *fond* of someone or something is to have a liking for that person or thing, but not as much of a liking as being *devoted* to that person or thing. Degree of difference relationship.

15. (b) To *quench* one's *thirst* is to put an end to it. To *quell* a *rebellion* is to end it.

16. (c) A *desiccant* is a drying agent, something that removes water or *dehydrates*. A *prevaricator* is one who *lies*. This is an agent-function relationship.

17. (a) Most of the passage is devoted to the dangers of majority rule that has no checks on the powers of the rulers. The word *tyranny* is used twice to describe these dangers.

18. (c) The passage, especially in the last paragraph, says that there is no redress from the decision of the majority, so choice (a) is wrong. The passage does not address itself to individual liberty, the statement in choice (b). The passage does not suggest that all governments are tyrannical but rather that governments with no checks on their powers are tyrannical; choice (d) is incorrect. While it criticizes majority rule, the passage never praises minority rule. The last sentence of the first paragraph says that we should no more give power without check to any group than we should to any individual. In effect, this is what choice (c) says.

19. (e) Choice (e) is correct; see paragraph two, which paraphrases the statement in choice (e). Choice (a) is incorrect: the passage speaks of the strength of American democratic institutions; it does not speak of the weakness of the government. Choice (b) is self-contradictory in expression. The conclusion for statement (c) is the opposite to that of the passage. The last clause in paragraph two says that excessive liberty is not as alarming as the lack of checks on the majority, so choice (d) is wrong.

20. (c) Paragraph one clearly indicates the correctness of choice (c).

21. (d) The author states, in the next-to-last paragraph that small firms will pursue innovation as stated in choice (d). Note that in the first

sentence of paragraph two, the author says we are told that monopoly power creates an environment supportive of innovation, but he indicates that this is said *despite* evidence to the contrary, negating choice (*a*). All the other choices are equally incorrect. Again, note that the passage makes a statement that seems to support choice (*e*), but the author goes on to offer a "but" that shows he does not accept that statement as true.

22. (*a*) Statement (*a*) appears in the third sentence of the third paragraph as a concept that the author can accept.

23. (*a*) First, the author points out that monopolistic industry did not invent its share of the innovations of the past. Second, the author points out that prodigious expenditures alone—note the huge federal expenditures—do not necessarily produce the inventions that improve the standard of living. Third, the author says that large-scale industry prefers the status quo and stable conditions, and that innovation threatens the status quo. Fourth, industrial giants have enormous capital investments which could be subject to obsolescence if changes were wrought. The only circumstance the author mentions under which big industry might spend large sums for innovations would be in a struggle with another industrial Goliath. With all these statements of doubt about the unwillingness or the inability of monopolistic industry to provide innovation, you can infer choice (*a*).

24. (*e*) Of the more than $35 billion spent on research in this country each year, the federal government spends almost two-thirds, or less than $24 billion. More than half of this $24 billion is spent, according to the second paragraph, on military research. The balance is spent on nonmilitary research, we must infer. Taking away more than half of $24 billion gives us less than $12 billion for the nonmilitary research.

25. (*b*) The passage indicates that most of the federal money is funneled into military research, but nothing is said about what sort of research is paid for with the balance.

26. (*b*) The first two sentences of the passage contrast the widespread belief that large companies spend enormous amounts on industrial research with the actuality that more than half the important inventions since 1900 have been produced by independent inventors. The passage then continues, indicating that giant corporations do not spend large sums on research at all unless forced to. As for the other choices, the passage does not advocate governmental support one way or the other, so choice (*a*) is wrong. Choice (*c*) is wrong; the passage does not describe the inadequacies of small firms. The passage merely says "we are told" of some inadequacy of small firms, but the fact that the author writes this does not make it his opinion. In fact, the passage makes clear that the author does not accept what "we are told." Choices (*d*) and (*e*) are not relevant to the passage.

27. (*d*) Choice (*a*) only tells us about the past. The industrial giants did not best serve the needs mentioned in the past; independent inventors did. Choice (*d*), however, does deal with the future. It tells us that large-scale enterprises prefer not to make changes. Striving for innovation must bring about change. Enterprises that tend to operate more comfortably in stable and secure circumstances will not undertake research that is certain to bring change. The other choices are not relevant. Choice (*b*) refers to the government, not large-scale industry; choice (*e*), in fact, refers to the only set of circumstances mentioned by the passage under which industrial giants might foster innovation. Choice (*c*) is completely unrelated to the question.

28. (*c*) *Chicanery*—deception, fraud; opposite—*probity* (integrity)

29. (*b*) *Propinquity*—closeness; opposite—*remoteness*

30. (*a*) *Choleric*—easily angered; opposite—*placid*

31. (*a*) *Tranquil*—calm, peaceful; opposite—*tumultuous*

32. (*e*) *Munificent*—extremely generous; opposite—*parsimonious* (frugal to excess)

33. (*c*) *Spurious*—bogus, fake; opposite —*authentic*

34. (*d*) *Impalpable*—intangible; opposite—*tangible* (real, material, capable of being touched)

35. (*b*) *Paramount*—chief in importance; opposite—*subordinate*

36. (*a*) *Derogate*—detract in estimation; opposite—*acclaim*

37. (*d*) *Contravene*—oppose, be in conflict with; opposite—*uphold*

38. (*e*) *Morbid*—suggesting an unhealthy mental state, unwholesomely gloomy; opposite—*wholesome*

SECTION III

1. (*c*) $40 (.3) = 12$ and $30 (.4) = 12$
So that the two quantities are equal.

2. (*a*) $(3n)^2 = 9n^2$ and n^2 is positive, so that $9n^2 > 3n^2$

3. (*d*) The length of the chord may vary from O to the length of the diameter. So that we cannot determine its relationship to the radius.

4. (*b*) Since $8.5 < 9$, then $\sqrt{8.5} < 3$
Since $28.2 > 27$, then $\sqrt[3]{28.2} > 3$
then, $\sqrt[3]{28.2} > \sqrt{8.5}$

5. (*a*) Since the indicated angles are vertical angles, then
$3g = 4h$
or
$g = \dfrac{4h}{3}$ so that $g > h$

6. (*b*) $\$80 (.70) = \$56.00$, (*a*)
$\$80 (.80) = \$64.00$
(first discount price)
$\$64 (.90) = \$57.60$ sale price (*b*)
Thus, (*b*) is greater than (*a*).

7. (d) $3x + 4y = 12$
When $x = 0$, $y = 3$ and $y > x$
When $y = 0$, $x = 4$ and $x > y$
Thus, the relationship cannot be determined.

8. (a) Area of circle $= \pi r^2$
Area of square $= (2r)^2 = 4r^2$
$t = \dfrac{\pi r^2}{4r^2} = \dfrac{\pi}{4} = \dfrac{3.14}{4} > \dfrac{3}{4}$

9. (d) Each interior angle $=$
$\dfrac{180° (n - 2)}{n}$
Each exterior angle $= \dfrac{360°}{n}$
We cannot determine which is greater unless we know the value of n.

10. (c) In parallelogram PSVT,
TV $=$ PS and PT $=$ SV
Perimeter of $\triangle$ PQR $=$
QR $+$ RS $+$ SP $+$ PT $+$ TQ
Perimeter of shaded region $=$
QR $+$ RS $+$ SV $+$ VT $+$ TQ
In view of the above equalities, the two perimeters are equal.

11. (a) Area of equilateral $\triangle$ PQR $=$
$\dfrac{d^2}{4} \sqrt{3} \approx \dfrac{1.73}{4} d^2 \approx .43d^2$
Area of semi-circle $=$
1/2 area of circle $=$
$\dfrac{1}{2} \pi \left(\dfrac{d}{2}\right)^2$
$= \dfrac{1}{2} \pi \dfrac{d^2}{4} = \dfrac{\pi}{8} d^2 \approx$
$\dfrac{3.14}{8} d^2 \approx .39d^2$
Thus the triangle is greater in area.

12. (c) $330 = 33 \times 10 = 11 \times 3 \times 5 \times 2$
(4 prime factors)
$210 = 21 \times 10 = 7 \times 3 \times 5 \times 2$
(4 prime factors)

The number of prime factors is the same in both cases.

13. (b) $\dfrac{p}{7} = \dfrac{7}{p}$
$p^2 = 49$
$p = -7$ since $p < 0$
$\dfrac{p}{14} = \dfrac{-7}{14} = -\dfrac{1}{2} < -\dfrac{1}{7}$

14. (d) If $rst = 0$, then at least one of the three factors is equal to zero. If $t = 0$, then $rt = st = 0$. Since we do not know the signs of r or s, we cannot compare rt and st in magnitude.

15. (d) If $y = 0$, the two expressions are equal.
If $y > 0$, $y(y + 2) = y^2 + 2y > y^2$
We cannot compare the two quantities.

16. (b) $y + \dfrac{2}{7} = \dfrac{5}{7}$
Subtract $\dfrac{2}{7}$ from both sides
$y = \dfrac{5}{7} - \dfrac{2}{7} = \dfrac{3}{7}$
$y + \dfrac{1}{7} = \dfrac{3}{7} + \dfrac{1}{7} = \dfrac{4}{7}$

17. (d) $17^2 = 289$
$18^2 = 324$ or $\sqrt{324} = 18$
Thus $\sqrt{340} > 18$ so that 18 is the greatest possible integer less than $\sqrt{340}$.

18. (c) $p = 12,000$
$q = 11,800$
$p - q = 200$

19. (e)

The side of the square is $\frac{36}{4} = 9$

The largest possible length of RS is obtained by making RS a diagonal of the square. In this case RS = $9\sqrt{2}$

20. (*d*) If he sold 2 apples, they would sell for 40¢, leaving $3.60 for the oranges. But $3.60 is not divisible by 25¢, so this is not possible. Try the other possible answers in this way. If he sells 5 apples, he gets $1.00, leaving $3.00 for the oranges. This number is divisible by 25¢, so that 5 is the least number of apples he could have sold.

21. (*a*) About 77 million people voted for President in 1972, while about 71 million voted for Representatives, approximately 90% of Presidential voters.

22. (*e*) This problem is best solved with a ruler or straight edge. Just measure the distance from the top of one election's bar to the top of the next election's: 1972–1974.

23. (*c*) This answer can be seen from the steepness of the line graph. 1970–1972 showed the largest increase of voting age citizens. Incidentally, this was caused by the lowering of the voting age from 21 to 18.

24. (*d*) About 72 million people voted for President in 1964, and about 114 million were eligible. The percent is 72/114 = 63%.

25. (*e*) Let r = radius of circle
$2\pi r = \pi r^2$
$r^2 = 2r$ Divide by r
$r = 2$
$C = 2\pi r = 4\pi$

26. (*d*) $\frac{5p^2 + 5q^2}{5} = \frac{5(p^2 + q^2)}{5} =$
$p^2 + q^2$
Thus, the 5's may be cancelled out. This is not true with any of the other expressions.

27. (*b*)

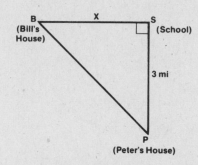

$PB = \sqrt{x^2 + 9} = (x + 3) - 1$
$x^2 + 9 = (x + 2)^2$
$x^2 + 9 = x^2 + 4x + 4$
$4x = 5$
$x = 1\frac{1}{4}$

28. (*a*) The least number is obtained by subtracting the largest of the three numbers from the smallest of them. Since r is the greatest number and t is the least quantity, then (t – r) is the least number of the five choices.

29. (*b*) The area of the rectangle in the figure is given by the formula
A = bh
b = 2 – (– 1) = 2 + 1 = 3
h = p – m
So that A = 3 (p – m)

30. (*d*) Area of RSTV = 25 (10) = 250
Area of two semicircles with same diameter = Area of one circle = $\pi r^2 = \pi (5)^2 = 25\pi$
Area of shaded region = 250 – 25π

1. (b) Since $\angle S = 90°$ and $\angle T = 30°$,
then $\angle R = 60°$
Thus, $ST > RS$.

2. (c) In a $30°–60°–90°$ triangle, the side opposite the $30°$ angle is equal to one-half the hypotenuse.
Thus, $RS = 1/2\ RT$

3. (a) Let $RT = x$, then $RS = \dfrac{x}{2}$ and

$ST = \dfrac{x}{2}\sqrt{3} = \dfrac{1.73x}{2} =$

$.86x > .75x$
Thus $ST > \dfrac{3}{4}\ RT$

4. (c) Since the diagonals of the parallelogram bisect each other, PM is a median of triangle PQS. A median divides a triangle into two triangles equal in area. Thus $\triangle PMS = \triangle PMQ$ in area.

5. (b) $RQ = PS$ and $RS = PQ$. Since it is given that $PQ > PS$, it follows that $RS > RQ$.

6. (a) $x°$ is the measure of an exterior angle of $\triangle MQR$. Thus, $x > y$.

7. (c) $y = z$ because these are the measures of alternate interior angles of parallel lines, PS and QR.

8. (b) In $\triangle PQR$, $PQ > QR$ since $QR = PS$.
Therefore, $y > t$ because the greater angle lies opposite the greater side.

9. (b) Since the four triangles with M as common vertex are all equal in area, $\triangle PQM = 1/4\ PQRS$ in area.
Thus, $\triangle PQM < 1/3\ PQRS$ in area.

10. (a) Since $PR + QR > PQ$, it follows that $PR > PQ - QR$

11. (d) There is no information as to the number of degrees in angle PQS. So we cannot determine the value of $x + t$.

12. (b) No. of seconds in 1 day = $60 \times 60 \times 24$
No. of hours in 20 years = $24 \times 365 \times 20$
Ignore the common 24. It is apparent that $365 \times 20 > 60 \times 60$.

13. (a) Multiply the two equations
$\dfrac{r}{s} = \dfrac{2}{5}$ and $\dfrac{s}{t} = \dfrac{3}{4}$
The result is
$\dfrac{r}{t} = \dfrac{2}{5} \times \dfrac{3}{4} = \dfrac{3}{10} < \dfrac{1}{3}$

14. (c) Surface area of cube of edge 6 = $6 \times 6^2 = 6^3$
Four times surface area of cube of edge 3 = $4 \times 6 \times 3^2 = 6 \times 6 \times 6 = 6^3$

15. (d) If $r = 0$, $s = 12/5$ and $s > r$
If $s = 0$, $r = 6$ and $r > s$
Comparison cannot be made.

16. (d) In 1967, the quantity of natural gas produced was $33 - 15 = 18$ quadrillion Btu.

17. (c) $55 - 37 = 18q$ Btu, out of a total of 60, or about 30%.

18. (b) Total production in 1976 was 60q Btu; in 1962 it was 44q Btu, for an increase of 16q Btu, or about 35%.

19. (d) The natural gas area clearly expanded from 1947 more than any other source.

20. (c) $x + y + z = 180$

$$z = \frac{x + y}{2}$$

or

$2z = x + y$

Substitute in first equation

$2z + z = 180$

$3z = 180$

$z = 60$

21. (b) He mows 4/5 of the lawn in 1⅓ hours. To do another 1/5 of the lawn will take $1/4 \times 4/3 = 1/3$ hour = 20 minutes

Thus, he will finish at 11:20 plus 20 minutes or 11:40 A.M.

22. (c) Grade B hard coal =
$$.70 \times .40 = .28$$
$$= 28\%$$

23. (a) Central angle = $.30 \times 360°$
$$= 108°$$

24. (d) Let x = cost of ticket before tax

then $.15x$ = tax

$1.15x = 11.50$

$115x = 1150$

$x = \$10$

Tax = $\$11.50 - \$10.00$

Tax = $\$1.50$

25. (e) The volume of the 2 cm. cube is given by

$V = e^3$

$\quad = 2^3$

$\quad = 8$ cubic centimeters

Weight = $8 \times 10 = 80$ grams

26. (c) $\quad 5\% = \dfrac{1}{20}$

Thus, $N = \dfrac{1}{20}x$

$\quad x = 20N$

27. (d) At 4:00, the minute hand is at the 12 and the hour hand at the 4; thus, the hands form an angle of $4 \times 30° = 120°$. In choices (a), (b), and (c),

the angle is always *slightly less* than 120°.

28. (a) There are $140 - 60 = 80$ studying French only; There are $180 - 60 = 120$ studying Spanish only.

Ratio = $\dfrac{120}{80} = \dfrac{3}{2} = 3:2$

29. (d) If a person picks 9 marbles, she may have 3 sets of 3 marbles of each color. If she picks one more marble, she must then have at least 4 marbles of the same color. Therefore, she must pick *at least* 10 marbles to be sure of having *at least* 4 of the same color.

30. (b) Average speed = $\dfrac{\text{total distance}}{\text{total time}}$

The trip going takes him $\dfrac{60}{40}$

$= 1\frac{1}{2}$ hours

The trip returning takes him $\dfrac{60}{30}$

$= 2$ hours

Total traveling time = $3\frac{1}{2}$ hours

Average speed = $\dfrac{120}{3\frac{1}{2}} = \dfrac{240}{7}$

$\quad = 34\dfrac{2}{7}$ m.p.h.

SECTION V

1. (a) A first-year student must choose two courses from the English, history, and sociology group. He or she may also take mathematics, a science, a language, and psychology. The maximum number of courses, therefore, is six.

2. (d) She needs a total of three more courses from the language group

and the humanities group. Diagram the choices as follows:

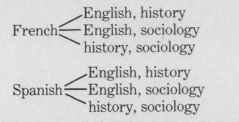

French — English, history
French — English, sociology
history, sociology

Spanish — English, history
Spanish — English, sociology
history, sociology

She may choose these three courses in six different ways.

3. (e) Diagram the choice of two additional courses as follows:

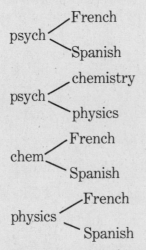

psych — French
psych — Spanish

psych — chemistry
psych — physics

chem — French
chem — Spanish

physics — French
physics — Spanish

He may choose these two courses in eight different ways.

4. (e) The only absolute constraint on the course selections of anyone, including a pre-med student, is that exactly two courses from the group of English, history, and sociology must be chosen. Anybody who takes only three courses must therefore take two courses from that group and one other course. Choice (e), however, lists two courses not included in the English, history, sociology group. A student choosing this schedule would be unable to take the two required courses from that group, making (e) the unacceptable schedule and, therefore, the correct choice.

5. (e) The argument is that the earth's resources must be conserved, and that the United States can "correct this" by not increasing its level of resource consumption. It is plain that this assumes that, as (e) states, curbing United States consumption will significantly retard world resource depletion. (a) and (b) are not necessarily assumptions of the argument's author. (c) is also not necessarily an assumption because it is not enough to assert that the United States uses more resources than any other country; the argument is that the United States can "correct" resource depletion by curbing its use of resources. Simply being the largest resource user does not imply having that much effect on resource depletion. (d) has no merit.

6. (b) This choice presents statistical evidence that the United States has a major effect on world resource consumption. As pointed out above, this does not prove the argument, but one-third is a large enough share of total resources use to lend credibility to the argument. (a) weakens the argument. (c) does not refer to resources and does not refer to the importance of the United States in causing world resource depletion. (d) also does not refer to the United States' role in resource depletion; if anything, the statement *weakens* the argument, for it is possible that the other countries' actions have curbed resource depletion. (e) is a poor choice because it does not refer to the

future; past United States action says nothing about what its future course should be.

7. (*a*) This choice points out that using resources does not necessarily imply a net loss of resources, paradoxical though it may seem. (The statement is, in fact, true: known oil reserves in the world have increased just about every year since oil was discovered, despite the great increase in oil use.) (*b*), (*c*), and (*d*) are irrelevant to the argument. (*e*) has little relevance, although it does evoke sympathy for the United States; the argument would have per capita United States resource consumption go down, as this choice points out. This does not greatly weaken the argument, however.

8. (*a*) After considering conditions 1, 2, 4, and 7, we can draw the following partial diagrams:

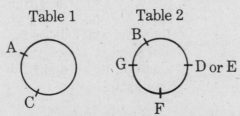

Next, note that someone must be between F and B (condition 5) and that D cannot be next to A (condition 6). The only possible way that D could be at the same table with A would be if E were between them; however, this is impossible, since that would leave F next to B. It follows that D and E must both be at table 2 with F, G, and B. Since D cannot be next to B (condition 3), E must be next to B, and the positions of D and F are interchangeable:

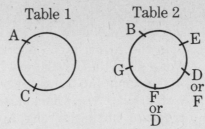

9. (*b*) As the discussion above shows, there are only two possible seating combinations.

10. (*d*) As the discussion above shows, B *must* be next to E. The other choices are either impossible or else possible but not definitely implied by the conditions given.

11. (*d*) Either Fred or Don could depart without violating the seating conditions. Neither Caryn, Arthur, nor Glenda could leave without violating the conditions that place them next to someone. Edward's leaving would place either Fred or Don next to Bertha.

12. (*b*) The relative strength of the teams' pitching and hitting must be listed separately. The statements regarding pitching say that the Engineers are worse than the Diamonds, the Diamonds are worse than the Cavaliers, the Cavaliers are worse than the Acorns, and the Acorns are worse than the Browns. This gives the following ranking from best to worst: B, A, C, D, E. The Fowls are better than the Cavaliers but worse than the Browns; whether they are better or worse than the Acorns is not stated. There are thus two possible rankings of the pitching strengths: either B, F, A, C, D, E or B, A, F, C, D, E.

In any case, the Browns have the best pitching, making (*b*) correct.

13. (b) The Browns have worse hitting than the Engineers, who are worse than the Acorns. The Acorns are worse than the Cavaliers, who are worse than the Fowls, who are worse than the Diamonds. The order of hitting strength, from best to worst, is, therefore: D, F, C, A, E, B.

The Browns have the worst hitting, making choice (b) the correct one.

14. (c) The Browns and Acorns both have better pitching and worse hitting than the Cavaliers.

15. (b) Both the Browns and the Acorns have worse hitting than the Fowls, but only the Browns definitely have better pitching than the Fowls, making (b), and not (d), the correct choice.

16. (c) As mentioned above, the relative strength of the pitching of the Acorns and Fowls is not given.

17. (e) The relative strength of the hitting of all teams is given.

18. (a) This is one of the most difficult sets of problems in the book. It can be solved only by organizing the data. One way is to set up a table:

Sheep
Ranch
Wolf
Owner

In this scheme, a given sheep, the ranch where that sheep lived, the wolf that killed the sheep, and the owner that killed the wolf are to be listed on the same vertical column. Note that, in accordance with condition (4), this chart does *not* match

an owner to his sheep (or to his ranch). The table may be started by arbitrarily listing sheep A, B, and C in that order. Conditions (2) and (5) give us:

Sheep	A	B	C
Ranch			Y
Wolf		2	
Owner			

Condition (1) gives us:

Sheep	A	B	C
Ranch	Z	X	Y
Wolf		2	
Owner			

The key point now is supplied by conditions (3) and (6): owner D killed wolf 1, and wolf 1, therefore, could not have killed sheep A—remember that no owner killed the wolf that killed his own sheep. This gives us:

Sheep	A	B	C
Ranch	Z	X	Y
Wolf		2	1
Owner			D

Filling in wolf 3 in the first column and noting the lack of information about owners E and F gives us the final table:

Sheep	A	B	C
Ranch	Z	X	Y
Wolf	3	2	1
Owner	E	E	D
	or	or	
	F	F	

The correct answer to question 18 is choice (a), since sheep A was on ranch Z.

19. (a) The table shows that statement I is the only correct one: owner D killed the wolf that killed sheep C. Statement II is clearly false, and state-

ment III may or may not be true; either owner E or owner F killed wolf 2.

20. (b) It is apparent that wolf 2 killed the sheep on ranch X. Choices (c) and (e) are true, and choices (a) and (d) are both possible.

21. (c) If we knew that owner E owned sheep B, then owner E would have to be put in the first column and owner F in the middle column. Statements I and II, on the other hand, provide information which we already know to be true.

22. (c) If owner E owned sheep B, owner E would be put in the column that did *not* include sheep B, which is the first column. He would also be owner of ranch X, leaving owner F to own ranch Y. Similarly, if owner F killed wolf 3, that would put him in the first column and owner E in the second column. If owner E were in the second column, he could not own sheep B, meaning that owner F must then be the owner of sheep B and ranch X. Statement III is false for the same reason that statement II is true.

23. (e) Statement (7) is redundant; we know from earlier statements that the wolf that killed sheep C was wolf 1, which was killed by owner D, not owner E.

24. (c) Choice (a) refers to weight as related to heart disease; the original passage makes no reference to weight. Choice (b) refers to cholesterol, which is also not mentioned in the original passage. Choice (d) refers to what people should do *after* getting heart disease; no mention is made of this in the original passage. Choice (c) points to the eating of fatty foods as the major cause of heart disease, which is the basic assumption in the argument presented. Choice (e) is irrelevant, since we are asked to assume, for the sake of argument, that Alan will refrain from fatty foods.

25. (d) The original statement indicates that price increases inevitably accompany a fall in interest rates. It does not state that a fall in interest rates follows stock price increases. Thus, choice (a) is not logically equivalent. Choices (b) and (c) are not logically equivalent to the original statement, because the original statement does not indicate what will happen if interest rates do *not* drop. Choice (e) is not equivalent, because the original statement does not indicate how stock prices will act if interest rates rise. Choice (d), however, is logically equivalent to the original statement. If stock market prices do not rise, interest rates must not drop.

SECTION VI

1. (e) The relationships described may simply be listed. From highest to lowest, the scores would run Q—RTSU. The dash indicates a gap that has not yet been occupied by any lettered grade.

2. (a) Since there is a 10 point difference between Q and R, V may lie between Q and R. Since R, T, S and U are each 5 points apart, there is no room for another passing score among them.

3. (e) Since W is lower than U, the seven grades mentioned may be listed from highest to lowest as QVRT SUW. Since there is a 5 point difference between each pair, W must be 70 and Q, 100.

4. (c) Statement I is correct because the argument makes no mention of, and needs no reference to, costs other than medical costs. Statement II, that all citizens are entitled to medical care, is not part of the argument's logical underpinnings. Statement III, that the private sector cannot control medical costs, is inherent in the argument that because costs have been rising so fast, government must provide all health care. If the private sector could control costs, the argument would not be valid.

5. (c) As explained in the previous answer, if the private sector can keep costs stable, then it does not follow that government should provide *all* health care. (c) is therefore an effective rebuttal. (a) is not relevant. (b) is not a good rebuttal, because it does not mention the *rate* of increase of medical costs in countries where government provides all health care. (d) refers to quality, not cost, and is thus not relevant. (e) has some logical force, but not much. Besides the point that railroads and health care are very different, the statement does not even imply that the government operates railroads poorly, for it could be that government loses less money on railroads than private enterprise.

6. (b) These questions are quite easy if the conditions are fully understood. Any situation which involves, or on a future move causes, an excess of Indians over cowboys somewhere is to be avoided.

One Indian cannot cross over on the first move, unless he were simply to cross right back, a situation to be ignored. If one Indian crossed, four Indians would be left on the other side. The second crossing would have to involve the cowboys, and could involve at most three of them, so that they would be outnumbered when they landed. Statement I therefore does not present a possible first crossing. Statement II is clearly impossible, for the two cowboys would be outnumbered by the five Indians when the cowboys landed. Statement III is quite possible, however. After three Indians cross, two cowboys could cross. The third crossing then involves one Indian and one cowboy. The fourth crossing then is of two Indians and two cowboys. The last two moves then involve two cowboys and then two Indians.

7. (c) As shown above, the first crossing must involve the Indians. Similarly, the second crossing involves the cowboys, not the Indians. Statement I is true; statement II is false. The most difficult choice involves statement III, which is true. It can be shown that the final crossing involves only Indians by showing that no cowboys may be involved: if cowboys were involved in the last crossing, they would be leaving a shore with five Indians, and would have been outnumbered there. Thus cowboys cannot be involved in the last crossing, and therefore it involves only Indians.

8. (c) If the final crossing involves only two Indians, the situation before that crossing looks like this: (* = boat, C = cowboy, I = Indian)

Shore 1   Shore 2
5C,2I*   3I

The only way that cowboys could have arrived at Shore 1 from Shore 2 is for three to have made the crossing, since there were three Indians on Shore 2.

9. (b) Using the same symbols as above, the crossings may be represented as follows:

Crossing number	Shore 1	Shore 2	Who crossed
0	5I*	5C	Original situation
1	3I	*2I,5C	Two Indians
2	3C,3I*	2I,2C	Three cowboys
3	2C,2I	*3I,3C	One Indian, one cowboy
4	5C,2I*	3I	Three cowboys
5	5C	*5I	Two Indians

Two additional moves beyond the first three are all that need be made.

10. (e) None may be assembled. Statement I (A, C, E) is precluded because if A works, F must work (stipulation #2). Statement II (A, F, G) is impossible because G will not work with A (stipulation #3). Statement III (B, D, G) is forbidden because any crew lacking person C must also lack B (stipulation #4).

11. (a) From (2), any crew containing A must contain F; choices B, C, and D may be quickly eliminated, since they do not contain F. A and F cannot be joined by B, since this would mean that C would not be working while B is working, in contradiction of stipulation (4).

12. (a) As seen above, no crew containing A can contain B, since A must be joined by F and B must be joined by C, making a three-person crew impossible.

13. (e) Statement I: We have seen that if B works, then C works. Since from (1), E must work if C works, it follows that B must work with C and E. It further follows that B can *only* work with C and E, and with no one else.
Statement II: This follows from the conclusion that B can work with no one but C and E.
Statement III: C must work with E and both C and E may work with F. F, who must work whenever A works, is not compelled to work with A; F is free to work with any two people who are free to work with him.
All three statements are true.

14. (b) From the previous discussions, it is clear that B must work with C and E, and that C must work with E. Both B and C are thus precluded from working with F and G. D, however, is free to work with F and G, making statement III the only true statement.

15. (e) The nine possible crews are as follows: A, D, F; A, E, F; B, C, E; C, D, E; C, E, F; C, E, G; D, E, F; D, E, G; and D, F, G.

16. (d) Before you delve into all the intricacies of a difficult problem such as this, start with the most straightforward facts and deductions. In this case, the information that 5 is in the middle, 9 is in the same row as 5, and that all rows and columns add to 15, means that 1 must be the

missing member of the row containing 5 and 9. This gives us:

1	5	9

It is clear from this alone that choice (*d*), which states that 5 and 1 must be adjacent, is correct. It will be clear from further discussion that the other pairs listed are not necessarily adjacent.

17. (*a*) We can now add to our table based on statement (7), which places 6 next to 1—whether above or below is irrelevant. Remembering that the diagonals add to 15 each, we may add the following numbers to the square:

		4
1	5	9
6		

This arrangement shows that 5 and 4 are *not* adjacent, since they are in different rows and columns, making choice (*a*) correct. The other pairs of cards listed either are or may be adjacent.

18. (*d*) The remaining cards have more than one set of possible locations, as the following reasoning demonstrates. The remaining cards are 2, 3, 7, and 8. The two that are in the unfinished diagonal with 5 must sum to 10. This means that either 2 and 8 or 3 and 7 must be at the unfilled corners. Two possible squares exist with 2 and 8 at the corners:

2	9	4
1	5	9
6	1	8

I

8	3	4
1	5	9
6	7	2

II

But possibility I cannot exist, for, in order to make the rows add to 15, cards marked with the numbers 9 and 1 would be needed. However, cards 9 and 1 have already been placed. Therefore, square II above is the only possible square with 8 and 2 at the corners.

Two possible squares with 3 and 7 at the corners are:

7	4	4
1	5	9
6	6	3

III

3	8	4
1	5	9
6	2	7

IV

Square III cannot exist, since it would mean using cards 4 and 6 twice each. Square IV, however, is entirely possible. This leaves only two possible arrangements:

8	3	4
1	5	9
6	7	2

II

and

3	8	4
1	5	9
6	2	7

IV

The middle column in square II and in square IV adds to 15. It cannot, therefore, add to either 10 or 20, making choice (d) correct for question 18.

19. (e) The answer to this question follows from the reasoning used above. The column with 6 in it adds to 15 in square II and to 10 in square IV. If it adds to 10, then it is false that 7 is in the middle column. The other choices present true statements.

20. (c) The same conclusions could have been drawn without the information that 6 is next to 1 (statement 7). Once the positions of 1, 5, and 9 are established, the knowledge that 4 is in the same column as 9 means that 4 and 5 are in the same diagonal. This in turn implies that 6 is also on the same diagonal (4 + 5 + 6 = 15) and is therefore next to 1. For these reasons, statement (7) could be omitted. Statement (8) could also be omitted; in fact, all our reasoning in the previous explanations has ignored this point. Clearly, however, eliminating the

requirement that the diagonals sum to 15 (statement 9) allows more possibilities; it may be remembered that this requirement was vital in the reasoning used in answering question 18. Without it, for example, the following squares would have been possible:

8	3	4
1	5	9
6	7	2

and

3	8	4
1	5	9
6	7	2

Thus, choice (d) is correct.

21. (a) We have seen that statement (8) is not essential. If it were omitted, the other conditions would still stand, including that mentioned in choice (a).

22. (e) The statement implies that since an economist, who studies money, does not have much money, he must be poor at his profession. Of the choices, that which most weakens this statement is choice (e), which points out that knowledge of economics and skill at handling one's own money are not necessarily related. The other statements are not as pertinent to the statement. Choice (d) is probably the second best answer, but since it only suggests an analogy between economists and psychiatrists, while choice (e) goes directly to the

point of the statement, choice (e) is better.

23. (a) The question has two pertinent logical features: it is answerable by "Yes" or "No," and either answer essentially concedes the point of the question. Even answering the question in the negative lends implicit assent to the premise that the present welfare system is inefficient and inhumane. Realizing this, one is essentially forced to answer "Yes"; a "No" response is not logically tenable. Choice (a) has the same features. Even answering "No" concedes that the ring is beautiful and that the "trinket" is repulsive, so that a "No" answer is not tenable. Obviously a beautiful ring is more attractive than a repulsive trinket.

Choice (b) is not a "Yes" or "No" question, and is incorrect for that reason alone. The other choices are answerable by "Yes" or "No," but are straightforward; without the catch in (a).

24. (b) The statement that if an object is a polar bear, then it is white, is logically identical to its contrapositive, that if an object is not white, then it is not a polar bear. Because of this logical equivalence, the author of the argument has reasoned that anything which supports the contrapositive must therefore also support the original statement. Choice (b) states the assumption underlying this conclusion.

25. (c) The argument being made is that because something (famines) has happened frequently in the past, it will happen again at some point. Choices (a) and (e) follow this line of

reasoning closely. Choice (d) is also implicit in this line of reasoning. Also implied is a lack of evidence that a famine is imminent, for it can be assumed that the speaker would have phrased his argument differently if he saw evidence of an imminent famine (choice b). Choice (c) is irrelevant to the argument; the speaker neither states nor implies anything about the relative goodness or evil of famine. This choice is therefore correct.

SECTION VII

1. (d) The Defense Department experts are obviously citing something that would justify their request for budgetary increases. A *disparity* (lack of equality), presumably favoring the potential enemies, would justify such a request. While the use of "contrast" (compare to show differences) would be acceptable, *disparity* is better because it is more specific about our lack of equality. The other words are too vague.

2. (a) Choices (d) and (e) are obviously wrong. One stirs up interest or *controversy*, but not indifference or restraint. The second word of choice (a), *unorthodox*, fulfills the meaning of the sentence. An unorthodox position would stimulate controversy.

3. (c) Since the president spoke somberly about the precarious position of the beleaguered troops, his viewers would not see the picture he painted as being "optimistic" or "auspicious." And while the picture could appear "believable," *ominous*

(threatening, or portending evil or harm) is more suitable, since the troops were described as being in a dangerous or precarious position. Choice (*e*), "redundant," is not suitable at all.

4. (*e*) An incandescent liquid mass would be white hot. It would not be "storing," "reducing," or "absorbing" heat. While the earlier belief could have been that the sun is "wasting" heat, it would not provide a meaning in opposition to the more recent theory. *Radiating* implies sending out energy, and the relatively fast using up of the incandescent liquid mass. This would be in opposition to the idea of a body that runs on an almost *infinite* amount of atomic fuel. We know that the older theory must be in opposition to the newer one because of the words "contrary" and "rather."

5. (*b*) Lester thought one thing, but the rest of us thought something else. The word "but" makes clear that this divergence of opinion is implied in the sentence. *Dissimulating* expresses Lester's view that they were pretending something when they embraced. The rest of us thought they were genuinely *affectionate*, not pretending that they were.

6. (*d*) Of the choices, what kind of care would be important for the severely disabled? "Preventive medicine" comes too late for them. "Surgery" might be important for some severely disabled people, but probably not as generally important as *physical rehabilitation*. The other options are not applicable.

7. (*a*) While other choices could fit into the first blank almost as well as *improved*, only *opened* applies as the correct verb for a Pandora's box. In the legend of Pandora's box, the box was not "concealed," "caused," or "devised"; it was *opened*. The word "impaired" does not fit the idea of contributing toward ending hunger and poverty.

8. (*c*) The *rabble* (lower classes or common people) may be characterized as *plebeian* (common). Similarly, the *intelligentsia* (artistic, social, or political elite) may be characterized as *elitist*.

9. (*b*) *Recapitulate* is a synonym for *synopsize*, just as *encumber* is a synonym for *burden*.

10. (*d*) *Embarrass* and *humiliate* are similar in meaning, but the latter is a stronger word. This is a degree of difference word relationship.

11. (*a*) *Explicate* means to explain or clarify. *Obfuscate* is opposite in meaning to explicate. So, too, *precipitate*, which means overly hasty or rash, is opposite in meaning to *deliberate*, which means unhurried or carefully considered.

12. (*d*) An *archaeologist* studies *artifacts* (objects made by man) of the past and analyzes them to learn about the cultures and peoples of the past. Similarly, a *paleontologist* analyzes *fossils* (any remains or traces of animals of a former geological age) to learn about the fauna of the past. A podiatrist examines or studies feet, but not to learn about the ancient past.

13. (e) An *anesthetic* relieves *pain*, just as a *stimulant* corrects and relieves *sluggishness*.

14. (e) A *pistol* is carried in a *holster*, where it is readily available when needed. A *sword* is carried in a *scabbard*, where it is readily available when needed. The word "looseleaf" is an adjective. Looseleaf paper can be carried in a binder, but even so, not so that it can be readily removed and put to use in the way that a weapon is.

15. (d) A *constellation* is the word that describes a *star* group. A *pride* is a word that refers to a *lion* group that live and hunts together. This is a whole and part word relationship.

16. (a) *Contiguous*, which means close to, bordering, almost touching, is opposite in meaning to *remote*. Similarly, *nonchalant*, which means coolly unconcerned, indifferent, or unexcited, is opposite in meaning to *excitable*.

17. (e) In the last paragraph, the author mentions the naturalist literary tradition of Dreiser and Defoe as a heritage of Capote and Mailer.

18. (c) Dreiser did not, of course, write tales of modern Brahmins; it was James who did. The lack of morality that the New Humanists accused Dreiser of was in connection with his examination of their accepted values, not of immoral relationships with others. Dreiser's sharp political differences with the New Humanists may have colored their view of him, perhaps, but it was not for his political differences

that they criticized him, according to the passage. None of the three statements is correct, and the answer is choice (c).

19. (a) The inferences here must be drawn from subtly shaded remarks. Capote and Mailer inherit a literary tradition from Dreiser and Defoe, a tradition with added strength. The implication is that Dreiser's contributions were a treasure on a par with Defoe's, and that his work had strengths to which good current writers could add. All this is contrasted with the insubstantial "gossamer" stories of nameless (thus unimportant) adherents of the Jamesian mode.

20. (b) The first two sentences of the passage say that sensory perceptions cannot be communicated except within the framework of what has already been experienced. To ask someone to bring in a champagne-colored blouse might get you a blouse of any one of hundreds of shades. However, once the other person has experienced the color of the champagne blouse you have in mind, you can communicate in terms of that color which you have both experienced.

21. (c) See paragraph two for the explanation of why statement I is wrong. Also in paragraph two lies an explanation of what would bridge the communication gap: statements II and III.

22. (c) Support for choice (c) is contained in the last sentence of the passage.

23. (b) The topic sentence and the first paragraph support choice (b). This

passage, while it deals with Darwin, was not written in order to set forth the view that Darwin's theory explains natural selection.

24. (a) While the passage does imply that Lord Kelvin believed that the sun was losing energy, it does not go on to say that the sun is *not* losing energy, or that it *is* losing energy. As for (b), the passage does state that Mendel's work was not recognized at the time of its original publication, and it implies that in the twentieth century, when Mendel's work was given recognition, it was as if he had been heard of for the first time. Though, of course, his work had never really been lost, it was as if it had been discovered again. The use of the quotation marks, in this case, indicates that Mendel was rediscovered only in a manner of speaking.

25. (e) The last paragraph of the passage indicates that Mendel's articulation of the particulate nature of inheritance is the current belief, and earlier in the passage it was indicated that the theory that held with blending inheritance was at odds with Mendel and with Darwin's original belief in this respect, so statement I can be inferred from this passage. Similarly for statement II, the Lamarckian theory of the transmission of somatic changes as the only way in which rapid change in a species could be accounted for is refuted by the Mendelian view. Statement III does not reflect anything in the passage.

26. (c) The last sentence of paragraph 4 supports choice (c).

27. (d) The last sentence of the passage refutes Jenkin's view as set forth in paragraph 3, and supports Darwin's conception of evolution through natural selection.

28. (d) *Profligate*—utterly and shamelessly immoral; opposite—*virtuous*

29. (b) *Circumscribed*—limited, restricted; opposite—*unchecked*

30. (c) *Profound*—pervasive, thorough; opposite—*superficial*

31. (d) *Littoral*—a region along the shoreline; opposite—*inland*

32. (b) *Flamboyant*—showy, strikingly bold; opposite—*austere*

33. (e) *Knavish*—dishonest; opposite—*unexceptionable* (offering no basis for objection, beyond criticism)

34. (a) *Blowzy*—frumpy, unkempt, not neat; opposite—*dapper*

35. (c) *Fugitive*—fleeting, transitory; opposite—*permanent*

36. (c) *Engrossed*—absorbed; opposite—*distracted*

37. (b) *Sepulchral*—tomblike, gloomy; opposite—*cheerful*

38. (c) *Insipid*—mindless, shallow; opposite—*sapient* (wise, knowledgeable)

Answer Sheet—Practice Test 3

When you have chosen your answer to any question, blacken the corresponding space on the answer sheet below. Make sure your marking completely fills the answer space. If you change an answer, erase the previous marking completely.

Section I

1 Ⓐ Ⓑ Ⓒ Ⓓ Ⓔ	11 Ⓐ Ⓑ Ⓒ Ⓓ Ⓔ	21 Ⓐ Ⓑ Ⓒ Ⓓ Ⓔ	30 Ⓐ Ⓑ Ⓒ Ⓓ Ⓔ
2 Ⓐ Ⓑ Ⓒ Ⓓ Ⓔ	12 Ⓐ Ⓑ Ⓒ Ⓓ Ⓔ	22 Ⓐ Ⓑ Ⓒ Ⓓ Ⓔ	31 Ⓐ Ⓑ Ⓒ Ⓓ Ⓔ
3 Ⓐ Ⓑ Ⓒ Ⓓ Ⓔ	13 Ⓐ Ⓑ Ⓒ Ⓓ Ⓔ	23 Ⓐ Ⓑ Ⓒ Ⓓ Ⓔ	32 Ⓐ Ⓑ Ⓒ Ⓓ Ⓔ
4 Ⓐ Ⓑ Ⓒ Ⓓ Ⓔ	14 Ⓐ Ⓑ Ⓒ Ⓓ Ⓔ	24 Ⓐ Ⓑ Ⓒ Ⓓ Ⓔ	33 Ⓐ Ⓑ Ⓒ Ⓓ Ⓔ
5 Ⓐ Ⓑ Ⓒ Ⓓ Ⓔ	15 Ⓐ Ⓑ Ⓒ Ⓓ Ⓔ	25 Ⓐ Ⓑ Ⓒ Ⓓ Ⓔ	34 Ⓐ Ⓑ Ⓒ Ⓓ Ⓔ
6 Ⓐ Ⓑ Ⓒ Ⓓ Ⓔ	16 Ⓐ Ⓑ Ⓒ Ⓓ Ⓔ	26 Ⓐ Ⓑ Ⓒ Ⓓ Ⓔ	35 Ⓐ Ⓑ Ⓒ Ⓓ Ⓔ
7 Ⓐ Ⓑ Ⓒ Ⓓ Ⓔ	17 Ⓐ Ⓑ Ⓒ Ⓓ Ⓔ	27 Ⓐ Ⓑ Ⓒ Ⓓ Ⓔ	36 Ⓐ Ⓑ Ⓒ Ⓓ Ⓔ
8 Ⓐ Ⓑ Ⓒ Ⓓ Ⓔ	18 Ⓐ Ⓑ Ⓒ Ⓓ Ⓔ	28 Ⓐ Ⓑ Ⓒ Ⓓ Ⓔ	37 Ⓐ Ⓑ Ⓒ Ⓓ Ⓔ
9 Ⓐ Ⓑ Ⓒ Ⓓ Ⓔ	19 Ⓐ Ⓑ Ⓒ Ⓓ Ⓔ	29 Ⓐ Ⓑ Ⓒ Ⓓ Ⓔ	38 Ⓐ Ⓑ Ⓒ Ⓓ Ⓔ
10 Ⓐ Ⓑ Ⓒ Ⓓ Ⓔ	20 Ⓐ Ⓑ Ⓒ Ⓓ Ⓔ		

Section II

1 Ⓐ Ⓑ Ⓒ Ⓓ Ⓔ	11 Ⓐ Ⓑ Ⓒ Ⓓ Ⓔ	21 Ⓐ Ⓑ Ⓒ Ⓓ Ⓔ	30 Ⓐ Ⓑ Ⓒ Ⓓ Ⓔ
2 Ⓐ Ⓑ Ⓒ Ⓓ Ⓔ	12 Ⓐ Ⓑ Ⓒ Ⓓ Ⓔ	22 Ⓐ Ⓑ Ⓒ Ⓓ Ⓔ	31 Ⓐ Ⓑ Ⓒ Ⓓ Ⓔ
3 Ⓐ Ⓑ Ⓒ Ⓓ Ⓔ	13 Ⓐ Ⓑ Ⓒ Ⓓ Ⓔ	23 Ⓐ Ⓑ Ⓒ Ⓓ Ⓔ	32 Ⓐ Ⓑ Ⓒ Ⓓ Ⓔ
4 Ⓐ Ⓑ Ⓒ Ⓓ Ⓔ	14 Ⓐ Ⓑ Ⓒ Ⓓ Ⓔ	24 Ⓐ Ⓑ Ⓒ Ⓓ Ⓔ	33 Ⓐ Ⓑ Ⓒ Ⓓ Ⓔ
5 Ⓐ Ⓑ Ⓒ Ⓓ Ⓔ	15 Ⓐ Ⓑ Ⓒ Ⓓ Ⓔ	25 Ⓐ Ⓑ Ⓒ Ⓓ Ⓔ	34 Ⓐ Ⓑ Ⓒ Ⓓ Ⓔ
6 Ⓐ Ⓑ Ⓒ Ⓓ Ⓔ	16 Ⓐ Ⓑ Ⓒ Ⓓ Ⓔ	26 Ⓐ Ⓑ Ⓒ Ⓓ Ⓔ	35 Ⓐ Ⓑ Ⓒ Ⓓ Ⓔ
7 Ⓐ Ⓑ Ⓒ Ⓓ Ⓔ	17 Ⓐ Ⓑ Ⓒ Ⓓ Ⓔ	27 Ⓐ Ⓑ Ⓒ Ⓓ Ⓔ	36 Ⓐ Ⓑ Ⓒ Ⓓ Ⓔ
8 Ⓐ Ⓑ Ⓒ Ⓓ Ⓔ	18 Ⓐ Ⓑ Ⓒ Ⓓ Ⓔ	28 Ⓐ Ⓑ Ⓒ Ⓓ Ⓔ	37 Ⓐ Ⓑ Ⓒ Ⓓ Ⓔ
9 Ⓐ Ⓑ Ⓒ Ⓓ Ⓔ	19 Ⓐ Ⓑ Ⓒ Ⓓ Ⓔ	29 Ⓐ Ⓑ Ⓒ Ⓓ Ⓔ	38 Ⓐ Ⓑ Ⓒ Ⓓ Ⓔ
10 Ⓐ Ⓑ Ⓒ Ⓓ Ⓔ	20 Ⓐ Ⓑ Ⓒ Ⓓ Ⓔ		

Section III

1 Ⓐ Ⓑ Ⓒ Ⓓ Ⓔ	9 Ⓐ Ⓑ Ⓒ Ⓓ Ⓔ	17 Ⓐ Ⓑ Ⓒ Ⓓ Ⓔ	24 Ⓐ Ⓑ Ⓒ Ⓓ Ⓔ
2 Ⓐ Ⓑ Ⓒ Ⓓ Ⓔ	10 Ⓐ Ⓑ Ⓒ Ⓓ Ⓔ	18 Ⓐ Ⓑ Ⓒ Ⓓ Ⓔ	25 Ⓐ Ⓑ Ⓒ Ⓓ Ⓔ
3 Ⓐ Ⓑ Ⓒ Ⓓ Ⓔ	11 Ⓐ Ⓑ Ⓒ Ⓓ Ⓔ	19 Ⓐ Ⓑ Ⓒ Ⓓ Ⓔ	26 Ⓐ Ⓑ Ⓒ Ⓓ Ⓔ
4 Ⓐ Ⓑ Ⓒ Ⓓ Ⓔ	12 Ⓐ Ⓑ Ⓒ Ⓓ Ⓔ	20 Ⓐ Ⓑ Ⓒ Ⓓ Ⓔ	27 Ⓐ Ⓑ Ⓒ Ⓓ Ⓔ
5 Ⓐ Ⓑ Ⓒ Ⓓ Ⓔ	13 Ⓐ Ⓑ Ⓒ Ⓓ Ⓔ	21 Ⓐ Ⓑ Ⓒ Ⓓ Ⓔ	28 Ⓐ Ⓑ Ⓒ Ⓓ Ⓔ
6 Ⓐ Ⓑ Ⓒ Ⓓ Ⓔ	14 Ⓐ Ⓑ Ⓒ Ⓓ Ⓔ	22 Ⓐ Ⓑ Ⓒ Ⓓ Ⓔ	29 Ⓐ Ⓑ Ⓒ Ⓓ Ⓔ
7 Ⓐ Ⓑ Ⓒ Ⓓ Ⓔ	15 Ⓐ Ⓑ Ⓒ Ⓓ Ⓔ	23 Ⓐ Ⓑ Ⓒ Ⓓ Ⓔ	30 Ⓐ Ⓑ Ⓒ Ⓓ Ⓔ
8 Ⓐ Ⓑ Ⓒ Ⓓ Ⓔ	16 Ⓐ Ⓑ Ⓒ Ⓓ Ⓔ		

Section IV

1 Ⓐ Ⓑ Ⓒ Ⓓ Ⓔ	9 Ⓐ Ⓑ Ⓒ Ⓓ Ⓔ	17 Ⓐ Ⓑ Ⓒ Ⓓ Ⓔ	24 Ⓐ Ⓑ Ⓒ Ⓓ Ⓔ
2 Ⓐ Ⓑ Ⓒ Ⓓ Ⓔ	10 Ⓐ Ⓑ Ⓒ Ⓓ Ⓔ	18 Ⓐ Ⓑ Ⓒ Ⓓ Ⓔ	25 Ⓐ Ⓑ Ⓒ Ⓓ Ⓔ
3 Ⓐ Ⓑ Ⓒ Ⓓ Ⓔ	11 Ⓐ Ⓑ Ⓒ Ⓓ Ⓔ	19 Ⓐ Ⓑ Ⓒ Ⓓ Ⓔ	26 Ⓐ Ⓑ Ⓒ Ⓓ Ⓔ
4 Ⓐ Ⓑ Ⓒ Ⓓ Ⓔ	12 Ⓐ Ⓑ Ⓒ Ⓓ Ⓔ	20 Ⓐ Ⓑ Ⓒ Ⓓ Ⓔ	27 Ⓐ Ⓑ Ⓒ Ⓓ Ⓔ
5 Ⓐ Ⓑ Ⓒ Ⓓ Ⓔ	13 Ⓐ Ⓑ Ⓒ Ⓓ Ⓔ	21 Ⓐ Ⓑ Ⓒ Ⓓ Ⓔ	28 Ⓐ Ⓑ Ⓒ Ⓓ Ⓔ
6 Ⓐ Ⓑ Ⓒ Ⓓ Ⓔ	14 Ⓐ Ⓑ Ⓒ Ⓓ Ⓔ	22 Ⓐ Ⓑ Ⓒ Ⓓ Ⓔ	29 Ⓐ Ⓑ Ⓒ Ⓓ Ⓔ
7 Ⓐ Ⓑ Ⓒ Ⓓ Ⓔ	15 Ⓐ Ⓑ Ⓒ Ⓓ Ⓔ	23 Ⓐ Ⓑ Ⓒ Ⓓ Ⓔ	30 Ⓐ Ⓑ Ⓒ Ⓓ Ⓔ
8 Ⓐ Ⓑ Ⓒ Ⓓ Ⓔ	16 Ⓐ Ⓑ Ⓒ Ⓓ Ⓔ		

Section V

1 Ⓐ Ⓑ Ⓒ Ⓓ Ⓔ	8 Ⓐ Ⓑ Ⓒ Ⓓ Ⓔ	14 Ⓐ Ⓑ Ⓒ Ⓓ Ⓔ	20 Ⓐ Ⓑ Ⓒ Ⓓ Ⓔ
2 Ⓐ Ⓑ Ⓒ Ⓓ Ⓔ	9 Ⓐ Ⓑ Ⓒ Ⓓ Ⓔ	15 Ⓐ Ⓑ Ⓒ Ⓓ Ⓔ	21 Ⓐ Ⓑ Ⓒ Ⓓ Ⓔ
3 Ⓐ Ⓑ Ⓒ Ⓓ Ⓔ	10 Ⓐ Ⓑ Ⓒ Ⓓ Ⓔ	16 Ⓐ Ⓑ Ⓒ Ⓓ Ⓔ	22 Ⓐ Ⓑ Ⓒ Ⓓ Ⓔ
4 Ⓐ Ⓑ Ⓒ Ⓓ Ⓔ	11 Ⓐ Ⓑ Ⓒ Ⓓ Ⓔ	17 Ⓐ Ⓑ Ⓒ Ⓓ Ⓔ	23 Ⓐ Ⓑ Ⓒ Ⓓ Ⓔ
5 Ⓐ Ⓑ Ⓒ Ⓓ Ⓔ	12 Ⓐ Ⓑ Ⓒ Ⓓ Ⓔ	18 Ⓐ Ⓑ Ⓒ Ⓓ Ⓔ	24 Ⓐ Ⓑ Ⓒ Ⓓ Ⓔ
6 Ⓐ Ⓑ Ⓒ Ⓓ Ⓔ	13 Ⓐ Ⓑ Ⓒ Ⓓ Ⓔ	19 Ⓐ Ⓑ Ⓒ Ⓓ Ⓔ	25 Ⓐ Ⓑ Ⓒ Ⓓ Ⓔ
7 Ⓐ Ⓑ Ⓒ Ⓓ Ⓔ			

Section VI

1 Ⓐ Ⓑ Ⓒ Ⓓ Ⓔ	8 Ⓐ Ⓑ Ⓒ Ⓓ Ⓔ	14 Ⓐ Ⓑ Ⓒ Ⓓ Ⓔ	20 Ⓐ Ⓑ Ⓒ Ⓓ Ⓔ
2 Ⓐ Ⓑ Ⓒ Ⓓ Ⓔ	9 Ⓐ Ⓑ Ⓒ Ⓓ Ⓔ	15 Ⓐ Ⓑ Ⓒ Ⓓ Ⓔ	21 Ⓐ Ⓑ Ⓒ Ⓓ Ⓔ
3 Ⓐ Ⓑ Ⓒ Ⓓ Ⓔ	10 Ⓐ Ⓑ Ⓒ Ⓓ Ⓔ	16 Ⓐ Ⓑ Ⓒ Ⓓ Ⓔ	22 Ⓐ Ⓑ Ⓒ Ⓓ Ⓔ
4 Ⓐ Ⓑ Ⓒ Ⓓ Ⓔ	11 Ⓐ Ⓑ Ⓒ Ⓓ Ⓔ	17 Ⓐ Ⓑ Ⓒ Ⓓ Ⓔ	23 Ⓐ Ⓑ Ⓒ Ⓓ Ⓔ
5 Ⓐ Ⓑ Ⓒ Ⓓ Ⓔ	12 Ⓐ Ⓑ Ⓒ Ⓓ Ⓔ	18 Ⓐ Ⓑ Ⓒ Ⓓ Ⓔ	24 Ⓐ Ⓑ Ⓒ Ⓓ Ⓔ
6 Ⓐ Ⓑ Ⓒ Ⓓ Ⓔ	13 Ⓐ Ⓑ Ⓒ Ⓓ Ⓔ	19 Ⓐ Ⓑ Ⓒ Ⓓ Ⓔ	25 Ⓐ Ⓑ Ⓒ Ⓓ Ⓔ
7 Ⓐ Ⓑ Ⓒ Ⓓ Ⓔ			

Section VII

1 Ⓐ Ⓑ Ⓒ Ⓓ Ⓔ	11 Ⓐ Ⓑ Ⓒ Ⓓ Ⓔ	21 Ⓐ Ⓑ Ⓒ Ⓓ Ⓔ	30 Ⓐ Ⓑ Ⓒ Ⓓ Ⓔ
2 Ⓐ Ⓑ Ⓒ Ⓓ Ⓔ	12 Ⓐ Ⓑ Ⓒ Ⓓ Ⓔ	22 Ⓐ Ⓑ Ⓒ Ⓓ Ⓔ	31 Ⓐ Ⓑ Ⓒ Ⓓ Ⓔ
3 Ⓐ Ⓑ Ⓒ Ⓓ Ⓔ	13 Ⓐ Ⓑ Ⓒ Ⓓ Ⓔ	23 Ⓐ Ⓑ Ⓒ Ⓓ Ⓔ	32 Ⓐ Ⓑ Ⓒ Ⓓ Ⓔ
4 Ⓐ Ⓑ Ⓒ Ⓓ Ⓔ	14 Ⓐ Ⓑ Ⓒ Ⓓ Ⓔ	24 Ⓐ Ⓑ Ⓒ Ⓓ Ⓔ	33 Ⓐ Ⓑ Ⓒ Ⓓ Ⓔ
5 Ⓐ Ⓑ Ⓒ Ⓓ Ⓔ	15 Ⓐ Ⓑ Ⓒ Ⓓ Ⓔ	25 Ⓐ Ⓑ Ⓒ Ⓓ Ⓔ	34 Ⓐ Ⓑ Ⓒ Ⓓ Ⓔ
6 Ⓐ Ⓑ Ⓒ Ⓓ Ⓔ	16 Ⓐ Ⓑ Ⓒ Ⓓ Ⓔ	26 Ⓐ Ⓑ Ⓒ Ⓓ Ⓔ	35 Ⓐ Ⓑ Ⓒ Ⓓ Ⓔ
7 Ⓐ Ⓑ Ⓒ Ⓓ Ⓔ	17 Ⓐ Ⓑ Ⓒ Ⓓ Ⓔ	27 Ⓐ Ⓑ Ⓒ Ⓓ Ⓔ	36 Ⓐ Ⓑ Ⓒ Ⓓ Ⓔ
8 Ⓐ Ⓑ Ⓒ Ⓓ Ⓔ	18 Ⓐ Ⓑ Ⓒ Ⓓ Ⓔ	28 Ⓐ Ⓑ Ⓒ Ⓓ Ⓔ	37 Ⓐ Ⓑ Ⓒ Ⓓ Ⓔ
9 Ⓐ Ⓑ Ⓒ Ⓓ Ⓔ	19 Ⓐ Ⓑ Ⓒ Ⓓ Ⓔ	29 Ⓐ Ⓑ Ⓒ Ⓓ Ⓔ	38 Ⓐ Ⓑ Ⓒ Ⓓ Ⓔ
10 Ⓐ Ⓑ Ⓒ Ⓓ Ⓔ	20 Ⓐ Ⓑ Ⓒ Ⓓ Ⓔ		

Practice 3
Test

GRE Practice Test 3

Time—30 minutes
38 Questions

For each of the numbered questions in this section, choose the best answer according to the instructions, and blacken the correspondingly numbered blank space on the answer sheet.

Each of the sentences below has one or more blank spaces indicating where a word or words have been omitted. Each sentence is followed by five words or sets of words lettered from (a) to (e). Select the lettered word or set of words which, inserted to replace the blanks, BEST fits in with and completes the meaning of the sentence as a whole.

1. While diligence is a trait much to be admired, it should not be confused with drudging, the unquestioning preoccupation with – – – routines.

   (a) daily
   (b) systematic
   (c) calcified
   (d) formal
   (e) menial

2. The Board of Directors – – – the Chairman's million-dollar salary by saying that the demand for top-flight profit-producing executives is growing enormously throughout the world, but the supply of high-– – – management talent is very limited.

   (a) justified . . . caliber
   (b) criticized . . . salaried
   (c) increased . . . rise
   (d) calculated . . . flying
   (e) measured . . . caliper

3. Over the years she had proven herself so wise, so concerned, so dedicated to the welfare of the community, that it was hardly surprising that everyone in it treated her with great – – –.

   (a) dignity
   (b) forebearance
   (c) sympathy
   (d) rectitude
   (e) deference

4. Although he had shown himself to be – – – in the most dangerous of situations in both war and peace, he revealed himself as – – – in the social atmosphere of the female-dominated drawing room.

   (a) reliable . . . self-assured
   (b) intrepid . . . craven
   (c) calm . . . cavalier
   (d) heroic . . . diehard
   (e) self-controlled . . . diplomatic

5. The air was bitter cold, the temperature well below the freezing point, yet they found themselves – – – freely as they clambered up the steep northern slope.

   (a) laughing
   (b) perspiring
   (c) disporting
   (d) shivering
   (e) confiding

6. Try as we may to eliminate personal – – – from our conclusions, we insensibly tend to take – – – stances, whether it be by favoring or by leaning over backward.

   (a) friendship . . . opposing
   (b) references . . . liberal
   (c) concerns . . . unpopular
   (d) bias . . . subjective
   (e) preferences . . . philosophical

7. I had never imagined that Mr. Hart could be guilty of – – –, but then he shocked me by announcing that he was appointing his son to the firm's presidency.

   (a) embezzlement
   (b) insubordination
   (c) nepotism
   (d) subornation
   (e) entropy

In each of the questions below, a related pair of words or phrases in capital letters is followed by five pairs of words or phrases, lettered from (a) to (e). Select the lettered pair that expresses a relationship that is MOST similar to that of the capitalized pair.

8. EDITOR : NOVELIST : : (a) receptionist : restaurant
   (b) surrogate : probate (c) director : playwright
   (d) psychiatrist : neurotic (e) priest : convert

9. PORTFOLIO : SECURITIES : : (a) bureau : commission
   (b) cabinet : carpentry (c) panel : jurors
   (d) portmanteau : sketches (e) silo : sheaves

10. NEUTRALITY : PARTICIPANT : :
    (a) passivity : activist (b) gender : sexuality
    (c) repose : synergist (d) complicity : culprit
    (e) entropy : philanthropy

11. IRRITANT : ANNOYANCE : :
    (a) stimulus : incitement (b) caustic : invigorate
    (c) soporific : sanctification (d) coagulation : glut
    (e) repercussion : inhibition

12. SWORD : SCABBARD : : (a) coal : furnace
    (b) clam : shell (c) caviar : champagne
    (d) corsage : box (e) arrow : quiver

13. VINDICTIVENESS : FELLOWSHIP : :
    (a) venality : probity (b) equanimity : stability
    (c) rancor : surliness (d) fortitude : patience
    (e) pollution : wastes

14. SHACKLES : FETTER : : (a) remuneration : munificent
    (b) emancipation : liberate (c) complicity : exonerate
    (d) meditation : elate (e) tether : unleash

15. SELDOM : RARELY : : (a) frequently : infrequently
    (b) often : usually (c) collectively : selectively
    (d) tantamount : equivalent (e) basic : fundamental

16. ERUPTION : VOLCANO : : (a) cannon : pistol
    (b) spate : tempest (c) broadside : retort
    (d) earthquake : fault (e) vindication : corroboration

In the series of selections below, each passage is followed by questions based on its content. Read the passage and choose the best answer for each question based on the contents of the passage. The questions must be answered on the basis of what is stated or implied in the reading passage.

All along the chain of biological evolution, the extinction of species appears to have been a stage in the process of adapting genetic lineages to changing environmental conditions. Although some catastrophic extinction occurred naturally, producing total loss of a genetic line, such catastrophes were comparatively rare. In modern times, however, human activities have altered the fundamental nature of this process, resulting in nearly total genetic losses.

It is not difficult to gain general agreement that man-induced increases in the endangerment and extinction of wildlife—whether due to habitat alteration or loss, pollution, insufficiently regulated hunting, or other factors—are undesirable. It is, however, more difficult to obtain consensus when consideration is given to the economic costs of correcting such trends, including natural habitat preservation, regulation of pesticides and other toxic substances, and wildlife and park management. Endangered species often are, in effect, competitors with humans for habitat and other resources which also provide other kinds of human uses and needs.

Measures needed to protect endangered species vary considerably in difficulty and cost. Of the approximately 400 invertebrate species which at present appear to be threatened, for example, about one-third could probably be restored by such inexpensive means as modifying the boundaries of designated natural areas, acquiring and protecting caves and other small areas which contain the particular species, and additional management of parks and refuges.

Another one-third of the endangered lower animal species are threatened principally by water pollution and could be protected by improved control, particularly of five southern rivers.

The remaining one-third of the 400 endangered shellfish species would be considerably more difficult to protect. These are threatened by complex factors, such as overcollecting, channelization, highway and housing development, dams, introduced species such as the Asian snail, dredging, quarry washing, poor erosion control, and lowering of water tables.

The identification of threatened species and other significant wildlife trends must precede any corrective measures, and our knowledge base for making such identification is deficient in many respects. Our present lists of threatened species and subspecies are known to be incomplete, except in those geographical areas which contain habitats of species that have important commercial or sports harvest value.

17. Which of the following is neither expressed nor implied in the passage as being a threat posed by man to wildlife preservation?

   (a) The discharge of chemical wastes into streams as a result of industrial development
   (b) Large-scale housing development
   (c) Poor coordination of international efforts at park and refuge management
   (d) Introduction of species into environments
   (e) Control of blights and pests which attack crops

18. It can be inferred from the passage that studies of endangered species

   (a) have revealed little of importance to improve wildlife preservation
   (b) are more likely to be carried out when a financially concerned interest group is involved
   (c) sometimes endanger the very species they hope to protect
   (d) show that endangered species can never be saved except at great cost
   (e) seldom arrive at a consensus

19. Which of the following statements is expressed or implied in the passage?

(a) Approximately 400 species of mollusk are on the current endangered species list.

(b) The Asian snail is a victim of overcollecting.

(c) It is not easy to arrive at a consensus on how to deal with situations in which humans compete with endangered species for habitat and other resources, especially when cost is a factor.

(d) Water pollution, which can be controlled at relatively low cost, threatens the majority of the endangered invertebrate species.

(e) Modification of boundaries of parks and other recreational areas is less effective in protecting endangered species than acquiring caves and refuges.

One of the many theories about alcoholism is the learning and reinforcement theory, which explains alcoholism by considering alcohol ingestion as a reflex response to some stimulus and as a way to reduce an inner-drive state such as fear or anxiety. Characterizing life situations in terms of approach and avoidance, this theory holds that persons tend to be drawn to pleasant situations or repelled by unpleasant ones. In the latter case, alcohol ingestion is said to reduce the tension or feelings of unpleasantness and to replace them with the feeling of euphoria generally observed in most persons after they have consumed one or more drinks.

Some experimental evidence tends to show that alcohol reduces fear in an approach-avoidance situation. Conger trained one group of rats to approach a food goal and, using aversive conditioning, trained another group to avoid electric shock. After an injection of alcohol the pull away from the shock was measurably weaker, while the pull toward food was unchanged.

The obvious troubles experienced by alcoholic persons appear to contradict the learning theory in the explanation of alcoholism. The discomfort, pain, and punishment they experience should presumably serve as a deterrent to drinking. The fact that alcoholic persons continue to drink in the face of family discord, loss of employment, illness, and other sequels of repeated bouts is explained by the proximity of the drive reduction to the consumption of alcohol; that is, alcohol has the immediate effect of reducing tension while the unpleasant consequences of drunken behavior come only later. The learning paradigm, therefore, favors the establishment and repetition of the resort to alcohol.

In fact, the anxieties and feelings of guilt induced by the consequences of excessive alcohol ingestion may themselves become the signal for another bout of alcohol abuse. The way in which the cue for another bout could be the anxiety itself is explained by the process of stimulus generalization: Conditions or events occurring at the time of reinforcement tend to acquire the characteristics of stimuli. When alcohol is consumed in association with a state of anxiety or fear, the emotional state itself takes on the properties of a stimulus, thus triggering another drinking bout.

The role of punishment is becoming increasingly important in formulating a cause of alcoholism based on the principles of learning theory. While punishment may serve to suppress a response, experiments have shown that in some cases it can serve as a reward and reinforce the behavior. Thus if the alcoholic person has learned to drink under conditions of both reward and punishment, either type of condition may precipitate renewed drinking.

Ample experimental evidence supports the hypothesis that excessive alcohol consumption can be learned. By gradually increasing the concentration of alcohol in drinking water, psychologists have been able to induce the ingestion of larger amounts of alcohol by an animal than would be normally consumed. Other researchers have been able to achieve similar results by varying the schedule of reinforcement; that is, by requiring the animal to consume larger and larger amounts of the alcohol solutions before rewarding it. In this manner, animals learn to drink enough to become dependent on alcohol in terms of demonstrating withdrawal symptoms.

20. The author's primary purpose in the passage is to

   (a) support Alcoholics Anonymous as a means of coping with alcoholism
   (b) present a learning paradigm which will help alcoholics and others to understand what causes their dependence upon alcohol
   (c) explain the application of a psychological approach to alcoholism
   (d) demonstrate the most effective new treatment of alcoholism
   (e) condition alcoholics to accept the learning and reinforcement theory

21. To which one of the following questions does the author provide enough information to formulate an answer?

   (a) Why do people who are alcoholics continue to drink even though the consequences of their drinking are very unpleasant?
   (b) How did Conger explain the behavior of alcoholics in terms of shock therapy?
   (c) Under what circumstances does an alcoholic benefit from anxiety attacks?
   (d) To what extent does stimulus generalization prevent alcohol ingestion from becoming the signal for another bout of alcohol abuse?
   (e) Which has proven more successful in the treatment of alcoholism, the use of aversive conditioning or the use of reinforcement?

22. Which of the following statements is not directly stated but can be inferred from the passage?

(a) The behavior of alcoholics contradicts the approach-avoidance theory.
(b) People may be taught by experience to become alcoholics.
(c) Punishment may become the stimulus for added drinking.
(d) The behavior of alcoholics seems to defy accepted psychological theories.
(e) Alcohol does help to reduce tensions.

23. According to the passage, the process of stimulus generalization

(a) explains why people tend to avoid behavior that is associated with painful experiences
(b) is responsible for the drive reduction that results from an attempt to avoid tension
(c) may cause the heavy drinking of a controlled alcoholic to diminish
(d) is responsible for the fact that alcoholics have a wide range of problems aside from their drinking problem
(e) is one in which the circumstances existing at the time of reinforcement tend to act as a stimulus as well

24. The description of Conger's experiment with two groups of rats was intended to

(a) show that ingestion of alcohol does not affect appetite
(b) corroborate the findings of other academic researchers
(c) show that alcohol minimizes fear
(d) disprove learning and reinforcement theory
(e) convince the reader of the usefulness of behavioral research

25. The author maintains that habituation to excessive alcohol consumption can be learned. The method employed to do so, experimentally, which uses reinforcement is

(a) the introduction of alcohol into the bloodstream by injection
(b) the stimulus generalization approach
(c) the increase of the concentration of alcohol in the subject's drinking water
(d) the use of anxiety in an avoidance-approach pattern
(e) increasing the amount of alcohol the subject must drink each time before giving it a reward

26. Which of the following, according to the passage, contribute to alcoholism?

I. The need to reduce tensions and anxieties
II. The anxieties resulting from guilt feelings about previous drinking bouts

III. Punishment for alcoholic behavior

(a) I only
(b) I and II only
(c) I, II, and III
(d) II only
(e) II and III only

27. A statement that is supported by the passage is

(a) if the pleasurable taste of whisky leads to an acquired taste for brandy, then stimulus generalization has occurred
(b) slapping a child for misbehaving over a period of time may encourage him to repeat his misbehavior
(c) if a person has learned to drink under two sets of conditions, both must be present in order to induce him to drink
(d) the troubles experienced by alcoholics as a result of their alcoholism tends to encourage them to abstain from drinking
(e) learning and reinforcement theory assumes that alcoholics knowingly damage themselves in order that they may satisfy more immediate inner urges

In each of the questions below, a capitalized word is followed by five words or phrases lettered from (a) through (e). Select the word or phrase most nearly OPPOSITE in meaning to the capitalized word.

Since some of the questions require that you distinguish fine shades of meaning, consider all choices carefully before you select your answer.

28. DISHEARTEN

(a) weaken
(b) buoy
(c) abash
(d) refute
(e) enable

29. DISCRETE

(a) intemperate
(b) hidden
(c) scrupulous
(d) fused
(e) authentic

30. TRADUCE

(a) appreciate
(b) malinger
(c) signify
(d) emancipate
(e) expedite

31. CONTUMACIOUS

(a) compliant
(b) defensive
(c) tranquil
(d) ruminative
(e) profound

32. PUISSANT

(a) lucid
(b) dull-witted
(c) virulent
(d) oblivious
(e) impotent

33. CONSONANT

(a) clumsy
(b) number
(c) discordant
(d) intrepid
(e) versify

34. INDIGENCE

    (*a*) hard-working
    (*b*) loquacious
    (*c*) current
    (*d*) affluence
    (*e*) obsolescence

35. CACOPHONOUS

    (*a*) loud
    (*b*) mysterious
    (*c*) harmonious
    (*d*) earth-shattering
    (*e*) fruitless

36. DEXTEROUS

    (*a*) witless
    (*b*) maladroit
    (*c*) two-handed
    (*d*) sinister
    (*e*) procrastinating

37. IRASCIBLE

    (*a*) propitiatory
    (*b*) reversible
    (*c*) comprehensible
    (*d*) limpid
    (*e*) neutral

38. UPRIGHT

    (*a*) rectangular
    (*b*) slack
    (*c*) unscrupulous
    (*d*) baseless
    (*e*) injudicious

STOP! Work only on this section until the time allowed is over.

SECTION II

Time—30 minutes
38 Questions

For each of the numbered questions in this section, choose the best answer according to the instructions, and blacken the correspondingly numbered blank space on the answer sheet.

Each of the sentences below has one or more blank spaces indicating where a word or words have been omitted. Each sentence is followed by five words or sets of words lettered from (a) to (e). Select the lettered word or set of words which, inserted to replace the blanks, BEST fits in with and completes the meaning of the sentence as a whole.

1. His credentials, which included years of top-level experience in related fields, should have given him preference over the other applicants, but Personnel decided that he was – –.–, and selected a – – – for the position.

   (a) overqualified . . . tyro
   (b) superannuated . . . veteran
   (c) disdainful . . . woman
   (d) unreliable . . . consultant
   (e) underage . . . youth

2. Realizing that his negative appraisal of her ability had stemmed from his too-hasty evaluation of her work, he offered her, as an act of – – –, a chance to work on the new skyscraper.

   (a) mercy
   (b) charity
   (c) friendship
   (d) desperation
   (e) contrition

3. People seem to be – – – stimulated by the death and havoc wrought in such great disasters as the destruction of the Hindenburg, the sinking of the Titanic, and the mass murders and suicides in Guyana.

   (a) morbidly
   (b) delightfully
   (c) understandably
   (d) intellectually
   (e) quietly

4. Miss Snell's rapid advancement in rank, which resulted directly from her industry and ability, was enviously – – – by some of her colleagues to luck and family connections.

   (a) inferred
   (b) imputed
   (c) accredited
   (d) blamed
   (e) implied

5. The opposition had – – – such strong arguments against his position on the issue that even his most loyal adherents deserted him, and he was forced to – – –.

   (a) fabricated . . . resist
   (b) instituted . . . falter
   (c) marshalled . . . acquiesce
   (d) tendered . . . concentrate
   (e) structured . . . reciprocate

6. The controversy surrounding the question of the effect of herbicides threatens not just to – – – the members of the scientific community, but to – – – them.

   (a) condemn . . . insult
   (b) infuriate . . . confuse
   (c) ostracize . . . criticize
   (d) divide . . . polarize
   (e) implicate . . . involve

7. Although the appearance of printed materials has – – – very little in the past forty years, the basic methods used to produce them have changed almost beyond – – –.

   (a) contributed . . . expectation
   (b) offered . . . television
   (c) developed . . . others
   (d) altered . . . recognition
   (e) diminished . . . comparison

In each of the questions below, a related pair of words or phrases in capital letters is followed by five pairs of words or phrases, lettered from (a) to (e). Select the lettered pair that expresses a relationship that is MOST similar to that of the capitalized pair.

8. IRREVERENT : PIOUS : : (a) courtly : interminable (b) cantankerous : argumentative (c) isolated : intimidated (d) commendatory : disapproving (e) current : regressive

9. IRRITATED : EXASPERATED : :
   (a) contemptuous : contemptible (b) abounding : glutted
   (c) overdone : redundant (d) pubescent : mature
   (e) stolid : sordid

10. DESULTORY : METHODICAL : : (a) integral : unified
    (b) plaintive : contemplative (c) dissipated : concentrated
    (d) attenuated : actuated (e) verbose : loquacious

11. RACE : FATIGUE : : (a) track : athlete
    (b) ant : bug (c) fast : hunger
    (d) walking : running (e) air : sleep

12. BALLAST : STABILITY : : (a) springs : resiliency
    (b) armor : obduracy (c) flotation : airiness
    (d) spinnaker : seaworthiness (e) fuel : thermals

13. FORTUITOUS : INHERENT : : (a) envious : desire
    (b) knowledgeable : incoherent (c) legible : indelible
    (d) rugged : endurable (e) gregarious : introverted

14. EQUIVOCATION : MISLEADS : :
    (a) misdirection : intrigues (b) elucidation : clarifies
    (c) interrogation : answers (d) extrapolation : reverses
    (e) rebuttal : confuses

15. BIRTHMARK : CONGENITAL : :
    (a) beauty spot : facial (b) baldness : hereditary
    (c) small pox : vaccine (d) fracture : incurred
    (e) obesity : overindulgence

16. OPAQUE : TRANSPARENT : :
    (a) concentrated : dissipated (b) turgid : swollen
    (c) imprisoned : incarcerated (d) forlorn : despondent
    (e) tepid : seething

In the series of selections below, each passage is followed by questions based on its content. Read the passage and choose the best answer for each question based on the contents of the passage. The questions must be answered on the basis of what is stated or implied in the reading passage.

Clinicians at a recent psychoanalytic conference brought forth interesting evidence that guilt, far from being the psychic impediment generally conceived, has the potential to inspire creativity, and enhance sensitivity.

Tests of prison inmates have shown significantly low scores on guilt scales, measured by psychologist-researcher Donald L. Mosher. The

Mosher scales measure the tendency to feel guilt in three forms: sex guilt, hostility guilt, and general guilt, called morality conscience. Prisoners who had committed sex crimes scored low on sex guilt; those who were imprisoned for violent crimes scored low on hostility guilt; those incarcerated for crimes against property scored low on morality conscience.

Other studies conducted in the armed forces corroborate the findings that men accused of brutality toward those they command feel little or no sense of remorse or guilt, but tend to defend vigorously the "correctness" of their actions.

That guilt can be a lonely and lacerating burden has long been known. The ancient Greeks understood the redemptive feelings and cathartic benefits of watching the tragic hero struggle with guilt. Hamlet plots to "catch the conscience of the King." O'Neill re-creates the ancient themes and adds to them contemporary guilts. The Judeo-Christian ethic transmits this heavy burden, commencing with "original sin" and continuing with the need for confession and atonement.

Although in the past many psychoanalysts, joined by a recent spate of authors, seem to have been dedicated to eliminating the sense of guilt, some clinicians hold that guilt is the necessary price for socialization.

Still others agree with Dr. Karl Menninger in the value of appropriate, or rational, guilt, and feel that a prime objective of therapeutic intervention should be to help the patient differentiate between guilt feelings that are unwarranted and unfounded, based perhaps on distorted perceptions of past occurrences, and those which are well-founded responses to real situations. The child, it is felt, should not be made to feel guilt about exploring his body, just as the adult should not be ashamed of his or her sexuality. But this freedom must not be viewed as license. When the individual's desires or needs can be fulfilled without coming into conflict with societal needs, the albatross of guilt can be shed.

It is this new approach, this compromise, which we find surfacing in twentieth-century literature. Herzog and Willy Loman battle their needless guilt, and their experiences help us all to cope.

17. A point that the passage emphasizes concerning guilt is, by inference, that

   (a) guilt serves to punish the person who commits offense against individuals or society
   (b) some people never suffer from feelings of guilt
   (c) unfortunately, many people who have been judged guilty of offenses against society do not recognize their acts as being wrong
   (d) crimes against property should not arouse guilt feelings in the perpetrator
   (e) sensitive people are guiltier than those who are less sensitive

18. According to the passage, a crucial concern of the therapist should be to

    (a) help patients evaluate appropriate and inappropriate responses of guilt feelings in their own lives
    (b) direct the patient to understand that guilt feelings are unwarranted and unfounded
    (c) intervene between the patient and society, so that the patient can fulfill his needs without societal interference
    (d) help the patient conquer guilt
    (e) show the patient how to manipulate feelings of guilt in interactions with others

19. The statement for which there is support in the passage is that

    (a) guilt is a psychic impediment
    (b) low scores on the Mosher scales are evidence of good mental health
    (c) the best military commanders feel little sense of guilt about carrying out their assignments even if it goes against their grain to do so
    (d) individuals should not feel guilty about fulfilling their own needs and desires as long as they do not act counter to the needs of society
    (e) we are all guilty, but we should learn to shed our feelings of guilt just as we shed our clothes

Changes in the volume of unemployment are governed by three fundamental forces: the growth of the labor force, the increase in output per man-hour, and the growth of total demand for goods and services. Changes in the average hours of work enter in exactly parallel fashion but have been quantitatively less significant. As productivity rises, less labor is required per dollar of national product, or more goods and services can be produced with the same number of man-hours. If output does not grow, employment will certainly fall; if production increases more rapidly than productivity (less any decline in average hours worked), employment must rise. But the labor force grows too. Unless gross national product (total final expenditure for goods and services corrected for price changes) rises more rapidly than the sum of productivity increase and labor-force growth (again modified for any change in hours of work), the increase in employment will be inadequate to absorb the growth in the labor force. Inevitably the unemployment rate will increase. Only when total production expands faster than the rate of labor force growth plus the rate of productivity increase and minus the rate at which average annual hours fall does the unemployment rate fall. Increases in productivity were more important than growth of the labor force as sources of the wide gains in output experienced in the period from the end of the war to the mid-sixties. These increases in potential production simply were not matched by increases in demand adequate to maintain steady full employment.

Except for the recession years of 1949, 1954, and 1958, the rate of economic growth exceeded the rate of productivity increase. However, in the late 1950s productivity and labor force were increasing more rapidly than usual, while the growth of output was slower than usual. This accounted for the change in employment rates.

But if part of the national purpose is to reduce and contain unemployment, arithmetic is not enough. We must know which of the basic factors we can control and which we wish to control. Unemployment would have risen more slowly or fallen more rapidly if productivity had increased more slowly, or the labor force had increased more slowly, or the hours of work had fallen more steeply, or total output had grown more rapidly. These are not independent factors however, and a change in any of them might have caused changes in the others.

A society can choose to reduce the growth of productivity, and it can probably find ways to frustrate its own creativity. However, while a reduction in the growth of productivity at the expense of potential output might result in higher employment in the short run, the long-run effect on the national interest would be disastrous.

We must also give consideration to the fact that hidden beneath national averages is continuous movement into, out of, between, and within labor markets. For example, 15 years ago, the average number of persons in the labor force was 74 million, with about 70 million employed and 3.9 million unemployed. Yet 14 million experienced some term of unemployment in that year. Some were new entrants to the labor force; others were laid off temporarily. The remainder were those who were permanently or indefinitely severed from their jobs. Thus, the average number of unemployed during a year understates the actual volume of involuntary displacement that actually occurs.

High unemployment is not an inevitable result of the pace of technological change, but the consequence of passive public policy. We can anticipate a moderate increase in the labor force accompanied by a slow and irregular decline in hours of work. It follows that the output of the economy—and the aggregate demand to buy it—must grow in excess of 4 percent a year just to prevent the unemployment rate from rising, and even greater if the unemployment rate is to fall further. Yet our economy has seldom, if ever, grown at a rate faster than 3.5 percent for any extended length of time.

We have no cause for complacency. Positive fiscal, monetary, and manpower policies will be needed in the future.

20. According to the passage, the rate of employment can be expected to rise when

   (a) productivity rises at the same rate as growth of the labor force.
   (b) productivity and labor force increase at a greater pace than output.
   (c) output exceeds productivity.
   (d) rate of economic growth is less than the number of man-hours required.
   (e) none of the above.

21. In the specific recession years noted in the passage, it can be inferred that

   (*a*) the rate of employment rose.
   (*b*) labor force growth exceeded final expenditure for goods.
   (*c*) full employment was attained.
   (*d*) more labor was required per dollar of national product.
   (*e*) the rate of unemployment grew.

22. The author's purpose in this passage is to

   (*a*) define the economic terms used in discussion of employment.
   (*b*) criticize the decisions of past administrations during recession years.
   (*c*) allay current fears about increasing unemployment.
   (*d*) document the rise of American productivity since the war.
   (*e*) call for the application of positive economic control policies in the years that lie ahead.

23. The statement that is supported by the passage is

   (*a*) as productivity rises, a greater amount of labor per dollar of national product can be expected.
   (*b*) unemployment falls when production expands faster than labor force growth plus productivity increase, minus the fall of average annual hours worked.
   (*c*) reduction in the growth of productivity and a cutback in potential output are in the national interest.
   (*d*) technological growth must, in the long run, increase unemployment.
   (*e*) the long-term rate of growth in our economy, if continued at the same rate as present into the future, will eventually decrease our unemployment rate.

24. It can be inferred from the passage that the author would

   (*a*) advocate a carefully managed economy.
   (*b*) prefer the unemployment rate to rise and fall with the value of the gross national product as a check on labor costs.
   (*c*) perceive high unemployment as undesirable but unavoidable.
   (*d*) contend that manipulation of the size of the labor force would have prevented recessions in the years noted.
   (*e*) oppose governmental interference in the interplay among the three forces affecting employment.

25. According to the author, gross national product is

    (*a*) total production less the decline in average hours worked.
    (*b*) the combined sum of all goods in the country.
    (*c*) manufactured goods plus the cost of personal services minus the cost of technological change.
    (*d*) the output of the economy decreased by the cost of social services and governmental costs.
    (*e*) total final expenditures for goods and services corrected for price changes.

26. According to the passage, national employment averages

    (*a*) do not reveal the actual volume of unemployment due to layoffs and discharges during a year.
    (*b*) have shown a steady increase in the cost of production over the last twenty years.
    (*c*) are the best indices for monitoring the actual effect of increased productivity on economic growth.
    (*d*) reveal that the recession years were really years of increased productivity and decreased employment.
    (*e*) are useless statistics as a basis for positive fiscal policy.

27. For which of the following questions does the author give enough information to provide an answer?

    (*a*) How can the rate of growth of the new entrants into the labor market be controlled?
    (*b*) Why has the rate of growth of the economy remained under 3.5 percent over the long run?
    (*c*) To what extent did the postwar economy reflect the impact of prewar economic policy?
    (*d*) At what rate must the economy grow in order to avoid a rise in the unemployment rate, if there is a moderate growth in the labor force and a decline in hours of work?
    (*e*) What impact would a freeze in the wage and price structure have on total demand for goods and services and productivity?

In each of the questions that follow, a capitalized word is followed by five words or phrases lettered (*a*) through (*e*). Select the word or phrase most nearly OPPOSITE in meaning to the capitalized word.

Since some of the questions require that you distinguish fine shades of meaning, consider all choices carefully before you select your answer.

28. RESCISSION

(a) disputation
(b) readmission
(c) neglect
(d) confirmation
(e) judiciousness

29. SANGUINE

(a) sugary
(b) hopeless
(c) judgmental
(d) pacific
(e) unintelligent

30. SYMMETRICAL

(a) unartistic
(b) shoddy
(c) euphonious
(d) subdued
(e) skewed

31. OVERT

(a) clandestine
(b) rectangular
(c) uncontested
(d) undiplomatic
(e) intricate

32. CONDIGN

(a) corroborate
(b) unsullied
(c) unprecedented
(d) inappropriate
(e) woebegone

33. BLATANT

(a) subjugated
(b) subdued
(c) pulsating
(d) infamous
(e) turbid

34. ABSTRUSE

(a) manifest
(b) positive
(c) darksome
(d) profane
(e) pitiless

35. SALUBRIOUS

(a) nonsaline
(b) sober
(c) unwholesome
(d) penurious
(e) contrite

36. DULCET

(a) onesided
(b) cancerous
(c) exemplary
(d) stentorian
(e) independent

37. ATTENUATE

(a) wait
(b) impregnate
(c) strengthen
(d) hinder
(e) dissipate

38. CACOPHONOUS

(a) amplified
(b) androgynous
(c) euphonious
(d) munificent
(e) contiguous

STOP! Work only on this section until the time allowed is over.

SECTION III

Time—30 minutes
30 Questions

The following questions each consist of two quantities, one in Column A and one in Column B. Compare the two quantities and on the answer sheet blacken oval

(a) if the quantity in Column A is greater;
(b) if the quantity in Column B is greater;
(c) if the two quantities are equal;
(d) if the relationship cannot be determined from the information given.

All letters such as x, y, and n represent real numbers. A symbol appearing in both columns represents the same quantity in Column A as it does in Column B.

In some questions, information concerning one or both of the quantities to be compared is centered above the two columns.

Figures are generally not drawn to scale, unless otherwise stated. You may assume these figures lie in a plane, unless it is indicated they represent solid figures.

Lines that appear to be straight may be assumed to be straight lines.

Column A	Column B
1. 30% of 70	70% of 30

2.
$$2 < p < 7$$
$$7 < q < 10$$

Column A	Column B
p	q

3.
r, s, and t are positive integers
$$r > 1$$

Column A	Column B
r(s + t)	rs + t
4. $\dfrac{1}{3} \times \dfrac{1}{4}$	$\dfrac{1}{3} \div \dfrac{1}{4}$

5.
$$r = 2s$$

Column A	Column B
6s + 3	2r + 3
6. $11 \times 180 \times 7$	$9 \times 180 \times 12$

		Column A			**Column B**

7.

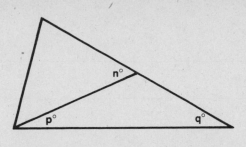

| n | | q |

---

8. Area of circle with diameter d | Area of square with side 3/4 d

---

Questions 9 and 10 refer to figure below.

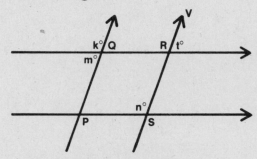

PQRS is a parallelogram.

9. k | n

10. m + k | n + t

$$r > s;\ r, s \neq 0$$

11. $\dfrac{1}{r}$ | $\dfrac{1}{s}$

Questions 12 and 13 refer to diagram below.

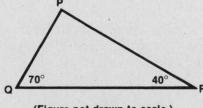

(Figure not drawn to scale.)

12. PQ | QR

13. PR | QR

	Column A	**Column B**
14.	$x \geq 0, y - 2x = 5$	
	x	y
15.	$\sqrt[3]{28.2}$	$\sqrt{8.92}$

Solve each of the following problems based on the information provided. Then indicate the best answer on your answer sheet.

16. How many thousandths are there in 2.7%?

    (*a*) .27
    (*b*) 2.7
    (*c*) 27
    (*d*) 270
    (*e*) 20.7

17. $.04 \div \dfrac{4}{.5} =$

    (*a*) .005
    (*b*) .05
    (*c*) .5
    (*d*) 5
    (*e*) .32

18. A loan library charges 10¢ for the first 3 days and 6¢ for each additional day a book is borrowed. If a borrower pays $1.18 for the loan of a book, for how many days was the book borrowed?

    (*a*) 15
    (*b*) 18
    (*c*) 20
    (*d*) 21
    (*e*) 24

19. An equilateral triangle three inches on each side is divided up into equilateral triangles one inch on each side. What is the maximum number of the smaller triangles that can be formed?

    (*a*) 3
    (*b*) 6
    (*c*) 9
    (*d*) 12
    (*e*) 15

20. The length of a rectangular court is 6 feet shorter than twice its width, W. The perimeter of the court is

   (a) 3W – 6
   (b) 6W – 6
   (c) 4W – 12
   (d) 3W – 12
   (e) 6W – 12

Questions 21–24 refer to the following graph.

**Advertising Expenditures
Outlays by Media**

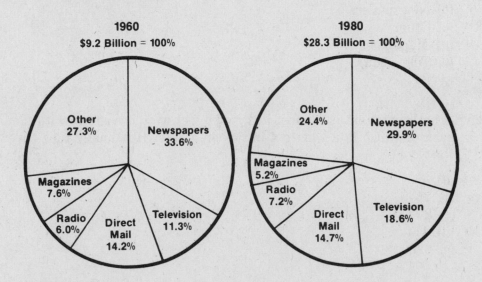

1960
$9.2 Billion = 100%

Other
27.3%

Newspapers
33.6%

Magazines
7.6%

Radio
6.0%

Direct
Mail
14.2%

Television
11.3%

1980
$28.3 Billion = 100%

Other
24.4%

Newspapers
29.9%

Magazines
5.2%

Radio
7.2%

Direct
Mail
14.7%

Television
18.6%

21. How much more was the outlay for newspaper advertising in 1960 than that for radio advertising in the same year?

   (a) $1.5 billion
   (b) $2.0 billion
   (c) $2.5 billion
   (d) $3.0 billion
   (e) $3.5 billion

22. Which of the following is the best approximation of the ratio of direct mail outlays in 1960 to direct mail outlays in 1980?

   (a) 1:3
   (b) 1:2
   (c) 1:1
   (d) 2:1
   (e) 3:1

23. Of all the categories of outlays shown on both graphs, what is the fourth largest outlay?

    (*a*) Direct mail—1980
    (*b*) Newspapers—1960
    (*c*) Radio—1980
    (*d*) Magazines—1980
    (*e*) Other—1960

24. Which medium experienced the greatest gain in total advertising outlays from 1960 to 1980?

    (*a*) Direct mail
    (*b*) Newspapers
    (*c*) Other
    (*d*) Magazines
    (*e*) Television

25. A bathroom that is 7⅔ feet long and 6 feet wide is covered with tiles, each of which is a square 4 inches on a side. How many tiles cover the floor?

    (*a*) 45
    (*b*) 75
    (*c*) 207
    (*d*) 414
    (*e*) 620

Questions 26–29 refer to the following graph.

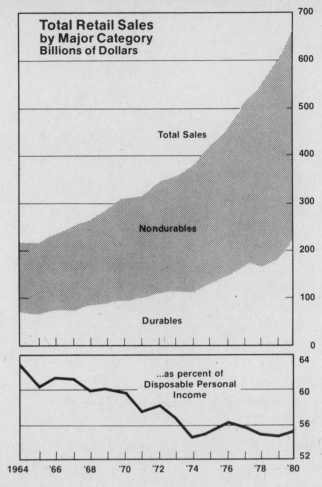

26. Approximately what was the total disposable income in 1969 in the United States?

   (a) $200 billion
   (b) $300 billion
   (c) $400 billion
   (d) $500 billion
   (e) $600 billion

27. Approximately how much greater were sales of nondurable goods than sales of durable goods in 1980?

   (a) $650 billion
   (b) $550 billion
   (c) $450 billion
   (d) $350 billion
   (e) $250 billion

28. Approximately what percent of disposable personal income was spent on durable goods in 1980?

(a) 17%
(b) 13%
(c) 10%
(d) 5%
(e) 30%

29. If disposable income was $500 billion in 1974, approximately how much was it in 1979?

(a) $350 billion
(b) $550 billion
(c) $750 billion
(d) $950 billion
(e) $1,150 billion

30.

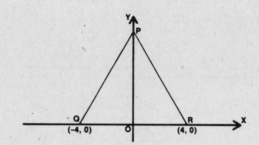

In the figure above, triangle PQR is equilateral. The coordinates of point P are

(a) $(0,4)$
(b) $(4\sqrt{3},0)$
(c) $(8\sqrt{3},0)$
(d) $(0,8\sqrt{3})$
(e) $(0,4\sqrt{3})$

STOP! Work only on this section until the time allowed is over.

SECTION IV

Time—30 minutes
30 Questions

The following questions each consist of two quantities, one in Column A and one in Column B. Compare the two quantities and on the answer sheet blacken oval

(a) if the quantity in Column A is greater;
(b) if the quantity in Column B is greater;
(c) if the two quantities are equal;
(d) if the relationship cannot be determined from the information given.

All letters such as x, y, and n represent real numbers. A symbol appearing in both columns represents the same quantity in Column A as it does in Column B.

In some questions, information concerning one or both of the quantities to be compared is centered above the two columns.

Figures are generally not drawn to scale, unless otherwise stated. You may assume these figures lie in a plane, unless it is indicated they represent solid figures.

Lines that appear to be straight may be assumed to be straight lines.

Column A	**Column B**

1. $$0 < k < 1$$

k^2	k

2.

f	$g - h$

Column A	Column B

3.

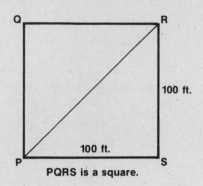

PQRS is a square.

The number of seconds it takes a man to walk from P to R directly at 5 feet per second

The number of seconds it takes a man to run from P to Q and Q to R at 8 feet per second

---

4.   r is the tens digit of (235 ÷ 5)
s is the tens digit of (342 × 273)

r   s

For questions 5–7

$$p = \left(-2\frac{1}{4}\right) \qquad q = \left(\frac{3}{4}\right) \qquad r = (3)$$

$$\begin{array}{ccccccccccccccccccc} & & & & & & & p & & & q & & r & & & & \\ -6 & -5 & -4 & -3 & -2 & -1 & 0 & \frac{1}{4} & \frac{1}{2} & \frac{3}{4} & 1 & 2 & 3 & 4 & 5 & 6 \end{array}$$

5. pq   −2

6. $-\dfrac{p}{r}$ $-\dfrac{r}{p}$

7. $p < t < q$
−q   t

Column A	Column B

Questions 8–11 refer to the diagram below.

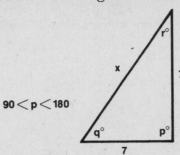

$90 < p < 180$

(Figure not drawn to scale.)

8. x | $7\sqrt{2}$

9. x | 14

10. $q + r$ | 90

11. Numerical value of the perimeter of the triangle | Numerical value of the area of the triangle

---

12. $1 < k < m$

2m | $k + m$

---

13. $\dfrac{1}{3} + \dfrac{1}{3} + \dfrac{1}{\pi}$ | 1

---

14. $3 < r \leq 6;\ 3 < s \leq 6$

The maximum possible value of $r - \dfrac{r}{s}$ | 5

15.

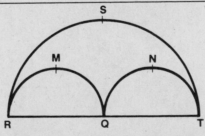

RST, RMQ and QNT are semicircles.

Length of arc RST | Length of arc RMQ + length of arc QNT

Solve each of the following problems based on the information provided. Then indicate the best answer on your answer sheet.

16. The time in city A is 3 hours later than in city B. A plane leaves city A at 5 P.M. for city B and arrives there 4 hours later. What time is it in city B upon arrival?

    (a) 6 A.M.
    (b) 6 P.M.
    (c) 2 P.M.
    (d) 3 P.M.
    (e) 4 P.M.

17.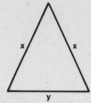

    In the figure above, $10 < x < 20$. Which of the following gives all possible values of y?

    (a) $0 < y < 20$
    (b) $0 < y < 40$
    (c) $5 < y < 20$
    (d) $10 < y < 40$
    (e) $20 < y < 80$

Questions 18–21 refer to the following graph.

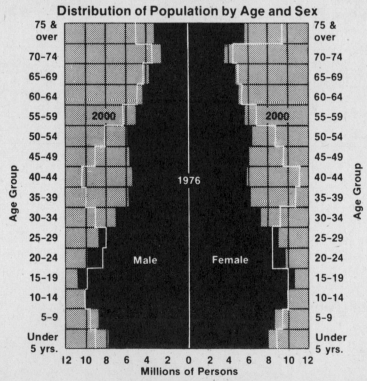

Distribution of Population by Age and Sex

18. According to the graph, which age group will have the largest population in the United States in the year 1981?

   (a) 10–14
   (b) 15–19
   (c) 20–24
   (d) 25–29
   (e) 30–34

19. Approximately how many teenagers (13–19 years old) were there in the United States in 1976?

   (a) 29.5 million
   (b) 20.6 million
   (c) 40.6 million
   (d) 48.3 million
   (e) 50.2 million

20. By what percent will the group of 45–49-year-old women increase from 1976 to 2000?

   (a) 10%
   (b) 20%
   (c) 40%
   (d) 60%
   (e) 80%

21. By approximately how many persons is the "under 25" age group expected to grow from 1976 to 2000?

   (a) 5 million
   (b) 0
   (c) 10 million
   (d) 15 million
   (e) 20 million

22. In a right triangle, the ratio of the legs is 2:3. If the area of the triangle is 75, what is the length of the hypotenuse?

   (a) 4
   (b) $4\sqrt{5}$
   (c) $13\sqrt{5}$
   (d) $5\sqrt{3}$
   (e) $5\sqrt{13}$

23. What is the surface area in square feet of a cube with a volume of 125 cubic feet?

   (a) 25
   (b) 27
   (c) 64
   (d) 100
   (e) 150

24.

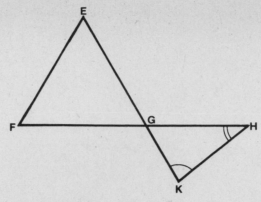

In the diagram above, EFG is an equilateral triangle. Sides FG and EG are extended through G to H and K and another triangle is formed. The sum of the measures in degrees of angles K and H is

(a) 60
(b) 120
(c) 135
(d) 140
(e) 150

25. If p = 4q and q = 2r, find r in terms of p.

(a) $\dfrac{p}{2}$

(b) $\dfrac{p}{4}$

(c) $\dfrac{p}{8}$

(d) 4p

(e) 8p

26. The price of ball point pens which originally sold for $24 a dozen is changed to $24 for 1½ dozen. This represents a

(a) 50% increase in price
(b) 50% decrease in price

(c) $66\dfrac{2}{3}$ % decrease in price

(d) $33\dfrac{1}{3}$ % increase in price

(e) $33\dfrac{1}{3}$ % decrease in price

27.

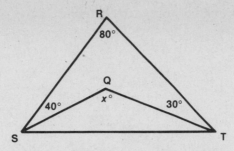

(Figure not drawn to scale)

In △ RST above, x =

(a) 160
(b) 150
(c) 140
(d) 135
(e) 120

28.

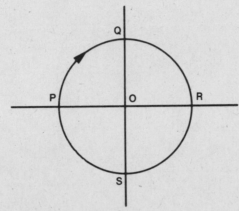

Starting at P in the figure above, a point rotates clockwise around circle O through 500°. The point is then

(a) between P and Q
(b) between Q and R
(c) between R and S
(d) between S and P
(e) at S

29. If $(r - s)^2 = 32$ and $rs = 4$, $r^2 + s^2 =$

(a) 18
(b) 24
(c) 30
(d) 32
(e) 40

30. If t tennis balls can be bought for d dollars, how many dollars would s tennis balls costs?

(a) $\dfrac{ds}{t}$

(b) $\dfrac{s - t}{d}$

(c) $\dfrac{dt}{s}$

(d) $\dfrac{t - s}{d}$

(e) $\dfrac{st}{d}$

STOP! Work only on this section until the time allowed is over.

SECTION V

Time—30 minutes
25 Questions

A written passage or set of statements precedes each question or group of questions in this section. Choose the best answer to each question. For some questions, you may find it useful to draw a diagram, graph, or other problem-solving aid.

Questions 1–4 refer to the following:

(1) Five people sat at a linear dais that had six seats.
(2) Arnold sat at one end, at chair #1.
(3) Celia and Earl were adjacent to each other.
(4) Fewer seats separated Bob from Celia than from Earl.
(5) Fewer seats separated Dorothy from Earl than from Arnold.

1. If Earl was at #2, then the empty seat was #

   (a) 4 only
   (b) 6 only
   (c) 4 or 5 only
   (d) 5 or 6 only
   (e) 4, 5, or 6 only

2. Which of the following deductions may be made?

   I.   Celia was not at #2.
   II. Celia was not at #4.
   III. Celia was not at #6.

   (a) I only
   (b) III only
   (c) I and II only
   (d) I and III only
   (e) I, II, and III

3. If Celia was at #5, then which statement is correct?

   (a) Dorothy was at #3.
   (b) Earl was at #4.
   (c) Bob was at #6.
   (d) All of the above are correct.
   (e) None of the above are correct.

4. If Dorothy was at #3, then which of the following is a possible seating arrangement for numbers 4, 5, and 6, in that order?

   I. Bob, Earl, Celia
   II. Earl, Celia, Bob
   III. Bob, Celia, Earl

   (a) I only
   (b) II only
   (c) I and II only
   (d) I and III only
   (e) II and III only

Questions 5-6 refer to the following:

Cancer is a dreaded disease that kills more and more people each year. Therefore the government should increase its funding for research into a cure for cancer.

5. The argument would be most strengthened if it were true that

   (a) failure to continue cancer research would lead to increased mortality rates
   (b) all forms of cancer are increasing in frequency
   (c) the federal government's budget is balanced
   (d) all forms of cancer will someday be shown to be curable
   (e) only the government is capable of funding increased cancer research

6. Which of the following is not an assumption made by the author of the argument above?

   (a) Deaths from cancer are increasing at least as fast as death from other causes.
   (b) All forms of cancer are usually fatal.
   (c) Cancer treatment will probably be improved as a result of cancer research.
   (d) The current level of government funding for cancer research is too low.
   (e) Adequate progress in the fight against cancer will not be made without government help.

Questions 7-10 refer to the following:

(1) Leslie, Lynn, and Gail are related.
(2) Leslie is the father of Gail's brother's wife.
(3) Lynn is a blood relative (related by birth) of Leslie.

(4) Gail's brother is a blood relative of Lynn.
(5) Three generations or fewer are involved.
(6) No marriage between blood relatives has occurred.

7. Which of the following must be true?

    I. Gail is Lynn's aunt or uncle.
   II. Leslie and Lynn are siblings.
  III. Lynn is younger than Gail.

(a) I only
(b) III only
(c) I and III only
(d) II and III only
(e) I, II, and III

8. Which of the following must be true of Lynn's mother?

    I. She is Gail's sister-in-law.
   II. She is Gail's brother's wife.
  III. Leslie is her father.

(a) I only
(b) III only
(c) I and II only
(d) II and III only
(e) I, II, and III

9. Which of the following must be true?

(a) Gail may be a blood relative of Leslie.
(b) Gail may be a blood relative of her brother's wife.
(c) Gail's brother is a blood relative of Leslie.
(d) Gail's brother's wife is a blood relative of Lynn.
(e) Gail has more than one brother.

10. Which of the six numbered statements may be omitted without changing the nature of the relationships being described?

(a) Statement (1)
(b) Statement (3)
(c) Statement (4)
(d) Statement (5)
(e) Statement (6)

Questions 11–15 refer to the following:

All S's are P's.
All T's are S's.
All R's are both P's and Q's.
Not all P's are S's.
Not all S's are T's.

11. Which of the following can be inferred from the statements above?

   (a) Some S's are Q's.
   (b) All T's are P's.
   (c) All P's are Q's.
   (d) Some S's are not R's.
   (e) All Q's are R's.

12. If a T is an R, it must also be which of the following?

   (a) a Q only
   (b) an S only
   (c) a P only
   (d) an S and a Q only
   (e) an S, a Q, and a P only

13. Given the information above, which of the following situations is not possible?

   (a) Some T's that are R's are not Q's.
   (b) Some S's that are R's are also Q's.
   (c) All T's are P's.
   (d) Some Q's are not P's.
   (e) Some T's are not Q's.

14. If all Q's are R's, it can be inferred that

   (a) all P's are Q's
   (b) all P's are R's
   (c) all Q's are P's
   (d) some R's are T's and Q's
   (e) some R's are S's and Q's

15. Which of the following statements must be true?

   I. There are more R's that are P's than are T's.
   II. There are more P's than R's.
   III. There are more P's than T's.

   (a) I only
   (b) III only
   (c) I and II only
   (d) II and III only
   (e) I, II, and III

Questions 16–22 refer to the following:

A certain archipelago is composed of seven islands, known as islands A, B, C, D, E, F, and G.

All excursions among the islands are by boat and begin from island A.

All boats go to island B from island A and take either 5, 10, or 15 minutes to do so.

If the trip from island A to island B takes 5 minutes, the boat goes next to island C; if the trip takes 10 minutes, the boat goes next to island D; if the trip takes 15 minutes, the boat goes next to island E.

The trips from island B to islands C, D, and E take 10, 15, and 20 minutes respectively.

The boat goes from island C to island F, taking 15 minutes.

The boat goes from island E to island G, taking 15 minutes.

The boat goes from island D to island E, taking 10 minutes.

The boat goes from island C to island D, taking 5 minutes.

The boat goes from island D to island F, taking 10 minutes.

The boat goes from island G to island A, taking 35 minutes.

The boat goes from island D to island G, taking 10 minutes.

No trips other than those listed above may occur.

16. How many minutes may be spent in traveling from island A to island D?

   I. 20
  II. 25
 III. 30

  (*a*) I only
  (*b*) III only
  (*c*) I or II only
  (*d*) II or III only
  (*e*) I, II, or III

17. How many different routes lead from island A to island E without stopping at any island twice?

  (*a*) 1
  (*b*) 2
  (*c*) 3
  (*d*) 4
  (*e*) 5

18. How many minutes long is the longest trip from island A to island F without stopping at any island twice?

  (*a*) 25
  (*b*) 30
  (*c*) 35
  (*d*) 40
  (*e*) 45

19. How many minutes does the shortest trip from island A to island G take?

(a) 30
(b) 35
(c) 40
(d) 45
(e) 50

20. How many different routes lead from island A to island G?

(a) 1
(b) 2
(c) 3
(d) 4
(e) 5

21. According to the conditions above, from which island is it impossible to return to island A?

(a) Island C
(b) Island D
(c) Island E
(d) Island F
(e) Island G

22. Which of the following statements is (are) correct?

I. If one travels from island A to island B in 5 minutes, one cannot reach island G.
II. If one travels from island A to island B in 10 minutes, one can reach any island without making a second stop at any island.
III. If one travels from island A to island B in 15 minutes, one cannot reach island F without first returning to island A.

(a) I only
(b) III only
(c) I and II only
(d) I and III only
(e) II and III only

23. Judging from its nature and source, which statement appears the most reasonable and trustworthy?

(a) Chemist: "This experiment will win me the Nobel Prize."
(b) Mother: "My child is the smartest in her grade."
(c) Auto mechanic: "This car needs a lot of work done on it."
(d) Doctor: "Mr. Cross came to my office July 14 complaining of persistent nosebleeds."
(e) Clerk: "The Fireball is the best car on the market."

24. Mickey: "Politicians are crooks."
    Minnie: "That's not so. I know of many businessmen who are terrible thieves."

    Minnie's response shows that she interpreted Mickey's remark as meaning that

    (*a*) no politicians are crooks
    (*b*) some politicians are not crooks
    (*c*) only politicians are crooks
    (*d*) only businessmen are honest
    (*e*) some politicians are businessmen

25. Descartes said, "I think, therefore I am." Descartes was confused when he said that, for although inanimate objects do not think, they clearly exist.

    The most appropriate response to the argument above would be to point out that

    (*a*) people who do not exist do not think
    (*b*) Descartes did not say, "A thing exists only if it thinks."
    (*c*) Descartes evidently did not believe that inanimate objects exist
    (*d*) philosophical statements are not always meant to be analyzed logically
    (*e*) even great thinkers sometimes make mistakes

STOP! Work only on this section until the time allowed is over.

SECTION VI

Time—30 minutes
25 Questions

A written passage or set of statements precedes each question or group of questions in this section. Choose the best answer to each question. For some questions, you may find it useful to draw a diagram, graph, or other problem-solving aid.

Questions 1–4 refer to the following:

The north-south avenues of Middletown are parallel and are one block apart.
Fir Avenue is five blocks west of Walnut Avenue.
Birch Avenue is one block west of Fir Avenue.
Oak Avenue is two blocks east of Fir Avenue.
Chestnut Avenue is two blocks east of Oak Avenue.
Walnut Avenue is two blocks east of Maple Avenue.

1. Maple Avenue must be

    (*a*) four blocks east of Fir Avenue
    (*b*) one block west of Birch Avenue
    (*c*) between Oak Avenue and Chestnut Avenue
    (*d*) between Fir Avenue and Oak Avenue
    (*e*) two blocks east of Chestnut Avenue

2. Another avenue, Palm Avenue, could be located in any of the following places except

    (*a*) one block west of Birch Avenue
    (*b*) one block east of Walnut Avenue
    (*c*) between Fir Avenue and Oak Avenue
    (*d*) two blocks east of Chestnut Avenue
    (*e*) three blocks west of Walnut Avenue

3. How many blocks from Fir Avenue is Chestnut Avenue?

    (*a*) 1
    (*b*) 2
    (*c*) 3
    (*d*) 4
    (*e*) 5

4. Which avenue is equally distant from Birch Avenue and Walnut Avenue?

(a) Fir
(b) Oak
(c) Palm
(d) Maple
(e) Chestnut

Questions 5–7 refer to the following:

Vitamin X is necessary for many essential bodily functions. Everyone should take vitamin X tablets to prevent vitamin-deficiency disease.

5. If *false*, which of the following statements would *invalidate* the above argument?

I. Vitamin X may be lacking in the diet.
II. Valid research showing the need for vitamin X has been done.
III. Vitamin X can be isolated in some manner.

(a) I only
(b) III only
(c) I and II only
(d) II and III only
(e) I, II, and III

6. The argument presented would be strongest if it were true that

(a) most common foods contain little or no vitamin X
(b) vitamin X deficiency has socially embarrassing but non-fatal symptoms
(c) some doctors take vitamin X tablets
(d) vitamin X deficiency is found only in the very young
(e) vitamin X is nontoxic

7. Which of the following, if true, would most weaken the argument?

(a) People have lived healthily until now without knowing about vitamin X.
(b) Every scientist who has tried to duplicate the experiment purportedly showing vitamin X's importance has failed.
(c) Some people can manufacture vitamin X in their bodies from ordinary nutrients found in all foods.
(d) The leading nutrition expert in the country does not take vitamin X tablets.
(e) People lacking vitamin X usually lack other vitamins as well.

Questions 8–10 refer to the following:

J, K, L, M, and N are seated around a circular table.
There is one seat between L and M.
J is not seated next to M.

8. Which of the following statements must be true?

    I. K is seated next to M.
   II. N is seated next to M.
  III. There is one seat between J and N.

(a) III only
(b) I and II only
(c) I and III only
(d) II and III only
(e) I, II, and III

9. Which of the following statements must be true?

    I. J is seated directly between K and L.
   II. If L is seated next to N, there is one seat between L and K.
  III. If L is seated next to K, there is one seat between L and N.

(a) II only
(b) I and III only
(c) II and III only
(d) I, II, and III
(e) neither I, II, nor III

10. If a sixth person, P, places a chair directly between L and K and joins the group, then

(a) there is one seat between P and M
(b) J is seated next to K
(c) K is seated next to N
(d) there is one seat between P and N
(e) J is seated next to M

Questions 11–14 refer to the following:

$$X*Y = \frac{X}{X + Y}$$

$$X@Y = \frac{X + Y}{Y}$$

When more than one operation is indicated, perform the operations from right to left. For instance, $1@1*1$ is found by solving $1*1$, which equals 1/2. Then $1@1/2$ is performed, giving a result of 3.

11. What is $2@2@2@2@2@2$?

(a) 1/2
(b) 0.8

(c) 1

(d) 2

(e) 8

12. What is 0*1*2*3*4*5@5?

(a) 0

(b) 31/53

(c) 1

(d) 2

(e) infinity

13. Which is greatest?

(a) 4*0

(b) 4*1*1

(c) 4*1

(d) 4*2

(e) 4*12@4

14. Which is least?

(a) 3*1

(b) 3*3

(c) 3*5

(d) 3@1

(e) 1@1

Questions 15–18 refer to the following:

(1) The members of a certain tribe are divided into three castes, known as the Hra, Cru, and Erg castes.

(2) A Hra woman cannot marry a Cru man.

(3) An Erg man cannot marry a Cru woman.

(4) A son takes the caste of his father; a daughter takes the caste of her mother.

(5) All marriages except those mentioned above are permitted.

(6) There are no children born out of wedlock.

15. It can be inferred from the conditions described that an Erg man

  I. cannot have a Cru grandmother
 II. cannot have a Cru mother
III. may have a Hra mother

(a) I only

(b) III only

(c) I and II only

(d) II and III only

(e) I, II, and III

16. A Hra woman marries and has three children, all of whom are members of the Hra caste. Which of the following must be true?

    I. If she were married to an Erg man, they have no male children.

    II. If she were married to a Hra man, they may have male children.

    III. If her fourth child is male, he may be a Cru.

  (*a*) I only

  (*b*) III only

  (*c*) I and II only

  (*d*) II and III only

  (*e*) I, II, and III

17. A Hra woman

  (*a*) may have a Cru grandson

  (*b*) may not have an Erg son

  (*c*) may not have an Erg grandson

  (*d*) may not have a Cru granddaughter

  (*e*) may have an Erg daughter-in-law

18. When two Crus are married, it is impossible for them to have

    I. Any female Hra descendants

    II. A Hra great-granddaughter

    III. A Hra granddaughter

  (*a*) I only

  (*b*) III only

  (*c*) I and II only

  (*d*) II and III only

  (*e*) I, II, and III

Questions 19–23 refer to the following:

Celia's school district offers adult education courses January through April. Courses are given either for an entire month or twice as intensively for half a month. Celia can take two one-month courses concurrently, but can take no other course while she takes a half-month course. She wishes to take courses in American literature, basket weaving, cooking, dance, and English literature.

American literature is offered in the first half of January and in March.

Basket weaving is offered in February and in March.

Cooking is offered in the second half of February and in April.

Dance is offered in the second half of January, in March, and in the second half of April.

English literature is offered in January, in the second half of February, in March, and in the first half of April.

Each course is a month-long course unless specifically stated to be otherwise.

19. In what month is the greatest number of courses offered?

    (a) January
    (b) February
    (c) March
    (d) April
    (e) March and April are equal in this regard.

20. In which month(s) is Celia limited to only one course?

    (a) January
    (b) February
    (c) April
    (d) January and February
    (e) January and April

21. If Celia is to take both literature courses before March, then how many schedules are available to her?

    (a) 0
    (b) 1
    (c) 2
    (d) 4
    (e) 6

22. If Celia takes no courses in January, then which of the following must she take if she is to take all five courses?

    (a) Cooking in February
    (b) English literature in February
    (c) Dance in March
    (d) English literature in March
    (e) Cooking in April

23. If Celia is to finish by the end of March, then which of the following courses must she take?

    I. American literature in January
    II. English literature in February
    III. Basket weaving in March

    (a) I only
    (b) II only
    (c) I and II only
    (d) I and III only
    (e) II and III only

24. Superior teachers are invariably inspiring. However, some superior teachers are also irritable, and irritable teachers are frequently disturbing to certain students.

Which of the following conclusions may properly be drawn from the statements above?

(a) Superior teachers are generally disturbing to students.
(b) Most inspiring teachers are disturbing to certain students.
(c) Irritable teachers are often superior teachers.
(d) Some inspiring teachers are frequently disturbing to certain students.
(e) Inspiring teachers tend to stimulate students to further learning.

25. History shows that economic expansion occurs only when government intervention in the economy is kept to a minimum. Since the economy is now in a period of stagnation, we should reduce the extent of governmental intervention in the economy right now.

The argument above would be most strengthened if it could be shown that

(a) the economy may actually be in a period of gradual decline
(b) the general public currently favors a decreased level of governmental intervention in the economy
(c) twenty years ago, when the economy was stronger, the extent of governmental intervention was smaller
(d) a reduction in the degree of governmental intervention may actually stimulate economic expansion
(e) governmental intervention in the economy is currently more extensive than ever

STOP! Work only on this section until the time allowed is over.

SECTION VII

Time—30 minutes
38 Questions

For each of the numbered questions in this section, choose the best answer according to the instructions, and then blacken the correspondingly numbered blank space on the answer sheet.

Each of the sentences below has one or more blank spaces indicating where a word or words have been omitted. Each sentence is followed by five words or sets of words lettered from (a) to (e). Select the lettered word or set of words which, inserted to replace the blanks, BEST fits in with and completes the meaning of the sentence as a whole.

1. With the inflationary spiral winding upward at double digit rates, the average wage earner, despite pay adjustments, remains frustrated by the – – – between income and the cost of living.

   (a) friction
   (b) division
   (c) upsurge
   (d) discrepancy
   (e) change

2. More women than ever are – – – to positions in middle management, but they are finding that traditional attitudes are still – – – their ambitions to obtain top jobs in the highest echelons of business.

   (a) aspiring . . . restraining
   (b) rising . . . thwarting
   (c) drawn . . . inspiring
   (d) retiring . . . dominating
   (e) attracted . . . condemning

3. Politicians parade their families before the public when campaigning, in the hope that voters will be – – – that a candidate who seems – – – to his or her family must also, of necessity, be devoted to the public good.

   (a) aware . . . lovable
   (b) doubtful . . . thoughtful
   (c) convinced . . . oblivious
   (d) satisfied . . . suitable
   (e) persuaded . . . devoted

4. Less than a generation ago, the computer was a tool – – – for the use of large businesses and research centers; today it is used not only by small businesses but by – – – as well, for a variety of purposes including self-instruction and recreation.

   (a) adapted ... stock brokers
   (b) equipped ... corporations
   (c) reserved ... individuals
   (d) intended ... institutions
   (e) fashioned ... scientists

5. The effectiveness of government depends upon the willingness of the governed to give up some degree of freedom and – – – the laws in return for the assurance of an orderly existence.

   (a) profit by
   (b) learn about
   (c) enforce
   (d) debate
   (e) abide by

6. Technology provides new means to combat crime, but technology is available to the criminal, too, and every new law-enforcement technique is – – – to advances in – – – methodology.

   (a) responsive ... systematic
   (b) impervious ... deleterious
   (c) helpful ... electronic
   (d) vulnerable ... criminal
   (e) equivalent ... scientific

7. His crime was so – – – that even Phillips, a judge noted for his – – –, could find no grounds for clemency.

   (a) meaningless ... dispassion
   (b) heinous ... leniency
   (c) impassioned ... temperament
   (d) reprehensible ... candor
   (e) premeditated ... perspicacity

In each of the questions below, a related pair of words or phrases in capital letters is followed by five pairs of words or phrases, lettered from (a) to (e). Select the lettered pair that expresses a relationship that is MOST similar to that of the capitalized pair.

8. MACHINE : FACTORY : : (a) product : formula
   (b) foreman : toolmaker (c) waste : conservation
   (d) boiler : coal (e) conveyor belt : assembly line

9. TURGID : INFLATE : : (a) grasp : release
(b) unclean : contaminate (c) rotund : ingest
(d) humid : ignite (e) languid : impair

10. MOROSE : ANIMATION : : (a) respectable : veneration
(b) lachrymose : misfortune (c) audacious : trepidation
(d) incongruous : anachronism (e) temperate : moderation

11. APPRECIATION : ADULATION : :
(a) scholarship : pedantry (b) bravery : intrepidity
(c) abstemiousness : pretentiousness (d) punctilio : formality
(e) caution : prudence

12. RENEGE : PROMISE : : (a) edit : manuscript
(b) convoke : conference (c) defile : mountain
(d) relegate : oblivion (e) default : obligation

13. CHAIR : THRONE : : (a) palace : castle
(b) cassock : miter (c) hat : crown
(d) horse : coach (e) sword : sceptre

14. DAGGER : SHEATH : : (a) arrow : quiver
(b) train : tunnel (c) cart : horse
(d) lance : shield (e) pin : pincushion

15. CORONATION : MONARCH : : (a) replication : sound
(b) divination : angel (c) ordination : priest
(d) inauguration : republic (e) enervation : invalid

16. PALM : VICTORY : : (a) star : virtue
(b) standing ovation : performance
(c) consolation : bereavement (d) white feather : cowardice
(e) ignominy : defeat

In the series of selections below, each passage is followed by questions based on its content. Read the passage and choose the best answer for each question based on the contents of the passage. The questions must be answered on the basis of what is stated or implied in the reading passage.

The newer classification system lists all of the more than 300,000 known plants in just two phyla, the Bryophytes and the Tracheophytes. Bryophytes, the mosses and liverworts, are usually soft and nonwoody in structure, take in water through short root-like filaments called rhizoids, and may have stems and simple leaves but, unlike the more complex Tracheophytes, do not have true roots or vascular tissue whose function it is to circulate water, food, and essential minerals throughout the organism.

Tracheophytes are divided into four sub-phyla: lycopsids, which number some 900 living species; sphenopsids, whose fossil species contributed to coal formation in the Carboniferous period, but which have few living species; psilopsids, an extinct group of relatively simple plants, which fossil studies show to have been more advanced than any of the mosses; and pterosids, subdivided into three classes, the ferns, the gymnosperms, and the angiosperms.

The angiosperms, the most highly developed and complex class of plants, reproduce by means of single and double seed leaves called cotyledons. Monocots, such as corn, wheat, lilies, and orchids, have leaves with parallel veins, while dicots, which include oaks, maples, roses, and thistles, among others, have net-veined leaves and stems with annual growth rings.

17. The author's primary purpose in this passage is to

   (a) demonstrate the complexity of plants in the phylum Bryophytes
   (b) illustrate the differences between the two phyla into which all plants are divided
   (c) set forth the broad outlines of the current plant classification system
   (d) explain the evolutionary chain that connects fossil plants with the angiosperms
   (e) show that fossil studies are the basis for understanding the current system of plant classification

18. According to the passage, all of the following statements are true except

   (a) Tracheophytes have true roots, woody stems, leaves, and vascular tissue which circulates food, water, and essential minerals throughout the plant
   (b) monocots are angiosperms with stems that do not have annual growth rings
   (c) the rhizoids found in Bryophytes are analogous to roots in that they take in water, but they lack vascular tissue
   (d) ferns are a species belonging to the sub-phylum Pteropsids of the phylum Tracheophytes
   (e) the world's present reserves of coal were created by fossil species of the sub-phylum sphenopsids

19. Which of the following statements most correctly characterizes the Bryophytes?

   (a) They are soft and woody in structure, but lack vascular tissue.
   (b) They are less complex than any of the Tracheophytes other than the psilopsids.
   (c) They may have stems, net-veined leaves, and rhizoids which function as true roots.

(d) Fossil studies show them to be more complex than the early Tracheophytes, which had only single seed leaves.

(e) Unlike the more complex Tracheophytes, their rhizoids are not true roots, and they lack vascular tissue.

In 1921, leading investigators in the field of intelligence, participating in a symposium, "Intelligence and Its Measurement," sponsored by the *Journal of Educational Psychology*, defined the title concept, producing almost as many definitions as there were definers, but reached no consensus. One contemporary observer was prompted to quip that intelligence seemed merely to be the capacity to do well on an intelligence test. Now, sixty years later, the situation seems little changed. As Yale's Robert J. Sternberg, an influential cognitive psychologist, warns, "If we are to seek genuine understanding of the relationship between natural intelligence and measured intelligence (IQ), there is one route that clearly will not lead us to the heart of the problem and that we must avoid at all costs. This route is defining away (rather than defining) intelligence as whatever it is that IQ tests measure."

The dominant approach followed by researchers attempting to define intelligence has been factor analysis, a statistical method that examines mental ability test scores with an eye to discerning constellations of test scores that are closely related to each other. The underlying thesis is that where a correlation appears among the scores of many people on tests of different mental abilities, a single factor of intelligence must be common to performance on those tests.

Charles Spearman, originator of factor analysis, held that two kinds of factors form the basis of intelligence: a general factor and specific factors. Subsequent theorists divided the general factor into two or more subfactors, the two most generally agreed upon being verbal-educational and practical-mechanical abilities. Factor analysis has listed many discrete mental abilities and produced models that show how they combine, but it has not suggested how these abilities work, nor has it been productive in dealing with adaptational ability or practical problem solving.

A more recent approach is process analysis or information processing, whose thrust is to analyze the processes of test performance rather than the products of test performance. Process analysts, says Dr. Sternberg, do not reject the findings of factor analysis but, rather, seek "to supplement our understanding of the factors of intelligence with an understanding of the processes that are responsible at least in part for the generation of these factors as sources of individual difference."

The counterpart of the factor as a unit of analysis is the component, described by Dr. Sternberg as "an elementary information process that operates upon internal representations of objects or symbols." Componential studies have been subjected to statistical analysis, and the findings have clarified how certain tasks are performed. However, like factor analysis, process analysis has so far provided few insights into practical problem solving and adaptation to real-world environments. Dr. Sternberg hopes that the application of componential analysis to simulations of real-world task performance will contribute to an understanding of how intelligence operates in that area of human activity.

Some in the field say that identifying factors and processes is worthwhile, but that doing so will not lead to a definition of intelligence. These critics warn that the models produced by such research may become the basis for some future statement that intelligence is what the models model.

20. It can be inferred from the first paragraph that

   (*a*) no progress has been made in the study of intelligence since 1921
   (*b*) intelligence is the capacity to do well in an intelligence test
   (*c*) Robert J. Sternberg was one of the participants in the 1921 symposium, "Intelligence and Its Measurement"
   (*d*) psychologists have not yet arrived at a generally accepted definition of intelligence
   (*e*) the consensus reached at the 1921 symposium was the basis for subsequent improvement in intelligence testing techniques

21. The author's primary purpose in the passage is to

   (*a*) prove that factor analysis provides a definitive explanation of the various skills which make up intelligence
   (*b*) contrast the techniques of factor analysis with those used in process analysis
   (*c*) explain the most recent developments in the field of cognitive theory
   (*d*) argue that intelligence will probably never be adequately defined
   (*e*) suggest that, despite the progress that has been made, the true nature of intelligence is not yet understood

22. According to the passage, process analysis

   (*a*) is fundamentally opposed to the concept of factor analysis
   (*b*) has shed light on how intelligence works in the performance of certain tasks
   (*c*) has contributed to an understanding of adaptational ability through the simulation of real-world task performance
   (*d*) concentrates on identifying the specific factors that form the basis of intelligence
   (*e*) emphasizes the analysis of the products of test performance

23. It can be inferred that which of the following represent(s) the kind of mental activity into which neither factor analysis nor process analysis has provided much insight?

    I. The acquisition of vocabulary
    II. Reading comprehension
    III. The selection of methods for achieving goals

    (a) I only
    (b) II only
    (c) III only
    (d) I and II only
    (e) I, II, and III

24. According to the passage, factor analysis

    (a) organizes mental processes and components into a single factor of intelligence
    (b) subjects mental ability test scores to statistical analysis to determine the correlations between the test scores of different mental abilities
    (c) simulates real-world problems in an attempt to isolate the factors that are common to all problem-solving techniques
    (d) arranges constellations of abilities into patterns that are the basis for well-designed intelligence tests
    (e) seeks to supplement the findings of the 1921 symposium with proof of the effectiveness of intelligence tests

25. It can be inferred from the passage that Dr. Sternberg

    (a) favors the information processing approach
    (b) disagrees with the factor analysis approach
    (c) rejects the use of simulations in componential analysis
    (d) agrees with Charles Spearman's two-factor theory of intelligence
    (e) believes that intelligence cannot be fully explained through cognitive theory

26. Which of the following is neither stated nor implied in the passage?

    (a) The symposium "Intelligence and Its Measurement" failed to produce a consensus.
    (b) In process analysis, the component is the basic unit of analysis.
    (c) The information processing approach has the greatest promise of providing an acceptable definition of intelligence.
    (d) Neither process analysis nor factor analysis has provided important insights into practical problem solving.
    (e) Charles Spearman's original theory of intelligence was modified by those who followed him.

27. Which of the following titles best summarizes the content of the passage?

   (a) Intelligence and Its Measurement
   (b) Factorial Theory and Its Impact on Cognitive Theory
   (c) The Effect of Information Processing on Test Performance
   (d) Recent Advances in the Field of Cognitive Thinking
   (e) Some Difficulties in Defining Intelligence

In each of the questions below, a capitalized word is followed by five words or phrases lettered (a) through (e). Select the lettered word or phrase that is most nearly OPPOSITE in meaning to the capitalized word.

Since some of the questions require that you distinguish fine shades of meaning, consider all choices carefully before you select your answer.

28. CONVENE

   (a) dissolve
   (b) extract
   (c) disseminate
   (d) obstruct
   (e) retract

29. IMPLICATE

   (a) inveigh
   (b) dissuade
   (c) correspond
   (d) exculpate
   (e) recriminate

30. OBSCURE

   (a) reinfect
   (b) reveal
   (c) amplify
   (d) distend
   (e) relegate

31. IMPOUND

   (a) savor
   (b) harass
   (c) retain
   (d) guarantee
   (e) release

32. ARROGATE

   (a) defy
   (b) waive
   (c) renovate
   (d) exemplify
   (e) interrogate

33. REMONSTRATION

   (a) endorsement
   (b) preview
   (c) recapitulation
   (d) ascension
   (e) ingenuity

34. MOOT

   (a) authentic
   (b) capricious
   (c) hyperbolic
   (d) contentious
   (e) indisputable

35. SATURNINE

   (a) exotic
   (b) orgiastic
   (c) blithe
   (d) martial
   (e) platonic

36. INSULAR

    (*a*) sympathetic
    (*b*) urban
    (*c*) cosmopolitan
    (*d*) incontinent
    (*e*) artistic

37. QUIXOTIC

    (*a*) literal
    (*b*) mercurial
    (*c*) practical
    (*d*) temperamental
    (*e*) far-sighted

38. EQUIVOCAL

    (*a*) unbalanced
    (*b*) categorical
    (*c*) epistolary
    (*d*) ubiquitous
    (*e*) untenable

STOP! Work only on this section until the time allowed is over.

Answer Key—Practice Test 3

SECTION I

1. *e*	9. *c*	17. *c*	25. *e*	33. *c*
2. *a*	10. *a*	18. *b*	26. *c*	34. *d*
3. *e*	11. *a*	19. *c*	27. *b*	35. *c*
4. *b*	12. *e*	20. *b*	28. *b*	36. *b*
5. *b*	13. *a*	21. *a*	29. *d*	37. *a*
6. *d*	14. *b*	22. *b*	30. *a*	38. *c*
7. *c*	15. *b*	23. *e*	31. *a*	
8. *c*	16. *d*	24. *c*	32. *e*	

SECTION II

1. *a*	9. *b*	17. *c*	25. *e*	33. *b*
2. *e*	10. *c*	18. *a*	26. *a*	34. *a*
3. *a*	11. *c*	19. *d*	27. *d*	35. *c*
4. *b*	12. *a*	20. *c*	28. *d*	36. *d*
5. *c*	13. *e*	21. *e*	29. *b*	37. *c*
6. *d*	14. *b*	22. *e*	30. *e*	38. *c*
7. *d*	15. *b*	23. *b*	31. *a*	
8. *d*	16. *a*	24. *a*	32. *d*	

SECTION III

1. *c*	7. *a*	13. *c*	19. *c*	25. *d*
2. *b*	8. *a*	14. *b*	20. *e*	26. *d*
3. *a*	9. *c*	15. *a*	21. *c*	27. *e*
4. *b*	10. *c*	16. *c*	22. *a*	28. *a*
5. *a*	11. *d*	17. *a*	23. *a*	29. *c*
6. *b*	12. *b*	18. *d*	24. *b*	30. *e*

SECTION IV

1. *b*	7. *d*	13. *b*	19. *a*	25. *c*
2. *a*	8. *a*	14. *c*	20. *d*	26. *e*
3. *a*	9. *b*	15. *c*	21. *b*	27. *b*
4. *b*	10. *b*	16. *b*	22. *e*	28. *b*
5. *a*	11. *d*	17. *b*	23. *e*	29. *e*
6. *b*	12. *a*	18. *c*	24. *b*	30. *a*

SECTION V

1. *e*	6. *b*	11. *b*	16. *c*	21. *d*
2. *d*	7. *a*	12. *e*	17. *c*	22. *b*
3. *e*	8. *e*	13. *a*	18. *c*	23. *d*
4. *b*	9. *d*	14. *c*	19. *a*	24. *c*
5. *e*	10. *a*	15. *b*	20. *e*	25. *b*

SECTION VI

1. *c*	6. *a*	11. *d*	16. *c*	21. *c*
2. *e*	7. *b*	12. *a*	17. *e*	22. *a*
3. *d*	8. *b*	13. *a*	18. *b*	23. *d*
4. *b*	9. *c*	14. *c*	19. *c*	24. *d*
5. *e*	10. *a*	15. *e*	20. *b*	25. *d*

SECTION VII

1. *d*	9. *b*	17. *c*	25. *a*	33. *a*
2. *b*	10. *c*	18. *e*	26. *c*	34. *e*
3. *e*	11. *a*	19. *e*	27. *e*	35. *c*
4. *c*	12. *e*	20. *d*	28. *a*	36. *c*
5. *e*	13. *c*	21. *e*	29. *d*	37. *c*
6. *d*	14. *a*	22. *b*	30. *b*	38. *b*
7. *b*	15. *c*	23. *c*	31. *e*	
8. *e*	16. *d*	24. *b*	32. *b*	

Explanatory Answers—Practice Test 3

SECTION I

1. (e) Diligence, the sentence says, should not be confused with drudging or with similarly characterized routines. The only word that is like drudging is *menial*.

2. (a) The Board of Directors would hardly be likely to "criticize" the Chairman's salary, since they are the ones who must have approved it. More likely, and correctly, they *justified* his salary, since to do otherwise would be to blame themselves for overpaying him.

3. (e) How would people treat someone they considered wise, concerned, and dedicated to their community? They would treat her with great respect, or *deference*.

4. (b) The word "although" leads us to expect that the subject of the sentence had shown himself to be one kind of person in dangerous situations, but an entirely different kind of person in the drawing room. The two words would have to be opposites. The only pair of opposites, *intrepid* and *craven*, correctly completes the sentence.

5. (b) They found themselves doing something freely despite the bitter cold. The only thing that they could be doing that would seem to be despite the cold is *perspiring*.

6. (d) While choices other than *bias* could fit into the first blank, only *subjective* works for the second blank. The sentence as completed

thus states that even though we try to be fair, we cannot be. We wind up responding to our biases either by giving in to them, or by reacting strongly against them.

7. (c) Appointing his own son to the firm's presidency is clearly an act of *nepotism*, favoritism in business or politics toward someone on the basis of family relationship. Even if Mr. Hart is not guilty of nepotism, the speaker feels him to be.

8. (c) The *editor* works with the *novelist* to get the latter's work into shape for presentation to the public. Similarly, the *director* works with the *playwright* to get the latter's work into shape for public presentation. This is an associational relationship.

9. (c) A *portfolio* is the entire group of *securities* a person holds for investment. A *panel* is a whole group of *jurors* from whom a jury is selected. A whole and part relationship.

10. (a) *Neutrality* does not characterize someone who is a *participant* in a fight or discussion, etc. *Passivity*, similarly, does not characterize someone who is an *activist* in dealing with social issues. This is a negative characterization.

11. (a) An *irritant* causes *annoyance*, and a *stimulus* causes *incitement*. Cause and effect relationship.

12. (e) Just as a *sword* is carried in a *scabbard*, an *arrow* is carried in a *quiver*. While it is true that a corsage can be carried in a box, the box does not serve as the permanent holder of the corsage; it serves only as a temporary container.

13. (a) *Vindictiveness* is not a characteristic of *fellowship*. Similarly, *venality* is not a characteristic of *probity*. Negative characterization relationship.

14. (b) Just as *shackles* serve to *fetter*, so too, *emancipation* serves to *liberate*.

15. (b) *Seldom* means not very often; *rarely* is more extreme than seldom because it means hardly ever. *Often* means quite frequently, but *usually* is more extreme in meaning than often because it means most of the time. This is a degree of difference relationship.

16. (d) An *eruption* results from the activity of a *volcano*, while an *earthquake* results from the activity of a geological *fault*.

17. (c) The passage does not address itself to any international aspects of protection of endangered species or park management. All the other choices are either expressed or implied. Choice (a) is implied in the last sentence of paragraph one, the first sentence of paragraph two, and in the reference to water pollution in paragraph four. Choice (b) is mentioned in paragraph five. Choice (d), introduced species, is mentioned in paragraph five as well. Choice (e) is implied in paragraph two, where regulation of pesticides is mentioned.

18. (b) The final sentence of the passage says that where commercial or sports harvesting of shellfish is of important value, the list of endangered species is complete; elsewhere, lists are incomplete. This contrast implies that research is carried out where wildlife preservation is a matter of financial concern to a particular group.

19. (c) The correct answer is clearly stated in the second and third sentences of the first paragraph. Choice (a) is wrong because the 400 endangered invertebrates may not all be mollusks—they could be members of the clam family, for instance. Choice (b) is wrong; the Asian snail is mentioned only as an introduced species. Choice (d) is incorrect; the passage refers to one-third of the 400 endangered shellfish as being the victims of pollution. No comparison is made in the passage concerning the relative effectiveness of the two approaches to improved preservation.

20. (b) The passage never addresses itself to Alcoholics Anonymous, so choice (a) is eliminated. There is no treatment of a psychological approach to alcoholism in the passage; choice (c), therefore, is wrong. Choice (d) is wrong; the passage does not speak of treatment for alcoholism. Choice (e) is wrong; the statement says, in effect, that the purpose of this passage is to teach alcoholics about learning theory, but the passage is

really meant to explain to alcoholics and others why people become and remain alcoholics.

21. (a) The answer to the question in choice (a) is in paragraph three, which says that even though drinking causes alcoholics to suffer, the immediate reduction of tension is more reinforcing for drinking than the subsequent discomfort is for abstinence. None of the other questions are answered by the passage.

22. (b) Choice (a) is wrong because the statement itself is different from what the passage says in paragraph three. The passage says only that it *seems* as if the behavior of alcoholics contradicts learning theory, and later it resolves the contradiction. Choice (c) is clearly stated, not implied, in the next to the last paragraph. Choice (d) is neither stated nor implied. Choice (e) is clearly stated in paragraph two, but the question calls for a statement that is not directly stated, but rather that can be inferred.

23. (e) See paragraph four, sentence two: "Conditions or events occurring at the time of reinforcement . . ."

24. (c) The second paragraph's topic sentence says that some experimental evidence tends to show that alcohol reduces fear. The rest of the paragraph tells of Conger's experiment. You can clearly infer that the rest of the paragraph is meant to substantiate the topic sentence.

25. (e) Sentence three in the last paragraph tells of two methods used experimentally to habituate the subject to excessive alcohol consumption. The first method is mechanical, increasing the concentration of alcohol in the animal's drinking water gradually. The second method uses reinforcement, the giving of a reward after drinking, and increasing the doses required to earn the reward.

26. (c) Sentence one says alcohol ingestion is a way to reduce an innerdrive state such as fear or anxiety, corroborating statement I. Statement II is corroborated by paragraph four. Paragraph five suggests that punishment can serve as a reward and reinforce the very behavior it is intended to suppress, which is a paraphrase of statement III.

27. (b) The statement in choice (a) is not an example of stimulus generalization (see paragraph four). Choice (c) misstates the last sentence in paragraph five which says "either," not "both." Choice (d) states the opposite of what appears in the passage in paragraph three. Choice (e) is wrong, too. The statement does not relate in any way to learning and reinforcement theory which, in effect, is about behavioral modification or conditioning. Choice (b) is an example of what the passage speaks of in paragraph five.

28. (b) *Dishearten*—discourage, depress; opposite—*buoy* (encourage)

29. (d) *Discrete*—separate; opposite—*fused* (blended together, as if melted)

30. (a) *Traduce*—malign; opposite—*appreciate*

31. (a) *Contumacious*—obstinately disobedient; opposite—*compliant*

32. (e) *Puissant*—mighty, powerful; opposite—*impotent*

33. (c) *Consonant*—harmonious, in agreement; opposite—*discordant*

34. (d) *Indigence*—poverty; opposite—*affluence*

35. (c) *Cacophonous*—having harsh or dissonant sound; opposite—*harmonious*

36. (b) *Dexterous*—skillful, adroit; opposite—*maladroit* (unskillful)

37. (a) *Irascible*—easily provoked to anger; opposite—*propitiatory*

38. (c) *Upright*—righteous, honest, just; opposite—*unscrupulous*

SECTION II

1. (a) The sense of the latter part of the sentence is that Personnel didn't like the applicant's qualifications in a particular respect and selected someone whose qualifications ran counter to the applicant's. Thus, if Personnel had decided he was "underage," they would have chosen someone older, someone reliable, not a "consultant"; if "disdainful," someone respectful, not a "woman"; if "superannuated," someone younger, not a "veteran." Since they decided he was *overqualified*, it is suitable for the sentence's meaning to select a *tyro*—novice—by way of contrast.

2. (e) He wished to make up for his "too-hasty evaluation" which had resulted in a "negative appraisal," and so, as an act of *contrition* (remorse or penitence) he offered her a chance to work on the new skyscraper. It is clear from the wording that he knew he had done something wrong, and the only word that indicates this understanding is choice (e).

3. (a) Concern with the gruesome and grisly is morbid. People interested in the gruesome and grisly aspects of great disasters are probably *morbidly* stimulated.

4. (b) While both "accredited" and *imputed* imply definite origin, the former has complimentary connotations, while the latter has come to have uncomplimentary connotations. Miss Snell's colleagues are certainly being uncomplimentary when they say that her rapid advancement comes from luck and family influence.

5. (c) To marshal means to array as for battle. *Marshalled* fits in very well for the first blank. The linguistic structure of the sentence indicates that the events of the first part caused the events of the second part of the sentence. Strong arguments arrayed against him by the opposition convinced even his most loyal followers that he was wrong. What would he have done? Just what the sentence says. He was forced to *acquiesce*.

6. (d) The sentence's context suggests that the word for the second blank will have the same implication as the word for the first blank, but it will be stronger in degree. Only *divide* and *polarize*, among the choices, fulfill the idea suggested.

7. (d) The only words that suit the first blank are "developed" and *altered*, but "others" fails to complete any meaning for the sentence, whereas *recognition* supplies meaning, and fits from the point of view of diction as well.

8. (d) An *irreverent* remark is the opposite of a *pious* one. Similarly, a *commendatory* remark is the opposite of a *disapproving* one.

9. (b) This is a degree of difference relationship. A person *irritated* very greatly would be *exasperated*. A market *abounding* with petroleum would have much petroleum, but not as much as one *glutted*, that is, filled to excess, with petroleum.

10. (c) This is an antonymous relationship. *Desultory* means without consistency or visible order, the opposite of *methodical*. So, too, *dissipated* means dispersed, the opposite of *concentrated*.

11. (c) The result of participating in a *race* is *fatigue*. The result of a *fast* is *hunger*. This is a cause and effect relationship.

12. (a) *Ballast* is heavy material which provides *stability* for a ship. *Springs* provide *resiliency* for a car. A function relationship.

13. (e) Something *fortuitous*, that is, produced by chance or accident, does not stem from *inherent*, that is inseparable, attributes. *Gregarious* acts are not characteristic of *introverted* people. The relationships are antonymous.

14. (b) This is a function relationship. *Equivocation*, the use of ambiguous or unclear expressions, usually *misleads*. Similarly, *elucidation*, throwing light upon something, usually *clarifies*.

15. (b) A *birthmark*, a blemish or mark on a person from birth, is characterized as *congenital*, which means existing from or at birth. *Baldness*, a physical trait which is transmitted genetically from a progenitor, is characterized as *hereditary*.

16. (a) *Opaque* (not allowing light to pass through) is the opposite of *transparent*, just as *concentrated* (clustered or gathered together closely) is the opposite of *dissipated* (scattered or dispersed). In choice (e), "tepid" is not the opposite of "seething"; it is merely different in degree. The other choices are incorrect because they are synonymous pairs, not opposites.

17. (c) Paragraph two, by saying that sex offenders scored low on having sex guilt, violent criminals scored low on hostility guilt, and thieves and robbers scored low on morality conscience, implies that criminals tend not to see their acts as something to feel guilty about. Paragraph three says that brutal people often see their brutality as correct behavior for the circumstances. Both imply the statement in choice (c). Note that (b) is incor-

rect because it never overstates the information given in the passage.

18. (*a*) Paragraph six says that the therapist should help the patient to differentiate between guilt feelings that are based on reality and those that are based on misperceptions of what has actually taken place—another way of phrasing the statement in choice (*a*).

19. (*d*) Sentence one says that guilt is far from being a psychic impediment; this eliminates choice (*a*). Since the Mosher scales, according to paragraph two, measure the tendency to feel guilt, not mental health, choice (*b*) can be judged as incorrect. The passage says nothing about the quality of military commanders in discussing guilt, so choice (*c*) is wrong. Feeling guilt and being guilty are two completely separate ideas. The passage does not discuss being guilty; it talks only of feeling guilt, so choice (*e*) is wrong. The support for choice (*d*) is to be found in the next to the last paragraph, last sentence.

20. (*c*) Sentence four, paragraph one, clearly states, "If output does not grow, employment will certainly fall." The opposite is also true, for the sentence concludes, "if production increases ... employment must rise."

21. (*e*) In paragraph one, the passage says that unless gross national product rises more rapidly than rate of productivity, the unemployment rate will increase. In paragraph two, the passage says

that in the recession years the economic growth rate did not exceed the rate of productivity increase. It can be inferred that the rate of unemployment grew in the recession years.

22. (*e*) The author, throughout the passage, writes of the various causes of unemployment, of the possibility of controlling the various forces, and concludes by saying that high unemployment is a consequence of passive public policy. In the very last sentence, the author says that positive policies will be needed in the future. (*a*) is incorrect because the passage is not merely a description of economic forces. (*b*) is wrong because the passage never refers to past administrations. (*c*) is wrong because the passage does not address itself to specifics like current unemployment. (*d*) is wrong because there is no overall documentation of any specific economic trend.

23. (*b*) Choice (*a*) is incorrect; the passage does not give enough information for arrival at the conclusion given. Support for (*b*) can be found in the fourth sentence, first paragraph. Paragraph four contradicts choice (*c*). The first sentence of the next to the last paragraph, contrary to choice (*d*), says that technological change need not inevitably result in high unemployment. As for choice (*e*), the long-term rate of growth in our economy, according to the next to the last paragraph, is about 3.5 percent, and that paragraph also says that a 4 percent annual rate of growth for our economy would

merely keep unemployment from increasing. A 3.5 percent rate, therefore, would increase our unemployment rate, not decrease it.

24. (a) Since the author so carefully sets forth the impact of each of the three forces that affect unemployment, and then speaks of the possibility of controlling those forces and the need for positive fiscal, monetary, and manpower policies, you can assume that he would favor controlling the forces so as to maintain growth and, at the same time, limit unemployment, or do whatever was thought to be in the public interest. The employment rate, according to the passage, does not rise and fall with the value of the gross national product alone, so (b) is incorrect. The passage says that unemployment is affected by several forces, and indicates that those forces can be manipulated. It is obvious, then, that the author does not feel that unemployment is inevitable or unavoidable as (c) states. The passage makes no reference at all to what might have prevented any recession, so (d) is incorrect. (e) is exactly the opposite of what the author would advocate.

25. (e) The definition for the gross national product appears in parentheses in the sixth sentence of the first paragraph.

26. (a) The only reference to national averages is in paragraph five. The conclusion of the paragraph is paraphrased by the statement in choice (a).

27. (d) The only reference to new entrants into the labor market appears in paragraph five, and it does not refer to controlling the rate of growth of new entrants into the market; choice (a) is, therefore, wrong. No explanation is offered for the rate of growth having remained so low for so long; choice (b) is incorrect. There is no treatment in the passage of prewar economic policy; choice (c) is incorrect. The passage does not deal with wage and price freezes, so (e) is wrong. Choice (d) is answered in paragraph six, sentences two and three.

28. (d) *Rescission*—the act of revoking or repealing; opposite—*confirmation*

29. (b) *Sanguine*—optimistic; opposite—*hopeless*

30. (e) *Symmetrical*—corresponding on either side of a line or plane; opposite—*skewed* (asymmetrical)

31. (a) *Overt*—not concealed or secret; opposite—*clandestine*

32. (d) *Condign*—merited or deserved; opposite—*inappropriate*

33. (b) *Blatant*—clamorous; opposite—*subdued*

34. (a) *Abstruse*—recondite, hard to understand; opposite—*manifest*

35. (c) *Salubrious*—wholesome; opposite—*unwholesome*

36. (d) *Dulcet*—melodious to the ear; opposite—*stentorian*

37. (c) *Attenuate*—weaken; opposite—*strengthen*

38. (c) *Cacophonous*—having a harsh or discordant sound; opposite—*euphonious* (pleasant in sound)

SECTION III

1. (c) 30% of 70 = .3 (70) = 2.1
70% of 30 = .7 (30) = 2.1

2. (b) Since all possible values of q are greater than all possible values of p, it follows that q > p.

3. (a) r(s + t) = rs + rt
Since r > 1 and s and t are positive, rs + rt > rs + t.

4. (b) 1/3 × 1/4 = 1/12
1/3 ÷ 1/4 = 1/3 × 4 = 4/3 = 16/12 > 1/12

5. (a) If r = 2s, then 2r = 2 (2s) = 4s. Then 6s + 3 > 4s + 3.

6. (b) Since 180 is common to both products, let us compare 11 × 7 = 77 with 9 × 12 = 96. Obviously 96 > 77.

7. (a) Since n is an exterior angle of the triangle containing angles p and q, it follows that n > q.

8. (a) Area of circle =
$$\pi r^2 = \pi \left(\frac{d}{2}\right)^2 =$$
$$\frac{\pi d^2}{4} \approx \frac{3.14 d^2}{4}$$
Area of square $= \left(\frac{3d}{4}\right)^2 = \frac{9d^2}{16}$
$$\frac{3.14}{4} \approx .78, \frac{9}{16} \approx .56$$

Therefore the area of the circle is greater.

9. (c) Angle k = angle PQR (vertical angles)
Angle n = angle PQR since they are opposite angles of a parallelogram
Therefore k = n

10. (c) m + k = 180° (supplementary)
n = ∠ QRV (corresponding angles of parallel lines)
∠ QRV + t = 180° (supplementary)
or
n + t = 180°
so that m + k = n + t

11. (d) If r > s, 1/r < 1/s if r and s are positive. However, this relationship will not hold if one or both of these variables are negative.

12. (b) Angle P = 180 – (70 + 40) = 180 – 110 = 70°
Therefore, QR > PQ since the longer side lies opposite the larger angle.

13. (c) Since ∠ P = ∠ Q = 70°, it follows that the sides opposite are equal, so PR = QR.

14. (b) y – 2x = 5, x ≥ 0
y = 2x + 5
Since y is 5 more than twice x and x ≥ 0, it follows that y > x.

15. (a) $\sqrt[3]{28.2} > \sqrt[3]{27} = 3$
$\sqrt{8.92} < \sqrt{9} = 3$
Since the item in column A > 3 and that in column B < 3, (a) must be the answer.

16. (c) 2.7% = .027 = 27 thousandths

Practice Test 3   429

17. (a) $.04 \div \dfrac{4}{.5} = .04 \times \dfrac{.5}{4}$

$\qquad = .04 \times \dfrac{5}{40} = .04 \times \dfrac{1}{8}$

$\qquad = \dfrac{.040}{8} = .005$

18. (d) Let n = the number of additional days after the first three.
$10 + 6n = 118$
$6n = 108$
$n = 18$
$n + 3 = 21$

19. (c)

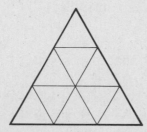

The figure above shows the division of the larger triangle into 9 smaller ones.

20. (e) Let w = width
then l = 2w − 6 (length)
perimeter = 2l + 2w
$= 2(2w - 6) + 2w$
$= 4w - 12 + 2w$
$= 6w - 12$

21. (c) Newspapers were 33.6% of the total; radio 6.0%, or a difference of 27.6%. The total outlay was $9.2 billion, so 27.6% of $9.2 billion is about $2.5 billion.

22. (a) This question provides two important lessons. First, look to see if an approximation is adequate. Direct mail outlays went from 14.2% to 14.7%, not really much of a change, so we can skip the step of calculating the actual amount and just take the total outlay ratio of $9.2 billion to $28.3 billion. Second, be sure you have read the question carefully. It's 1960 to 1980, not 1980 to 1960; i.e., 1:3.

23. (a) Obviously, newspapers, other, and television in 1980 are numbers one, two, and three. The next choice is either direct mail—1980, or newspapers—1960; the rest can be eliminated. In 1960 newspapers were about 1/3 of $9 billion or $3 billion. In 1980 direct mail was about 15% of $30 billion or $4.5 billion or perhaps a bit less, but still greater than $3 billion.

24. (b) Don't jump to the conclusion that it was television right away. Television went from 11% of $9 billion, or about $1 billion, to 19% of $28 billion, or about $5.3 billion, up $4.3 billion. Newspapers went from 1/3 of $9 billion, or about $3 billion, to 30% of $28 billion or about $8.4 billion, up about $5.4 billion.

25. (d) Each tile is 4/12 or 1/3 ft. on a side.
The number of tiles lengthwise is $7\frac{2}{3} \div 1/3 = 23/3 \times 3 = 23$
The number of tiles along the width is $6 \div 1/3 = 6 \times 3 = 18$
The total number of tiles is $23 \times 18 = 414$

26. (d) In 1969 total retail sales was approximately 60% of disposable personal income and at the level of about $300 billion.
$300 = .6x$, $x = \$500$ billion

27. (e) Total sales were about $650 billion, durables were about $200 billion, so nondurables were about $450 billion, so they were $250 billion greater.

28. (*a*) Durable sales in 1980 were about $200 billion out of a total of $650 billion, or 20/65 or 4/13. Total sales were about 55% of disposable personal income, so durable sales were 4/13 × 55 or 17% approximately.

29. (*c*) Retail sales as a percentage of disposable personal income did not change from 1974 to 1979, so it is safe to assume that disposable personal income rose by the same percent as did retail sales. They were almost $400 billion in 1974 and $600 billion in 1979, an increase of 50%. Disposable personal income then, also rose 50%, from $500 billion to $750 billion.

30. (*e*) Triangle OPR is a 30° – 60° – 90° triangle.
Since OR = 4, PR = 8 and OP = $4\sqrt{3}$
The coordinates of P are $(0, 4\sqrt{3})$

SECTION IV

1. (*b*) If $0 < k < 1$, then $k^2 < k$, since the squaring of a positive fraction less than 1 produces a still smaller positive fraction.

2. (*a*) Since the sum of two sides of a triangle is greater than the third side, $f + h > g$
Subtracting h from both sides, we get $f > g - h$

3. (*a*) PR = $100\sqrt{2} \approx 100 (1.41) \approx 141$ ft
Walking PR at 5 feet per second takes about 141/5 = 28.2 seconds. PQ + QR = 200 ft. so that running from P to Q and Q to R takes 200/8 or 25 seconds.
So that A > B

4. (*b*) 235 ÷ 5 = 47 so that r = 4
$$\begin{array}{r} 342 \\ \times 273 \\ \hline 1026 \\ 2394 \\ 684 \\ \hline 93366 \end{array}$$ so that s = 6
Thus s > r

5. (*a*) $p = -2\frac{1}{4}$, $q = 3/4$
$$pq = -\frac{9}{4}\left(\frac{3}{4}\right) = -\frac{27}{16} > -2$$

6. (*b*) $-\dfrac{p}{r} = -\left(\dfrac{-2\frac{1}{4}}{3}\right) =$
$$\frac{9}{4} \times \frac{1}{3} = \frac{3}{4}$$
$$-\frac{r}{p} = \frac{4}{3} > \frac{3}{4}$$

7. (*d*) If t is between $-2\frac{1}{4}$ and 3/4, it may be greater than, less than, or equal to $-q = -3/4$.

8. (*a*) If p were 90, x would be $7\sqrt{2}$
Since $p > 90$, $x > 7\sqrt{2}$

9. (*b*) $x < 14$ since the sum of two sides of a triangle must be greater than the third side.

10. (*b*) Since the sum of the angles of a triangle is 180° and $p > 90$, then $q + r < 90$

11. (*d*) The wide variation of x and the wide variation of p make it impossible to compare the numerical values of the perimeter and area of the triangle.

12. (*a*) Since $k < m$
$k + m < m + m$
$k + m < 2m$

13. (b) Since $\pi > 3$, $\dfrac{1}{\pi} < \dfrac{1}{3}$

and $\dfrac{1}{3} + \dfrac{1}{3} + \dfrac{1}{\pi} < 1$

14. (c) The maximum possible value of
$r - \dfrac{r}{s}$ is $6 - \dfrac{6}{6} = 6 - 1 = 5$

15. (c) Let $RQ = QT = 1$

$\overset{\frown}{RMQ} + \overset{\frown}{QNT} = \pi(1) = \pi$

$\overset{\frown}{RST} = \dfrac{1}{2}\pi(2) = \pi$

16. (b)

(3 hrs. later)

A ├────────────────────┤ B

leaves 5 P.M.

When the plane leaves city A at 5 P.M., it is 3 hours earlier in city B, or 2 P.M. Four hours later it is 6 P.M. upon arrival.

17. (b) $y < 2x$ so that $y < 40$. But y can have a minimum value as close to zero as we wish to make it, so that $0 < y < 40$

18. (c) In 1976 the largest age group is $15 - 19$. By 1981 this group will be 20–24 years old.

19. (a) The 15–19-year-old group includes approximately 10.5 million girls and 11 million boys. The 10–14-year-old group includes approximately 10 million of each, but only about 2/5 of this group are 13 and 14, so $10.5 + 11 + 4 + 4 = 29.5$ million.

20. (d) It was 6 million in 1976 and it will be about 9.6 million by 2000, an increase of 3.6 or 60%.

21. (b) The group is not expected to grow at all: under 5's and 5–9's will grow, 10–14's will remain the same, and 15–19's and 20–24's will shrink by approximately the same amount as under 5's and 5–9's will grow.

22. (e) Let the legs be 2x and 3x.
Area $= 1/2\,(2x)(3x) = 75$
$3x^2 = 75$
$x^2 = 25$
$x = 5$

The legs are 10 and 15. Let hypotenuse = h.
Thus $h = 10^2 + 15^2 = 100 + 225 = 325$
$h = \sqrt{325} = \sqrt{25 \times 13} = 5\sqrt{13}$

23. (e) If e is the edge of the cube, then
$V = e^3 = 125$
$e = 5$
$S = 6e^2$
$ = 6(5)^2$
$ = 6(25)$
$ = 150$

24. (b) Angle HGK = angle EGF = 60°
So that $\angle H + \angle K = 120°$

25. (c) $p = 4q$ and $q = 2r$, so that
$p = 4(2r) = 8r$
Therefore, $r = \dfrac{p}{8}$

26. (e) $24 per dozen $= \dfrac{24}{12}$
$= \$2$ each;

$24 per 1½ dozen $= \dfrac{24}{18}$
$= \$1\dfrac{1}{3}$ each.

This represents a reduction of $\$\dfrac{2}{3}$ on each pen.

% decrease $= \dfrac{2}{3} \div 2$

$= \dfrac{1}{3}$ or $33\dfrac{1}{3}$%.

27. (b)

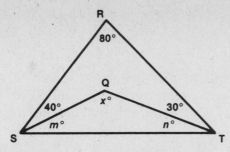

From the figure, x = 180 − (m + n)
In △RST, 80 + 40 + 30
$$+ m + n = 180$$
$$m + n = 30$$
$$x = 180 − 30 = 150$$

28. (b) A 360° rotation brings the point back to P. It then rotates another 140° (500° − 360° = 140°). This will put the point between Q and R.

29. (e) (r − s)² = 32 and rs = 4
$$r^2 − 2rs + s^2 = 32$$
$$r^2 − 2(4) + s^2 = 32$$
$$r^2 + s^2 = 40$$

30. (a) Let x = cost of s tennis balls.
$$\frac{t}{d} = \frac{s}{x}$$
Cross multiply:
$$tx = ds$$
$$x = \frac{ds}{t}$$

SECTION V

1. (e) Since Arnold is at #1, if Earl is at #2, from statement 3 Celia is at #3. This may be drawn as follows.

A	E	C	—	—	—
#1	#2	#3	#4	#5	#6

Bob may be at any of the remaining seats in order to satisfy statement 4. Similarly, Dorothy may be at any of the remaining seats to satisfy statement 5. Since Bob and Dorothy may have any seating relation to each other, they may occupy two of seats #4, #5, and #6 in any order, leaving any of them unoccupied.

2. (d) If Celia is at #2, then Earl would be at #3.

A	C	E	—	—	—
#1	#2	#3			

There is no way in this situation to fulfill statement 4, in which Bob is said to be closer to Celia than to Earl. Statement I is therefore correct; Celia was not at #2. Celia could well be at #4, so that statement II is incorrect. An example follows.

A	—	E	C	B	D
#1	#2	#3	#4	#5	#6

Statement III is correct, for Celia could not have been at #6. If she was, then Earl was at #5, and Bob could then not have been closer to Celia than to Earl.

A	—	—	—	E	C
#1				#5	#6

3. (e) The way to solve the problem is to draw Arnold and Celia at #1 and #5, and then try Earl at #4 and #6. If Earl was at #4, then the following situation existed.

A	—	—	E	C	—
#1	#2	#3	#4	#5	#6

It is apparent that in this situation, Bob must have been at #6 in order to have been nearer Celia than Earl, and Dorothy must have been at #3 in order to have been nearer Earl than Arnold. Earl, however, could have been at #6. In that case, the following situation existed.

$$\frac{A}{\#1} \quad \frac{\quad}{\#2} \quad \frac{\quad}{\#3} \quad \frac{\quad}{\#4} \quad \frac{C}{\#5} \quad \frac{E}{\#6}$$

The conditions could then have been fulfilled with Bob at #3 and Dorothy at #4. It is clear, then, that choices (a), (b), (c), and (d) are correct *only if* Earl was at #4. Since he could have been at #6, they are incorrect.

4. (b) Statements I, II, and III describe the following three situations.

I. $\dfrac{A}{} \ \underline{\quad} \ \dfrac{D}{} \ \dfrac{B}{} \ \dfrac{E}{} \ \dfrac{C}{}$

II. $\dfrac{A}{} \ \underline{\quad} \ \dfrac{D}{} \ \dfrac{E}{} \ \dfrac{C}{} \ \dfrac{B}{}$

III. $\dfrac{A}{} \ \underline{\quad} \ \dfrac{D}{} \ \dfrac{B}{} \ \dfrac{C}{} \ \dfrac{E}{}$

#1 #2 #3 #4 #5 #6

Only the second arrangement is valid. The other two are not in accord with the rules because in each, Dorothy is not closer to Earl than to Arnold, and in the first, Bob is not closer to Celia than to Earl.

5. (e) The argument is essentially that because a certain evil (cancer) is spreading, the government must aid the fight against this evil. There are clearly certain links missing in this chain of reasoning. One is the point that only the government can adequately underwrite the battle against cancer. Unless this is true, the argument would then properly be only that *someone* should fund increased research.

Choice (a) is the next best answer, and with a slightly different argument, this would be the proper choice. However, the thrust of the argument was that the *government* should act. Since choice (e)

addresses this point, it is a better choice.

6. (b) The argument does not suggest that all forms of cancer are usually fatal, only that deaths from cancer are increasing. The author does imply that cancer is an increasingly important cause of mortality; that increased research will benefit cancer treatment; that increased government funding is necessary; and, as mentioned above, that government action is needed for adequate progress against cancer to occur.

7. (a) From statement (2), we can draw the following diagram of the characters' relationships.

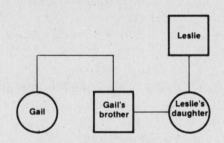

This shows that Gail's brother is married to Leslie's daughter. In order for both Gail's brother and Leslie to be blood relatives of Lynn, Lynn must be a product of the marriage between Gail's brother and Leslie's daughter. This is seen because, from statement (6), Gail's brother is unrelated to Leslie or his daughter, except by marriage. Since no more than three generations are involved, Lynn must be the offspring of Leslie's daughter and Gail's brother. The family may be drawn as the following:

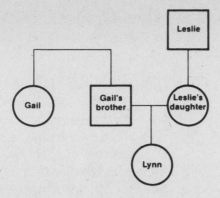

Statement I is correct, as the diagram above shows. Note that Gail's sex is not given in the question and since some males are named Gail, the statement correctly identifies Gail as Lynn's aunt or uncle. Statement II is incorrect; Leslie is Lynn's grandfather. Statement III need not be correct; Gail's brother could have fathered Lynn at, say, the age of seventeen, while Gail would have been born when her brother was twenty.

8. (e) As the diagram shows, all three statements are true.

9. (d) It is clear from the diagram that Gail's brother's wife (labeled "Leslie's daughter") is a blood relative of Lynn (that is, her mother). Choices (a), (b), and (c) are excluded by the rule against incest. Choice (e) may or may not be true, but the question calls for a statement which *must* be true.

10. (a) Statements (2), (3), and (4) make it quite clear that Leslie, Lynn, and Gail are related, making statement (1) unnecessary. The other statements are all necessary to define the possible relationships among the people mentioned.

11. (b) The relationships described in the statements may be diagrammed by means of overlapping and concentric circles. Each circle represents a category of things. Concentric circles represent one category completely contained within another; overlapping circles represent two categories with some, but not all, members in common. The first two and last two statements yield this diagram:

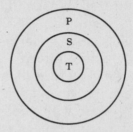

We can't tell for certain how the third statement should be diagrammed. We do know that the category of R's is completely contained within both the P and the Q categories, but we don't know whether or not the Q category is contained within the P category. Here are three of the possible diagrams:

(1)

(2)

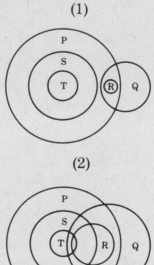

(3)

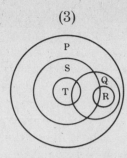

In all three of the diagrams, we see that all T's are P's. Choices (c) and (e) are not true in any of the three diagrams. Choice (a) is true in diagrams (2) and (3), but not in diagram (1). Hence, it cannot be definitely inferred. Choice (d) is true in all three diagrams, but we may draw a fourth diagram in keeping with the statements to show that it need not be true:

(4)

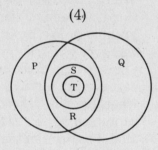

12. (e) Diagram (4) above illustrates the truth of (e). The word "only" in choices (a), (b), (c) and (d) makes these statements incorrect answers.

13. (a) We can see from all four diagrams that any T's that are R's must also be Q's, since all R's are Q's. Thus (a) is not possible. From diagrams (1) and (2) we can see that (b), (c), (d), and (e) are possible.

14. (c) If all Q's are R's, then the category Q would be *identical* with the category R, and all Q's would be P's. Choices (a) and (b) cannot be inferred, as shown in all four dia-

grams. Choices (d) and (e) cannot be inferred, as shown in diagram (1).

15. (b) Only statement III, that there are more P's than T's, is necessarily true. As the diagrams show, all T's are within S, and all S's are within P, meaning that P's are more numerous than either S's or T's. Statement I asserts that more R's are P's than are T's, but this would be false if all R's were T's, a possibility which is not precluded by the instructions. Statement II, that there are more P's than R's, sounds plausible, since all R's are P's. It is not necessarily true, however, because all P's could also be R's; that is, the categories P and R could be identical.

16. (c) Before answering the questions, draw a map outlining the various trips described:

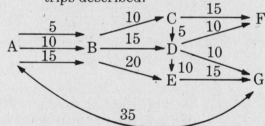

It may be seen that there are two ways to get to D. The boat may follow the route A–B–C–D, in which case the total time would be 5 + 10 + 5 = 20 minutes. It also may follow the route A–B–D, in which case the trip would take 10 + 15 = 25 minutes. Statements I and II, which correspond to these two possibilities, are given in choice (c), which is correct.

17. (c) The three possible routes to E are A–B–C–D–E, A–B–D–E, and A–B–E.

18. (c) F is reachable only from D or C. As mentioned in the answer to question 16 above, the longer trip to D takes 25 minutes. Add on the 10-minute trip to F for a total trip of 35 minutes. The route to F via C takes 15 minutes to get to C plus 15 minutes to get from C to F, for a total of 30 minutes.

19. (a) G is reachable from either D or E. The shorter trip to D takes 20 minutes, and the 10-minute trip to G gives a total of 30 minutes. The trip A–B–E–G takes 50 minutes, and the trip A–B–C–D–E–G takes 45 minutes.

20. (e) There are five different routes leading to G: A–B–C–D–E–G, A–B–C–D–G, A–B–D–E–G, A–B–D–G, and A–B–E–G.

21. (d) It is possible to get to island G and thus ultimately to A from any island except F, from which there is no way back to A.

22. (b) Statement I is false; a 5-minute trip to B means the next stop is C, from which G is easily reached. Statement II is also false; a 10-minute trip to B means the next stop is D; this makes it impossible to visit C without returning to A and setting out anew. Statement III is true. A 15-minute trip from A to B means the next trip is to E, from which point F cannot be reached without first returning to A.

23. (d) The doctor's statement was factual, reasonably phrased, and seemingly unbiased. Choices (a), (b), and (c) are clearly self-serving. Choice (e) is obviously a loose statement, not one that should be interpreted as being fact.

24. (c) Minnie's counter-example was that businessmen are sometimes thieves. This makes sense if she believed that Mickey had implied that no businessmen are thieves or crooks. Choice (c) expresses this misinterpretation, that Mickey meant that "only politicians are crooks." The other choices do not reasonably explain Minnie's response.

25. (b) The statement "I think, therefore I am" is logically similar to statements like "The light is on, therefore it is bright inside." This statement does not imply that the only condition under which it can be bright inside is if the light is on; it merely says that if the light is on, then it is bright inside. By this reasoning, Descartes's statement may be interpreted to mean "If I think, then I exist." It need not mean that the only reliable proof of existence is thought. The best rejoinder, then, is given by choice (b), which raises this point and thus refutes the original argument.

SECTION VI

1. (c) From the information given, we can diagram the locations of the avenues.

Birch
_____

Fir
_____

_____

Oak
_____

Maple
_____

Chestnut
_____

Walnut
_____

Note that one avenue has not been given a name. Since Walnut is two blocks east of Maple, Maple must be between Oak and Chestnut.

2. (e) Three blocks west of Walnut brings us to Oak Avenue. Thus Palm Avenue cannot be located there. All other choices are possible locations.

3. (d) We see from the diagram that it is four blocks from Fir Avenue to Chestnut Avenue.

4. (b) From the diagram, we see that Oak Avenue is three blocks from Birch and also three blocks from Walnut.

5. (e) All three statements must be true for the argument to be valid (though their truth does not imply that the argument is valid). If vitamin X is not lacking in the diet, then taking tablets of it is unnecessary and the argument is invalid. Statement I therefore, if false, would invalidate the argument. Similarly, if valid research showing the need for vitamin X had not been done, the claim could not be made that it is necessary for many bodily functions. The falsity of statement II would therefore invalidate the argument. If vitamin X cannot be isolated in some manner, then tablets of it cannot be produced. The validity of the argument therefore also depends on the truth of statement III.

6. (a) If most foods contain more than small amounts of vitamin X, then supplemental tablets would be unnecessary. Choice (a), if true,

would therefore support the argument by demonstrating that taking in very little vitamin X is easy to do. The other statements do not strengthen the argument. (d) in particular may be tricky. If vitamin X deficiency is found only in the very young, then *only the very young* should take vitamin X supplements. The argument, however, is that *everyone* should take vitamin X tablets.

7. (b) The failure of scientists to repeat the experiment allegedly demonstrating the need for vitamin X greatly weakens the argument. (a) is not a good choice because it does not refer to all people, just to people in general. Some people may have lived unhealthily until now because of vitamin X deficiency, and taking tablets may in the future prevent such cases. (c) is not relevant unless it is known which people can manufacture vitamin X. Such knowledge would mean that some people need not take the vitamin, undercutting the argument. (d) and (e) are irrelevant and should be unpersuasive to you.

8. (b) Under the given conditions, we can diagram four possible arrangements.

(1)

(2)

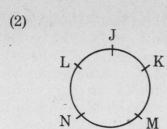

(3)

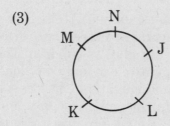

(4)

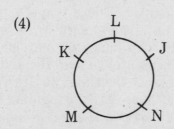

From these diagrams, we see that K always sits next to M (I) and N always sits next to M (II). However, in diagrams (3) and (4), there is no seat between J and N (III). Thus the answer is I and II only.

9. (c) In diagrams (3) and (4) above, J does not sit between K and L (I). In diagrams (1) and (2), L sits next to N and there is one seat between L and K (II). In diagrams (3) and (4), L sits next to K and there is one seat between L and N. Thus, the answer is II and III only.

10. (a) P can place a chair between L and K only in diagrams (3) and (4) above. There is then one seat between P and M. None of the other choices is true.

11. (d) The directions are clear. The oper-

ations must be performed carefully, but the questions are uncomplicated.

$2@2 = \dfrac{2 + 2}{2} = 2$. Since

$2@2 = 2, 2@2@2@2\ldots = 2$.

12. (a) Since operations are to be performed from right to left, the final operation is "0* something" (zero star something). Zero star anything is equal to zero divided by some number, the result of which always equals zero. The complicated expression therefore reduces to zero. The other operations should *not* be performed. Doing so wastes valuable time.

13. (a) This problem may be solved without any calculations once it is noted that all choices present fractions of the form $\dfrac{4}{4 + Y}$. Since Y is never negative, $4 + Y$ is greater than 4 for choices (b), (c), (d), and (e), making the total fraction less than 1. Choice (a) gives the expression 4/4, or 1, which is greater than the other choices.

If you work out the exact values for each choice, you'll get:

(a) $\dfrac{4}{4 + 0} = \dfrac{4}{4} = 1$

(b) $4 * \dfrac{1}{1 + 1} = 4 * \dfrac{1}{2} =$

$\dfrac{4}{4 + \frac{1}{2}} = \dfrac{8}{9}$

(c) $\dfrac{4}{4 + 1} = \dfrac{4}{5}$

(d) $\dfrac{4}{4 + 2} = \dfrac{4}{6} = \dfrac{2}{3}$

(e) $4 * \dfrac{12 + 4}{4} = 4 * \dfrac{16}{4} =$

$4 * 4 = \dfrac{4}{4 + 4} = \dfrac{4}{8} = \dfrac{1}{2}$

14. (c) Choices (a), (b), (c), (d), and (e) equal, in order, 3/4, 3/6, 3/8, 4, and 2. Choice (c) is thus the least.

15. (e) It is apparent from rule (4) that an Erg man must have an Erg father. Since this father cannot have married a Cru woman, statement II is correct. Since the father must also have had an Erg father, there could also have been no Cru grandmother, making statement I correct. Since an Erg man, including the father, may marry a Hra woman, there may be a Hra mother, making statement III correct. Choice (e) is therefore the proper one.

16. (c) Statement I is correct. A Hra woman may marry an Erg man. If she has three children all of her caste, there must be no males among them, for they would have the father's caste and thus be Erg. Statement II is also correct. Were she and her husband both Hra, all their children would be Hra, no matter what their sex was. Statement III is false; a Hra woman cannot marry a Cru man and thus she cannot have a Cru son.

17. (e) A Hra woman can have an Erg son if she marries an Erg man, so (b) is false. She can therefore have an Erg grandson, so (c) is false. If she has a Hra son, he may marry a Cru woman and produce a Cru granddaughter, so (d) is false. There is no way that a Hra woman can have a Cru grandson, however. Her daughter must be Hra and ineligible to marry a Cru man, so there can be no Cru grandson through the daughter; hence (a) is false. The woman's sons can be either Hra or Erg. They clearly cannot produce a Cru grandson for her. Choice (d) is therefore also false. Choice (e) is true, however. A Hra woman's Erg or Hra sons may marry Erg women if they wish.

18. (b) Only statement III is correct. A marriage between two Crus produces only Cru children. The Cru daughter can only produce Cru granddaughters. The Cru son cannot marry a Hra woman, and thus also cannot produce a Hra granddaughter. There may be a Hra great-granddaughter, however. The Cru daughter may marry a Hra man and have a Hra son. This male can then marry a Hra woman and have a Hra daughter. Statements I and II are therefore possible.

19. (c) The key to answering the five questions in this problem is to draw out the schedule of course offerings. The following table presents this, with an "X" representing times when a course is available. Each course is abbreviated to its first initial.

	A	B	C	D	E
January 15-	X			x	X
February 14-		X	x		x
March 15-	X	X		X	X
April 15-			X	x	X

Course duration is indicated by the size of the crosses. The large "X's" represent month-long courses, small "X's" half-months.

As we can see, four courses are offered in March, more than in any other month.

20. (*b*) In February, Celia is limited to only one course. Any combination of two courses would involve taking a half-month course along with another course, something which is not allowed.

21. (*c*) The only way Celia can take both literature courses before March is to take American literature in January and English literature in February. This necessitates taking cooking in April, since the only other time cooking is offered conflicts with English literature in February. Similarly, basket weaving must be taken in March, to avoid a conflict with English literature. Dance may be taken either in January or in March, giving the two possibilities.

22. (*a*) This moderately difficult problem may be solved using information gleaned in the previous question. Celia is to take no courses in January and can only take one course in February. She must therefore take two courses in both March and April. The only way to take two courses in April is to take dance and English literature then. The other courses must be taken in February or March. Since cooking is not offered in March, it must be taken in February, so that (*a*) is correct. American literature and basket weaving must be taken in March.

23. (*d*) Celia is to take no courses in April and, as we have seen, can only take one course in February. She must therefore take two courses in both January and March. The only way to take two courses in January is by taking American literature and dance then. Since cooking is not given in March, it must be taken in February, leaving basket weaving and English literature to be taken in March. Statements I and III are therefore correct; statement II is incorrect.

24. (*d*) The original statement indicates that some superior teachers, although inspiring, are also irritable and tend to disturb certain students. This is essentially what statement (*d*) says. Statement (*a*) transforms the word "some" to "generally," which is not justifiable. In choices (*b*) and (*c*) the use of the words "most" and "often" lead to similarly erroneous conclusions. Statement (*e*) is irrelevant.

25. (*d*) The weakness of the original argument lies in its assumption that a correlation—the occurrence of two events together—is the same as a cause/effect relationship. To bolster the argument, it would be necessary to show not merely that economic expansion and governmental nonintervention have occurred together in the past, but that the one can be *caused by* the other. Only choice (*d*) addresses this fundamental issue.

SECTION VII

1. (*d*) If the average wage earner is frustrated by the inflationary spiral, we can infer that there must be a disparity, a gap, or a *discrepancy*

between income and the cost of living.

2. (b) Eliminate choice (d). The word "retiring," in this context, could only be satirical or sarcastic, and there is no evidence to suggest such an intent. Choices (a), (c), and (e) all provide similar first words that suggest only that women would like to have middle management positions, not that they are achieving their goals. If they are not, their ambitions to obtain higher level positions would be irrelevant. Choice (b), however, makes sense of the sentence. The words "traditional attitudes" suggest attitudes that oppose the concept of women competing with men in business. Women may be *rising* to middle management positions despite traditional attitudes (held, it is implied, by men), but these traditional attitudes are still *thwarting* (blocking) their ambitions to obtain the highest jobs.

3. (e) The sentence implies that a candidate's attitude toward his family may be seen by the voters as indicative of his attitude toward the public good. In choices (a) and (d), however, the words "lovable" and "suitable" do not describe the candidate's attitude toward his family, but rather his family's attitude toward him. These choices should be eliminated. If the candidate were "oblivious" to his family, the voters would hardly be convinced that he would be devoted to the public good, so choice (c) can be eliminated. Choice (b) is incorrect, since a candidate would hardly do things to make voters "doubtful." The remaining possibility, choice (e), is correct. Politicians hope that voters will be *persuaded* that a candidate *devoted* to his family would also be devoted to the public good.

4. (c) The two clauses of this sentence both suggest a contrast between the past and the present. Less than a generation ago, the computer was used only by big business; today it is used by small business. The only choice that completes the idea of the contrast is choice (c), *reserved . . . individuals*.

5. (e) *Abide by*, in this context, would mean "submit to" or "agree to," and would complete the sense of the sentence.

6. (d) The use of the word "but" warns us to expect a reversal of what we have been told. Technology may combat crime, but . . . . The "but" in this case is that criminals can use technology, too. Every law-enforcement innovation is followed by some criminal innovation. Therefore, choice (d) is correct.

7. (b) The sentence suggests that Phillips might have been expected to find grounds for clemency. We can infer, therefore, that Phillips is noted for his *leniency*. The description of the crime as *heinous* (utterly reprehensible) explains why even Phillips could find no grounds for clemency. The first word of choice (d) would have been acceptable, but the second word, "candor" (honesty or frankness) is not as appropriate as "leniency."

8. (*e*) A *machine* is part of a *factory* in just the same way that a *conveyor belt* is part of an *assembly line.*

9. (*b*) A balloon or similar object will become *turgid* if you *inflate* it. Similarly, water or food, among other things, will become *unclean* if you *contaminate* it.

10. (*c*) To be *morose* (sullen or sulky) is to be lacking in *animation.* In like manner, to be *audacious* (extremely bold or recklessly brave) is to be lacking in *trepidation* (tremulous fear).

11. (*a*) *Appreciation* is respect, but *adulation* is excessive devotion or servile admiration. The second feeling is similar to the first except for the fact that it is excessive. Similarly, *scholarship* is the accumulation and display of learning, but *pedantry* is the undue or excessive display of learning. Again, the second term is similar to the first except for the fact that it is excessive.

12. (*e*) To *renege* is to go back on one's word or to fail to fulfill a *promise.* In the same way, to *default* is to fail to perform an *obligation.* In each of the two word relationships, the first term is one that denotes failure to perform, and the second term is one that denotes the act that is not performed.

13. (*c*) A *throne* is the kind of *chair* used by a monarch, just as a *crown* is the kind of *hat* worn by a monarch.

14. (*a*) A *dagger* is contained in a *sheath,* a close-fitting cover or case, just as an *arrow* is contained in a *quiver.*

15. (*c*) A *coronation* is the ceremony or rite at which a person is crowned or officially proclaimed a *monarch.* Similarly, an *ordination* is the ceremony or rite at which a person is ordained or officially recognized as a *priest* or clergyman. Note that choice (*d*) would be correct if the second term were "president" rather than "republic."

16. (*d*) The *palm* is a symbol of *victory.* The *white feather* is a symbol of *cowardice.*

17. (*c*) To determine the author's purpose, look to see what the passage mainly concerns itself with. The first paragraph sets forth the two phyla and some characteristics of one of them. The second paragraph sets forth the subdivisions of the other phylum. The third paragraph deals with a single class of one of those sub-phyla. The answer which summarizes this logical structure is choice (*c*).

18. (*e*) In paragraph 2, the passage states that sphenopsids *contributed to* coal formation in the Carboniferous period, but choice (*e*) says that the world's coal reserves *were created by* the sphenopsids. Choice (*e*) is incorrect because it implies that no other phyla contributed to the formation of the coal beds, while the passage states only that the sphenopsids contributed, which implies to assist along with others.

19. (*e*) Choice (*a*) is incorrect because paragraph 1 states that the Bryophytes are nonwoody in structure. Choice (*b*) is wrong; paragraph 2 says that the psilopsids were more advanced than any of the mosses,

and the mosses are Bryophytes. Choice (c) is incorrect on two counts: paragraph 2 states that the Bryophytes may have simple leaves (not net-veined leaves), but not true roots. Choice (d) has no support in the passage.

20. (d) Since Dr. Sternberg is quoted, sixty years later, on the problems of defining intelligence, we can infer that cognitive psychologists have not yet arrived at a generally accepted definition of intelligence.

21. (e) Paragraph 3 indicates that factor analysis has not succeeded in explaining mental abilities, so choice (a) can be eliminated. The passage deals with the nature of intelligence. It briefly describes some of the contributions made by factor analysis and process analysis, but only in connection with how far they have led to an understanding of the nature of intelligence. Choices (b) and (c) can, therefore, be ruled out. And while the passage concludes that the true nature of intelligence is not yet understood, it does not go so far as to say that intelligence will never be adequately defined. Choice (d) is incorrect, and we are left with choice (e) as the author's primary purpose.

22. (b) Paragraph 5 clearly states that process analysis has clarified our understanding of how certain mental tasks are performed, and this is what choice (b) says. Choice (a) is incorrect since paragraph 4 states directly that process analysis does not reject the findings of factor analysis. Choice (c), too, is incorrect; paragraph 5 states that

Dr. Sternberg *hopes* that the application of componential analysis will contribute to an understanding of adaptational ability, but does not indicate that it has made that contribution as yet. As to choices (d) and (e), it is factor analysis, not process analysis, that identifies specific factors that form the basis of intelligence and analyzes the products of test performance.

23. (c) In paragraphs 3, 4, and 5, the passage suggests that factor analysis and process analysis have made progress in understanding verbal-educational abilities, but not in understanding adaptational or practical problem-solving abilities. Items I and II are examples of verbal-educational abilities. Item III is an example of adaptational or practical problem-solving ability, and, according to the passage, neither factor analysis nor process analysis has offered much understanding in this area.

24. (b) The first sentence in paragraph 2 is a paraphrase of the statement in choice (b) and provides the correct answer.

25. (a) Since most of the material about process analysis in the passage is either in the form of direct or indirect quotation from Dr. Sternberg, and since that material is positively expressed, we can infer that Dr. Sternberg subscribes to the information processing approach.

26. (c) Choice (a) is incorrect, since that statement is made in the first sentence of the passage. The first sen-

tence of paragraph 5 supports the statement in choice (*b*), so that is not the correct answer. The second sentence of paragraph 5 supports the statement that neither process analysis nor factor analysis has provided important insights into the area of practical problem-solving, so choice (*d*) is incorrect. The second sentence of paragraph 3 indicates that subsequent theorists modified Spearman's theory of factor analysis, so choice (*e*) is incorrect. There is no support, direct or implied, for the statement in choice (*c*), so that is the correct answer.

27. (*e*) Best title questions really ask you to select the choice that best describes what the passage as a whole is about. Although this passage deals with factor and process analysis, it does so only to show that neither approach has been successful in defining intelligence. Both the opening and closing paragraphs of the passage also deal with the difficulty of defining intelligence, and that is why choice (*e*) is the "title" that best summarizes the content of the passage.

28. (*a*) *Convene*—to convoke, to cause to assemble; opposite—*dissolve* (to order the temination of [an assembly])

29. (*d*) *Implicate*—to involve (a person) in a charge or accusation; oppo-site—*exculpate* (to clear from a charge of guilt or fault)

30. (*b*) *Obscure*—to hide or cover; opposite—*reveal*

31. (*e*) *Impound*—to seize or shut up in a pound, as a stray animal; opposite—*release*

32. (*b*) *Arrogate*—to claim or appropriate to one's self without right; opposite—*waive* (to renounce a claim or right to)

33. (*a*) *Remonstration*—a pleading in protest or objection; opposite—*endorsement* (a statement of acceptance or approval)

34. (*e*) *Moot*—debatable, doubtful; opposite—*indisputable*

35. (*c*) *Saturnine*—gloomy; opposite—*blithe* (merry or gay)

36. (*c*) *Insular*—narrowly exclusive, provincial; opposite—*cosmopolitan*

37. (*c*) *Quixotic*—visionary, impractical; opposite—*practical*

38. (*b*) *Equivocal*—doubtful, questionable; opposite—*categorical* (absolute, unqualified and unconditional)

Answer Sheet—Practice Test 4

When you have chosen your answer to any question, blacken the corresponding space on the answer sheet below. Make sure your marking completely fills the answer space. If you change an answer, erase the previous marking completely.

Section I

1 Ⓐ Ⓑ Ⓒ Ⓓ Ⓔ	11 Ⓐ Ⓑ Ⓒ Ⓓ Ⓔ	21 Ⓐ Ⓑ Ⓒ Ⓓ Ⓔ	30 Ⓐ Ⓑ Ⓒ Ⓓ Ⓔ
2 Ⓐ Ⓑ Ⓒ Ⓓ Ⓔ	12 Ⓐ Ⓑ Ⓒ Ⓓ Ⓔ	22 Ⓐ Ⓑ Ⓒ Ⓓ Ⓔ	31 Ⓐ Ⓑ Ⓒ Ⓓ Ⓔ
3 Ⓐ Ⓑ Ⓒ Ⓓ Ⓔ	13 Ⓐ Ⓑ Ⓒ Ⓓ Ⓔ	23 Ⓐ Ⓑ Ⓒ Ⓓ Ⓔ	32 Ⓐ Ⓑ Ⓒ Ⓓ Ⓔ
4 Ⓐ Ⓑ Ⓒ Ⓓ Ⓔ	14 Ⓐ Ⓑ Ⓒ Ⓓ Ⓔ	24 Ⓐ Ⓑ Ⓒ Ⓓ Ⓔ	33 Ⓐ Ⓑ Ⓒ Ⓓ Ⓔ
5 Ⓐ Ⓑ Ⓒ Ⓓ Ⓔ	15 Ⓐ Ⓑ Ⓒ Ⓓ Ⓔ	25 Ⓐ Ⓑ Ⓒ Ⓓ Ⓔ	34 Ⓐ Ⓑ Ⓒ Ⓓ Ⓔ
6 Ⓐ Ⓑ Ⓒ Ⓓ Ⓔ	16 Ⓐ Ⓑ Ⓒ Ⓓ Ⓔ	26 Ⓐ Ⓑ Ⓒ Ⓓ Ⓔ	35 Ⓐ Ⓑ Ⓒ Ⓓ Ⓔ
7 Ⓐ Ⓑ Ⓒ Ⓓ Ⓔ	17 Ⓐ Ⓑ Ⓒ Ⓓ Ⓔ	27 Ⓐ Ⓑ Ⓒ Ⓓ Ⓔ	36 Ⓐ Ⓑ Ⓒ Ⓓ Ⓔ
8 Ⓐ Ⓑ Ⓒ Ⓓ Ⓔ	18 Ⓐ Ⓑ Ⓒ Ⓓ Ⓔ	28 Ⓐ Ⓑ Ⓒ Ⓓ Ⓔ	37 Ⓐ Ⓑ Ⓒ Ⓓ Ⓔ
9 Ⓐ Ⓑ Ⓒ Ⓓ Ⓔ	19 Ⓐ Ⓑ Ⓒ Ⓓ Ⓔ	29 Ⓐ Ⓑ Ⓒ Ⓓ Ⓔ	38 Ⓐ Ⓑ Ⓒ Ⓓ Ⓔ
10 Ⓐ Ⓑ Ⓒ Ⓓ Ⓔ	20 Ⓐ Ⓑ Ⓒ Ⓓ Ⓔ		

Section II

1 Ⓐ Ⓑ Ⓒ Ⓓ Ⓔ	11 Ⓐ Ⓑ Ⓒ Ⓓ Ⓔ	21 Ⓐ Ⓑ Ⓒ Ⓓ Ⓔ	30 Ⓐ Ⓑ Ⓒ Ⓓ Ⓔ
2 Ⓐ Ⓑ Ⓒ Ⓓ Ⓔ	12 Ⓐ Ⓑ Ⓒ Ⓓ Ⓔ	22 Ⓐ Ⓑ Ⓒ Ⓓ Ⓔ	31 Ⓐ Ⓑ Ⓒ Ⓓ Ⓔ
3 Ⓐ Ⓑ Ⓒ Ⓓ Ⓔ	13 Ⓐ Ⓑ Ⓒ Ⓓ Ⓔ	23 Ⓐ Ⓑ Ⓒ Ⓓ Ⓔ	32 Ⓐ Ⓑ Ⓒ Ⓓ Ⓔ
4 Ⓐ Ⓑ Ⓒ Ⓓ Ⓔ	14 Ⓐ Ⓑ Ⓒ Ⓓ Ⓔ	24 Ⓐ Ⓑ Ⓒ Ⓓ Ⓔ	33 Ⓐ Ⓑ Ⓒ Ⓓ Ⓔ
5 Ⓐ Ⓑ Ⓒ Ⓓ Ⓔ	15 Ⓐ Ⓑ Ⓒ Ⓓ Ⓔ	25 Ⓐ Ⓑ Ⓒ Ⓓ Ⓔ	34 Ⓐ Ⓑ Ⓒ Ⓓ Ⓔ
6 Ⓐ Ⓑ Ⓒ Ⓓ Ⓔ	16 Ⓐ Ⓑ Ⓒ Ⓓ Ⓔ	26 Ⓐ Ⓑ Ⓒ Ⓓ Ⓔ	35 Ⓐ Ⓑ Ⓒ Ⓓ Ⓔ
7 Ⓐ Ⓑ Ⓒ Ⓓ Ⓔ	17 Ⓐ Ⓑ Ⓒ Ⓓ Ⓔ	27 Ⓐ Ⓑ Ⓒ Ⓓ Ⓔ	36 Ⓐ Ⓑ Ⓒ Ⓓ Ⓔ
8 Ⓐ Ⓑ Ⓒ Ⓓ Ⓔ	18 Ⓐ Ⓑ Ⓒ Ⓓ Ⓔ	28 Ⓐ Ⓑ Ⓒ Ⓓ Ⓔ	37 Ⓐ Ⓑ Ⓒ Ⓓ Ⓔ
9 Ⓐ Ⓑ Ⓒ Ⓓ Ⓔ	19 Ⓐ Ⓑ Ⓒ Ⓓ Ⓔ	29 Ⓐ Ⓑ Ⓒ Ⓓ Ⓔ	38 Ⓐ Ⓑ Ⓒ Ⓓ Ⓔ
10 Ⓐ Ⓑ Ⓒ Ⓓ Ⓔ	20 Ⓐ Ⓑ Ⓒ Ⓓ Ⓔ		

Section III

1 Ⓐ Ⓑ Ⓒ Ⓓ Ⓔ	9 Ⓐ Ⓑ Ⓒ Ⓓ Ⓔ	17 Ⓐ Ⓑ Ⓒ Ⓓ Ⓔ	24 Ⓐ Ⓑ Ⓒ Ⓓ Ⓔ
2 Ⓐ Ⓑ Ⓒ Ⓓ Ⓔ	10 Ⓐ Ⓑ Ⓒ Ⓓ Ⓔ	18 Ⓐ Ⓑ Ⓒ Ⓓ Ⓔ	25 Ⓐ Ⓑ Ⓒ Ⓓ Ⓔ
3 Ⓐ Ⓑ Ⓒ Ⓓ Ⓔ	11 Ⓐ Ⓑ Ⓒ Ⓓ Ⓔ	19 Ⓐ Ⓑ Ⓒ Ⓓ Ⓔ	26 Ⓐ Ⓑ Ⓒ Ⓓ Ⓔ
4 Ⓐ Ⓑ Ⓒ Ⓓ Ⓔ	12 Ⓐ Ⓑ Ⓒ Ⓓ Ⓔ	20 Ⓐ Ⓑ Ⓒ Ⓓ Ⓔ	27 Ⓐ Ⓑ Ⓒ Ⓓ Ⓔ
5 Ⓐ Ⓑ Ⓒ Ⓓ Ⓔ	13 Ⓐ Ⓑ Ⓒ Ⓓ Ⓔ	21 Ⓐ Ⓑ Ⓒ Ⓓ Ⓔ	28 Ⓐ Ⓑ Ⓒ Ⓓ Ⓔ
6 Ⓐ Ⓑ Ⓒ Ⓓ Ⓔ	14 Ⓐ Ⓑ Ⓒ Ⓓ Ⓔ	22 Ⓐ Ⓑ Ⓒ Ⓓ Ⓔ	29 Ⓐ Ⓑ Ⓒ Ⓓ Ⓔ
7 Ⓐ Ⓑ Ⓒ Ⓓ Ⓔ	15 Ⓐ Ⓑ Ⓒ Ⓓ Ⓔ	23 Ⓐ Ⓑ Ⓒ Ⓓ Ⓔ	30 Ⓐ Ⓑ Ⓒ Ⓓ Ⓔ
8 Ⓐ Ⓑ Ⓒ Ⓓ Ⓔ	16 Ⓐ Ⓑ Ⓒ Ⓓ Ⓔ		

Section IV

1 Ⓐ Ⓑ Ⓒ Ⓓ Ⓔ	9 Ⓐ Ⓑ Ⓒ Ⓓ Ⓔ	17 Ⓐ Ⓑ Ⓒ Ⓓ Ⓔ	24 Ⓐ Ⓑ Ⓒ Ⓓ Ⓔ
2 Ⓐ Ⓑ Ⓒ Ⓓ Ⓔ	10 Ⓐ Ⓑ Ⓒ Ⓓ Ⓔ	18 Ⓐ Ⓑ Ⓒ Ⓓ Ⓔ	25 Ⓐ Ⓑ Ⓒ Ⓓ Ⓔ
3 Ⓐ Ⓑ Ⓒ Ⓓ Ⓔ	11 Ⓐ Ⓑ Ⓒ Ⓓ Ⓔ	19 Ⓐ Ⓑ Ⓒ Ⓓ Ⓔ	26 Ⓐ Ⓑ Ⓒ Ⓓ Ⓔ
4 Ⓐ Ⓑ Ⓒ Ⓓ Ⓔ	12 Ⓐ Ⓑ Ⓒ Ⓓ Ⓔ	20 Ⓐ Ⓑ Ⓒ Ⓓ Ⓔ	27 Ⓐ Ⓑ Ⓒ Ⓓ Ⓔ
5 Ⓐ Ⓑ Ⓒ Ⓓ Ⓔ	13 Ⓐ Ⓑ Ⓒ Ⓓ Ⓔ	21 Ⓐ Ⓑ Ⓒ Ⓓ Ⓔ	28 Ⓐ Ⓑ Ⓒ Ⓓ Ⓔ
6 Ⓐ Ⓑ Ⓒ Ⓓ Ⓔ	14 Ⓐ Ⓑ Ⓒ Ⓓ Ⓔ	22 Ⓐ Ⓑ Ⓒ Ⓓ Ⓔ	29 Ⓐ Ⓑ Ⓒ Ⓓ Ⓔ
7 Ⓐ Ⓑ Ⓒ Ⓓ Ⓔ	15 Ⓐ Ⓑ Ⓒ Ⓓ Ⓔ	23 Ⓐ Ⓑ Ⓒ Ⓓ Ⓔ	30 Ⓐ Ⓑ Ⓒ Ⓓ Ⓔ
8 Ⓐ Ⓑ Ⓒ Ⓓ Ⓔ	16 Ⓐ Ⓑ Ⓒ Ⓓ Ⓔ		

Section V

1 Ⓐ Ⓑ Ⓒ Ⓓ Ⓔ	8 Ⓐ Ⓑ Ⓒ Ⓓ Ⓔ	14 Ⓐ Ⓑ Ⓒ Ⓓ Ⓔ	20 Ⓐ Ⓑ Ⓒ Ⓓ Ⓔ
2 Ⓐ Ⓑ Ⓒ Ⓓ Ⓔ	9 Ⓐ Ⓑ Ⓒ Ⓓ Ⓔ	15 Ⓐ Ⓑ Ⓒ Ⓓ Ⓔ	21 Ⓐ Ⓑ Ⓒ Ⓓ Ⓔ
3 Ⓐ Ⓑ Ⓒ Ⓓ Ⓔ	10 Ⓐ Ⓑ Ⓒ Ⓓ Ⓔ	16 Ⓐ Ⓑ Ⓒ Ⓓ Ⓔ	22 Ⓐ Ⓑ Ⓒ Ⓓ Ⓔ
4 Ⓐ Ⓑ Ⓒ Ⓓ Ⓔ	11 Ⓐ Ⓑ Ⓒ Ⓓ Ⓔ	17 Ⓐ Ⓑ Ⓒ Ⓓ Ⓔ	23 Ⓐ Ⓑ Ⓒ Ⓓ Ⓔ
5 Ⓐ Ⓑ Ⓒ Ⓓ Ⓔ	12 Ⓐ Ⓑ Ⓒ Ⓓ Ⓔ	18 Ⓐ Ⓑ Ⓒ Ⓓ Ⓔ	24 Ⓐ Ⓑ Ⓒ Ⓓ Ⓔ
6 Ⓐ Ⓑ Ⓒ Ⓓ Ⓔ	13 Ⓐ Ⓑ Ⓒ Ⓓ Ⓔ	19 Ⓐ Ⓑ Ⓒ Ⓓ Ⓔ	25 Ⓐ Ⓑ Ⓒ Ⓓ Ⓔ
7 Ⓐ Ⓑ Ⓒ Ⓓ Ⓔ			

Section VI

1 Ⓐ Ⓑ Ⓒ Ⓓ Ⓔ	8 Ⓐ Ⓑ Ⓒ Ⓓ Ⓔ	14 Ⓐ Ⓑ Ⓒ Ⓓ Ⓔ	20 Ⓐ Ⓑ Ⓒ Ⓓ Ⓔ
2 Ⓐ Ⓑ Ⓒ Ⓓ Ⓔ	9 Ⓐ Ⓑ Ⓒ Ⓓ Ⓔ	15 Ⓐ Ⓑ Ⓒ Ⓓ Ⓔ	21 Ⓐ Ⓑ Ⓒ Ⓓ Ⓔ
3 Ⓐ Ⓑ Ⓒ Ⓓ Ⓔ	10 Ⓐ Ⓑ Ⓒ Ⓓ Ⓔ	16 Ⓐ Ⓑ Ⓒ Ⓓ Ⓔ	22 Ⓐ Ⓑ Ⓒ Ⓓ Ⓔ
4 Ⓐ Ⓑ Ⓒ Ⓓ Ⓔ	11 Ⓐ Ⓑ Ⓒ Ⓓ Ⓔ	17 Ⓐ Ⓑ Ⓒ Ⓓ Ⓔ	23 Ⓐ Ⓑ Ⓒ Ⓓ Ⓔ
5 Ⓐ Ⓑ Ⓒ Ⓓ Ⓔ	12 Ⓐ Ⓑ Ⓒ Ⓓ Ⓔ	18 Ⓐ Ⓑ Ⓒ Ⓓ Ⓔ	24 Ⓐ Ⓑ Ⓒ Ⓓ Ⓔ
6 Ⓐ Ⓑ Ⓒ Ⓓ Ⓔ	13 Ⓐ Ⓑ Ⓒ Ⓓ Ⓔ	19 Ⓐ Ⓑ Ⓒ Ⓓ Ⓔ	25 Ⓐ Ⓑ Ⓒ Ⓓ Ⓔ
7 Ⓐ Ⓑ Ⓒ Ⓓ Ⓔ			

Section VII

1 Ⓐ Ⓑ Ⓒ Ⓓ Ⓔ	8 Ⓐ Ⓑ Ⓒ Ⓓ Ⓔ	14 Ⓐ Ⓑ Ⓒ Ⓓ Ⓔ	20 Ⓐ Ⓑ Ⓒ Ⓓ Ⓔ
2 Ⓐ Ⓑ Ⓒ Ⓓ Ⓔ	9 Ⓐ Ⓑ Ⓒ Ⓓ Ⓔ	15 Ⓐ Ⓑ Ⓒ Ⓓ Ⓔ	21 Ⓐ Ⓑ Ⓒ Ⓓ Ⓔ
3 Ⓐ Ⓑ Ⓒ Ⓓ Ⓔ	10 Ⓐ Ⓑ Ⓒ Ⓓ Ⓔ	16 Ⓐ Ⓑ Ⓒ Ⓓ Ⓔ	22 Ⓐ Ⓑ Ⓒ Ⓓ Ⓔ
4 Ⓐ Ⓑ Ⓒ Ⓓ Ⓔ	11 Ⓐ Ⓑ Ⓒ Ⓓ Ⓔ	17 Ⓐ Ⓑ Ⓒ Ⓓ Ⓔ	23 Ⓐ Ⓑ Ⓒ Ⓓ Ⓔ
5 Ⓐ Ⓑ Ⓒ Ⓓ Ⓔ	12 Ⓐ Ⓑ Ⓒ Ⓓ Ⓔ	18 Ⓐ Ⓑ Ⓒ Ⓓ Ⓔ	24 Ⓐ Ⓑ Ⓒ Ⓓ Ⓔ
6 Ⓐ Ⓑ Ⓒ Ⓓ Ⓔ	13 Ⓐ Ⓑ Ⓒ Ⓓ Ⓔ	19 Ⓐ Ⓑ Ⓒ Ⓓ Ⓔ	25 Ⓐ Ⓑ Ⓒ Ⓓ Ⓔ
7 Ⓐ Ⓑ Ⓒ Ⓓ Ⓔ			

Practice Test **4**

GRE Practice Test 4

SECTION I

Time—30 minutes
38 Questions

For each of the numbered questions in this section, choose the best answer according to the instructions, and blacken the correspondingly numbered blank space on the answer sheet.

Each of the sentences below has one or more blank spaces indicating where a word or words have been omitted. Each sentence is followed by five words or sets of word lettered from (a) to (e). Select the lettered word or set of words which, inserted to replace the blanks, BEST fits in with and completes the meaning of the sentence as a whole.

1. Although he acted as if he were completely absorbed in copying the material, he really found the work extremely – – –, and he completed it only by virtue of sheer determination.

    (a) revealing
    (b) appealing
    (c) interesting
    (d) tedious
    (e) woeful

2. Prepared though I was to be impressed by the magnificence of the Grand Canyon, when I actually stood at its brink, I was – – – by the magnitude of its scale and astonished and – – – by the sheer grandeur of its beauty.

    (a) awestruck . . . dumbfounded
    (b) numbed . . . inhibited
    (c) bored . . . imbued
    (d) unaffected . . . repelled
    (e) effected . . . stricken

3. It was probably to – – – for the searing privation he had endured as a youngster brought up in Appalachia, that he so fondly indulged his children's every whim.

    (a) recriminate
    (b) compensate

(c) reciprocate
(d) arrogate
(e) retroact

4. The improvement in the finances of Hutchner and Sons came so quietly, and in such modest – – –, that none of their competitors was aware of the change in their fortunes until the day that young Victor Hutchner announced the – – – of that giant of the industry, Giddings and Clark.

(a) doses . . . reorganization
(b) guise . . . bankruptcy
(c) development . . . opposition
(d) increments . . . acquisition
(e) circumstances . . . collapse

5. The announcement by two major oil companies that gasoline deliveries would be – – – next month highlights the uncertainty of future gasoline availability, optimistic federal projections notwithstanding.

(a) curtailed
(b) maintained
(c) continued
(d) augmented
(e) increased

6. Microsurgery, in just one decade, has progresed from being a research – – – to becoming a clinical – – –.

(a) necessity . . . luxury
(b) possibility . . . probability
(c) curiosity . . . reality
(d) hypothesis . . . desideratum
(e) technique . . . experiment

7. It is – – – that people who would be considered poor credit risks by most banks can accumulate total credit card debts—in reality, – – – loans—far beyond what they would be granted if they were to apply for a loan.

(a) dangerous . . . defaulted
(b) scandalous . . . interest-free
(c) understandable . . . unregistered
(d) fortunate . . . demand
(e) ironical . . . unsecured

In each of the questions below, a related pair of words or phrases in capital letters is followed by five pairs of words or phrases lettered from (a) to (e). Select the lettered pair that expresses a relationship that is MOST similar to that of the capitalized pair.

8. DIRTY : FILTHY : : (a) rapacious : ravishing (b) inept : skilled (c) courteous : polite (d) disorderly : disobedient (e) elevated : exalted

9. COUNTERMAND : ORDER : : (a) rescind : decree (b) defy : commmand (c) repeal : principle (d) override : approve (e) contradict : revoke

10. COMPASSION : SUFFERING : : (a) alienation : association (b) compunction : wrongdoing (c) indifference : comprehension (d) fervor : disease (e) arrogance : righteousness

11. REAM : SHEET : : (a) check : balances (b) battery : cannon (c) aggregation : parishioners (d) ounce : pound (e) bottle : fluid

12. INDOLENCE : BEAVER : : (a) joviality : hyena (b) passivity : cow (c) ferocity : lamb (d) elegance : peacock (e) wisdom : owl

13. MISUNDERSTANDING : ALTERCATION : : (a) discord : amiability (b) banality : stimulation (c) disgrace : arrogance (d) accommodation : reconciliation (e) bias : fairness

14. PREDILECTION : AVERSION : : (a) pretension : contention (b) cyclical : cylindrical (c) penitent : unregenerate (d) disdainful : scornful (e) aberrant : antipathy

15. DILETTANTE : CONNOISSEUR : : (a) aesthete : ascetic (b) duffer : beginner (c) researcher : laureate (d) amateur : professional (e) convert : apostate

16. COMPTROLLER : FINANCES : : (a) projectionist : disbursements (b) actuary : realities (c) demographer : exorcisms (d) immunologist : measurements (e) quartermaster : materiel

In the series of selections that follows, each passage is followed by questions based on its content. Read the passage and choose the best answer for each question based on the contents of the passage. The questions must be answered on the basis of what is stated or implied in the reading passage.

The source of endrin contamination in the river could not have been the nearby sugar cane fields, because the biggest kills occurred in late autumn, and the fields were sprayed in the spring. Investigation revealed no Louisiana industries discharging insecticide wastes into the river. It was concluded that the endrin must have been carried into Louisiana by the river's current from the north.

The symptoms which affected the fish in the widespread kills were described by the scientists as sub-acute. It was proposed therefore that the fish were receiving small doses of endrin resulting from dilution over a long distance in the immense flow of the river. The investigation zeroed in, therefore, on a plant 500 miles up river in Memphis, Tennessee, which manufactured endrin.

The job of the investigative team was to collect information on the manufacture of endrin, and to obtain samples of the mud and water from the immediate vicinity of the plant. The United States Public Health Service team did not find themselves very welcome at the plant. The manager refused to answer any specific questions about endrin and its byproducts, tersely suggesting that the questioners read the patents for particulars about the manufacturing processes. Moreover, the company officials insisted upon selecting the sites from which the soil and water samples were to be taken. In short, the investigators were treated more like spies from an alien government than like officers of the United States Public Health Service.

17. Which of the following pieces of information was of no use in determining the source of the endrin contamination?

    (a) an analysis of the soil and water samples from the immediate vicinity of the plant
    (b) the sugar cane fields being sprayed in the spring
    (c) the sub-acute nature of the symptoms which affected the fish killed in the spills
    (d) an investigation revealing that no Louisiana industry was discharging insecticide wastes into the river
    (e) the kills occurring in the late autumn

18. The use of the word "sub-acute" to describe the symptoms that affected the fish in the widespread kills, implies that

    (a) only small amounts of fish were killed
    (b) the symptoms were undiscernable
    (c) the fish showed comparatively mild symptoms of poisoning
    (d) symptoms were localized
    (e) the symptoms were brief in duration

19. It can be inferred from this passage that endrin

   (a) is no longer used as a pesticide
   (b) should not be used near rivers
   (c) would be considered a suitable substitute for DDT and other pesticides whose use has been banned
   (d) is stored in the tissues of fish and is passed on in the food chain
   (e) is a very potent chemical even in very weak concentrations

   In developing a model of cognition, we must recognize that perception of the external world does not always remain independent of motivation. While progress toward maturity is positively correlated with differentiation between motivation and cognition, tension will, even in the mature adult, militate towards a narrowing of the range of perception and in the lessening of the objectivity of perception.

   Cognition can be seen as the first step in the sequence of events leading from the external stimulus to the behavior of the individual. The child develops from belief that all things are an extension of its own body to the recognition that objects exist independent of his perception. He begins to demonstrate awareness of people and things which are removed from his sensory apparatus and initiates goal-directed behaviors. He may, however, refuse to recognize the existence of barriers to the attainment of his goals, despite the fact that his cognition of these objects has been previously demonstrated.

   In the primitive being, goal-directed behavior can be very simply motivated. The presence of an attractive object will cause an infant to reach for it; its removal will result in the cessation of that action. Studies have shown no evidence of the infant's frustration; rather, it appears that the infant ceases to desire the object when he cannot see it. Further indications are that the infant's attention to the attractive object increases as a result of its not being in his grasp. In fact, if he holds a toy and another is presented, he is likely to drop the first in order to clutch the second. Often, once he has the one desired in his hands, he loses attention and turns to something else.

   In adult life, mere cognition can be similarly motivational, although the visible presence of the opportunity is not required as the instigator of response. The mature adult modifies his reaction by obtaining information, interpreting it, and examining consequences. He formulates an hypothesis and attempts to test it. He searches out implicit relationships, examines all factors, and differentiates among them. Just as the trained artist can separate the values of color, composition, and technique, while taking in and evaluating the whole work, so, too, the mature person brings his cognitive learning strengths to bear in appraising a situation.

   Understanding that cognition is separate from action, his reactions are only minimally guided from conditioning, and take into consideration anticipatable events.

The impact of the socialization process, particularly that of parental and social group ideology, may reduce cognitively directed behavior. The tension thus produced, as for instance the stress of fear, anger, or extreme emotion, will often be the overriding influence.

The evolutionary process of development from body schema through to cognitive learning is similarly manifested in the process of language acquisition. Auditing and speaking develop first, reading and writing much later on. Not only is this evident in the development of the individual human being from infancy on, but also in the development of language for humankind.

Every normal infant has the physiological equipment necessary to produce sound, but the child must first master their use for sucking, biting, and chewing before he can control his equipment for use in producing the sounds of language. The babble and chatter of the infant are precursors to intelligible vocal communication.

From the earliest times, it is clear that language and human thought have been intimately connected. Sending or receiving messages, from primitive warnings of danger to explaining creative or reflective thinking, this aspect of cognitive development is also firmly linked to the needs and aspirations of society.

20. It can be inferred from this passage that the author would support the attitude towards art appreciation that

(a) a work of art should not be analyzed.
(b) analysis of a work of art makes for greater understanding of it.
(c) understanding the life of the artist helps us to understand his work.
(d) all mature people can understand art equally well.
(e) an holistic approach to art is never valuable.

21. The statement which is neither implied nor stated in this passage is:

(a) The child is concerned only with his own body.
(b) The child learns to act in a way that will serve his desires.
(c) The infant's attention can be distracted from an object by simply concealing it.
(d) The infant finds it difficult to focus attention on more than one object at a time.
(e) The child may continue to be aware of his mother's existence even after she has moved out of his presence.

22. It may be inferred from the passage that the effects of society on learning may be

(a) to enhance the individual's motivation to learn as quickly as possible.
(b) to deter learning by reason of anxiety about possible conflict with ideology.
(c) to bring man's knowledge within the scope of all.
(d) to keep all learning at the same stage of development.
(e) to increase appreciation of art forms.

23. It can be inferred from the passage that language acquisition and general cognition

    (*a*) develop in similar fashion.
    (*b*) are parallel in development but independent of thought process.
    (*c*) are both responsive to society's mores.
    (*d*) differ in that the latter is more firmly tied to parental influence.
    (*e*) are dissimilar in their lessening of objective perception.

24. The major thesis of the author includes the following elements:

    I. Lessening of subjectivity accompanies maturation.
    II. Goal-directed behavior is the hallmark of juvenile behavior.
    III. Anxiety about conflict may impair learning.

    (*a*) I only
    (*b*) I and II only
    (*c*) I and III only
    (*d*) II only
    (*e*) III only

25. It can be inferred from the passage that an educational approach which the author would be likely to support would be one in which

    (*a*) all children are taught the same things at the same age level.
    (*b*) a developmental approach is used taking into consideration the stage of development of each individual child.
    (*c*) many stimuli are presented simultaneously so that the child is highly motivated.
    (*d*) parents are involved in daily instruction.
    (*e*) the child is taught the nature of his body.

26. The passage implies that

    (*a*) speech is acquired through direct teaching.
    (*b*) the infant should be taught not to babble.
    (*c*) infants who do not chatter will never learn to speak.
    (*d*) infants are born with the ability to speak but the ability to do so depends upon development of physical functions through non-verbal activities.
    (*e*) primitive speech did not communicate.

27. It would appear from the passage that it would be useful for the parent of the newborn to

    (*a*) give the infant what he needs before he cries.
    (*b*) teach the infant how to speak as quickly as possible.
    (*c*) model speech sounds and encourage the infant to produce them.
    (*d*) refuse the infant's demands until he makes them clear.
    (*e*) allow nature to take its course.

In each of the following questions, a capitalized word is followed by five words or phrases lettered (*a*) through (*e*). Select the word or phrase most nearly OPPOSITE in meaning to the capitalized word.

Since some of the questions require that you distinguish fine shades of meaning, consider all choices carefully before you select your answer.

28. PROFANE

    (a) intercede
    (b) execute
    (c) perpetuate
    (d) consecrate
    (e) secrete

29. CHIMERICAL

    (a) feasible
    (b) mystical
    (c) choleric
    (d) altruistic
    (e) uninquisitive

30. PIVOTAL

    (a) square
    (b) peripheral
    (c) immobile
    (d) diminutive
    (e) prodigal

31. CELERITY

    (a) unknown
    (b) convenience
    (c) discordance
    (d) deliberateness
    (e) emergency

32. EGREGIOUS

    (a) hermetic
    (b) parsimonious
    (c) inconsequential
    (d) atheistic
    (e) sordid

33. PLACABLE

    (a) ruthless
    (b) covetous
    (c) enigmatical
    (d) execrable
    (e) contrite

34. FLACCID

    (a) defiled
    (b) weakened
    (c) wiry
    (d) requited
    (e) impetuous

35. RECONDITE

    (a) original
    (b) reclusive
    (c) piquant
    (d) secular
    (e) superficial

36. CLEAVE

    (a) knife
    (b) unite
    (c) depredate
    (d) permit
    (e) launch

37. DISINTERESTED

    (a) informal
    (b) resigned
    (c) arranged
    (d) biased
    (e) deterred

38. JOCULAR

    (a) grave
    (b) contemptuous
    (c) reverent
    (d) familiar
    (e) sedulous

STOP! Work only on this section until the time allowed is over.

SECTION II

Time—30 minutes
38 Questions

For each of the numbered questions in this section, choose the best answer according to the instructions, and blacken the correspondingly numbered blank space on the answer sheet.

Each of the sentences below has one or more blank spaces indicating where a word or words have been omitted. Each sentence is followed by five words or sets of words lettered from (a) to (e). Select the lettered word or set of words which, inserted to replace the blanks, BEST fits in with and completes the meaning of the sentence as a whole.

1. If it had not been for that strange sequence of coincidences, that almost eerie – – – of events, they would never have undertaken the expedition that recovered the sunken treasure.

    (a) comedy
    (b) concatenation
    (c) convocation
    (d) concordance
    (e) consummation

2. He was – – – for his – – –, puffing up even his most casual conversations with polysyllabics and unnecessary verbiage, never using a simple sentence or expression where a complex one would do.

    (a) notorious . . . grandiloquence
    (b) nefarious . . . eloquence
    (c) esteemed . . . concision
    (d) reputed . . . sententiousness
    (e) admired . . . sobriety

3. The fear of inflation is not a mere apprehension on the part of the elderly, many of whom live on fixed incomes derived from pensions, social security, or investments; rather, that fear is very – – –, for inflation is already reducing their standard of living.

    (a) illusory
    (b) explicit
    (c) revealing
    (d) substantial
    (e) terrifying

4. Since preserving, cooking, and storing can destroy much of the vitamins in foods, those of us who depend heavily on precooked conve-

nience foods, or canned fruits and vegetables, may well be – – – on diets which are markedly – – – in the vitamins we need.

(a) relying . . . prolific
(b) battening . . . lacking
(c) repining . . . abundant
(d) indulging . . . weak
(e) subsisting . . . deficient

5. He was considered a rogue and gambler, hardly a model of probity and rectitude, but his code of personal behavior was so – – – that I would have taken his word before that of many a – – – pillar of society.

(a) amiable . . . sober
(b) complex . . . reverent
(c) punctilious . . . self-proclaimed
(d) pious . . . reliable
(e) zealous . . . steadfast

6. His self-control was such that even when he was brought before the Council and forced to undergo a most rigorous cross-examination before patently hostile judges, he remained – – –.

(a) imperturbable
(b) indefatigable
(c) incorruptible
(d) ineffable
(e) implacable

7. Hedonistic where I was ascetic, materialistic where my leanings were spiritual, egocentric where I tended to be altruistic, Martin represented the – – – of everything I believed in, and yet, instead of – – –, what developed between us was deep understanding and friendship.

(a) apotheosis . . . suspicion
(b) antithesis . . . antipathy
(c) crystallization . . . amity
(d) dissimulation . . . dissension
(e) negation . . . disparity

In each of the questions below, a related pair of words or phrases in capital letters is followed by five pairs of words or phrases lettered from (a) to (e). Select the lettered pair that expresses a relationship that is MOST similar to that of the capitalized pair.

8. LACKADAISICAL : INVIGORATE : :
(a) dispirited : animate (b) overbearing : subordinate
(c) lackluster : redouble (d) depressed : illuminate
(e) besieged : relieved

9. LABYRINTHINE : INTRICATE : :
   (a) terpsichorean : elegant (b) lachrymose : ebullient
   (c) unflappable : impartial (d) pachydermous : thick-skinned
   (e) quixotic : imperturbable

10. BACKSLIDING : SIN : : (a) reneging : treachery
    (b) importuning : radiometry (c) commutating : travel
    (d) recidivism : crime (e) proselytizing : sports

11. JURIST : PREDISPOSITION : :
    (a) advocate : unprejudiced (b) athlete : competitive
    (c) ballerina : graceful (d) ambassador : diplomatic
    (e) scholar : erudite

12. PRONE : SUPINE : : (a) leaning : limpid
    (b) ventral : dorsal (c) effecting : affecting
    (d) dominant : reflective (e) vengeful : vindictive

13. ASCETIC : CARNAL : : (a) acidulous : meaty
    (b) beautiful : beastly (c) voluptuary : spiritual
    (d) self-denying : carnivorous (e) austere : sumptuary

14. PIANO : PERCUSSIVE : : (a) anvil : sledge
    (b) vise : incisive (c) tympani : marimbas
    (d) clarinet : reedy (e) speech : stammering

15. PERJURY : TESTIMONY : :
    (a) mortality : eternity (b) compulsion : willingness
    (c) intimidation : cooperation (d) theft : trust
    (e) counterfeiting : mintage

16. HYPOTHETICAL : CONJECTURAL : :
    (a) discovered : unproven (b) demonstrated : undoubted
    (c) restricted : unbiased (d) eventual : happenstance
    (e) decorous : actual

In the series of selections that follows, each passage is followed by questions based on its content. Read the passage and choose the best answer for each question based on the contents of the passage. The questions must be answered on the basis of what is stated or implied in the reading passage.

When a people have no sufficient value for, and attachment to, a representative constitution, they have next-to-no chance of retaining it. Representative institutions necessarily depend for their permanence upon the readiness of the people to fight for them in case of their being endangered. If too little valued for this, they are almost sure to overthrow, as soon as the head of the government, or any party leader who can muster a force for a *coup de main*, is willing to run some small risk for absolute power.

These considerations relate the first two causes of failure in a representative government. The third is, when the people lack either the will or the capacity to fulfill the part which belongs to them in a representative constitution.

When nobody, or only some small fraction, feels the degree of interest in the general affairs of the state necessary to the formation of a public opinion, the electors will seldom make any use of the right of suffrage but to serve their private interest, or the interest of their locality, or of someone with whom they are connected as adherents or dependents. The small class who, in this state of public feeling, gain the command of the representative body, for the most part use it solely as a means of seeking their fortune.

17. The primary purpose of this passage is to

    (a) warn people away from representative government.
    (b) advocate greater involvement in political affairs on the parts of all the governed.
    (c) defend the constitution by warning against democratic abuse.
    (d) present arguments for and against representative government.
    (e) oppose the extension of suffrage to those with private interests.

18. It can be inferred from the passage that the author would encourage

    (a) resistance of the electorate to strong party leaders.
    (b) the institution of a poll tax on all voters to insure that only those interested enough to pay would vote.
    (c) compulsory registration for voting.
    (d) broad dissemination of news, educational programs in public affairs, and grass-roots participation in government.
    (e) a strong central government, a first-class permanent army, and rigid property requirements for enfranchisement.

19. The statement that expresses the view of the author is that

    (a) those who run the government are not to be trusted to follow the will of the people.
    (b) those who believe in representative government and institutions must be prepared to fight for their beliefs.
    (c) those who are at the head of representative governments would not put their private interest ahead of the public interest.
    (d) public opinion is opposed to the establishment of a representative constitution that limits the right of suffrage.
    (e) people who are not willing to go to war will inevitably fall prey to the heads of government who seek absolute power.

In a reaction against a too-rigid, overrefined classical curriculum, some educational philosophers have swung sharply to an espousal of "life experience" as the sole source of learning. Using their narrow interpretation of John Dewey's theories as a base for support, they conclude that only through "doing" can learning take place. Spouting such phrases as, "Teach the child, not the subject," they demand, without sensing its absurdity, an end to rigorous study as a means of opening the way to learning. While not all adherents to this approach would totally eliminate a study of great books, the influence of this philosophy has been felt in the public school curricula, as evidenced by the gradual subordination of great literature.

What is the purpose of literature? Why read, if life alone is to be our teacher? James Joyce states that the artist reveals the human situation by re-creating life out of life; Aristotle that art presents universal truths because its form is taken from nature. Thus, consciously or otherwise, the great writer reveals the human situation most tellingly, extending our understanding of ourselves and our world.

We can soar with the writer to the heights of man's aspirations, or plummet with him to tragic despair. The works of Steinbeck, Anderson, and Salinger; the poetry of Whitman, Sandburg, and Frost; the plays of Ibsen, Miller, and O'Neill: all present starkly realistic portrayals of life's problems. Reality? Yes! But how much wider is the understanding we gain than that attained by viewing life through the keyhole of our single existence.

Can we measure the richness gained by the young reader venturing down the Mississippi with Tom and Huck, or cheering Ivanhoe as he battles the Black Knight; the deepening understanding of the mature reader of the tragic South of William Faulkner and Tennessee Williams, of the awesome determination—and frailty—of Patrick White's Australian pioneers?

This function of literature, the enlarging of our own life sphere, is of itself of major importance. Additionally, however, it has been suggested that solutions of social problems may be suggested in the study of literature. The overweening ambitions of political leaders—and their sneering contempt for the law—did not appear for the first time in the writings of Bernstein and Woodward; the problems, and the consequent actions, of the guiltridden did not await the appearance of the bearded psychoanalyst of the twentieth century.

Federal Judge Learned Hand has written, "I venture to believe that it is as important to a judge called upon to pass on a question of constitutional law, to have at least a bowing acquaintance with Thucydides, Gibbon, and Carlyle, with Homer, Dante, Shakespeare, and Milton, with Montaigne and Rabelais, with Plato, Bacon, Hume, and Kant, as with the books which have been specifically written on the subject. For in such matters everything turns upon the spirit in which he approaches the questions before him."

But what of our dissenters? Can we overcome the disapproval of their "life experience classroom" theory of learning? We must start with the field of agreement—that education should serve to improve the individual and society. We must educate them to the understanding that the voice of human experience should stretch our human faculties, and open us to learning. We must convince them—in their own personal language perhaps—of the "togetherness" of life and art; we must prove to them that far from being separate, literature is that part of life which illumines life.

20. According to the passage, the end goal of great literature is

   (a) the recounting of dramatic and exciting stories, and the creation of characters
   (b) to create anew a synthesis of life that illumines the human condition
   (c) the teaching of morality and ethical behavior
   (d) to write about tragedy and despair
   (e) to portray life's problems

21. In the author's opinion, as seen in this passage, one outcome of the influence of the "life experience" adherents has been

   (a) the gradual subordination of the study of great literature in the schools
   (b) a narrowed interpretation of the theories of John Dewey
   (c) a sharp swing over to "learning through doing"
   (d) an end to rigorous study as a way of learning
   (e) an expansion of the curriculum to include experiential units

22. As the author sees it, one of the most important gains from the study of great literature is

   (a) enrichment of our understanding of the past
   (b) broadening of our approaches to social problems
   (c) that it gives us a bowing acquaintance with great figures of the past
   (d) that it improves our understanding of the young reader
   (e) that it provides us with vicarious experiences which provide a much broader experience than we can get from experiences of simply our own lives *alone*

23. The author's purpose in this passage is to

   (a) list those writers who make up the backbone of a great literature curriculum
   (b) compare the young reader's experience with literature to that of the mature reader
   (c) advocate the adoption of the "life experience" approach to teaching
   (d) plead for the retention of great literature as a fundamental part of the curriculum
   (e) overcome the opposition of Dewey's followers to the inclusion of current literature in the curriculum

24. The author's reason for quoting Judge Hand is to

   (a) call attention to the writing of Thucydides and Carlyle
   (b) support the thesis of the author that literature broadens our understanding and stretches our faculties
   (c) point out that constitutional law is a part of the great literature of our past
   (d) show that everyone, including judges, enjoys reading
   (e) rebut the dissenters

Can man be credited with choosing the right path when he knows only one? Can he be congratulated for his wise decision when only one judgment is possible? If he knows nothing of vice, is he to be praised for adhering to virtue?

From the day when the first man tasted the forbidden fruit, he has been struggling with the choice between good and evil, but without his full awareness of the pleasing taste of that apple, or even of its existence, would he be worthy of praise for forebearing to eat it?

Wisdom consists of the deliberate exercise of judgment; knowledge comes in the discrimination between those known alternatives. Weighing these alternatives is the way of maturity. Only then does man have the strength to follow his choice without wavering, since that choice is based firmly on knowledge rather than on an uncertain, dangerously shallow foundation of ignorance.

25. The writer of this passage disputes the contention that

   (a) it is possible to judge right from wrong
   (b) the taste of the apple was reason enough to judge it evil
   (c) virtue lies in following the ethically and morally right path
   (d) the intelligent are usually more virtuous
   (e) the choice between good and evil has always been with us

26. The major point made by the author in this passage is that

    (*a*) one can only be credited with a wise decision when one has chosen from among known alternatives

    (*b*) the wise man will always know what is right

    (*c*) original sin stemmed from the tasting of the forbidden fruit

    (*d*) decision should be subjected to an expert's appraisal

    (*e*) knowledge should be concrete, not abstract

27. It can be inferred from the passage that the author would favor

    (*a*) strict censorship of all reading materials

    (*b*) a prescribed list of informational materials, graded as to content, for high school use

    (*c*) the widest possible range of reading materials to be placed on library shelves

    (*d*) selection of reading materials from among books with approved moral and ethical viewpoints

    (*e*) selections that advocate the triumph of religion over sinners

In each of the questions below, a capitalized word is followed by five words or phrases lettered (*a*) through (*e*). Select the word or phrase most nearly OPPOSITE in meaning to the capitalized word.

Since some of the questions require that you distinguish fine shades of meaning, consider all choices carefully before you select your answer.

28. EVANESCENT

    (*a*) transparent
    (*b*) cloudy
    (*c*) poignant
    (*d*) integrated
    (*e*) perpetual

29. SIMILITUDE

    (*a*) disparity
    (*b*) gregariousness
    (*c*) precocity
    (*d*) agitation
    (*e*) verisimilitude

30. DISSONANT

    (*a*) penitent
    (*b*) assertive
    (*c*) narrative
    (*d*) euphonious
    (*e*) beautiful

31. EUPHORIA

    (*a*) transience
    (*b*) depression
    (*c*) void
    (*d*) difficulty
    (*e*) complacency

32. SALUTARY

    (*a*) valedictory
    (*b*) deleterious
    (*c*) abstemious
    (*d*) remorseful
    (*e*) aggravating

33. GERMANE

    (*a*) biotic
    (*b*) nephritic
    (*c*) penitent
    (*d*) irrelevant
    (*e*) irresponsible

34. SANGFROID

(a) perturbation
(b) warmth
(c) spinelessness
(d) divinity
(e) malice

35. TORPOR

(a) animation
(b) lucidity
(c) contrition
(d) laziness
(e) antipathy

36. COMITY

(a) diffusion
(b) separation
(c) tragedy
(d) dissension
(e) parity

37. ANOMALOUS

(a) bazaar
(b) organized
(c) regular
(d) maculate
(e) impertinent

38. CENSURE

(a) delete
(b) commend
(c) dismiss
(d) elect
(e) repent

STOP! Work only on this section until the time allowed is over.

SECTION III

Time—30 minutes
30 Questions

The following questions each consist of two quantities, one in Column A and one in Column B. Compare the two quantities and on the answer sheet blacken oval

- (*a*) if the quantity in Column A is greater;
- (*b*) if the quantity in Column B is greater;
- (*c*) if the two quantities are equal;
- (*d*) if the relationship cannot be determined from the information given.

All letters such as x, y, and n represent real numbers. A symbol appearing in both columns represents the same quantity in Column A as it does in Column B.

In some questions, information concerning one or both of the quantities to be compared is centered above the two columns.

Figures are generally not drawn to scale, unless otherwise stated. You may assume these figures lie in a plane, unless it is indicated they represent solid figures.

Lines that appear to be straight may be assumed to be straight lines.

Column A	Column B
1. $\dfrac{10}{21}$	$\dfrac{8}{15}$
2. $2\sqrt{6}$	6

3.   p and q are positive numbers

$\dfrac{4p + q}{pq}$	$\dfrac{4 + \dfrac{q}{p}}{q}$

4. $\dfrac{r}{3} = \dfrac{s}{4}$

$4r$	$3s$
5. $\left(\dfrac{7}{15} + \dfrac{16}{33}\right) \times 423$	423

Column A		**Column B**

6.

$$\frac{x}{y} = \frac{4}{7}$$

x		y

7.

k is an integer

The remainder when $k^2 + k$ is divided by 2		0

8.

t > 0

t^3		t

Questions 9–13 refer to the figure below.

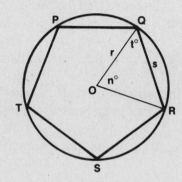

PQRST is a regular pentagon inscribed in circle O with side s.

Point O represents the center of circle O.

9. n		72
10. t		n
11. s		r
12. Area of pentagon PQRST		28
13. Length of arc QR		Length of QR

14.

6x = 5k, 4y = 3k, k > 0

x		y

15. $\sqrt{.09}$		$\dfrac{\pi}{7}$

Solve each of the following problems based on the information provided. Then indicate the best answer on your answer sheet.

16. A metal rod 8 feet long weighs 44 pounds. What is the weight in pounds of a rod 10 feet long of the same diameter and composed of the same metal?

    (a) 48
    (b) 51
    (c) 55
    (d) 58
    (e) 62

17. If $\dfrac{3p}{q} = 5$, find the value of $\dfrac{3p - q}{q}$.

    (a) 3
    (b) 4
    (c) 5
    (d) $4\frac{3}{5}$
    (e) It is impossible to find with the information given.

18. If t is the average of 2, 3, 5, 8 and t, find the value of t.

    (a) $2\frac{1}{2}$
    (b) 3
    (c) $3\frac{1}{2}$
    (d) 4
    (e) $4\frac{1}{2}$

19. A stock 40 inches long is cut into two pieces so that the length of one piece is 2/3 the length of the other piece. How many inches are there in the shorter piece?

    (a) 16
    (b) 18
    (c) 22
    (d) 24
    (e) 28

20. The diagonal of a rectangle is 15 centimeters and its height is 9 centimeters. Find the area of the rectangle in square centimeters.

    (a) 54
    (b) 86
    (c) 98
    (d) 108
    (e) 125

Questions 21–26 refer to the following graph.

Borrowing in International Markets

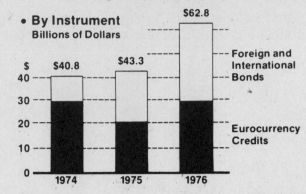

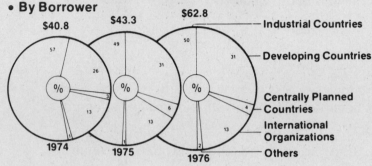

21. Approximately how many dollars of Eurocurrency credits were borrowed by industrial countries in 1976?

    (*a*) $31 billion
    (*b*) $15 billion
    (*c*) $63 billion
    (*d*) $10 billion

    (*e*) Impossible to determine from the information provided

22. By approximately how much did the total borrowings of developing countries increase from 1975 to 1976?

    (*a*) $6 billion
    (*b*) $12 billion
    (*c*) $20 billion
    (*d*) $30 billion
    (*e*) $35 billion

23. The funds from foreign and international bonds could support the borrowings of which of the following groups in 1976?

    (*a*) Industrial countries
    (*b*) Developing countries
    (*c*) Centrally planned countries

(d) International organizations

(e) Each of the above

24. By what percent did the borrowings of international organizations increase from 1974 to 1976?

(a) 31%

(b) 54%

(c) 13%

(d) 25%

(e) 8%

25. By approximately how much did the total borrowings of the "others" group increase from 1974 to 1976?

(a) $.2 billion

(b) $.4 billion

(c) $.6 billion

(d) $.9 billion

(e) $2.3 billion

26. Which of the following groups experienced the largest relative increase in borrowings from 1975 to 1976?

(a) Industrial countries

(b) Developing countries

(c) Centrally planned countries

(d) International organizations

(e) Others

27. All of the following have the same value except

(a) 5/8

(b) .625

(c) 15/24

(d) 45/70

(e) $\sqrt{25/64}$

28. Which of the following integers cannot be written as the sum of two *prime* numbers?

(a) 16

(b) 23

(c) 24

(d) 28

(e) 30

29. In a given sequence of numbers, the first term is 2 and each successive term is formed by taking 1/4 of the cube of the preceding term. What is the eleventh term of the sequence?

    (a) 1
    (b) 3/2
    (c) 2
    (d) 18
    (e) 180

30. If p is 50% more than q, then q is what percent less than p?

    (a) 66⅔%
    (b) 50%
    (c) 40%
    (d) 33⅓%
    (e) 25%

Time—30 minutes
30 Questions

The following questions each consist of two quantities, one in Column A and one is Column B. Compare the two quantities and on the answer sheet blacken oval

    (*a*) if the quantity in Column A is greater;
    (*b*) if the quantity in Column B is greater;
    (*c*) if the two quantities are equal;
    (*d*) if the relationship cannot be determined from the information given

All letters such as x, y, and n represent real numbers. A symbol appearing in both columns represents the same quantity in Column A as it does in Column B.

In some questions, information concerning one or both of the quantities to be compared is centered above the two columns.

Figures are generally not drawn to scale, unless otherwise stated. You may assume these figures lie in a plane, unless it is indicated they represent solid figures.

Lines that appear to be straight may be assumed to be straight lines.

Column A	Column B

$$n > 0$$

1. The average of
5n, 3n and 7

                                   The average of
2n, 6n and 9

2.

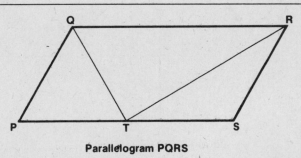

Parallelogram PQRS

Perimeter of
parallelogram PQRS

                                   Perimeter of
triangle QRT

3.
$$\frac{x^3}{y^6} = \frac{1}{8}$$

2x

                                   y^2

Column A	Column B

4.   P is a set of 3 consecutive odd integers
       Q is a set of 3 consecutive even integers

The greatest integer in P	The greatest integer in Q

5. The edge of a cube of volume 216 | The edge of a cube of surface area 150

6.   1 kilometer = 5/8 mile

60 km | 40 miles

7. $3\sqrt{3}$ | $\sqrt[3]{130}$

8. The probability of throwing a "twelve" with a pair of dice | The probability of throwing a "two" with a pair of dice

9. $\dfrac{p}{q} = \dfrac{7}{10}, q \neq 0$

p | q

Questions 10–13 refer to the diagram below

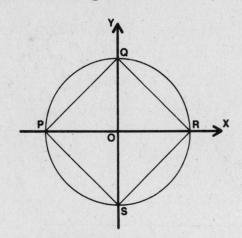

Square PQRS is inscribed in circle O. The area of the square is 64. Point O is to be considered (0, 0) on the graph.

Column A	Column B

10. Perimeter of square PQRS   30

11. Ordinate of point Q   6

12. Numerical value of the area of circle O   Twice the numerical value of the circumference of circle O

13. Number of degrees in angle QSR   Number of degrees in angle QPR

---

14.   k an integer

$(2k)^3$ $2k^3$

---

15. The sum of all the possible factors of 28 including 1 and 28   56

Solve each of the following problems based on the information provided. Then indicate the best answer on your answer sheet.

16. A gallon of oil is poured into a cubical container 7 inches on an edge. About how high, in inches, does the oil rise in the container? (1 gallon = 231 cu. in.)

(a) 3.8
(b) 4.2
(c) 4.7
(d) 5.2
(e) 5.6

Questions 17–18 refer to the following graph.

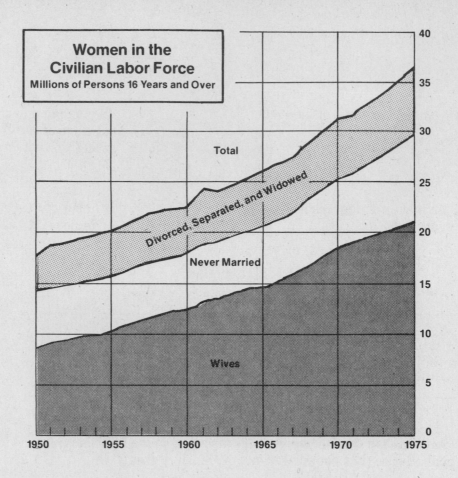

Women in the Civilian Labor Force
Millions of Persons 16 Years and Over

Total

Divorced, Separated, and Widowed

Never Married

Wives

17. Approximately what percent of the female labor force in 1955 was made up of women who were or had been married?

 (a) 75%
 (b) 55%
 (c) 35%
 (d) 25%
 (e) 15%

18. By approximately what percent did the total number of single women (never married, divorced, separated or widowed) in the work force increase from 1950 to 1975?

 (a) 50%
 (b) 35%
 (c) 20%
 (d) 5%
 (e) 0%

19. The diagonal of a rectangular door is 6-1/2 feet long. The longer side of the door is 6 feet. What is the area of the door in square feet?

    (*a*) 156
    (*b*) 60
    (*c*) 39
    (*d*) 17
    (*e*) 15

20. If a vehicle goes 300 miles on 15 gallons of gas, how many more miles per gallon must it get to go the same 300 miles on 12 gallons?

    (*a*) 1
    (*b*) 3
    (*c*) 5
    (*d*) 7
    (*e*) 9

Questions 21–24 refer to the following graph.

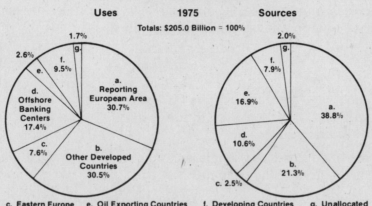

Estimated Size of the Eurocurrency Market

Uses   1975   Sources

Totals: $205.0 Billion = 100%

c. Eastern Europe   e. Oil Exporting Countries   f. Developing Countries   g. Unallocated

Note: Eurocredit outstanding through the banks of 8 reporting European countries.

21. In which of the following areas were the sources of Eurocurrency in 1975 greater than the uses?

    (*a*) Reporting countries in Europe
    (*b*) Other developed countries
    (*c*) Eastern Europe
    (*d*) Offshore banking centers
    (*e*) Developing countries

22. How many Eurodollars were used by European countries in 1975?

    (*a*) $16 billion
    (*b*) $63 billion
    (*c*) $78 billion
    (*d*) $89 billion
    (*e*) $205 billion

23. The Eurodollars supplied by non-European developed countries could support which using areas?

   (*a*) Reporting European area
   (*b*) Other developed countries
   (*c*) Offshore banking centers plus Eastern Europe
   (*d*) Eastern Europe plus developing countries plus oil exporting countries plus unallocated
   (*e*) Offshore banking centers plus oil exporting countries

24. Which of the following areas had the greatest deficit (uses to sources) of Eurodollars in 1975?

   (*a*) Developing countries
   (*b*) Offshore banking centers
   (*c*) Eastern Europe
   (*d*) Other developed countries
   (*e*) Oil exporting countries

25. A teacher drives 40 miles to her office every morning in 55 minutes. If she leaves 7 minutes late one morning, how many miles per hour must she drive to arrive at the time she normally does?

   (*a*) 42
   (*b*) 45
   (*c*) 48
   (*d*) 50
   (*e*) 54

26. The base of an isosceles triangle is 10, and each of the equal sides is 13. What is the area of the triangle?

   (*a*) 30
   (*b*) 45
   (*c*) 60
   (*d*) 65
   (*e*) 130

27. Tony buys a radio for $60.00 after receiving a discount of 20% on the list price. What was the list price?

   (*a*) $72.00
   (*b*) $75.00
   (*c*) $78.00
   (*d*) $80.00
   (*e*) $82.50

28. The average of 4 numbers p, q, r, and s is n. The value of $(n - p) + (n - q) + (n - r) + (n - s)$ is

    (a) -2
    (b) -1
    (c) 0
    (d) 2
    (e) 4

29. A prime number is an integer which has no integral factors other than itself and one. One is usually not considered a prime number. Which of the following numbers may be written as the sum of exactly two prime numbers?

    (a) 17
    (b) 23
    (c) 27
    (d) 29
    (e) 32

30. If the radius of a cylinder is doubled while its height is divided by 2, its volume

    (a) remains the same
    (b) is doubled
    (c) is divided by 2
    (d) is quadrupled
    (e) is divided by 4

STOP! Work only on this section until the time allowed is over.

SECTION V

Time—30 minutes
25 Questions

A written or set of statements precedes each question or group of questions in this section. Choose the best answer to each question. For some questions, you may find it useful to draw a diagram, graph, or other problem-solving aid.

Questions 1–4 are based on the following:

(1) Seven people sit at a round table on which the hours of a clock face are marked. (No two people may sit at the same position; all sit precisely on an hour mark.)
(2) Andrew sits at 6 o'clock.
(3) Bernice and Dora each sit 3 hours from Andrew.
(4) Clark sits 3 hours from Dora.
(5) Edward and Flora sit 6 hours apart.
(6) George sits 2 hours from Flora.
(7) George sits less than 3 hours from Clark.
(8) George sits more than 2 hours from Andrew.

1. Which statement repeats information presented elsewhere?

 (a) 3
 (b) 4
 (c) 5
 (d) 6
 (e) 7

2. How many seating arrangements may exist?

 (a) 2
 (b) 4
 (c) 6
 (d) 8
 (e) 12

3. If George sits five hours from Bernice, then Edward and Flora sit at hours which add up to

(a) 8
(b) 10
(c) 16
(d) 8 or 16
(e) 10 or 14

4. If George sits at 10 o'clock, Flora *must* sit

(a) at 12 o'clock
(b) next to Dora
(c) at 2 o'clock
(d) two hours from Andrew
(e) at none of the above locations

Questions 5–6 are based on the following:

It is disgraceful that some people who make $1,000,000 a year are legally able to pay no taxes that year. Such people should be forced to pay something in taxes.

5. The preceding argument implies which of the following?

I. The present tax laws are unjust.
II. Everyone should pay at least some tax.
III. The tax rules which allow business losses to be deducted from present income should be eliminated.

(a) I only
(b) II only
(c) I and II only
(d) II and III only
(e) I, II, and III

6. Which of the following statements, if true, would most weaken the above argument?

(a) Some people earning $900,000 per year pay no tax.
(b) Some people who earn $1,000,000 one year are not wealthy.
(c) Some people earning $1,000,000 per year pay several hundred thousand dollars in tax for that year.
(d) Most people earning $1,000,000 a year pay tax.
(e) It is possible to earn $1,000,000 a year from interest on municipal bonds, income which everyone agrees should be tax-exempt.

Questions 7–10 refer to the following:

A college basketball coach must form a five-member team selected from a group of three juniors, players P, Q, and R, and four seniors, players J, K, L, and M. There must be at least two juniors on the team.

Q will not play with J.
R will not play with L.
K will not play with J or L.

7. If both Q and R are on the team, which other players must be on the team with them?

    (a) P, J, and M
    (b) P, K, and M
    (c) P, J, and K
    (d) P, K, and L
    (e) P, L, and M

8. If K is on the team, which other players must be on the team with K?

    (a) P, Q, R, and M
    (b) P, R, J, and L
    (c) P, R, J, and M
    (d) Q, R, L, and M
    (e) Q, R, J, and M

9. If L is not on the team, which of the following groups of players can form a team?

    (a) P, Q, R, J, and M
    (b) P, Q, R, J, and K
    (c) P, Q, J, K, and M
    (d) P, Q, R, K, and M
    (e) P, R, J, K, and M

10. If P cannot play, how many different teams can be formed?

    (a) 4
    (b) 3
    (c) 2
    (d) 1
    (e) none

Questions 11–16 refer to the following:

Five automobiles, known by the letters A, B, C, D, and E, were rated with respect to durability, cost, and styling.

A was more durable than B, less expensive than C, and less stylish than B.
B was less durable than C, more expensive than A, and more stylish than E.

C was less durable than A, more expensive than E, and more stylish than D.
D was less durable than E, less expensive than A, and more stylish than B.
E was less durable than B, more expensive than B, and more stylish than A.

11. Which car was rated as most durable?

    (a) A
    (b) B
    (c) C
    (d) D
    (e) E

12. Which of the following cars was (were) both more durable and more expensive than E?

    (a) A only
    (b) B only
    (c) C only
    (d) D only
    (e) C and D

13. Which of the following cars was (were) both more durable and more stylish than D?

    (a) A only
    (b) B only
    (c) C only
    (d) B and C
    (e) C and E

14. Which of the following cars was (were) rated as both more expensive than A and more stylish than E?

    (a) B only
    (b) B and C
    (c) C only
    (d) D only
    (e) B and D

15. Points are awarded based on a car's ranking in each category, with 1 the highest and 5 the lowest score. The highest-rated car is

    (a) A
    (b) B
    (c) C
    (d) D
    (e) E

16. Under the rating system described in the previous question, how many points are awarded to E?

(a) 7
(b) 8
(c) 9
(d) 10
(e) 11

Questions 17–22 refer to the following:

(1) All P's are Q's; some Q's are not P's.
(2) Some T's are P's; some T's are not P's; some P's are not T's.
(3) All P's are either A's or B's.
(4) No Q's are C's.

17. If at least some T's are not Q's, then

(a) some Q's may be both T's and A's
(b) no P's may be T's
(c) some T's are A's
(d) some T's are neither A's nor B's
(e) none of the above is true

18. If all T's are either U's or V's, then

(a) some Q's are either U's or V's without being P's
(b) some U's or V's are not Q's
(c) any A's or B's that are also U's or V's are also P's
(d) some Q's are either U's or V's without being either A's or B's
(e) none of the above is true

19. Which of the following statements must be *false*?

  I. All Q's are T's.
 II. Some P's are C's.
III. Some Q's are A's or B's.

(a) I only
(b) II only
(c) I and III only
(d) II and III only
(e) I and II only

20. If some C's are A's, then which of the following statements must be true?

  I. Some T's are A's.
 II. Some C's are not T's.
III. Some A's are not Q's.

(a) I only
(b) III only
(c) I and II only
(d) II and III only
(e) I, II, and III

21. It can be inferred that

  I. no T's are either A's or B's
  II. some T's are either A's or B's
  III. some T's are Q's

(a) I only
(b) III only
(c) I and II only
(d) II and III only
(e) I, II, and III

22. Which of the following statements must be true?

(a) Some C's are P's.
(b) Some Q's are T's.
(c) Some C's are Q's.
(d) Some C's are T's.
(e) The P's which are not T's are not Q's.

23. Democrats support social welfare programs. Wendy supports social welfare programs. Therefore, Wendy is a Democrat.

Which of the following arguments is most similar to the argument above?

(a) Insects have six legs. Spiders have eight legs. Therefore, spiders are not insects.
(b) Equilateral triangles have three equal sides. Triangle PQR is equilateral. Therefore, Triangle PQR has three equal sides.
(c) Vegetarians do not eat meat. Brenda eats meat. Therefore, Brenda is not a vegetarian.
(d) Rodents are gnawing mammals. Squirrels are gnawing mammals. Therefore, squirrels are rodents.
(e) Republicans favor budget cuts. Eli does not favor budget cuts. Therefore, Eli is not a Republican.

24. Victor must be a Hindu; he always wears a turban.

The argument above would be valid if it were true that

(a) all Hindus wear turbans
(b) all male Hindus wear turbans
(c) only Hindus wear turbans
(d) turbans are a common form of head dress for Hindus
(e) few non-Hindus wear turbans

25. If the territory of Kanamara votes to join the U.S., then Congress will undoubtedly vote to accept it as a state.

The statement above may be inferred from which of the following statements?

(a) Any territory that votes to join the U.S. will be accepted by Congress as a state.
(b) Kanamara will vote to join the U.S.
(c) Kanamara's oil reserves are coveted by several U.S. corporations.
(d) Kanamara will vote either to join the U.S. or to join Canada.
(e) Congress has the constitutional authority to either accept Kanamara as a state or to reject it.

STOP! Work only on this section until the time allowed is over.

Time—30 minutes
25 Questions

A written passage or set of statements precedes each question or group of questions in this section. Choose the best answer to each question. For some questions you may find it useful to draw a diagram, graph, or other problem-solving aid.

Questions 1–4 refer to the following:

A man was driving in an area where all roads ran either north-south or east-west, forming a grid. All parallel adjacent roads were separated by one mile.

1. The man started at the intersection of Elm St. and Maple St. He drove two miles north, two miles west, and three miles south. Which further route could get him back to his starting point?

    I. Two miles east, then one mile south
    II. One mile north, then two miles east
    III. Three miles north, then two miles east, then two miles south

    (a) I only
    (b) III only
    (c) I and II only
    (d) II and III only
    (e) I, II, and III

2. The man in the previous question, after driving as described above, did not return to his starting point, but instead then drove three miles east and one mile north. Which of the following statements about his new location may be made?

    (a) He was on Elm St.
    (b) He was on Maple St.
    (c) He was on either Elm St. or Maple St., but not at their intersection.
    (d) He was equidistant from Elm St. and Maple St.
    (e) He was on neither Elm St. nor Maple St., and was not equidistant from them.

3. Starting at the intersection of Elm St. and Maple St., the man drives two miles on Elm, then three miles east, three miles north, and five miles west, ending up on Maple St. It can be concluded that

    I. Elm St. runs east-west
    II. the man goes east at the start of the maneuvers described in question 3
    III. Maple St. is at least three miles long

    (*a*) I only
    (*b*) III only
    (*c*) I and II only
    (*d*) I, II, and III
    (*e*) Neither I, II, nor III

4. After following the route described in question 3, how many miles from Elm St. did the man end up?

    (*a*) none
    (*b*) one mile
    (*c*) three miles
    (*d*) five miles
    (*e*) either one or five miles

Questions 5–7 refer to the following:

A study has shown that on a wide variety of representative psychological tests, children reared entirely in groups by professional workers fared the same as children brought up entirely by their own parents. This supports the argument that day-care facilities for children of working parents should be increased.

5. The truth of which of the following statements is needed to validate the above line of reasoning?

    (*a*) More women work than ever before.
    (*b*) Government should provide more day-care facilities.
    (*c*) Professionals should take care of children in day-care facilities.
    (*d*) Mothers would rather work than take care of their children.
    (*e*) A parent who does not work should not be allowed to put his or her child in a day-care facility.

6. The argument would be most strengthened by pointing out that

    (*a*) single working mothers favor the argument presented
    (*b*) there are long waiting lists for most day-care facilities
    (*c*) some day-care facilities are not crowded

(d) the study referred to was done carefully

(e) eight different psychological qualities were measured in the study

7. The argument would be most weakened by pointing out that

(a) no one attempted to duplicate the study
(b) a similar study on animals yielded somewhat different results
(c) most parents have no professional training in child rearing
(d) the study is not especially relevant to the author's conclusion, since children at day-care facilities are raised both by workers there and by their parents
(e) the study's results were completely unexpected

Questions 8–10 refer to the following:

H, J, K, L, M, and N are seated in a row.
L sits at one end of the row.
M does not sit next to N.
J sits next to K.
H sits at one end of the row.

8. Which of the following is a possible seating order from left to right?

(a) HJMKNL
(b) LMJNKH
(c) LJMKNH
(d) HMJKNL
(e) LKNJMH

9. Based on the information given above, how many different seating orders are possible?

(a) four
(b) five
(c) six
(d) seven
(e) eight

10. Which of the following must be true of the seating order in this row?

(a) There must be two persons seated between M and N.
(b) K is not seated next to N.
(c) J is not seated next to M.
(d) M is seated next to H.
(e) N is seated next to L.

Questions 11–16 refer to the following:

(1) A number is <u>bre</u> if it is divisible by 6.
(2) A number is <u>erb</u> if it is divisible by 5.
(3) A number is <u>ber</u> if it is divisible by 4.
(4) A number is <u>reb</u> if it is divisible by 3 and is not <u>bre</u>.
(5) A number to which more than one of the above names apply may be called by a compound name; e.g., a number divisible by both 5 and 6 is <u>erbbre</u>, and a number twice divisible by 4 (e.g., 16 = 4 × 4) is <u>berber</u>.
(6) For every <u>bre</u> that can be in its name, a number receives 6 points; for every <u>erb</u>, 5 points; for every <u>ber</u>, 4 points; for every <u>reb</u>, 3 points. For example, a number that is <u>rebreberb</u> is worth 3 + 3 + 5 or 11 points.

11. How would 20 be described?

   (a) <u>rebber</u>
   (b) <u>erbber</u>
   (c) <u>erbbre</u>
   (d) <u>berbererb</u>
   (e) <u>erberbbre</u>

12. How many points is 24 worth?

   (a) 4
   (b) 7
   (c) 9
   (d) 10
   (e) 13

13. Which number is worth the most points?

   (a) 12
   (b) A number that is <u>erberb</u>
   (c) 24
   (d) A number that is <u>berberber</u>
   (e) 30

14. What is the smallest number that is <u>rebreberb</u>?

   (a) 9
   (b) 15
   (c) 30
   (d) 45
   (e) 90

15. Of the following three numbers, which is worth the most points?

   I. 180
   II. 300
   III. 375

(a) I only
(b) II only
(c) III only
(d) I and II (tied)
(e) II and III (tied)

16. According to the rules, which of the following names cannot occur?

   I. rebbre
  II. rebber
 III. erbber

(a) I only
(b) III only
(c) I and II only
(d) II and III only
(e) I, II, and III

Questions 17–22 refer to the following:

There are five men in a room.
Leon is tall and wears black shoes.
Martin is short and has long hair.
Nelson is of medium height and wears white shoes.
Oscar is bald and wears brown shoes.
Paul has a crew cut.
One person wears boots.
Two people are of medium height and two are short.
No one with long hair wears boots.
A tall person has a crew cut.
A man with brown shoes is of medium height.

17. How many men in the room have a crew cut?

(a) 1
(b) 2
(c) 3
(d) 1 or 2
(e) 2 or 3

18. It may be inferred that any man in the room wearing brown shoes is

(a) tall
(b) of medium height
(c) short
(d) either short or of medium height
(e) either tall or of medium height

19. It may be inferred that one of the men in the room is a

   (a) tall bald man with brown shoes
   (b) short man with a crew cut and boots
   (c) short man with long hair and boots
   (d) short bald man with brown shoes
   (e) bald man of medium height with white shoes

20. The statements above give no information about which of the following?

   I. Leon's hairstyle
   II. Martin's footwear
   III. Nelson's hairstyle

   (a) I only
   (b) III only
   (c) I and II only
   (d) II and III only
   (e) I, II, and III

21. Which of the following statements may be inferred?

   I. Oscar may be short, but only if Paul has brown shoes.
   II. Paul may be of medium height, but only if he wears brown shoes.
   III. The man wearing boots is short.

   (a) I only
   (b) III only
   (c) I and II only
   (d) II and III only
   (e) I, II, and III

22. How many people's height, hairstyle, and footwear are all known?

   (a) None
   (b) 1
   (c) 2
   (d) 3
   (e) 4

Questions 23–24 refer to the following:

The doctors claim that an electrocardiogram is a *good* indicator of the *health* of the heart. But I would point to the fact that *many* people have walked out of their doctor's office with normal electrocardiograms only to drop dead of a heart attack. This *shows* the doctor's claim to be *suspect*.

23. The author's method of questioning the doctors' claim is to

    (a) question the doctors' motives
    (b) assert that doctors are poorly trained
    (c) demonstrate that they are rarely correct
    (d) present contradictory evidence
    (e) suggest an alternative view

24. The author's argument could be improved by changing one of the italicized words. Which substitution would effect the greatest improvement in the argument?

    (a) *perfect* instead of *good*
    (b) *unhealthiness* instead of *health*
    (c) *some* instead of *many*
    (d) *indicates* instead of *shows*
    (e) *incorrect* instead of *suspect*

25. XYZ Widget Company has embarked upon a new program designed to restore the firm's profitability. XYZ is offering a 15% discount to all potential customers, hoping to make up in volume what it sacrifices in profit per widget.

    The above strategy is likely to prove successful only if

    (a) sales can be increased by 50% or more
    (b) prior attempts to raise prices have resulted in sharply falling sales
    (c) widget sales are sensitive to fluctuations in price
    (d) costs are cut at the same time prices are cut
    (e) XYZ's widgets are as good as those produced by the competition

STOP! Work only on this section until the time allowed is over.

1. If $6 \times 6 \times t = 18 \times 18 \times 18$, then $t =$

   (a) 3
   (b) 9
   (c) 54
   (d) 108
   (e) 162

2. The temperature at the bottom of a ski lift is 12° and at the top is −18°. How many degrees higher is the temperature at the bottom than at the top?

   (a) 6°
   (b) −6°
   (c) 30°
   (d) −30°
   (e) 40°

3. How many 9–inch pieces of molding can be cut from a 6–foot piece?

   (a) 2/3
   (b) 1½
   (c) 4½
   (d) 8
   (e) 12

4.

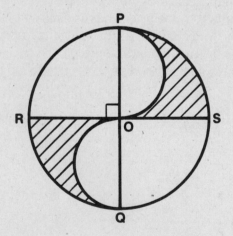

In the figure at the bottom of the preceding page, the circle with center at O has a radius of 2. Diameters PQ and RS are perpendicular. Semicircles are drawn with diameters PO and OQ as shown. Find the shaded area.

(a) π

(b) $\dfrac{\pi}{2}$

(c) 2π

(d) $\dfrac{3\pi}{2}$

(e) 4π

5. A boy runs 4/5 of the distance around a circular track in m minutes. How many minutes does it take him to run around the entire track at the same rate?

(a) $\dfrac{m}{4}$

(b) $\dfrac{5m}{4}$

(c) $\dfrac{4m}{5}$

(d) $\dfrac{5}{4m}$

(e) $\dfrac{4}{m}$

6. An aircraft flies 3 miles in 15 seconds. What is its speed in miles per hour?

(a) 440
(b) 520
(c) 600
(d) 720
(e) 800

7. In a class of 30 students, the average on a certain test is p. The teacher decides to raise each mark 10 points. What is the new average?

(a) p + 10
(b) p + 30
(c) p + 300
(d) 10p
(e) p + 3

8.

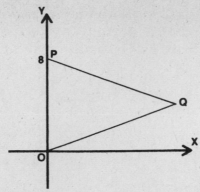

In the graph above, the area of the triangle OPQ is 64. Find the altitude from Q to OP

(a) 8
(b) 10
(c) 12
(d) 14
(e) 16

Questions 9–14 refer to the following graph.

**DISTRIBUTION OF SELECTED INDUSTRIES
IN THE UNITED STATES**
(by number of companies)

{ F—Manufacturing
G—Finance
H—Agriculture
J—Service
K—Real Estate

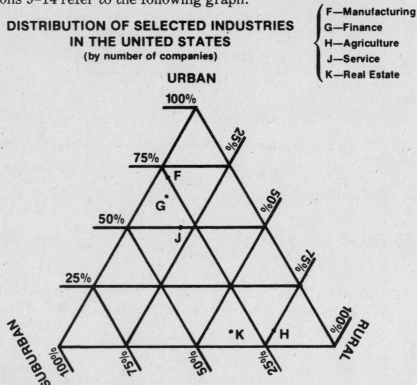

The triangular graph above shows the percentages of five industry groupings in the United States, broken down by type of area: urban, suburban and rural. The letters on the graph represent each particular industry. The vertices of the triangle represent 100%, and the base lines opposite each vertex represent zero%. For example, of all manufacturing companies in the United States, approximately 70% of them are located in urban areas, 5% in rural areas, and 25% in suburban areas.

All the questions which follow refer only to information which can be read from the graph.

9. Approximately what percent of the service companies are found in suburban areas?

   (a) 90%
   (b) 70%
   (c) 50%
   (d) 30%
   (e) 10%

10. Which industry is distributed approximately evenly between urban and suburban areas?

   (a) Real Estate
   (b) Service
   (c) Finance
   (d) None of the above
   (e) It cannot be determined from the information given

11. Which of the following ratios is the best approximation of the number of companies in the finance industry in suburban areas to the number of finance companies in urban areas in the United States?

   (a) 1/6
   (b) 1/2
   (c) 1/1
   (d) 2/1
   (e) 6/1

12. Both urban and suburban areas taken together are the locales of 25% of which industry?

   (a) Manufacturing
   (b) Finance
   (c) Agriculture
   (d) Service
   (e) Real Estate

13. In which industry is the number of companies located in urban areas at least as great as the number of companies located in suburban and rural areas combined?

   (a) Finance
   (b) Service
   (c) Manufacturing
   (d) All of the above
   (e) It cannot be determined from the information given

14. Which of the following ratios is the best approximation of the number of companies in the finance business in urban areas to the number of companies in the real estate business in urban areas?

(a) 3/1
(b) 4/1
(c) 5/1
(d) 6/1
(e) It cannot be determined from the information given.

15.

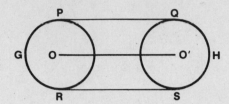

A conveyor belt 6 feet long is drawn tightly around two circular wheels each 1 foot in diameter. What is the distance in feet between the centers of the two wheels (O and O' in the figure above)?

(a) π

(b) $6 - \pi$

(c) $\dfrac{\pi - 6}{2}$

(d) $\dfrac{3\pi}{2}$

(e) $\dfrac{6 - \pi}{2}$

16. Which of the following has no finite value that can be determined?

(a) $\dfrac{0}{3}$

(b) 3×0

(c) $0 - 3$

(d) $\dfrac{3}{0}$

(e) None of these

17. John has half as much money as Bob. If Bob gives John $5, John will have $4 less than Bob has then. How much money did John and Bob have together originally?

(a) $23
(b) $27
(c) $42
(d) $48
(e) $51

18.

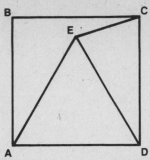

In the figure above, ABCD is a square and ADE is an equilateral triangle. How many degrees in ∠ ECD?

(a) 75
(b) 70
(c) 65
(d) 60
(e) 55

19.

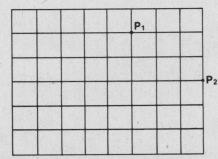

In the figure above, the coordinates of P_1 are (2,4). What are the coordinates of P_2?

(a) (2,5)
(b) (5,2)
(c) (2,2)
(d) (5,1)
(e) (5,5)

20. If r + s = 100 and $\frac{r}{s} = \frac{1}{4}$, then s – r =

(a) – 100
(b) 30
(c) 50
(d) 60
(e) 75

21. What is the surface area of a cube with a volume of $64k^3$?

(a) $16k^2$
(b) $96k^2$
(c) $64k^2$
(d) $16k^3$
(e) $256k^3$

22. If the tax on a suit priced at $125 is $20, at the same rate how much should the tax be on a suit priced at $175?

    (a) $16
    (b) $24
    (c) $28
    (d) $32
    (e) $35

23. If p is an integer, which of the following cannot equal zero?

    I. p − 1
    II. p + 1
    III. $p^2 - 1$
    IV. $p^2 + 1$

    (a) only II and IV
    (b) only III
    (c) only IV
    (d) only I and III
    (e) only II, III and IV

24. If the radius of circle P is 60% of the radius of circle Q, the area of circle P is what percent of the area of circle Q?

    (a) 36%
    (b) 40%
    (c) 64%
    (d) 80%
    (e) 120%

25.

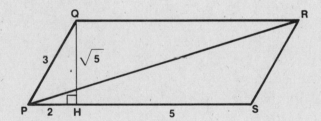

    In the figure above, PQRS is a parallelogram with measurements as shown. The length of diagonal PR is

    (a) $\sqrt{5}$
    (b) 3
    (c) 7
    (d) $\sqrt{58}$
    (e) $\sqrt{86}$

STOP! Work only on this section until the time allowed is over.

Answer Key — Practice Test 4

SECTION I

1. *d*	9. *a*	17. *a*	25. *b*	33. *a*
2. *a*	10. *b*	18. *c*	26. *d*	34. *c*
3. *b*	11. *b*	19. *e*	27. *c*	35. *e*
4. *d*	12. *c*	20. *b*	28. *d*	36. *b*
5. *a*	13. *d*	21. *a*	29. *a*	37. *d*
6. *c*	14. *c*	22. *b*	30. *b*	38. *a*
7. *e*	15. *d*	23. *a*	31. *d*	
8. *e*	16. *e*	24. *c*	32. *c*	

SECTION II

1. *b*	9. *d*	17. *b*	25. *c*	33. *d*
2. *a*	10. *d*	18. *d*	26. *a*	34. *a*
3. *d*	11. *a*	19. *b*	27. *c*	35. *a*
4. *e*	12. *b*	20. *b*	28. *e*	36. *d*
5. *c*	13. *c*	21. *a*	29. *a*	37. *c*
6. *a*	14. *d*	22. *e*	30. *d*	38. *b*
7. *b*	15. *e*	23. *d*	31. *b*	
8. *a*	16. *b*	24. *b*	32. *b*	

SECTION III

1. *b*	7. *c*	13. *a*	19. *a*	25. *d*
2. *b*	8. *d*	14. *a*	20. *d*	26. *e*
3. *c*	9. *c*	15. *b*	21. *e*	27. *d*
4. *c*	10. *b*	16. *c*	22. *a*	28. *b*
5. *b*	11. *a*	17. *b*	23. *e*	29. *c*
6. *d*	12. *d*	18. *e*	24. *b*	30. *d*

SECTION IV

1. *b*	7. *a*	13. *c*	19. *e*	25. *d*
2. *a*	8. *c*	14. *d*	20. *c*	26. *c*
3. *c*	9. *d*	15. *c*	21. *a*	27. *b*
4. *d*	10. *a*	16. *c*	22. *c*	28. *c*
5. *a*	11. *b*	17. *a*	23. *e*	29. *e*
6. *b*	12. *a*	18. *a*	24. *d*	30. *b*

SECTION V

1. *e*	6. *e*	11. *a*	16. *d*	21. *d*
2. *d*	7. *b*	12. *c*	17. *a*	22. *b*
3. *e*	8. *a*	13. *c*	18. *a*	23. *d*
4. *d*	9. *d*	14. *b*	19. *e*	24. *c*
5. *a*	10. *e*	15. *c*	20. *b*	25. *a*

SECTION VI

1. *d*	6. *b*	11. *b*	16. *c*	21. *b*
2. *c*	7. *d*	12. *d*	17. *e*	22. *d*
3. *d*	8. *d*	13. *d*	18. *d*	23. *d*
4. *c*	9. *e*	14. *d*	19. *b*	24. *a*
5. *c*	10. *a*	15. *a*	20. *d*	25. *c*

SECTION VII

1. *e*	6. *d*	11. *b*	16. *d*	21. *b*
2. *c*	7. *a*	12. *c*	17. *c*	22. *c*
3. *d*	8. *e*	13. *d*	18. *a*	23. *c*
4. *a*	9. *d*	14. *e*	19. *b*	24. *a*
5. *b*	10. *d*	15. *e*	20. *d*	25. *e*

Explanatory Answers—Practice Test 4

SECTION I

1. (*d*) The word "although" tells us that despite acting as if he were "completely absorbed" he did not really find the work absorbing. The only word that suggests that the work was not absorbing is *tedious*, choice (*d*).

2. (*a*) The word "though" suggests that the subject was, despite his expectations, either unimpressed or even more deeply impressed when he actually saw the Grand Canyon. Since in addition to his reaction, as expressed by the word for the first blank, he was also "astonished," you can assume that he was very strongly impressed. Only *awestruck* and "numbed" express a feeling of deep impression, but "inhibited," the word that is paired with "numbed," is meaningless in the context, while *dumbfounded*, the second word of choice (*a*), completes the meaning of astonished.

3. (*b*) The context suggests that the subject endured privation when young, and that later he indulged his children. The causal relationship between these two ideas seems to be that he indulged them to make up for or *compensate* for the privation he once endured.

4. (*d*) If Hutchner and Sons experienced improvement in its finances, the only announcement that Victor could have made that would seem related to that improvement is the *acquisition* of Giddings and Clark.

Any other announcement would be about the financial condition of Giddings and Clark, and that firm is not the subject of this sentence. Furthermore, *increments*, or increases, completes the meaning of the first part of the sentence.

5. (*a*) Federal projections of gasoline availability are optimistic in this sentence, yet the announcement of the two oil companies highlights the uncertainty of future gasoline availability. The announcement obviously was that deliveries would be *curtailed*.

6. (*c*) The key word in this sentence is "progressed." In addition, the phrase "in just one decade" implies that the progress has been great for so short a period. The only pair of words that expresses great progress is *curiosity* and *reality*.

7. (*e*) Without filling in the blanks, you can arrive at the following: people who would be considered poor credit risks can accumulate debts far beyond what they would be granted if they were to apply for a loan. While such a situation could be "dangerous" or "scandalous," credit card loans cannot be called "defaulted" or "interest-free." However, *ironical*, which suggests a contradictory situation, is suitable for filling the first blank, and *unsecured* loans does describe the nature of credit card debt.

8. (e) *Dirty* is a lower degree of uncleanliness than *filthy*. Similarly, *elevated*, which means raised in regard or esteem, is a lower degree of promotion or advancement than *exalted*. This is a degree-of-difference relationship.

9. (a) To *countermand* is to revoke or cancel an *order*, in just the same way as to *rescind* is to revoke or cancel a *decree*.

10. (b) *Compassion* is a feeling engendered by someone's *suffering*. In somewhat the same way, *compunction*, which means remorse or a feeling of misgiving, is engendered by our own *wrongdoing*.

11. (b) A *ream* is a specific quantity of paper; a *sheet* is a single unit of a ream. A *battery* is a number of pieces of artillery used for combined action; a *cannon* is a single unit of a battery. This is an example of a part-whole relationship.

12. (c) *Indolence* is the opposite characteristic of that usually symbolized by the *beaver*. Similarly, *ferocity* is the opposite characteristic of that usually symbolized by the *lamb*.

13. (d) A *misunderstanding* may lead to an *altercation* between the participants in a discussion. Similarly, *accommodation*, acting so as to conform to others, may lead to *reconciliation* between people who are arguing.

14. (c) *Predilection*, which means an inclination or predisposition to something, is opposite in meaning to *aversion*. In the same way, *penitent*, which means feeling or expressing sorrow for sin or wrongdoing, is opposite in meaning to *unregenerate*.

15. (d) A *dilettante* is one who takes up an art or activity simply for amusement, while a *connoisseur* is one who is especially competent to pass judgment or criticize in art or matters of taste. An *amateur* is one who engages in an activity for pleasure, while a *professional* is one who is highly competent in a particular art or activity.

16. (e) The function of a *comptroller* is to administer *finances*. In the same manner, the function of a *quartermaster* (in the armed services) is to administer *materiel*.

17. (a) The analysis of the soil and water in the immediate vicinity of the plant depended upon the plant's already having been found. The information in choice (b) eliminated pesticide spraying in the cane fields. The information in choice (c) indicated that the endrin was very diluent, and suggested that it had come from a long way up the river. (d) eliminated all Louisiana sources of contamination, and (e) corroborated the point made in (b).

18. (c) Sub-acute connotes less than acute. Acute means severe in effect. Sub-acute implies that the symptoms are less than severe, or relatively mild. The suggestion that the dose was diluent would imply that the symptoms would have been more severe if the drug had been more concentrated.

19. (e) There is no indication in the passage that endrin use has been stopped or curtailed, so choice (a) is wrong. Although the endrin seems to have been carried in the river, the article no more implies

that endrin should not be used near rivers than it does that the kill was unavoidable, so (b) is incorrect. Choice (c) is wrong; the passage does not compare endrin with DDT. The passage does not deal with endrin's relationship to the food chain, so choice (d) is wrong.

20. (b) Paragraph four of the passage refers to the way in which the trained artist evaluates a work of art, and goes on to say that a mature adult brings his cognitive skills to bear in the same way, implying that the use of such skills would increase understanding and appreciation.

21. (a) The passage says that the child starts with physical self-involvement, but does not in any way indicate that he continues to be self-involved. The word "only" makes the statement one that is not implied nor expressed in the passage.

22. (b) Paragraph one says that tension militates toward narrowing the range of perception. Paragraph six says the socialization process may reduce cognitively directed behavior by increasing tension. These two statements imply choice (b).

23. (a) Paragraph seven implies that language acquisition and general cognition develop similarly. Choice (b) is wrong, since the last paragraph says that language and thought are intimately connected. The passage does not deal with society's mores, so choice (c) is wrong. No inference concerning

choice (d) is possible, since the passage's only reference to parental influence does not refer to language acquisition. Choice (e) is opposite to what can be inferred from paragraph seven.

24. (c) Statement I's gist is contained in paragraph two: the child develops from awareness only of self to objects independent of his perception, increasing in objectivity, lessening subjectivity. Statement III is implied by sentence one, paragraph six. Statement II is incorrect. The passage does not make any judgment about the relative maturity of goal-directed behavior.

25. (b) Cognition, the passage indicates, is related to maturation. It can be inferred that learning is related to the level of physical and mental development. Since such development is at different rates for different individuals, the author would probably feel that an educational approach that takes individual differences into account would be desirable. Choice (a) is exactly the opposite of this. Choice (c) goes counter to the implication in the passage that children are highly distractable. There is nothing in the passage to support choice (d). In fact, paragraph six implies that such involvement might reduce cognitively directed behavior. Paragraphs two and seven suggest that the child develops beyond exploring his own body; teaching the child about his body might impede the developmental process, so choice (e) is wrong.

26. (*d*) The next-to-last paragraph paraphrases choice (*d*). The infant learns to speak by developing the other physical functions of the equipment that he will later use to produce sounds.

27. (*c*) Choice (*a*) goes counter to what the passage describes of the development of speech ability, as contained in paragraph eight. Choice (*b*) implies a disregard for the infant's physical development. Choice (*d*) punishes the child for failure to develop, but does nothing to speed that development. Choice (*e*), allowing nature to take its course, presupposes that nature's course takes place in a vacuum. Choice (*c*) supplies stimuli that encourage cognitive learning.

28. (*d*) *Profane*—treat with irreverence, defile anything revered or respected; opposite—*consecrate* (declare sacred)

29. (*a*) *Chimerical*—vainly or idly fanciful; opposite—*feasible*

30. (*b*) *Pivotal*—of critical importance; opposite—*peripheral* (not really essential)

31. (*d*) *Celerity*—speed, alacrity, dispatch; opposite—*deliberateness*

32. (*c*) *Egregious*—glaring, flagrant, remarkably bad in some way; opposite—*inconsequential*

33. (*a*) *Placable*—forgiving, capable of being appeased; opposite—*ruthless*

34. (*c*) *Flaccid*—soft and limp, flabby; opposite—*wiry* (lean and sinewy)

35. (*e*) *Recondite*—very profound; opposite—*superficial*

36. (*b*) *Cleave*—to split or divide, as by a cutting blow; opposite—*unite*

37. (*d*) *Disinterested*—absence of prejudice, lack of bias; opposite—*biased*

38. (*a*) *Jocular*—facetious, waggish, given to joking or jesting; opposite—*grave* (serious, earnest, solemn)

SECTION II

1. (*b*) To concatenate is to link in a series or chain. A sequence would be a *concatenation*.

2. (*a*) A user of excessive verbiage would not be "admired," "esteemed," or "reputed" for this attribute, nor would such an attribute be characterized as "eloquence." He probably would be *notorious*—widely but not favorably known—for his *grandiloquence* or lofty, pompous style of speech.

3. (*d*) An apprehension is a fear of what is to come. As such, it is not concrete in a certain sense. When an apprehension becomes a reality, as in this case where inflation is already reducing the standard of living of the elderly, the fear becomes concrete or *substantial*.

4. (*e*) Those who depend upon pre-cooked foods may be on vitamin-*deficient* diets. If they are not getting enough vitamins to meet their daily requirements, they are *subsisting*, or maintaining, them-

selves. They are not "battening," because battening means thriving. Choice (c) and (d) are wrong because "repining" means grumbling or complaining, and "indulging" does not take the preposition "on". Choice (a) is incorrect because cooked foods would not be "prolific" in vitamins, even if that word were suitable from the point of view of diction.

5. (c) The word "but" should lead you to expect that his code of personal behavior was much different from what his reputation would lead you to believe it to be. The only word that fits is *punctilious*—strict in the observation of formalities of conduct. Furthermore, the speaker of the sentence would have taken the rogue's word before that of a pillar of society. The word that would characterize the sort of pillar of society whose word you would likely not take is *self-proclaimed*. Certainly you would not take the word of a rogue and gambler over that of a "reliable" pillar of society, so choice (d) is incorrect.

6. (a) The first part of the sentence clearly indicates that the subject of the sentence retained his self-control even though he was subjected to a rigorous cross-examination. You can conclude that he remained unruffled or *imperturbable*. None of the other choices make sense.

7. (b) The paired descriptives at the beginning of the sentence are contrasting attributes; Martin represents the opposite of everything that the speaker of the sentence believes in. "Apotheosis" is incorrect since it means the glorification of an idea. Martin's beliefs do not glorify the subject's beliefs. "Crystallization" is incorrect for almost the same reason. "Dissimulation" means disguising or concealing under a false appearance. The sentence does not imply that Martin pretended to the subject's views. "Negation" could be used in the first blank, but the second word of choice (e), "disparity," could not be used to fill the second blank. Disparity could not develop between two people in the sense of this part of the sentence. Choice (b) is correct. *Antithesis* means the direct opposite, and *antipathy* means aversion or repugnance. These two words complete the sentence completely and correctly.

8. (a) A person will not act in a *lackadaisical* manner if you *invigorate* him. Similarly, a person will not act in a *dispirited* manner if you *animate* him. The relationship is like cause and effect, except that the effect is opposite to the cause.

9. (d) Something *labyrinthine* is by definition *intricate*. Similarly, something *pachydermous* is by definition *thick-skinned*. This is a characterization relationship.

10. (d) *Backsliding* is falling back into *sin* after having been led back to the paths of righteousness. *Recidivism* is a falling back into *crime* after having been released from prison as rehabilitated.

11. (a) It would be inappropriate or worse for a *jurist* to have a *predisposi-*

tion—a tendency to make a disposition before he heard a case. Similarly, it would be inappropriate for an *advocate* to be *unprejudiced* in pleading for a cause—he should certainly be biased in favor of that which he advocates.

12. (*b*) *Prone*, which means to lie on one's stomach, is the opposite of *supine*, which means to lie on one's back. *Ventral*, which means situated on the abdominal side, is the opposite of *dorsal*, which means situated on the back.

13. (*c*) An *ascetic*, one who denies one's self, would not be interested in *carnal* or fleshly matters. Similarly, a *voluptuary*, one devoted to the pursuit of sensual pleasure, would not be interested in *spiritual* matters.

14. (*d*) A *piano* is an instrument that produces sound when its hammers strike its strings. It can be characterized as *percussive*. A *clarinet* produces sound through the passage of air over a vibrating reed. It can be characterized as *reedy*.

15. (*e*) *Perjury* is false *testimony*. Similarly, *counterfeiting* is false *mintage*.

16. (*b*) A *hypothetical* case is *conjectural* in nature, since it is based on assumption rather than proof. A *demonstrated* case is *undoubted*, since it is based upon actual proof.

17. (*b*) Paragraph three says that unless more than a small fraction of the people care enough about the general affairs of state and create a climate of public opinion, those in office will feel free to seize power, or at least act only in their own interest. Therefore, it behooves the people to involve themselves in political affairs, as stated in choice (*b*). The passage does not attack representative government, nor does it present the pros and cons of representative government. The passage does not bear upon the question of extension of suffrage to any group.

18. (*d*) The thrust of the passage is that the survival of representative government depends upon the involvement of the people in public affairs. It can be inferred that the author would favor actions or programs that would strengthen public interest in such affairs. The other choices do not bear on the main purpose of the passage. Choice (*a*) implies that strong party leaders are necessarily opposed to representative government, but that is an implication that is not necessarily true. Choice (*b*) would restrict large scale participation in government, and the author would be unlikely to encourage such an approach. Choice (*c*) might increase voting, but it would not necessarily increase public interest, so it too is incorrect. Choice (*e*)'s proviso concerning rigid property requirements for enfranchisement is wrong because it would have the same effect as choice (*b*).

19. (*b*) Choice (*b*) is closely paraphrased in the first two sentences of the passage, and expresses the view of the author that representative government can survive only if the people are ready to fight to

preserve it from those who would either seize it by force (last sentence of paragraph one), use it to serve their private interests (sentence one, paragraph three), or use it to seek their fortune (last sentence of the passage).

20. (b) Paragraph two supports choice (b), referring to Joyce's and Aristotle's views. See sentences two and three. Nowhere in the passage is there support for choice (a) or choice (c). As to choices (d) and (e), the passage says that great literature deals with life's problems, and great writers write about tragedy and despair, but it does not say that the end goal of literature is to do so. It clearly means to say that great literature uses life's problems and tragedy and comedy in order to illuminate the human situation.

21. (a) The last sentence of paragraph one supports choice (a). The passage does not say, as choice (d) suggests, that one outcome has been an end to rigorous study as a way of learning. What it does say is that these advocates are asking for an end to rigorous study.

22. (e) See the end of paragraph three for concrete support for choice (e), and paragraph five, sentence one for additional evidence. Choices (a) and (b) are mentioned as possible gains from the study of great literature, but only choice (e) is supported in unequivocal terms as a function of major importance.

23. (d) The paragraph concluding the passage advocates choice (d). Choice (e) is incorrect because it speaks only of the inclusion of current literature, and the passage does not make that reservation.

24. (b) The passage uses the common rhetorical device of quoting a famous and respected person who agrees with the author's point of view as a means of influencing the reader. Judge Hand, in the quote, points out that literature broadens the reader's outlook, a necessity for one who must make the important decisions of a federal judge.

25. (c) The author disagrees with the statement in choice (c), maintaining that doing the "right thing" is meaningful only if one does it as a choice between the right and the wrong. He does not, however, say that it is not possible to judge right from wrong, as in choice (a), nor does he deal in any way with the contention contained in choice (b).

26. (a) The author asks in paragraph one whether a man should be praised for a wise decision when he really has made no choice. He asks the same question in paragraph two. In paragraph three, he says that wisdom is the power to discriminate among known alternatives, paraphrasing choice (a).

27. (c) As you have seen in the two previous questions, the author believes that people should choose among known alternatives, and that only then does a person develop judgment. The author would not, therefore, favor any of the choices that limit the range of people's experience. Only with choice (c) could a person make choices based firmly on knowledge, as suggested in the last sentence.

28. (e) *Evanescent*—fleeting, short-lived; opposite—*perpetual*

29. (a) *Similitude*—likeness; opposite—*disparity*

30. (d) *Dissonant*—discordant, harsh in sound; opposite—*euphonious* (pleasant sounding)

31. (b) *Euphoria*—feeling of well-being; opposite—*depression*

32. (b) *Salutary*—wholesome, healthful; opposite—*deleterious* (harmful)

33. (d) *Germane*—relevant; opposite—*irrelevant*

34. (a) *Sangfroid*—composure; opposite—*perturbation*

35. (a) *Torpor*—lethargy, a state of suspended physical activity; opposite—*animation*

36. (d) *Comity*—mutual civility; opposite—*dissension* (discord)

37. (c) *Anomalous*—deviating from the common type; opposite—*regular*

38. (b) *Censure*—to condemn or blame; opposite—*commend* (to praise)

SECTION III

1. (b) Since $\frac{10}{20} = \frac{1}{2}$, $\frac{10}{21} < \frac{1}{2}$

Since $\frac{8}{16} = \frac{1}{2}$, $\frac{8}{15} > \frac{1}{2}$

so that $\frac{8}{15} > \frac{10}{21}$

2. (b) $6 = \sqrt{6}\,\sqrt{6}$
Since $\sqrt{6} > 2$, then $\sqrt{6}\,\sqrt{6} > 2\,\sqrt{6}$, that is, $6 > 2\,\sqrt{6}$

3. (c) $\dfrac{4 + \dfrac{q}{p}}{q} = \dfrac{4p + q}{pq}$
(Multiply numerator and denominator by p)

4. (c) $\dfrac{r}{3} = \dfrac{s}{4}$
(Cross-multiply or simply remember that the product of the means is equal to the product of the extremes in all ratios.) $4r = 3s$

5. (b) 7/15 and 16/33 are each less than 1/2.
Thus, (7/15 + 16/33) must be less than 1.
So that (7/15 + 16/33) 432 < 423

6. (d) $\dfrac{x}{y} = \dfrac{4}{7}$
$7x = 4y$
$y = \dfrac{7}{4}x$
However, we do not know if x and y are each positive or negative numbers. Thus we cannot compare their magnitudes.

7. (c) $\dfrac{k^2 + k}{2} = \dfrac{k(k + 1)}{2}$
k and (k + 1) are consecutive integers and one of them must be even (divisible by 2). Thus the remainder is equal to zero.

8. (d) If $t > 1$, then $t^3 > t$
If $t = 1$, then $t^3 = t$
If $0 < t < 1$, then $t^3 < t$
Thus, comparison cannot be made.

9. (c) $QOR = \dfrac{1}{5}(360°) = 72°$
$n = 72$

10. (b) In triangle OQR, n + 2t = 180
72 + 2t = 180
2t = 108
t = 54
So that n > t

11. (a) In triangle OQR, QR is opposite the largest angle n. So that QR > OQ, or s > r.

12. (d) There is not enough information to determine the area of the pentagon since we do not know the value of r or s.

13. (a) Arc QR is longer than line segment QR since a straight line is the shortest distance between two points.

14. (a) 6x = 5k, 4y = 3k
$x = (5/6)k, y = (3/4)k$

Since k > 0, $\frac{5}{6}k =$

$\frac{10}{12}k > \frac{9}{12}k = \frac{3}{4}k$

So that x > y

15. (b) $\sqrt{.09} = .3$

$\frac{\pi}{7} \approx \frac{3.14}{7} \approx .45$

So that $\frac{\pi}{7} > \sqrt{.09}$

16. (c) Let x = weight in pounds of 10-foot rod. Then 8/44 = 10/x; cross multiply.
8x = 440
x = 55

17. (b) $\frac{3p - q}{q} = \frac{3p}{q} - \frac{q}{q} = 5 - 1 = 4$

18. (e) $\frac{2 + 3 + 5 + 8 + t}{5} = t$

18 + t = 5t
18 = 4t
t = 4½

19. (a) Let y = length of longer piece in inches
Then (2/3)y = length of shorter piece in inches
y + (2/3)y = 40
Multiply both sides by 3
3y + 2y = 120
5y = 120
y = 24 (longer piece)
(2/3)y = (2/3)(24) = 16 (shorter piece)

20. (d)

PQ = 15 = 3(5), QR = 9 = 3(3)
Thus, triangle PQR is a 3–4–5 right triangle multipled by 3, or a 9–12–15 triangle.
Therefore, b = 12 and the area of the rectangle is 12 × 9 = 108 sq. cm.

21. (e) It is impossible to tell. Although $30 billion in Eurocurrency credits were borrowed, and industrial countries borrowed 50% of all funds, this does not imply that they necessarily borrowed 50% of the Eurocurrency credits.

22. (a) This question is an exercise in speed technique. Rather than take 30% each of $43 billion and $63 billion, and subtracting, take the difference between $43 billion and $63 billion first, $20 billion, and take 30% of that, $6 billion. You can do this because the percentage remained constant.

23. (e) They could support the borrowings of any one of them. Note that

the bonds part of the bar graph is obviously greater than 50% of the total, and the group with the greatest share of the funds, industrial countries, borrowed only 50% of that total.

24. (*b*) First note that the percent of the total for international organizations remained constant at 13%, so the total borrowings figures can be used directly without calculating 13% of them. Second, note that the years are 1974 to 1976: $62.8 billion minus $40.8 billion equals $22 billion, about a 54% increase over $40.8 billion.

25. (*d*) In this case the totals have to be calculated beforehand. 1% of $40.8 billion is approximately $.4 billion. 2% of $62.8 billion is approximately $1.3 billion, an increase of $.9 billion.

26. (*e*) The largest *relative* increase is the one which increased the most in terms of its original amount. All groups increased somewhat (excepting centrally planned countries, which remained roughly constant), but the "others" group more than doubled.

27. (*d*) $.625 = \frac{5}{8}, \frac{15}{24} =$
$\frac{5}{8}, \sqrt{\frac{25}{64}} = \frac{5}{8}$
$\frac{45}{70} = \frac{9}{14}$ which is not equal to $\frac{5}{8}$

28. (*b*) $16 = 13 + 3$
$24 = 19 + 5$
$28 = 23 + 5$
$30 = 23 + 7$
23 cannot be written as the sum of two primes.

29. (*c*) First term = 2
Second term = $(1/4)2^3$
$(1/4)8 = 2$
Third term = $(1/4)2^3$
All terms of the sequence are 2

30. (*d*) Let q = 100
then p = q + .50q
p = 100 + .50(100) = 150
q is now 50 less than p
$\frac{50}{150} = \frac{1}{3} = 33\frac{1}{3}\%$
So that q is 33⅓% less than p

SECTION IV

1. (*b*) Average of 5n, 3n, and 7 =
$\frac{8n + 7}{3}$
Average of 2n, 6n, and 9 =
$\frac{8n + 9}{3}$
Since n > 0, 8n + 9 > 8n + 7
So that the average in column B > average in column A

2. (*a*) In triangle PQT, PQ + PT > QT
In triangle RST, SR + ST > RT
Thus, the perimeter of the parallelogram is greater than the perimeter of triangle QRT.

3. (*c*) Take the cube root of both sides of $\frac{x^3}{y^6} = \frac{1}{8}$, yielding $\frac{x}{y^2} = \frac{1}{2}$
or $2x = y^2$
Note that $x^3 = (1/8)y^6$; since y^6 is positive, x^3, and therefore x, is positive. No problem of signs is in question here.

4. (*d*) We do not know where each set begins or ends, so that we cannot compare integers in P and Q.

5. (a) $V = e^3 = 216$
    $e = 6$ (edge of cube in Column A)
    $S = 6e^2 = 150$
    $e^2 = 25$
    $e = 5$ (edge of cube in Column B)

6. (b) $60 \text{ km} = \dfrac{5}{8} (60 \text{ miles})$

    $= \dfrac{300}{8}$

    $= 37.5 \text{ miles} < 40 \text{ miles}$

7. (a) Cube the two quantities in columns A and B.
    $(\sqrt[3]{130})^3 = 130$
    $(3\sqrt{3})^3 = 27(3\sqrt{3})$
    $\qquad = 81\sqrt{3}$
    $\qquad \approx 81(1.73)$
    $\qquad \approx 140 > 130$

8. (c) To throw a "twelve" with a pair of dice, one must get two "sixes." To throw a "two," one must get two "ones." The probabilities of these two events are the same, because in each case there is only one combination that will yield it.

9. (d) $\dfrac{p}{q} = \dfrac{7}{10}$

    $p = \dfrac{7}{10} q$

    Since we do not know the signs of p and q, we cannot compare their size from the above.

10. (a) The side of the square is 8 and its perimeter is $8(4) = 32 > 30$.

11. (b) In right triangle QRS, $QS = 8\sqrt{2}$ and $QO = 4\sqrt{2}$. Thus, the ordinate of Q is $4(1.414) \approx 5.6 < 6$.

12. (a) Area of circle $= \pi(4\sqrt{2})^2 = 32\pi$
    Twice the circumference
    $= 2\pi(8\sqrt{2})$
    $= 16\pi\sqrt{2}$

$\qquad \approx 16\pi (1.4)$
$\qquad \approx 22.4\pi$

13. (c) Angles QSR and QPR are inscribed in the same arc and are therefore equal to each other.

14. (d) $(2k)^3 = 8k^3$
    This cannot be compared to $2k^3$ since we do not know the sign of k or if $k = 0$.

15. (c) The factors of 28 are 1, 2, 4, 7, 14 and 28. The sum of these is 56.

16. (c) Let the oil rise to a height of h inches
    Then $7 \times 7 \times h = 231$. Divide by 7.
    $7h = 33$
    $h \approx 4.7$ inches

17. (a) The total female labor force in 1955 was about 20 million, of which wives accounted for about 10 million and divorced, separated, or widowed women accounted for about 5 million, for a total of 15 million out of 20 million, or 75%.

18. (a) The number of single women (never married, divorced, separated, or widowed) rose from about 10 million (18 million minus 8 million) to about 15 million (37 million minus 22 million), an increase of 5 million, or 50%.

19. (e)

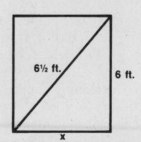

$6\frac{1}{2} = \frac{13}{2}, 6 = \frac{12}{2}$

So that x = 5/2 (5–12–13 triangle where each side is divided by 2)

Area = $6\left(\dfrac{5}{2}\right)$ = 15 sq. ft.

20. (c) $\dfrac{300}{15}$ = 20 miles per gallon

$\dfrac{300}{12}$ = 25 miles per gallon

Thus, 5 miles more per gallon

21. (a) Reporting countries in Europe (a) is the only sector where the sources percentage (38.8%) is greater than the uses percentage (30.7%).

22. (c) Eastern Europe plus the reporting European countries = 7.6% + 30.7% = 38.3% of $205 billion ≈ $78 billion.

23. (e) Other developed countries supplied 21.3% of the Eurodollars. Simply add up the choices:
(a) Reporting European area: 30.7%
(b) Other developed countries: 30.5%
(c) Offshore banking centers plus Eastern Europe: 17.4% + 7.6% = 25%
(d) Eastern Europe plus developing countries plus oil exporting countries plus unallocated = 7.6% + 9.5% + 2.6% + 1.7% = 21.4%
(e) Offshore banking centers plus oil exporting countries = 17.4% + 2.6% = 20%

24. (d) Developing countries:
9.5% – 7.9% = 1.6%
Offshore banking centers:
17.4% – 10.6% = 6.8%

Eastern Europe:
7.6% – 2.5% = 5.1%
Other developed countries:
30.5% – 21.3% = 9.2%
(greatest deficit)
Oil exporting countries:
Surplus.

25. (d) She must now drive 40 miles in 55 – 7 = 48 minutes = 48/60 or 4/5 hour.

Rate = $\dfrac{\text{Distance}}{\text{Time}}$

$= 40 \div \dfrac{4}{5} = \dfrac{40}{1} \times \dfrac{5}{4}$

$= 10 \times 5 = 50$ mph

26. (c)

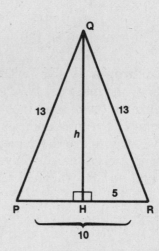

HR = ½(10) = 5
In right △ QRH, h² = 13² – 5²
$= 169 - 25$
$= 144$
h = 12
Area △ PQR = ½(bh)
$= ½(10)(12) = 60$

27. (b) Let x = the list price.
If the discount was 20%, Tony paid 100% – 20% = 80% of the list price.
.8x = 60
8x = 600
x = $75

28. (c) $n = \dfrac{p + q + r + s}{4}$

or $p + q + r + s = 4n$

$(n - p) + (n - q) + (n - r) + (n - s)$
$= 4n - (p + q + r + s)$
$= 4n - 4n = 0$

29. (e) $32 = 19 + 13$

Both 19 and 13 are prime numbers. The other four choices cannot be written as the sum of exactly two prime numbers.

30. (b)

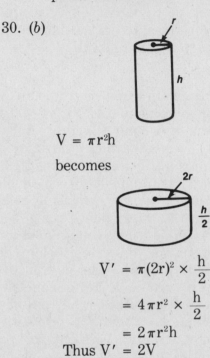

$V = \pi r^2 h$

becomes

$V' = \pi (2r)^2 \times \dfrac{h}{2}$

$= 4 \pi r^2 \times \dfrac{h}{2}$

$= 2 \pi r^2 h$

Thus $V' = 2V$

The volume is doubled.

SECTION V

1. (e) Statements 1–4 lead to the following diagram, in which each person's initial is used instead of his or her name:

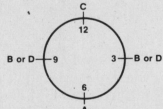

Statements 5 and 6 provide further possibilities. Statement 7 narrows the possible range of seats for George, as does statement 8.

Statement 7 limits George's location to either 1, 2, 10, or 11 o'clock. Since Bernice and Dora are at 3 and 9 o'clock, statement 8 also limits George to 1, 2, 10, or 11 o'clock. Statements 7 and 8 therefore repeat each other.

2. (d) Remembering that Bernice and Dora are interchangeable, we may draw all possibilities satisfying statements 5–7 consistent with the diagram in the answer to Question 1.

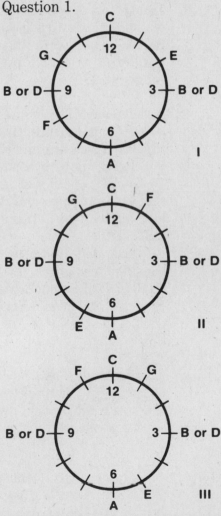

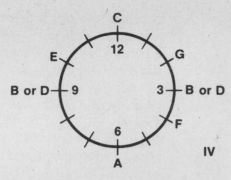

The easiest way to draw these possibilities is to place George at each of his four possible locations. Only one location exists for Flora at each location of George.

The diagrams show that four possibilities exist with regard to George, Flora, and Edward. Since each of these may be associated with either of two possibilities for Bernice and Dora, there are a total of (4 × 2) or 8 possible arrangements.

3. (e) Arrangement I shows George five hours from Bernice. There, Edward is at 2 o'clock and Flora is at 8 o'clock, numbers which sum to 10. There is another arrangement that works, however. If Bernice is at 9 o'clock and Dora is at 3 o'clock, the locations of George, Edward, and Flora that fit the question are given by arrangement IV. There, Edward and Flora are at 4 and 10 o'clock, for a total of 14. Choice (e), 10 or 14, is thus correct.

4. (d) Arrangement I is the only one with George at 10 o'clock. In it, Flora is at 8 o'clock, two hours from Andrew. She may be next to either Dora or Bernice.

5. (a) The author's argument is clearly that the present tax laws are un-

just because they allow some people with very large incomes to escape paying any income tax. Statement I is therefore correct. Statement II, that everyone should pay some tax, is not implied by the argument, because the argument referred only to people with high incomes. People with low or no incomes are not necessarily required by the author to pay tax. Statement III is much too specific to be implied by the author's statement, although he might well agree with it.

6. (e) This choice presents a possible way for someone to earn $1,000,000 a year in a manner which "everyone" agrees should yield tax exemption. Choice (a) is consistent with the argument. (b) is both implausible and not completely relevant, because simply being not wealthy is insufficient grounds for not paying any taxes. Being not wealthy is quite different from being poor. (c) and (d) offer no rebuttal to the author, who has only claimed that "some" people earning a million dollars pay no tax, not that most or all such people do not pay tax.

7. (b) If both Q and R are on the team, then J and L cannot be on the team, since they will not play together. This leaves P, K, and M as the only possible teammates for Q and R.

8. (a) Since K will not play with J or L, the only other possible team members are P, Q, R, and M.

9. (d) If L is not on the team, then juniors P, Q, R, and seniors K and M can make up a team of five. Choices (a), (b), and (c) are not possible because Q and J cannot be on the same team. Choice (e) is not possible because K and J cannot be on the same team.

10. (e) If P cannot play, no teams can be formed. Since K will not play with J or L, a five-member team cannot be formed.

11. (a) The problems in this set may be solved by arranging the cars in three lists corresponding to the three categories:

Durability
A
C
B
E
D

Expense
C
E
B
A
D

Styling
C
D
B
E
A

The above information is derived solely from the five statements. If you had any difficulties, go through the process of arranging the cars in the proper order to understand how it is done; there is nothing tricky at all about it.

It is apparent that A was rated the most durable car.

12. (c) C was the only car rated as both more durable and more expensive than E.

13. (c) C was also the only car rated as both more durable and more stylish than D.

14. (b) Both B and C were rated as both more durable than A and more stylish than E.

15. (c) C is by far the best-rated car overall, receiving 2 points for durability and 1 point each for expense and styling. No other car approaches its total of 4 points.

16. (d) E is fourth in durability, second in expense, and fourth in styling, for a total of 10 points.

17. (a) From statement I we may draw the following.

From statement 2 we may draw the following two possibilities.

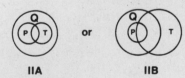

We shall note statement 3 and draw the possibilities which statement 4 adds to statements 1 and 2.

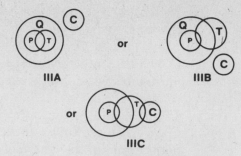

IIIA   or   IIIB

or   IIIC

The premise in this question refers to diagram IIB, in which some T's are not Q's. From statement 3, it is clear that some T's may be A's. In that case, some Q's would be both A's and T's. Choice (a) is correct, then. A glance at the diagrams shows choice (b) to be incorrect. (c) is wrong because all T's could be B's; all we know is that some P's are A's or B's. We do not know that the P's that are T's are also A's; the P's that are T's might be only B's. (d) is wrong because, as stated above, there is no reason given why all T's could not be A's, B's, or both.

18. (a) The set of T's is here divided into subsets of U's and V's. (a) is clearly correct, since some Q's are not P's and some T's are Q's but not P's. Diagrams IIA and IIB make that point. According to the question the members of T are U's or V's. From the reasoning above, the Q's that are T's but not P's must also be U's or V's. Diagram IIA shows that all U's or V's could be Q's, so that (b) is incorrect. (c) is incorrect because some A's or B's could be not P's; there is no stipulation that all A's or B's are P's. So, the boundaries of sets A or B could intersect those of U or V elsewhere than within P. (d) is incorrect because it claims that some Q's are neither A's nor B's. As shown

above, it is possible that all Q's are either A's or B's.

19. (e) Statements I and II are false. Statement I cannot be correct because, as diagrams IIA and IIB show, there must be some Q's that are P's that are not T's; therefore, not all Q's can be T's. Remember that P's are contained within Q's but that some P's are not T's. Diagrams IIIA, IIIB, and IIIC show that statement II is false. Since all P's are Q's but no Q's are C's, no P's may be C's. Statement III is correct, since some Q's are P's and all P's are either A's or B's.

20. (b) If some C's are A's, clearly some A's are not Q's, since no members of C are Q's. Thus statement III is correct. Statement I could be false, as shown by this diagram adding to diagram IIIA.

There is no reason why all C's could not all be T's, and therefore statement II is not necessarily true.

21. (d) Since some T's are P's, and all P's are either A's or B's, some T's are either A's or B's. Therefore, statement I is false and statement II is true. Since all P's are Q's, it also follows that at least some T's are Q's, making statement III true. Since statements II and III are true, choice (d) is correct.

22. (b) By similar reasoning to that used for the previous question, we may conclude that some T's are Q's,

and *vice versa*, making choice (*b*) correct. Choices (*a*), (*c*), and (*d*) are all false because the conditions listed give no positive information about what C *is*; all they state is that Q's and C's have no members in common. Choice (*e*) is false because all P's are Q's.

23. (*d*) The original argument deals with a class (Democrats) that has a certain property (supporting social welfare programs). It then refers to an individual (Wendy) who exhibits that property and concludes that the individual must be a member of the class. Argument (*d*) follows the same pattern; arguments (*a*), (*b*), and (*c*) do not. Argument (*e*) varies from the original argument in that the second statement describes an individual who does *not* exhibit the property described.

24. (*c*) If only male Hindus wear turbans, and Victor wears a turban, then he must be a Hindu. Statement (*c*) gives the needed support for the original conclusion. The other statements leave open the possibility of people other than Hindus wearing turbans.

25. (*a*) The questions asks which of the choices logically implies the statement in question. Choice (*a*) does this. It says that Congress will accept any territory which votes to join the U.S. If this is true, it *must* follow that if Kanamara votes to join the U.S., Congress will accept it as a state. The other choices have no logically compelling relationship to the original statement.

SECTION VI

1. (*d*) Note that to answer these questions, it is unnecessary to know in which directions Elm St. and Maple St. run.

The man originally drove two miles north and later three miles south; overall, he drove one mile south. He also drove two miles west. Any route which reverses those two directions and brings him one mile north and two miles east brings him back to his starting point. Clearly statement II does this, but statement I does not. Statement III is equivalent to statement II, for it has the man going three miles north and two miles south, for a net change of one mile north. Both II and III have the driver simply going two miles east.

A graphic representation of this problem is wasteful of time and need not be done except as a check on the reasoning above. If it were done, it would be done as follows:

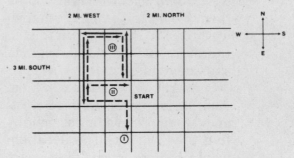

2. (*c*) The man this time began two miles west and one mile south of the intersection of Elm St. and Maple St. He traveled three miles east, bringing him a total of one mile east of that intersection. He also traveled one mile north, bringing him on the same north-south location as the intersection (that is, on

the same east-west road). He therefore ended up on either Elm St. or Maple St., depending on which ran north-south and which east-west. Diagrammatically, his position is determined this way:

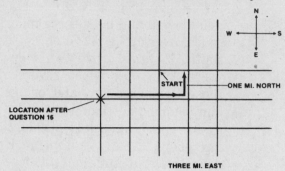

3. (d) The question does not specify which way Elm runs or in which direction the man drove on Elm. Trial and error can answer the question, however. Suppose Elm runs north-south. If the man initially drives south, then his complete set of maneuvers will take him two miles south plus three miles north = one mile north, and three miles east plus five miles west = two miles west. This route, then, would leave him north and west of his starting point, and therefore off both his original starting roads.

Similarly, if he starts north on Elm, he will go three miles west and two plus three miles north = five miles north. This location would also be away from both original roads.

It can thus be deduced that the man proceeds either east or west on Elm. If he starts east, then the net effect of his travels will be to take him two miles east plus three miles east + five miles west = no change in direction east or west. This will put him back on Maple, three miles north of his starting

point (see map below). This route is therefore possible.

If he starts west on Elm, he will go two miles west plus three miles east plus five miles west = four miles west, as well as three miles north, which will take him off both Elm and Maple. Therefore, it can be concluded that he goes east on Elm and ends up three miles north of Elm on Maple, making all the statements correct.

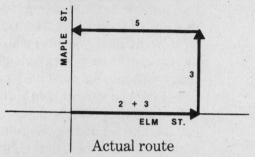

Actual route

4. (c) As explained under question 3, the man ends up three miles from Elm.

5. (c) The study referred to examined the results of professionals taking care of children. The only way the argument would be valid would be if similar conditions held in day-care facilities as in the study. The other choices are not relevant to the argument's validity.

6. (b) Day-care facilities should be increased if there are not enough to go around, a condition expressed by choice (b). That single working mothers favor the proposal is not surprising and is not persuasive unless (b) is also correct. (c) weakens the argument to some degree. (d) and (e) are good to know, but are not especially important to the argument. They provide further evidence that the study actually did show what the

author claims it showed, but neither goes so far as to indicate a need for more day-care facilities.

7. (*d*) Even if day-care facilities had professionals, the situation there would be very different from the one in the study. In the study children were raised only by one person (or small group of persons) and were compared to children raised only by their parents. Children raised *both* by their parents and by people in a day-care facility could well be different from children raised by either one or the other. The other choices are either barely relevant ((*a*) and (*b*)) or completely irrelevant ((*c*) and (*e*)).

8. (*d*) H and L must be at either end. If J sits next to K, and M does not sit next to N, J and K must take the two middle seats. Thus, of the possible choices given, only (*d*) is acceptable.

9. (*e*) Using the information given, we can list all the possible seating orders. With J and K in the middle and H and L at each end, the possible orders are as follows:

H M J K N L
H N J K M L
H M K J N L
H N K J M L
L M J K N H
L N J K M H
L M K J N H
L N K J M H

Thus, there are eight possible arrangements.

10. (*a*) From the possible seating orders listed above, we see that M and N must always have two students

between them (J and K). This holds true in all possible arrangements.

11. (*b*) The instructions to this set are clear but complex, and the symbols reb, erb, ber, and bre were obviously chosen to be confusing but should not have seriously impeded your progress to the solutions. In the first question, 20 = 5 × 4 = erbber (or backwards, bererb).

12. (*d*) 24 = 6 × 4 = 10 points. Although 24 is divisible by 3, it is not reb, because a number is reb only if it is not bre (divisible by 6).

13. (*d*) 12 is divisible by 6 once and by 4 once, and is thus breber and is worth 6 + 4 or 10 points. Though divisible by 3, 12 is not reb because it is bre. Choice (*b*), a number that is erberb, gets 5 points for each erb and is thus worth 5 + 5 or 10 points. Choice (*c*), 24, is worth 10 points, as shown in the previous explanation. Choice (*d*), a number that is berberber, gets 4 points for each ber and is therefore worth 4 + 4 + 4 or 12 points. Choice (*e*), 30, is divisible by 6 once and by 5 once, and is thus breerb. 30 is not divisible by 4 and is not reb because, though divisible by 3, it is bre. 30 is worth 6 points for being bre and 5 points for being erb and is thus worth 6 + 5 or 11 points. Choice (*d*), a number that is berberber, is worth the greatest number of points, 12, and is the correct answer.

14. (*d*) According to the instructions, a number that is rebreberb is divis-

ible by 3, by 3 again, and by 5, since reb stands for 3 and erb stands for 5. In other words, the number is a product of 3, 3, and 5. The smallest number divisible by 3, 3, and 5 is 3 × 3 × 5 or 45.

15. (a) 180 is worth 21 points. 300 is worth 20 points. 375 is worth 18 points. Methods for determining these follow.

$$\overset{30}{6)\overline{180}}$$

$$\overset{36}{5)\overline{180}}$$

$$\overset{45}{4)\overline{180}}$$

$$\overset{5}{6)\overline{30}}$$

The divisors of 180 are 6, 6, 5, and 4, for a total of 6 + 6 + 5 + 4 or 21 points.

$$\overset{50}{6)\overline{300}}$$

$$\overset{60}{5)\overline{300}}$$

$$\overset{75}{4)\overline{300}}$$

$$\overset{12}{5)\overline{60}}$$

The divisors of 300 are 6, 5, 5, and 4, for a total of 6 + 5 + 5 + 4 or 20 points.

$$\overset{75}{5)\overline{375}}$$

$$\overset{125}{3)\overline{375}}$$

$$\overset{15}{5)\overline{75}}$$

$$\overset{3}{5)\overline{15}}$$

The divisors of 375 are 5, 5, 5, and 3, for a total of 5 + 5 + 5 + 3 or 18 points.

16. (c) Condition (5) states that a number can be reb only if it is not bre, so that no number can be rebbre. Statement I is therefore a name which cannot occur. Statement II also cannot occur, for a more subtle reason. Statements (3) and (4) imply that a number that is rebber is divisible by 4 and by 3, but not divisible by 6 (not bre). These conditions are self-contradictory, however. Any number that is divisible by both 4 and 3 is divisible by 4 × 3 = 12 and is therefore divisible by 6. For this reason, a number cannot be rebber. Erbber (statement III) is a number divisible by both 4 and 5, which is entirely possible, making statements I and II the only correct ones. Choice (c) is therefore correct.

17. (e) Attempt to solve a complex problem such as this at the outset, attacking the problem as a whole. Certain things are known about each man (L = Leon, M = Martin, N = Nelson, O = Oscar, and P = Paul):

	Height	Hair-style	Foot-wear
L	tall		black
M	short	long	
N	medium		white
O		bald	brown
P		crew	

Since two people are known to be short and two of medium height (based on the eighth fact listed), either Oscar or Paul is of medium height, while the other is short. It is also known that someone who does not have long hair is wearing boots. By exclusion, this means that Paul is wearing boots.

We also know that someone with brown shoes is of medium height; since Paul is now known to be wearing boots, it must be Oscar who is of medium height. Paul, therefore, must be short. The table now looks like this:

	Height	Hair-style	Foot-wear
L	tall		black
M	short	long	
N	medium		white
O	medium	bald	brown
P	short	crew	boots

The only other bit of information given in the problem concerns a tall person who has a crew cut. This must be Leon. The final table is:

	Height	Hair-style	Foot-wear
L	tall	crew	black
M	short	long	?
N	medium	?	white
O	medium	bald	brown
P	short	crew	boots

It is clear that at least two people, and possibly three, have crew cuts—Leon and Paul certainly do, and Nelson is unknown. Choice (e), then, is correct.

18. (d) It is known that Oscar, of medium height, is wearing brown shoes. It is possible that Martin, who is short, may also be wearing brown shoes, so that the most specific thing that can be said is that any man wearing brown shoes is either short or of medium height.

19. (b) The description of a short man with a crew cut and boots fits Paul; the other choices do not exactly fit any of the people described.

20. (d) Martin's footwear and Nelson's hairstyle are the only items which cannot be deduced, making statements II and III correct.

21. (b) The man wearing boots is Paul, who is short. Thus statement III is correct. Statements I and II are incorrect, for the information presented prevents Oscar from being short and Paul from being of medium height.

22. (d) The height, hairstyle, and footwear of three people—Leon, Oscar, and Paul—are completely known.

23. (d) The author does not question the doctor's motives, assert that doctors are poorly trained, demonstrate that they are rarely correct, or suggest an alternative view of the value of an electrocardiogram. His method of questioning the doctors' claims is to present what he believes to be evidence contradicting the claim that the electrocardiogram is a good indicator of the heart's health.

24. (a) The author's argument is actually that the electrocardiogram is not a *perfect* indicator of the heart's health. He makes no attempt to show that it is usually not a *good* indicator. His use of the phrase "many people" is misleading because a huge number of people have had electrocardiograms. The substitution of *unhealthiness* for *health* (b) would not affect the argument. Using *some* instead of

many (c) would weaken the argument to some degree. (d), the substitution of *indicates* for *shows,* is irrelevant to the argument. Substituting *incorrect* for *suspect* (e) would weaken the argument by making an already weak argument more extreme. The original argument merely casts doubt upon the doctors' claim; the substitution of *incorrect* would assert that their claim is definitely wrong. The argument does not support this assertion.

25. (c) The question asks for a condition which must be true if XYZ's strategy is to work; it does not ask that that condition be sufficient. Thus the correct answer will be a condition without which the strategy will surely fail, but which need not guarantee success or even make it likely. Looking at the question this way, it is easy to see that the strategy of cutting the selling price in order to turn a profit will work only if the sale of widgets is sensitive to changes in their price. The other choices are all relevant to the situation and, if true, may work in favor of XYZ's strategy, but the strategy might work in their absence.

SECTION VII

1. (e) $6 \times 6 \times t = 18 \times 18 \times 18$
   Divide both sides of the equation by 6×6
   $t = 3 \times 3 \times 18$
   $t = 162$

2. (c) $12 - (-18) = 12 + 18$
   $= 30$

3. (d) 9 inches = 9/12 foot = 3/4 foot
   $6 \div 3/4 = 6 \times 4/3 = 8$

4. (a) Area of circle O = $\pi r^2 = \pi(2)^2$
   $= 4\pi$
   Area of quadrant POS + quadrant ROQ = $\frac{1}{2}(4\pi) = 2\pi$.
   Since the radius of the smaller semicircles is 1, then the area of the two small semicircles = $2(\pi/2)$
   $= \pi$.
   The shaded area = $2\pi - \pi = \pi$.

5. (b) If he does around 4/5 of the track in m minutes, then he runs 1/5 of the track in m/4 minutes, since 1/5 = 1/4 of 4/5. Thus, to run the entire track would take m + m/4 = 4m/4 + m/4 = 5m/4 minutes.

6. (d) If it flies 3 miles in 15 seconds, then it flies 12 miles in 60 seconds (1 minute). If it flies 12 miles in 1 minute, then it flies 12 × 60 or 720 miles in 60 minutes or one hour.

7. (a) The sum total of the 30 scores is 30p. If each mark is raised 10 points the sum total becomes 30p + 30(10) = 30p + 300
   The average is then
   $\frac{30p + 300}{30} = p + 10$

8. (e) Area of triangle OPQ = (1/2)(OP × altitude)
   $64 = (1/2)8h$
   $64 = 4h$
   $h = 16$

9. (d) The point for service companies on the graph, J, is exactly on the 50% line for urban areas. Turning the graph clockwise a half-turn, you can measure where J falls on the suburban scale: somewhat above 25%, or about 30%. Turning the graph counterclockwise a

half-turn, you can measure J on the rural scale: a bit below 25%, or 20%.

Remember that on this graph, the percentages for each industry will all add up to 100%. That is, while there may be industries *not* depicted on the graph, all *areas* of the United States are included.

10. (*d*) None of the above. The breakdowns, in tabular form, are as follows:

Finance (G):
60% urban areas
30% suburban areas
10% rural areas

Agricultural (H):
5% urban areas
20% suburban areas
75% rural areas

Service (J):
50% urban areas
30% suburban areas
20% rural areas

Real Estate (K):
10% urban areas
30% suburban areas
60% rural areas

Manufacturing (F):
70% urban areas
25% suburban areas
5% rural areas

11. (*b*) 30% of the finance companies are located in suburban areas, and 60% of them are located in urban areas; hence 1/2 is the ratio of the number in suburban areas to the number in urban areas.

12. (*c*) Agriculture (H). This question requires adding up several sets of percentages. Since only 25% is the sum we are looking for, it pays to start looking for an industry with small percentages in urban (5%)

and suburban (20%) areas. The most obvious first guess would be agriculture. You can check this answer by observing that H represents 75% in rural, leaving only 25% for urban and suburban combined.

13. (*d*) All of the above. Note the figures for urban areas given in the answer to question 10: finance, 60%, service, 50%, and manufacturing, 70%.

14. (*e*) It cannot be determined from the information given. The percentages on this graph show the distribution of any particular industry among the different areas of the country. It says nothing about the total number of companies in each industry. For example, there could be only 1,000 finance companies and more than 25,000 real estate companies in the United States.

15. (*e*) Let $OO' = x$, then
$PQ = RS = x$ (external tangents)
Then $\overset{\frown}{PGR}$ and $\overset{\frown}{QHS}$ are semicircles and their sum is equal to the circumference (C) of one of the circles. $C = \pi D = \pi$ feet
$6 = x + x + \pi$
$6 = 2x + \pi$
$6 - \pi = 2x$
$x = \dfrac{6 - \pi}{2}$

16. (*d*) Since we cannot divide by 0, the fraction 3/0 has no finite value that can be determined.

17. (*c*) Let x = Bob's original amount in dollars.
Then $(1/2)x$ = John's original amount in dollars.

x − 5 = Bob's new amount
(1/2)x + 5 = John's new amount
(1/2)x + 5 = (x − 5) − 4
(1/2)x + 5 = x − 9
Multiply both sides by 2·
x + 10 = 2x − 18
x = 28 (Bob's original amount)
(1/2)x = 14
(John's original amount)
$28 + $14 = $42
(amount together)

18. (a) Since ∠ ADE = 60° and
∠ ADC = 90°
then ∠EDC = 90 − 60 = 30°.
Since ED = DC, the base angles
of triangle EDC are each
$$\frac{180 - 30}{2} = \frac{150}{2} = 75°$$

19. (b) To locate the origin from P_1, go
left 2 units and down 4 units. It
can be seen that P_2 is 5 units to the
right of the origin and 2 units up.
So that the coordinates of P_2 are
(5,2).

20. (d) If $\frac{r}{s} = \frac{1}{4}$, then 4r = s
Substitute 4r for s in the equation
r + s = 100
r + 4r = 100
5r = 100
r = 20
s = 4r = 80
So that s − r = 80 − 20 = 60

21. (b) The volume V and surface area S
of a cube are given by the formulas
$V = e^3$ and $S = 6e^2$ where e is the
edge of the cube.
The problem states:
$V = 64k^3$
$V = (4k)^3$
But $V = e^3$
So e = 4k
And $e^2 = 16k^2$
Thus $S = 6(16k^2) = 96k^2$

22. (c) Let t = tax on a suit priced at $75
then
$$\frac{125}{20} = \frac{175}{t}$$
125t = 3500
t = 28

23. (c) p^2 must be positive so that $p^2 + 1$
must be a positive number. The
other choices have at least one
value of p for which they can equal
zero.

24. (a) Let the radius of circle Q = 1
Then the radius of circle P = .6
Area of circle Q = $\pi(1)^2 = \pi$
Area of circle P = $\pi(.6)^2 = .36\pi$
Thus, the area of circle P is 36% of
the area of circle Q

25. (e) Drop a perpendicular RT from R
to PS extended. Then triangle
PQH ≅ triangle SRT, so that RT
= QH = $\sqrt{5}$ and ST = PH = 2. In
right triangle PTR, $\overline{PR^2} = \overline{PT^2} +$
$\overline{RT^2} = 9^2 + (\sqrt{5})^2 = 81 + 5 = 86$.
PR = $\sqrt{86}$.

PART VIII

Vocabulary List for the GRE

How to Use the GRE Vocabulary List

Vocabulary strength is an important asset when you deal with the verbal problems on the GRE General Test. A large percentage of the questions on the test are purely vocabulary knowledge questions. The vocabulary section that follows presents a list of words which are typical of those that have appeared on previous examinations, and although no list of words can promise to cover all the vocabulary you will find on the GRE, familiarity with the words on this list should prove to be of great value to you.

The vocabulary list is arranged alphabetically for easy reference. Following each word, printed in boldface, you will find synonyms and/or short definitional phrases. Where both are given, the synonyms usually precede the definitional phrases. Where a satisfactory range of synonyms is listed, definitional phrases may be omitted.

We have listed antonyms for many of the bold-faced words where appropriate to our purpose. The antonym, where it is provided, appears in boldface and indented on the line below the given word:

Circumspect. Discreet; cautious; prudent.
    Indecorous. Improper; indiscreet; unseemly.

In the example given, *indecorous* is the antonym for *circumspect*. Each of the two words is followed by its synonyms.

In many instances, the most commonplace synonyms or definitions for a word are omitted on the assumption that you know those meanings already. The synonyms and antonyms that do appear are those that are most likely to apply to that word in a test problem.

PRACTICAL STUDY SUGGESTIONS FOR LEARNING THE WORDS

1. Check your knowledge of the words on this vocabulary list by self-testing. Do not eliminate a word from the list unless you know *all* the listed meanings!

2. Divide the list into groups of fifteen or twenty words and study the synonyms and antonyms for each word. Test yourself by writing the synonyms for each word.

3. After you have gone through the entire list once or twice, pick out the words and their synonyms with which you are still not fully familiar. Make up an index card for each word, with the word itself in capitals on the front and the synonyms on the back. Include the antonym, in capitals, on the back. (The antonym should be in capitals so it will not be confused with the synonyms.) Use the index cards as self-testing flash cards.

4. Since different people learn differently, try various approaches to studying until you find the one or ones that suit you best:
   a. Cover the column of synonyms with a sheet of paper and see how many of those given you can recall.
   b. Copy a group of words and their synonyms each day until you have exhausted the list.
   c. Compose sentences for those words that seem most elusive.
   d. Read a word and its synonyms several times.
   e. Have someone quiz you orally by giving you the key word and having you respond with the listed synonyms and antonyms.
   f. Use any or all of the above singly or in combination.

However you attack the problem of learning the vocabulary list, be aware that you do not know the listed word until you are easily familiar with all the meanings of the word. Also note that each of these words has other forms. If the adjective form is given, be aware that the adverbial, noun, or verb forms may be different. The word *prey* is related to *predator*, *predatory*, *predacious*, and *preying*. Familiarize yourself with common adjectival, adverbial, verbal, and noun endings.

In addition to learning the words on this list, you should make an effort to strengthen your vocabulary skills by noting unfamiliar words that you come across in your readings, or that you hear in classes or in the oral media. Use the index card method for compiling lists of such words and check the dictionary and a thesaurus for synonyms and antonyms.

The GRE Vocabulary List

Abaft. Behind; to the rear of.
  Forward. Ahead; up ahead; in front of.
Abeam. At right angles to a ship's keel
Abecedarian. *See* **Abstruse.**
Abhorrence. Repugnance; loathing; detestation.
  Adoration. Idolatry; worship: veneration.
Abnegation. Self-denial; relinquishment; rejection.
Aborigine. Original inhabitants; primitive tribesman, especially of Australia.
Abrogate. Nullify; abolish.
  Enact. Put into effect; establish.
Absolve. Exculpate; pardon; clear.
  Implicate. Involve; incriminate; imply.
Abstain. Refrain voluntarily (usually from something considered improper); refrain from voting.
  Indulge. Yield to desire; gratify oneself.
Abstemious. Sparing; moderate; abstinent.
  Gluttonous. Voracious; greedy; insatiable.
Abstinent. Abstemious; self-restrained; self-denying, forbearing from any indulgence of appetite.
Abstruse. Recondite; esoteric; profoundly difficult.
  Abecedarian. Rudimentary; elementary; primary.
Accelerate. *see* **Decelerate.**
Accolade. Award; expression of praise.
Acetic. Vinegary; derived from vinegar.
Acrimony. Sharpness, harshness, or bitterness of nature, speech, or disposition.
Acquiescing. *see* **Averse.**
Acrophobia. Pathological fear of high places.
Acumen. Superior mental acuteness; keen insight.

Credulity. Gullibility; readiness to believe or trust without proper evidence.
Adamant. Unyielding; grim; stubborn.
  Relenting. Bending; yielding; giving in.
Adroit. Dexterous; deft; adept; cleverly skillful.
  Inept. Clumsy; ungainly; awkward; bungling.
Adulation. Excessive devotion; servile flattery.
  Disparagement. Belittlement; deprecation; speak slighting about.
  Revilement. Abusing verbally.
Aerial. *See* **Amphibian.**
Aesthetic. A love of beauty.
Affinity. Having a natural attraction to.
  Antipathy. Aversion; basic or habitual repugnance.
Affluent. Prosperous; wealthy.
  Indigent. Impoverished; destitute; needy.
  Penurious. Extremely poor.
Agreeable. *see* **Pugnacious.**
Aggressive. Boldly assertive; taking the offensive; initiating a quarrel; making inroads.
  Submissive. Compliant; subdued; resigned; obedient; yielding.
Alchemy. Magic; medieval form of chemistry, concerned with transmuting baser metals into gold; finding a universal solvent; making an elixir of life.
Alert. *See* **Lethargic.**
Alien. *See* **Indigenous.**
Allusive. Having reference to something implied or suggested.
Alluvial. Of or pertaining to alluvium; sandy soil deposited by running water.
Alpinism. Mountain climbing.
  Spelunking. Cave exploring.
Altruism. Selfless concern for others.

Egoism. Selfishness; opposed to *altruism;* self-interest.

Ambiguous. *See* **Explicit.**

Ambivalent. Having simultaneous feelings of attraction toward and repulsion from.

   Single-minded. Having a single purpose.

Amenable. Tractable; agreeable; answerable.

   Averse. Opposed; unwilling.

Amity. *See* **Animosity.**

Amniotic. Of the amnion, the inner fetal membrane.

Amphibian. Living/operating on land and in water.

   Aquatic. Living in water.

   Terrestrial. Living on land.

   Arboreal. Living in trees.

   Aerial. Living in the air.

Ample. Adequate or more than adequate in extent, size, etc.

   Meager. Scanty; insufficient.

Anachronistic. Set in the wrong time or period; misdated.

Analogous. Similar; comparable; corresponding.

   Disparate. Dissimilar; incongruous.

Anathema. A curse; a formal ecclesiastical curse involving excommunication; a thing accursed.

Anile. Like a weak old woman.

   Senile. Referring to loss of faculties due to old age.

Animated. Lively; spirited.

   Lethargic. Drowsy; sluggish; apathetic.

Animosity. Ill will; hostility; antagonism.

   Amity. Friendship; harmony.

Anneal. Toughen; temper.

Annihilate. Ruin; destroy utterly.

Annular. Ring-shaped.

Anodyne. Pain reliever.

Antipathy. *See* **Affinity.**

Apathetic. Impassive; unresponsive.

Responsive. Reacting readily; concerned.

Aphelion. The point in a planet's orbit that is farthest from the sun.

   Perihelion. The point, as above, that is nearest the sun.

Apiary. A bee house (contains several hives).

Aplomb. Imperturbable self-possession; great poise.

   Perturbation. Agitation; excitability; nervousness.

Apocalyptic. Revelatory; prophetic.

Apogee. The point in a satellite's orbit when it is farthest from the earth.

   Perigee. The point, as above, that is nearest the earth.

Apostate. One who deserts his religion or principles.

Aquatic. *See* **Amphibian.**

Aquiline. Hooked; eaglelike.

Arachnid. Spider, scorpion, tick, mite, etc.

Arboreal. *See* **Amphibian.**

Ardor. Fervor; zeal; passion.

Apathy. Indifference; lack of emotion.

Arthropod. Segmented invertebrate, such as insect, arachnid, crustacean, etc.

Ascetic. Austere; rigorously abstinent; one who practices extreme self-denial or self-mortification.

   Hedonist. One who devotes himself to pleasure.

Assiduity. Diligence; industry.

   Sloth. Indolence; laziness.

Assuage. Appease; satisfy; mollify; pacify; soothe.

   Perturb. Disturb; irritate; agitate.

Astute. Sagacious; shrewd; ingenious.

   Injudicious. Ill-advised; foolish; asinine.

Asunder. In pieces; apart.

Attenuate. Weaken; make slender; reduce in force or intensity.

   Enlarge. Increase; expand; amplify.

Audacious. Brazen; impudent; extremely bold or daring.

  Timorous. Fearful; cautious; nervous; apprehensive.

Aurora. Radiant emissions; polar lights; **Aurora Borealis**—northern lights; **Aurora Australis**—southern lights.

Auspicious. *See* **Sinister.**

Austral. Southern.

  Boreal. Northern.

Autarchy. Absolute sovereignty; autocratic government.

Authoritarian. Domineering; autocratic; favoring complete subjection to authority.

Autocrat. Domineering person; one who exercises absolute power.

Avarice. Greed; inordinate desire to gain and hoard wealth.

Averse. Antipathetic; opposed; loath; unwilling.

  Acquiescing. Agreeing; going along with; complying.

Avuncular. Pertaining to uncles.

Azimuth. The arc of the horizon; angle of horizontal deviation.

Azure. Sky blue; unclouded sky.

Balmacaan. A type of man's overcoat.

Banal. Hackneyed; trite; commonplace; inane; insipid; pointless.

  Original. Inventive; creative.

Batten. Thrive; grow fat; fatten; cover to make watertight.

Beatific. Blissful; saintly.

Bedeck. Adorn; deck out; to ornament.

Bedizen. Adorn in showy, gaudy, vulgar manner.

Bellicose. Pugnacious; ready to fight.

  Pacific. Peaceful.

Benefactor. Kindly helper; one who confers a benefit; one who makes a bequest or endowment. *See* **Malefactor.**

Beneficial. *See* **Deleterious.**

Benevolent. *See* **Rancorous.**

Benign. Gracious, favorable; kindly; salubrious; gentle.

  Malignant. Dangerous; harmful; deadly: malevolent; spiteful.

Bevy. Flock of quail or larks; group of girls or women.

Bifurcate. Forked; divided into two branches.

Biota. Animal and plant life of a region or period.

Biserrate. Notched, with the notches also notched.

Blackbirding. Kidnapping for selling into slavery.

Blasphemer. Impious one; irreverent one; one who speaks evil.

Blunt. Gruff; bluff; brusque; dull; insensitive; obtuse.

  Keen. Sharp; perceptive; sensitive.

Blurt. Utter suddenly; inadvertently.

Bolo. Machete; large single-edged military knife.

Boorish. Rude; crude; unmannerly; loutish; rustic; oafish.

  Urbane. Suave; polished; sophisticated; elegant.

Boreal. Northern; pertaining to the north wind.

  Austral. *See* **Austral.**

Bovine. Stolid; dull; oxlike; cowlike; cow or ox.

Boycott. To abstain from buying or using; to combine in abstaining, as a means of coercion.

Brusque. Blunt; unceremonious; abrupt in manner.

  Suave. Smooth; agreeably urbane.

Buccal. Of the cheek; of the sides of the mouth.

Bucolic. Pastoral; idyllically rural.

Bumble. Bungle; blunder; muddle; stumble; botch; mumble.

Bumptious. Offensively aggressive and self-assertive.

Diffident. Timid; shy; self-effacing.

Burnoose. Hooded mantle or cloak, as that worn by Arabs. *See* **Caftan, Djellabah.**

Cabal. Clique; group of plotters.

Cacophonous. Harsh or discordant sound.

Mellifluous. Sweetly flowing; sweet-sounding; honeyed.

Cadaver. Dead body; corpse (esp. one used for dissection).

Caduceus. Winged staff entwined with two serpents; emblem of medical profession and U.S. Army Medical Corps; carried by Mercury as a messenger of the gods..

Caftan. A long coatlike garment tied at the waist with a sash.

Caliber. Diameter of bore of gun; degree of merit, competence, or importance.

Calibrate. Mark with gradations, graduations, etc.; check the graduation of instrument giving quantitative measurements.

Calliope. Muse of heroic poetry; musical instrument consisting of steam whistles that are activated by a keyboard.

Calumny. Slander; defamation.

Panegyric. Formal commendation; eulogy; formal speech of praise.

Candid. Frank; outspoken; open; sincere.

Disingenuous. Insincere; deceitful.

Canine. Of or like a dog; a dog; a cuspid or eyetooth.

Canon. Church law; body of principles; criterion; standard; officially recognized set of sacred books; the body of works of an author; a contrapuntal musical composition.

Canonize. Glorify; treat as sacrosanct; declare someone to be a saint.

Capon. A castrated rooster.

Captious. Faultfinding; exaggerating trivial defects.

Cardiac. Pertaining to the heart.

Cardinal. Of prime importance.

Caries. Dental decay.

Carnal. Fleshly; sensual; worldly.

Spiritual. Ethereal; incorporeal; other-worldly.

Carnivore. Flesh-eater: dogs, cats, lions, etc.

Herbivore. Plant-eater: hoofed mammals, etc.

Omnivore. Plant and meat eaters; humans, bears, etc.

Carom. Strike and rebound.

Carping. Captious; petulant; faultfinding.

Carrion. Dead and putrefying flesh.

Castigate. Correct by punishing; criticize severely.

Extol. Glorify; exalt.

Catenary. Cable running above the track, from which trolley wire is suspended.

Catholic. Universal; all-encompassing; wide-ranging.

Provincial. Narrow; illiberal; unsophisticated.

Parochial. Provincial; narrow.

Caustic. Severely critical; sarcastic; capable of burning, corroding, destroying living tissue.

Emollient. Soothing to living tissue.

Cauterize. Burn for curative purposes with iron, fire, caustic.

Cavalier. Haughty; disdainful; unceremonious; supercilious.

Cavil. Carp; nitpick; raise inconsequential objections.

Censure. Strong expression of disapproval; reproach harshly; reprimand vehemently.

Commend. Approve; applaud; praise.

Central. *See* **Peripheral.**

Cerulean. Deep blue; azure; sky blue.

Cervine. Deerlike; of deers or the deer family.

Chaff. Mock; tease; banter; husks separated from grain during threshing; worthless matter; refuse.

Chagrin. Vexation from humiliation or disappointment.

Chandler. Candle maker or merchant; dealer in supplies and provisions.

Charlatan. Quack; impostor; mountebank; fraud.

Chasm. Gorge; abyss; fissure; interruption or gap.

Chaste. *See* **Salacious.**

Chastise. Discipline; punish.
  Reward. Commend; applaud.

Chauvinist. Zealous, belligerent patriot; prejudiced devotee to any attitude or cause.

Chesterfield. Type of overcoat; type of sofa; *see* **Balmacaan and Ulster.**

Chiaroscuro. Distribution of light and shade in a picture.

Chide. Scold; rebuke; reprove; find fault.
  Approve. Sanction; acclaim; credit.

Chiromancy. Palmistry; fortune telling through palm reading.

Chromatic. Of colors; in music, progressing by semitones.

Circumspect. Discreet; cautious; prudent.
  Indecorous. Indiscreet; improper; unseemly.

Clarify. *See* **Obfuscate.**

Clio. Greek Muse of history.

Coalesce. Unite; blend; fuse; grow into one.
  Disintegrate. Disjoin; separate; decompose.

Cob. Male swan; short-legged, thick-set horse.

Cockle. Bivalve mollusk; light shallow boat.

Codicil. Supplement to a will; any similar supplement; an appendix; clause with change or modification.

Deletion. Removal; erasure; eradication.

Coercion. Intimidation by threat or duress; forceful compulsion.
  Persuasion. Inducing belief through appeal to reason and understanding.

Coeval. Of the same age or duration; contemporary with.

Cogent. To the point; relevant.
  Irrelevant. Not pertinent.

Cohort. Companion; associate.

Colliery. A coal mine, complete with buildings and works.

Comatose. In a coma; lethargic; lacking energy.

Comely. Pretty; fair; pleasing in appearance.
  Homely. Unattractive; plain; unpretentious; not beautiful.

Commodious. Spacious; roomy.
  Cramped. Confined; contracted; narrow.

Commutator. Device for reversing direction of electrical current.

Compunction. Contrition; uneasiness or hesitation about the rightness of an action; remorse for wrongdoing.
  Conscienceless. Remorseless; unscrupulous.

Concatenation. A linking together.
  Discontinuity. Unlinked; gap or break; interrupted connection.

Conciliatory. *See* **Contentious.**

Concise. Succinct; terse.
  Prolix. Long-winded; wordy; verbose.

Concur. Agree; coincide; work together.
  Demur. Object (esp. on grounds of scruples); take exception.

Conflagration. Large, destructive fire.

Conflagrative. Combustible; flammable; inflammable.
  Incombustible. Not flammable.

Connoisseur. Expert in art, the fine arts, and/or in matters of taste.

Consonant. *See* **Dissonant.**

Contentious. Quarrelsome; disputatious; tending to strife.

  Conciliatory. Propitiating; placatory; pacific.

Continent. Restrained in regard to desires or passions, especially to sexual desires.

  Lustful. Unrestrained in regard to sexual desires; motivated by lust, greed, or the like.

Contumacious. Contrary; refractory; stubbornly perverse; obstinately rebellious or disobedient.

  Pliant. Unresisting; compliant.

Contumely. Humiliating insult; insulting display of contempt.

Conundrum. A puzzle; riddle whose answer involves a pun.

Coolie. Unskilled, low-paid laborer in or from the Orient.

Cooper. Maker of casks or barrels.

Copious. Abundant; fullness, as of thoughts and words.

  Scanty. Inadequate; meager; insufficient.

Coronary. Of the heart, with respect to health; crownlike.

Corpuscular. Made up of particles.

Corroborate. Confirm; substantiate; verify: make more certain.

  Contradict. Gainsay; dispute; controvert; deny directly and categorically; assert the opposite of.

Coruscate. Sparkle; scintillate; gleam; emit vivid flashes of light.

Cosmopolitan. Belonging to all the world; free from local, provincial, or national ideas, prejudices, or attachments; a citizen of the world.

  Provincial. *See* **Catholic.**

Coterie. Clique; set; group of associates who are close because of common social purposes or interests.

Covetous. Greedy; grasping; avaricious; inordinately or wrongfully desirous.

Credulity. *See* **Acumen.**

Crescendo. Gradual increase in force, volume, loudness.

  Diminuendo. Gradual decrease in force, etc.

Crestfallen. Dejected; dispirited; depressed.

  Exuberant. Abounding in vitality; extremely joyful.

Crustacean. Chiefly aquatic arthropods with typical hard-shelled body covering, such as lobsters, crabs, etc.

Cryogenics. Branch of physics dealing with very low temperatures.

Crystallography. Science of crystallization, forms and structure of crystals.

Cuneiform. Wedge-shaped; writing with wedge-shaped characters of the ancient Assyrians and Babylonians.

Cupidity. Avarice; greed; covetousness.

  Unselfishness. Liberality; magnanimity.

Cupola. A dome; structure used as belfry or belvedere.

Curmudgeon. Churl; irascible person.

Cygnet. Young swan.

Cynosure. Center of interest; something that strongly attracts attention by its brilliance, interest, etc.

Dearth. Scarcity; shortage; lack; famine.

  Plenitude. Abundance; fullness; adequacy.

Debacle. Sudden collapse; general breakup; violent rush of waters or ice.

Decalogue. Ten Commandments.

Decelerate. Slow down.

  Accelerate. Speed up.

Deciduous. Transitory; not permanent; shedding leaves annually.

Coniferous. Evergreen cone bearers; not leaf shedding.

Decorous. Proper; seemly; sedate; characterized by propriety.

Unseemly. Inappropriate; unbecoming.

Decry. Belittle; disparage; discredit.

Delete. Erase; remove; expunge.

Insert. Put in.

Deleterious. Hurtful; harmful; injurious.

Beneficial. Helpful; advantageous; conferring benefits.

Deliquesce. Melt away; become liquid by absorbing moisture from the air.

Deluge. Flood; downpour; great flood; anything that overwhelms like a flood.

Demography. Science of vital and social statistics.

Demur. *see* **Concur.**

Depilate. Remove hair from.

Deplete. Exhaust or decrease seriously.

Deploy. Spread out or array strategically.

Desiccate. Dehydrate; dry thoroughly; remove moisture from.

Despondent. *See* **Ebullient.**

Destitute. Indigent; poor; without means of subsistence.

Affluent. Prosperous; wealthy.

Desultory. Disconnected; fitful; random; lacking in order.

Concatenate. Linked together.

Dexterous. Skillful; adept.

Inept. Clumsy; unskilled.

Dialectic(s). Logical argumentation.

Diametrical. Direct; absolute; complete; pertaining to or along a diameter.

Diaphanous. Very sheer; almost transparent or translucent; delicately hazy.

Opaque. Not transparent; not transmitting light; not lucid.

Diatribe. Tirade; bitter, abusive denunciation.

Panegyric. Eulogy; oration in praise.

Didactic. Intended for instruction; too inclined to teach, preach, lecture, moralize.

Diffident. Timid; shy; lacking in self-confidence.

Bold. Resolute; confident; self-assured.

Diffuse. Disseminate; spread out; scatter widely.

Focus. Concentrate.

Dilatory. Delaying; procrastinating; tardy; slow.

Expeditious. Quick; speeded up; prompt.

Dilemma. Perplexing problem; situation requiring a choice between equally undesirable alternatives.

Dilettante. Dabbler; one who takes up an art, activity, or subject merely for amusement; a lover of an art, especially a fine art, or a science.

Diminuendo. *See* **Crescendo.**

Disburse. Expend; pay out; distribute.

Disconsolate. Inconsolable; cheerless; gloomy; sad; melancholy; miserable.

Discreet. Judicious; circumspect; tactful; diplomatic.

Discrete. Separate; distinct; discontinuous.

Disingenuous. *See* **Candid.**

Disparagement. *See* **Adulation.**

Disparate. *See* **Analogous.**

Disport. To display oneself; to divert or amuse oneself.

Dissonant. Discordant; disagreeing or harsh in sound; out of harmony.

Consonant. In agreement; corresponding in sound; in harmony.

Dissuade. Persuade not to do something.
Persuade.

Djellabah. A loose-fitting hooded gown or robe of North Africa. *See* **Caftan** and **Burnoose.**

Doctrinaire. Dogmatic; authoritarian; merely theoretical.

Liberal. Favoring the maximum individual freedom possible.

Pragmatic. Having a practical point of view.

Doldrums. State of inactivity or stagnation; low spirits; dull, listless, depressed mood.

Dolt. Blockhead; dull, stupid person.

Dorsal. Situated on the back.

  Ventral. Situated on the abdominal side.

Doting. Bestowing excessive love or fondness on.

Doughty. *See* **Pusillanimous.**

Draconian. Rigorous; unusually severe or cruel; characteristic of Draco or his code of laws.

Dregs. Lees; grounds; a small remnant; the least valuable parts of anything; the sediment of liquors.

Duplicity. Deceitfulness; double-dealing; a double state or quantity.

  Straightforwardness. Honesty; lack of deceit.

Duress. Coercion; constraint; forcible restraint; compulsion by threat.

Dysphoria. *See* **Euphoria.**

Ebullient. High-spirited; overflowing with enthusiasm; boiling up.

  Despondent. Morose; depressed; low-spirited.

Eccentric. Person with unusual or odd personality, set of beliefs, or behavior pattern; something unusual, peculiar, or odd.

Ecclesiastical. Clerical; not lay; of the church or clergy.

  Laic. Not clerical.

Eclectic. Selecting; choosing from various sources.

Eclogue. A pastoral poem.

Ecstatic. Rapturous; delighted.

Edema. Swelling; effusion of serous fluid into body cavities.

Educe. Infer; deduce; draw forth; bring out.

Effeminate. *See* **Virile.**

Effete. *See* **Puissant.**

Effulgent. Radiant; shining forth brilliantly.

Effusive. Unduly demonstrative; pouring out; overflowing.

  Reserved. Reticent; distant; cold; self-restrained.

Egregious. Flagrant; notorious; remarkable in some bad way.

Élan. Dash; impetuous ardor.

Elation. Great joy or gladness; high spirits; exultant gladness.

  Somberness. Gloom; depression; extreme gravity.

Elegiac. Expressing sorrow or lamentation.

Elegy. A lament for the dead.

Elixir. Panacea; cure-all; quintessence or absolute embodiment of anything; sweetened solution of alcohol and water used as a vehicle for medicinal substances.

Ellipsis. The omission from a sentence of a word or words that would complete the construction.

Emanate. Emit; send forth; flow out; issue forth.

Emancipate. Free from bondage; free from restraint or influence.

  Enslave. To put into bondage; to make a slave of.

Emetic. Inducing vomiting; something that induces vomiting.

Emollient. *See* **Caustic.**

Empathy. Identification with or vicarious experiencing of the feelings, thoughts, etc., of another.

Empiricism. Belief based on experience or observation.

Encomium. *See* **Slander.**

Encumber. Impede; hinder; hamper; retard; fill with what is obstructive or superfluous; burden or weigh down.

Enervate. Weaken; enfeeble; exhaust; deprive of nerve, force or strength; destroy the vigor of.

Enigma. A puzzle; a person of contradictory traits.

Enjoin. Direct or order someone to do something.

Ennui. Boredom; weariness or discontent stemming from satiety or lack of interest.

Enslavement. *See* **Emancipate, Manumission.**

Entomologist. One who studies insects.

Ephemeral. Transitory; short-lived; lasting a very short time.

> **Enduring.** Long-lasting.

Epicure. Connoisseur; one who cultivates a refined taste.

Epiphany. An appearance or manifestation.

Equine. Of horses; horselike; a horse.

Equinox. Time of equal day and night, about March 21 and September 21.

Equitable. Reasonable; just and right.

> **Unfair.** Inequitable.

Eradicate. To root out; remove completely; annihilate.

Erato. Greek Muse of lyric and love poetry.

Erudite. Learned; scholarly.

> **Unlettered.** Uneducated; illiterate; ignorant.

Esoteric. Recondite; known only to a few.

> **Commonplace.** Known to many; ordinary.

Essence. Core; soul; intrinsic nature.

Estivate. To spend the summer, as at a specific place; to pass the summer in a torpid state.

> **Hibernate.** To spend the winter in a dormant state; to withdraw to seclusion; to retire.

Ethereal. Light; airy; tenuous; heavenly; celestial; of the upper regions of space; extremely delicate or refined.

Earthy. Direct; robust; unaffected; realistic; practical; coarse; unrefined.

Etiology. Study of causation; the study of the cause of diseases.

Etymologist. One who studies derivations of words; one who studies the history of linguistic change.

Eulogy. High praise; encomium; speech or writing that praises.

Euphony. Pleasant sounds.

Euphoria. A feeling of well-being, esp. one without basis.

> **Dysphoria.** State of dissatisfaction, restlessness, anxiety.

Euthanasia. Mercy killing; painless death to relieve suffering.

Euthenics. Science of improving the environment.

Evanescent. Vanishing; fleeting; tending to become imperceptible.

> **Enduring.** *See* **Ephemeral.**

Evoke. Elicit; summon; call up.

Exacerbate. *See* **Mollify.**

Exculpate. Absolve; vindicate; free from blame.

> **Incriminate.** *See* **Absolve.**

Exegesis. Critical explanation or interpretation.

Exemplar. Model; pattern; typical example or instance.

Exhort. Urge; advise; admonish.

Exhume. Disinter; bring to light; revive.

> **Inter.** *See* **Inter.**

Exigency. Emergency; something that needs prompt attention.

Exiguous. Scanty; meager; small.

Exodus. Departure; emigration (usually of a large number of people); the flight from Egypt; second book of the Bible.

Exonerate. Free from blame; exculpate.

> **Incriminate.** *See* **Absolve.**

Exoteric. Popular; simple; commonplace; suitable for the general public.

  Esoteric. *See* **Esoteric.**

Expectoration. Spitting; hawking phlegm.

Expedite. Hasten; dispatch; quicken; accelerate; hurry; to speed up the progress of.

  Delay. To hold back; retard; defer; postpone.

Expiration. Termination; ending; breathing out; emission of air from the lungs.

Explicate. Explain; interpret; unfold; make plain; to develop a principle or theory.

  Obfuscate. Muddle; perplex; cloud; to make obscure.

Explicit. Unequivocal; unambiguous; definite; precise; exact; fully and clearly expressed.

  Implicit. Not fully and clearly expressed; implied.

  Ambiguous. Indefinite; unclear.

Expunge. Erase; efface; wipe out; destroy; blot out.

Extemporize. To improvise; to deliver impromptu; to do in a makeshift way.

Extol. *See* **Castigate, Objurgate.**

Extricate. Disengage; liberate from combination; to free or release from entanglement.

Extrinsic. *See* **Intrinsic.**

Exuberant. *See* **Crestfallen.**

Exultation. Triumphant joy; jubilation.

Fabulous. Incredible; almost unbelievable; marvelous; superb; known through myths and legends.

  Historical. Of history, as opposed to legend or fiction.

Factitious. Artificial; contrived; not spontaneous.

  Genuine. Authentic; free from pretense.

  Spontaneous. Unpremeditated; resulting from natural impulse.

Fain. Glad; content; pleased; willing.

Fallible. Liable to err.

  Infallible. Exempt from error; unfailing in effectiveness.

Farrago. Hodgepodge; medley; mishmash; confused mixture.

Fathom. Understand fully; measure by sounding; unit of length equal to six feet.

Fatuous. Inane; silly; illusory; complacently foolish.

  Judicious. Wise; sensible; characterized by good judgment.

Fauna. Animals of a given region or period.

Fawn. Young deer; seek favor by servile behavior.

Fealty. Sworn allegiance to a lord; fidelity.

Feasible. Workable; practicable; suitable.

Feckless. Feeble; ineffective; worthless; lazy; valueless.

Fecund. Creative; fruitful; fertile; productive.

Feign. Simulate; affect; concoct; pretend.

Ferment. Seethe with agitation or excitement; inflame or foment; biochemical change, brought on by yeasts, molds, enzymes, certain bacteria, etc.

Fervor. Ardor; intensity; passion.

  Sobriety. Gravity; restrained behavior.

Fetid. Stinking; having an offensive odor.

Fetish. Amulet; object believed to have magical power.

Fidelity. Accuracy; faithfulness; loyalty.

  Perfidy. Faithlessness; a deliberate breach of trust.

Fiduciary. A trustee; of the relationship between a trustee and his principal.

Filly. A young female horse.

Fission. Cleaving or splitting into parts.

Flag. Diminish in vigor; droop; pave with flagstones.

Flagellate. Whip; scourge; flog; lash.

Flaunt. Parade or display ostentatiously.

Flock. Animals, such as birds, sheep and goats, keeping together in large numbers. Terms used for other animal groupings include: pack of wolves; gaggle of geese; pride of lions; herd of elephants; bevy of quail; covey of partridges; exaltation of larks; shoal of fish; pod of whales; swarm of bees, etc..

Flora. Plants of a particular region or period.

Flout. Treat with disdain, scorn, or contempt; scoff at; mock.

Flux. Continuous change; instability; fusion.

 Stability. Resistance to change; permanence.

Foment. Instigate; foster (rebellion, etc.).

Footpad. Robber who goes on foot.

Foreboding. Presentiment; portent.

Forensic. Rhetorical; adapted to argumentation.

Fortissimo. *Mus.* very loud.

 Pianissimo. *Mus.* very soft.

Fripperies. Geegaws; trifles; empty display; ostentation.

Frivolous. *See* **Grave.**

Furtive. Stealthy; sly; shifty.

Fusion. Uniting by melting together.

Galvanize. Startle into sudden activity; to coat with zinc.

Gambrel. Type of roof. Other types: gable, hip, mansard, lean-to.

Gamut. Entire scale or range.

Gander. Male goose.

Garrulous. Verbose; wordy; excessively talkative.

 Taciturn. Reserved in speech; reticent.

Gauche. Awkward; tactless; lacking social grace.

Gauge. Appraise; estimate; measure; device for measuring; distance between a pair of wheels on an axle.

Geegaws (also Gewgaws). Bauble; trifle.

Gelding. Castrated male horse.

Gentle. *See* **Truculent.**

Geoponics. The art or science of agriculture.

Geotropism. Movement or growth oriented by force of gravity.

Germane. Relevant; pertinent.

Germinate. To begin to grow; to begin to develop.

Gerontology. Study of the aging and their problems.

Gestalt. Unified whole whose value differs from the values derived from the sum of the parts; pattern; configuration.

Glaucoma. A disease of the eye characterized by increased pressure within the eyeball.

Glissando. A musical effect performed by sliding or gliding the fingers over the keys or strings.

Glutton. Excessive eater; one with a great capacity for doing something.

Gondola. Venetian boat powered by single oarsman in stern; car of a dirigible.

Gosling. Young goose.

Gourmand. Gourmet; epicure; glutton.

Gourmet. Connoisseur of fine food and wine; epicure.

Grave. Solemn; serious; sedate; dignified; staid.

 Frivolous. Lack of seriousness or sense; paltry; trivial.

Gregarious. Sociable; fond of company.

Hagiology. Literature dealing with lives and legends of the saints; a biography of a saint or saints.

Halcyon. Peaceful; calm; tranquil; joyful; carefree; wealthy; prosperous.

 Turbulent. State of agitation; tumultuous.

 Ill-omened. Ill-fated; unlucky.

Hallucinate. Experience something sensorily that does not exist outside the mind.

Harbinger. Herald; omen; a foreshadow; advance man.

Harking. Listening; hearing.

Hauteur. Haughtiness.

Hectare. A metric measure equal to 100 ares, 10,000 square meters or 2.471 acres.

Hedonist. *See* **Ascetic.**

Heinous. Hateful; odious; abominable; totally reprehensible.

Hellene. A Greek.

Herbivore. *See* **Carnivore.**

Heretic. A professed believer who holds opinions contrary to those of his church; anyone who does not conform with an established attitude, doctrine, or principle.

Orthodox. Conforming to attitudes, doctrines, or principles that are generally approved.

Herpetologist. One who studies reptiles and amphibians.

Hiatus. Gap; missing part; break in continuity; lacuna.

Hibernate. *See* **Estivate.**

Hierarchy. Any system of persons or things rated one above the other.

Hieroglyphic. Pictographic script, esp. ancient Egyptians'; hard to decipher.

Hip (slang). Informed; knowledgable; up on the latest.

Histrionics. Acting; theatricals; artificial behavior or speech done for effect.

Hodge-podge. Jumble; heterogeneous mixture.

Holocaust. Devastation; a sacrifice totally consumed by fire.

Holography. Making of true three-dimensional photographs by use of laser beams.

Homely. *See* **Comely.**

Homologous. Corresponding; having same or similar relation.

Homophone. Word pronounced the same as, but differing in meaning from another, whether spelled the same way or not.

Hone. Sharpen.

Hubbub. Tumult; uproar; loud, confused noise.

Hullabaloo. Uproar; clamorous noise or disturbance.

Humble. *See* **Pompous.**

Hurly-Burly. Uproar; tumult; commotion.

Hybrid. Anything derived from heterogeneous sources; offspring of two animals or plants of different races, breeds, varieties, species, or genera.

Hydraulics. Study of water or other liquids in motion.

Hydroponics. Cultivation of plants in liquid nutriments.

Hydrotropic. Turning toward or away from moisture.

Hyperbola. Curve with two distinct and similar branches.

Hyperbole. Intentional or obvious exaggeration; excess.

Understatement. Less strong expression than the facts would bear out; expressed in restrained or weak terms.

Hyperborean. Arctic; frigid; northern; polar.

Hypercritical. Captiously critical; excessively fault-finding.

Ichthyology. Study of fishes.

Iconoclast. Destroyer of images; attacker of traditions.

Iconolater. Worshipper of idols or images.

Idol. Favorite; pet; any person or thing devotedly or excessively admired; an image or object worshipped as a deity.

Idolater. Hero worshipper; worshipper of idols; devotee.

Igneous. Of or about fire; produced under intense heat.

Illicit. Unlicensed; unlawful.

Legal. Permitted by law; licit.

Imago. An adult insect.

Imbroglio. Bitter disagreement; confused state of affairs.

Immiscible. Incapable of being mixed.

Mixable. Capable of being mixed.

Immutable. Unchangeable; unalterable; changeless.

Impeccable. Faultless; irreproachable; not liable to sin.

Impermeable. Impenetrable; impassable.

Impervious. Incapable of being impaired; impermeable.

Implicate. *See* **Absolve.**

Imply. Hint; indicate without express statement.

Impolitic. Unwise; inexpedient; injudicious.

Judicious. *See* **Fatuous.**

Impress. Force (into public service); seize (for public use).

Impromptu. Extemporaneous; improvised; unprepared; made or done without previous preparation.

Planned.

Imprudent. *See* **Judicious.**

Impudent. Rude; saucy; presumptuous; brazen; bold; shameless.

Courteous.

Inadvertent. Heedless; unintentional; negligent; thoughtless.

Provident. Proceeding from foresight; acting with prudence.

Inane. Pointless; silly; foolish.

Incarcerate. Imprison; confine; enclose; constrict.

Incarnadine. Blood-red; crimson; flesh-colored; pale pink.

Inception. Outset; start; origin; beginning.

Inchoate. Rudimentary; incipient; not organized.

Incinerate. Burn; reduce to ashes.

Incipient. Initial; beginning.

Incite. Foment; provoke; goad; arouse.

Discourage.

Incombustible. *See* **Conflagrative.**

Incorporeal. Unsubstantial; not material.

Incorrigible. Bad beyond reform; uncorrectible; impervious to punishment.

Incorruptible. *See* **Venal.**

Incriminate. Inculpate; implicate; accuse; charge with a crime or fault.

Exculpate. *See* **Exculpate.**

Incumbent. Obligatory; holder of an office; leaning upon.

Indecorous. *See* **Circumspect.**

Indigenous. Native; natural; innate; aboriginal; inherent.

Alien. Strange; noncitizen; not native.

Indigent. Destitute; impoverished; needy.

Indisputable. *See* **Moot.**

Ineffable. Inexpressible; unutterable; indescribable.

Ineluctable. Inescapable; incapable of being evaded.

Inept. *See* **Dexterous.**

Inexorable. Implacable; relentless; unyielding.

Flexible.

Merciful.

Infallible. *See* **Fallible.**

Infamous. Disreputable; notorious; scandalous; nefarious.

Infer. Conclude; deduce.

Ingenious. Bright; gifted; able; inventive.

Ingenuous. Artless; innocent; naive; candid.

Inherent. Innate; native; inbred; ingrained.

Iniquitous. Sinful; wicked; nefarious; base.

Injudicious. *See* **Astute.**

Inordinate. Immoderate; disproportionate.

Reasonable.

Insidious. Crafty; wily; deceitful; intended to beguile.

Insipid. Pointless; vapid; flat; dull.

Inspiration. Inhalation; taking of air into lungs; stimulus.

Insular. Detached; isolated; illiberal; of an island.

Insulated. Covered; surrounded; separated with nonconducting material; isolated.

Intangible. *See* **Tactile.**

Integral. Entire; whole; essential.

Discrete. *See* **Discrete.**

Inter. Bury.

Exhume. *See* **Exhume.**

Interdiction. Prohibition; prevention from participation in certain sacred acts.

Intern. Restrict; confine; impound; apprentice.

Intrepid. Fearless; dauntless.

Timorous. Fearful; timid; pusillanimous.

Intrinsic. Innate; true; natural.

Extrinsic. Extraneous; external.

Inundation. Deluge; flood; anything overwhelming.

Inure. Toughen; harden; habituate.

Invertebrate. Without a backbone; spineless; without strength of character.

Invidious. Offensive; injurious.

Irascible. Testy; touchy; irritable; choleric.

Irreconcilable. *See* **Placable.**

Jayhawker. Plundering marauder.

Jejune. Immature; juvenile; dull; deficient in nutrient value; insipid.

Joule. A measure of work or energy.

Jubilation. Exultation; rejoicing.

Judicious. Prudent; wise; sagacious; reasonable.

Imprudent. Improvident; not wise; indiscreet.

Kinetic. Of motion; characterized by motion.

Kleptomania. Irresistible impulse to steal.

Knobkerrie. Stick or club with knob on the end, used by South African natives for striking or throwing.

Kudos. Praise; glory.

Labial. Of the lips.

Laconic. Concise; terse; succinct; expressing much in few words.

Verbose. Wordy.

Lacuna. Gap; hiatus.

Laic. *See* **Ecclesiastical.**

Lariat. Lasso; long, noosed rope.

Larva. Immature stage of an insect; any animal in an analogous immature form.

Lascivious. Lewd; wanton; arousing sexual desire.

Laud. Praise; extol.

Lax. Careless; negligent; loose; vague; not rigid.

Leeward. *See* **Windward.**

Leonine. Of or about lions; resembling a lion.

Lepidopterist. One who studies butterflies and moths.

Lethargic. Drowsy; sluggish; apathetic.

Alert. Keen; vigilantly attentive.

Levity. Lightness of character, mind, or behavior.

Lewd. Obscene; vulgar; low; characterized by lust.

Libel. Written defamation; anything defamatory.

Limpid. Clear; transparent (as water or air); pellucid; lucid; completely calm.

Lipid. Fat; other esters with analogous properties.

Lissome. Supple; nimble; agile; limber.

Lithe. Pliant; flexible; easily bent.

Lithograph. Print made from a plane surface on which the image to be printed is ink-receptive and the background ink-repellent (on stone, zinc, aluminum, or other substances).

Littoral. Of the shore; a coastal region.

Loquacious. Talkative; garrulous.

  Laconic. *See* **Laconic.**

Low. Mean; base; to moo; the deep sustained sound of cattle; deficient in vital energy.

Lozenge. Figure with four equal sides, two acute, and two obtuse angles; diamond; something so shaped, like a small tablet or candy.

Lucid. Clear; bright; shining; pellucid; easily understood.

Ludicrous. Laughable; ridiculous; laughably incongruous.

Lugubrious. Mournful; dismal; gloomy; excessively sorrowful (sometimes feigned).

Luminescent. Characterized by light not caused by incandescence.

Lustful. Lecherous; zestful; passionately yearning; motivated by greed or sexual appetite.

Lycanthrope. Werewolf; wolf-man.

Machete. Heavy knife used for cutting undergrowth or cane.

Macroscopic. Large enough to be observed by the naked eye.

  Microscopic.

Malefactor. Criminal; evildoer; offender; culprit.

  Benefactor. *See* **Benefactor.**

Malfeasance. Wrongdoing; official misconduct; illegal deed.

Malign. Defame; vilify, calumniate; slander; having an evil disposition; sinister; baleful.

  Benign. *See* **Benign.**

Malignant. *See* **Benign.**

Malingering. Shirking; avoiding duty through pretense of illness.

Mandate. Command; to authorize; fiat; injunction; decree.

Mansard. Type of sloped roof.

Manumission. Freeing; release; releasing from slavery.

  Enslavement. *See* **Emancipate.**

Marital. Connubial; conjugal; of or about marriage.

Marrow. Inmost or essential part; tissue in the inner cavity of bones.

Marsupial. Pertaining to an abdominal pouch; any mammal that nurses or carries young in a marsupium.

Martial. Warlike; soldierly; pertaining to war.

Martinet. Strict disciplinarian.

Mature. *See* **Puerile.**

Maudlin. Mawkish; fuddled; emotionally silly; effusively sentimental.

Mauve. Pale bluish purple; lilac.

Meager. Sparse; scanty; spare; exiguous; lacking richness.

  Opulent. Rich; affluent; abundant.

Medieval. Of the Middle Ages.

Mercenary. Venal; acquisitive; covetous; hired for service; acting only for reward; a professional soldier serving in a foreign army solely for pay.

  Altruist. *See* **Altruism.**

Mercurial. *See* **Stolid.**

Meridian. Highest point; midday; period of greatest splendor or prosperity; circle of the earth passing through the poles and any given point on earth's surface.

Metamorphosis. Mutation; transformation; transmutation; complete change or alteration.

  Stasis. Equilibrium; inactivity caused by opposing equal forces.

Mete. Dole; measure out; parcel out; deal; allot; boundary; limiting mark.

Metonymy. Figure of speech: use of name of one object (or concept) for that of another to which it is related or of which it is a part.

Miasma. Noxious exhalations; foreboding influence.

Microscopic. *See* **Macroscopic.**

Microtome. Instrument for slicing materials for microscopic examination.

Millennium. Thousand years; period of general happiness, esp. in the indefinite future.

Mellifluous. *See* **Cacophonous.**

Misanthropy. Hatred or distrust of mankind.

Miscegenation. Marriage between those of different races.

Misogamy. Hatred of marriage.

Misogynist. Woman-hater.

Mixable. *See* **Immiscible.**

Mollify. Pacify; appease; mitigate; reduce.

  Exacerbate. Aggravate.

Moot. Doubtful; debatable; hypothetical; purely academic; unsettled.

  Indisputable. Incontrovertible; incontestable; undeniable.

Moraine. A deposit of gravel and other materials carried by a glacier.

Morass. Marsh; bog.

Morbid. Gruesome; grisly; unwholesomely gloomy; pertaining to diseased parts.

  Wholesome.

Mordant. Sarcastic; caustic.

Moribund. Dying; stagnant; on the verge of extinction.

Mufti. Civilian dress as worn by one who usually wears a uniform; religious head of a Muslim community.

Mummer. Actor; pantomimist.

Mundane. Common; ordinary; banal; of everyday concerns of the world.

Munificent. Very generous.

  Parsimonious. Stingy.

Mutant. Result of change or alteration from forebears; sudden departure from parent type.

Mystical. Occult; mysterious; spiritually symbolic.

Nadir. Lowest point.

  Zenith. Highest point.

Naive. Unsophisticated; ingenuous; lacking experience.

  Sophisticated. Worldly-wise; deceptive; misleading; complex; intricate.

Napery. Table linens; any household linens.

Nebulous. Hazy; vague; indistinct.

Necromancy. Magic; witchcraft; conjuration; divination through communication with the dead.

Necropolis. A cemetery.

Nefarious. Iniquitous; extremely wicked; heinous; vile.

Nephrologist. Kidney specialist.

Nepotism. Favoritism or patronage based on family relationship.

Nescient. Ignorant; agnostic.

Neurotic. One affected with an emotional disorder involving anxiety, compulsion, etc.

Niggardly. Stingy.

Niobe. Mythological figure symbolizing sorrow.

Noisome. Offensive; disgusting; harmful noxious; stinking.

  Healthful. Salubrious.

Nonfeasance. Omission of some act which ought to have been performed.

Nostrum. Quack medicine; pet scheme; favorite remedy.

Notorious. Widely, but unfavorably known; recognized.

Nugatory. Trifling; trivial; frivolous; useless; ineffective.

  Significant. Important; weighty; momentous.

Numismatist. Coin and medal collector.

Obdurate. Stubborn; unyielding; unmovable; persistently impenitent.

Obedient. *See* **Obstreperous.**

Obese. Corpulent; overweight; excessively fat.

Obfuscate. Confuse; cloud; make obscure; stupefy.

  Clarify. Make clear.

Objurgate. Berate sharply; reproach vehemently.

  Extol. Glorify; exalt.

Obliterate. Destroy completely; expunge; efface; remove all traces.

Obloquy. Bad repute; reproach; aspersion; disgrace.

Obsequious. Fawning; servilely deferential; sycophantic.

Obsidian. Dark volcanic glass, usually transparent.

Obstreperous. Unruly; clamorous; boisterous; uncontrolled.

  Obedient.

Obtuse. *See* **Perspicacious.**

Officious. Meddling; interfering; objectionably forward in offering unrequested help or advice.

  Retiring. Shy; withdrawing.

Olfactory. Of the sense of smell.

Oligarchy. Government by the few, or by a dominant clique.

Ominous. Threatening; portentous; portending evil or harm.

  Propitious. Auspicious; favorable.

Omniscient. All-knowing.

Omnivore. *See* **Carnivore.**

Oncologist. Specialist in tumors and cancer.

Opalescent. Having a milky iridescence.

Opaque. Not transmitting light; dull; impenetrable; hard to understand.

  Transparent. Easily seen through; transmitting light so that bodies situated beyond or behind can be distinctly seen.

Ophidian. Of or about snakes.

Ophthalmology. Study of the functions and diseases of the eye.

Opprobrium. Infamy; disgrace resulting from outrageously shameful conduct.

Opulent. *See* **Meager.**

Ordain. Decree; destine; prescribe; confer holy orders upon.

Ornithologist. One who studies birds.

Orthodox. *See* **Heretic.**

Ostracism. Banishment; exile; exclusion from society, privileges, etc., by general consent.

Otiose. Indolent; futile; superfluous; ineffective; leisured; slothful.

Otologist. Ear specialist.

Ottoman. A Turk; a cushioned footstool.

Ovine. Of or about sheep.

Oviparous. Producing eggs that mature and hatch outside of the body.

Paean. *See* **Tirade.**

Paleontology. Study of past life forms through fossils.

Palindrome. A word, line, verse, etc., reading the same backward as forward.

Palmistry. *See* **Chiromancy.**

Panegyric. Encomium; formal eulogy or commendation.

Parabola. A conic section; the intersection of a right circular cone with a plane parallel to an element of the cone.

Paradigm. Model; pattern; standard; paragon; a set of forms containing the same element.

Paradox. Seeming self-contradiction that may be true; a statement contrary to accepted opinion.

Paraffin. An inflammable waxy substance used for preserving.

Pariah. Outcast; person despised by society; member of a low caste in southern India.

Parochial. *See* **Catholic.**

Parricide. Murder of one's parent.

Parsimonious. Stingy; penurious; frugal to excess.

  Munificent. *See* **Munificent.**

Parthenogenetic. Reproduced through the development of an unfertilized egg.

Parvenu. Upstart; one with recently acquired wealth or position who lacks the proper social qualifications.

Pathos. Pity; evoking pity or compassion; the quality in art forms that evokes pity or compassion.

Patrician. Aristocratic; noble; of high birth.

  Plebeian. Common; commonplace; vulgar; belonging to the common people.

Patrimony. Heritage from one's father or other ancestor.

Pecuniary. Financial; monetary; relating to money.

Pedantry. Slavish attention to details; didacticism; excessive formalism; ostentatious display of learning.

Pedodontia. Dealing with care of children's teeth.

Pelage. Hair, fur, wool, or other soft covering of a mammal.

Pelt. Hide or skin of an animal; attack; assail; beat; pound; throw; hurry.

Pensive. Reflective; meditative; dreamily or sadly thoughtful.

Penurious. *See* **Affluent.**

Peremptory. Arbitrary; dogmatic; arrogant; incontrovertible; imperious; decisive; leaving no chance for refusal or denial.

Perfidy. *See* **Fidelity.**

Perigee. *See* **Apogee.**

Perihelion. *See* **Aphelion.**

Periodontia. Dentistry dealing with the gums and connective tissue and bone surrounding a tooth.

Peripatetic. Wandering; roving; vagrant; itinerant; pertaining to Aristotelian school of philosophy.

Peripheral. External; outside; superficial; not concerned with the essential.

  Central. At the core.

Peristaltic. Movement through a tubular muscular system resulting from a progressive wave of contraction and relaxation, as food through the alimentary canal.

Perjure. Swear falsely; lie under oath.

Perquisites. Fringe benefits or bonuses granted an employee; incidental gain additional to regular wages.

Perspicacious. Shrewd; discerning; perceptive; acute; astute.

  Obtuse. Dull.

Peruke. A wig, esp. of a kind worn by men in the 17th and 18th centuries; a periwig.

Peruse. Read; read critically or thoroughly.

  Skim. To read in a cursory way.

Pessimistic. *See* **Sanguine.**

Pestle. An implement for pulverizing substances in a mortar; to pound, pulverize, mix.

Pewter. Any alloy having tin as its chief constituent.

Philatelist. One who collects and studies stamps.

Philogyny. Fondness for women.

  Misogyny. Hatred of women.

Physiognomy. The face; external aspect; countenance.

Pianissimo. *See* **Fortissimo.**

Pious. *See* **Sanctimonius.**

Piquant. Pungent; spicy; provocative; pleasantly sharp or tart.

  Insipid. *See* **Insipid.**

Pique. Offense; dudgeon; fit of resentment; provoke; nettle; challenge; goad; arouse resentment.

Pisces. Twelfth sign of the zodiac—the Fishes; class of vertebrates comprising the fish.

Piscine. Of or like fish or fishes.

Pithy. Concise; substantial; succinct; tersely cogent.

　Prolix. *See* **Concise; Verbose; Garrulous.**

Placable. Conciliatory; forgiving; appeasable.

　Irreconcilable. Firmly opposed; incapable of being made to compromise.

Placebo. Substance having no pharmacological effect given to soothe or appease the patient.

Plebeian. *See* **Patrician.**

Plenitude. *See* **Dearth.**

Plethora. Excess; abundance; state of being overfull.

　Dearth. *See* **Dearth.**

Pleura. Serous membrane investing the lung and also lining the thorax.

Pliant. *See* **Contumacious.**

Pointillism. A technique of painting using dots of color, associated with the impressionist Seurat.

Polyhymnia. The Muse of the sacred music and dance.

Pompous. Showy; ostentatious; self-important.

　Humble. Modest; courteously respectful; unpretentious.

Portentous. Ominous; momentous; significant; inauspicious.

　Propitious. *See* **Ominous.**

Poser. Puzzle; baffling question; one who poses.

Potlatch. Distribution of gifts, ceremonial in nature, among American Indians of the northwest coast.

Practicable. Possible; feasible; usable; capable of being put into practice.

Pragmatism. Philosophy stressing practical consequences and values; character or conduct which stresses practicality.

Predatory. Rapacious; living by plunder; preying upon other animals.

Preemptive. Appropriating; usurping; acquiring before someone else.

Presto. Rapid; immediately; at a rapid tempo.

Primeval. Primordial; of the first ages (of the earth).

Prism. A transparent solid body used for dispersing light into a spectrum or for reflecting rays of light..

Proboscis. An elephant's trunk; any long, flexible snout.

Procrastination. Deferring; delaying; putting off till another time.

Prodigal. Spendthrift; profligate; wastefully extravagant; wastrel; waster.

　Thrifty.

Prodigy. One with extraordinary talent or ability; something wonderful; something monstrous.

Prognosticate. Forecast; foretoken; prophesy.

Proliferation. Excessive, rapid spread.

Prolix. *See* **Concise.**

Propitious. *See* **Ominous.**

Proscribe. Denounce; condemn; prohibit; outlaw.

Prosthesis. An artificial part to supply a defect of the body.

Protean. Variable; readily assuming different shapes.

Provenance. Source; place of origin.

Provident. *See* **Inadvertent.**

Provincial. *See* **Catholic.**

Prudery. Excessive modesty.

Psychotic. Person with a severe mental disorder, or having a disease affecting the total personality.

Puce. Dark or brownish purple.

Puerile. Childishly foolish; boyish; juvenile.

Mature.

Pugnacious. Quarrelsome; argumentative; contentious; excessively inclined to fight.

Agreeable.

Puissant. Powerful; mighty; potent.

Effete. Decadent; lacking in wholesome vigor; worn out; sterile; unable to produce.

Pullulate. Sprout; teem; breed; multiply; swarm; germinate.

Pulmonary. Of the lungs.

Pulverize. Demolish; crush; reduce to dust by pounding or grinding.

Pupa. Stage between larva and imago in an insect.

Purblind. Dim-sighted; partially blind; slow in imagination, understanding, and vision.

Purveyance. Act of supplying provisions.

Purview. Range of authority; scope; range of vision, sight, or understanding.

Pusillanimous. Cowardly in spirit; timorous; fearful.

Intrepid. *See* **Intrepid.**

Doughty. Steadfastly courageous and resolute.

Pyromania. Compulsion to set things on fire.

Quack. Charlatan; fraudulent pretender to medical skill.

Quaff. Drink copiously and heartily.

Quagmire. A bog; a situation from which extrication is very difficult.

Qualm. Misgiving; compunction; pang of conscience; sudden onset of illness, esp. nausea.

Quarter. Region or district; one-fourth; one of the four principal points of the compass; to lodge and feed; mercy or indulgence; to traverse ground from left to right and from right to left while advancing.

Quell. Suppress; vanquish; subdue; extinguish.

Quench. Slake, satisfy, or allay thirst, hunger, passions, etc.; extinguish; cool suddenly; overcome.

Querulous. Complaining; peevish; petulant; testy.

Quirk. Peculiarity; evasion; sudden twist or turn; mannerism.

Quotidian. Daily; everyday; ordinary; recurring daily.

Raconteur. One skilled in telling stories or anecdotes.

Raglan. Loose overcoat; *see* **Balmacaan, Chesterfield, Ulster.**

Raillery. Banter; badinage; satirical pleasantry; good-humored ridicule.

Rallentando. Gradually slowing tempo.

Rancorous. Intensely malignant; vehemently antagonistic; filled with spite or ill will; full of enmity.

Benevolent. Kind hearted; benign; charitable; characterized by goodwill; desiring to do good to others.

Reata. *See* **Lariat.**

Rebuke. Reprove; reprimand; censure; admonish.

Recalcitrant. Rebellious; opposed; resistant; refractory.

Recidivism. Repeated or habitual relapse; chronic tendency toward repeated criminal or antisocial behavior patterns.

Rehabilitation. Restoration of good reputation and or standing; restore to a condition of good health, or the like.

Recondite. Abstruse; deep; difficult; profound; obscure; little known; beyond ordinary understanding; esoteric.

Commonplace. *See* **Esoteric.**

Redemption. Deliverance; rescue; repurchase; salvation; recovery of something pledged; conversion.

Regicide. Killing of a king; killer of a king.

Rejuvenate. Restore to youthful vigor; refresh; renew.

Relinquish. Renounce; surrender; yield; resign; abdicate.

Remonstrate. Object; expostulate; plead in protest.

Renal. Of or about the kidneys.

Repine. Grumble; fret; complain.

Replenish. Supply with fresh fuel; refill.

Reprehend. Rebuke; censure; blame; reproach; admonish; chide; upbraid.

Repugnance. Aversion; objection; antipathy.

    Attraction.

Rescind. Abrogate; annul; revoke; repeal; invalidate by later action.

Resuscitation. Revival, especially from apparent death.

Retiring. *See* **Officious.**

Revilement. *See* **Adulation.**

Rickshaw. Jinrickisha; a small two-wheeled passenger vehicle drawn by one person.

Rodomontade. Bragging; vainglory; vainglorious boasting; pretentious, blustering talk.

Roister. Revel noisily; swaggering boisterous manner.

Ruminant. Contemplative; cud-chewing; any even-toed, cloven-hoofed, cud-chewing quadruped.

Sagacious. Wise; sage; discerning; showing acute mental discernment.

    Injudicious. *See* **Astute, Impolitic.**

Salacious. Lustful; lecherous; obscene; grossly indecent; lewd; pornographic.

    Chaste. Decent; undefiled; stainless; virtuous; not obscene.

Salubrious. Healthful; wholesome; favorable to health.

    Noisome. *See* **Noisome.**

Salutatory. Greeting; welcoming address at a commencement, delivered by the salutatorian.

Samisen. Guitarlike Japanese stringed musical instrument.

Sanctimonious. Hypocritical; pietistic; hypocritical show of piety or righteousness.

    Pious. Devout; reverent; godly.

Sanction. Authorize; approve; allow; ratify; confirm; enact as a penalty for disobedience, or as a reward for obedience.

Sanguinary. Bloodthirsty; characterized by bloodshed.

Sanguine. Cheerful; hopeful; confident; reddish; ruddy.

    Pessimistic. Gloomy; hopeless; anticipating only the worst.

Sardonic. Biting; mordant; contemptuous; characterized by scornful derision.

Sartorial. Of or about tailors or tailoring.

Saturnine. Gloomy; sluggish in temperament; suffering from lead poisoning.

Satyr. A lecher; a lascivious man; a woodland deity, part human, part goat attendant on Bacchus.

Savanna. Grassland with scattered trees; a plain with coarse grasses, usually in tropical or subtropical regions.

Scathing. Injurious; searingly harmful; bitterly severe.

Scavenger. Animals that feed on dead organic matter; a street cleaner.

Scepter. A rod—emblem of regal power; sovereignty.

Scintilla. Minute trace; jot; a spark; a minute particle.

Scour. Range over; move rapidly; cleanse or polish by rubbing; remove dirt.

Scourge. Whip; lash; punish; chastise; criticize severely; the cause of affliction or calamity.

Scruple. Qualm; compunction; a very small amount; an apothecary's unit of weight; moral or ethical restriction that acts as a restraining force.

Seething. Surging; foaming; boiling; steeping; soaking; act of being agitated or excited; frothing.

Seismograph. Device for measuring and recording the vibrations of an earthquake.

Senile. *See* **Anile.**

Serif. A small line used to finish off the main stroke of a letter.

Serigraph. A print made by the silk-screen process.

Servile. Obsequious; fawning; cringing; sycophantic; slavishly submissive.

  Aggressive. *See* **Aggressive.**

Significant. *See* **Nugatory.**

Similitude. Likeness; resemblance; semblance; comparison; parable or allegory.

Sinister. Portending evil; threatening; malevolent; on the left; unfavorable.

  Auspicious. Favorable; propitious.

Sitar. A lute of India.

Skim. *See* **Peruse.**

Slander. Defame orally; defamation; calumny.

  Encomium. Formal expression of high praise; eulogy.

Sloth. Indolence; laziness; habitual disinclination to exertion; a sluggish arboreal animal; a tropical American edentate.

Slough. Swamp; mire; marshy pool; condition of degradation; the outer layer of the skin of a snake; a discard; get rid of; dispose of; shed; molt.

Sobriety. *See* **Fervor.**

Solecism. Breech of good manners or etiquette; error in propriety or consis-

tency; substandard grammatical usage.

Soliloquy. Talking as if alone; utterance by a person talking to himself.

Soma. Body, as opposed to psyche.

Somber. Grave; gloomily dark; shadowy; dull; murky; sunless; melancholy.

  Exuberant. Extremely joyful; jubilant.

Sophisticated. *See* **Naive.**

Soporific. Causing sleep; of or about sleep; drowsy.

Sordid. Dirty; squalid; wretchedly poor; morally ignoble or base; vile; degraded; self-seeking; mercenary.

  Honorable.

  Cheerful.

Sororicide. Killing of one's sister; one who kills one's sister.

Spatula. An implement with a broad, flat, usually flexible blade.

Spectrum. An ordered array of entities; an array; band of colors produced when sunlight is passed through a prism; a broad range of varied but related ideas.

Spelunking. Cave exploration.

Spirited. *See* **Vapid.**

Spoor. A track or trail of an animal.

Squall. A sudden violent wind, often accompanied by rain, snow, or sleet; a sudden disturbance or commotion; to cry; to scream violently.

Stable. *See* **Volatile.**

Stability. *See* **Flux.**

Stannary. Tin-mining region or district; a tin smeltery.

Stasis. *See* **Metamorphosis.**

Steer. A castrated bull.

Stigmatize. Mark with a brand; set a mark of disgrace upon; characterize in marked manner as unfavorable; to produce stigmata, marks, etc.

Stoical. Impassive; imperturbable; characterized by calm, austere fortitude.

Stolid. Unemotional; immovable; dull; stupid; not easily stirred; phlegmatic.

Mercurial. Active; lively; sprightly; volatile; changeable; fickle; flighty; erratic.

Stratum. Layer; level; single bed of sedimentary rock; one of a number of parallel levels.

Stringent. Strict; severe; compelling; urgent; forceful; exacting; rigorously binding.

Lax. Slack; not rigid; lenient.

Strop. Sharpen; strip, usually of leather, used for sharpening razors.

Suavity. Sophistication; worldliness; smoothly agreeable manners; courteous actions.

Sumptuary. Pertaining to regulation of expense.

Sumptuous. Splendid; superb; luxuriously fine; entailing great expense.

Supine. Inactive; passive; inert; lying on the back.

Supplant. Replace; remove; succeed; overthrow.

Suppliant. Petitioner; supplicant.

Surreptitious. Stealthy; sneaky; clandestine; secret; unauthorized; underhanded.

Tacit. Unspoken; silent; implicit; indicated.

Explicit. Fully and clearly expressed; unequivocal; leaving nothing merely implied.

Taciturn. Uncommunicative; reticent; dour; stern; habitually silent.

Loquacious. Talkative; verbose; garrulous; wordy; voluble.

Tactile. Tangible; perceptible to the touch; of or about touch.

Intangible. Incorporeal; incapable of being perceived through the sense of touch.

Tangential. Divergent; digressive; erratic; merely contiguous; only slightly connected.

Taxonomy. Classification, especially of plants and animals; laws and principles of such classification; science dealing with naming, identification, and classification.

Tedium. Boredom; ennui; irksomeness; tediousness.

Teem. Be prolific; abound; produce; to empty; to pour out; to discharge.

Teleology. The belief that design is apparent in nature, and that final causes exist.

Temerity. Audacity; effrontery; cheek; hardihood; rashness; nerve; unreasonable contempt for danger.

Temporal. Secular; of or limited by time; transitory; civil or political; pertaining to the present life, or this world.

Tendentious. Showing a definite tendency, bias, or purpose.

Tendril. A shoot; a sprout; a leafless organ of climbing plants.

Tepid. Lukewarm; moderately warm.

Terpischore. The Greek Muse of dancing and choral song.

Terrain. Milieu; environment; a tract of land, esp. with reference to its natural features, military advantages, etc.

Terrestrial. *See* **Amphibian.**

Tetrahedron. A solid figure; a triangular pyramid.

Therapeutic. Curative; treatment and curing of disease.

Thrifty. *See* **Prodigal.**

Timorous. Fearful; timid; cowardly.

Intrepid. *See* **Intrepid.**

Tirade. Harangue; diatribe; long vehement speech; bitter, outspoken denunciation.

Paean. Song of praise, joy, or triumph.

Tithe. Any tax, levy, or the like; one-tenth; a tenth part set aside as an offering to

God, for works of mercy or the like; a tenth part or small part of anything.

Tittle. A particle; jot; whit; a dot or other small mark used as a diacritic mark in writing or printing.

Tonsure. The shaven crown or patch worn by monks or ecclesiastics; the act of cutting the hair; the act of shaving the head, or some part of it, as a religious practice or rite.

Torpid. Lethargic; dull; inert; apathetic; sluggish; dormant.

Torque. That which produces rotation or torsion.

Tort. A civil wrong (except for breach of contract) for which the injured party is entitled to compensation.

Totem. A natural object assumed as the emblem of a clan or group; an object with which a clan or sib considers itself closely related.

Toxology. Study of poisons and antidotes.

Tractable. Obedient; docile; malleable; easily controlled.

   Recalcitrant. *See* **Recalcitrant.**

Transitory. *See* **Ephemeral.**

Transparent. *See* **Opaque.**

Triptych. A picture or carving in three compartments, side by side.

Truculent. Savage; cruel; fierce.

   Gentle.

Turbid. Muddy; roiled; clouded; having the sediment disturbed.

Turbulent. *See* **Halcyon.**

Turncoat. Renegade; traitor.

Tyrannical. Despotic; oppressive; dictatorial; imperious; domineering; unjustly severe in government.

Tyro. Novice; amateur; beginner in learning.

Ukase. Edict; proclamation by an authority; imperial order; official decree.

Ulster. A type of overcoat. *See* **Balmacaan, Chesterfield, Raglan.**

Ululate. Howl; wail; hoot, as an owl.

Unctuous. Smug; oily; greasy; oily or soapy to the touch; suave; excessively pious; excessively smooth.

Ungulate. Hooflike; of or about hoofed mammals; any of the hoofed mammals.

Unique. Single; sole; strange; unequalled; matchless.

Unlettered. *See* **Erudite.**

Urban. Citified; of or comprising a city or a town.

   Rustic. Simple; artless; unsophisticated; uncouth; boorish; rude; a country person; an unsophisticated country person; of or pertaining to living in the country; rural.

Urbane. *See* **Boorish.**

Ursine. Bearlike; of or about bears.

Usury. The lending of money with an excessive charge for its use; unconscionable or exorbitant amount of interest.

Valedictory. A farewell; an occasion of leave-taking; a farewell address or oration.

Vapid. Insipid; spiritless; inane; having lost life or zest.

   Spirited. Showing mettle, courage, vigor; liveliness.

Vector. Direction or course followed by an airplane, a missile, or the like.

Vehement. Forceful; impetuous; furious; ardent; eager; impassioned; deeply felt.

Venal. Mercenary; corruptible; open to corrupt influence or bribery; capable of being bought.

   Incorruptible. Incapable of being bribed or perverted.

Vendetta. Feud; rivalry; contention.

Venial. Excusable, trifling, or minor, as a sin; capable of being forgiven.

Ventral. *See* **Dorsal.**

Verbose. Wordy; loquacious; talkative; prolix.

  Taciturn. *See* **Taciturn.**

  Laconic. Terse; concise.

Vilify. Defame; slander; calumniate; disparage; malign.

  Commend. Praise; laud.

Vindicate. Exculpate; defend; avenge; punish; justify; sustain; exonerate.

Virago. A shrew; an ill-tempered scolding woman.

Virile. Vigorous; masculine; characteristic of, and befitting, a man.

  Effeminate. Delicate to an unmanly degree in traits, tastes, habits.

Vivacious. Lively; animated; sprightly.

Viviparous. Producing living young from the body instead of from eggs.

Volatile. Changeable; fickle; evaporating rapidly.

  Stable. Resistant to sudden change or deterioration; reliable; steady; enduring; permanent.

Voracious. Gluttonous; rapacious; ravenous; insatiable; immoderate; greedy.

Vulpine. Cunning; crafty; foxlike; of or about foxes.

Wane. Diminish; abate; decrease, as the waning of the moon from the full moon to the new moon.

  Wax. To grow; increase; enlarge; dilate.

Whence. From what place; source; origin; cause.

Wholesome. *See* **Morbid.**

Windward. Toward the direction from which the wind blows; the side from which the wind blows.

  Leeward. The side toward which the wind blows; the sheltered side.

Wreak. Inflict; exact; execute.

Wright. Constructive workman.

  Wheelwright. Wheel maker.

  Cartwright. Cart maker.

  Boatwright. Boat maker.

  Millwright. Worker who erects the machinery for a mill.

  Wainwright. Wagon maker.

Wrought. Pt. and pp. of *work;* worked; elaborated; embellished; beaten with a hammer.

Xanthic. Yellow; yellowish color.

Xenophobia. Hatred of foreigners or that which is strange.

Zealot. Fanatic; bigot; excessively zealous person.

Zenith. *See* **Nadir.**